Acts

ΠΑΙΔΕΙΑ ▣ paideia
COMMENTARIES ON
THE NEW TESTAMENT

Acts

MIKEAL C. PARSONS

Baker Academic
a division of Baker Publishing Group
Grand Rapids, Michigan

Published by Baker Academic
a division of Baker Publishing Group
P.O. Box 6287, Grand Rapids, MI 49516-6287
www.bakeracademic.com

Printed in the United States of America

Library of Congress Cataloging-in-Publication Data
Parsons, Mikeal, Carl, 1957–
    Acts / Mikeal C. Parsons.
      p. cm. — (Paideia : commentaries on the New Testament)
    Includes bibliographical references and indexes.
    ISBN 978-0-8010-3188-5 (pbk.)
    1. Bible. N. T. Acts—Commentaries. I. Title.
BS2625.53.P37 2008
226.6'07—dc22   2008034284

In memory of
Cronje B. Earp
and
in honor of
Dean M. Martin
R. Alan Culpepper
Charles H. Talbert

Contents

List of Figures   ix

List of Figures

Foreword

Paideia: Commentaries on the New Testament is a series that sets out to comment on the final form of the New Testament text in a way that pays due attention both to the cultural, literary, and theological settings in which the text took form and also to the interests of the contemporary readers to whom the commentaries are addressed. This series is aimed squarely at students—including MA students in religious and theological studies programs, seminarians, and upper-divisional undergraduates—who have theological interests in the biblical text. Thus the didactic aim of the series is to enable students to understand each book of the New Testament as a literary whole rooted in a particular ancient setting and related to its context within the New Testament.

The name "Paideia" reflects (1) the instructional aim of the series—giving contemporary students a basic grounding in academic New Testament studies by guiding their engagement with New Testament texts; (2) the fact that the New Testament texts as literary unities are shaped by the educational categories and ideas (rhetorical, narratological, etc.) of their ancient writers and readers; and (3) the pedagogical aims of the texts themselves—their central aim being not simply to impart information but to form the theological convictions and moral habits of their readers.

Each commentary deals with the text in terms of larger rhetorical units; these are not verse-by-verse commentaries. This series thus stands within the stream of recent commentaries that attend to the final form of the text. Such reader-centered literary approaches are inherently more accessible to liberal arts students without extensive linguistic and historical-critical preparation than older exegetical approaches, but within the reader-centered world the sanest practitioners have paid careful attention to the extratext of the original readers, including not only these readers' knowledge of the geography, history, and other context elements reflected in the text but also to their ability to respond correctly to the literary and rhetorical conventions used in the text. Paideia commentaries pay deliberate attention to this extratextual repertoire in order to highlight the ways in which the text is designed to persuade and move its readers. Each rhetorical unit is explored from three angles: (1) introductory matters; (2) tracing the train of thought or narrative or rhetorical flow; and (3) theological issues raised by the text that are of interest to the contemporary Christian. Thus the primary focus remains on the text and not its historical context or its interpretation in the secondary literature.

Our authors represent a variety of confessional points of view: Protestant, Roman Catholic, and Greek Orthodox. What they share, beyond being New Testament scholars of national and international repute, is a commitment to reading the biblical text as theological documents within their ancient contexts. Working within the broad parameters described here, each author brings his or her own considerable exegetical talents and deep theological commitments to the task of laying bare the interpretation of Scripture for the faith and practice of God's people everywhere.

Mikeal C. Parsons
Charles H. Talbert

Preface

Biblical commentaries belong to a genre distinctive to the study of scriptures, texts held to be sacred and authoritative for the faith and practice of religious communities. As such, they demand something from the interpreter that other genres of writing rarely require, namely, attention to each and every paragraph—if not to every word—of the text. Thus commentary writing, which attempts to follow the argument and logic of "another" and to present that argument as transparently as possible, demands a different kind of discipline than the academic monograph, whose writer attempts to present his or her own logic as lucidly and clearly as possible. Submitting myself to the discipline of this kind of analysis, that is, tracing the narrative logic of the ancient writer who produced the Acts of the Apostles, has been both rewarding and challenging. One is forced to comment on texts the meaning of which may not be readily apparent to the interpreter!

I have worked on Acts for more than twenty-five years, producing various articles and monographs, with a goal, eventually, of producing a full-length commentary. The actual writing of the commentary took place during the 2006–2007 academic year and was especially intense during the spring and summer of 2007, during which time I had a research leave. Taking up my post in a small cubicle in my university's library, I spent eight or more hours each day engaging with and engaged by the narrative of Acts. My sustained experience with this portion of scripture has profoundly deepened my respect for the literary skills and theological vision of the author who produced it. That respect stands in contrast to the critical reception of Acts among those (perhaps many) who still view the Lukan corpus as the unwanted stepchild among the New Testament writings. That disregard was encapsulated for me in a throw-away comment by a colleague in the field, who, upon learning that I was writing a commentary on Acts, quipped: "You have the best story with the worst theology in the New Testament!" I must now register my strong disagreement with the latter part of this assessment; Luke's literary skills in communicating his story are matched if not exceeded by the theological vision that undergirds that story. If this commentary in some small way makes that theological vision a bit more transparent to the modern reader, then it will have achieved my aspirations for it.

One feature of the commentary is the attention paid to the ways in which the Christian scriptures, in this case Acts, shape the theological reflection and moral habits of its Christian readers; hence the title of the commentary series, *Paideia*. I am glad also to confess that over time this moral vision has captured my own theological imagination, and I humbly count myself in the "company of St. Luke," that is, among those who continue to be "schooled" in matters of Luke's vision of the Christian Way. The discipline required in commentary writing thus has produced another kind of discipline, this one a kind of spiritual discipline that frankly came upon me in unexpected but welcome ways.

The format of the commentary does not allow me to register in each passage the deep debt I owe to those who have sought to comment on the Acts of the Apostles from beginning to end. I have learned so much about Luke's Acts from these writers, from Chrysostom and the Venerable Bede to—among others— Joseph Fitzmyer, Beverly Gaventa, Justo González, Ernst Haenchen, Luke Timothy Johnson, John Polhill, Gerhard Schneider, Scott Spencer, Ben Witherington, and my colleague, Charles Talbert, even—perhaps especially— when I found myself disagreeing with them.

I have also profited from the growing body of secondary literature, monographs, articles, and especially doctoral dissertations that have grappled with specific aspects of Acts. In particular, I should like to mention the community of doctoral students at Baylor University who over the years have produced significant contributions in seminar papers and dissertations (some published, some unpublished, and some still in progress) to my understanding of the Lukan corpus: Andrew Arterbury, Kenneth Bass, Martin Culy, Norfleete Day, Derek Dodson, Stan Harstine, Chad Hartsock, Derek Hogan, Dennis Horton, Ira Jolivet Jr., David Matson, Jim McConnell, Kathy Maxwell, Alicia Myers, Mark Proctor, Keith Reich, Jesse Robertson, William Shiell, Julien Smith, Josh Stigall, and Jason Whitlark. In addition to sharing their work with me, several of them also read and interacted with parts of the commentary. It has been an extraordinary blessing to live and work among such a talented and committed community of young scholars, who along with my colleagues in New Testament, Sharyn Dowd, Naymond Keathley, Charles Talbert, and now Lidija Novakovic, have contributed to an environment that is both nurturing and challenging. I especially wish to thank Jim McConnell, who worked with extraordinary patience and diligence in tracking down sources and putting the manuscript in proper format.

I have used the translation produced with Marty Culy for *Acts: A Handbook on the Greek Text*, published by Baylor University Press (2003). Translations are already acts of interpretation and, in those cases where readers want fuller explanation for the translation (as well as technical discussions of grammar and text-critical issues), they are encouraged to turn to the *Handbook* for more details. Appreciation is expressed to my coauthor, Marty Culy, and to Dr. Carey Newman, director of Baylor University Press, for permission to use the translation in the commentary.

I am grateful to Baylor University, and especially Provost Randall O'Brien and my departmental chair, Bill Bellinger, for their continued expressions of support, in particular for making possible the aforementioned research leave in spring 2007. James Ernest of Baker Academic first proposed the idea of the series in which this commentary appears and extended the invitation to me to serve not only as an author but also as series coeditor with Charles Talbert. From that initial conversation years ago at a regional SBL meeting has come an impressive collection of authors among whom I am proud to be counted. For James's gentle spirit and firm editorial hand, I am most thankful, and I look forward to the time when the series is complete!

As always, my family has been my primary source of support and encouragement. For the undeserved joy that Heidi and my children bring to my life, I once again express my deep gratitude. Final revisions to the manuscript were made during the summer of 2007 while we were in Florence, Italy. Thanks especially to Heidi for helping each of us make Italy our home away from home!

Like Luke's audience, I have been schooled by "masters" in matters of faith, and it is to four of those mentors that I dedicate this book: Cronje B. Earp—blessed be his memory—taught me, as an undergraduate, how to read classical and Hellenistic Greek. Dean M. Martin, first as my undergraduate adviser and later as a colleague, taught me how to read critically and think theologically. R. Alan Culpepper, first through his seminars and later as a colleague, and Charles H. Talbert, first through his writings and later as a colleague, taught me the art of "theological exegesis" in interpreting the Greek New Testament, and Luke/Acts in particular. It has been my distinct privilege to be "taught more accurately about the Way" by these Christian intellectuals, and for those opportunities I will be forever in their debt. I offer this commentary and a humble and grateful heart as a poor return for their investment of time and friendship over the years.

Mikeal C. Parsons
Baylor University
Lent 2008

Acknowledgments

Appreciation is expressed to the following publishers for permission to reproduce portions of these publications:

Fortress Press for permission to reproduce portions of chapter one in Mikeal C. Parsons and Richard I. Pervo, *Rethinking the Unity of Luke and Acts* (Minneapolis: Fortress, 1993).

Baker Academic for permission to reproduce portions of chapters 7 and 8 of *Body and Character in Luke and Acts: The Subversion of Physiognomy in Early Christianity* (Grand Rapids: Baker Academic, 2006).

Baylor University Press for permission to reproduce portions of the introduction and the translation found in *A Handbook on the Greek Text of Acts* (Waco, TX: Baylor University Press, 2003).

Hendrickson Publishers for permission to reproduce portions of chapter 7 of *Luke: Storyteller, Interpreter, Evangelist* (Peabody, MA: Hendrickson, 2007).

Mercer University for permission to reproduce portions of "Acts," pp. 1–64 in *Acts and Pauline Writings* (Mercer Commentary on the Bible 7; edited by Watson E. Mills, Richard F. Wilson, et al.; Macon, GA: Mercer University Press, 1997).

The National Association of Baptist Professors of Religion for permission to reproduce portions of "Nothing Defiled AND Unclean: The Conjunction's Function in Acts 10:14," *Perspectives in Religious Studies* 27 (2000): 263–74.

Abbreviations

General

b.	Babylonian Talmud	NT	New Testament
ca.	circa	OT	Old Testament
chap(s).	chapter(s)	sp.	spurious
esp.	especially	*t.*	Tosefta
m.	Mishnah	*y.*	Jerusalem Talmud
MSS	manuscripts		

Bible Texts and Versions

KJV	King James Version	NRSV	New Revised Standard Version
LXX	Septuagint		
NA[27]	*Novum Testamentum Graece*. Edited by [E. and E. Nestle and] B. Aland et al. 27th rev. ed. Stuttgart: Deutsche Bibelgesellschaft, 1993	RSV	Revised Standard Version
		TEV	Today's English Version
		UBS[4]	*The Greek New Testament.* Edited by B. Aland et al. 4th ed. Stuttgart: Deutsche Bibelgesellschaft and United Bible Societies, 2001.
NIV	New International Version		
NJB	New Jerusalem Bible		

Ancient Corpora

OLD TESTAMENT

		Deut	Deuteronomy
1–2 Chr	1–2 Chronicles	Esth	Esther
Dan	Daniel	Exod	Exodus

Ezek	Ezekiel	1–2 Tim	1–2 Timothy

Ezek   Ezekiel

Gen   Genesis

Hab   Habakkuk

Isa   Isaiah

Jer   Jeremiah

Josh   Joshua

Judg   Judges

1–2 Kgs   1–2 Kings

Lev   Leviticus

Mal   Malachi

Mic   Micah

Nah   Nahum

Neh   Nehemiah

Num   Numbers

Prov   Proverbs

Ps/Pss   Psalm/Psalms

1–2 Sam   1–2 Samuel

Zech   Zechariah

Zeph   Zephaniah

DEUTEROCANONICAL BOOKS

Ep Jer   Epistle of Jeremiah

Jdt   Judith

1–4 Macc   1–4 Maccabees

Sir   Sirach

Tob   Tobit

Wis   Wisdom of Solomon

NEW TESTAMENT

Col   Colossians

1–2 Cor   1–2 Corinthians

Eph   Ephesians

Gal   Galatians

Heb   Hebrews

Matt   Matthew

1–2 Pet   1–2 Peter

Phil   Philippians

Phlm   Philemon

Rev   Revelation

Rom   Romans

1–2 Thess   1–2 Thessalonians

1–2 Tim   1–2 Timothy

DEAD SEA SCROLLS AND RELATED WRITINGS

CD   *Damascus Document*

1QM   *War Scroll*

1QpHab   *Pesher on Habakkuk*

1QS   *Rule of the Community*

4QFlor   *Florilegium*

TARGUMIC TEXTS

Tg. Ps.-J.   *Targum Pseudo-Jonathan*

RABBINIC LITERATURE

Abod. Zar.   *Abodah Zarah*

Exod. Rab.   *Exodus Rabbah*

Lev. Rab.   *Leviticus Rabbah*

Meg.   *Megillah*

Naz.   *Nazir*

Nid.   *Niddah*

'Ohal.   *'Ohalot*

Pesah.   *Pesahim*

Shabb.   *Shabbat*

Sanh.   *Sanhedrin*

Sheqal.   *Sheqaliim*

OLD TESTAMENT PSEUDEPIGRAPHA

As. Moses   *Assumption of Moses*

2 Bar.   *2 Baruch* (Syriac Apocalypse)

1 En.   *1 Enoch* (Ethiopic Apocalypse)

2 En.   *2 Enoch* (Slavonic Apocalypse)

Jos. Asen.   *Joseph and Aseneth*

Jub.   *Jubilees*

LAB   *Liber antiquitatum biblicarum* (pseudo-Philo)

Let. Aris.   *Letter of Aristeas*

Ps.-Phoc.   *Pseudo-Phocylides*

Pss. Sol.   *Psalms of Solomon*

Sib. Or.   *Sibylline Oracles*

T. Ab.   *Testament of Abraham*

T. Jac.	Testament of Jacob
T. Job	Testament of Job
T. Jos.	Testament of Joseph
T. Levi	Testament of Levi
T. Naph.	Testament of Naphtali
T. Reu.	Testament of Reuben
T. Sim.	Testament of Simeon

APOSTOLIC FATHERS

Barn.	Barnabas
1 Clem.	1 Clement
Did.	Didache
Herm. Mand.	Shepherd of Hermas, Mandates
Herm. Vis.	Shepherd of Hermas, Visions
Ign. Eph.	Ignatius, To the Ephesians

Ign. Magn.	Ignatius, To the Magnesians
Ign. Pol.	Ignatius, To Polycarp
Ign. Rom.	Ignatius, To the Romans
Mart. Pol.	Martyrdom of Polycarp
Pol. Phil.	Polycarp, To the Philippians

NEW TESTAMENT APOCRYPHA AND PSEUDEPIGRAPHA

Acts Andr.	Acts of Andrew
Acts Paul	Acts of Paul and Thecla
Acts Pil.	Acts of Pilate
Acts Thom.	Acts of Thomas
Ep. apost.	Epistula apostolorum
Gos. Pet.	Gospel of Peter

NAG HAMMADI CODICES

Apoc. Pet.	Apocalypse of Peter

Ancient Authors

ACHILLES TATIUS

Leuc. Cli.	Leucippe et Clitophon

ADAMANTIUS

Physiogn.	Physiognomonica

AELIUS ARISTIDES

Hier. log.	Hieroi logoi (Sacred Tales)

AESCHINES

Tim.	In Timarchum

AESCHYLUS

Ag.	Agamemnon
Eum.	Eumenides
Prom.	Prometheus Bound

ALBINUS

Epit.	Epitome doctrinae Platonicae

APHTHONIUS

Prog.	Progymnasmata

APOLLODORUS

Bibl.	Bibliotheca

APOLLONIUS RHODIUS

Argon.	Argonautica

APPIAN

Bell. civ.	Bella civilia
Hist. Rom.	Fragmenta historiae Romanae (Ab urbe condita)

APULEIUS

Apol.	Apologia
Dogm. Plat.	De dogma Platonis
Metam.	Metamorphoses (The Golden Ass)

ARATUS

Phaen.	Phaenomena

ARISTIDES, PUBLIUS AELIUS

Or.	Orationes

ARISTOPHANES

Eq.	Equites

ARISTOTLE

Eth. Nic.	Ethica Nichomachea
Physiogn.	Physiognomia (sp.)

Poet.	*Poetica*		*De or.*	*De oratore*
Pol.	*Politica*		*Dom.*	*De domo suo*
Rhet.	*Rhetorica*		*Flac.*	*Pro Flacco*
Rhet. Alex.	*Rhetorica ad Alexandrum* (dub.)		*Inv.*	*De inventione rhetorica*
			Leg.	*De legibus*
ARRIAN			*Off.*	*De officiis*
Anab.	*Anabasis*		*Phil.*	*Orationes Philippicae*
			Quint. fratr.	*Epistulae ad Quintum fratrem*
ARTAPANUS			*Rhet. Her.*	*Rhetorica ad Herennium* (sp.)
Jud.	*De Judaeis* (fragments)		*Top.*	*Topica*
ARTEMIDORUS			*Tusc.*	*Tusculanae disputationes*
Onir.	*Onirocriticon*		*Verr.*	*In Verrem*
ASCONIUS			**CLEMENT OF ALEXANDRIA**	
Pis.	*In Senatu contra L. Pisonem*		*Strom.*	*Stromata (Miscellanies)*
ATHENAEUS			**CURTIUS RUFUS**	
Deipn.	*Deipnosophistae*		*Hist. Alex.*	*Historiae Alexandri Magni*
AUGUSTINE			**DEMETRIUS**	
Bapt.	*De baptismo contra Donatistas*		*Eloc.*	*De elocutione* (sp.)
Conf.	*Confessiones*		**DEMOSTHENES**	
AULUS GELLIUS			*Mid.*	*In Midiam*
Noct. Att.	*Noctes Atticae (Attic Nights)*		*Or.*	*Orationes*
			4 Philip.	*Philippica 4* (sp.)
AURELIUS VICTOR			**DIDYMUS**	
Vir. illustr.	*De viris illustribus*		*In Gen.*	*In Genesim*
BEDE			**DIO CASSIUS**	
Comm. Acts	*Commentary on the Acts of the Apostles*		*Hist. Rom.*	*Historia Romana*
CALLISTHENES			**DIO CHRYSOSTOM**	
Alex.	*Vita Alexandri* (sp.)		*Alex.*	*Ad Alexandrinos*
CHARITON			*Cel. Phryg.*	*Celaenis Phrygiae*
Chaer.	*De Chaerea et Callirhoe*		*Charid.*	*Charidemus*
			Consuet.	*De consuetudine*
CICERO			*Dei cogn.*	*De dei cognitione*
Amic.	*De amicitia*		*Grat.*	*De gratitudo*
Att.	*Epistulae ad Atticum*		*Hom. Socr.*	*De Homero et Socrate*

Lyb. myth.	*Lybicus mythus*
Or.	*Orationes*
Rhod.	*Rhodiaca*
1 Tars.	*Tarsica prior*
Ven.	*Venator*

DIODORUS SICULUS

Hist.	*Bibliotheca historica*

DIOGENES LAERTIUS

Vit. phil.	*Vitae philosophorum*

DIONYSIUS OF HALICARNASSUS

1–2 Amm.	*Epistulae ad Ammaeum i–ii*
Ant. Rom.	*Antiquitates Romanae*
Comp.	*De compositione verborum*
Dem.	*De Demosthenis dictione*
Isocr.	*De Isocrate*
Pomp.	*Epistula ad Pompeium geminum*

EPICTETUS

Diatr.	*Diatribai*

EPICURUS

Ench.	*Enchiridion (Ratae sententiae)*

EPIPHANIUS

Pan.	*Panarion (Refutation of All Heresies)*

EURIPIDES

Bacch.	*Bacchae*
Herc. fur.	*Hercules furens*
Iph. Taur.	*Iphigenia Taurica*

EUSEBIUS

Hist. eccl.	*Historia ecclesiastica*
Praep. ev.	*Praeparatio evangelica*

HELIODORUS

Aeth.	*Aethiopica*

HERMOGENES

Invent.	*De inventione*
Meth. dein.	*Peri methodou deinotēs (On Method of Forceful Speaking)* (sp.)
Prog.	*Progymnasmata* (sp.?)

HERODIAN

Hist.	*Historiae*

HERODOTUS

Hist.	*Historiae*

HESIOD

Theog.	*Theogonia*
Op.	*Opera et dies (Works and Days)*

HIPPOLYTUS

Trad. ap.	*Traditio apostolica*

HOMER

Il.	*Ilias*
Od.	*Odyssea*

HORACE

Carm.	*Carmina*
Sat.	*Satirae*

IAMBLICHUS

Vita	*Vita Pythagorica*

IRENAEUS

Haer.	*Adversus haereses*

JEROME

Nom. Hebr.	*De nominibus Hebraicis*

JOHN CHRYSOSTOM

Hom. Act.	*Homiliae in Acta apostolorum*

JOHN OF DAMASCUS

Vit. Barl.	*Vita Barlaam et Joasaph* (sp.)

JOSEPHUS
- Ant.   *Antiquitates Judaicae*
- BJ   *Bellum Judaicum*
- C. Ap.   *Contra Apionem*

JULIAN
- Or.   *Orationes*

JUSTIN
- 1 Apol.   *Apologia I*
- Dial.   *Dialogus cum Tryphone*

JUSTINIAN
- Dig.   *Digesta*

JUVENAL
- Sat.   *Satirae*

LACTANTIUS
- Inst.   *Divinarum institutionum libri VII*

LIBANIUS
- Or.   *Orationes*

LIVY
- Hist.   *Historiae (Ab urbe condita)*

LONGUS
- Daphn.   *Daphnis et Chloe*

LUCIAN
- Alex.   *Alexander*
- Bis acc.   *Bis accusatus*
- Demon.   *Demonax*
- Eunuch.   *Eunuchus*
- Hermot.   *Hermotimus*
- Hist. conscr.   *Quomodo historia conscribenda sit*
- Icar.   *Icaromenippus*
- Jupp. conf.   *Juppiter confutatus*
- Nav.   *Navigium*
- Nigr.   *Nigrinus*
- Peregr.   *De morte Peregrini*
- Philops.   *Philopseudes*
- Rhet. praec.   *Rhetorum praeceptor*
- Sacr.   *De sacrificiis*
- Somn.   *Somnium*
- Tox.   *Toxaris*

MACROBIUS
- Comm. somn.   *Commentarii in somnium Scipionis*

MANETHO
- Apot.   *Apotelesmatica*

MENANDER (COMICUS)
- Dysk.   *Dyskolos*

MENANDER (RHETOR)
- Epid.   *Peri epideiktikōn*

MINUCIUS FELIX
- Oct.   *Octavius*

NICOLAUS
- Prog.   *Progymnasmata*

ORIGEN
- Cels.   *Contra Celsum*

OVID
- Fast.   *Fasti*
- Metam.   *Metamorphoses*

PAUSANIAS
- Descr.   *Graeciae descriptio*

PETRONIUS
- Sat.   *Satyricon*

PHILO
- Abr.   *De Abrahamo*
- Conf.   *De confusione linguarum*
- Decal.   *De decalogo*
- Flacc.   *In Flaccum*
- Ios.   *De Iosepho*
- Legat.   *Legatio ad Gaium*

Migr.	De migratione Abrahami
Mos.	De vita Mosis
Praem.	De praemiis et poenis
Spec.	De specialibus legibus
Virt.	De virtutibus

PHILO OF BYZANTIUM

Sept.	De septem orbis spectaculis

PHILOSTRATUS

Vit. Apoll.	Vita Apollonii
Vit. soph.	Vitae sophistarum

PHOEBAMMON

Fig.	De figuris

PINDAR

Pyth.	Pythionikai

PLATO

Apol.	Apologia Socratis
Ep.	Epistulae
Euthyphr.	Euthyphro
Leg.	Leges
Phaedr.	Phaedrus
Resp.	Respublica
Symp.	Symposium

PLINY THE ELDER

Nat.	Naturalis historia

PLINY THE YOUNGER

Ep.	Epistulae
Ep. Tra.	Epistulae ad Trajanum

PLUTARCH

Adul. amic.	Quomodo adulator ab amico internoscatur
Aem.	Aemilius Paullus
Alex.	Alexander
Caes.	Caesar
Eum.	Eumenes
Garr.	De garrulitate
Luc.	Lucullus

Marc.	Marcellus
Mor.	Moralia
Num.	Numa
Per.	Pericles
Princ. iner.	Ad principem ineruditum
Pyrrh.	Pyrrhus
Rom.	Romulus
Virt. prof.	Quomodo quis suos in virtute sentiat profectus

POLEMO

Physiogn.	Physiognomonica

POLLUX

Onom.	Onomasticon

POLYBIUS

Hist.	Historiae

QUINTILIAN

Inst.	Institutio oratoria

SALLUST

Bell. Cat.	Bellum Catalinae

SALLUSTIUS

De deis	De deis et mundo

SENECA (THE ELDER)

Con.	Controversiae

SENECA (THE YOUNGER)

Ep.	Epistulae morales
Nat.	Naturales quaestiones

SILIUS ITALICUS

Pun.	Punica

SOCRATES

Ep.	Epistulae (sp.)

STRABO

Geogr.	Geographica

SUETONIUS

Claud.	Divus Claudius
Nero	Nero
Rhet.	De rhetoribus
Tib.	Tiberius
Tit.	Divus Titus

TACITUS

Ann.	Annales
Hist.	Historiae

TERTULLIAN

Apol.	Apologeticus (Apology)
Praescr.	De praescriptione haereticorum
Ux.	Ad uxorem

THEMISTIUS

Or.	Orationes

THEON

Prog.	Progymnasmata

THEOPHILUS OF ANTIOCH

Autol.	Ad Autolycum

THUCYDIDES

Hist.	Historiae

TYCONIUS

Comm. Apoc.	Commentarium in Apocalypsim

VEGETIUS

Epit.	Epitoma rei militaris

VIRGIL

Aen.	Aeneid

XENOPHON OF EPHESUS

Ephes.	Ephesiaca

XENOPHON THE HISTORIAN

Anab.	Anabasis
Hell.	Hellenica
Mem.	Memorabilia

Ancient Collections and Anonymous Works

Anon. Lat.	Anonymous Latin treatise De physiognomonia	Epigr. Gr.	Epigrammata graeca
Anth. Pal.	Anthologia Palatina	Ps.-Clem.	Pseudo-Clementine Homilies
Const. ap.	Constitutiones apostolicae		

Series, Collections, and Reference Works

ACM	*Ancient Christian Magic: Coptic Texts of Ritual Power.* Edited by Marvin Meyer and Richard Smith. San Francisco: HarperSanFrancisco, 1994.
AG	*Anthologia graeca.* Edited by H. Beckby. 4 vols. 2nd ed. Munich: Heimeran, 1965–1968.
ANF	*The Ante-Nicene Fathers.* 10 vols. Repr. ed. Grand Rapids: Eerdmans, 1957.
BDAG	Frederick William Danker. *A Greek-English Lexicon of the New Testament and Other Early Christian Literature.* 3rd ed. Chicago: University of Chicago Press, 2000.
BDF	F. Blass, A. DeGrunner, and R. W. Funk. *A Greek Grammar of the New Testament and Other Early Christian Literature.* Chicago: University of Chicago Press, 1961.

CCF   *Creeds and Confessions of Faith in the Christian Tradition.* Edited by J. Pelikan and V. Hotchkiss. 3 vols. New Haven: Yale University Press, 2003.

Corp. Herm.   *Corpus Hermeticum.* Edited by A. D. Nock and A.-J. Festugière. Vol. 1. Paris: Belles Lettres, 1946.

I.Eph.   *Die Inschriften von Ephesos.* Edited by H. Engelmann, H. Wankel, and R. Merkelbach. 8 vols. Inschriften griechischer Städte aus Kleinasien 11–17. Bonn: Habelt, 1979–1984.

IG   *Inscriptiones graecae, consilio et auctoritate Academiae Litterarum Borussicae editae.* Edited by F. Hiller von Gaertringen et al. Berlin: Walter de Gruyter, 1873.

L&N   Johannes P. Louw and Eugene A. Nida. *Greek-English Lexicon of the New Testament: Based on Semantic Domains.* 2 vols. 2nd ed. New York: United Bible Societies, 1989.

NPNF[2]   *Nicene and Post-Nicene Fathers.* Second series. Edited by P. Schaff and H. Wace. 14 vols. Repr. ed. Peabody, MA: Hendrickson, 1994.

NTA   *New Testament Apocrypha.* Edited by Wilhelm Schneemelcher. English translation by R. McL. Wilson. 2 vols. Louisville: Westminster John Knox, 1991.

OGIS   *Orientis graeci inscriptiones selectae. Supplementum Sylloges inscriptionum graecarum.* Edited by W. Dittenberger. 2 vols. Leipzig: Hirzel, 1903–1905.

OTP   *The Old Testament Pseudepigrapha.* Edited by James H. Charlesworth. 2 vols. Garden City, NY: Doubleday, 1983–1985.

P.Col.   *Columbia Papyri.* Edited by W. L. Westermann et al. 11 vols. New York: Columbia University Press, 1929–1954; Missoula, Atlanta: Scholars Press, 1979–1998.

PG   Patrologia graeca [= Patrologiae cursus completus: Series graeca]. Edited by J.-P. Migne. 162 vols. Paris, 1857–1886.

PL   Patrologia Latina [= Patrologiae cursus completus: Series graeca]. Edited by J.-P. Migne. 221 vols. Paris, 1844–1865.

P.Herc. 1018   *Storia dei filosofi: La Stoà da Zenone a Panezio (PHerc. 1018).* Edited by Tiziano Dorandi. Leiden: Brill, 1994.

P.Herc. 1021   *Storia dei filosofi: Platone e l'Academia (PHerc. 1021 e 164).* Edited by Tiziano Dorandi. Naples: Bibliopolis, 1991.

P.Lond.   *Greek Papyri in the British Museum.* Edited by F. G. Kenyon, H. I. Bell, and T. C. Skeat. 5 vols. Oxford: Oxford University Press, 1893–1974.

P.Magd.   *Papyrus de Magdola.* Edited by J. Lesquier. Paris: Leroux, 1912.

P.Oslo   *Papyri Osloenses.* Edited by S. Eitrem and L. Amundsen. 3 vols. Oslo: Jacob Dybwad, 1936.

P.Oxy.   *The Oxyrhynchus Papyri.* London: Egypt Exploration Fund, 1898.

P.Ryl.   *Catalogue of the Greek Papyri in the John Rylands Library, Manchester.* Edited by J. M. Johnson et al. Manchester: Manchester University Press, 1911–1952.

SIG[3]   *Sylloge inscriptionum graecarum.* Edited by W. Dittenberger. 3rd ed. Leipzig: Hirzel, 1920.

Acts

Introduction

"A storm center" (Unnik 1966). "Shifting sands" (Talbert 1976). "A fruitful field" (Gasque 1988). These are but a few of the epithets used to describe the scholarly interpretation of the Acts of the Apostles in the twentieth century. The spate of commentaries and collected essays during the past two decades suggests continued and sustained interest in Acts (commentaries: Schneider 1980; Johnson 1992; Polhill 1992; Barrett 1994–1998; Spencer 1997; Talbert 1997, 2005; Fitzmyer 1998; Witherington 1998; González 2001; Gaventa 2003; Bock 2007; collected essays: Tyson 1988; Keathley 1990; Richard 1990; Neyrey 1991; Parsons and Tyson 1992; Marconi and O'Collins 1993; Witherington 1996; Marshall and Peterson 1998; Thompson and Phillips 1998; Moessner 1999; Verheyden 1999).

This introduction aims at addressing topics necessary to orient the reader in using the commentary as a guide for interpreting Acts. Some of these issues are typically associated with critical introductions (authorship, date, place, etc.); others are not. The focus of the introduction, as with the commentary, is the text and its interpretation, and as such, the history of the interpretation of Acts (available elsewhere; see Gasque 1975) yields to a focus on the work itself (though a volume on the reception history of Acts is in the works: see Parsons and Hornik, forthcoming).

Since issues typically associated with a commentary introduction are scattered throughout this introduction, it may be useful to state succinctly the perspective taken on those issues in this work. The author of Acts, traditionally known as "Luke," wrote what became known as the "Acts of the Apostles" as a sequel to a plurality of gospels then currently in use of which the Third Gospel (which "Luke" also wrote) stands as the "first among equals." The Third Gospel was written in the '80s (or '90s), followed some years later by Acts (within the first two decades of the second century, ca. AD 110).

Little can be known for certain regarding the identity of the author of Acts; what is clear is that the text presents the early Christian movement, known as "the Way," within the context of first-century Judaism(s), and that first-century Judaism(s), as well as the spread of the Christian movement, must be understood within the larger first-century Greco-Roman context. In his composition of Acts, Luke demonstrated command of a number of rhetorical conventions and techniques, drew on various cultural and social scripts, and blended multiple genres of writing (including, but not limited to, elements of ancient biography, historiography, novel, and perhaps epic). Acts is a "charter" document of Christian self-identity and legitimation, written, not for a specific "Lukan community," but rather for a general audience of early Christians living in the ancient Mediterranean world. Inaccessible—and fortunately for our purposes, irrelevant—is the provenance of Luke at the time of composition (although Ephesus seems to be of special interest to the author). It is difficult to distinguish when Luke's writing reflects things as they were when they happened, or as they were in Luke's day at the time of his writing, or as Luke hoped they would be. Luke's primary purpose in writing is to "school" his intended audience in the moral and theological implications of the Christian vision by telling the story of the first followers of the movement's founder. For contemporary Christians to adopt the point of view of the authorial audience (with the nuances necessary for a document set in circumstances nineteen hundred years ago) is to share in this Christian vision; it is to be theologically formed by the perspectives of this part of the Christian canon.

To orient the user of this commentary it is helpful to speak of the now familiar relationship between author, text, and audience. These rubrics were popularized during the emergence of literary studies of the biblical text (see especially Culpepper 1983; Rhoads and Michie 1982) and were based on communication models that assumed that meaning was conveyed through the interaction of these three elements (cf. Chatman 1978).

A communication model appropriate for biblical narrative is at the same time simpler and more complex than most previous models. It is simpler in the sense that ancient writers rarely if ever employed narrators whose voice was in conflict with the ideology of the implied or real author (contra Dawsey 1986) as is sometimes the case in a modern novel. The biblical model is more complex because the process of composing texts often involved a scribe whose participation in the process may have varied from that of being a kind of human "word processor," who simply wrote down everything dictated by the author, to the role of coauthor of the document. The roles of the scribe have been rather fully explored in Pauline studies (Murphy-O'Connor 1995). It is assumed for purposes of this commentary that if Luke did use a scribe it would have been for the purposes of writing down his dictation.

The other end of the model likewise represents a complicated situation. It is widely recognized in NT studies that the early Christian literature would have been read to a congregation or gathering of Christians by one appointed to that task, usually referred to as the "reader" or "lector" (see Shiell 2004). The role of the reader was later institutionalized in the church in the form of the lector, a minor office in the church (see Tertullian, *Praescr.* 41; Hippolytus, *Trad. ap.* 1.12). We find references to "readers" and "public reading" in the various types of literature in the NT (Mark 13:14; 1 Tim 4:13; Rev 1:3; cf. Gamble 1995, 218–24). At the beginning of the Christian movement, then, those tapped for the task of public reading, whether of the Jewish scriptures or emerging Christian literature, would have been chosen on the basis of their gifts for public speaking. In addition to being literate, readers would need the gifts of a strong voice and most likely some training in rhetoric. Among the rhetoricians, a strong voice was a natural gift. The reader of early Christian texts presumably had the "gift" of public speaking. This idea that speaking is a natural gift was easily translated by Christians as evidence of a spiritual gift (*Const. ap.* 8.22).

In the Roman period, training in rhetoric began in elementary school and continued, for those interested in pursuing a career in politics, through several advanced levels. We may assume that the first lectors or readers of early Christian literature were among those most highly trained in the practice of rhetoric. One bit of evidence for this is found in Irenaeus, who claims that some heretics "do not know how to read Paul" and gives as an example the need to clarify the use of *hyperbaton*, the transposition of words, in 2 Thess 2:8 (*Haer.* 3.7.2). Irenaeus, at least, presumes that the "orthodox" reader will have enough rhetorical training to avoid some basic mistakes in delivery.

Relatively little attention is paid in this commentary to the actual "performance" of Acts by the reader or lector (though cf. the comments on the lector's gestures at 13:16; 24:10; 26:1, and the sidebar at 21:40), but the user of the commentary is well advised always to keep this fact in mind: the author of Acts expected his audience to experience the text aurally and communally (see also Shiell 2004). For this reason, the commentary refers to "audience" or "authorial audience" rather than "reader" not only to respect the role reserved for the "reader" or "lector" who "performs" the text by reading (or reciting) it aloud, but also to underscore the aural and communal context within which Luke expected his work to be experienced, and within which, in practice, it was. One imagines, then, a social context of early Christian worship in which Acts, as one among several early Christian texts, was read aloud as part of a Christian meeting, perhaps after a meal (following the pattern of the Hellenistic symposium), both for edification and for entertainment. The use of Acts as the textual basis for Christian proclamation did not arise until much later (although the second-century writers Irenaeus and Tertullian most certainly knew Acts; Ephraem the Syrian in the fourth century and John Chrysostom in the fifth produced the earliest extant collections of commentaries or homilies on Acts).

In its application to biblical studies, the communication model has often suffered from an overly optimistic view of the autonomy of the text, based on the (often unstated) assumption of what was then known as New Criticism, that a text could be understood best quite apart from its particular social and historical location and was independent of its "author's intentions" (the so-called intentional fallacy; cf. Wimsatt and Beardsley 1954). The gains of this approach in NT studies, especially in terms of refocusing the interpreter's attention on the final form of the text as we have it, rather than historical events, or literary or oral sources, or the evangelist's mind, are well documented and thoughtfully critiqued (Moore 1989). The communication model, however, presumes a closer cultural and historical relationship between author, text, and audience, and if we rightfully demur from the notion of "authorial intention" as being too fraught with psychological overtones, we may nonetheless still speak of the "intention of the text" (*intentio operis*; cf. Eco 1992) as a way to emphasize the primacy of that first communication between Luke the author and his "intended audience," the authorial audience.

The aim of this commentary, in keeping with the overall goals of the series in which it is published, is to read the final form of Acts within the early second-century historical, cultural, rhetorical, and theological contexts in which it was composed (as well as the mid-first-century contexts, which it purports to recount). The focus here is on the earliest reception of the final form of Acts. As such, the rubrics of author, text, and audience serve as helpful reminders of the importance of the first communication between author and audience in the form of a written text within its historical context. Exploring the author, in terms of issues of composition, and the audience, in terms of its reception and formation, allows the focus to remain on the text itself, not as an autonomous entity removed from its historical moorings but rather as a written communication between author and audience deeply embedded and implicated within its historical circumstances. The history of interpretation plays a role, in the sense that knowledge of it can give clues as to the important issues raised by the text as they have been understood over the history of the reception of Acts within the Christian community. Contextualizing the text in this way also allows theological issues of interest to contemporary Christian communities to arise naturally out of the exegetical treatment.

The Author and Issues of Composition

Most discussions of the authorship of Acts center on the author's identity (see, e.g., Parsons 2001, 12–21, 54–55). Such debates typically assess the reliability of the traditions associating Acts with "Luke the Beloved Physician" and the problems of identifying the author's ethnic identity (Gentile, Jew, or a God-fearing Jewish sympathizer). Luke's ethnic identity is less important for interpretation than acknowledging that he situates the Christian community within the larger Jewish debate about self-identity. Here, clearly, Luke understands the Way to be a movement within first-century Judaism (see below and especially Theological Issues on 9:32–11:18).

Luke as Historian and Theologian

Surveyors of the Lukan landscape typically categorize the scholarship on Acts in terms of interest in Luke the historian, Luke the theologian, and, more recently, Luke the litterateur. The move from form and source criticism (Dibelius 1956 et al.), which focused on Luke as historian, to redaction criticism (Conzelmann 1960 et al.), which focused on Luke as theologian, to the newer literary studies (Tannehill 1986–1990 et al.), which focused on Luke as creative writer, have been well documented in the surveys of Acts research (see esp. Powell 1991). The attention Acts has generated has not always been positive. As a historian, though he had his defenders (see Ramsay 1906, Gasque 1975, Hemer 1989, Marshall 1990), Luke was routinely criticized for his unreliable depictions of various characters (e.g., Vielhauer 1966, 33–50, on Paul) and events (e.g., Knox 1950 on the Jerusalem conference). As a theologian Luke was accused, among other things, of advocating a triumphalistic "theology of glory" that was inferior to Paul's "theology of the cross" and of replacing the pristine eschatology of early Christianity with a three-stage salvation history—an "early Catholicism" shaped by the delay of the parousia that represented a degenerative step away from the primitive Christian kerygma, which proclaimed the imminent return of Jesus (so Käsemann 1982, 89–92). Even Luke's abilities as a writer have been called into question from time to time (see Dawsey 1986).

While these issues are pursued in more detail at specific points in the commentary, suffice it to say here that Luke's theological agenda is rich and nuanced and can hold its own in comparison with Pauline or Johannine theology, against which it is often measured and found lacking. Luke tells the story of the first followers of Jesus in such a way as to highlight that community's heritage in the scriptures and experience of Israel and at the same time to chronicle the new thing God has done through the death and resurrection of Jesus, Israel's Messiah, especially in terms of the inclusion of the Gentiles into the newly constituted people of God. Luke's use of Jewish scriptures and covenantal, especially Abrahamic, language and concepts are addressed throughout the commentary (see especially Theological Issues on 3:1–4:31; 6–7). This community is called to bear faithful witness to the resurrected Lord, even as it suffers for that witness throughout the Roman Empire.

In terms of Luke as historian, Acts suggests an author deeply committed to historical verisimilitude, a commitment that rests in part on Luke's determination to get the story straight. A modern reader, however, must recognize that getting the story straight in an ancient context does not imply that Luke "got it right" historically in terms of every detail (though neither is Luke free simply to "make stuff up"). Rather, Luke's commitment to verisimilitude is just as much a reflection of Luke's training in rhetoric as it is a reflection of his knowledge of ancient historiography. Quintilian wrote, "It is possible to make sound use of anything that is naturally sound" (*Inst.* 2.10.3, trans. Brett Butler, 1921).

Luke and Rhetoric

To understand Luke either as theologian or historian, we must first understand his skills as a writer. And while modern literary criticism has been successful in raising the question of Luke as litterateur, it has not yet been able to circumscribe it fully. In part this is due to reliance on categories and concepts based on the modern novel and not categories and concepts derived from antiquity. To understand the historical verisimilitude and theological message of Acts, one must first understand the rhetorical strategies and conventions employed by the author. Thus issues of composition are of singular significance in this commentary and mark its distinctive, and perhaps most important, contribution to the interpretation of Acts.

This conclusion is based firmly on the assumption that the historical and theological content of Acts—the "what" of Luke's message—is irreducibly shaped by and inextricably interwoven with the "how" of Luke's message,

Species of Ancient Rhetoric

George Kennedy gives a concise and clear summary of the different kinds of rhetorical speech practiced in antiquity:

"There are three species of rhetoric, a theory formulated by Aristotle (Rhet. 3.1.1358a) and universally found in subsequent writers: judicial, deliberative, and epideictic. Although these categories specifically refer to the circumstances of classical civic oratory, they are in fact applicable to all discourse. The species is judicial when the author is seeking to persuade the audience to make a judgment about events occurring in the past; it is deliberative when he seeks to persuade them to take some action in the future; it is epideictic when he seeks to persuade them to hold or reaffirm some point of view in the present, as when he celebrates or denounces some person or some quality."

Kennedy further recognizes that "in a single discourse there is sometimes the utilization of more than one species, and the definition of the species as a whole can become very difficult" (Kennedy 1984, 19). This is certainly the case with some of the speeches in Acts, although it is a helpful exercise to attempt to understand the rhetorical conventions at work in the individual speeches.

that is, the ways in which Luke has shaped Acts into a well-formed narrative, drawing upon all the figures of speech and literary conventions at his disposal through his training in ancient rhetoric.

Studies of the speeches in Acts show that Luke was more than competent in the handbook tradition, and it is possible to analyze the speeches in Acts in terms of their rhetorical species (cf. Kennedy 1984, 114–40; Neyrey 1984, 210–23; Black 1988, 1–8; Morgenthaler 1993; Satterthwaite 1993, 337–79; Soards 1994). Scholars, for the most part (though cf. Taylor 1946), have been reluctant to apply these insights to the narrative portions of Acts. One reason for hesitation has been the recognition that the rhetorical handbook tradition represented by Cicero, Quintilian, and others is aimed at training orators for declamation; that is, their focus is on delivering oral speeches, not on writing narratives. This reading of the handbooks, of course, fails to appreciate that Quintilian, Cicero, and the others generously quote examples from various Greek and Latin epics, histories, poetry, and other works. Still, the reluctance is understandable.

Based on the speeches, it is fair to conclude also that Luke would have cut his rhetorical teeth, as it were, on the *progymnasmata* tradition. The *progymnasmata* were "handbooks that outlined 'preliminary exercises' designed to introduce students who had completed basic grammar and literary studies to the fundamentals of rhetoric that they would then put to use in composing speeches and prose" (Braun 1995, 146). As such, these graded series of exercises were probably intended to facilitate the transition from grammar school to the more advanced study of rhetoric. Four of these *progymnasmata* from the first to fifth centuries AD have survived: Theon (first century?), Hermogenes (second century), Aphthonius (fourth), and Nicolaus (fifth) (collected and translated in Kennedy 2003).

What is important about these writings is that some of the exercises in the *progymnasmata* are clearly intended to embrace both written and oral forms of communication. For example, in his chapter "On the Education of Young Students," Aelius Theon remarks:

> So then, I have presented these things, not thinking that they are all suitable for all beginners, but in order that we might know that training in the exercises is absolutely necessary, not only for those who are going to be orators, but also if anyone wishes to practice the art of poets or prose-writers, or any other writers. These things are, in effect, the foundation of every form of discourse. (*Prog.* 70.24–30, trans. Kennedy 2003, 13)

Thus though the rhetorical handbooks and the *progymnasmata* often address the same topics, the *progymnasmata*, aimed as they are in equipping young students with the building blocks of communication, both written and oral, serve as a kind of filter for the handbooks to sift out what comments might be more appropriate for written communication.

Furthermore, George Kennedy observes:

> The curriculum described in these works, featuring a series of set exercises of increasing difficulty, was the source of facility in written and oral expression for many persons and training for speech in public life. . . . Not only the secular literature of the Greeks and Romans, but *the writings of early Christians beginning with the gospels* and continuing through the patristic age, and of some Jewish writers as well, *were molded by the habits of thinking and writing learned in schools.* (emphasis added; Kennedy 2003, ix)

If the last part of Kennedy's comment is true and if Luke at least, among the gospel writers, was familiar with the rhetorical exercises similar to those discussed by Theon and others, then a thoroughgoing investigation into the rhetorical conventions of Luke is warranted. Throughout the commentary (often in sidebars), the rhetorical strategies, conventions, and figures of speech

---

Identifying Figures of Speech

Cataloging the rhetorical figures of speech helps contemporary readers understand how the rhetoric functions in Acts. Luke's audience would not necessarily have been able to identify these figures by their technical names. But they were used to listening to speeches and hearing texts read aloud and would have responded appropriately to these figures.

Consider the "I Have a Dream" speech delivered August 28, 1963, by Martin Luther King Jr. from the steps of the Lincoln Memorial in Washington, DC. The speech is replete with rhetorical figures and devices. In addition to allusion, metaphor, alliteration, hendiadys, and so on, the speech makes especially effective use of epanaphora (cf. *Rhet. Her.* 4.13.19), the repetition of a word or phrase at the beginning of a sentence. In addition to the repetition of the title phrase, "I have a dream," the speech repeats the phrase "let freedom ring" eight times. Furthermore, the speech ends with an effective use of transplacement, the reintroduction of a word or phrase "so as to render the style more elegant" (*Rhet. Her.* 4.14.20): "Free at last, free at last, thank God Almighty, we are free at last." Few modern hearers could name the rhetorical figures at work in King's speech, but the power of its rhetoric is undeniable, and looking at the rhetorical figures helps explain that power.

The analysis of rhetorical figures and devices in the commentary is aimed at helping the modern reader recover some sense of the rhetorical effect on the ancient audience. We may apply to rhetorical figures in general the words of an ancient rhetorical treatise regarding figures involving repetition: "There inheres in the repetition an elegance which the ear can distinguish more easily than words can explain" (*Rhet. Her.* 4.14.21, trans. Caplan 1954, 281).

and thought reflected in Luke's composition of Acts are explored. The analysis is by no means exhaustive, but rather limited to those instances in which knowledge of the relevant rhetorical device sheds additional exegetical light on the passage's meaning. This leads to a discussion of the text and issues of intertextual relationships.

The Text of Acts and Issues of Intertextuality

Narrowly speaking, discussions of the "text" of Acts as a matter of critical introduction usually refer to issues related to the manuscript evidence for the writing and issues of textual criticism. While the term is used here more broadly to speak of issues related to the work itself (rather than the author or audience), it is wise to begin with this more narrow understanding.

The Textual Traditions of Acts

To speak of the "final form" of the text of Acts is to engage in the issue of the distinctive textual traditions of Acts, most commonly referred to as the "Alexandrian" and "Western" texts. The so-called Western text is most commonly identified with, but not exclusively limited to, Codex Bezae (D in Acts). It is approximately 8 percent longer than the Alexandrian tradition. We can illustrate the character of many of the Western readings by considering the four verses in Acts that are now omitted in most critical Greek editions and English translations:

And Philip said, "If you believe with all your heart, you may." And he replied, "I believe that Jesus Christ is the Son of God" (8:37; a Western addition found in E, many minuscules, it[gig, h] vg[mss] syr[h with *] cop[G67] arm; Codex D is not extant for 8:29–10:14).

But it seemed good to Silas that they remain, and Judas journeyed alone (15:34; Codex D; cf. the Majority Text, which reads: "But it seemed good to Silas to remain there").

And we would have judged him according to our law. But the chief captain Lysias came and with great violence took him out of our hands, commanding his accusers to come before you (24:6b–8a; a Western addition found in E, 1739, it[gig] vg, etc.; Codex D is not extant from 22:29 to the end).

And when he had said these words, the Jews departed, holding much dispute among themselves (28:29; a Western addition found in 383 614 it[gig, p] vg[mss] syr[h with *]; Codex D is not extant from 22:29 to the end).

In each case, these additions attempt to expand upon or clarify the immediate context. In all four verses the Western tradition was taken up into the Byzantine or Majority Text, which was the basis for the earliest English translations with versification, including the Authorized or "King James" Version. This association with the Majority Text (and not necessarily their connection to the Western tradition) accounts for the inclusion of the verses in early Greek editions and English translations of Acts. Once it was determined that the variants in question were not part of the "original" text, the editors and translators of the various Greek editions and English translations, rather than renumbering the verses from that point forward, opted rather to omit the verses altogether (as they did in other places in the NT). Thus these variants are chosen to illustrate the differences in the Western tradition of Acts, not because they are the most important, exegetically speaking, nor the most controversial, but simply because these are the first places at which a contemporary reader of Acts in translation is most likely to encounter the issue of textual traditions.

Despite arguments that the Western tradition holds priority over, or at least equal footing with, the Alexandrian text (Clark 1933; Boismard and Lamouille 1984; Strange 1992), this commentary, for the most part, accepts the critical consensus regarding the generally secondary and derivative nature of the Western text of Acts, and follows the critical edition of NA^{27}/UBS^4, which itself is based primarily on the Alexandrian tradition (cf. the history and evaluation of the textual traditions of Acts by Head 1993, 415–45). Occasionally the commentary will treat textual variants as they might shed light on the meaning of a particular passage (for more detailed treatment, see Culy and Parsons 2003).

Acts, Luke, and the Other Gospels

This excursion into textual criticism raises questions regarding the relationship between Acts and Luke (interest in the question of unity has reemerged since Parsons and Pervo 1993; see Rowe 2005, 2007; Johnson 2005; Bockmuehl 2005; Bird 2007; Spencer 2007). Perhaps it is best to begin with what textual criticism can *not* tell us about that relationship. Contra Kirsopp Lake (1933) and the various versions of this argument by Amos Wilder (1943), Hans Conzelmann (1960), and Philippe Menoud (1962), there is no manuscript evidence to support the contention that the ascension narrative in Luke 24 was added after the two works were separated (Menoud actually argued that both ascension accounts were interpolations after Luke and Acts were divided upon acceptance into the canon).

Each document has its own distinct reception history (see Gregory 2003, 300–301), a point that speaks against a precanonical "narrative" unity of the two documents. For example, the evidence of early gospel collections fails to support an original unity (Parsons and Pervo 1993). The oldest copy of the fourfold Gospel, P[45] (ca. AD 200), also contains Acts, but has the gospels in the traditional order: Matthew, Mark, Luke, and John. Codex Bezae preserves the so-called Western order of the two apostles (Matthew and John), followed by the two "apostolic companions" (Luke and Mark). Here Luke and Acts could easily have been placed together, but Mark stands between Luke and Acts. Thus a great opportunity was missed to place Luke last in the order and alongside Acts, preserving both the *Tetraevangelium* and the unity of Luke and Acts. The Cheltenham Canon (c. 360) and the stichometry of Codex Claromontanus (seventh century) place Luke last among the gospels, but Acts comes after the Pauline epistles in the former and at the end of the NT books in the latter. P[74] (seventh century) puts Acts with the General Epistles (see Parsons and Pervo 1993, 22). The inescapable conclusion is that there is simply no manuscript evidence in which Luke and Acts appear side by side, ready for reading as a continuous whole. Some have countered that the reception history does not necessarily reflect authorial intention, and in the case of Luke/Acts most certainly does not (Johnson 2005). But is this necessarily the case?

The fact that the textual history of Acts is distinct from Luke's other volume, the Third Gospel, is not always fully appreciated in discussions of the relationship between Luke and Acts from the point of view of *intentio operis*. As Bruce Metzger notes, "The text of the book of the Acts of the Apostles circulated in the early church in two quite distinct forms, commonly called the Alexandrian and the Western" (Metzger 1994, 222). The same has not, and indeed cannot be said about Luke's gospel. Furthermore, while the Western tradition of Acts shares with Luke (as well as the other gospels and Pauline corpus) "minor variants that seek to clarify and explain the text and make it smooth . . . there are variants of another kind, peculiar to the Western text of Acts" (Metzger 1994, 233). These variants

> include many additions, long and short, of a substantive nature that reveal the hand of a reviser. . . . The reviser, who was obviously a meticulous and well-informed scholar, eliminated seams and gaps and added historical, biographical, and geographical details. Apparently, the reviser did his work at an early date, before the text of Acts had come to be generally regarded as a sacred text that must be preserved inviolate. (Metzger 1994, 233)

Regardless of how one accounts for the origins of these two textual traditions of Acts (Metzger 1994, 225–32), their existence provides further support for the conclusion that Acts has its own distinctive transmission history and points to a circulation of the text of Acts, independent of the Third Gospel.

The little evidence that we do have, then, does not suggest that these two documents, Luke and Acts, were "published" together by Luke as one volume or even published at the same time, only later to be separated from one another with the emergence of the fourfold Gospel. Rather, the manuscript traditions suggest two distinct transmission histories, one for the Gospel and one for Acts. This implies at least that the two were published and disseminated separately, and quite probably at different times.

The prologue to the Third Gospel (1:1–4) suggests that Luke writes, in part, because he thinks that previous attempts at gospels have proven unsuccessful in producing a rhetorically persuasive narrative (see Parsons 2007). On the basis of Luke's reference to "many" other attempts to write accounts of Jesus' life, it seems that a plurality of gospels was already a reality by the time the Third Gospel was written (probably in the '80s or early '90s). The number and content of these other "gospels" is unknown; the "many" (even if hyperbolic) may have included "heretics" who "used traditional material in the interest of their own perverse propaganda" (Danker 1988, 24). In this sense, Luke may have been partially successful in replacing some of these previous "attempts," of which he is critical (and thus contributed to the loss of some early accounts that are no longer extant). Nevertheless, Luke probably did not think his version of the Jesus story would replace *all* other versions. And even if he did, he knew better by the time he published Acts. His account of "the things accomplished" had taken its place alongside other versions. Thus Luke writes Acts in the full knowledge that it would be read as a "sequel," not just to the Third Gospel, but to a plurality of narratives about Jesus, what would later be dubbed simply "the gospel" (of which there emerged four authoritative versions, but still of *one* gospel). These gospels (Luke and Mark and an indeterminate number of others) were already being read together in Christian worship by the time Acts was published.

We should not dismiss those other "attempts" at writing a gospel as possible *sources* for Acts (cf., e.g., Mark 14:57–58/Acts 6:13–14 *et passim*), but Luke used the Third Gospel as the primary narrative for structuring Acts, thus accounting for the many parallels between Luke and Acts (cf. Talbert 1974). In other words, with Acts, Luke follows up the basic plot of the Third Gospel, while presuming knowledge on the audience's part of at least some of the "many" who undertook to write a narrative about Jesus (some of which are perhaps no longer extant; cf. the *agraphon* in Acts 20:35). We should not be surprised, then, to find Acts following the basic plot and structure of the "primary" narrative, Luke, while echoing other "Jesus-stories," only some of which are still accessible to the modern reader.

From a plurality of gospels would eventually emerge the notion of one gospel in four versions, indirectly attested by the longer ending of Mark, which presumes a fourfold Gospel in the early second century (see Kelhoffer 2000). When canonizers/collectors placed Acts after the fourfold Gospel (whether in the "Eastern" or "Western" order), they were actually fulfilling the *intentio operis* that Acts be read as the sequel to the "Gospel" (albeit in ways Luke could not perhaps have fully anticipated) and not somehow distorting it.

Thus, from the point of view of the authorial audience (see below), Acts is read and heard as a follow-up to the Jesus story. Acts is written before this plurality of Jesus stories is textualized (possibly reduced in number, then collected and published) in the fourfold Gospel, but after the public use of multiple gospels in liturgical settings. In other words, the fourfold Gospel is the culmination of an earlier liturgical practice and theological reality of multiple gospel usage in local congregations. In sum, the question of Luke's intent and the audience's reception are perhaps much closer than usually allowed; at least we would do well to resist a facile conclusion that the canonizers "botched" the job. As a result, it is a minor (some twenty non-Lukan gospel parallels or echoes are noted), but distinctive, aspect of this commentary to note, at least in passing, the non-Lukan materials in Acts that are parallel to the extant gospels (and an occasional conjecture regarding a now "lost echo") and their effect on the reading of Acts.

Acts and Genre

Another debated issue of text and intertextuality is the question of the genre of Acts (for a helpful survey, see Phillips 2006). The Acts of the Apostles has been variously compared to the genre of ancient biography (Talbert 1974, 1977, 1992), the ancient novel (Pervo 1987), ancient epic, whether Roman (Bonz 2000) or Greek (MacDonald 2003), or most frequently with some type of historiography (e.g., general history, Aune 1987; political history, Balch 1985, 1987, 1990; Deuteronomistic history, Brodie 1990; or apologetic history, Sterling 1992). No one of these arguments has emerged as the critical *opinio communis*; rather the emerging consensus seems to be that Acts represents a blending of genres (Phillips 2006, 384–85), a consensus that even includes some of those who had earlier advocated a specific generic designation (see Talbert and Stepp 1998, 178–79; Pervo 1999, 135; Balch 2003, 141). Understanding Acts as a foundational or charter document for the Christian community— that is, as a document that seeks to establish the identity of its constituency as legitimate and true heirs of Moses within the larger panoply of ancient Greco-Roman religions and philosophies—requires it to be read in conversation. That conversation must include not just one other genre of literature but rather all those documents that share or contest its field of vision, regardless of generic designation.

Acts and the Pauline Letters

What more may we say of the relationship of Luke to Paul? Long ago Philipp Vielhauer raised the historical issue regarding whether Acts gives evidence that Luke knew and was influenced by Paul. Over against the still dominant conclusion that there is little connection between the Paul of Acts and the Paul of the Epistles (Vielhauer 1966) a number of protests have been lodged (inter alia, Walker 1985, 1998; Porter 1999). Whether or not the "historical" Luke knew and traveled with the "historical" Paul (cf. Fitzmyer 1989, 1–26), the literary issue of the relationship of the book of Acts to Paul's letters remains. This is a related, but nonetheless slightly different issue than the one posed by Vielhauer. Richard Pervo has recently offered compelling evidence that Luke was familiar with Paul's life and thought through a collection of some of his extant letters (see Pervo 2006).

How then would an audience familiar with Paul through his letters hear Luke's story of Paul in Acts? This question is addressed intermittently throughout the second half of the commentary. To anticipate the conclusion, the overall picture of Paul in Acts is not exactly identical to the Paul of the letters (who, we do well to remember, is itself a projected rhetorical persona), but there are nonetheless similarities between the two portraits (cf. Parsons 2007, 123–37).

Dating Acts

These comments also touch upon the issue of the date of Acts. As we suggested, the separate transmission histories of Luke and Acts, as well as the separation of the two works in all known collections and lists, make it more likely that the two documents were published and disseminated at different times than that an original single work (for which we have no external evidence) was subsequently divided. Knowledge of a collection of Paul's letters would push the *terminus a quo* for the dating of Acts to the beginning of the second century (see Pervo 2006; also Tyson 2006). If we grant the critical consensus that the Third Gospel was written in the last quarter of the first century (in the '80s or '90s), and accept Luke's knowledge of Paul's letters (see above and throughout the commentary), then we arrive at a *terminus a quo* for Acts of no earlier than the beginning of the second century (Pervo 2006). Thus twenty to thirty years lapsed between the publication of the two documents. What can be said about a *terminus ad quem* for Acts?

In his *Letter to the Philippians*, Polycarp refers to Jesus "whom God raised, loosening the birth pangs" of Hades (1.2). The phrase occurs verbatim at Acts 2:24, in which Peter refers to Jesus "whom God raised, loosening the birth pangs" of Death (or Hades, so D and some Latin, Syriac, and Coptic MSS). What is striking is that the distinctive phrase "loosening the birth pangs" is found nowhere else in the LXX (though it alludes to Ps 18:4–6) or any other extant Jewish or early Christian literature. As Andrew Gregory has observed: "It is certainly unlikely that Luke and Polycarp would each have adopted the form independently" (Gregory 2003, 314). Rather than appeal to an earlier and hypothetical testimony book (so Barrett 1994, 36), the simplest solution is to conclude that Polycarp knew Acts (see Zahn 1909, 2:186; Berding 2002, 39–40; Hartog 2002, 185). Other possible allusions then fall into place with this conclusion (cf. Pol. *Phil.* 2.1 / Acts 10:42; *Phil.* 2.3 / Acts 20:35; *Phil.* 3.2

/ Acts 16:12–40; *Phil.* 6.3 / Acts 7:52; *Phil.* 12.2 / Acts 26:18; 8:21; cf. Barrett 1994, 36–37; Gregory 2003, 314 n. 24).

The disputed composition history of Polycarp's letter, however, further complicates the situation. Those who follow P. N. Harrison's multiple letter theory (Harrison 1936) would date Polycarp, *Philippians* 1–12, to about AD 135; in this scenario Acts could be dated as late as AD 120–130. William Schoedel (1967), however, has argued cogently for the unity of the letter. The letter was written shortly after the martyrdom of Ignatius, which, following Eusebius (*Hist. eccl.* 3.36.1), is traditionally dated toward the end of Trajan's reign (ca. AD 110–117, and possibly connected with Trajan's eastern trip in 114). The date for Polycarp's letter would then be about AD 115 (see Hartog 2002, 60, 169). The date of Ignatius's martyrdom, however, is by no means certain since the accuracy of Eusebius's report, given his apologetic interests in securing as early a date as possible for Ignatius, cannot simply be assumed (on the difficulties of dating the martyrdom, cf. Foster 2006). Others prefer a date of about 125 for Ignatius's martyrdom, during Hadrian's reign (AD 117–138; cf. Pervo 2006, 17–20). Michael Holmes prudently concludes: "Perhaps the most that can be said with any degree of confidence is that Ignatius probably died sometime during the first third of the second century" (Holmes 2006, 62). Thus I would place the date of the publication of Acts at about AD 110, though a release anytime within the first two decades of the second century (ca. AD 100–120) would have provided sufficient time for Polycarp's knowledge of the book.

In this scenario Acts is published several decades after the publication of the Third Gospel. In the intervening period, the liturgical use of a plural-form Gospel would be securely in place and a collection of (an indeterminate number of) Paul's letters would be widely known. It is within this historical framework that I place the first reception of the final form of Acts.

The Overall Structure of Acts

In its final form, Acts divides into halves, 1–12 and 13–28. The first half of the book deals with the people and places of the Jerusalem church; the second half focuses on the missionary activities of Paul. Additionally, each half is subdivided into two sections: 1–12 consists of 1:1–8:3 and 8:4–12:25; 13–28 is composed of 13:1–19:41 and 20:1–28:31. Luke has used the rhetorical device called chain-link interlock to connect these four units of Acts (Lucian, *How to Write History* 55; Quintilian *Inst.* 9.4.129; cf. Longenecker 2005). Part 1 (Acts 1–7) is linked to part 2 (Acts 8–12) by 8:1–3. Part 2 (Acts 8–12) is linked to part 3 (Acts 13–19) via 11:27–12:25; and part 3 (Acts 13–19) is linked to part 4 (Acts 20–28) by 19:21–41. Furthermore, each of these major units may be segmented into smaller units. The two halves are symmetrical (but not perfectly so). Acts 1–12 is constructed of nine text segments or episodes (five in the first section and four in the second) and comprises 43.6 percent

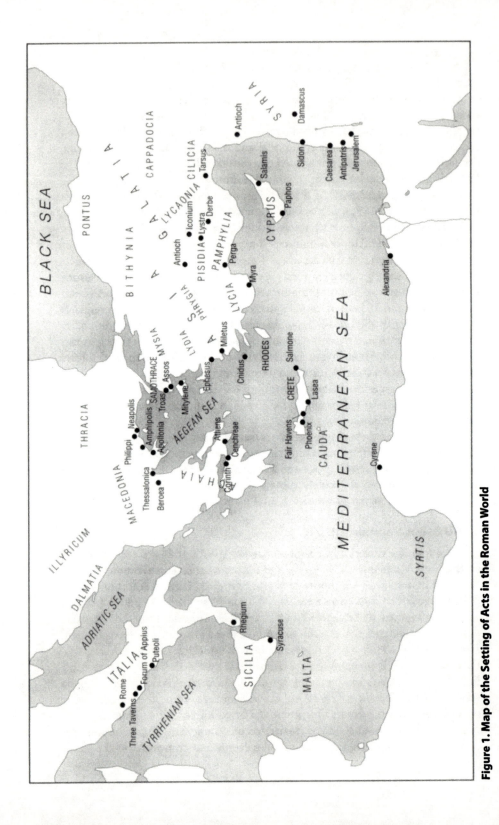

Figure 1. Map of the Setting of Acts in the Roman World

of the Greek text; Acts 13–28 has nine segments (five in the third section and four in the fourth), constituting 56.4 percent of the text. The accompanying outline shows the structure of Acts; throughout the commentary more detailed outlines will show this structure in closer detail.

The Audience of Acts and Issues of Reception and Formation

Interest in the "reader(s)" or "audience" of biblical texts has soared in recent decades (see Fowler 1991; Powell 1990). Understanding the terminology of reader-oriented interpretations, however, is not always easy. This commentary attempts to consider two kinds of readers or audiences: the constructed "authorial audience" and real, flesh-and-blood contemporary Christian communities, although the focus in the commentary proper is clearly on the former.

The Authorial Audience of Acts

This commentary is written from the perspective of the authorial audience, that is, the reception of the text by the audience that the author had in mind when he wrote his Gospel (cf. Rabinowitz 1987; Carter 1996; Talbert 1998, 2003; Parsons 2007). It is important to tease out the implications of this fact for understanding the impact of Luke's writings upon his authorial audience, which presumably also knew how to respond appropriately (if unconsciously) to the effects of persuasive rhetoric, with an eye toward how they might illuminate our understanding of how Luke told his story of Jesus' first followers; that is, the rhetorical strategies and literary conventions he employed and the ways they might have been understood by his audience.

An Outline of Acts

The people and places of the Jerusalem church (1–12)

  The sense of a beginning (1–7)

    The beginning of the church (1)

    The miracle and meaning of Pentecost (2)

    The healing of a lame man (3:1–4:31)

    Tensions within and without (4:32–5:42)

    Stephen and the Seven (6–7)

  Beyond Jerusalem: Philip, Saul, Peter, and others (8–12)

    Philip: a man on a mission (8)

    Saul and Ananias: conversion and call (9:1–31)

    Peter: his words and deeds (9:32–11:18)

    Barnabas, Peter, and Herod (11:19–12:25)

The missionary activities of Paul (13–28)

  Paul's mission to the Gentile world (13–19)

    Paul's initial missionary campaign (13–14)

    The Jerusalem conference (15:1–16:5)

    Paul in Macedonia (16:6–17:15)

    Paul in Achaia (17:16–18:17)

    Paul in Ephesus (18:18–19:41)

  Paul's farewell journey (20–28)

    Paul's last journey to Jerusalem (20:1–21:16)

    Paul in Jerusalem (21:17–23:35)

    Paul before Felix, Festus, and Agrippa (24–26)

    The sea voyage to Rome (27–28)

Thus the commentary attempts to understand the ways in which the final form of the Acts of the Apostles was received by the authorial audience. The authorial audience is not a real flesh-and-blood audience; it is nonetheless historically circumscribed. The effort, then, is both historical and hermeneutical, and it is important to outline the parameters of that historical task. First, Luke's authorial audience is not to be mistaken for a specific second-century community; in other words, there was no "Lukan community" per se whose interests and needs we can tease from between the lines of Luke's Gospel (Johnson 1979). Rather, Acts (and Luke) were addressed to a general Christian audience, living in the Roman Empire at the turn of the second century (Bauckham 1998, 9–48). Thus Acts is read in its historical context, but as Richard Bauckham says, "That context is not the evangelist's community. It is the early Christian movement in the late first century" or, as we presume, early second century (Bauckham 1998, 46). For this reason, attempts to locate the provenance of either the author or the audience have failed to create a critical consensus, and more telling, have proven mostly irrelevant for interpreting the text.

For purposes of the commentary I assume that both Luke and the authorial audience of Acts were familiar with the cultural scripts and rhetorical conventions of the larger Greco-Roman world, scripts and conventions that were extant in specific documents that they may or may not have known. The audience is also familiar with the basic themes of the Jewish scriptures (especially regarding the inclusion of the "righteous Gentile"), other Second Temple Jewish literature (or at least the prominent themes that those documents preserve and reflect), and other early Christian literature, including an early collection of Paul's letters, some gospels (certainly Mark, possibly Matthew), and perhaps some other writings.

The commentary focuses on how the authorial audience heard Acts within the web of other texts and contexts familiar to that audience. We ask, "What would be the rhetorical impact of such 'intertextuality' on the authorial audience?" The issue is the way in which these cultural scripts and rhetorical conventions are echoed and reconfigured in this new text. This kind of intertextual exploration takes into account the rhetorical conventions, social scripts, and theological concepts reflected in those texts and with which the audience would likely have been familiar.

Luke also understood his task as having hermeneutical implications. Education, or *paideia*, in the ancient world (not unlike today in many quarters) "was based on the transmission of an established body of knowledge, about which there was wide consensus" (Cribiore 2001, 8). The transmission of traditional values included also the formation of the moral character of the students (or audience) (Penner 2003, 425–39). Theon of Alexandria, author of the earliest of the extant *progymnasmata*, confirms this point several times: "Surely the exercise . . . not only creates a certain faculty of speech but also good character [*ethos*], while we are being exercised in the moral sayings of the wise" (Theon, *Prog.* 60.18, trans. Kennedy 2003, 4; see also 71.6; 78.9). Beyond acquiring facility in grammar and rhetoric, a fortunate by-product of the rhetorical exercises from the teacher's point of view was the shaping of moral habits that reflected the prevailing cultural values of the day.

At the same time that Luke acquired the ability to read and write through his rhetorical education, he also learned *ethos* argumentation, that is, how to shape the moral character of his audience and thus how to inculcate those values in the student/audience's moral vision. The moral vision propagated by the progymnasmatists was elitist, racist, and sexist. The ideal was the free, male Roman citizen; all others were deemed inferior (Gleason 1995). While Luke invokes the methods and categories of rhetorical argument, he often does so only to subvert or overturn them, a rhetorical move of *ethos* argumentation that he no doubt learned from the very teachers of grammar and rhetoric whose moral vision he so severely challenges (Parsons 2007). In its place, Luke offers a vision of God's family that is inclusive of Jew and Gentile, rich and disenfranchised, male and female, slave and free, the physically whole and the physically disabled. Luke's use of rhetoric is aimed at forming the moral character and theological vision of the Christian community so that the followers may more faithfully imitate the founder, Jesus the Christ (for a similar argument, see Bockmuehl 2006).

The Contemporary Christian Audience(s) of Acts

The contemporary Christian community is invited to participate in this vision, to adopt the point of view of the authorial audience Luke had in mind. Of course, such imitation of the authorial audience by a real contemporary Christian community, removed by space and time, can only be approximate at best, and may entail, from time to time, acknowledging contextual differences. For example, the contemporary Christian reader, living in a post-Holocaust context, must acknowledge the difficulty and difference in hearing Luke's story of the conflict between the first followers of Jesus and other Jewish groups, as Luke intended it, as an intra-Jewish debate (see Theological Issues on Acts 9:32–11:18).

The contemporary Christian readers of Acts are also implicated in their own web of texts and cultural scripts. In addition to, and perhaps more important than, the history of Acts scholarship, with which the contemporary reader may (or may not) be familiar, is the liturgical and aesthetic contexts within which many modern Christians experience Acts, if only indirectly. Furthermore, within those Christian communities that adhere explicitly to some form of Christian confession or creed, it is interesting to note that in the Pelikan and Hotchkiss collection of nearly three hundred creeds and statements of faith from a wide variety of confessional communities there are nearly twelve hundred references to Acts (Pelikan and Hotchkiss 2003). Such theological issues are raised explicitly in the commentary only on occasion (see, e.g., the discussion of the Triune God in Theological Issues on 20:1–21:16), but it is helpful to recall constantly how Acts "has been prayed and sung in [the church's] liturgy, confessed in its creeds and confessions of faith, [and] defended by its seven ecumenical councils" (Pelikan 2005, 26), since these are the liturgical and confessional contexts within which we most often encounter the Acts of the Apostles.

The liturgical and creedal use of Acts may seem foreign to those contemporary Christians who come from a "low church" background. This unfamiliarity with the explicit liturgical use of Acts should not, however, be mistaken for the absence of Acts from their own distinctive forms of worship. The worship and theology of Pentecostals, for example, are profoundly shaped by a particular appropriation of the book of Acts. Furthermore, the hymnody of "free church" traditions draws deeply from the rich resources of Acts (cf. for example, the nearly thirty references to Acts in the scripture index of *The Baptist Hymnal*, 1991). Rarely if ever does this contemporary context take the forefront in the exegetical section of the commentary, but it forms a useful background against which to read and use the commentary.

The Theological Issues sections of the commentary draw on interpretive issues of interest to the contemporary Christian community, whose "preunderstanding" of Acts is shaped to varying degrees by these diverse liturgical and theological influences. Luke's own commitment to this formation of Christian character functions as the springboard for these reflections. Sometimes the "theological issues" involve the context of the larger Christian canon. At other times, the history of the interpretation of the text is brought to bear. As the meaning(s) of the text for the authorial audience comes into focus, the implications for the contemporary faith community become more transparent. This is not to suggest that the Theological Issues sections exhaust the possible topics for consideration; rather, they should be viewed as "conversation starters," and as attempts to extend Luke's spiritual formation of his audience into faithful disciples who can know more fully the truth of the matters in which they have been instructed.

The Sense
of a Beginning

The first part, Acts 1–7, centers primarily on the activities of Jesus' followers in and around Jerusalem. It traces events involving key persons in the early Christian movement: Peter and the apostles, the selection of the Seven, and the martyrdom of Stephen. It is clear from the opening pages that the movement known as "the Way" was one of several expressions of first-century Judaism(s).

Acts 1–7 in Context

The people and places of the Jerusalem church (1–12)

▶ The sense of a beginning (1–7)

The beginning of the church (1)

The miracle and meaning of Pentecost (2)

The healing of a lame man (3:1–4:31)

Tensions within and without (4:32–5:42)

Stephen and the Seven (6–7)

Beyond Jerusalem: Philip, Saul, Peter, and others (8–12)

The missionary activities of Paul (13–28)

Paul's mission to the Gentile world (13–19)

Paul's farewell journey (20–28)

Acts 1

The Beginning of the Church

⊡

Introductory Matters

The opening chapter of Acts serves not only to set the stage for the emergence and spread of the earliest Christian community; it constantly refers back to the previous story of the founder of that community, Jesus of Nazareth. Acts 1:1–14 functions as the introduction to the book. The remainder of the first chapter (1:15–26) is devoted to the accounts of the defection of Judas from the circle of the Twelve and the selection of his successor.

Tracing the Narrative Flow

Introduction (1:1–14)

The surface structure of 1:1–14 falls into three parts: Acts 1:1–5 represents the literary preface—the introduction proper—and includes several formal features common to prefaces of antiquity. Acts 1:6–11 describes the departure of Jesus and the response of his disciples and borrows elements from Greco-Roman and Jewish assumption scenes. Acts 1:12–14 forms a summary statement at the end of the episode and

> **Acts 1 in the Narrative Flow**
>
> **The people and places of the Jerusalem church (1–12)**
>
> **The sense of a beginning (1–7)**
>
> ▶ The beginning of the church (1)
>
> Introduction (1:1–14)
>
> Preface to Acts (1:1–5)
>
> Departure of Jesus and response of the disciples (1:6–11)
>
> Narrative summary (1:12–14)
>
> Death of Judas and election of Matthias (1:15–26)

as such represents a common literary convention employed by Luke to provide transition from one episode to the next.

1:1–5. The presence in 1:1–5 of a "secondary" preface (which refers to an earlier work) does not, in and of itself, demonstrate narrative unity. Sequential books in antiquity employed any one of three types of prologues (see Palmer 1987, 427–38): (1) Some writers presented a summary of the preceding book and an outline of what was covered in the present volume (see Polybius, *Hist.* 2.1.4–8; 3.1.5–3.3; see also his explanatory note in the fragments of book 11; Diodorus Siculus, *Hist.* 1.4.6–5.1; Philo, *Mos.* 2.1). (2) Others give a retrospective summary of the preceding book and move directly into the contents of the present work (see Xenophon, *Anab.*; Josephus, *Ant.*; Herodian, *Hist.*). (3) Still others give a prospective summary, but do not mention the previous volume (see Appian, *Hist. Rom.* 1.13–15; Diodorus Siculus, *Hist.* 2.1; Eusebius, *Hist. eccl.* 7.praef.). Luke apparently followed the first pattern of a retrospective summary and an outline of what was to follow. Acts contains a brief, retrospective summary, which describes the contents of the Third Gospel as what **Jesus began to do and teach until the very day he was taken up** (1:2). A prospective outline of the contents of Acts is given in 1:8. This prefatory summary was, as we have seen, a typical literary convention of antiquity (Lucian, *Hist. conscr.* 23).

Thus the narrator has chosen to present a retrospective summary and a prospective outline of the contents of Acts, similar to, but not in exact correspondence with, the first option. By crediting Jesus with the outline and by shaping it into the form of a promise, the narrator creates audience expectations that the witness to the gospel will be fulfilled "to the end of the earth." Are these expectations fulfilled?

In addition, Acts 1:1–5 exhibits several literary conventions typical not just of sequels but generally characteristic of narrative beginnings in late antiquity. The first is the presence of a first-person narrator in the preface (see Philo, *Mos.* 1.1; Diodorus Siculus, *Hist.* 1.3.1). Such narration is used in both Luke and Acts to provide a frame for the story (see Luke 1:1–4; 5:14; Acts 23:22; for a similar rhetorical device, see also Josephus, *BJ* 1.76; *Ant.* 1.100; Arrian, *Anab.* 5.11.4; John 3:15–16). First-person narration facilitates the move of the audience from a point of view external to the story to an internal point of view—the audience moves from the position of arm-chair spectator to full participant in the story.

A second convention is the naming of **Theophilus** (1:1) as addressee. Historically, these names in antiquity are believed, in many cases, to represent a benefactor/client relationship between the named person and the author (see Aelius Aristides, *Hier. log.* 51.63; Horace, *Carm.* 1; *Sat.* 2; Josephus, *C. Ap.* 1.1; Dionysius of Halicarnassus, *1 Amm.*1.2; Hermogenes, *Invent.* 3.1). Regardless of the historical background, from a literary perspective Theophilus functions to circumscribe the reception of Acts. To imitate the authorial audience of Acts, the real reader must assume the posture of Theophilus, a "lover of God." Theophilus, then, functions as a hermeneutical bridge between the narrative world of the text and the "real world" of the audience. The naming of Theophilus here in Acts 1, of course, also recalls the mention of Theophilus in Luke 1. Evoking Theophilus at the beginning of the narrative is a literary strategy that reminds the audience of the previous volume, Luke, and provides the authorial audience with entry to the narrative world of Acts.

The authorial audience recognizes that the command not to **depart from Jerusalem but to wait for what the Father had promised** (1:4) echoes Luke 24:49, but Jesus' note that **John baptized with water, but you will be baptized with the Holy Spirit** (1:5) more closely resembles the Markan form (Mark 1:8) of that saying than either Matt 3:11 or Luke 3:16 (both of which add "and fire" to "Holy Spirit").

1:6–11. The ascension account in Acts 1:6–11 borrows its formal features primarily from Greco-Roman assumption stories, while its terminology is heavily dependent on the assumption stories of Elijah. The ascension of Jesus contains several features common to Greco-Roman (and some Jewish) assumption stories: (1) A mountain as the site of the assumption is one common element found in many Greco-Roman assumption stories (Lucian, *Hermot.* 7; Apollodorus, *Bibl.* 2.7.7; Minucius Felix, *Oct.* 22.7; Diodorus Siculus, *Hist.* 3.60.3; Aurelius Victor, *Vir. illustr.* 2.13; see Acts 1:12). (2) Clouds are typical elements in both Greco-Roman and Jewish assumption stories (Apollodorus, *Bibl.* 2.7.7; Dionysius of Halicarnassus, *Ant. Rom.* 1.77.2; Plutarch, *Num.* 2.23; *T. Ab.* 8.3; 10.2; 12.1, 9; *4 Ezra* 5.7; see Acts 1:9). (3) Appearances by the ascended one figure in several Greco-Roman heavenly assumptions (Plutarch, *Rom.* 28:13; Livy, *Hist.* 1.16.58; Ovid, *Fast.* 2.499–509; Lucian, *Peregr.* 40; Philostratus, *Vit. Apoll.* 8.31).

> ### Litotes
>
> In Acts 1:5, Luke uses *litotes*, a favorite rhetorical device in which a statement is made by negating the opposite idea (see *Rhet. Her.* 4.38.50). Here "not after many days" means "very soon" (for other examples of Lukan litotes, see Acts 4:20; 5:26; 12:18; 14:28; 15:2; 17:4, 12; 19:11, 23, 24; 20:12; 21:39; 25:6; 26:19, 26; 27:14, 20; 28:2; cf. Clark 2004).

In addition to these formal similarities, the ascension account in Acts 1 has several striking parallels with the assumption of Elijah. Especially noteworthy is the use of *analambanō* to describe the assumption of Elijah (2 Kgs 2:9–11; 1 Macc 2:58; Sir 48:9) and the ascension of Jesus (Acts 1:2, 11, 22).

Whether Jewish or Greco-Roman, these assumption stories accentuate the elevated status of their subjects. Likewise, the ascension of Jesus functions to underline the exaltation of Jesus. It is the fitting conclusion to the ministry of Jesus (so Luke 24:50–53); more important here, it is the foundation of the church, which makes the life of the church both possible and intelligible.

Ironically the departure of Jesus inaugurates the beginning of the church—the gift of the Holy Spirit at Pentecost and the beginning of the worldwide mission.

In addition to the significance of the ascension for Luke's story and theology, these opening verses focus as much on the response of the disciples to Jesus as they do on his words and deeds. This second section contains two parts, and each concludes with a reproof of and a promise to the disciples. In Acts 1:7–8, Jesus responds with a reproof: **It is not for you to know the times or seasons that the Father has established by his own authority** (1:7; cf. Matt 24:36); and a promise: **But you will receive power when the Holy Spirit comes upon you and you will be my witnesses** (1:8a; see Talbert 1984, 6–7). The promise of the Holy Spirit for empowering the witness of the disciples is found also in John 15:26–27. This empowerment will enable the disciples to engage in a worldwide mission, **beginning in Jerusalem, throughout Judea and Samaria, and to the end of the earth** (1:8b; cf. Matt 28:19–20).

Likewise, at the conclusion of 1:9–11 we read the angelic response in two parts: a reproof, **Galileans, why are you standing (there) staring at the sky?** (1:11a), and a promise, **This Jesus, who was taken up from you into the sky, will come (back) in the very same manner that you saw him go into the sky** (1:11b; cf. Luke 21:27).

Despite the reproaches, both dialogues end with promises to the disciples, thus inviting a favorable judgment of the disciples by the audience. In fact, from this group Peter emerges as the protagonist for much of the first half of the narrative. The identification of the audience with the disciples has already been strengthened in what precedes the ascension narrative. At 1:2 we learn that Jesus chose the apostles through the Holy Spirit. In Acts 1:3, we find that Jesus appeared to them for forty days. The specific reference to "forty days" may be explained by recognizing: (1) the number forty has a rich Jewish heritage (see Exod 24:12–18; *2 Bar.* 76.1–4); and (2) the dating of the Pentecost requires that the hiatus between Easter and Pentecost be filled—Luke fills the gap with the forty days of instruction and the (implied) ten days in which the disciples pray and choose a successor for Judas. Jesus' response does not indicate that the restoration of Israel is impossible, but it does challenge the norms of the disciples and the audience. The burning issue is not "When will the kingdom be restored to Israel?" Rather, it is "Who is commissioned to spread the good news on worldwide missions?"

Through being taught by the risen Lord, praying together with one accord, and performing the delicate and crucial task of selecting Judas's replacement without incident, the formal features of the opening scene depict the disciples as informed, spiritually mature, and administratively equipped—all signs that they are prepared to undertake the task of worldwide mission that lies before them (cf. Matt 28:19–20).

Jesus' ascent into heaven is described in "earth-bound" terms, not as a heavenly journey in which the narrator accompanies the hero (as is the case in many heavenly journeys in late antiquity). Luke employs the rhetorical figure of *conversio* (*antistrophē*), that is, the repetition of the same word or group of words at the end of successive clauses, sentences, or lines (*Rhet. Her.* 4.13.19). The phrase "into the sky" (or "heaven") occurs four times in rapid succession, emphasizing that Jesus is taken from the eyes of the disciples and thus from the audience's "visual" field.

Another literary device employed by Luke is the rhetorical question (Quintilian, *Inst.* 9.2.7). In Acts 1:11 the two messengers ask: **Galileans, why are you standing (there) staring at the sky?** Again, just as the disciples' question to Jesus in 1:6 seemed reasonable, so also their actions seem most natural. What else should one do when Jesus ascends except stand and look into heaven after him? But idly gazing into heaven is an inappropriate response to Jesus' ascension. The messengers assure the disciples (and audience) that Jesus will return in just the same way he left.

1:12–14. The Mount of Olives is the locale of Jesus' departure (1:12–14; contra Bethany in Luke 24:50). The fact that Bethany was located on the Mount of Olives, while easing historical concerns, serves only to heighten the literary significance of the variation. Though both narratives tell of the disciples' return to Jerusalem, they differ in regard to their specific destination and the activity that occupies them. In Luke the disciples return with joy to the temple and are incessantly blessing God. In Acts, on the other hand, the disciples return to the upper room where they **devoted themselves together to prayer** (1:14). The reference in Luke to Bethany is appropriate because it closely links the closing scene with the triumphal entry scene at 19:28–40. The closing scene of the Gospel, set as it is in Bethany, becomes Jesus' triumphal exit. In the same way that the triumphal entry closes the journey of Jesus to Jerusalem, so the triumphal exit brings an end to Jesus' exodus.

The reference to the Mount of Olives as the site of the ascension in Acts (1:12) not only recalls the triumphal entry scene (19:29, 37), but also Luke 21:37 and 22:39.

Contentio

In Acts 1:11, Luke uses the rhetorical figure of *contentio* (anthithesis) to make his point regarding Christ's return. *Contentio* is the juxtaposition of contrasting words or ideas. The author of *Rhetorica ad Herennium* cites several examples, including: "In a situation requiring all your coolness, you are on fire; in one requiring all your ardour, you are cool" (4.15.21, trans. Caplan 1954, 283). He concludes: "Embellishing our style by means of this figure we shall be able to give it impressiveness and distinction."

Such distinction (and impressiveness) is evident in Luke's use of the figure in 1:11: "This Jesus, who was taken up from you into the sky, will come (back) in the very same manner that you saw him go into the sky."

The reference at 21:37 is to Jesus teaching in the temple during the day and lodging at the Mount of Olives at night. Luke alone of the evangelists records that the place to which Jesus returned was the Mount of Olives (Luke 22:39). Important here is the narrator's effort to inform the audience that the Mount of Olives was a familiar place to Jesus. The specific reference to "the place" (Luke 22:40) indicates he has prayed here before.

The next (and last) reference to the Mount of Olives in the Lukan writings is in this passage. By means of redundancy the narrator has brought to mind the prayer scene on the mountain. Jesus has again taken his disciples to a favorite place—here is an element of repetition. This time, however, when they return from Jerusalem they do what they were unable to accomplish prior to the arrest—they pray. Again the authorial audience is assured of the disciples' readiness and competence to be witnesses of the gospel.

The disciples return to the **upstairs room** (1:13a). This word is not the same used to describe the room where Jesus ate the Passover meal with his disciples (Luke 22:12), yet the identification of the two seems most natural, and the reference here serves to strengthen the connection made above between the prayer scene on the Mount of Olives and the ascension in Acts.

Luke provides a "laundry list" of the disciples who have gathered together in the upper room (cf. Luke 6:13–16). The names of the disciples in Acts 1 are the same as those in Luke 6, though the order is slightly different: Luke's list—"Simon, whom he named Peter, and Andrew his brother, and James and John"—is shuffled in Acts to read **Peter, John, James, Andrew** (1:13b). The shift may be the result of a kind of "pecking order"—an observation supported by the fact that only the first three named in Acts receive any attention beyond this list (on Peter and John, see Acts 3–4; the only further mention of James, brother of Zebedee, is the brief notice regarding his death in 12:2). A similar phenomenon occurs in the list of the seven Hellenists in Acts 6 where only the first two mentioned, Stephen and Philip, receive any attention in the narrative. The omission of Judas's name from the list, of course, prepares the audience for the legend of Judas's death and the choice of his replacement.

To list the successors or followers of a leader was a common device in ancient literature (see, e.g., Diogenes Laertius, *Vit. phil.*; *Aristippus*, 2.85–86; *Plato* 3.46–47; *Zeno* 7.36–38; *Pythagoras* 8.45–46; *Epicurus* 10.22–28). The list of followers is extended in Acts to include women and the family of Jesus, inviting the audience perhaps to revise the definition of disciple and the understanding of who was present at the ascension. To mention **women** is unusual for a succession list. **Mary, the mother of Jesus** (1:14) stands as a bridge figure between the women who followed Jesus (see Luke 8:2; 23:49, 55; 24:10) and the family of Jesus, which (except for James) receives no further mention in the text.

Luke concludes this section with the first of a series of summary statements (see comments on 2:41–47). Following the ascension, Acts 1:12–14 depicts the disciples as fully instructed and appropriately pious—they pray. To be sure, the disciples are not perfect, but the result is that when Jesus exits from the scene, the authorial audience is still left with a group of characters who have been chosen by Jesus through the Holy Spirit, who have been witnesses of his postresurrection appearances and ascension, who have been deputized as ambassadors with a divine mandate, and who, in a short while, will receive what Jesus promised—the gift of the Holy Spirit. In these early chapters, the narrator uses the disciples to shape the audience's view toward a particular understanding of discipleship. The summary here serves both as an expanded conclusion to the ascension story and as a prefatory note that sets the stage for the selection of a replacement for Judas.

Death of Judas and Election of Matthias (1:15–26)

Before Luke can narrate the fulfillment at Pentecost of Jesus' promise that the disciples will be empowered by the Holy Spirit, he must address what for him is a problem of the first magnitude. The circle of the Twelve has been broken and must be restored (Johnson 1977, 175). Acts 1:15–26 divides into three parts: (1) introduction (1:15); (2) Peter's speech (1:16–22); and (3) Election of Matthias (1:23–26).

1:15. Peter stands in the midst of the believers to address this problem of the fall of Judas from the circle of the Twelve (1:15). The situational irony of this first apostolic speech within the post-Easter community should not be lost, an irony created by the similarities in the pre-Easter actions of Judas and Peter. Judas betrayed Jesus (Luke 22:47), thus fulfilling Jesus' prophecy (Luke 22:21–22). Peter denied knowing Jesus three times before three different persons in the courtyard of the high priest (Luke 22:54–62), thus fulfilling Jesus' prophecy (Luke 22:34). The actions of both Judas and Peter are associated with the work of Satan (Luke 22:3; 22:31). And so in Acts 1:15, we have the ironical predicament of the one who denied Jesus retelling the story of the one who had betrayed him.

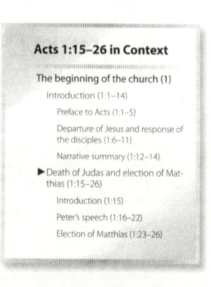

Acts 1:15–26 in Context

The beginning of the church (1)

Introduction (1:1–14)

Preface to Acts (1:1–5)

Departure of Jesus and response of the disciples (1:6–11)

Narrative summary (1:12–14)

▶ Death of Judas and election of Matthias (1:15–26)

Introduction (1:15)

Peter's speech (1:16–22)

Election of Matthias (1:23–26)

Though the actions of both are somehow related to Satan, there is a sharp distinction. "Satan entered Judas" (Luke 22:3) indicates that Judas's actions were under the jurisdiction of the "power of darkness" (Luke 22:53). His act of betrayal and subsequent demise fulfill Jesus' pronouncement of curse: "woe to that one by whom he is betrayed!" (Luke 22:22). In the case of Peter, Jesus' warning, "Simon, Simon, listen! Satan has demanded to sift all of you like wheat," is followed by an exhortation, "when once you have turned back, strengthen your brothers" (Luke 22:31–32). The difference between the two is in the revelation of Jesus to Peter: "but I have prayed for you that your own faith may not fail" (Luke 22:32). The appearance of Jesus to Peter (Luke 24:34; [24:12?]) provides Peter the opportunity to "turn again." The situation of having the "rehabilitated" denier of Jesus speak of the divine necessity for the one who betrayed Jesus to go to his "own place" is certainly justified from the perspective of the narrator. If Judas fulfills the woe of Jesus when he bursts asunder in the field that he has purchased, then Peter fulfills the exhortation of Jesus to "strengthen your brethren" when he stands in their midst and expounds upon the divine imperative of the scripture regarding the fate of Judas and the election of his replacement.

The narrator uses an aside (see Sheeley 1992) to address the audience directly about the size of the assembly gathered with Peter: **the crowd of people together numbered one hundred and twenty people** (1:15). The number is significant since one hundred and twenty is not only a multiplication of the Twelve but also since one hundred and twenty *men* are necessary to constitute a local sanhedrin (*Sanh.* 1.6). Even if Luke is not making the point that the early church is also a "properly constituted" community (see Conzelmann 1987, 10), it is still clear from the narrative that in this newly formed community, women count (see 1:14; also Luke 8:1–3; 23:49).

1:16–22. Because Peter recommends an action in the very near future, namely the replacement of Judas in the circle of the Twelve, his speech (1:16–22) falls into the rhetorical species of deliberative discourse (see "Species of Ancient Rhetoric," p. 8). The speech turns upon the OT quotation cited in 1:20. The first half of the quotation, taken from Ps 69:25, deals with the demise of Judas; the second half, which is a citation of Ps 109:8, addresses the election of Judas's successor. The double use of the *dei* of divine necessity is the textual clue to this division. The shift in tense from imperfect to present also supports the view that the first half of the quotation is addressed by Peter's story of Judas and the second quotation anticipates fulfillment in the election narrative (see Dupont 1961, 41–51).

What Would Peter Say?

That Peter's first speech (1:16–22) is in keeping with his character as developed elsewhere in Acts is not surprising given the fact that one of the progymnasmatic exercises practiced in antiquity was that of *prosōpopoeia*, or speech in character (elsewhere known as *ethopoeia*; cf. Hermogenes, *Prog.* 20, trans. Kennedy 2003, 84; Aphthonius, *Prog.* 34 R, trans. Kennedy 2003, 115), whereby the author attributes to a person words that "are suitable to the speaker and have an indisputable application to the subject discussed" (Theon, *Prog.* 115, trans. Kennedy 2003, 47). In order to present a speech that is suitable, Theon argues that "one should have in mind what the personality of the speaker is like, and to whom the speech is addressed" (Theon, *Prog.* 115, trans. Kennedy 2003, 47).

Peter's story of Judas's demise summarizes the bare essentials of Judas's betrayal found in the Third Gospel and then adds new information presumably not known to Luke's authorial audience. The contrasts between Matthew's version of Judas's demise (Matt 27:1–10) and Luke's account helpfully instruct regarding the distinct perspective of the Lukan Peter. Matthew's account includes: (1) Judas repented and returned the money (27:3–4). (2) The priests are responsible for buying the field for burial (27:7). (3) The name of the field is the result of the use made of the money. (4) Matthew cites scripture (Zech 11:12–13; Jer 32:8–9) to explain the price of the land, not to speak of Judas's fate.

Peter depicts the defection of Judas and his subsequent judgment with the use of money. In the Third Gospel (contra Matthew), Judas does not repent and return the money, but rather, according to Acts 1:18, purchased a field (*chōrion*) with the betrayal money. Such a self-serving purchase not only stands in sharp contrast to the way the believers sold their fields and laid the proceedings at the apostles' feet (see 4:32–35) but also is juxtaposed to the narrator of this story, Peter, who along with James and John "left everything" to follow Jesus (see Luke 5:11). Judas has traded his inheritance (*klēron*) in the apostolic ministry (1:17) for a farm, a symbol of his apostasy from the circle of the Twelve.

Ironically, Judas dies on this same property, according to Acts: **this man purchased a field using the money earned from his unjust deed and after becoming prostrate he burst open in the middle and all his insides poured out** (1:18). The phrase "becoming prostrate" or "falling headlong" (*prēnēs genomenos*) recalls conceptually the prophecy of Simeon that Jesus would be "set for the *fall* and rising of many in Israel" (2:34). There is no hint of suicide here (contra Matt 27); the death is the result of divine judgment and fits into the theme of "the death of the opponent of God" (Conzelmann 1987, 11), and like the account of Herod (cf. Acts 12:20–23) is conveyed in vivid, "ekphrastic" language, meant as much for the eye as for the ear (see Acts 2:1–5). Because Judas meets his death on this property, it is called the **Field of Blood** (1:19). And just as the purchasing of a field symbolized Judas's defection, so also the fact that his property is doomed to perpetual desertion (1:20) is a sign of his judgment.

Appositio

The rhetorical figure of *appositio*, the addition of an adjacent, coordinate, explanatory or descriptive element (Quintilian, *Inst.* 8.6.40–43), has occurred twice now (1:15 and 1:18–19). In the case of Acts 1:18–19, the name "Field of Blood" is explained by Judas's actions. Furthermore, the use of foreign language (here the Aramaic term "Akeldama" or "Field of Blood"), from a rhetorical point of view, is considered a barbarism (*barbarismus*; Quintilian, *Inst.* 1.5.5–33), but nonetheless necessary for Luke. The effect for the audience is to supplement or correct Matthew's explanation of the name.

1:23–26. The account in 1:23–26 presupposes that the authorial audience of Acts is familiar with the practice of casting lots (see Num 26:55; Prov 16:33; 1QS 5.3; Livy, *Hist.* 23.3.7). The crucial feature of this scene is that the number of the Twelve is full again. **Joseph** and **Matthias** (1:23) are put forward, and the assembly prays for divine guidance in the selection process. The result of the prayer is that Matthias is chosen as the replacement.

Note the play on words throughout this scene: Judas has forfeited his share (*klēron*) in the apostolic ministry and goes to his own place (*topos*). In contrast, the lot (*klēron*) now falls to Matthias, and he takes his place (*topos*) alongside the Eleven in the apostolic ministry (on the rhetorical device of using words with multiple meanings, see the sidebar on Acts 4:22). The scriptures are fulfilled, the circle of the Twelve is reconstituted, the stage is set for Pentecost.

Theological Issues

Only Luke and Acts in the NT narrate the departure/ascension of Jesus. By repeating the departure of Jesus in Acts, the narrator has identified the story of Jesus with the story of the church. These two accounts share several common elements. The characters are the same—Jesus and the disciples. In both accounts, this scene is the last appearance of Jesus to his followers. Both stories report Jesus' commission to his disciples to preach "to all the nations" or to "the end of the earth." The command to wait in the city for the promise of the Father is also found in both accounts.

Nevertheless, the variations between the two accounts are striking. The narrative contexts in which these two stories are placed explain several of the variations. The ascension story in Luke functions in its narrative context to bring closure to the Gospel, while the ascension narrative in Acts serves in its context as a narrative beginning (see Parsons 1986b). The role of each account in its respective narrative context largely accounts for the differences in detail.

The most obvious discrepancy is the chronological difference between Luke and Acts. The Gospel appears to date the final departure of Jesus on Easter Sunday; Acts allows a period of forty days during which Jesus appeared to the disciples. From a historical point of view, the difference of the forty days between Luke and Acts is intolerable. The temporal tension, however, is readily explained on literary grounds. To end the Gospel with a reference to forty days of appearances by the risen Lord would destroy the rhetorical effect of the ending of Luke. The end of Luke's gospel is a "close-up" ending with no temporal gap between the body of the narrative and its conclusion. The departure of Jesus occurs on the same day as his resurrection. No epilogue describing the time after the resurrection rounds off the story (as in John). In the narrative context of Acts, however, forty days of appearances are entirely appropriate. Establishing the disciples as reliable and legitimate successors of

Jesus is a major task of the narrative beginning of Acts. The period of forty days is needed to assure the audience that the disciples are "fully instructed" (see Acts 20:20, 27, 31). During this period of time, then, Jesus was "telling them things about the kingdom of God" (1:3).

There is no dialogue in the Gospel account; one sees but cannot hear the action. The scene at the end of Luke is a silent scene. The significance of this silence is that it creates distance between the audience and the characters and facilitates closure. The audience can "see" Jesus and the disciples but is unable to hear them. This framing device creates the literary illusion of space between audience and story and effectively assists the audience in leaving the story world.

In Acts, however, more than half of the account is dialogue. Two speeches by Jesus anticipate the unfolding of the rest of the narrative. First, Jesus promises the disciples that "you will be baptized with the Holy Spirit, not many days from now" (Acts 1:5). This word finds fulfillment in the Pentecost narrative (see Acts 2). Second, in response to the disciples' question about the kingdom, Jesus gives his commission, which effectively serves to outline the rest of the narrative. The unfolding of Acts is in accordance with Jesus' promise that the disciples would be "witnesses in Jerusalem, throughout Judea and Samaria, and to the end of the earth" (Acts 1:8).

The "raising of hands" and the repeated references to "blessing" in Luke are missing from Acts. The "raising of the hands" and the blessing at the end of the Gospel draw a full circle around the story. In the first episode of the Gospel, Zechariah is incapable of discharging his duties as priest; he is unable to bless the people who patiently await his service. He returns home, unable to speak, task unfinished (1:23). At the end of the Gospel, Jesus raises his hands in Levitical fashion (see Lev 9:22; Sir 50:20–22) and blesses his disciples who are also waiting. In effect, Jesus completes what Zechariah could not do; he blesses the people of God. These elements are strong closural devices appropriate to the context of Luke 24:50–53 as a narrative ending, but they are missing in Acts 1:1–11. The variation again occurs because what is appropriate or necessary for a narrative ending is not always appropriate or necessary for a narrative beginning. The benediction at the end of Luke becomes an invocation at the beginning of Acts. The narrator of Luke and Acts has employed the ascension narrative to bring closure to one narrative and provide entrance into its sequel.

There is no need, however, to speak of an "absentee Christology" in Acts. The influence of Jesus throughout the rest of the narrative is profound even though he is absent as a character from the narrative of Acts after chapter 1 (except for appearances in visions). His name occurs no less than sixty-nine times in Acts. He is at the center of the church's controversy with the Jews. He guides the church in its missionary efforts. He empowers the disciples to perform miracles. The ascended and exalted Christ, though absent as a character, is nonetheless present throughout the narrative.

Acts 2

The Miracle and Meaning of Pentecost

Introductory Matters

A. R. C. Leaney nicely summarized the various ways in which Acts 2 has been interpreted as the "reversal of Babel, the proclamation of the New Law, the fulfillment of the prophecy of Joel, of the threat of John the Baptist, and of the promise of Jesus, and an earnest of the spread of the gospel throughout the world" (Leaney 1968, 419). Although the lectionary tradition links Acts 2 with Gen 11, there is little from the ancient historical and religious context to suggest that Luke or his audience would have made such a connection, despite the theological attractiveness of seeing Pentecost as the reversal of Babel.

There is more evidence for linking the Pentecost event with the renewal of the Sinai covenant. Pentecost, or the Feast of Weeks, in the OT was a festival associated with the wheat harvest (Exod 23:16; Deut 16:9–12). The writer of *Jubilees* (second century BC), however, states that Moses is given the law at Sinai in the third month of the year (1.1) and later states that Pentecost (or *Shebuot*) is a festival observed during the third month of the calendar (6.1), thus suggesting an implicit link between the giving of the law and Pentecost, an allusion that is made explicit by the time of rabbinic Judaism (*b. Pesaḥ.* 68b: "It [Pentecost] is the day on which the Torah was given"). Clues in Acts 2 suggest Luke stands in this stream of thought that moves from *Jubilees* to rabbinic Judaism (see Talbert 2005, 23–24; Fitzmyer 1998, 233–35). The sound, fire, and speech in the Pentecost narrative were phenomena associated with the Sinai theophany (Exod 19:16–19; cf. Philo, *Decal.* 9:33), which itself suggests that Luke thinks of Pentecost in terms of a "new covenant" (Talbert

2005, 26). This "new covenant" was foretold by Jesus at the Last Supper (Luke 22:20) and echoes the "new covenant" of Jeremiah (31:31–34). In his speech, Peter makes it clear that receiving the Holy Spirit at Pentecost is the fulfillment of the ancestral promise given to Abraham (Gen 12:3; 22:18). The gift of the Spirit fulfills the promise not only for Peter's Jewish audience (and their children; cf. 2:39), but now "all the nations of the earth," whom Peter calls "all those in the future" who are also blessed (Acts 2:39; cf. Acts 3:25; 22:21; see Dunn 1970, 47).

Just as the Holy Spirit descended on Jesus at the outset of his public ministry (Luke 3:22; 4:1, 14), so now the Holy Spirit comes upon the disciples at the inauguration of their public mission (cf. John 20:19–23). The second chapter of Acts is comprised of three parts: the narrative recounting the Pentecost event itself and its witnesses (2:1–13), Peter's interpretation of Pentecost (2:14–40), and a summary statement, which brings this section to a close (2:41–47).

Tracing the Narrative Flow

The Miracle of Pentecost (2:1–13)

The story of Pentecost fills a gap created when Jesus instructs the disciples to stay in the city for an indeterminate length of time until "they receive power when the Holy Spirit has come upon them" (1:8). We learn in 2:1 that the length of time is fifty days. It has not been idle time for the disciples—they spend forty days being instructed about the kingdom of God by the Risen Lord (1:3) and an unspecified time electing Judas's replacement. Acts 2:1–13 divides into two parts: the event of Pentecost (2:1–4) and the witnesses of Pentecost (2:5–13).

2:1–4. What is the nature of the miracle recorded here in Acts 2:1–4? The coming of the Spirit is joined by two manifestations: a noise from the sky, like a strong blowing wind (2:2), and divided tongues (that looked) like fire (2:3). In describing the event as accompanied by these natural phenomena, Luke is echoing the theophany scenes of the OT, in which God's presence is accompanied by similar signs (Exod 19:16; Judg 5:4–5; cf. Ps 18:7–15; 29:3–9).

Luke is also using the rhetorical strategy of *ekphrasis*, that is, employing language that appeals as much to the eye as to the ear. Theon defines *ekphrasis* as "bringing

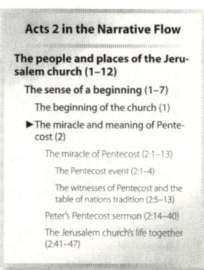

Acts 2 in the Narrative Flow

The people and places of the Jerusalem church (1–12)

The sense of a beginning (1–7)

The beginning of the church (1)

▶ The miracle and meaning of Pentecost (2)

The miracle of Pentecost (2:1–13)

The Pentecost event (2:1–4)

The witnesses of Pentecost and the table of nations tradition (2:5–13)

Peter's Pentecost sermon (2:14–40)

The Jerusalem church's life together (2:41–47)

what is portrayed clearly before the sight." What is portrayed could be "of persons and events and places and periods of time" (*Prog.* 118, trans. Kennedy 2003, 45). An *ekphrasis* of an event could include a description of "war, peace, a storm, famine, plague, an earthquake" (*Prog.* 118, trans. Kennedy 2003, 45). Often an *ekphrasis* was a detailed, verbal description of a visual artifact (e.g., the shield of Achilles in Homer, *Il.* 18.478–608; Dido's murals in Carthage in Virgil, *Aen.* 1.642–699; the canopy over the bed of Anthia and Habracomes Xenophon of Ephesus, *Ephes.* 1.2.5–8), but it is by no means limited to such description.

Given the rather extravagant, even excessive, use of vivid language in many descriptions labeled as *ekphraseis*, some might object to applying that label here to Acts 2:1–4. Theon himself, however, uses the brief description of Eurybates as "round-shouldered, swarthy-skinned, woolly-haired" in Homer (*Od.* 19.246) as an example of an *ekphrasis* of a person (*Prog.* 118). Even if we concede that the Pentecost description is not a full-blown *ekphrasis*, there is no denying the use of "ekphrastic" language, which is similar to what the rhetorical handbooks call *demonstratio*. Pseudo-Cicero defines *demonstratio* as "when an event is so described in words that the business seems to be enacted and the subject to pass vividly before our eyes" (*Rhet. Her.* 4.50.68, trans. Caplan 1954, 405).

The function of *ekphrasis* or ekphrastic language in a narrative is often to draw attention to the significance of the event thus described for the overarching argument of the narrative (Krieger 1992, 7). Such is certainly the case with the use of ekphrastic language in Luke and Acts, in which vivid language is used at key moments in the life of Jesus. At Jesus' baptism, Luke alone reports, "the Holy Spirit descended upon him *in bodily form* like a dove" (Luke 3:22; my emphasis). At the transfiguration scene, "the appearance of [Jesus'] face changed, and his clothes became dazzling white" (9:29). Later in the same scene "a cloud came and overshadowed" Jesus and his disciples (9:34). In the ascension scene described in Acts, Jesus is taken from his disciples' sight by a cloud (1:9), and two men "in white robes" stood by, rebuking the disciples for staring into heaven after Jesus (1:10–11). The ekphrastic language in the Pentecost scene underscores the continuity between the founder of the "Way" and his followers. Significant events in Jesus' life and ministry were depicted in language that appealed to the eye more than the ear. The beginning of the disciples' "public ministry" described in similarly vivid language, marking the disciples' reception of the Holy Spirit.

2:5–13. In 2:5–13, Luke lists witnesses to Pentecost in connection with a list of nationalities reminiscent of the Gen 10 "table of nations." He reports, **A crowd of people came together and . . . heard them speaking in their own language** (2:6). For Luke, Pentecost is as much a "miracle of hearing" as it is of "speaking," a point Peter will later underscore in his sermon (2:33; cf. also the use of "hear" [*akouō*] in 1:7 and 11). Even so, not all hear with understanding in their own native language (2:13).

In Acts 2:5, we read that there were Jews living in Jerusalem, pious men from every nation under heaven. In Acts 2:9–11, representative nations are listed: Parthians, Medes, Elamites, those living in Mesopotamia, Judea, Cappadocia, Pontus, Asia, Phrygia, Pamphylia, Egypt and the parts of Libya adjacent to Cyrene, those who live in Rome—both Jews and proselytes—Cretans and Arabs. While surely no random ordering of nations (pace Fitzmyer 1998, 240), efforts to explain the specific sequence of nations in the list have failed to convince (see Cumont 1909; Metzger 1970, 123–33). The list of nations in Acts 2:9–11 may be taken as an "update" of the table-of-nations tradition found in Gen 10, a point rarely examined by interpreters (though see Scott 1994, 2:483–544). The authorial audience has already been introduced to the table-of-nations tradition in Luke 10:1 in the so-called mission of the Seventy. The mission of the Seventy foreshadows the Gentile mission. From a very early point, then, the audiences (the scribes) connected the mission of the Seventy(- Two) with the table of nations in Gen 10 to symbolize that their mission

Ratiocinatio

The response of the crowd present at Pentecost (2:9–11) is linked to the list of nations present at Pentecost through the rhetorical figure of reasoning by question and answer (*ratiocinatio*). According to the *Rhetorica ad Herennium*, through this figure "we ask ourselves the reason for every statement we make" (*Rhet. Her.* 4.16.23). In this figure persons typically reason with themselves by asking and answering their own questions (hence, this figure is unlike the "rhetorical question," which expects no explicit answer; cf. Quintilian, *Inst.* 9.2.7). *Ad Herennium* lists several examples, including:

> "It is a good principle which our ancestors established, of not putting to death any king captured by force of arms. Why is this so? Because it were unfair to use the advantage vouchsafed to us by fortune to punish those whom the same fortune had but recently placed in the highest station." (*Rhet. Her.* 4.16.23, trans. Caplan 1954, 287)

The author goes on to commend the use of this figure because "it is exceedingly well adapted to a conversational style, and both by its stylistic grace and the anticipation of the reasons, holds the hearer's attention" (*Rhet. Her.* 4.16.24).

Likewise, in Acts, the crowd asks, "Aren't all of these people who are talking Galileans? So how is it that each of us hears (them speaking) in our own native language?" To this they give their own answer by listing the nations present and claiming that the result of the phenomenon is that "we hear them speaking of God's greatness in our own languages!" (2:7–8, 11).

was a universal one. The list of nations also highlights the role of Jerusalem because Jews, living in every nation, have returned there, whether temporarily for the festival or for permanent residence (cf. Acts 6:9). Furthermore, the list of nations given in Acts 2:9 reflects different directions as viewed from Jerusalem: east (Parthians, Medes, Elamites, and residents of Mesopotamia); center (Judea); north (Cappadocia, Pontus, Asia, Phrygia, and Pamphylia), southwest (Egypt and Libya); west (Rome and Crete); and south (Arabia) (Bauckham 1995, 417–27; Alexander 2005, 79).

The authorial audience of Luke/Acts may have been aware of several different streams of tradition, which located Jerusalem in relationship to the rest of the world (for details, see Parsons 2007). From the time of Isa 66:18–20 through writings just prior to (*Jubilees*) or contemporary with Luke (e.g., Philo, Josephus), the table-of-nations tradition had been updated, albeit in varying ways. For the authorial audience familiar with these traditions, the text of Luke/Acts does not explicitly refer to Jerusalem as the "center" of the world, as *Jubilees* 8.12 does (although see the comment above on the geographical directions of the list of nations), nor does Acts limit its role to the land of Israel only, as Josephus does (*BJ* 3.52). Neither does Luke make any explicit use of the tradition that Jerusalem would be (re-)established as the center of the universe in the eschaton (*1 En.* 26.1; *Pss. Sol.* 11.1–7; cf. Isa 66:17–20; Ezek 38:10–12). Luke is closest perhaps to those who claim that Jerusalem is rightly called the "mother city" because Jews live in every part of the inhabited world (so Philo, *Legat.* 281–282), though Luke falls short of ever explicitly referring to Jerusalem as the navel or mother city of the world.

For the authorial audience, presumed to be conversant with these various options for "locating" Jerusalem, Luke locates Jerusalem by drawing on a familiar "thesaurus"; the audience recognizes (1) Luke's use of the table-of-nations tradition (with *Jubilees*, Isaiah, and Josephus); (2) the appeal (with Philo) to the Diaspora to establish Jerusalem's place; and (3) the eschatological setting of many references to Jerusalem (with Ezekiel, *Psalms of Solomon*, *1 Enoch*, and the *Sibylline Oracles*). But Luke's view presents the audience with another alternative, which may be stated negatively: in the final analysis, Jerusalem does not stand in the center of Luke's symbolic world.

If not at the center, then where does Jerusalem stand? It stands at the *end* of the story of Jesus as the goal of his journey and at the *beginning* of the story of the church as the starting point for Christian witness in the world. For Luke, Jerusalem is not the city of the end-time. His symbolic world does not picture the nations swarming to Jerusalem to receive the gospel. Jerusalem is associated with the end only in the sense that it stands at the beginning of the end, the beachhead for the Gentile mission. Thus at the end of Luke's Gospel Jesus commands his disciples, "Thus it is written, that the Messiah is to suffer and to rise from the dead on the third day, and that repentance and forgiveness of sins is to be proclaimed in his name to all nations, *beginning from Jerusalem*. You are witnesses of these things" (24:46–48, emphasis added).

Peter's Pentecost Sermon (2:14–40)

Peter's interpretation of the Pentecost experience is nearly three times longer than the narrative account detailing the event itself. The speech divides into two main parts (2:16–21; 2:22–36), with an introduction (2:14–15) and conclusion (2:37–40). George Kennedy (1984, 117) has further suggested that the speech consists of two species of rhetoric (see the sidebar "Species of Ancient Rhetoric" in the introduction): judicial (with a refutation of the charge of drunkenness, 2:14–21, and an indictment of the Jews for their participation in Jesus' death, 2:22–36) and deliberative (taking the end of the speech, 2:37–40, to demand a decision in the near future).

2:14–15. In 2:14–15, Peter stands again to strengthen the brothers and sisters (see Luke 22:32). His initial address, or proem, is formal and polite: "Men of Judea" (Kennedy 1984, 117). The narrator's introduction (2:14a) anchors the speech firmly within the narrative framework of 2:1–13. The linguistic connections are strong. Peter **raised his voice** (*phonē*, 2:14) in harmony with the sound (*phonē*, 2:6) that had drawn the multitudes to the company of believers in the first place. Furthermore, the word Luke uses to describe the address of Peter to the crowd (**declared**, *apophthengomai*) is the same used to describe the inspired

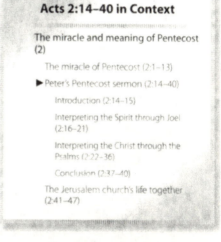

Acts 2:14–40 in Context

The miracle and meaning of Pentecost (2)

   The miracle of Pentecost (2:1–13)

  ▶ Peter's Pentecost sermon (2:14–40)

     Introduction (2:14–15)

     Interpreting the Spirit through Joel (2:16–21)

     Interpreting the Christ through the Psalms (2:22–36)

     Conclusion (2:37–40)

   The Jerusalem church's life together (2:41–47)

speech that the Spirit gave to the believers who were speaking in "other tongues" (see 2:4). The effect is to underline not only that the speech of Pentecost is divinely inspired, but that Peter's interpretation of that event is likewise authoritatively inspired.

The introit of the speech likewise establishes points of contact with the preceding narrative and argues that Peter's sermon is a continuation of the Pentecost event. Peter addresses the **Judeans and all who live in Jerusalem** (2:14b; see 2:5). His sermon is a response to the exasperated question that some of them are posing to each other: "What does this mean?" Some gathered there have already ventured to express their interpretations of the Pentecost experience, and this diverse group of Jews (see the catalog of nations in 2:9–11) is further divided by their understanding.

Refutatio

In Acts 2:15, Peter rejects the charge that the disciples are drunk by use of the common rhetorical strategy of *refutatio*, "an overturning of some matter at hand" (Aphthonius, *Prog.* 101). Students of rhetoric could refute a narrative, *chreia*, or thesis by demonstrating that the claim was incredible with respect to person, action, place, time, manner, and/or cause (Theon, *Prog.* 93–94). Peter refutes the claim that the apostles are drunk on the basis of time (and perhaps also custom; see Theon, *Prog.* 121–122): "These people are not drunk as you suppose, for it is only 9:00 AM!" (2:15). People don't drink at this hour of the day except in the worst cases of debauchery, as in this example referred to by Cicero: "But how many days did you most disgracefully carouse in that villa! From the third hour there was drinking, gaming, vomiting" (*Phil.* 2.41.104; cf. Talbert 2005, 27; Fitzmyer 1998, 251).

If Peter refutes the mockery of some that the believers are drunk (2:15; see 2:13), in the remainder of his speech he affirms the understanding of others that the believers are rehearsing "God's greatness" (2:11). In fact, Peter's sermon is a retelling of salvation history, which now includes a new chapter on the mighty deeds, wonders, and signs, which God has worked through Jesus.

2:16–21. In Acts 2:16–21, the citation of Joel 3:1–5 (LXX) bridges from what precedes to what follows. In addition to functioning as the text for Peter's subsequent interpretation in 2:17–36, the Joel prophecy serves as the authoritative interpretation of the Pentecost event. The sermon proper begins with a pesher-like statement, **this is what was spoken** (2:16), in which Peter asserts that the events narrated in 2:1–12 are the fulfillment of the ancient prophecy.

This radical new community about which Joel speaks and which Peter says is realized in the earliest Christian community is remarkably inclusive. It is gender inclusive: **your sons** and **your daughters** (2:17); **servants—both male and female** (2:18). It is age inclusive: **your young men** and **your old men** (2:17). And if we are to take seriously the opening (**all people**) of this citation, then this community is also destined to be ethnically inclusive.

The Joel citation has been modified by the addition of several significant terms and phrases. That this new community itself is an eschatological sign is underscored by the change from the rather nondescript "after these things" (*meta tauta*) in the LXX text of Joel to **in the last days** (2:17). The Pentecost event is recast here as one of those wonders and signs (2:19) that will precede the coming of **the great and marvelous day of the Lord** (2:20).

That this sermon is inspired, authoritative speech is further underscored by adding **says God** (2:17). Peter had assumed the role of the narrator in this speech, but quickly yields the floor to Joel who, in turn, defers to God. The effect of these narrative layers—"Luke said that Peter said that Joel said that God said"—is to reinforce the utterly reliable and authoritative character of the speech here. The Christian prophet, Peter, stands in direct continuity with the prophet of old, Joel, who stands directly in line with God who is, we learn, the speaker. The Word of the Lord is directly from God (see 7:6 and 15:17–18). This point is underscored by the next Lukan addition to the quotation at the end of 2:18: **and they will prophesy.** This promise is fulfilled not only in the Pentecost event; Peter is fulfilling it himself in this very speech (see comments on 2:14 above).

Another element added to the Joel citations, **signs** (*sēmeia*, 2:19), is perhaps the most significant addition and certainly strengthens the point made above. The further additions of **above** and **below** are needed to complete the parallelism that the narrator has introduced with the addition of "signs."

The phrase "wonders and signs" or "signs and wonders" is a refrain throughout the first half of Acts (see O'Reilly 1987). Of course, it first recurs in the context of this very speech in which Peter refers three verses later to "Jesus the Nazarene—a man who was commended to you by God through miracles, wonders, and signs which God did through him in your midst" (2:22). Jesus

---

Topoi

Cicero, refining Aristotle's categories, defines a *topos* as "the region of an argument, and an argument as a course of reasoning which firmly establishes a matter about which there is some doubt" (*Top.* 2.7–8; see McConnell 2006). Cicero divides *topoi* into intrinsic and external categories and further subdivides the latter into human and divine testimony. About the topos of divine testimony he writes:

"The testimony of the gods is covered thoroughly enough by the following: first, utterances, for oracles get their name from the fact that they contain an utterance (oratio) of the gods; secondly, things in which are embodied certain works of the gods. First, the heavens themselves and all their order and beauty; secondly, the flight of birds through the air and their songs; thirdly, sounds and flashes of fire from the heavens, and portents given by many objects on earth, as well as the foreshadowing of events which is revealed by the entrails (of sacrificial animals). Many things also are revealed by visions seen in sleep. The testimony of the gods is at times adduced from these topics in order to win conviction." (Top. 20.76–77)

Thus a writer may appeal to divine words or deeds in order to persuade the audience to accept his argument. In the Pentecost narrative Luke does both: (1) through *ekphrasis* of "sounds and flashes of fire from the heavens" (as Cicero says), Luke provides divine testimony through a sign; (2) through the quotation of scripture, whose ultimate author, Peter claims, is God himself, Luke appeals to divine testimony through words. Both forms of divine testimony are marshaled by Luke to convince the audience of the importance of the Pentecost event and the reliability of the characters—the disciples—who participated in it.

is the primary referent to God's prophecy that he would work wonders and signs as eschatological portents of the coming "day of the Lord." But Jesus is not the only referent. Others who perform signs and wonders include: the apostles (cf. 4:30; 5:12); Stephen (6:8); Moses (7:36); Philip (8:6, though note the absence of "wonders"); and Paul and Barnabas (14:3; see 15:12; 19:11). Signs and wonders, then, accompany the ministries of the leaders of God's community in unbroken succession, from Moses to Jesus (who is a prophet like Moses, see 3:22), the Twelve, Stephen the Hellenist, and Paul and Barnabas, the leaders of the Gentile mission.

Luke seeks to demonstrate, not that the church is the "new Israel," but rather that it is the "true Israel"; that is, the early church has been more faithful to the traditions of Moses than other Jewish sects making the same claims. Universality is another hallmark of the "true Israel" (see Acts 10–11), and membership in this radically inclusive community is restricted in only one way (and even this restriction is stated in the most open and positive of ways): **And everyone who calls upon the name of the Lord will be saved** (2:21). The identity of this "Lord" is explored in the second part of this sermon (2:22–36), and the call to "be saved" is the focus of the invitation at the end (2:37–40).

2:22–36. The second part of the speech is introduced with a second proem (or introduction): **Israelites, listen to these words!** (2:22). Acts 2:22–36 is also marked with several other appeals for attention that serve as indicators of rhetorical shifts (forming the following chiastic structure; see Krodel 1986, 83):

A The kerygma (2:22–24)
   B Proof from scripture (2:25–28)
      C Interpretation of scripture (2:29–31)
         D The resurrection and exaltation of Jesus and the mediation of the Holy Spirit (2:32–33)
      C′ Interpretation of scripture (2:34a)
   B′ Proof from scripture (2:34b–35)
A′ The kerygma (2:36)

Sections A and A′ set out the christological kerygma (2:22–24, 36). Just as the Lukan narrator of Acts tells the story of Peter and the apostles' time, so now Peter rehearses the story of Jesus' time. The first and longer kerygma includes not only the brief narrative of Jesus' death and resurrection (see 2:23–24); it also refers to the public ministry of Jesus, characterized by **miracles, wonders, and signs** (2:22). This reference not only resumes the theme of signs and wonders noted above (see 2:19); it also echoes Peter's first speech in that among the qualifications for Judas's replacement he includes having been one of those who were associated with Jesus "beginning with the baptism of John until the day he was taken up from us" (1:22; see also 1:2).

Despite the emphasis on the death and resurrection of Jesus, this christological formula has a thoroughly theocentric character. God performed the
mighty works and wonders and signs *through* Jesus (2:22); God **destroyed
the pains of death** and raised Jesus from the dead (2:24). And even though,
Peter says to his audience, **you crucified and killed** [Jesus] **by the hands of
lawless** [Romans], in reality even in Jesus' death, God is in control: this Jesus
was delivered up according to the **fixed intention and foreknowledge of God**
(2:23; on the use of an encomium/invective *synkrisis* here, see the comments
on Acts 3:13–15).

The point that Jesus' death is the result of divine activity is reaffirmed in
the second kerygmatic statement at the end of this section. Here again, Peter's audience is reminded of their culpability in the death of Jesus, **this Jesus
whom you crucified** (2:36). But this kerygmatic statement, like the earlier one,
is thoroughly theocentric: God has made this crucified Jesus **both Lord and
Christ.** This last statement picks up on several previous narrative strands. The
mighty deeds of God (2:11), which were being rehearsed by the spirit-filled
believers (2:11), Peter explains, now include what God has done in and through
Jesus of Nazareth, the crucified one. And finally the ambiguous "Lord" upon
whom all must call for salvation (2:21) is clearly identified as Jesus.

Sections B and B′ offer proof from scripture (2:25–28, 34b–35). The Lukan
Peter arrives at this conclusion in his sermon by employing two proofs, both
quotations from the Psalter. The first is from Ps 16, a psalm quoted elsewhere
in the NT only in Acts 13:35. Though not immediately apparent, the speaker
in this quotation is the Messiah, speaking through the mouth of David, in an
analogous way to God speaking through the prophecy of Joel. The expressions of confidence here echo the last words of Jesus in Luke. There we have
no cry of dereliction (cf. Mark 15:34), but Jesus speaking words of assurance
in the language of the psalmist: "Father, into your hands I commit my spirit"
(Luke 23:46). The Messiah's soul was not abandoned to Hades (Acts 2:27a),
but rather entered Paradise (see Luke 23:43; Krodel 1986, 85–86). And the
key phrase in this citation for Peter is that God did not **allow** [his] **holy one
to experience decay** (2:27b).

The other citation is from Ps 110, a text quoted frequently in the NT. Unlike
the Joel citation, neither of the citations departs significantly from the LXX,
and the importance of these passages is to be found in the interpretation that
the Lukan Peter assigns to them.

Sections C and C′ provide interpretations of scripture (2:29–31, 34a). Why does
Peter choose these two Psalms to support his interpretation of the Joel citation? A
clue may be provided in Peter's reference to David, who **was a prophet and knew
that God had sworn an oath to him to put one of his offspring on his throne** (2:30).
Psalm 16 echoes yet another OT text, 2 Sam 7:13, 16, in which God, through
Nathan, makes the unconditional promise that "the throne" of David would be
established "forever." As a prophet, David not only **foresaw this and spoke of the**

resurrection of the Christ (2:31), he stands in continuity with the other prophets—Moses, Jesus, Peter and the apostles, Stephen, and Paul—to whom God made and kept promises. Hence, both of the supporting proofs from scripture which Peter marshals in his attempt to identify this "Lord" mentioned in the Joel citation (see 2:21) come from the corpus of material traditionally assigned to David: the Psalter.

In Acts 2:29–31, Peter's basic argument is to deny the identity of the "holy one" as David. After all, the death of David is recorded in history, and David's tomb is a matter of public record. He could not be the referent of Ps 16. Rather, Peter argues, David prophesied "the resurrection of the Christ."

Peter makes the same point in the very brief interpretation that precedes the citation of Ps 110: **For David did not go up into heaven, but he himself says, "The Lord said to my Lord, 'Sit at my right hand until I put your enemies under your feet'"** (Acts 2:34–35). In both passages, the interpretation uses a *via negativa* argument to assert that David is not the referent of the two citations. And in the case of the first interpretation, Peter offers the alternative interpretation that the referent is none other than the Messiah. Peter has identified the "Lord" of the Joel citation as the "Messiah"; the way is now left open for him further to identify this messianic figure.

The heart of the Pentecost sermon is to be found in section D, 2:32–33. These verses reverberate in both directions. First, Peter identifies the unnamed Christ who was **neither abandoned in Hades nor did his body see corruption** (2:31) as Jesus (2:32). Here Peter uses *correctio*, a rhetorical figure of speech, which involves amending a term or phrase just employed, often by indicating what something is *not* (*Rhet. Her.* 4.26.36). Further explanation of "resurrection/raised up" is given by describing what it is *not*, namely *not* being abandoned to Hades or corruption of the flesh.

What distinguishes Luke's messianic exegesis from that of his Jewish contemporaries is his identification of this Messiah with Jesus. David foresaw and spoke of the resurrection (*anastaseōs*) of Christ; that is, **God raised this Jesus** (*anestēsen*, 2:32a). These verses also point in the other direction with the link of exaltation language of sitting at the right hand (see 2:33, 34).

Finally, the verses also serve to link the speech with the Pentecost narrative and its interpretive framework provided by the Joel citation. The reference in Acts 2:33 to the **promise** (*epangelion*) that Jesus received **from the Father** recalls the Pentecost event in the same way that Jesus himself anticipated it in Luke 24:49: "And behold, I send the promise (*epangelion*) of my Father upon you." Acts 2:33 further identifies that promise as the **Holy Spirit** (taking the *tou pneumatos* to be an epexegetical genitive explaining the character of the promise; Culy and Parsons 2003, 42). That Jesus **poured him out, as you yourselves see and hear** (2:33) echoes the Joel prophecy ("I will pour out my Spirit") and explicitly interprets Pentecost as a miracle of both sight and sound. Jesus and God seem interchangeable: both are credited with pouring out the Spirit (cf. 2:17 and 2:33). Jesus then fulfills his promise to the disciples that they will be "enclothed with power from on high" (Luke 24:49).

2:37–40. Peter's conclusion to his sermon leads up to Luke's conclusion to this episode. The speech itself is interrupted by the audience, which is cut to the heart and asks Peter and the rest of the apostles, **What should we do?** (2:37). The question is an exact verbal parallel to the question the crowds put to John the Baptist (Luke 3:10). The interruption by the audience is a common device in the speeches in Acts (e.g., Acts 7:54; 22:22; and elsewhere in ancient literature: Appian, *Bell. civ.* 3.51–61; Curtius Rufus, *Hist. Alex.* 6.9.2–24; 7.1.10–40; Tacitus, *Ann.* 16.31) and provides Peter with the opportunity to offer a soteriological conclusion to his sermon: **Repent, [he said,] and be baptized, each of you, in the name of Jesus Christ for the forgiveness of your sins** (2:38a). His invitation echoes the preaching of John the Baptist, who preached "a baptism of repentance for the forgiveness of sins" (Luke 3:3). He also promises that they too will **receive the gift of the Holy Spirit** (2:38b). This **promise** (*epangelia*, 2:39; see 2:33) is not only for Peter's audience, but for their children and **for all those in the future** (2:39). There is a rich ambiguity in this phrase; it may be a temporal reference to future generations, or a spatial reference to Diaspora Jews living in areas beyond Jerusalem and Judea, or, more likely, as an ethnic designation referring to Gentiles who will now be included in God's mercies of salvation (see above and the similar phrase in Acts 22:21). In fact, from the narrator's perspective, all these are true and will, in varying degrees of success, be fulfilled by the narrative's end. The final phrase of Peter's speech, **as many as the Lord our God calls to himself** (2:39), takes the last phrase of the Joel citation (2:21) and turns it on its head. The invitation to salvation is reciprocal: those "who will call upon the name of Lord" will be those whom "the Lord our God calls to himself." Luke indicates that Peter continued his soteriological invitation by bearing witness **with many other words**, which Luke sums up in the *peroratio* (or final exhortation): **Be**

saved from this crooked generation! (2:40), which reiterates the conclusion of the Joel quotation (2:21; see Witherington 1998, 139).

The Jerusalem Church's Life Together (2:41–47)

Luke concludes this section with the first of a series of long summary statements (2:41–47). Some summaries, like Acts 1:12–14, are brief (see 6:7; 8:14; 9:31–32; 11:19–20); others, such as 2:41–47, are longer and more detailed (4:32–35; 5:12–16). These summaries are quite common in the early chapters of Acts and serve a double purpose of dividing and connecting. They divide the narrative into segments, but serve also as connective tissue or "narrative glue," shaping the episodes into a continuous narrative. In that sense, the summaries are Janus-like "revolving doors" that look back at the previous unit and at the same time anticipate the next scene.

In this particular summary the first major section of the narrative beginning of Acts is brought to a close. Jesus departs from the disciples, but only after fully instructing them. The circle of the Twelve is restored with the election of Matthias, and the new eschatological community is formed and sealed with the giving of the Holy Spirit. This new community is the true Israel, a community populated by Jews from every nation under the heavens and a community marked by gender, age, and racial inclusiveness.

The summary begins and ends with reference to the numerical growth of the community (2:41b; 2:47b). In between, the narrator depicts the shared life of the community, which for Luke is the life of the Spirit. The believers who accepted the word and were baptized now devote themselves (2:46; see 1:14) **to the teaching of the apostles and to fellowship, to the breaking of bread and to prayer** (2:42). These four elements characterize the life of the Spirit and are illustrated by the examples given in 2:43–47 (see Johnson 1977, 183–90).

In 2:43, the teaching of the apostles is linked with the signs and wonders that they performed, recalling the opening verse of this narrative, which itself recalled the "first book," which recorded all that Jesus began "to do and to teach" (1:1). The authority of the apostles, as we noted earlier, stands in the prophetic tradition of Moses and the prophet like Moses, Jesus, and fills the believers with reverent awe.

The term *koinōnia* (2:44), here translated "common life," is far more "muscular" in the narrative of Acts than in its popular, contemporary Christian parlance. The first statement denotes a general, universal practice: **All those who believed were in the same place and shared everything** (2:44). The unity of community is empirically demonstrated by their sharing of all possessions (see comments on 1:15–23); it also echoes the practice and custom of ancient friendship, in which "friends have all things in common" (Aristotle, *Eth. Nic.* 9.8.2; see also Plutarch, *Adul. amic.* 65A; cf. Mitchell 1992). This practice is fleshed out in 2:45: **They were selling their properties and possessions and**

distributing (the proceeds from) them to all, as anyone had a need. At this point the apostles presumably play no role in this redistribution (see 4:32–35).

Breaking . . . bread (2:46) is Lukan shorthand for the Lord's Supper and refers to one aspect of the corporate worship of the early church. For Luke, the Eucharist is a revelatory experience with the Risen Lord and the reference here echoes the Emmaus narrative in which the two with whom Jesus ate report to the disciples how Christ was "made known to them in the *breaking of the bread*" (Luke 24:35, emphasis added). Furthermore, by partaking of food with gladness and humility, the community was following the example of Jesus. More than any of the other gospel accounts, the Third Gospel regularly depicts Jesus at table. As one commentator has put it, in the Gospel of Luke, Jesus is "either going to, coming from, or at a meal!" (Karris 1985, 47).

That the believers devoted themselves to prayer (2:42d) is given content here: **They praised God and had favor** (2:47). Their prayer has a vertical dimension in the community praising God (see Luke 24:53), and a horizontal dimension in prayer directed outward to **all the people.** That the inward experience of prayer is confirmed to the community by their dealings with outsiders is a common theme in these opening chapters of Acts. This section ends with the phrase *epi to auto*, which has become the refrain throughout the first two chapters for the deep unity experienced in the community. They are indeed "all together."

Theological Issues

Few, if any, biblical events have lent their name to describe a religious movement, yet this is the case for Pentecost. The full-scale movement known as Pentecostalism dates from the series of meetings held in Azusa Street, Los Angeles, beginning in 1906. Pentecostalism was (and is) grounded on the belief, drawn from its interpretation of Acts 2, that speaking in tongues is the physical manifestation of a person's having received the baptism of the Holy Spirit, an experience that is distinct from and subsequent to conversion and that empowers believers for witness (Dunn 1970, 2). Pentecostalism continues to be a major force in global Christianity, flourishing in all quarters of the world. Not only has Pentecostalism expressed itself in various denominational structures—the Assemblies of God, for example—but Pentecostal experience and theology have swept through all the mainline Protestant denominations and Catholicism as well. For many later Pentecostals, these early beliefs about the "baptism in the Holy Spirit" have hardened into rigid doctrines that tend to require speaking in tongues as a necessary sign of salvation.

On the other hand, resistance to Pentecostalism has caused others to deny the ongoing effects of Pentecost, claiming that the "tongues" described in Acts 2 were not a permanent endowment but were rather limited to the apostolic period as a necessary sign for the inauguration of the church's public ministry, not a practice that was required nor even allowed in modern times (Carver 1916, 24). This view, called "cessationism," also reads the "foundation of the apostles and prophets" in Eph 2:20 as referring to the role of the apostles (including their miracle-working role and use of tongues) as foundational but not continuing. With the passing of the last apostle (or in some variations, with the writing of the NT) miracles and glossolalia ceased. The classic exposition of this view is by B. B. Warfield (1918). A. T. Robertson went so far as to dismiss "modern so-called tongues" as nothing but "jargon and hysteria" (Robertson 1933, 3.22; cf. modern popular critiques of Pentecostalism by Gaffin [1979]; for a critique of cessationism, see Ruthven [1993]).

How do we navigate among these various opinions? The place to begin is with the Pentecost narrative itself. When the apostles speak "in other tongues" (2:4) are they speaking in ecstatic, unintelligible speech (cf. 1 Cor 12–14) or are they speaking in the languages of the many foreign peoples gathered together there? Is this the distinction Paul seeks to make in 1 Cor 13:1 when he refers to the tongues "of humans" (intelligible foreign language) or "angels" (unintelligible, ecstatic speech)? If so, which does Luke intend? There is evidence for both interpretations. Those gathered there heard in their own languages (2:6–7), but others mistakenly believed the disciples were drunk (2:13), suggesting that at least for some the apostles' speech was unintelligible. Some have observed that the miracle at Pentecost was one of hearing not of speaking, in which case Luke may have intended to convey that ecstatic speech was "translated" by the Holy Spirit into language intelligible to the audience—that is, into whatever language they spoke. So the Venerable Bede suggests:

> Was the marvel rather the fact that the discourse of those who were speaking were understood by everyone of the hearers in his own language? So, for example, when any one of the apostles were talking in the assembly (for one person had to speak while the rest were silent, and one discourse had to come within the hearing of everyone) that very discourse had within itself the power that, when there were hearers of diverse nations, each of them would perceive what they heard in terms of his own language and would grasp the meaning of that one and the same discourse which had been uttered by the apostle. (Bede, *Comm. Acts* 2, trans. L. Martin 1989, 60; cf. PL 92.947)

Whatever the nature of glossolalia in the book of Acts, did Luke understand the Pentecost event to be a "once for all" phenomenon? The answer here is simply "No." Filling with the Holy Spirit occurs throughout Acts (cf. 4:31 *et passim*). Likewise, glossolalia is sometimes depicted as the public display of the gift of the Holy Spirit (cf. 10:46; 19:6). But it would be equally mistaken to suggest that tongues are a necessary evidence of baptism in the Holy Spirit (cf. 8:17) or that there is any clear sequence of baptism and reception of the Holy Spirit in Acts. Sometimes baptism precedes reception of the Spirit (8:12–17);

Figure 2. Giotto di Bondone, *Pentecost*, c. 1305. Fresco cycle. Scrovegni Chapel, Padua, Italy.

In this Pentecost fresco, Giotto depicts the descent of the Holy Spirit as shafts of light falling on the heads of the apostles. The apostles are seated within an enclosed space, as in Giotto's earlier depiction of the Last Supper. His depiction of Pentecost as part of a life-of-Christ cycle is unusual in the history of art but in keeping with the role it plays within the Lukan narratives. As C. K. Barrett observed: "In Luke's thought, the end of the story of Jesus is the Church; and, the story of Jesus is the beginning of the Church" (Barrett 1961, 57).

sometimes baptism follows reception of the Spirit (10:44–48); sometimes it accompanies baptism in the name of Jesus and the laying on of hands (19:5–6). All this is to suggest that our current context calls for a middle way that affirms the reality of Pentecostal experience while correcting aspects of extreme expressions of Pentecostal theology.

Acts 3:1–4:31

The Healing of a Lame Man

Introductory Matters

In the history of interpretation, the story of the healing of a lame man (Acts 3:1–4:31) has raised interesting questions with regard to historicity, Luke's presumed use of medical terminology, and literary structure.

Questions of Historicity

Miracle stories such as this one have inevitably circulated at the eye of historical-critical storms. Gerd Lüdemann's representative skepticism toward miracle is still the dominant view in modern NT scholarship: "There is no historical nucleus to the tradition of the miracle story in vv. 1–10. Those who are lame from their childhood are (unfortunately) not made whole again" (Lüdemann 1989, 54). For a defense of the historicity of miracles in Acts, generally, see Colin Hemer (1989, 439–43). On the question of miracles in Acts, see the balanced presentation by Charles Talbert (1997, 251–53).

Purported Medical Terminology

A related issue regarding the healing of the lame is its purported use of medical terminology that "demonstrates" that the author was Luke the physician. Acts 3:7 was a favorite among those who advanced the thesis that Luke's so-called medical vocabulary proved that the author was a physician. W. K. Hobart was probably not the first to comment on this verse, but he surely made more of it than most have. About "feet" he observed that the word was employed to "show that the writer was acquainted with medical phraseology, and had investigated the nature of the disease under which the man suffered" (Hobart 1882; reprint 1954, 35). In typical fashion, he cites Galen and others in support of this claim. Furthermore, he claims that "ankles" (*sphydra*) is "the technical term for the ankles, thus defined by Galen" (Hobart 1882; reprint 1954, 35; cf. Harnack 1907, 191).

By showing the widespread usage of vocabulary in Hellenistic writings that Hobart and Harnack had labeled uniquely or distinctly medical terminology, Henry Cadbury dismantled the thesis that one could "prove" that the author of Luke/Acts was a physician by this medical terminology (Cadbury 1920). Cadbury notes that the term "feet" (*basis*), for example, occurs elsewhere in Plato, Aristotle, Josephus, Philostratus, Aelius, the LXX, and Apollodorus (Cadbury 1920, 13). A search of the Thesaurus Linguae Graecae database for this term produces over sixteen hundred references, confirming Cadbury's general point. A similar search yields well over a hundred references to "ankle" (*sphydron*). It is more profitable to explore this story (and the terms for "ankles" and "feet") in light of the theories and practice of ancient physiognomy (Parsons 2006).

Literary Structure of Acts 3:1–4:31

Acts 3:1–4:31, according to Robert Funk, is a narrative stretch "readily isolated from what precedes and what follows" (Funk 1988, 83). This section is clearly set off from the rest of Acts by narrative summaries on either side (2:41–47; 4:32–37), which are unfocused in terms of spatial definitions and temporal duration. The passage itself displays a certain internal coherence and is divided into four segments or scenes that may be detected by shifts in space, time, and participants. (See figures 3 and 4.) The first two scenes take place in and around the temple: the first (3:1–10) is set at the gate of the temple; the second (3:11–4:4) is set at Solomon's Portico. Both these scenes

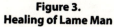

**Figure 3.
Healing of Lame Man**

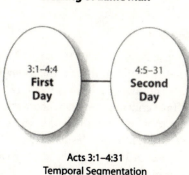

Acts 3:1–4:31
Temporal Segmentation

After Funk 1988, 86

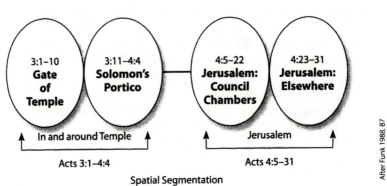

Figure 4.
Healing of Lame Man

Spatial Segmentation

occur on the same day and are united by this common temporal period. After a nocturnal pause between 4:4 and 4:5, the second half of the narrative is set more generally in Jerusalem, but certainly not in the temple area: the council chambers of the religious leaders is the locale of the third scene (4:5–22); the place at which the friends of Peter and John are gathered is the setting for the fourth (4:23–31).

A shift of participants corresponds to these shifts in time and setting. These changes in time, setting, and characters provide clear rhetorical markers for dividing the text into four segments, which are also united by several thematic narrative links. The theme of healing is found in every scene, either with specific reference to the lame man at the Beautiful Gate (3:7, 16; 4:9–10, 22) or to healing in general (4:30). Likewise, references to the name of Jesus are found throughout this stretch of narrative on the lips of Peter (3:6, 16; 4:10, 12), the religious leaders (4:7, 17–18), and the community of believers (4:30).

Tracing the Narrative Flow

At the Beautiful Gate (3:1–10)

Peter and John, like Jesus before them (Luke 5:17–26), and Paul who will follow them (Acts 14:8–18), command the lame to walk, confirming and extending the programmatic ministry of Jesus (Luke 7:22). The healing of a lame man at the Beautiful Gate contains the characteristics typical of a miracle story: statement of the problem ("crippled since the time of his birth," 3:2); description of the cure ("in the name of Jesus Christ of Nazareth, [get up and] walk!" 3:6); and the response to the sign ("and they were utterly astonished at what had happened to him," 3:10b; see Talbert 1984, 18).

3:1–2. The opening verses particularize the general description of the community of believers found in the preceding narrative summary in which "many signs and wonders were being done through the apostles" (2:43) and the believers were daily "(meeting) together in the temple" (2:46). Now two of these apostles, Peter and John, are going to worship in the temple on a specific day at a specific time: the ninth hour, the hour of prayer. With the setting, time, and characters in place, the stage is set for a specific sign of healing (cf. 4:22).

3:3–7. A beggar sits at the Beautiful Gate of the temple doing the only thing he knows to do: begging for alms. An exchange of glances leads the lame man to expect to receive something, but surely not that which he does receive. He begs for "alms" or human kindness and receives the mercies of God. **I do not have any silver or gold,** Peter says, but quickly adds, **but I will give you what I have. In the name of Jesus Christ of Nazareth, [get up and] walk!** (3:6).

> **Acts 3:1–4:31 in the Narrative Flow**
>
> **The people and places of the Jerusalem church (1–12)**
>
> The sense of a beginning (1–7)
>
> The beginning of the church (1)
>
> The miracle and meaning of Pentecost (2)
>
> ▶ The healing of a lame man (3:1–4:31)
>
> At the Beautiful Gate (3:1–10)
>
> Introduction (3:1–2)
>
> The healing (3:3–7)
>
> Reactions to the healing (3:8–10)
>
> In Solomon's Portico (3:11–4:4)
>
> Before the Sanhedrin (4:5–22)
>
> Reunited with friends (4:23–31)

The name of Jesus Christ is here introduced into this story and will remain the focus of attention throughout this section of narrative. The lame man's feet and ankles are made strong. Why mention this detail? The physiognomic handbooks from antiquity provide some illumination.

In the ancient world it was a commonplace to associate outer physical characteristics with inner qualities, a world in which it was assumed that one can, as it were, judge a book by its cover. The study of the relationship between the physical and the moral was known as "physiognomy." In the earliest extant treatise on this topic, the author of the pseudo-Aristotelian tractate claims: "The physiognomist takes his information from movements, shapes, colors, and traits as they appear in the face, from the hair, from the smoothness of the skin, from the voice, from the appearance of the flesh, from the limbs, and from the entire stature of the body" (806a.28–34). This method is based on the assumption that "soul and body react on each other; when the character of the soul changes, it changes also the form of the body, and conversely, when the form of the body changes, it changes the character of the soul" (808b.12–15).

Feet and ankles are also the object of physiognomic consideration. About ankles, pseudo-Aristotle writes:

> Those who have strong and well-jointed ankles are brave in character; witness the male sex. Those that have fleshy and ill-jointed ankles are weak in character; witness the female sex. (*Physiogn.* 810a.25–29)

Adamantius, likewise, comments on the importance of ankles:

> Perfect, solid ankles belong to a noble man, those which are soft and smooth to a more unmanly man and those which are very thin to a cowardly and intemperate man. All those who have thick ankles, thick heels, fleshy feet, stubby toes, and thick calves are for the most part stupid or mad. (Adamantius, *Physiogn.* 7, trans. Swain 2007, 521)

The comments about feet (here the more familiar *podes*) are similar:

> Those who have well-made, large feet, well-jointed and sinewy, are strong in character; witness the male sex. Those who have small, narrow, poorly-jointed feet, are rather attractive to look at than strong, being weak in character; witness the female sex. Those whose toes of the feet are curved are shameless, just like creatures which have curved talons; witness birds with curved talons. (ps.-Aristotle, *Physiogn.* 810a15–22)

In Polemo, we find another description:

> If you see contracted, strong feet, and their tendons are straight and strong, and their joints are evenly proportioned, these are the signs of powerful and mighty men. If the feet are very fleshy and soft, they indicate weakness, softness, and laxity. (*Physiogn.* 5.15–19, trans. Swain 2007, 397)

In a culture pervaded by the "physiognomic consciousness," "well-made" ankles and feet are a sign of a "robust character"; conversely, the lame man's weak ankles would have been viewed as an outward physical sign of his inner weak moral character, his *malakos* ("soft," "timid," "cowardly," or "effeminate") nature. This weakness is confirmed by his presentation in the narrative as a passive participant. The lame man "is carried"; "he is laid daily at the gate"; "Peter took him by the right hand" and "raised him up."

That the audience would have viewed the lame man negatively is further confirmed by the attitude in antiquity toward the disabled generally and the lame specifically. The disabled, especially the lame, were objects of ridicule and derision. As an example of this kind of ribald and denigrating humor, consider also Plutarch who "informs us that the typical kinds of commands which an insensitive symposiarch or master of drinking might give to test the guests' ability to hold their liquor included ordering a stammerer to sing, a bald man to comb his hair, *or a lame man to dance on a greased wineskin*" (*Mor.* 621E; emphasis added).

Whether lame worshipers were formally and ritually excluded from the first-century temple is a hotly debated and probably irresolvable issue (see Jeremias 1969, 117; Gaventa 2003, 84; Olyan 1998, 218–27). Nonetheless, the location of the lame man at the threshold of the temple enclosure suggests that the authorial audience would have inferred from this reference that the man was socially ostracized, lying, as it were, "outside" the boundaries of institutional religion.

The physiognomic understanding of weak ankles and feet combined with the reality of the derision of the disabled in Greco-Roman society, and the possible social exclusion hinted at by his location "outside" the gate would have caused the audience of Acts 3–4 to view the lame man as a thoroughly negative character, a morally weak and passive man, who is unable to stand on his own two feet.

The strengthening of the lower extremities would be an outward sign of his newly found inner moral strength of character, what pseudo-Aristotle calls *eurōstos* ("stout," "strong," or "robust"). Though Luke does not use the term *eurōstos*, he shows the restored "vigor" and "robustness" of the lame man's character through the physical manifestations of standing and walking (Acts 3:9). The outer physical healing thus provides empirical proof for the inner moral and spiritual transformation, a point underscored by the double sense of *sōzō* in 4:9 as both "heal" in a physical sense and "save" in a moral/spiritual sense, a double entendre that conforms nicely to physiognomic expectations.

3:8–10. What are we to make of the lame man's actions? He jumped up, stood (there), and then began walking. He went with them into the temple, walking and leaping and praising God (3:8). Form-critically this action is typically labeled the "demonstration of healing," but it certainly goes beyond the typical demonstration (cf. Luke 5:25; Acts 14:10). The references to leaping and praising God should, in the first instance, be taken as a spontaneous

Commutatio in Acts 3

In 3:8, Luke highlights the healed man's action through the use of the rhetorical figure of speech known as *commutatio* ("reciprocal change"), a kind of repetition of contrasting ideas in a chiastic pattern: "He jumped up (*exallomenos*) . . . then began walking (*periepatei*) . . . walking (*peripatōn*) and leaping (*allomenos*)."

Compare with the anonymous *Rhetorica ad Herennium*'s examples: "You must eat to live, not live to eat. . . . A poem ought to be a painting that speaks; a painting ought to be a silent poem." The author of this treatise comments: "One cannot deny that the effect is neat when in juxtaposing contrasting ideas the words are also transposed" (4.28.38).

response of exhilarating joy at having his body restored and being able, for the first time, to become ambulatory. The leaping is also symbolic of the restoration of Israel (see below), and finally, by moving from total inactivity to excessive activity, in his joy the lame man breaks physiognomic convention. He does not "walk like a man" but rather leaps in grateful response to this benefaction of God.

More than one commentator has focused on the intertextual echoes with Isa 35:5–6. In that eschatological vision we hear that "the eyes of the blind shall be opened, and the ears of the deaf unstopped; then the *lame shall leap like a deer*" (cf. Acts 3:9). The image is of the restoration of Israel as part of the vision of God as cosmic king (Conrad 1991, 145). As in Isaiah, the lame man in Acts symbolizes the potential restoration of Israel (see Acts 1:6) as part of the establishment of God's cosmic reign, inaugurated by Jesus and continued through the ministry of the apostles and Paul. In this light it is difficult to resist giving symbolic value to the more than forty years of the lame man's illness in terms of the exiled and restored Israel (pace Spencer 2004, 57; contra Johnson 1992, 79).

But there is yet more to the story, and here the physiognomy texts shed further light. It was the walk of the lion that, in the zoological shorthand of physiognomy, represented the ideal male, a sentiment echoed by pseudo-Aristotle in his description of the lion as "the most perfect share of the male type" (*Physiogn.* 809a15–16). After describing the fine features of the lion's head and back, the author proceeds to speak of the lion's lower body:

> His legs are strong and muscular, his walk is vigorous, and his whole body is well-jointed and muscular. . . . He moves slowly with a long stride and swings his shoulders as he moves. These then are his bodily characteristics; in character he is generous and liberal, magnanimous and with a will to win; he is gentle, just, and affectionate towards his associates. (*Physiogn.* 809b.30–36)

By contrast, Polemo describes the effeminate or cowardly: "You may recognize him by his provocatively melting glance and by the rapid movement of his intensely staring eyes. . . . his loins do not hold still, and his slack limbs never stay in one position. He minces along with little jumping steps" (see Gleason 1995, 63).

The lame man, "inadequate" though he may have been, does not thus simply conform to the physiognomic standards of the day and immediately comport himself with a slow, dignified gait, showing that he is a man of courage or vigorous character, in other words, a "manly man." Rather, Luke shows that the formerly lame man, by leaping and praising God, is an enthusiastic and grateful member of the eschatological community of God. It is more important, in Luke's opinion, for one to respond appropriately to the benefaction of God than to worry about whether or not one's gait is conventionally masculine.

The authorial audience experiences both continuity with and discontinuity from physiognomic conventions, as Luke subverts them in the name of Jewish eschatological expectation.

A third group of participants now enter the scene, **all the people**, who recognize him as the one who sat for alms (3:9). For the second time the Beautiful Gate of the temple is mentioned. Historical reconstruction has failed to locate this gate. With this second reference one wonders if the narrator may be working a word play between the repetition of "hour" (*hōra*—"hour of prayer, the ninth [hour]," 3:1) and the Beautiful (*Hōraia*) Gate. Within the semantic domain of *hōraia* is the meaning, "the opportune moment" or "timely" (see Rom 10:15, quoting Isa 52:7). Could the narrator be hinting that this ninth hour, the hour of prayer, is the "timely" moment of opportunity for this lame man who sits begging, ironically, at the Gate of Opportunity (see Hamm 1986, 317)?

In Solomon's Portico (3:11–4:4)

The change in locale from the "Beautiful" Gate to Solomon's porch indicates a scene change (3:11). The rest of this scene (3:11–4:4) comprises Peter's speech (3:12–26) and the subsequent arrest of Peter and John (4:1–4). All these events occur on the same day as the healing itself.

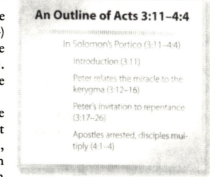

An Outline of Acts 3:11–4:4

In Solomon's Portico (3:11–4:4)

Introduction (3:11)

Peter relates the miracle to the kerygma (3:12–16)

Peter's invitation to repentance (3:17–26)

Apostles arrested, disciples multiply (4:1–4)

3:11. The sequel to the healing repeats the pattern of Pentecost: a miraculous event (3:1–10, echoing 2:1–4) draws a crowd (3:11, recalling 2:5–12), and Peter delivers a speech (3:12–26, like 2:14–40). The people whom Peter will address are brought into sharper focus: **all the people ran together to them** (3:11). Rather than an "amorphous mass" they "come into focus as a single, cohesive group" who can be addressed as "People of Israel" and given "a unified function in Peter's speech" (Funk 1988, 94). Luke conveys the amazement of the crowd at the healing by transposing **amazed** to the end of the sentence. This device of "upsetting" the word order is the rhetorical figure of *transgressio* (hyperbaton) and is achieved in this case by means of transposition (*Rhet. Her.* 4.32.44; cf. Quintilian, *Inst.* 8.6.65).

3:12–16. The first half of Peter's speech interprets the miracle of healing by means of traditional christological kerygma. The outer frame of this part of the speech deals with the healing of the lame man (3:12, 16). The inner layer is a traditional christological kerygmatic statement (3:13–15). We will deal with the inner frame first. The christological kerygma is arranged in a chiastic pattern:

A *The God of Abraham and of Isaac and of Jacob . . . glorified his servant Jesus* (3:13a)

B *whom you handed over and disowned before Pilate* (3:13b)

B′ *You rejected the holy and righteous one . . . you killed the author of life* (3:14–15a)

A′ *whom God raised from the dead* (3:15b)

This chiastic pattern underscores the fundamental difference between the act of Peter's audience, which is responsible for the death of Jesus, and the mighty deed of God, who is responsible for his resurrection (cf. 2:23–24). The "you" (plural) addressed by Peter in this speech are the Jerusalem Jews who had gathered at the temple at the time of prayer and who, the Lukan Peter believes, have participated in the death of Jesus.

The Lukan Peter again uses the popular rhetorical strategy of *synkrisis* to bring the culpability of his audience to the fore. Here the *synkrisis* is a comparison between "dissimilar things, of lesser things to greater" (Hermogenes, *Prog.* 18, trans. Kennedy 2003, 83). This *synkrisis* is an encomium/invective contrast in which "we blame one thing completely and praise the other" (Hermogenes, *Prog.* 19, trans. Kennedy 2003, 84). Here God's actions in raising Jesus are praised while the audience's participation in Jesus' death is criticized. The language of Peter's invective in 3:13–15 is direct and highly charged, typical of ancient invective: Peter's audience **handed over and disowned** [Jesus] **before Pilate** (3:13); **rejected the holy and righteous one** (3:14); and **killed the author of life** (3:15). Peter attacks the character of the audience, claiming that they "acted in ignorance" (3:17). Ignorance is no excuse for their actions (contra Longenecker 1995, 93; Bruce 1986, 90; Marshall 1980, 92; Johnson 1992, 73; pace Talbert 2005, 39; Witherington 1998, 183). This interpretation fits with pseudo-Cicero's view that stupidity was a valid category for invective and vituperation (*Rhet. Her.* 3.18.15). Peter's accusations here should be understood both within the general Greco-Roman rhetorical category of invective (in which emotionally charged language and hyperbole is normal) in both theory and practice (see Demosthenes, *Mid.*; Aeschines, *Tim.*; Juvenal, *Sat.* 1.69–80) and in polemics in intra-Jewish debates in particular (see Johnson 1989, 419–41). The loaded christological titles "servant" (3:13), "holy and righteous one" (3:14), and "author of life" (3:15) sharpen the contrast between "God and his Messiah, on the one hand, and, on the other, the deeds of the audience that acted out its sinfulness in the passion of Jesus" (Krodel 1986, 101). The contrast between the plan of God and the actions of the audience also shows that the purpose of the invective was not simply to discredit the audience's character. Rather, the invective is employed to persuade the audience of the error of their ways in order that they might change.

The christological titles, along with the traditional kerygma, also provide the foundation for the correct interpretation of the healing of the lame man (3:12–16). While it is certainly feasible that some observers of this sign might conclude that Peter and John by their **own power or piety . . . have made him walk** (3:12), Peter denies this interpretation and argues rather that **the faith that comes through him gave him this perfect health before all of you** (3:16b). The closing sentence to this outer frame is fraught with interpretive difficulties. Apparently **the faith in his name, which has strengthened this man** (3:16a), was the faith of the apostles, not the lame man. This view is supported by the presence in 3:15b of the brief phrase **whose witnesses we are**, which serves as the bridge from the christological kerygma to the interpretation of the healing. Still, a certain ambiguity shrouds any clear identification of the referent of this faith. What is clear is that Peter here "places great emphasis on faith and on Jesus' name as the keys to the healing of the lame man" (Tannehill 1990, 224; cf. Schneider 1980, 1:320–21).

3:17–26. The second half of Peter's sermon is signaled by a rhetorical clue: **And now, brothers** (3:17). Here Peter extends an invitation to repentance, undergirded by various citations of and allusions to scripture. He begins by acknowledging that his audience, though culpable for the death of Jesus, **acted in ignorance, just as your leaders did** (3:17). This ignorance produces a guilt that stands in need of repentance (3:19).

Peter then quotes one of the **holy prophets**, Moses: **The Lord your God will raise up for you a prophet like me from your brothers** (3:22). Peter has now used Davidic (chap. 2) and Mosaic resources to disclose the identity and vocation of this Jesus. These benefits carry with them a certain responsibility: **Obey him in everything that he says to you** (3:22). The addition of the words "to you" in this quotation from Deut 18:15–20 is a rhetorical device the Lukan Peter employs to sharpen his challenge to his audience. The speech ends on a salvation-historical note: **God raised up his servant, first of all for your benefit**

Refining

The importance of repentance ("repent and turn [to God]" [3:19]) in Peter's speech is underscored by the rhetorical device of *expolitio* (refining). Refining, according to *Rhet. Her.* 4.42.54–55, allows the rhetor to dwell on a topic by expressing an idea once and then by repeating "it once again or oftener in other, equivalent terms." The call to "turn" is accompanied by the promise of a number of benefits: "refreshing times may come from the Lord's presence" (3:20); Jesus, who is "the Christ who has been chosen for you" (3:20); and the subsequent restoration of all things (see 1:6), which "God spoke of through the mouth(s) of his holy prophets long ago" and which will accompany the Christ's parousia (3:21).

(3:26), hinting at least at the Gentile mission that will soon follow in Acts, led by Peter himself (see Acts 10).

4:1–4. In this second scene's concluding verses we learn that Peter's speech was not finished but interrupted (4:1). New participants are introduced—priests and the captain of the temple and the Sadducees—who take Peter and John into custody because they were **teaching the people and proclaiming, with respect to Jesus, the resurrection from the dead** (4:2). It is late, so their interrogation must wait until the next day. The major temporal break between the first two scenes and the last two does not occur, however, before we learn in a brief aside that **many of those who had heard the message believed. Indeed, the number of men (that believed) was about 5,000** (4:4). Even in the face of danger, the community of believers continues to grow.

Before the Sanhedrin (4:5–22)

The third and fourth scenes take place on the following day. The third scene (4:5–22) is set in Jerusalem. Peter and John are questioned before the Sanhedrin, threatened, and then released. The scene concludes with new information about the lame man who was made to walk.

Acts 4:5–22 in Context

The healing of a lame man
(3:1–4:31)

  At the Beautiful Gate (3:1–10)

  In Solomon's Portico (3:11–4:4)

▶ Before the Sanhedrin (4:5–22)

    Introduction: the opponents
    gather (4:5–6)

    Apostolic benefaction (4:7–14)

    The Sanhedrin deliberates
    (4:15–17)

    Apostolic witness (4:18–21)

    Conclusion: the sign of healing
    (4:22)

4:5–6. A formidable group of religious leaders assembles on the next day for the interrogation of Peter and John. In fact, the narrator provides a rather detailed list of specific names of those who were among the entourage of **leaders, elders, and scribes** (4:5). These include **Annas, the high priest, Caiaphas, John, Alexander, and all those who were from the high priestly family** (4:6). The credentials and pedigrees of these interrogators stand in bold contrast to the apostles who "lacked education and were laymen" (4:13).

4:7–14. The apostles are set in the midst of their accusers (4:7). The inquiry of the Jewish leaders links with Peter's previous speech: **By what power** (see 3:12) **or by what name** (see 3:16) **did you do this?** Before recording Peter's response, the narrator reports that Peter was **filled with the Holy Spirit** (4:8), recalling Jesus' words of encouragement to the disciples: "When they bring you before the synagogues, the rulers, and the authorities, do not worry about how you are to defend yourselves or what you are to say; for the Holy Spirit will teach you at that very hour what you ought to say" (Luke 12:11–12). Thus, filled with the Holy Spirit, Peter recapitulates his previous speech. **Whom you crucified but God raised**

from the dead (4:10) echoes the traditional kerygma (see 3:13, 15). With **This [Jesus] is the stone that was despised by you, the builders, that has become the cornerstone** (4:11) he reiterates the rejection of Jesus by his audience (see 3:13, 14). He also underscores the fact that the healing was **by the name of Jesus Christ of Nazareth** (4:10; see 3:16).

Peter introduces a new element into his summary; he identifies the healing as a **good deed** (4:9) or "benefaction" (*euergesia*). This is the technical word associated with the benefaction system so prominent in the social structures of the ancient Greco-Roman world (Danker 1982). Benefactors gave support, financial and otherwise, to individuals, groups, and sometimes whole cities. In return the beneficiaries of such benefaction pledged and gave their loyalty to these benefactors. This system permeated all levels of society: there were official benefactor structures such as the emperor cult, but informal benefaction structures were also present, often based along kinship lines.

Later in Acts, Peter will characterize the healing ministry of the earthly Jesus as "doing good" or "benefaction" (10:38). In the Third Gospel, Luke used the rhetoric of "benefactor" language to make his message palpable to a Hellenized audience (Jew and Gentile), which understood well the workings of the benefactor. Now in Acts we learn that the disciples have taken over the role of benefactor, though, like Jesus, that which they have to give—wholeness of life—is far more precious than the benefits of "silver and gold" so typical of most benefactors.

We see this point born out in the narrative as well. The lame man moves from inactivity to walking, from paralysis to praise. He also moves from sitting to clinging (Acts 3:11), to standing unassisted alongside Peter and John. As such he shares in the **boldness** (*parrēsia*) of the apostles (4:13).

The boldness of the apostles was noted long ago by John Chrysostom: "Great was the boldness of the man; that even in the judgement-hall he has

---

Boldness

Some rhetoricians identify *parrēsia* ("boldness") as the Greek name for a figure of speech known in Latin as *licentia* (*Rhet. Her.* 4.36.48; though see Quintilian, *Inst.* 9.2.27; 9.3.99). According to pseudo-Cicero, "frankness of speech" (*parrēsia*) occurs "when, talking before those to whom we owe reverence or fear, we yet exercise our right to speak out, because we seem justified in reprehending them, or persons dear to them, for some fault" (*Rhet. Her.* 4.36.38).

Peter displays just this kind of "frankness of speech" when he accuses the "rulers of the people and elders" of being the builders who rejected the cornerstone, Christ (4:11; cf. Ps 118:22).

not left them [Peter and John]. For had they said that the fact was not so, there was he to refute them" (*Hom. Act.* 10, *NPNF*). Chrysostom, building on the use of the word "see" (*theōreō*) in Acts 4:13, in which the religious authorities "saw" the apostles' boldness, also claims that this boldness was not confined to words, but rather was "seen" in the apostles' physical appearance: "[Not only by their words,] but by their gesture also, and their look and voice, and, in short, by everything about them, they manifested the boldness with which they confronted the people." So even though he does not speak, the lame man's boldness is seen also in his "body language," as he boldly takes his stand in solidarity with the persecuted apostles, and his transformation is complete.

4:15–17. Peter's speech causes the Jewish leaders to identify Peter and John as companions of Jesus who were bold and uneducated (4:13). Unable to rebuke Peter and John because the lame man stood beside the apostles as empirical proof of the truth of Peter's words, they order them outside the Sanhedrin and take counsel as to what they should do. This scene heightens in tension when the Jewish leaders reach the conclusion that they should warn the apostles **not to speak in this name any more with anyone** so that this deed (and the apostles' reputation) **may not spread further among the people** (4:17).

4:18–21. The apostles are called back in and warned that under **no condition were they to speak or teach in the name of Jesus** (4:18). They respond with the boldness the Sanhedrin has already observed: **For we simply must tell about the things we have seen and heard!** (4:20). The narrator depicts Peter and John speaking these words in choruslike unison (4:19), highlighting the unity of the apostolic witness.

This is the first time the content of John's speech is overtly reported. For most of this narrative sequence, John has been the silent partner, fading into the background as Peter acts as spokesperson on their behalf (3:6, 12; 4:8). Twice after Peter has finished speaking, the audience learns that somehow John was involved in the speech as well—"while they were speaking to the people" (4:1); "when they saw the boldness of Peter and John" (4:13)—subtle reminders that John has not abandoned Peter. That John now joins Peter in this "apostolic duet" seems to underscore the importance of the witness being brought here in the face of possible persecution. The Sanhedrin further threatens them and then releases them, unable to follow through on their threats **on account of the people** and their celebration over **what had happened** (4:21).

4:22. This scene ends in 4:22 with a reference to the event of 3:1–10. The audience learns that the man was **more than forty years old** (4:22), though the narrator does not disclose the significance of that reference. Is he old enough to be a reliable witness to the event? Does his age underscore the miraculous nature of the healing of this one who had been "crippled since the time of his birth" (3:2)?

More significant, perhaps, is the reference to this event as a **sign of healing**, linking this miracle closely to the signs and wonders done through the

Bede's Interpretation of the Healing of the Lame Man

For a symbolic reading of the lame man's illness of forty years (Acts 4:22), consider the comments of the Venerable Bede:

"According to the historical sense, this [age] shows that the man's mature age [made him] invincible to detractors. Allegorically, however, [the passage signifies that] the people of Israel . . . in the land of promise continued always to limp along [claudicabat] with the rites of idols together with those of the Lord." (Comm. Acts 4.22, trans. L. Martin 1989)

Bede (ca. 673–735) was an English monk and scholar. Remembered primarily as the "father of English history," he was also a biblical scholar who wrote commentaries reflecting the influence of Augustine, Jerome, and others, but also offering original interpretations.

apostles (2:43). The Sanhedrin had just acknowledged that this healing was "an extraordinary sign" (4:16). And earlier Peter had made the connection between this man who had been cured (*sōzō*; 4:9) "by the name of Jesus" and his soteriological conclusion that "there is no other name under heaven that has been given to people by which we must be saved" (*sōzō*; 4:12). Employing this same word, *sōzō*, which bears the double meaning of "cure" and "save," suggests that for Peter (and the narrator) this healing story is more than a miracle

Double Meaning

If Luke is playing on the double meaning of *sōzō* in 4:22, he is defying rhetorical convention. Theon cautions against the use of the "homonym," which "is a single word pronounced in the same way but with different significations" (Theon, *Prog.* 81, trans. Kennedy 2003, 31). But Luke has a penchant for this rhetorical ambiguity, seen not only in his use of *sōzō* ("save" or "heal"; Acts 4:9, 12) and *hōraia* ("beautiful" or "timely"; Acts 3:10) or *klēros* ("share" or "lot"; Acts 1:23–26), but he also uses the term *pais* ("child" or "servant") in Acts 4:25, 27, 30, once of David and twice of Christ. Does the community's prayer refer to David and Christ as "child" or "servant" (cf. various English translations of this passage; note also in 4:29 the community refers to themselves as "servants" but uses a different word, *douloi*)? Interestingly, as his only example of a homonym to be avoided, Theon cites *"pais* ('boy'); for it means a son and a young child and a slave" (Theon, *Prog.* 81, trans. Kennedy 2003, 31). While we have seen repeated instances in which Luke follows rhetorical convention of the day to make his point more persuasive, these examples suggest that there were certain rhetorical conventions he was willing to break for the same reasons.

devoid of theological content; the healed lame man is the continuing symbol of the salvation for all offered in Jesus' name. Further, for Peter's audience this salvation does not mean healing of lameness but the gifts of repentance, release of sins, and the blessings of the messianic kingdom (see 2:38–40).

The narrator has now added a third perspective on this healing: it is a **sign** (4:22). The healed lame man has become the paradigm of salvation through Jesus' name in Acts. Dennis Hamm has astutely observed: "In the Gospel of John, where believing is symbolized as a kind of seeing, it is clear why the fourth evangelist makes his most elaborate healing story the cure of a man born blind (John 9). Similarly, in Acts, where much stress is given to journey narratives, it should come as no surprise that great emphasis falls upon the healing of a man born lame" (Hamm 1986, 305).

Reunited with Friends (4:23–31)

The finale (4:23–31) to this episode is set in some unnamed place in Jerusalem and comprises a single scene: the believers pray (4:24–30). As the final curtain falls on this first skirmish with the Jewish authorities, the community of believers is gathered in prayer.

4:23–24a. The apostles return to **their own people** (4:23) and report to them what the audience already knows, namely the threats of the chief priests and elders (4:23–24a). This recapitulation prompts the community to pray with one voice to God in a show of solidarity with their beleaguered colleagues.

4:24b–4:30. The prayer begins with an *epideictic proem* (Soards 1994, 47), which is an invocation of praise for the sovereign who is the Creator, using language that echoes the heart of creation theology (see Exod 20:11; Ps 146:6 *et passim*; see Downing 1982, 546–49). Psalm 2 is interpreted in light of the passion of Jesus. The kings (Herod and Pontius Pilate) and rulers (by inference, the Sanhedrin; see 4:5, where the Sanhedrin is referred to as "leaders") gathered with the Gentiles and the peoples of Israel against the Lord and his Anointed. Of course, even these acts are according to God's hand and plan, which he **foreordained to happen** (4:28; see 2:23).

But this Psalm, interpreted in light of the present circumstances of the believers, is used as part of a rhetorically deliberative prayer for help (Kennedy 1984, 120). The believers pray that the Lord will **take note of their threats and allow your servants to speak your message with great boldness** (4:29). The final verse of the prayer is a neat précis of many of the issues addressed in

---

Acts 4:23–31 in Context

The healing of a lame man
(3:1–4:31)

  At the Beautiful Gate (3:1–10)

  In Solomon's Portico (3:11–4:4)

  Before the Sanhedrin (4:5–22)

▶ Reunited with friends (4:23–31)

  Introduction (4:23–24a)

  The community at prayer
  (4:24b–4:30)

  Conclusion: speaking with boldness
  (4:31)

---

this episode (indicated here with italics): **by stretching out your hand so that there will be** *healing* **and** *signs and wonders through the name of your holy servant Jesus* (4:30).

4:31. The entire episode is brought to a close with this final verse: **While they were praying the place where they had gathered began to shake, and all of them were filled with the Holy Spirit** (4:31, echoing the Pentecost experience, 2:1–4). The second petition that many signs and wonders be performed is fulfilled in the summary statement in Acts 5:12–16 (Talbert 1984, 20). And the first part of their petition, "to speak your message with great boldness" (4:29), is also fulfilled in the immediate context: **all of them . . . began speaking the message of God with boldness** (4:31). In fact, this theme of speaking the word of God with "boldness" or "openness" (*parrēsia*) is another dominant theme not only in this episode (see 4:13, 29; and here in 4:31), but throughout the book of Acts (see 2:29; 9:28; 13:46; 14:3; 18:26; 26:26), most often in connection with the preaching of Paul. In the very last scene of Acts the audience is left with the image of Paul not only preaching and teaching "without hindrance," but "boldly" (28:31). Such boldness will surely be needed as the believers face conflict both within and without the community in the next episodes.

Theological Issues

Luke is often depicted as writing to a primarily "Gentile audience," in contrast to Matthew, who writes for a predominantly "Jewish audience." There is, of course, some truth to these characterizations. Matthew begins his Gospel with a genealogy that details the Davidic lineage of Jesus. Furthermore, Matthew uses a fulfillment formula throughout his Gospel (but especially in the infancy narrative) to show how certain events from the life of Jesus fulfill prophecies found in Israel's scriptures (Stendahl 1968). He also notes that Jesus' public ministry was confined to "the lost sheep of the house of Israel" (Matt 10:5–6; cf. 15:24). Finally, many think that Matthew has presented Jesus as a "new Moses" and has collected the speeches and parables of Jesus into five discourses (chaps. 5–7; 10; 13; 18; 24–25) that parallel the five books of Moses (Meier 1979).

Matthew's gospel is also interested in the role of Gentiles in salvation history. From the non-Israelite women mentioned in the genealogy (Tamar, Rahab, Ruth, and Bathsheba), to the Gentile magi who venerate the newborn King, to the Great Commission at the end of the Gospel, through which Jesus commissions his disciples to "make disciples of all the nations/Gentiles," there is an eye toward the place of the Gentiles in the people of God. Thus it would be a mistake to infer from its label as the "Jewish gospel" that Matthew has no interest in Gentiles. David Garland has also noted that, in addition to this interest in the fate of Gentiles, Matthew's "anti-Jewish" material (21:43;

23:32–35; 27:25) prohibits one from concluding "too quickly that Matthew was primarily for Jews" (Garland 1993, 2).

Likewise, it would be a mistake to think that Luke, the "Gentile gospel," has no interest in things Jewish. The Gospel begins in the vicinity of the temple and refers to the Jewish piety of Zechariah and Elizabeth. The Gospel also ends with expressions of Jewish piety (Luke 23:50–56; 24:52–53). Between we find Jesus preaching, teaching, and healing in the synagogue (Luke 4:16–30; 6:6; 13:10). Furthermore, Luke understands that the "plan of God" (*boulē tou theou*) includes a mission to the Gentiles, a mission that is grounded in the scriptures of Israel, and specifically is a fulfillment of the Abrahamic covenant in the text cited in our section (Acts 3:25).

Furthermore, Luke is aware of other covenants between God and his people in Israel's scriptures. In fact, in addition to the Abrahamic covenant, Luke mentions or alludes to the Noahic covenant, the Mosaic covenant, the Davidic covenant, and the "new covenant" of Jeremiah. It is helpful to explore briefly the roles of these other covenants in Luke's narrative before turning to the Lukan function of the Abrahamic covenant (also helpful is to compare Luke's view of the covenants outlined here with Paul's view of the covenants; on Paul, see Talbert 1987, 299–313).

Noahic Covenant

In addition to God's promise not to destroy the earth again by means of a flood, the Noahic covenant imposes certain dietary restrictions on God's people:

> God blessed Noah and his sons, and said to them, "Be fruitful and multiply and fill the earth. The fear and dread of you shall rest on every animal of the earth, and on every bird of the air, on everything that creeps on the ground, and on all the fish of the sea; into your hand they are delivered. Every moving thing that lives shall be food for you; and just as I gave you the green plants, I give you everything. Only, you shall not eat flesh with its life, that is, its blood." (Gen 9:1–4; cf. Lev 17:13)

This dietary restriction to avoid meat with blood in it seems to be echoed in the Apostolic Decree of Acts 15, and provides a compromise between the sect of the Pharisees and the advocates of the Gentile mission: "Instead, (we should simply) write them a letter in order that they might abstain from things defiled by idols, from sexual immorality, from (eating the meat of animals that have been) strangled, and from (eating/drinking) blood" (Acts 15:20; cf. 15:29). While Gentiles do not have to be circumcised they should follow (among other things) the Noahic prohibition to abstain from meat of strangled animals (see Bockmuehl 1995). Otherwise, the Noahic covenant is given scant attention in the pages of Luke/Acts.

Mosaic Covenant

The Mosaic covenant is central to Israel's understanding of its relationship with Yahweh and likewise holds an important, if ambiguous, place in Luke's writings (Wilson 1983). Exodus 34:27–28 gives a brief summary of the covenant with Moses:

> The LORD said to Moses: Write these words; in accordance with these words I have made a covenant with you and with Israel. He was there with the LORD forty days and forty nights; he neither ate bread nor drank water. And he wrote on the tablets the words of the covenant, the ten commandments.

We find a number of references to the law of Moses in Luke/Acts, some positive, others less so. In Jesus' response to the rich ruler's question, "What must I do to inherit eternal life?" (Luke 18:18), Jesus responds, "You know the commandments: 'You shall not commit adultery; You shall not murder; You shall not steal; You shall not bear false witness; Honor your father and mother'" (Luke 18:20; cf. 1:6; 10:25–27). Presumably here Jesus endorses following the Mosaic law, though he points out that in the case of the rich ruler, one thing is still missing.

Of course, in the debate with Jewish leaders, the Christians were accused of ignoring, or worse, abrogating the law of Moses. This was one of the charges brought against Stephen, and later Paul: "For we have heard him saying that this Jesus, the Nazarene, will tear down this place and change the customs that Moses handed down to us" (Acts 6:14; cf. 21:21). The Lukan Paul exposes what he considers to be the soteriological inadequacy of the law: "by this man all who believe will be justified from all the things from which you could not be justified by the law of Moses" (Acts 13:39). Certainly it would be fair to say that Luke (like Paul) had an ambivalent attitude toward the Jewish law. It clearly had a positive role in maintaining community boundaries, but seemed to have lost its soteriological function.

Davidic Covenant

As in much of early Christianity, the Davidic covenant was crucial for understanding Jesus' role in salvation history in Luke (Strauss 1995). Isaiah 11 gives a brief summary of the expectations of David's heir:

> A shoot shall come out from the stump of Jesse, and a branch shall grow out of his roots. The spirit of the LORD shall rest on him, the spirit of wisdom and understanding, the spirit of counsel and might, the spirit of knowledge and the fear of the LORD. His delight shall be in the fear of the LORD. . . . With righteousness he shall judge the poor, and decide with equity for the meek of the earth; he shall strike the earth with the rod of his mouth, and with the breath of his lips he shall kill the wicked. (Isa 11:1–4)

Jesus' Davidic pedigree was made known from the beginning in Luke. Zechariah proclaims: "Blessed be the Lord God of Israel, for he has looked favorably on his people and redeemed them. He has raised up a mighty savior for us in the house of his servant David" (Luke 1:68–69; cf. 1:32). Furthermore, through his adopted father, Joseph, Jesus was of Davidic lineage (Luke 3:23–38; cf. 1:27). The blind man of Jericho recognizes Jesus as "son of David" (Luke 18:38, 39). The Lukan Jesus himself alludes to his Davidic lineage when he asks, "How can they say that the Messiah is David's son? For David himself says in the book of Psalms, 'The Lord said to my Lord, "Sit at my right hand, until I make your enemies your footstool."' David thus calls him Lord; so how can he be his son?" (Luke 20:41–44).

In Acts 2:34–36, Peter cited this same Psalms passage (110:1) in support of his argument that Jesus is the Messiah, the Christ; he is both David's descendant and his Lord. Luke's understanding of Jesus as the Christ is fundamentally through the lens of the Davidic covenant and its concomitant messianic expectations.

New Covenant of Jeremiah

Consider also Jeremiah's "new covenant":

> The days are surely coming, says the LORD, when I will make a new covenant with the house of Israel and the house of Judah. . . . This is the covenant that I will make with the house of Israel after those days, says the LORD: I will put my law within them, and I will write it on their hearts; and I will be their God, and they shall be my people. (Jer 31:31–33)

This covenant does not receive much explicit attention in Luke/Acts, but Jesus does allude to it in a key passage: "And he did the same with the cup after supper, saying, 'This cup that is poured out for you is the new covenant in my blood'" (Luke 22:20). Though the language of "new covenant" is not prominent in the rest of Luke/Acts, the concept is certainly present, especially at Pentecost in Acts 2 (see Introductory Matters on Acts 2). Thus Jeremiah's "new covenant" is important in understanding Lukan soteriology. But the most important covenant for understanding Luke's ecclesiology, his view of the church, and especially its mission is the Abrahamic covenant to which we now turn our attention.

Abrahamic Covenant

The Abrahamic covenant (Gen 12:2) is explicitly cited in Peter's speech in Acts 3, in the context of the story of the healing of the lame man: "You are descendants of the prophets and members of the covenant that God established with your ancestors when he said to Abraham, 'All the families of the earth will be blessed through your seed'" (Acts 3:25).

70

Allusions to the covenant appear throughout Luke/Acts (see Dahl 1976; Brawley 1999). The Abrahamic covenant was *foretold* in the coming of Christ. Consider Simeon's speech: "For my eyes have seen your salvation, which you have prepared in the presence of all peoples, a light for revelation to the Gentiles and for glory to your people Israel" (Luke 2:30–32). The Abrahamic covenant was *inaugurated* in Jesus' sermon in Nazareth, where the central recipients of God's mercy, the widow in Zarephath and Naaman the Syrian, were non-Israelites (Luke 4:25–27). The Abrahamic Covenant was *declared* by Peter in his Pentecost sermon: "For the promise is for you and your children and for all those in the future, as many as the Lord our God calls to himself" (Acts 2:39). The Abrahamic covenant is actually *cited* in his speech before the Sanhedrin (Acts 3:25). Finally, the Abrahamic covenant *undergirds* Paul's Gentile mission: "Then the Lord said to him, 'Go, for I have chosen this man as an instrument to carry my name before the Gentiles, kings, and the people of Israel. I will show him how much he must suffer for the sake of my name'" (Acts 9:15–16). The Abrahamic covenant provides for Luke scriptural warrant for the Gentile mission and Luke's understanding of conversion and the reconstitution of the people of God must be read in light of it.

> ## Inflection
>
> That God directly benefits Peter's audience through the Abrahamic covenant is made clear through the rhetorical device of inflection (*polyptoton* or *klisis*; Theon, *Prog.* 74.24–35, ed. Patillon 1997, 33; 48; 85.29–31; Quintilian, *Inst.* 9.1.34), in which the key term, in this case "you" (i.e., the audience), is inflected in all cases at least once to draw attention to the subject:
>
> *"You [hymeis, nominative case] are descendants of the prophets and members of the covenant that God established with your [hymōn, genitive case] ancestors when he said to Abraham, 'All the families of the earth will be blessed through your seed.' God raised up his servant, first of all for your [hymin, dative case; lit. "first to you"] benefit, and sent him to bless you [hymas, accusative case] by turning each of you from your [hymōn, genitive case] wicked ways." (Acts 3:25–26)*

Acts 4:32–5:42

Tensions Within and Without

🔲

Introductory Matters

The next rhetorical section, 4:32–5:42, consists of two units: 4:32–5:11, which address issues of conflict within the community, and 5:12–42, which looks at issues of conflict from outside the community. The life of the community is marked both by great unity of purpose and signs of opposition, both within and without.

Tracing the Narrative Flow

Tensions Within (4:32–5:11)

Following yet another summary statement (4:32–35), expressing a utopian vision of the Christian community grounded in a common understanding of the intricate web of accountability found in views of ancient friendship (see Mitchell 1992), Luke employs the rhetorical device of *synkrisis* in the form of an encomium/invective (see 3:13–15). An encomium/invective *synkrisis* contrasts two persons, ideas, or things and represents an attempt to "blame one thing completely and praise the other"

72

(Hermogenes, *Prog.* 19, trans. Kennedy 2003, 84). Here the actions of Barnabas, "son of encouragement" (4:36–37), are contrasted starkly with the actions of Ananias and Sapphira (5:1–11).

4:32–35. In a narrative summary (4:32–35), Luke reiterates the shared life of the believers that was symbolized by their shared possessions. In many ways, this summary repeats the point of emphasis of the previous summary in 2:41–47: "The community of possessions functions in the first place as a manifestation of spiritual unity; the way the believers disposed of their possessions showed that they were one heart and soul" (Johnson 1977, 199). Echoing Deut 15:4, the narrator informs the audience that **there was not anyone in need among them** (4:34).

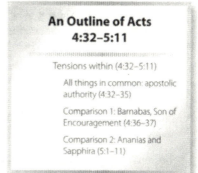

An Outline of Acts 4:32–5:11

Tensions within (4:32–5:11)

All things in common: apostolic authority (4:32–35)

Comparison 1: Barnabas, Son of Encouragement (4:36–37)

Comparison 2: Ananias and Sapphira (5:1–11)

This summary also provides some interesting variations to the themes found in 2:41–47. Now we learn that the **apostles** are responsible not only for **testifying to the resurrection of the Lord Jesus** (4:33) but also for the distribution of those funds **to each person as needs arose** (4:35). If we take the narrative flow of Acts seriously, only now do the apostles have responsibility for the distribution of resources within the community, which may explain, at least in part, why Peter could say to the lame man, "I have no silver or gold" (3:6). At any rate, this new administrative responsibility of the apostles will soon be reassigned (6:1–7).

The believers took the proceeds from their sales and laid it **at the feet of the apostles** (4:35). To assume the posture of being at another's feet is a gesture of submission in the OT (Josh 10:24; 1 Sam 25:24, 41; 2 Sam 22:39; Pss 8:6; 110:1). Luke also employs this language of being at another's feet as a symbol of submission (Luke 7:38, 44–46; 8:35, 41; 10:39; 17:16; 20:43; Acts 2:35; 10:25; 22:3). So here in 4:35, laying the proceeds at the apostles' feet is more than just a way of taking care of an administrative detail; it is a symbolic gesture of submission to apostolic authority (Johnson 1977, 202). Thus while the authority of the apostles was being challenged from without, it was being affirmed by those, like Barnabas, who laid their possessions at the feet of the apostles as a sign of loyalty.

4:36–37. Joseph, who was called Barnabas (4:36a), **sold a field and laid the money at the apostles' feet** (4:37). Like Paul (Acts 7:58), Barnabas makes a cameo appearance before assuming the center stage of the Gentile mission (9:27). He provides a concrete example of those believers who demonstrated their commitment to the faith and loyalty to the apostles' authority (4:35). We are provided with several interesting details about Barnabas; he is a **Levite** (who in the OT had no portion in the land; see Deut 12:12; 14:29) **and a native of Cyprus** (4:36a).

Reduplication

Luke underscores the importance of the authority of the apostles by using the rhetorical figure of reduplication (*conduplicatio*), which "is the repetition of one or more words for the purpose of amplification or appeal to pity" (*Rhet. Her.* 4.28.38, trans. Caplan 1954, 325). The author of *Ad Herennium* cites the following example: "You now even dare to come into the sight of these citizens, traitor to the fatherland? Traitor, I say, to the fatherland, you dare come into the sight of these citizens?" (ibid.).

Likewise, three times in the course of five verses (Acts 4:35, 37; 5:2), Luke states that proceeds from a sale were laid "at the apostles' feet." The repetition will serve to further the contrast between Barnabas and Ananias and Sapphira.

The impact of this figure is, as pseudo-Cicero's definition suggests, both informational and emotive: "The reiteration of the same word makes a deep impression on the hearer and inflicts a major wound upon the opposition—as if a weapon should repeatedly pierce the same part of the body" (*Rhet. Her.* 4.28.38).

The most important detail is his surname, Barnabas. That the apostles have given this name is another indication that Barnabas has submitted himself to the authority of the apostles. Peter is the only other apostle to receive a new name, and his is given by Jesus. The name itself is also interesting, or more specifically the translation that the narrator provides for this name, **son of encouragement** (4:36b; on the rhetorical figure of *appositio* [Quintilian, *Inst.* 8.6.40–43], see p. 33). The significance lies less in the etymology of the aramaic *bar-anaba* than in the role Barnabas will play later in this story. Here is an interesting character study; the same spirit of submission and liberality—"of encouragement"—is seen throughout the subsequent scenes in which Barnabas appears.

While the Jews plot to kill Saul and the believers are afraid of him and doubt that he is a disciple (9:23–27), Barnabas takes the risk of befriending him, bringing him before the apostles, and confirming his Damascus Road experience (9:27). When the church in Jerusalem heard about Greeks "turning to the Lord" in Antioch (11:19–21), they sent Barnabas to Antioch, and he "*encouraged* them all to remain faithful to the Lord with steadfast purpose" (11:23, emphasis added; cf. 4:36). When the disciples decide to send relief "to the brethren who lived in Judea," they sent it by the hands of Barnabas and Saul (11:30). Barnabas is a sign both of submission to the apostles and encouragement to fellow believers.

But his submission to apostolic authority is not blind loyalty. When Barnabas turns his attention to the Gentile mission, he is sent out, not by the apostles, but by the Holy Spirit (13:4; on Barnabas's role in the Gentile mission, see 13:43, 46, 50). And Barnabas plays an active role in the debate with the Judaizers who taught that circumcision was indispensable for salvation (15:1–2). The compromise of the Apostolic Conference (chap. 15) testifies to the way Barnabas (and Paul) held respect for the apostles' authority in tension with their submission to the guidance of the Holy Spirit. And Barnabas, ever wishing to encourage, will part company with Paul, the apostle to the Gentiles himself, because Barnabas is willing to take a second chance on young John Mark, who had earlier withdrawn from their work (15:36–40).

5:1–11. Not everyone submitted themselves to the authority of the apostles, as our second case study (5:1–11) indicates. Though this story is linked linguistically to the previous two scenes by the words **at the feet of the apostles** (5:2; cf. 4:35, 37), this unit depicts a negative example of community life described in 4:32–37 and fulfills the threat of Peter's sermon: "every person who does not obey that prophet will be cut off from the people" (3:23; cf. Josh 7).

Ananias and Sapphira sell a piece of property but they mock the community's Spirit of unity and usurp the authority of the apostles when they lay only a part of the proceeds at the feet of the apostles. Peter assumes the role of the prophet when he confronts Ananias with the conspiracy: **Ananias, why has Satan filled your heart so that you tried to deceive the Holy Spirit?** (5:3). Like Judas (Luke 22:3), Ananias has fallen prey to Satan, and like Judas, Ananias will not live to enjoy the material gains of his deceit (5:5; cf. 1:17–18). Though Ananias has not lied verbally, the act of conspiracy itself falsified the Holy Spirit (Johnson 1977, 207–8).

The remainder of Peter's questioning makes it clear that Ananias and Sapphira were not required to dispose of their property in this way, but could retain **authority** over it (5:4). By taking this duplicitous action, they did, in fact, usurp the authority of the apostles. The offense was not simply against the community, Peter argues; it was against God. The problem was not simply a human one; it had serious spiritual dimensions, and as Ananias soon found out, serious repercussions. Upon hearing Peter's words, **he dropped dead** (5:5).

After the disposal of Ananias and an interval of **about three hours** (5:7), Peter confronts Sapphira in what resembles a juridical trial. The story is rich with irony because the audience has knowledge that Sapphira does not possess; the conspiracy is broken. Unknowingly she compounds the conspiracy with a verbal lie. Yes, she tells Peter, they sold the land **for such an amount** (5:8). Peter's role as prophet becomes even more active when he predicts that this one who conspired against the community and God with her husband would now suffer the same fate as he (5:8). In a final note of irony Sapphira falls dead at Peter's feet. She who had feigned to lay her possessions at the apostles' feet now falls at Peter's feet herself. The submission to apostolic authority, which she failed to give while alive, she now gives permanently in death. This time Peter's "strengthening of the brethren" begins to look like a sifting of the disciples like wheat. It is no wonder that **great fear came upon the whole church and upon all those who heard about these things** (5:11).

Tensions Without (5:12–42)

The last phrase of 5:11, "all those who heard about these things," points the audience outside the community of believers, and in fact the final episode in chapter 5 (vv. 12–42) depicts the life of the community from an outsider's perspective. Here many of the themes found in 3:1–4:31 are repeated: the apostles are found healing the sick (5:12–16; cf. 3:1–10), which prompts the religious authorities to arrest them again and to bring them before the Sanhedrin for their second interrogation (5:17–42; cf. 3:11–4:22). As the community is marked by unity and tension within, so it is characterized by challenges from without.

5:12–16. A third and final summary describing the Jerusalem church (cf. 1:12–14; 2:41–46) recalls the previous episode (3:1–4:31) in several ways. First, there is the setting of Solomon's Portico, which was the site of Peter's speech and the apostles' arrest (3:11–4:4). Second, the other half of the believers' prayer that "signs and wonders" be performed (4:30) is now fulfilled when the narrator reports: **Many signs and wonders were being performed through the hands of the apostles among the people** (5:12). Finally, the healing of one man in chapter 3 has now been intensified and multiplied so that people from the outskirts of Jerusalem, as well as Jerusalemites, carried their **sick into the streets** (5:14–15), where the apostles continue their benefaction (see 4:9), and **all were being healed** (5:16). And, of course, the narrator does not miss an opportunity to record that **those who believed in the Lord were (regularly) being added, large groups of both men and women** (5:14). The reference to the church's growth precedes the account of the healings so that Luke can make clear that church growth is not the result of miracles. Note also again the emphasis on the gender inclusive character of the community: both men and women can lie to the community, and both men and women can become believers.

This summary is, however, distinct from the previous two in at least one important way. In contrast to the previous summaries (2:41–47; 4:32–35), "which looked inward at the internal life of the community, Luke's new summary looks outward at the public effect of the apostles on the Jewish people"

Acts 5:12–42 in Context

Tensions within and without (4:32–5:42)

  Tensions within (4:32–5:11)

    All things in common: apostolic authority (4:32–35)

    Comparison 1: Barnabas, Son of Encouragement (4:36–37)

    Comparison 2: Ananias and Sapphira (5:1–11)

  ▶ Tensions without (5:12–42)

    Healings again (5:12–16)

    Before the council again (5:17–42)

(Krodel 1986, 124). And so we learn that **none of the rest (of the people there) dared to join them, but the people spoke well of them** (5:13).

5:17–42. The public character of this summary scene is presumed in the closing episode of chapter 5 (vv. 17–42). The audience now learns of another response to the apostles than that of the people who "spoke well of them." The high priest and the party of the Sadducees were **filled with jealousy** (5:17). This response also explains further the timidity of the people who dared not join the believers (5:13).

There is remarkable redundancy between this episode and Acts 4:1–22. Both include the arrest of the apostles, their appearance before the Sanhedrin, short speeches highlighting the apostolic witness to Jesus and their commitment to obey God rather than the Sanhedrin, deliberation by the Sanhedrin out of the presence of the apostles, and the determination to release the apostles with the warning not to preach in Jesus' name. Variations in detail between these two accounts serve to heighten the tension of the narrative between the believers and the religious establishment. How will the church respond to these challenges from without?

In 5:17–26, Luke recounts divine intervention on behalf of the apostles. The conflict has broadened; all the apostles are placed in prison, not just Peter and John (cf. 4:3). The narrator winks at the audience when he reports that the apostles are released from prison by an angel, whose very existence the Sadducees deny (see 23:8). The next morning, the officers find the prison guards standing watch over an empty cell (5:23). The liberated apostles are found teaching in the temple as they were instructed to do (5:20), and they are quietly returned to the Sanhedrin (5:25–26).

The stage is set for the second interrogation and the apostles' witness (5:27–32). The old charge of teaching **in this name** (cf. 4:7) is coupled with a new reaction by the Sadducees to the accusation that the apostles' teaching is intended to **bring this man's blood upon us** (5:28). The stakes have gotten considerably higher since the last confrontation. In a judicial speech (Kennedy 1984, 120), Peter responds with a confession similar to the one he made at the first interrogation (see 4:19): **It is necessary to obey God rather than men** (5:29). But now what was a conditional sentence, "If it is right to listen to God rather than you, you must judge," becomes a divine imperative, "It is necessary for us to obey God rather than men." And the duet of Peter and John now becomes an apostolic chorus led by Peter.

The apostles then employ the christological kerygma typical of the previous speeches (2:23–24, 36; 3:13–15; 4:10): **The God of our ancestors raised up Jesus whom you had seized and murdered by crucifying him** (5:30). But rather than calling down this man's blood upon the Sadducees as the high priest suggested, the apostles claim that the exalted Jesus is the **Leader and Savior** who gives **repentance** and **forgiveness of sins** (5:31). The speech concludes with the apostles' marshalling their role as witnesses as a "proof" in

Chreia

According to Theon, "a chreia is a brief saying or action making a point, attributed to some specific person or something corresponding to a person" (Theon, *Prog*. 96, trans. Kennedy 2003, 15). Furthermore, according to Theon (*Prog*. 97–98, trans. Kennedy 2003, 16–17), *chreiai* may be expressed in speech, action, or a mixture of the two. Verbal *chreiai* may be declarative (some statement volunteered by the speaker) or responsive (in response to a question or inquiry or in response to some statement). *Chreiai* attributed to Jesus in the gospels have been the subject of much investigation (see Robbins and Mack 1989).

In Acts, however, Jesus' followers speak in *chreiai* much less frequently. Acts 5:29 ("We must obey God rather than any human authority") seems to fit Theon's description and would qualify as an utterance made in response to the council's chastisement of Peter and the apostles. Acts 5:30–31 elaborates this memorable *chreia* by providing its rationale. Verse 30 first offers the cause: "The God of our ancestors raised up Jesus." If Jesus has been raised up, he is the one to be obeyed. The second half of the verse gives the rationale for not obeying the human authority, in this case the council: "You had [Jesus] seized and murdered by crucifying him." Verses 31 and 32 offer arguments from example for the truth of the *chreia*: God has exalted Jesus; the apostles (and the Holy Spirit) are witnesses to these things. This call to radical obedience to God gives the auditors echoes of statements by Jesus (cf. the negative form in Mark 7:8: "You leave the commandment of God, and hold fast to human tradition"). The *chreia* serves to highlight in memorable fashion the radical claim of Peter (and the apostles) that they must follow God's commandments rather than the authority that threatens them.

their defense, along with the Holy Spirit whom God gave to those who obey him (5:32).

In 5:33–39, human intervention unexpectedly appears. The apostles' insistence on the culpability of the religious leaders in Jesus' death, the need for Israel's repentance, and the reference to the gift of the "spirit" (in which the Sadducees also did not believe; see 23:8) now cause the Sadducees not merely to be "annoyed" (see 4:2); they were furious and wanted to kill them (5:33). Abruptly, a Pharisaic member of the council, Gamaliel, who was respected by all the people (5:34) stands up and orders that the apostles be taken outside. He then offers a brief deliberative speech marked by restraint and caution (Kennedy 1984, 120–21; Soards 1994, 53; Witherington 1998, 239). Citing the historical examples of Theudas and Judas the Galilean who were leaders of revolutionary movements that came to nothing (5:36), Gamaliel advises the council that if this plan or this deed is of human origin it will be destroyed. But if (on the other hand) it is from God, you will not be able to destroy them (5:38–39). Of course, Luke's authorial audience already knows from the divine intervention, the miraculous healings, and the signs and wonders, that "this plan" and "this deed" are indeed "of God." The only conclusion to draw for the one who would identify with the narrator's point of view is that the Sanhedrin has already been found to be fighting God (5:39). Just as the angel had intervened on behalf of the apostles in freeing them from prison, so now the agent of intervention is a human who compels by the wisdom of his argument.

A summary of teaching and preaching Jesus as the Christ concludes the section (5:40–42). The Sanhedrin takes Gamaliel's advice and releases the apostles (5:40). Again, the religious leaders charge them not to speak in the name of Jesus (see 4:18), but the conflict is heightened as the threats turn into beatings. By rejoicing at their shame and suffering, the apostles fulfill the beatitude of Jesus (Luke 6:22–23). Once again, the apostles boldly defy the Sanhedrin's instructions, and every day in their expressions of corporate worship, publicly in the temple and privately at home (see 2:46), the apostles **did not stop teaching and preaching the good news that Jesus was the Christ** (5:42). This plan and this deed must surely be of God! That faithful witness continues even when, in the story of Stephen (6:11–8:1), the persecution moves beyond threats and beatings to martyrdom. But that is another part of the story.

Theological Issues

In a powerfully evocative turn of phrase borrowed from Martin Luther, Ernst Käsemann argued that Luke had exchanged Paul's theology of the cross for a theology of glory (Käsemann 1969, 92). This view of a Lukan theology of glory—a triumphalist attitude that depicts the gospel steamrolling through the Mediterranean basin converting anything that moves—was widely influential (Haenchen 1971, 563; Pervo 1990, 22; Kümmel 1973, 132). Even those who finally object to this characterization of Luke's theology admit to "triumphalist accents" in Acts (Marguerat 2002, 38). Ultimately, however, it is a mistake to label Lukan theology as a *theologia gloriae*, for, in Luke, to bear testimony to the redemptive work achieved by God through Christ more often than not involves a dimension of suffering. Jesus' followers were not only witnesses *to* the suffering of the Messiah (Luke 24:46–48), they were to participate *in* the suffering of the Messiah (Moessner 1990, 165–95). Luke has a theology not of glory but of providence, in which even the failures of the mission result in the expansion of the mission (Squires 1993, 37–77). As Daniel Marguerat observed: "Success for the Word does not grow independently of the suffering of the messengers, but because of it" (Marguerat 2002, 39).

We see this throughout the book of Acts, but especially in this unit 4:32–5:42, in which the church experiences persecutions from those outside its immediate community, a persecution and suffering that will be foundational for the Gentile mission. Certainly much of Paul's suffering in Acts is the direct result of his missionary activities, but his suffering is not limited to the Gentile mission. The last few chapters of Acts describe the journey of Paul, faithful witness to the gospel, to Rome, a place where there are already believers (cf. 28:14), yet he suffers and bears witness nonetheless (for more on Paul's suffering, see Theological Issues on Acts 21:17–23:35).

Further, Luke's "theology of glory" is often coupled with the assertion, drawing on Luke 4:32 (cf. also 2:41–42), that Luke presents an idyllic and idealized view of the early Christian community as being always "in one accord" (Krodel 1986, 117), thus glossing over any conflict within the community. It would be a mistake, however, to accuse Luke of smoothing over tensions within the community. Certainly the story of Ananias and Sapphira gives one pause in this regard. Luke bears witness to the necessity of bearing witness, whether within the community as Peter does to and about Ananias and Sapphira, or to those outside the community, as Peter and John do to the religious authorities. At times, such apostolic witness involves evangelizing the unconverted Gentiles; at other times, as with Stephen, James, and Paul, it involves bearing witness to a suffering Messiah by participating in the messianic suffering of the church. For Luke, the "theology of providence" is fulfilled just as much by Peter's admonition to the community regarding the distribution of possessions as by Peter's bold witness to the Sanhedrin, as much by Stephen in his martyrdom as by Paul in the Gentile mission, as much by Paul in his suffering journey to Rome as by Peter's conversion of Cornelius.

Acts 6–7

Stephen and the Seven

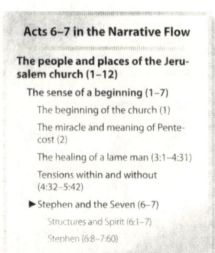

Introductory Matters

The next rhetorical unit in Acts, 6–7, continues the theme of tensions and conflicts both internal and external to the Christian community. In the first section (6:1–7), the issue of ministry to the needy within the community is resolved; in the second and longer section (6:8–7:60), Luke records conflict between one of the Seven and some fellow Jews who have accused Stephen and his companions of distorting the temple and the law. This conflict results in the first recorded martyrdom of the early church. Beginning with the story of Stephen, the next few chapters of Acts (up through chapter 12) explore personalities more than places. The adventures of Stephen, Philip, Paul, Peter, and Barnabas fill these pages. Of course, the success of the gospel in overcoming problems in the community is still the underlying theme that holds these stories together (see the *inclusio* formed by the references to "the message of God spread" in 6:7 and 12:24), but these middle chapters provide the best justification for the title assigned to this work in the second century, "The Acts of the Apostles."

> **Acts 6–7 in the Narrative Flow**
>
> **The people and places of the Jerusalem church (1–12)**
>
> The sense of a beginning (1–7)
>
> The beginning of the church (1)
>
> The miracle and meaning of Pentecost (2)
>
> The healing of a lame man (3:1–4:31)
>
> Tensions within and without (4:32–5:42)
>
> ▶ Stephen and the Seven (6–7)
>
> Structures and Spirit (6:1–7)
>
> Stephen (6:8–7:60)

Tracing the Narrative Flow

Structures and Spirit (6:1–7)

Acts 6:1–7 is a self-contained unit. It begins and ends with general references to the "increasing" of "the number of disciples" (6:1, 7). Luke also begins with a summary-like phrase, "in those days," which he has used before, most notably in the introduction to the selection of the Twelve in the Gospel (Luke 6:12; see also 1:39; 23:7; 24:18) and the replacement for Judas (Acts 1:15; also 11:27; cf. the similar but not identical phrase in 7:41 and 9:37). So the phrase is used frequently but not exclusively in conjunction with the selection of community leaders.

The passage serves two purposes: to provide another example of how conflict in the early Christian community is resolved (and schism thus avoided) and to introduce Stephen and Philip into the narrative. To fulfill the first purpose, Luke employs a narrative pattern remarkably similar to the OT form for choosing auxiliary leadership (Exod 18 and Num 27): (1) statement of the problem (Acts 6:1–2; cf. Exod 18:14–18; Num 27:12–14); (2) the proposed solution and qualifications for leadership (Acts 6:3–4; cf. Exod 18:19–23; Num 27:15–21); (3) setting apart the new leadership (Acts 6:5–6; cf. Exod 18:25; Num 27:22–23; for a slightly different construal of this pattern, see Talbert 2005, 58). The unit also reflects a common rhetorical figure, *distributio*, to describe the division of labor (see below).

An Outline of Acts 6:1–7

Structures and Spirit (6:1–7)
  The problem (6:1–2)
  The solution (6:3–4)
  Setting apart the leaders (6:5–6)
  Restoring unity (6:7)

6:1–2. The problem in Acts 6 occurs when a **complaint among the Hellenists** that **their widows were being overlooked** (6:1) disrupts the unity of the church. As such, this passage stands as another example of conflict/resolution stories so common in Acts (see, e.g., 5:1–11; 8:18–24; 9:26–28; 11:1–18; 15:1–35; 21:20–26). The word Luke uses for the dispute, a "complaint" (*gongysmos*) is not only an example of *onomatopoeia* (*Rhet. Her.* 4.31.42) but also echoes the Israelites' complaining or grumbling against Moses and God (see Exod 16:7–12; Num 11:1; 14:2, 27, 36; 17:25) and occurs only here in Luke or Acts (appropriately, since ps.-Cicero cautions that "this figure is to be used rarely"; 4.31.42).

Though there is still some debate, the **Hellenists** most likely are not Gentile "Greeks" but Greek-speaking Jews from the Diaspora, who in this case are believers, while the **Hebrews** are Aramaic-speaking Jews who are also believers (see Acts 21:40; 22:2; 26:14; cf. also Philo, *Conf.* 129). Thus the Hellenists are Diaspora Greek-speaking Jews, here Christian believers, whose widows are **being overlooked in the daily distribution.** The "daily distribution" could, as some translations assume, refer to food, in which case "tables" (*trapezai*) in the apostles' response (6:2) would refer to the tables upon which food is spread (cf. Acts 16:34; also Luke 16:21; 22:21). Alternatively, it could refer to "money," in which case the "table" means a "banker's bench" (Luke 19:23; cf. Matt 21:12; Mark 11:15; John 2:15; Plutarch, *Caes.* 28.4; 67.1). Both food and money are very important to Luke. That the grumbling of the Israelites, which Acts 6:1 echoes, is over food ("manna") is instructive but not decisive. What is at stake here is spiritual authority. The fact that the Seven are entrusted with serving tables, whether the banker's bench or the soup kitchen, is consistent with Luke's pattern elsewhere in which authority over material possessions represents spiritual authority (see Acts 4:32–5:11; see also below). They are certainly not glorified "bus boys" or bank tellers!

Another question lingers: who are these widows? Though little attention is given to widows in the other gospels (widows are mentioned three times in Mark 12, once in Matt 23, and not at all in John), audiences of Luke and Acts have already formed a rather full image of widowhood (nine occurrences in Luke; three in Acts): the widow is pious (Luke 2:36–38), generous (Luke 21:1–4), and loyal (Acts 9:39). But widowhood in Luke and Acts is also characterized by grief (Luke 7:11–17), poverty (Luke 18:1–8), and a vulnerability to exploitation (Luke 20:47). Care for the widow was also a tradition in the audience's OT (Exod 22:22; Deut 10:18; 14:29; 16:11, 14; 24:17, 19–21; 26:12–13; Ps 146:9). In the symbolic world of Acts, a "widow is in a precarious situation in regard to her 'shame' because she has no male to defend her and the honor of her children and household" (Malina and Neyrey 1991, 63). To fail to care for its widows not only stripped the women of their honor but shamed the entire community (see Spencer 1994). Though Luke knows of women who move outside the private sphere of the home (see Acts 16), the need to preserve the collective honor of the community lies in the background of Acts 6. A solution is sorely needed.

6:3–4. The problem to be addressed in 6:3 is that Greek-speaking Jewish-Christian widows were being excluded from table fellowship. What solution is proposed? The Twelve's calling does not include "serving tables," so they propose a division of labor within the leadership, in which seven would be appointed to meet this need. Luke employs the rhetorical device of *distributio* ("distribution") to delineate the responsibilities of the Seven and the Twelve. According to pseudo-Cicero, "Distribution occurs when certain specified roles are assigned among a number of things or persons" (*Rhet. Her.* 4.35.46, trans. Caplan 1954, 347). For example, "The Senate's function is to assist the state with counsel; the magistracy's is to execute, by diligent activity, the Senate's will; the people's to choose and support by its votes the best measures and the most suitable men" (*Rhet. Her.* 4.35.46). So here the responsibilities in the early church are disaggregated: the Twelve are to devote themselves to **prayer and the ministry of the word** (6:4) and the newly appointed auxiliary leadership should be responsible for the "service" of tables (6:2). Like the people in

Adiunctio

In Acts 6:4, Luke uses the figure of speech known as *adiunctio* ("adjunction," Greek *epizeugma*), in which "the verb holding the sentence together is placed at the beginning or the end" (*Rhet. Her.* 4.27.37). In verse 6 the verb "we will devote ourselves" occurs at the end of the sentence, highlighting the specific duties of "prayer and the ministry of the word," to which the Twelve have committed themselves.

pseudo-Cicero's example, who are to choose and support the "most suitable men" for office, so the **brothers** are to **look for seven respected men** (6:3) to serve in this capacity. The figure of *distributio* "has richness, for it embraces much in little and, by assigning to each his duty, severally distinguishes a number of entities" (*Rhet. Her.* 4.35.47).

It would be a mistake, however, to think that Luke views this division as either absolute or hierarchical. It is not absolute, because in the next two episodes two of the Seven, Stephen and Philip, are depicted not as serving tables but rather fulfilling the "service of the word" (Acts 7 and 8). Nor is "serving tables" in any sense inferior to the "service of the word," particularly in light of Jesus' saying, "For who is greater, the one who is at the table or the one who serves? Is it not the one at the table, but I am among you as one who serves" (Luke 22:27). The issue for Luke is that of spiritual authority, and for that reason, Luke is not interested in delineating the division of labor between serving tables and serving the word in the subsequent narrative.

What are the qualifications for this new leadership? Luke mentions several explicitly in 6:3: they are to **be respected men among yourselves who are full of the Spirit and wisdom.** Being full of the Spirit is a recurrent theme in Acts, and being full of wisdom echoes one of the characteristics assigned to the development of Jesus (Luke 2:40, 52). But Luke also implies another qualification through the list of names. Most, if not all, of the Seven, judging from their Greek names, came from the part of the church that had complained about mistreatment of some of its constituency. "Not only did they need to have a good reputation (being wise and spiritual), they also needed to represent the interests of the neglected (the Hellenists)" (Talbert 2005, 60–61).

6:5–6. The Seven are set apart by prayer and the laying on of hands. The syntax of 6:5 is ambiguous. It is not clear whether the apostles only or the entire congregation prayed and laid on hands. The context (especially 6:3), however, suggests that the entire congregation selected, prayed for, and **laid their hands** (6:6) on the Seven and that the apostles confirmed this choice. The laying on of hands is similar to the commissioning of Saul and Barnabas (13:3). Of the seven men named only **Stephen** and **Philip** (6:5) are given any attention in the subsequent narrative, supporting the earlier contention that one purpose of this story is to introduce Stephen.

6:7. This unit ends with a second reference to the way in which **the number of disciples in Jerusalem increased greatly** (6:7; cf. 6:1). The point is further emphasized by the notice that **the message of God spread** (on this phrase, see the comments at 12:24). The narrator goes on to add that **a large group of priests became obedient to the faith.** The upshot for Luke, of course, is that despite the conflicts that threaten the unity of the fledgling community, the church solves its problems and continues to grow.

Stephen (6:8–7:60)

Stephen is a significant character in Acts. The first named of the Seven, he is also the first named martyr of the early church. The episode about Stephen divides into three scenes: the controversy between Stephen and some of the Greek-speaking Jews (6:8–7:1); the speech of Stephen (7:2–53; the longest speech in Acts, which is further divided into five subscenes); and the martyrdom of Stephen and widespread persecution of the church (7:54–60). That the narrator will return to Stephen twice more in the remainder of the narrative (11:19; 22:20) indicates his importance for the larger story.

6:8–7:1. The tensions between the followers of Jesus and the leaders of the Jewish community that were recounted in Acts 4 and 5 now continue with the story of Stephen, one of the Seven. This unit divides into two brief and closely related scenes: (1) Stephen's debate with the Synagogue of the Freedmen (6:8–10); and (2) the charges against Stephen (6:11–7:1).

1. Exercising his evaluative mode, the narrator again reminds the audience that Stephen is **full of grace and power** (6:8; cf. the parallel constructions, employing "full of" in 6:3, in which the Seven, of whom Stephen is a member, are to be "full of the Spirit and of wisdom"; also 6:5 in

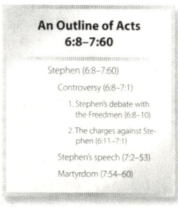

An Outline of Acts
6:8–7:60

Stephen (6:8–7:60)

Controversy (6:8–7:1)

  1. Stephen's debate with the Freedmen (6:8–10)

  2. The charges against Stephen (6:11–7:1)

Stephen's speech (7:2–53)

Martyrdom (7:54–60)

which Stephen is said to be "full of faith and the Holy Spirit"). This "grace and power" were made manifest in the **great wonders and signs** that Stephen performed (on the function of "signs and wonders," see the note on 2:22). That he performed these signs and wonders **among the people** is also important to show that Stephen, though a Hellenist, is working among the Jewish "people" in Jerusalem (*laos* almost always refers to the Jews, e.g., 2:47; 3:12; 4:1, 10; 5:12 *et passim*; though see 15:14 [also 18:10?] in which the word *laos* refers to Gentiles, while still maintaining the sense of "the people of God").

Stephen is soon engaged in a dispute with some Greek-speaking Jews: **certain men from the so-called "Synagogue of the Freedmen"—Cyrenians, Alexandrians, and those from Cilicia and Asia—came forward** to debate with

Stephen (6:9). Jews of the Diaspora engage Stephen in argument. Anywhere from one to five synagogues may be meant. The content seems to support one synagogue, "of the Freedmen," populated by Jews from Cyrene, Alexandria, Cilicia, and Asia, while the grammar suggests two distinct groups (separated by the definite article, *tōn*)—a synagogue of the "Freedmen," composed of Cyrenians and Alexandrians, and a second group of Jews who came from Cilicia and Asia.

The word "Freedmen" is a transliteration of the Latin *libertinus* and functions differently from the other names, which are of geographical regions. It is the title of the synagogue (not surprising to the audience who might know that some synagogues did take titles; cf. the inscriptional evidence at Corinth and Jerusalem, as well as the literary evidence in *y. Meg.* 73d.35; *b. Meg.* 26a; and *t. Meg.* 3.6) and suggests that at least some members of this synagogue had at one time been enslaved by the Romans (a typical practice; cf. Philo, *Legat.* 155; Tacitus, *Ann.* 2.85).

Each of the four geographical places mentioned, Cyrene, Alexandria, Cilicia, and Asia, plays a role elsewhere in Acts. Cyrenian Jews are mentioned in the catalog of nations in Acts 2:10 as being present at the Pentecost event, and Cyrenian Jewish Christians, along with the Cyprians, were responsible for bringing the Christian message to the Gentiles in Antioch (11:20). Individuals from Cyrene, Lucius and Simon, are named in Acts and the Gospel (Luke 23:26; Acts 13:1). Believers in Cilicia are mentioned in Acts 15:23 and 41; and, of course, the most famous resident of Cilicia is Saul of Tarsus (21:39; 22:3; 23:34).

Apollo is the only Alexandrian mentioned in Acts (18:24), but Asia plays an important role. In addition to being included in the catalog of nations in Acts 2:9, Asia is an important site of Paul's missionary activities (especially in and around Ephesus; Asia is mentioned specifically at 16:6; 19:10, 22, 26; 20:18). Named traveling companions of Paul, Tychicus and Trophimus, are from Asia (20:4; Trophimus is later more specifically identified as an "Ephesian"; cf. 21:29). Most noteworthy are the references in 21:27 and 24:19, which indicate that Asian Jews continue to attempt to stir up trouble for Paul as they did for Stephen. Finally, Acts 19:10, 27, and 31 are also interesting because they indicate that such opposition is not limited to Asian Jews, but includes Asian Gentiles who feel threatened by Paul as well (see comments on Acts 19).

These opponents **were not able to overcome the spiritual wisdom with which he spoke** (6:10). Reference to Stephen's "wisdom" and possession of "the Spirit" continue the positive portrait the narrator is seeking to paint. The "Spirit" recalls the quality possessed by all of the Seven (6:3) and specifically Stephen (6:5). Stephen's "wisdom" provides even richer fare. All four occurrences of "wisdom" appear in Acts 6 and 7. First, as with the "Spirit," "wisdom" is a defining characteristic of the Seven (6:3). Second, "wisdom" here is associated with Stephen's speech, which signals something to the audience to the effect that Stephen's interpretation of scripture demonstrates his "wisdom." Third, Stephen's wisdom is linked closely to the wisdom of two of the prominent figures in his speech, Joseph and Moses (7:10, 22). Finally, the note that his accusers could not withstand Stephen's wisdom fulfills a prediction by Jesus: "So make up your minds not to prepare your defense in advance; for I will give you words and a wisdom that none of your opponents will be able to withstand or contradict" (Luke 21:14–15; on "withstanding" cf. Acts 6:10).

2. In 6:11–7:1, Luke recounts the charges against Stephen. Unable to withstand the words of Stephen, these Diaspora Jews **bribed men to say, "We have heard him speak blasphemous words against Moses and God"** (6:11). Stephen's opponents at this point in the conflict resort to the rhetorical strategy of negative labeling to discredit or dishonor Stephen in an effort to render his message impotent among the people. Specifically, Stephen is charged with speaking "blasphemous words against Moses and God." "Blasphemy" elsewhere in Acts can refer to slanderous words spoken against the followers of Jesus (more negative labeling; see Acts 13:45; 18:6), but here refers to attempts to abrogate the authority of God or the Torah, charges made more specific in 6:13–14 (on Moses as a cipher for the Torah, see Acts 3:22; 15:1, 21; 21:21; 26:22; and on the unusual phrase, "blasphemous words against Moses," cf. Josephus, *BJ* 2.145; *Ant.* 3.307; *C. Ap.* 1.279). This negative labeling stands in direct contrast to the narrator's positive evaluation of Stephen (who spoke with wisdom and through the Spirit), and the audience is surely not expected to accept these Diaspora Jews' assessment. Further, Stephen himself will interrupt the labeling process with a few well-placed rhetorical flourishes of his own (see comments on 7:51–53).

The scene quickly intensifies: **They stirred up the people, the elders, and the scribes and then went and seized (Stephen) and brought him to the Council** (6:12). Placing Stephen before the Sanhedrin creates a more formal juridical setting. The Sanhedrin setting also parallels the encounters of the apostles with the council (cf. chaps. 4 and 5). One significant variation, however, heightens the drama. In the previous conflict scenes the "people" sided with the apostles (cf. 4:21; 5:26); here the people are stirred up against Stephen, thus removing the buffer that had previously protected the apostles (see Tannehill 1990, 84).

Instead, the scene now more closely echoes the arrest and trial of Jesus. The charge of blasphemy and the reference to false witnesses echo the passion of Jesus preserved in Mark 14:56–57, 64 (cf. Matt 26:59–60, 65). The passage also echoes Luke's gospel. Like Jesus, Stephen is led into the Sanhedrin (Acts 6:12; Luke 22:66) and the people are stirred first against Jesus, now against Stephen (Luke 23:13–25). The tension has escalated here in Acts to unprecedented proportions.

The charge of blasphemy against Stephen (cf. Luke 5:21) is specified by false witnesses (a practice condemned by Exod 20:16): **This man never stops saying things against the holy place and the law. For we have heard him saying that** this Jesus, the Nazarene, will tear down this place and change the customs that Moses handed down to us (6:13–14). The negative labeling is now extended to include Jesus as well; the use of "this" in reference to both Stephen and Jesus is derisive. Stephen will ultimately address both charges leveled against him, namely that he is saying things against "this holy place and the law" (see comments on the speech below). These charges do not die with Stephen; they will resurface later against Paul (21:28).

Whether the narrator views the words uttered against Jesus as false because Jesus never said them or because Stephen never repeated them is unclear. Jesus did, in fact, make similar claims, at least about the temple, in the Third Gospel:

> When some were speaking about the temple, how it was adorned with beautiful stones and gifts dedicated to God, he [Jesus] said, "As for these things that you see, the day will come when not one stone will be left upon another; all will be thrown down." (Luke 21:5–6)

> Jerusalem will be trampled on by the Gentiles, until the times of the Gentiles are fulfilled. (Luke 21:24)

While the authorial audience might reasonably conclude that Jesus himself does not claim here to destroy the temple and thus is not guilty of the false witnesses' charge in Acts 6:14, the narrator nowhere uses this argument to vindicate Jesus.

The charge that Jesus is changing "the customs that Moses handed down to us" is also problematic. Certainly in the Third Gospel Jesus appears to challenge Mosaic regulations, especially regarding Sabbath observance (Luke 6:1–11; 13:10–17; 14:1–6). So Jesus would appear to be open to charges of "changing" Mosaic regulations "even if he regarded his changes as fulfillment rather than destruction" (Barrett 1994, 1:329). "Customs" here certainly have a broader usage than the written Torah in Acts. The word is used variously to refer to both Jewish (see Acts 15:1; 21:21; 28:17) and Gentile practices (Acts 16:21; 25:16). Here the reference seems to be to "ritual obligations specific to Jews as part of their ancestral heritage" (Johnson 1992, 110).

Was Jesus guilty of changing these Jewish rituals? Not according to Luke. In many ways, the question for many Jewish groups in the first century was, "Who is most faithfully keeping the customs of Moses?" This would be just the way an authorial audience, familiar with the Greco-Roman rhetorical conventions, would have framed the issue. The question of keeping customs was not limited to Jewish concerns (see Dionysius of Halicarnassus, *Ant. Rom.* 7.70–73; Balch 1995). The narrator of Acts, through Stephen's speech, will reverse the charges of the Diaspora Jews and argue that *their* ancestors are the ones guilty of changing the customs of Moses, not the followers of Jesus.

Having made these charges **all those sitting in the Council watched (Stephen) closely and saw that his face looked like the face of an angel (6:15).** Understated but not entirely missing is the note of irony found in the fact that Stephen's face appears like that "of an angel," for many of those sitting in the council were no doubt Sadducees who denied the existence of angels (see Acts 23:8). This change in countenance echoes other Jewish texts (Dan 3:92 LXX; Gen 33:10 and the Palestinian Targum on that passage; 1 Sam 29:9; Exod 34:29–35; cf. *Jos. Asen.* 14.9), and, as in the transfiguration of Jesus, emphasizes the divinely endowed authority of the speaker. Finally, the high priest asked him: **Are these things true?** (7:1). In response to the high priest's question regarding the validity of these charges, Stephen speaks.

7:2–53. The speech of Stephen is important in understanding the nature of the conflict within the Jewish community about the role and purposes of Jesus. It falls into the category of judicial speech (Kennedy 1984, 121;

Simile

In 6:15, where members of the council see Stephen's face "looking like the face of an angel," we have an instance of the well-known figure of speech of *imago* ("simile"; Greek *eikōn*). "Simile is the comparison of one figure with another, implying a certain resemblance between them. This is used either for praise or censure" (*Rhet. Her.* 4.49.62). Certainly the authorial audience would have heard this description as one of positive praise, whatever those portrayed in the text may have thought.

Refutatio in Acts 7

In Stephen's speech, Luke employs the much used and highly regarded rhetorical strategy of *refutatio* in response to the charge that followers of Jesus want to change the customs of Moses.

According to Aphthonius, "Refutation is an overturning of some matter at hand" (*Prog.* 27, trans. Kennedy 2003, 101). On the importance of refuting or "destroying" the argument of one's opponent, Aphthonius comments further, "this *progymnasma* [refutation] includes in itself all the power of the art (of rhetoric)" (*Prog.* 28, trans. Kennedy 2003, 101). Pseudo-Cicero expresses a similar sentiment: "The entire hope of victory and the entire method of persuasion rest on proof and refutation, for when we have submitted our arguments and destroyed those of the opposition, we have, of course, completely fulfilled the speaker's functions" (*Rhet. Her.* 1.10.18, trans. Caplan 1954, 33).

Along with refutation of charges, however, Stephen develops an encomium of those from Israel's past worthy of praise, so that a kind of encomium/invective *synkrisis* runs through the speech. For more on the effect of *synkrisis*, see Theological Issues below.

Soards 1994, 58), but it is not a defense or apologia. Rather, Stephen goes on the offensive against his opponents (Witherington 1998, 260), employing the rhetorical strategy of *refutatio*. The speech is actually one continuous unit. On the basis of content, however, the speech may be divided into five parts: (1) the story of Abraham (7:2–8); (2) the story of Joseph and the patriarchs (7:9–16); (3) the story of Moses in three parts of forty years each (7:17–29, 30–34, 35–43); (4) the story of the tent and the temple (7:44–50); and finally (5) the invective against Stephen's listeners (7:51–53). All the parts fit together to make up Stephen's Christian interpretation of Jewish history.

1. Stephen begins his speech with an exordium, identifying with his audience: **Brothers . . . listen** (7:2a; by now a familiar opening; see 1:16; 2:29, 37; and later, 13:15, 26, 38; 15:7, 13; 23:1, 6; 28:17), thus framing the discourse as an intra-Jewish debate. Stephen here adds **and fathers**, not only showing respect to his audience, but also introducing a phrase repeated throughout the speech (translated "our ancestors" in the NRSV), which continually reminds Stephen's audience (and Luke's) that Stephen is himself a Jew who shares in this story (see 7:11, 12, 15, 32, 38, 39, 44; the significant shift to "your fathers" at 7:51, 52 will be dealt with below). The next reference to "our ancestor" is in the very next phrase: **The glorious God appeared to our ancestor Abraham** (7:2).

The story of Abraham is portrayed positively and invites Stephen's listeners (and Luke's audience) to identify with this shared story and the values it embodies, and thus also with the storyteller's point of view. The Lukan Stephen will draw on and modify a variety of traditions from Gen 11 and 15 to tell this part of the story. The focus of this unit, however, is neither on Abraham nor his faithfulness (cf. Gen 15:6). In fact, Abraham is a rather passive recipient.

Rather, God is the active focus of this scene. The phrase "glorious God" (7:2b) begins the speech proper (the *narratio* in rhetorical terms) and is unusual, appearing in the OT only at Ps 28:3 LXX (though cf. also *1 En.* 25.7); here it forms an *inclusio* with "God's glory" in 7:55. With the exception of **settled** in 7:4a, God is the subject of every main verb in 7:2–8a: God **appeared** (7:2), **said** (7:3), **resettled** [Abraham] (7:4b), **did not give** (7:5a), **promised** (7:5b), **spoke** (7:6), **said** (7:7), and **gave** (7:8a). The story is also framed by direct discourse from God (7:3, 7). This first episode is thoroughly theocentric and thus is a forceful, if indirect, response to the charge that Stephen spoke "blasphemous words against . . . God" (6:11). Stephen speaks wisely and Spirit-filled in behalf of God; he is represented as the divine mouthpiece.

Acts 7:2–53 in Context

Stephen (6:8–7:60)

   Controversy (6:8–7:1)

▶ Stephen's speech (7:2–53)

   1. Abraham (7:2–8)

   2. Joseph and the patriarchs (7:9–16)

   3. Moses in three parts of forty years each (7:17–43)

   4. The story of the tent and the temple (7:44–50)

   5. The invective against Stephen's listeners (7:51–53)

Martyrdom (7:54–60)

By noting that God appeared to Abraham **while he was in Mesopotamia before he settled in Haran** (7:2c), Stephen departs from any of the other versions that may have been known to the authorial audience (in addition to Gen 12, also *Jub.* 12.12–15; *LAB* 8.1–3; Josephus, *Ant.* 1.154; though see possibly Philo, *Abr.* 67). In those versions, Abraham had already migrated with his father, Terah, to Haran before God directed him to a new land. In Stephen's version, Abraham is still in Mesopotamia when God said to him, **Leave your country and your relatives and come to the land I will show you** (7:3; this address is a near verbatim citation of Gen 12:1). Mesopotamia becomes the point of origin for Abraham's divinely directed journey, perhaps because "he wanted to show his listeners that the call to a new land (to worship God) was at the very root of Abraham's earliest migration" (Kilgallen 1976, 42).

Abraham obeyed and **left the land of the Chaldeans and settled in Haran, and from there, after his father died, God resettled him in this land in which you now live** (7:4). Stephen apparently departs from biblical tradition again. A close reading of Gen 11:26–12:4 suggests that Abraham was born when his father, Terah, was seventy (11:26); Abraham left Haran at the age of seventy-five (Gen 12:4), when, by inference his father was 145 years old. Terah would then have lived sixty more years in Haran before dying there at the age of 205 (Gen 11:32). Perhaps Luke "paraphrases" his source by simply reading sequentially from Gen 11:32 (which records the death of Terah) to Gen 12:1 (which records the call of Abraham) and was not overly concerned with chronological accuracy. Certainly this detail has caught the attention of most modern commentators, but was most likely not an issue of concern for the ancient audience. Chrysostom, one of the earliest readers whose written reflections on Acts are extant, commented: "And how, it may be asked, does the scripture say this concerning Abraham's father? Because it does not trouble itself about matters that are not very essential. What was useful for to learn, this only has it taught" (variant reading in Chrysostom, *Hom. Act.* 15).

More important is Stephen's assertion that "God resettled him in this land in which you now live" (7:4). Two points are noteworthy. The use of "resettled" is striking and occurs in the NT only here and later in Stephen's speech at 7:43. Here it reinforces the theocentric

> ### Inflection in Acts 7
>
> The argument could be made that God is the subject, not only of this first episode 7:2–8, but of the entire speech. The Lukan Stephen uses the rhetorical device of "inflection" (*polyptoton* or *klisis*), in which the subject is inflected in all cases (Theon, *Prog.* 74.24–35, ed. Patillon 1997, 33; 85.29–31, ed. Patillon 1997, 48; Quintilian, *Inst.* 9.1.34). Stephen uses the word "God" (*theos*) seventeen times in his speech, twelve times in the nominative (7:2, 6, 7, 9, 17, 25, 32 [twice], 35, 37, 42, 45), three times in the genitive (7:43, 46, 56), and once each in the dative (7:20) and accusative (7:40).

focus of the passage. Abraham's migration was the result of divine fiat. The note that Abraham moved "in this land in which you now live" is curious since Stephen lives there as well. The rhetoric tends to distance Stephen from his audience and perhaps also downplays the importance of "place," which (from Stephen's point of view) has become disproportionately significant for his opponents. Here may well be the first hint of a polemic by Stephen against his audience (see Soards 1994, 62).

This implicit critique continues in the next verse: **He [God] did not give him a portion of it, not even a foot of space** (7:5a). Echoing the language of Deut 2:5 ("foot's length"), Stephen claims that Abraham received no land at this point but only a promise: **although he still did not have children, (God) promised to give it to him and to his descendants after him as a possession** (7:5b). Thus, in Stephen's retelling (which echoes Gen 12:7; 13:15; 15:2; 16:1; 17:8; and 48:4), when Abraham receives the promise from God, he is both landless and childless. The word "promise" does not occur in the Abraham story in the Greek OT and in fact is rather rare in the rest of the OT (see 2 Macc 2:17–18). The concept of "promise" is important for Luke, however (see Acts 1:4; 2:33, 39; 13:23, 32; 26:6; also Luke 24:49), and is referred to again in Stephen's speech at 7:17, where he introduces Moses' story by making reference to the impending fulfillment of the promise to Abraham.

Before the promise can be fulfilled, Stephen argues, Abraham's descendants must experience slavery and mistreatment: **God spoke in this way because his descendants would be temporary residents in a foreign land and (the citizens of that land) would enslave them and mistreat them for four hundred years. But God said, "I will punish the nation to whom they will be enslaved; and after these things they will come out and worship me in this place"** (7:6–7). The structure is similar to 7:48–50, which quotes Isa 66:1–2 using a "double speech formula" in which the first introduces the quotation and the second is inserted toward the end of the citation (see Richard 1978, 184). These verses are the heart of this opening unit. They serve as a précis for the general outline of the remainder of the speech: the suffering in Egypt (7:6, anticipating 9–22, esp. 17–21); the judgment on and exodus from Egypt (7:7a–b, anticipating 23–43, esp. 34, 36) and the subsequent Israelite worship (7:7c, anticipating 44–50, esp. 44, 47). These verses are also a quotation of Gen 15:13–14 (in 7:6–7a) and Exod 3:12 (in 7:7b), though not without modification, significant for Stephen's argument. The quote from Gen 15:13 changes the pronoun "they will enslave *them*" to literally "they will enslave *it*," where the antecedent is "seed" (*sperma*). The use of the singular underscores Stephen's point that the posterity of Abraham is preserved not through a group of persons but rather through "a series of individuals (e.g., Joseph, Moses, Joshua, David), culminating in the coming of the Just One (Acts 7:52)" (Richard 1978, 50).

The Lukan Stephen also paraphrases the quotation from Exod 3:12. First, note that a quotation from Exodus has been retrojected into the time of

Abraham, to explain that the act of Israel's worship went right back to the time of the Abrahamic covenant. Second, the phrase in Exod 3:12, "on this mountain," has been replaced with **in this place** as the site of the returning exiles' worship (7:7). In the immediate context, "this place" is to be understood as referring to "the land" promised to Abraham (Johnson 1992, 116), but the connection back to the accusation in 6:13–14 ("this man never stops saying things against this holy place"; "we have heard him saying that this Jesus, the Nazarene, will tear down this place") cannot be missed. First, Stephen again forcefully but indirectly addresses one of the charges against him. He acknowledges that the command to worship in the temple goes back to the very origins of Israelite faith. By making such a positive statement about the temple Stephen creates more tension: "How could the same God command the Israelites to worship Him in this place (indeed, he set them free so that they could do this) and then, at the high point of Israel's history (in Christian eyes), intend the destruction of the holy place of worship?" (Kilgallen 1976, 39). Stephen's explanation and resolution of this problem will come later in the speech.

Acts 7:8 functions as the transition to the next unit: **And he gave the covenant of circumcision to him; and consequently he had a son, Isaac, and circumcised him on the eighth day, and Isaac did the same to Jacob, and Jacob to the twelve patriarchs.** The reference to the "covenant of circumcision" is unusual ("covenant" occurs only here and at 3:25; the act of circumcising is mentioned in a speech again only in 21:21). It looks back to and resolves the problem of childless Abraham: he now has an heir, Isaac. "He gave" in 7:8a implies "God" as subject in continuity with 7:2, 5–6. Conversely, the shift in subject from God to Abraham and Isaac in 7:8b marks a shift away from the thoroughly theocentric character of the Abraham episode and points toward the next unit. Similarly the narrator "fast forwards" through a significant segment of Israelite history to arrive in the time of the patriarchs. Ending 7:8 and beginning 7:9 with the same term, "patriarchs," also serves both to link these two units together and to shift the focus to the time of Joseph.

2. The next unit in Stephen's speech, Acts 7:9–16, refers selectively to the story of Joseph and his brothers found in Gen 37–50. Though Joseph is the subject of much Second Temple literature (see *Jub.* 39–40; *LAB* 8; Josephus, *Ant.* 2.87–94; *T. Jos.*; *Jos. Asen.*; Philo, *Ios.*), only here in chapter 7 is Joseph ever the focus of the narrator of Acts (7:9, 13 [twice], 14, 18). Unlike the first section, however, there are no direct quotations from the OT, though the language and rhetoric clearly echo biblical idiom. The unit divides into three subunits: (1) the betrayal and rescue of Joseph (7:9–10); (2) Joseph and Jacob in Egypt (7:11–15a); and (3) the burial tradition (7:15b–16).

Perhaps the most important of the three subunits of Stephen's speech is the first: **The patriarchs were jealous of Joseph so they sold him into (slavery in) Egypt; but God was with him. He rescued him from all his troubles and gave** him favor and wisdom before Pharaoh, king of Egypt. He had him appointed ruler over Egypt and over Pharaoh's entire household (7:9–10). The beginning of the passage continues the polemic begun in the Abraham episode. "Patriarchs" is substituted for "brothers" (found in Gen 37:11) and underscores the point that Joseph's betrayers are none other than the founders of the tribes that later constitute Israel. They are culpable for selling Joseph into slavery in Egypt (contra Gen 37:28, 36, which claim that the Midianites, not Joseph's brothers, sold him into slavery), "because of jealousy" (note that other summaries of Joseph omit any reference to his brothers' jealousy; see Ps 104:17 LXX). Such an act of jealousy on the part of Joseph's brothers would have constituted for the authorial audience a severe case of censurable injustice (see Aristotle, *Rhet.* 1296a19–24). Stephen here responds for the first time to the charges that his Christian community was not keeping "the customs of Moses": he implies that from the beginning—indeed, even before Moses— the patriarchs had abandoned the "customs" by committing a censurable act of injustice, selling their brother into slavery (cf. Josephus, *Ant.* 4.146, 148; Athenaeus, *Deipn.* 6.22e–f).

Stephen's criticism continues in the implicit but sharp contrast between these "patriarchs" and Joseph (see Richard 1978, 186). God delivered Joseph from "all his troubles" (*thlipseōn*; 7:10), while "great suffering" (*thlipsis*) fell upon all of Canaan, including the patriarchs (7:11). God was with Joseph (7:9); by inference, he was not with the patriarchs. God appointed him ruler over Egypt (7:10; cf. Gen 45:8); the patriarchs (now called "our fathers") could not even find food (7:11).

Further, the specific characterization of Joseph is reminiscent of other characters in Acts. Stephen spoke with "wisdom" and was full of grace; Joseph was given **favor** and displayed **wisdom** (7:10). By use of an encomiastic *synkrisis*, Stephen highlights parallels between Joseph and Jesus (noted as long ago as Chrysostom, *Hom. Act.* 15; on encomiastic *synkrisis* or comparison, see Acts 3:13–15). About Joseph the audience is told: **God was with him** (7:9); Peter will later say the same about Jesus: "God was with him" (10:38). Likewise, Jesus is the first, according to the Third Gospel, to have both "wisdom" and "grace" (Luke 2:40, 52). Finally, the rhetoric and shape of the discourse echo the story of Jesus. God **rescued** (7:9) Joseph from all his afflictions and then enabled him to become the rescuer of his people. This rejected-yet-redeemed theme is prominent in the speeches in Acts: "This is the man who, delivered by the fixed intention and foreknowledge of God, you crucified and killed by the hands of lawless men. (He is the one) whom God raised up" (Acts 2:23–24; cf. also 2:31–33; 3:15–16; 4:10–12; 5:30–31; 10:39–40; 13:27–31; 26:23). As with Christ, so with Joseph, "the one who saves is the one who has been rejected, he saves those who rejected him precisely through their having rejected him" (Kilgallen 1976, 186).

The story of the famine (recorded in Gen 41–42) sets the context for the second subunit (7:11–15a). **Then a famine came over the whole (land) of Egypt and Canaan, (causing) great suffering, and our ancestors were unable to find food** (7:11). At this point, Stephen introduces a second character into the story, Jacob: **when he heard that there was grain in Egypt, he sent our ancestors** on their first trip (7:12; cf. Gen 42:2). The scene quickly passes from the "first" visit to the "second": **On their second trip, Joseph allowed himself to be recognized by his brothers and Joseph's racial background became known to Pharaoh. Then Joseph sent (someone) and summoned his father Jacob and all his relatives—seventy-five people in all. So Jacob went down to Egypt** (7:13–15a). If 7:9–10 records the salvation of Joseph, then 7:11–15a tells of the salvation of the "ancestors" through Joseph. Further, in all the versions of the Joseph cycle (see list above), the numbering of the visits as "first" and "second" is unique to Luke (see Johnson 1992, 118). "Already in the Joseph story, therefore, Luke shows the pattern that will be developed even more fully in his description of Moses, and which will structure his portrayal of Jesus as the prophet like Moses; the rejected and rescued savior, the double visitation with the possibility of further acceptance or rejection" (Johnson 1992, 122).

The reference to the burial site of the ancestors (7:15b–16) raises historical problems, which any modern commentary addresses. This much at least is clear: the ancestors received honorable burial because of the intercession of Joseph on their behalf. The burial notice also serves as the initial fulfillment of a "promised" land of "inheritance." Reminding his "Zionist" audience that the final resting place of the ancestors was ironically in hated Samaritan Shechem (and not in Jerusalem or even Hebron) gives Stephen no little pleasure (and prepares the authorial audience for the movement of the Christian gospel into Samaria in chap. 8). Finally, the story of Joseph explains how the people of Israel ended up in bondage in Egypt and why it was necessary for God to raise up a deliverer for the people, Moses.

3. Moses receives more attention in the speech than any other OT character. In 7:17–43, his life is divided into three periods of forty years each (17–29; 30–34; 35–43), presumably based on the tradition that Moses lived 120 years (see Deut 34:7). Assuming the authorial audience knows the primary account of Moses in the OT, comparison of redundancies and variations with these accounts may serve to highlight the importance the Lukan Stephen attached to each period.

Acts 7:17–29 recounts Moses' stay in Pharaoh's house. The section on Moses begins by recalling the promise to Abraham (cf. 7:6b): **As the time related to the promise that God had declared to Abraham drew near** (7:17a). Despite the fact that the fulfillment of the promise was still separated by 120 years (see 7:23, 30, 36; cf. 7:5), filled with the unspeakable death of Israelite infants, the exodus, the unfaithfulness of Israel, and the wilderness wanderings, the time of the promise had drawn near in the birth of Moses (7:20).

The second part of 7:17b–18, **the people multiplied and increased in Egypt until another king came to power over Egypt who did not know Joseph,** paraphrases Exod 1:7–8. The change from "sons of Israel" to "the people" reflects Luke's avoidance of using the name "Israel" for "Jacob" in this speech (cf. 7:8, 12, 14, 15, 32, 46; though cf. 7:42) and the narrator's preference in the rest of Acts for "the people" to refer to the Jews. The phrase "multiplied and increased" also echoes other occurrences in Acts in which the phrase refers to the growth of the church (cf. 6:7; 12:24). Even in the face of oppression, Israel in the early days in Egypt experienced the favor of God as did the early church in the face of persecution (Polhill 1992, 194).

The ancestors' oppression is expressed more fully in 7:19: **This man cunningly exploited our people and treated our ancestors cruelly, forcing them to abandon their babies so that they would die.** Again Stephen's speech draws on and abbreviates Exod 1:9–22. Verbal echoes with the OT are heard with the words "cunningly exploited" (see Exod 1:10), "treated cruelly" (Exod 1:11), and "so that they would die" (see Exod 1:22). Stephen employs a technical term (cf. Manetho, *Apot.* 6.52) for the exposure of infants (in Exodus only the male children are drowned; Stephen refers simply to the "babies"; on this story see also Josephus, *Ant.* 2.205–208).

At that very time (7:20a), that is, both the time of oppression and the time when the fulfillment of the Abrahamic promise was drawing near, **Moses was born.** The childhood of Moses is then summarized by Stephen: **and he was very pleasing to God. For three months he was raised in his father's house. But when he was abandoned, Pharaoh's daughter picked him up and raised him as her own son** (7:20b–21). Reference to Moses being "raised" or "nurtured" departs significantly from other descriptions of Moses' early infancy (in addition to Exod 2:3–4, see *Jub.* 47.3; Josephus, *Ant.* 2.218; Philo, *Mos.* 1.9; *LAB* 9.12). The explanation for the variation may be that Stephen employs "nurture" because it is the second part of the "classic biographical triad of 'birth, nurture, education'" (Johnson 1992, 125; see Plato, *Crito* 50E; 51C; Philo, *Mos.* 2.1; *Flacc.* 158). The Lukan Paul will use this same triad later in his "autobiographical" summary (Acts 22:3). After Moses was exposed (see Philo, *Mos.* 1.12), Pharaoh's daughter literally "picked him up" (as a technical term for "adoption," see Epictetus, *Diatr.* 1.23.7) and "raised him up as her own son."

Stephen's description of Moses' childhood ends with this summary: **And Moses was trained in all the wisdom of Egypt, and his words and deeds were powerful** (7:22). The word "trained" or "educated" completes the classical triad. The authorial audience may have been familiar with other traditions regarding Moses' prowess in Egyptian wisdom and culture (see Josephus, *Ant.* 2.233–235; Artapanus, *Jud.* frag. 3; [and later] Origen, *Cels.* 3.46; and esp. Philo, *Mos.* 1.20–24, who claims the child Moses actually surpassed his Egyptian and Greek teachers in knowledge; though cf. *LAB* 9.16 and *Jub.* 47.9, which emphasize his

Jewish education). A much "louder" echo is found, however, between this verse and Luke's earlier description of the childhood of Jesus: "And Jesus increased in wisdom and in stature, and in divine and human favor" (Luke 2:52). This parallel in description between Jesus and Moses would also explain the latter part of Acts 7:22, in which Stephen says that Moses was "powerful in his words and deeds." This phrase is a near-verbatim parallel to Luke's description of Jesus as "powerful in deed and word" (Luke 24:19; cf. Acts 2:22). Given this encomiastic *synkrisis* and the way in which the future greatness of Moses parallels that of Jesus, and taking into account the cumulative positive portrayal of Moses in the traditions (preserved in Torah and the subsequent accounts cited above), the authorial audience could easily comprehend Stephen's claim that Moses was "powerful in word" despite Moses' own claim to the contrary (see Exod 4:10).

The word "pleasing" or "beautiful" (cf. Exod 2:2) may also be explained on the basis of this Moses-Jesus *synkrisis*. While the tradition that Moses possessed remarkable physical qualities was widespread (cf. Philo, *Mos.* 1.9, 18; Josephus, *Ant.* 2.224; Heb 11:23), the word "beautiful," with the reverential dative of respect "before God," may also be a way of describing Moses' future greatness: "he was pleasing in God's eyes." The conceptual parallel to the childhood of Jesus ("and Jesus increased . . . in divine favor," Luke 2:52) is striking.

The second part of this first subscene passes over the youth of Moses to the time **when he was forty years old** (7:23). At that time, **an idea formed in his mind to visit his countrymen, the Israelites** (7:23b). The verb "visit" is used elsewhere in Luke and Acts to speak of God visiting his people (Luke 1:68; 7:16; Acts 15:14) or of Christian leaders looking after the churches they established (Acts 15:36); so here also, Moses "visits" his fellow Israelites as "God's emissary" (Polhill 1992, 195). What does Moses see? Stephen reports: **When he saw one of them being mistreated, he came to his aid and took revenge for the person who was mistreated by killing the Egyptian** (7:24).

While Stephen is very selective in his presentation of Israel's history, focusing almost exclusively on Abraham, Joseph, and Moses, in 7:23–29 he actually elaborates a story, giving more details about Moses' slaying of the Egyptian than appear in the Exodus account (Exod 2:11–15). Keeping the Exodus version in mind, Stephen adds and omits details in a way that justifies Moses' actions. Exodus simply says that Moses "saw an Egyptian beating a Hebrew" while Stephen argues that one of the Israelites was "being mistreated" and thus "took revenge for the person who was being mistreated by killing the Egyptian" (7:24). Stephen omits the detail in Exodus that Moses looked both ways and saw no one before striking the Egyptian, which gives the act a clandestine and perhaps even sinister sense. Also missing is the note in Exodus that when he is confronted by his fellow Hebrews about the death of the Egyptian, "Moses was afraid and thought, 'Surely the thing is known'" (Exod 2:14). Instead,

Moses is depicted as one who literally "made justice" on behalf of one who was "oppressed." Moses is also "powerful in deed" (7:22) and the killing of the Egyptian, from Stephen's perspective, is not only justifiable; it is a laudably just act. According to Greek rhetorical handbooks, injustice is the primary vice to be censured (see *Rhet. Alex.* 1421b37; Aristotle, *Rhet.* 1366a35–36).

The key to this section is found in 7:25: **Now he was thinking that his countrymen would see that God was bringing salvation to them through his efforts; but they did not see it that way.** Missing entirely from the OT story, the passage turns on the interplay between "see" (or "understand") and "not see" (or "not understand"). Rejection as the result of ignorance is found elsewhere in Acts (see 3:17; 28:26–27). What was it that his kinsfolk did not understand? Stephen claims Moses' kinsfolk did not understand that "God was bringing salvation to them through his efforts." By so interpreting the actions of Moses in Exod 2, Stephen here makes a very significant point: the action of Moses is more than an act of filial kindness; it is the righteous action of God's emissary intended to effect God's salvation for his people (cf. Acts 7:35).

In this way Stephen explains the next events that happen to Moses: **on the following day he unexpectedly came upon them—men who were fighting!—and he tried to make peace between them by saying, "Men! You are brothers! Why are you mistreating one another?" But the one who was mistreating his neighbor refused to listen and said, "Who appointed you as ruler and judge over us? Surely you're not planning to do away with me in the same way that you did away with the Egyptian yesterday?"** (7:26–28). Any cloud of doubt on Moses' character hinted at in Exodus is now shifted to overshadow the character of the people who do not understand Moses' role as their liberator. Here the Christian interpretation is most evident: it is necessary for Stephen to remove any aspersions about this episode in the life of Moses in order that the parallel between Moses the rejected prophet and Jesus the rejected prophet may be complete.

This unit ends with a reference to Moses' flight from Egypt: **When he heard this, Moses fled and became a temporary resident in the land of Midian, where he had two sons** (7:29). In the OT version, Moses leaves Egypt out of fear of Pharaoh; in Stephen's version, Moses is forced to flee because his kinsfolk do not comprehend his role as their liberator (cf. the various renditions of Moses' flight available to the authorial audience; *Jub.* 47.12; Artapanus, *Jud.* frag. 3; Josephus, *Ant.* 2.254–256; Philo, *Mos.* 1.43–46; and *LAB* 9.6–10.1, who omits any reference to the flight). The note that he became a "temporary resident" (cf. 7:6) in Midian where he fathered two sons not only fills the gap between the flight from Egypt and the following episode of the burning bush; it emphasizes "that but for the divine call Moses would have good reason to remain in Midian" (Barrett 1994, 1:360).

The second subunit of the Moses episode (7:30–34) begins with another temporal reference, **after forty years had passed** (7:30a). The scene comes to rest in the desert of Mount Sinai where an angel . . . appeared to Moses in the flame of a burning bush (7:30b). The verse recalls the event narrated in Exod 3:1–2. Angels appear in God's service and for the benefit of his people in 7:30, 35, 38, and 53. Moses' response is described in the barest of narrative detail: When Moses saw this, he was amazed at the sight, and when he approached it to get a closer look, (he heard) the voice of the Lord (7:31). The end of the verse changes the "angelophany" to a "theophany": Moses hears the very voice of the Lord.

The voice declares: I am the God of your ancestors, the God of Abraham, Isaac, and Jacob (7:32a). This time Moses began to tremble and did not dare look any closer (7:32b; cf. 7:31). The Lord then commanded him, Take off your sandals, for the place where you are standing is holy ground (7:33). The reference to "holy ground" is significant in the context of Stephen's speech. Identifying this place on Mount Sinai as "holy" relativizes the claims about "this holy place" that formed part of the charge against Stephen (Acts 6:13). "'Holy,' he suggests, is where the presence of God is" (Johnson 1992, 128).

This subunit ends with Moses' commission: I have surely seen the mistreatment of my people in Egypt and I have heard their groaning, and I have come down to take them away (from there). Now come, let me send you to Egypt (7:34). This verse recalls the outline at the beginning of Stephen's speech in which he reports that God declared: "I will judge the nation that they serve . . . and after that they shall come out" (7:7). God confirms what Moses had thought: Moses is the one "sent" or "commissioned" by God (see Luke 1:19; 4:18; 7:27; 9:2; 10:1; 11:49; Acts 3:20, 26) to "rescue" them (cf. 7:25).

The last subunit (7:35–43) addresses two issues. First, it begins by answering the question posed by the Israelite to Moses: Who appointed you as ruler and judge? (7:35b; cf. 7:25). The answer, of course, is "God." In fact, Stephen delares that Moses is the one God sent as both ruler and deliverer with the help of the angel who appeared to him in the bush (7:35c). The shift from singular to plural in This Moses—whom they had rejected (7:35a) indicates that the rejection of Moses was not limited to one indignant Israelite; rather, the Israelite mentioned in 7:25 was representative of the rejection of Moses by the nation. This act of disobedience toward a ruler is another censurable deed by which the ancestors have not kept the "customs of Moses" (on praising or censuring a city or a people according to their willingness to be ruled, see Menander, *Epid.* 3.360.10; Dionysius of Halicarnassus, *Ant. Rom.* 2.9.2; Josephus, *C. Ap.* 110–111; *Ant.* 4.186–190).

The term deliverer is introduced here for the first time (in place of "judge"; cf. 7:25, 35a) and recalls Luke 24:21, in which the two on the road to Emmaus lament that Christ had been the "one who was going to deliver Israel." Finally, the emphatic "this" in 7:35a ("this Moses") recurs in this is the one (7:35b), this man (7:36), this is the Moses (7:37), and this is the man (7:38) and may point to a kind of "Moses hymn" (cf. the Christ hymn of Col 1:13–20), with several distinct elements:

1. The man rejected by the people becomes ruler and deliverer (7:35).
2. He becomes deliverer through signs and wonders given by God (7:36).
3. He is both prophet and prototype of the Coming One (7:37).
4. He is mediator between God and people in the "assembly" (7:38a; note the use of *ekklēsia*, which is also commonly used to refer to the gathering of Christians).
5. He is the receiver and giver of words of life (7:38b; cf. 5:20).
6. His people reject him (7:39; see Barrett 1994, 1:362–63).

Whether understood as an actual hymn or not, these points highlight the continuing parallels between Moses and Jesus. Both Jesus and Moses accomplished an "exodus" (7:36; cf. Luke 9:31) and performed signs and wonders (7:36; see 2:22; along with Stephen; see 6:8). Both Moses and Jesus are prophets. The typology is made explicit in Moses' words to the Israelites, **God will raise up for you a prophet like me from your brothers** (7:37). This theme of Jesus as the "prophet like Moses" (see 3:22) is the most important parallel and lies at the heart of the Stephen speech. The ignorance of the people regarding Moses' call (7:25) and their subsequent rejection of him (7:35) foreshadow the rejection of Jesus by the people (7:52).

The rejection of the representatives of God is no less than a rejection of God himself: **Our ancestors were unwilling to obey him, but rejected (him) and, and in their hearts, returned to Egypt** (7:39). That is the point made in the second part of this episode (7:40–43). This turning of their hearts is mobilized into action. Not knowing what had happened to Moses (7:40), the people turned to idolatry, **made a calf** (cf. 7:41), **offered a sacrifice to the idol** (7:41a), and they **began to celebrate what they had made** (7:41b). This act of impiety is omitted by Josephus (see *Ant.* 3.90), but labeled by Philo as Israel's "great backsliding from the ways of their fathers" (*Mos.* 2.270).

God's response is twofold: First, God turned away from them and **handed them over to worship the stars of the sky** (7:42; cf. Wis 11:15). The worship of the "stars of the sky" is part of their punishment. Then God punishes them by removing them **beyond Babylon** (7:43). Here Luke paraphrases his source, Amos, from "beyond Damascus" to "beyond Babylon" to summarize the history of Israel from the wilderness wanderings to the exile as one of idolatry. The quotation of Amos 5:25–27 in Acts 7 reads: **Did you bring offerings and sacrifices to me for forty years in the wilderness, people of Israel? (No!) But you took along the tent of Molech and the star of [your] God Rephan, the images you made to worship, so I will deport you beyond Babylon** (Acts 7:42b–43). With the first part of the Amos passage, Stephen claims that the Israelites did, in fact, offer sacrifices to God in true acts of worship. The next verse (7:43), however, supports the accusation that the idolatry was not limited to the construction of a calf, but included the false worship of Molech and the astral idolatry of the star of Rephan. Stephen's addition of "to worship" to Amos also serves to underscore the counterfeit nature of Israel's worship. The punishment, then, of being removed "beyond Babylon" (reversing Abraham's transport in 7:4 from "beyond Babylon" to Palestine), from Stephen's point of view, is fully justified.

The Moses episode also contains Stephen's second indirect response to the accusation that Stephen had claimed that Jesus would change the "customs of Moses" (6:14). The rhetoric of Stephen's argument indicates that the Jewish leadership, not the followers of Jesus, are responsible for abandoning Moses and the law through acts of impiety (7:39; cf. 7:53). From Stephen's perspective, the Christian community is the "true Israel," that is, the group within Judaism who is authentically preserving the "customs of Moses" as they reflected the purpose and destiny of the people of God.

4. The next unit (7:44–50) addresses the second charge against Stephen, that he claimed that Jesus would destroy "this place" (i.e., the temple). The passage begins with a cluster of terms (italicized in the following translation) found in the preceding quotation from Amos: **Our ancestors had the *tent*** (cf. 7:43) **of testimony in the *wilderness*** (cf. 7:42b), **just as he who spoke to Moses commanded (him) to make it according to the *pattern*** (cf. 7:43b) **he had seen** (7:44). The cumulative effect of the cluster is to underscore the indictment that at the same time the ancestors were engaging in impious acts of idolatry, the "tent of testimony" that Moses had made was available to them. Further, this "tent," precursor to the temple, was divinely authorized (7:44b). This is an important note, since Stephen's complaint, as we shall see, is not against the existence of the temple per se.

Stephen then quickly summarizes the period between the wilderness wandering and the time of David: **Our ancestors inherited it and brought it with Joshua when they took possession of the nations that God drove out from the presence of our ancestors until the days of David** (7:45). Mention of Joshua's name (*Iēsou*) must surely have caused the audience to think, at least momentarily, about Jesus (also *Iēsou*), whose name has not been explicitly mentioned (nor shall it be) in Stephen's speech (see Soards 1994, 67). Reference to "took possession" recalls and fulfills the promise God made to Abraham to give the land as his "possession" (see 7:5).

But according to Stephen it was David who, like Jesus (Luke 2:52) and Moses (7:20), **found favor before God and asked to find a dwelling place for the descendants [or God] of Jacob** (7:46). Again there is no criticism here of seeking a "dwelling place" for God. It is only when Solomon "built a house for him [i.e., God's dwelling to be used by the house of Jacob]" (7:47) that Stephen offers what amounts to a prophetic critique: **Yet the Most High certainly does not live in something made by human hands, as the prophet says, "Heaven is** my throne, and the earth my footstool. What sort of house will you build for me?" says the Lord. "Or what will be my place of rest? Didn't my hand make all of these things?" (Acts 7:49–50; cf. Isa 66:1). The criticism is not directly leveled against the temple per se, but rather against the view that God's presence is limited to a particular place, a view that Stephen implies is connoted by the term "house." Only here in 7:46–47 in all of Acts does "house" refer to the temple. The word "house" in this context seems to limit God's self-disclosure to the temple. Such a view, for Stephen, is idolatrous, as evidenced by his assertion that the Most High does not dwell in "handmade" places, a term that elsewhere refers to the idolatrous practices of pagans (see Isa 16:12 LXX; Acts 17:24). The citation of Isa 66:1–2 supports Stephen's claim: God, whose throne is heaven and whose footstool is earth, transcends the temple, and any claim that God is limited to the temple is to be rejected.

Though Stephen does not make explicit the consequences for violating the purposes of the temple as he did the claim that God would judge the people's misunderstanding of Moses and his "customs" (7:42–43), the authorial audience hears this invective against the background of the destruction of the temple. Stephen's speech is not only drawing on the content of OT Israel's history; he is implicitly employing the familiar pattern of the Deuteronomistic History of disobedience, punishment, and call to repentance to make sense of the temple's destruction. The people had defied the purpose of temple worship and suffered the destruction of that institution. But the Lukan Stephen is not content only to offer critique of what he considers an inadequate view of the temple's purpose; he also redefines the social institution of the "house." It is not a way to limit the presence of God, but rather functions now for the Christian community in the way the temple had been intended for Israel, as the place where the people of God gather to worship.

5. The climax of the speech, the peroration, occurs here at the end (7:51–53). **You stiff-necked people! Uncircumcised in heart and in ears! You always resist**

Antithesis

The Lukan Stephen strengthens the contrast between the heavenly God and the earthly temple (7:49–50) by use of the rhetorical figure of *contentio* (antithesis), which according to pseudo-Cicero "is built upon contraries, as follows: 'Flattery has pleasant beginnings, but also brings on bitterest endings.' Again: 'To enemies you show yourself conciliatory, to friends inexorable'" (*Rhet. Her.* 4.15.21, trans. Caplan 1954, 283; cf. Quintilian, *Inst.* 9.3.81). Pseudo-Cicero concludes that "embellishing our style by means of this figure" will "give it impressiveness and distinction" (*Rhet. Her.* 4.15.21). So Stephen contrasts the limited view of a God who dwells in a house made with hands with the Isaianic God whose throne is heaven and whose footstool is the earth (7:49; Isa 66:1).

the Holy Spirit; as your ancestors did, so do you! (7:51). The rhetoric of this invective is harsh, and Stephen interrupts the negative labeling of his opponents with a little negative labeling of his own. Stephen calls his audience "stiff-necked" (cf. Exod 33:3, 5; Deut 9:6, 13, 27) and "uncircumcised in heart and ears" (cf. Lev 26:41; Jer 4:4; 6:10; 9:26; Ezek 44:7, 9). By referring to them as "uncircumcised," Stephen implies they have rejected in the deepest sense the covenant of circumcision, which God had given to Abraham (cf. 7:8). Thus the speech functions as a double invective, condemning both Stephen's audience and their ancestors (on the appeal to ancestors in an invective, see Aphthonius, *Prog.* 22R, trans. Kennedy 2003, 108). Further, the shift from "our ancestors" to "your ancestors" is startling and sharp; Stephen distances himself from both the ancestors and his contemporaries who were guilty of "forever opposing the Holy Spirit" (7:51). How had they done so? Stephen responds with a question: **Which of the prophets did your ancestors not persecute? They killed those who foretold the coming of the Righteous One, whose betrayers and murderers you have now become—you people who received the law through decrees given by angels, but did not keep it!** (7:52–53). They had rejected the prophets from Joseph to Moses to Jesus, the Righteous One (cf. Acts 3:14; cf. Luke 11:47–51 // Matt 23:34–36; Luke 13:34–35 // Matt 23:37–39), and they had an inadequate understanding of where and how they were to worship. By their acts of impiety, injustice, and disobedience, they had rejected the laws and customs of Moses. Their rejection of the Holy Spirit was to continue right through the speech of Stephen, who was full of the Holy Spirit (6:5) and spoke with the Holy Spirit (6:10). They had not kept these things that had been "ordained by angels" (7:53) and now they were about to reject the one whose "face was like the face of an angel" (6:15).

7:54–60. If the emotionally charged language of the speech's conclusion is designed to provoke a response from the hearer, Stephen's speech certainly achieves its goal: it results in his stoning (7:54–60). Earlier in the Pentecost sermon, Peter had leveled similar accusations against his listeners, which "cut to the heart" and led to their repentance. Here those whose hearts and ears are "uncircumcised" (7:51) harden their hearts and **cover their ears** (7:57) and drag Stephen out of the city to stone him, with one Saul aiding and abetting them.

This violent action only occurs after Stephen has recounted his vision of **the Son of Man standing at the right hand of God** (7:56; thus repeating the action of 7:55 and employing the rhetorical figure of *conversio* [*antistrophe*] in which the phrase [in this case "the right hand of God"] is repeated at the end of each line for emphasis; see *Rhet. Her.* 4.13.19 and the note on Acts 1:11). The term "Son of Man" (see Dan 7:13) occurs only here outside the Gospels, and the curious detail that the Son of Man is standing rather than sitting (see Luke 22:69) may be taken both in a juridical sense, in which Jesus stands in advocacy for Stephen before God (see Gen 18:22; Exod 8:20; 9:13; Jer 18:20;

Pronominatio

In 7:51, Stephen uses the figure of diction *pronominatio* (*antonomasia*) to heighten the emotional content of the invective. According to pseudo-Cicero, *pronominatio*

> "*designates by a kind adventitious epithet a thing that cannot be called by its proper name: for example . . . if someone speaking of his adversary should say: 'See now, men of the jury, how your Sir Swashbuckler [Plagioxiphus, lit. "flat of the blade"] there has treated me.' In this way we shall be able, not without elegance, in praise and in censure, concerning physical attributes*, qualities of character *or external circumstances, to express ourselves by using a kind of epithet in place of a precise name.*" (*Rhet. Her.* 4.31.42, trans. Caplan 1954, 335; emphasis added)

The audience that Stephen had originally addressed as "brothers and fathers" (7:2) has now become "stiff-necked" and "uncircumcised in heart and ears."

Zech 3:1–8), and as a posture of hospitality, in which Jesus stands to welcome Stephen in response to his plea to "receive my Spirit" (Luke 21:36; see Johnson 1992, 139). The last words of Stephen continue the parallels with Jesus begun in 6:8–15. Stephen's **Lord Jesus, receive my spirit** (7:59) is reminiscent of Jesus' word from the cross, "Father, into your hands I commend my spirit" (Luke 23:46), and Stephen's final words, **Lord, do not count this sin against them** (Acts 7:60) echo Jesus' prayer, "Father, forgive them, for they know not what they do" (Luke 23:34, though textually dubious and the parallel may run in the other direction; see Whitlark and Parsons 2006). Stephen, like Jesus in the Third Gospel, dies the death of an innocent martyr and thus takes his place as yet another example of a prophet who, because he spoke of "the coming of the Righteous One" (Acts 7:52), is the victim of "stiff-necked people" who continue to persecute the representatives of God.

Theological Issues

The use of the OT in the NT has been the focus of much recent study (see especially Hays 1989); nor has analysis of Luke's use of the OT been ignored (e.g., Rese 1969; Bock 1987; Sanders and Evans 1993). The issues, both textual (what OT text the NT writer is quoting) and hermeneutical (how the NT use of the OT informs contemporary Christian appropriation of scripture), raised by these studies are important, but too often these studies are too narrowly or, conversely, too broadly conceived to be of real use. For example, older (and some recent) studies focus almost exclusively on the issues attendant to the question on which OT text the NT writer is following: Is the underlying text

Figure 5. Annibale Carracci, *The Martyrdom of St. Stephen*, 1603–1604. Oil on canvas. Museé du Louvre, Paris.

The Italian artist Annibale Carracci contrasts the chaos of Stephen's frenzied opponents, who are about to stone him, with the serene Stephen. He assumes a posture of prayer and looks to the heavens, where he sees the Son of Man on the Father's right side.

Réunion des Musées Nationaux / Art Resource, NY

from the Hebrew or the Greek? If the text is from the Greek, which version? How do we explain the discrepancies and variations between the OT text and the version cited by the NT? Is the author using a text no longer extant, or quoting from memory, or making creative use of scripture?

When we examine Stephen's speech and its use of the OT in light of the rhetorical handbooks, our questions take on another, more historically plausible, alternative, namely, that Luke's citation of texts reflects rhetorical conventions of dealing with quoted material. For example, in his chapter on paraphrasing, Theon suggests that there are four main kinds: "variation in syntax, by addition, by subtraction, and by substitution, plus some combinations of these" (*Prog.* 108P, trans. Kennedy 2003, 70). Specifically with regard to word difference, Theon notes on "substitution": "We replace the original word with another; for example, *pais* or *andrapodon* for *doulos* (slave)" (*Prog.* 109P, trans. Kennedy 2003, 70). Thus slight changes in words might be due to neither of the reasons most often suggested (a different text or quotation from memory), but rather simply an expected compositional technique in the ancient world. Theon's emphasis is similar to what Quintilian says with regard to the orators' citation or paraphrase: "I would not have paraphrase [*conversio*] restrict itself to the bare interpretation of the original; its duty is rather to rival and vie with the original in the expression of the same thoughts" (*Inst.* 10.5.5, trans. Butler 1921). Remember that, according to the Hermogenic Corpus, adaptation occurs "whenever, after quoting part of the verse, one in his own words expresses the rest in prose and then quoting another verse adds something of his own, so that it becomes a single idea" (*Meth. dein.* 30, trans. Kennedy 2003, 252–55).

The Lukan Stephen has adapted his authoritative source to offer a persuasive "single idea." The speech is not a comprehensive retelling of Jewish history; in fact, it is very selective, with direct quotations from Genesis, Exodus, Deuteronomy, Amos, and Isaiah and scores of allusions to many other OT works (in addition to those already cited, Leviticus; Numbers; Joshua; 1 Kings; 1 Chronicles; 2 Chronicles; Nehemiah; Psalms; Jeremiah; Hosea; and possibly *Assumption of Moses*). As such it stands in a long line of summaries of Jewish (see Deut 6:20–24; 26:5–9; Josh 24:2; Neh 9:6–31; Pss 77; 104; 105; 135; Ezek 20; Jdt 5:6–18; Wis 10; Sir 44–50; Josephus, *BJ* 5.377–400) and Greek history (Herodotus, *Hist.* 9.26–27; Thucydides, *Hist.* 1.3.68–70; 2.6.35–47; like Acts, using the medium of the retrospective speech). Like those predecessors this story is not a dispassionate, neutral account; unlike them, it is history told from a Christian perspective. As is the case in so many discourses, both oral and written, the purpose of Stephen's recounting of Israel's history comes into focus only at the end of the speech. At the end of the speech (the peroration), Stephen accuses his listeners of "opposing the Holy Spirit, just as your ancestors used to do" (7:52). Specifically, just as the ancestors had persecuted the prophets, so now their descendants had betrayed and murdered the Righteous One whose coming the prophets had foretold (7:52). Both ancestors and contemporaries had rejected the law they had received. In short, Stephen argues that the death of Jesus fits into the overall pattern of rejection that was characteristic of Israel's history. All that goes before this part of the speech leads, in one way or another, to this climax.

The narrative context makes clear that Stephen is rehearsing Israel's history in order to refute the charges against him, namely that he and his compatriots are blaspheming both temple and law. Refutation requires great literary creativity in order to be persuasive to the audience. The effective refutation will draw on all available resources (including authoritative texts and stories), but cannot be handcuffed by following set formal arguments. On this point, Quintilian remarks:

Let it [the refutation] therefore travel not by the narrow paths, but over the open plains, not like a scanty spring conveyed in narrow pipes, but like the mightiest rivers that fill the whole valleys. If it does not find a way prepared for it, let it make one for itself. What is more debilitating than these petty rules, which make us behave like little children tracing the shapes of the letters or (as the Greeks say) carefully keeping to the clothes that mother gave? (*Inst.* 5.14.13–31, trans. Butler 1921)

Running parallel with this theme of refutation, however, is Stephen's paraphrase of the OT text and story in order to highlight the exemplars from Israel's past who are worthy of praise (see Penner 2004, 289–90). In other words, for every negative example there is a positive one, a kind of overarching *synkrisis* that may be summarized as in table 1. The rhetorical point of Stephen's speech was to employ Israel's story and canon in order to refute the charges that the Christian "Way" represents a radical departure from the worship of and covenant with God. But claiming that the opponents' version of the story was false was not enough; Stephen needed also to supply a competing version of the story that was coherent and compelling. And so he does: throughout their shared history, Stephen counters, exemplars who followed God's way can be found. Luke's ability to replace what he regarded as a false story with his own is no mean accomplishment. As Theon noted, "Not only to refute such mythologies, but also to show how such a distorted story originated, is a matter for a more mature skill than most have" (Theon, *Prog.* 95, trans. Kennedy 2003, 41–42).

Table 1.
Paired Positive and Negative Exempla in Stephen's Speech
(Reich 2005)

Encomium for Those Accepting God's Message and Messengers	Invective against Those Rejecting God's Message and Messengers
7:2–8 Abraham (obeys God; receives promise)	7:2–8 Egyptians (unnamed but represent nation who enslaved and ill-treated Abraham's seed for four hundred years)
7:9 Joseph (God was with him)	7:9–10 Joseph's brothers (patriarchs who were jealous and thus sold Joseph, rejecting God's representative)
7:30–39 Moses (God sends him to liberate Jewish slaves; raised up as a prophet; received living oracles)	7:35–41 Israelites in wilderness (reject Moses; in disobedience, make a golden calf to worship; reject worship of God)
7:52 Prophets (prophesied the coming of the Righteous One)	7:52 Ancestors (killed the prophets, thus rejecting God's representatives)
7:52 The Righteous One (God's appointed one)	7:52 Stephen's audience (betrayed and murdered the Righteous One, God's representative)
7:54–60 Stephen (representing the church; full of faith and Spirit [6:5]; sees vision of God; martyr's death)	7:54–60 Stephen's audience (kills Stephen, God's representative)

Understanding Stephen's speech as a *synkrisis* that draws on Israel's history for both positive and negative examples has important theological implications.

Some interpreters, hearing only the refutation, see anti-Jewish overtones in the speech, especially in its conclusion. Jon Weatherly writes:

> Do various details of the text indicate that Luke holds all Israel responsible for Stephen's death, and so also for its parallel, the crucifixion of Jesus? Does Stephen's speech, especially with its negative survey of Israel's history and possible disparagement of the temple, suggest a condemnation of the entire Jewish nation? Or does the structure of the narrative indicate that the Stephen episode is a watershed, marking the decisive rejection of the gospel by the Jews? (Weatherly 1994, 129)

Reading the speech through the lens of *synkrisis*, however, yields a different conclusion. Stephen is not pitting Christianity over against Judaism; rather, he is aligning himself and his group with what he considers to be the "best" in Jewish history. And throughout this argument, the Lukan Stephen appeals constantly to Israel's scripture and story. Luke's use of the OT, especially in constructing the argument of Acts 7, must be understood within a larger rhetorical and theological framework. There are in his version of Israel's history two Jewish groups: those who accept God's message and messengers and those who reject. The *synkrisis* Stephen develops in Acts 7 aligns Stephen and the church with Abraham, Joseph, the prophets, and Jesus. His opponents are aligned with the Egyptians, Joseph's brothers, the rebellious in the wilderness who disobeyed Moses, and the ancestors who killed the prophets. For Luke, rather than rejecting God's house or God's law, the church is in line with the faithful in Jewish history who have sought to keep covenant with God.

Beyond Jerusalem: Philip, Saul, Peter, and Others

The second section of Acts (chaps. 8–12) focuses on specific persons (Philip, Saul, Peter) and their part in spreading the good news of Jesus beyond the borders of Judea. The accounts of these missionary activities are interspersed with reports of struggles within the community over the conversions of Saul (who will be called "Paul" beginning in 13:9) and Cornelius to Christianity (chaps. 9, 11) and persecutions of the church by the Roman authorities (chap. 12).

Acts 8–12 in Context

The people and places of the Jerusalem church (1–12)

   The sense of a beginning (1–7)

▶ Beyond Jerusalem: Philip, Saul, Peter, and others (8–12)

    Philip: a man on a mission (8)

    Saul and Ananias: conversion and call (9:1–31)

    Peter: his words and deeds (9:32–11:18)

    Barnabas, Peter, and Herod (11:19–12:25)

The missionary activities of Paul (13–28)

   Paul's mission to the Gentile world (13–19)

   Paul's farewell journey (20–28)

Acts 8

Philip: A Man on a Mission

Introductory Matters

Luke has used the rhetorical device of the chain-link interlock to connect the various units of Acts (Longenecker 2005; see introduction). Here the two parts of the first half of the books of Acts (chaps. 1–7 and 8–12) are linked by 8:1–3. (See the details below under Tracing the Narrative Flow.)

What is a chain-link interlock? Lucian (c. AD 125–180) offered the following advice to writers about connecting text units:

> Though all parts must be independently perfected, when the first is complete the second will be brought into essential connection with it, and attached like one link of a chain to another; there must be no possibility of separating them; no mere bundle of parallel threads; the first is not simply to be next to the second, but part of it, their extremities intermingling. (*Hist. conscr.* 55; Longenecker 2005, 12)

Quintilian seems to describe a similar phenomenon when he suggests that an orator's speech should reflect

> a certain continuity of motion and connection of style. All its members are to be closely linked together, while the fluidity of its style gives it great variety of movement; we may compare its motion to that of people who link hands to steady their steps, and lend each other mutual support. (*Inst.* 9.4.129; Longenecker 2005, 13)

These ancient writers draw on existing convention, and while the chain-link interlock is not much discussed in the rhetorical handbooks and *progymnasmata*, its practice among ancient writers seems widespread and includes a number of early Christian writers (Longenecker 2005, 15–18). The pattern of a chain link is A b a B, resulting in "the overlapping of material (via content repetition or a gesture of some kind) at the boundary of two text units" (Longenecker 2005, 19).

Tracing the Narrative Flow

Luke uses chain-link interlock in 8:1–3 to connect Acts 1–7 with Acts 8–12. Then, having made his transition from events in the Jerusalem church to the activities of those dispersed, he turns his attention to a more detailed analysis of the efforts of one of those scattered, Philip, in Samaria (8:4–25) and beyond (8:26–40).

Table 2.
Chain-Link Interlock at Acts 8:1b–3
(Longenecker 2005, 194)

TEXT-UNIT "A"	INTERLOCKED "b" (anticipatory)	INTERLOCKED "a" (retrospective)	TEXT-UNIT "B"
Acts 1:1–8:3	Acts 8:1b, 3	Acts 8:2	Acts 8:4–12:25

Transition (Interlock) (8:1–3)

Luke concludes the episode of Stephen's speech and martyrdom with the notice that this persecution was not limited to Stephen; rather, that day, a severe persecution broke out against the Jerusalem church, and all except the apostles were scattered throughout the regions of Judea and Samaria (8:1b). The reference to the "scattered" anticipates the preaching activity of the scattered that will be introduced in 8:4. At this point Luke inserts an anticipatory link to the story of Paul's conversion in Acts 9: But Saul was devastating the church; he was going from house to house, dragging off both men and women, and delivering them to prison (8:3). These two verses, 8:1b and 8:3, then, anticipate the narratives of Philip and Paul, immediately following (8:4–40; 9:1–31). Sandwiched between them is a retrospective conclusion of the Stephen episode: **(Some) devout men buried Stephen and mourned loudly for him** (8:2). Stephen is given proper burial by "devout persons," a sign of the esteem in which he was held by fellow believers (see Luke 23:50), as is the note that "they mourned deeply for him" (8:2; cf. Luke 23:27, 48).

Philip and Simon Magus (8:4–25)

Acts 8:4–25 is marked off by an *inclusio* in Acts 8:4 and 8:25. Both summary statements refer to "preaching" and the "word/message." Within the *inclusio* are two panels of the same story.

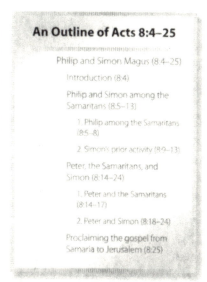

An Outline of Acts 8:4–25

Philip and Simon Magus (8:4–25)

Introduction (8:4)

Philip and Simon among the Samaritans (8:5–13)

1. Philip among the Samaritans (8:5–8)

2. Simon's prior activity (8:9–13)

Peter, the Samaritans, and Simon (8:14–24)

1. Peter and the Samaritans (8:14–17)

2. Peter and Simon (8:18–24)

Proclaiming the gospel from Samaria to Jerusalem (8:25)

8:4. **Those who had been scattered traveled around preaching the word** (8:4) leads into the first scene (8:5–13), which presents the Samaritan mission of Philip. The second scene (8:14–24), featuring the Samaritan activity of the Jerusalem apostles Peter and John, will close with their "preaching the gospel in many Samaritan villages" (8:25) as they travel back to Jerusalem.

8:5–13. The first scene divides into two parts: (1) Philip's activity among the Samaritans (8:5–8); and (2) the prior activity of a "certain man named Simon" among these same Samaritans (8:9–13). The ministry of Philip, as one of those scattered (see 8:4), is directly linked to the persecution of the Jerusalem church mentioned in 8:1. The first step in fulfilling Jesus' commission (Acts 1:8) is an ironic one. Philip, a member of the Seven and not an apostle, is the first to step beyond Judean borders to proclaim the Christian message in Samaria.

1. Philip's ministry in **Samaria** (8:5) is the culmination of an elaborate portrayal of Samaria/Samaritans, which began in Luke and continues in Acts. The uneasy alliance between the Jews and Samaritans in rejecting the mission of Jesus has been broken. Now when the gospel is preached to the Samaritans, **the crowds, without exception, paid close attention to the things that Philip was saying** (Acts 8:6). Even when the message that Jesus is the Messiah, the Christ (8:5), goes against Samaritan expectations for a *taheb*, who would restore the true worship on Gerazim, the Samaritans are receptive "without exception" (*homothymadon*; cf. 1:14).

Samaria/Samaritans are ambiguously located in the overlap between Jew and Gentile. Luke does not try to clarify the Samaritans' status; he is content to claim that despite the ambivalent role of Samaria, they are worthy of hearing the gospel. So Philip goes to the no-man's-land between Jew and Gentile, to an unnamed city of Samaria, and in that "polluted" place proclaims to them the Messiah.

Many of those healed are described as having **unclean spirits** (8:7), which come out **screaming in a loud voice** (see Gen 39:14 LXX), a typical sign accompanying exorcisms (cf. Luke 4:33–35; 8:28–33; 9:39–42; and Lucian, *Philops.* 16). This "ekphrastic" language (cf. 2:4) may also explain how the crowds not only **saw** but also **heard** the signs that Philip was performing (8:6).

2. But the unclean and the outcasts are not the only ones who come to hear Philip preach and perform signs. According to Acts 8:10, the crowd that was astonished by the magic of Simon included **the least to the greatest**, most likely a social designation to refer to those who have (or do not have) honor, influence, or power (see also Acts 26:22). So here, in a city that blurred the ethnic distinctions between Jew and Gentile, is gathered a cross-section of the city's populace, which transgressed the established economic, gender, and purity codes. This makes Luke's earlier note that the crowds were attentive "without exception" (8:6) even more remarkable. Philip's ministry had profound social implications, and as a result, **there was great joy in that city** (8:8).

One of Luke's purposes in recording Philip's encounter with Simon (8:9–13) was to respond to charges that the signs and wonders performed by early Christian missionaries were indistinguishable from the magical practices of antiquity. Luke concedes (contra later apologists) that outwardly there are similarities between Christian miracle workers and magicians, but then argues that the similarities are only superficial—at a deeper level there are profound differences between "Christian miracles" and "pagan magic." This story is the first of three in Acts (cf. also Acts 13:4–12; 19:11–20) that form a type-scene in which a Christian missionary (Philip, Paul) encounters and defeats the practice of magic, and which Luke associates with the realm and work of Satan, explicitly in the last two stories and implicitly here.

Luke begins by introducing **a certain man named Simon [who] had lived in the city for some time, practicing magic and amazing the nation of Samaria** (8:9). By the end of the episode, this reference to Simon the magician would have been viewed quite negatively. In fact, the pejorative use of "magic" was a quite common rhetorical device of negatively labeling and therefore marginalizing the practices of a rival group (see *Letters of Apollonius of Tyana* 1, 2, 5, 8, 16, 17). Jews (Juvenal, *Sat.* 6.542–547), Moses (Pliny the Elder, *Nat.* 30, 2, 11), and Jesus (Origen, *Cels.* 1.6, 28, 38) were also accused of practicing magic (see Johnson 1992, 147).

As a result of his activities, Simon was **claiming to be someone great** (8:9). The use of the relative pronoun (*tis*) here with an adjective is rhetorically emphatic and ironic (see Robertson 1933, 743). Simon was somebody great in his own mind. He had also convinced the Samaritans, for they designate him with a divine title as the **power of God which is called "Great"** (8:10). The title "Great Power" was a Samaritan name for Yahweh (Fossum 1985, 171–72). Luke uses this epithet ironically, to censure Simon on account of his self-aggrandizement (on the conventional use of the epithet, *pronominatio*, in rhetoric, see the sidebar on p. 104).

The title stands in direct contrast to Luke's depiction of Jesus. From Luke's perspective, the "power of God" was in Jesus, or upon Jesus, or with Jesus, but the power of God was always distinct *from* Jesus. That Simon does not reject this title (as Paul and Barnabas do in Acts 14:11–15), but rather encourages it through his magic, places him in the tradition of the "false prophets" who throughout Jewish history reject the way of God in favor of idolatry (cf. Luke 6:22–23; Acts 5:36; 7:51–52; 12:23).

Philip and Simon are both active in a Samaritan city (8:5, 8, 9). They both perform wondrous deeds (8:6–7, 9, 11) and make speeches (8:6, 9). Large numbers of the Samaritans **paid close attention** to both of them (8:6, 10, 11). Simon is called the "Great Power" (8:10) and **amazes** (8:9, 11) the Samaritans, while Philip works **great miracles** (8:13) and **amazes** Simon (8:13; see Spencer 1992b, 88–89).

The similarities between Simon and Philip serve only to bring out in bolder relief their differences. Luke uses an encomium/invective *synkrisis* in which to praise Philip and his message while condemning Simon (cf. Acts 3:13–15; Hermogenes, *Prog.* 19, trans. Kennedy 2003, 84).

Simon's deeds point to himself in an act of self-aggrandizement and self-gain (8:9, 19); Philip's signs point to the kingdom of God and corroborate his proclamation of the Christian gospel (8:5–6). What was the content of this message? Luke fills it out later in the narrative claiming that Philip **was preaching about the kingdom of God and the name of Jesus Christ** (8:12). So to preach the gospel for Philip was to proclaim that Jesus was the "Christ," the one God had anointed "for doing good and healing all who were oppressed by the devil" (as Peter would put it in 10:38). Hence, Philip's signs and wonders—the healings and exorcisms—were outward signs reinforcing his message: Satan is being overcome, and the kingdom of God is being established (Garrett 1989, 65).

Philip's preaching and wonder-working ministry are empowered by God, and his motive is neither for self-gain nor self-glory. Simon, on the contrary, is explicitly motivated by his own self-advancement and implicitly is an agent of the demonic. For Luke, this is the difference between Christian miracle and pagan magic: outwardly, the deeds may appear to be the same, but the source of the Christian miracle is in the power of God, not the missionary; the motive for the miracle is to proclaim in deed the coming kingdom of God.

The Samaritans believe what Philip has been preaching (and demonstrating) about the kingdom of God and the name of Jesus Christ and they are baptized. Simon is also baptized. The "Great Power" sees the "great powers" performed by Philip and becomes his devotee. Luke ends this scene by claiming that Simon was "amazed" at Philip's signs and great miracles. In none of the instances where the word occurs in Acts (here and 2:7, 12; 9:21; 10:45; 12:16) does this "amazement" have the substance of "faith." Simon, then, though he has been baptized, reveals his faith's lack of depth through his amazement with Philip's deeds (Garrett 1989, 69).

8:14–24. This second scene also divides into two parts: (1) Peter (and John) and the Samaritans (8:14–17); and (2) Peter (and John) and Simon (8:18–24).

1. In the first part (8:14–17), **the apostles in Jerusalem heard that the people of Samaria had received the message of God and they sent them Peter and John** (8:14). The interest shown in the Samaritan situation by the Jerusalem apostles confirms that the unity achieved between the "Hebrews" and the "Hellenists" (represented here by Philip) continues even after Stephen's death.

Peter and John discover that the Samaritans have not yet received the Holy Spirit because **they had only been baptized in the name of the Lord Jesus** (8:15–16). Philip and Peter have distinct, but not incompatible, roles: Philip is the initiator of the Samaritan mission; Peter is its verifier (Tannehill 1990, 102–12). Unlike the encomium/invective comparison of Philip and Simon, the comparison of Peter and Philip is a double encomium *synkrisis* in which "the subjects under discussion are both equal to each other or . . . one is greater than the other" (Nicolaus, *Prog.* 60, trans. Kennedy 2003, 162).

Philip initiates the Samaritan ministry by casting out the unclean spirits; Peter and John complete it by delivering the Holy Spirit to these same believers in an event that has aptly been described as the Samaritan Pentecost (8:17).

2. The second half of this scene (Acts 8:18–24) begins with the notice that **Simon saw that the Spirit was given through the laying on of the apostles' hands** (8:18a). The narrator is more interested in Simon's response to these signs than he is in the signs themselves: **he [Simon] offered them money and said, "Give me this power also so that whoever I lay (my) hands on will receive the Holy Spirit"** (8:18b–19). This detail confirms the earlier impression that Simon is portrayed as a false prophet, an agent of Satan. Magicians practiced their art for money, and as Hermas noted the false prophet "accepts rewards for his prophecy, and if he does not receive them he does not prophesy" (*Mand.* 11.12; cf. Plato, *Leg.* 909A, B; Philo, *Spec.* 3.100–101; Lucian, *Philops.* 15, 16; Juvenal, *Sat.* 6.546; Philostratus, *Vit.*

Antistrophe in Acts 8

The emphasis on the Holy Spirit is underscored by Luke's use of the rhetorical figure of *antistrophe*, in which the last word or phrase is repeated in successive phrases (*Rhet. Her.* 4.13.19). In Acts 8:15, 17, and 19, each verse ends with the words *pneuma hagion* (Holy Spirit). For pseudo-Cicero, *antistrophe* joins other figures of repetition (cf. *Rhet. Her.* 4.13.19–4.14.21) in which there "inheres in the repetition an elegance which the ear can distinguish more easily than words can explain" (4.14.21). Thus the figure both embellishes the content (focusing the ear on what is most important) as well as amplifies the style with charm (see *Rhet. Her.* 4.13.19).

Apoll. 8.7). If Simon is willing to pay money for the use of the Spirit, clearly he will later accept payment when he employs its power (see Garrett 1989, 70). In contrast, the audience knows what Simon cannot: Peter had earlier made it clear that the apostles would never take money for what they do (see 3:6). The Holy Spirit is a gift (cf. Acts 2:33), not an item of merchandise to be purchased and manipulated.

The syntax and rhetoric of Peter's invective (see 7:51–53) is harsh and reminiscent of OT curses of idolatry (8:20–23; cf. esp. Deut 29:17–19; see Acts 13:11 and 23:3 for other curses). Only here in the NT a present optative is used expressing a strong wish, perhaps best translated, "To hell with you and your money" (see Haenchen 1971, 304). Peter continues: **You have absolutely no part or share in this matter, for your heart is not right before God!** (8:21). The word "share" has a special role in Acts. It may refer, on the one hand, specifically to a "share" or "lot" in the apostolic ministry (see Acts 1:17, 26; pace Johnson 1992, 149) or, on the other hand, more generally to the share of salvation promised to all believers (Garrett 1989, 146; cf. also Deut 12:12). Thus not only does Simon have no place or share in the apostolic ministry; he is in severe danger of having no place or share in salvation at all.

The specific shape of Peter's accusation comes out in the intertextual echoes heard in 8:23: **For I can see that you are full of bitterness and bound by (your) evil ways.** Both phrases, "full of bitterness" and "bound by (your) evil ways" allude to Deut 29:17, which is a curse against those who turn away from God to serve other gods (Garrett 1989, 71). This idolatry is like a root growing with "gall" or "poison" and "bitterness" and will incur the severe judgment of the Lord (Deut 29:19).

As an idolater, Simon is still under the authority of Satan; he is, in Peter's words, "bound" (Acts 8:23; cf. Isa 58:6) or entrapped by Satan's authority (cf. Luke 4:18–19; Acts 10:38), and has not fully experienced Philip's message of liberation from sin (Garrett 1989, 72). His punishment will apparently be destruction.

A comment in Peter's speech, however, gives the audience pause before concluding that Simon, like others who have blasphemed against the Spirit (cf. Judas, Ananias and Sapphira, Herod) will be destroyed. In Acts 8:22, Peter exhorts: **Therefore, repent of this wickedness of yours, and pray to the Lord that he might perhaps forgive the intention of your heart.** Likewise, Simon's response at the end is also surprising; he entreats Peter and John: **You must pray to the Lord on my behalf so that none of what you have said will come upon me!** (8:24). Codex Bezae adds to the drama by noting that Simon "wept much." Has Simon repented?

The ambiguity surrounding Simon's fate arises because, in effect, he faces two futures: as a human, he still has opportunity for repentance, but as Satan's servant, he has been defeated and reduced to shame. Peter holds out repentance and salvation as a possibility for Simon. Luke knows that magic can be renounced (see Acts 19:18–19), and the audience is aware that the bonds of Satan can be broken (Luke 13:10–17; Herm. *Mand.* 12.6), so Simon as an individual may yet repent (see Garrett 1989, 148).

More importantly, Peter has perceived that Simon is an idolater and agent of Satan; he is "full of bitterness" (8:23). Simon's plea for intercession brings to mind again the encounter between Moses and Pharaoh, during which Pharaoh repeatedly asks Moses to pray for him (Exod 8:8, 28 [8:4, 24 LXX]; 9:28; 10:17) and then "hardens his heart" once Moses fulfills the request (Exod 8:15, 32; 9:35; 10:20). Luke leaves no real trace that this "idolater" and "evil-doer," Simon, has repented or been forgiven. Luke here portrays Simon as "a cornered criminal, frightened at the prospect of punishment although not obviously remorseful over his crimes" (Garrett 1989, 72).

Satan, in the person of Simon, has been defeated by those who come in the authority and power of the Holy Spirit (such conflict is common in Jewish [*T. Job* 27] and Christian texts [Herm. *Mand.* 11.14]; see Garrett 1989, 73). The conflict between pagan magic and Christian miracles is, for Luke, an opportunity to demonstrate that Christian miracles are a testimony, not to the abilities of the individual performing them, but to the power and authority of God, which even now is overcoming the powers of darkness in the world.

8:25. The opening notice (8:4) indicated that the scattering of believers gave opportunity for the spread of the gospel. With the defeat of the devil, the path is cleared for the preaching of the gospel in Samaria (8:25). Irony comes in the form of John, to whom (with Peter) the continued Samaritan mission is entrusted. Earlier, during the ministry of Jesus, John had offered to call fire down to consume the Samaritans (Luke 9:54). Now John, with Peter, is found testifying, speaking the word of the Lord, and indeed, **preaching the gospel in many Samaritan villages** on the way back to Jerusalem (8:25).

Philip and the Ethiopian Eunuch (8:26–40)

Acts 8:25 also serves as the transition to this new section, 8:26–40, which again involves Philip. The story is foundational to Luke's theology and certainly is most exotic in its details. The verses that frame it (8:25, 40) exhibit a chiastic structure. In this outline A, B, and C give the wording in 8:25, and A′, B′, and C′ give the wording in 8:40, in each case following the Greek word order:

A they returned to Jerusalem
  B to many villages of the Samaritans
    C they [Peter and John] preached
    . . .
    C′ he [Philip] preached
  B′ to all the cities
A′ until he came to Caesarea

118

The ellipsis represents 8:26–39. At the center of the section (8:35) lies the quotation of Isa 53:7–8 and the eunuch's questions. Philip uses this OT text to tell "the good news about Jesus." We will return to the heart of this passage, but first let us allow Luke to introduce the characters and setting.

8:26–29. An angel of the Lord directs Philip to go along the road from Jerusalem to Gaza (8:26). The rest of this opening unit is given over to a description of the man whom Philip meets: **an Ethiopian man, a eunuch and a minister of the Candace, queen of the Ethiopians, who was in charge of all her treasure (8:27),** who was returning from a trip to Jerusalem to worship.

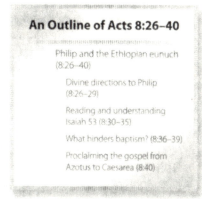

An Outline of Acts 8:26–40

Philip and the Ethiopian eunuch
(8:26–40)

Divine directions to Philip
(8:26–29)

Reading and understanding
Isaiah 53 (8:30–35)

What hinders baptism? (8:36–39)

Proclaiming the gospel from
Azotus to Caesarea (8:40)

Each of those words conveys very important cultural information about this character. He is an Ethiopian, which informs the audience of the geographic and ethnographic significance of this conversion. Ethiopia was viewed by people of antiquity as lying at the southernmost end or limit of the earth (see, e.g., Homer, *Il.* 23.205–297; Herodotus, *Hist.* 3.114–115; Strabo, *Geogr.* 1.2.27–28; 2.2.2). Second, in antiquity, skin color was an Ethiopian's most distinctive feature (Homer, *Od.* 19.244–248; Herodotus, *Hist.* 2.29–32; 3.17–24; 4.183, 197; and Seneca, *Nat.* 4A.218). What is the ethnographic significance of the Ethiopian's conversion? Clarice Martin (1989, 114) argues that "the story of a black African . . . from what would be perceived as a distant nation to the south of the empire is consistent with the Lukan emphasis on 'universalism,' a recurrent motif in both Luke and Acts, and one that is well known."

The allusion, however, may not have been altogether positive; it certainly was not in the physiognomic handbooks. About Ethiopians, pseudo-Aristotle says, "Those who are too swarthy are cowardly; this applies to Egyptians and Ethiopians" (*Physiogn.* 812a12–13). If this negative view of Ethiopia/Ethiopians is in the cultural repertoire of Luke's audience, Luke encourages the setting aside of those prejudices.

The Ethiopian is also a eunuch, but what did that term mean in late antiquity? Although there is some evidence for the view that "eunuch" is simply a royal title (see Gen 39:1 LXX), the Ethiopian eunuch here is most likely to be understood as a reference to a physically mutilated man. His service as a close adviser to a queen, the Candace, makes it likely he was castrated: male attendants for female royalty were often castrated (see Herodotus, *Hist.* 8.105; Esth 2:3, 14; 4:4–5). Further, for the remainder of the story the official is referred to not as an Ethiopian (an exotic, dark-skinned fellow), or as a "minister or official" (signifying power and wealth), but simply as the "eunuch" (8:34, 36,

38, 39). If this is his dominant, defining characteristic, then two questions emerge: What was the status of eunuchs in the Mediterranean world of late antiquity? How would Luke's audience have understood this text in light of the larger cultural script for eunuchs?

Eunuchs in antiquity "belonged to the most despised and derided group of men" (Spencer 1992a, 156). This claim would certainly find support in the writings of Polemo, who notes that "eunuchs are an evil people, and in them is greed and an assembly of various (evil) qualities" (*Physiogn.* 1.162F). This attitude was prevalent among Greek-speaking Jews of the first century as well (Josephus, *Ant.* 4.290–291).

Why were eunuchs thus demonized and ostracized in antiquity? In part, the answer lies in their ambiguous sexual identity. Lucian of Samosata argued that a eunuch "was an ambiguous sort of creature like a crow, which cannot be reckoned either with doves or with ravens . . . neither man nor woman but something composite, hybrid and monstrous, alien to human nature" (*Eunuch.* 6–11; cf. Josephus, *Ant.* 4.291; cf. Philo, *Spec.* 1.324–325). In a culture in which honor was gender-based, to be sexually ambiguous was to blur clear-cut gender roles and expectations and thus to bring shame upon oneself and one's community (see Spencer 1992a, 157).

Further, eunuchs, by belonging neither to the cultural expectations of male nor female, had violated purity codes. This was especially true in Judaism, which prohibited the physically defective, like eunuchs, from entering the temple and interacting with the larger social body: "No one whose testicles are crushed or whose penis is cut off shall be admitted to the assembly of the Lord" (see Deut 23:1). Within Judaism there existed the eschatological vision of Isaiah that eunuchs and foreigners and other outcasts would be reincorporated in the end days (Isa 56:4–6), but that was a vision to be fulfilled in the future. In the Acts passage, the eunuch has just returned from Jerusalem where he had gone to worship and was, no doubt, relegated to the outermost chambers of the temple. The eunuch was impure and filled with shame.

The fact that many eunuchs, despite their social stigmatization, held important offices, were literate, and had access to material wealth only made them that much more socially ambiguous (see again Lucian, *Eunuch.* 6–11). Crossing socioeconomic borders between the elite and the outcast only made the eunuch that much more of a liminal figure—trusted, yet treated with suspicion; prosperous, yet ostracized; the "powerful" whose access to power, ironically, came only through his humiliation (cf. Luke 1:48). It is this kind of person whom Philip is directed by the Spirit to approach (8:29)—a social outcast, living on the liminal in terms of his sexual identity, his religious identification, and his socioeconomic status.

8:30–35. Philip approaches the chariot and **heard him reading Isaiah the prophet** (8:30; on reading aloud cf. Augustine, *Conf.* 6.3). In a clever play on words, Philip asks the eunuch: **Do you really understand what you are**

reading? (*ginōskeis ha anaginōskeis*). The eunuch replies with a rhetorically sophisticated question (using a rare potential optative), which underscores again the privileged aspect of his position: **How can I possibly (understand), unless someone guides me?** (8:31). As a sign of his authority (cf. also 8:38), the eunuch commands, rather than invites, Philip to join him in his oxcart.

Why was the eunuch reading from Isa 53? The social location of the eunuch discussed above is a crucial key for interpreting the citation of Isaiah within the social and literary world of Acts. The passage of scripture that the eunuch was reading was a verbatim quotation of a Greek version of Isa 53:7–8: **Like a sheep led to the slaughter, and like a lamb before its shearer is silent, so he does not open his mouth. In [his] humiliation, justice was withheld from him. Who can list his descendants? For his life was taken up from the earth** (Acts 8:32–33). As has been frequently noted, the passage quoted here takes up just after the reference to the servant's vicarious suffering ("and the LORD has laid on him the iniquity of us all"; Isa 53:6) and ends just before a similar note in Isa 53:8 ("For he was cut off from the land of the living, stricken for the transgression of my people"). Rather than enter a debate at this point on Luke's understanding (or lack thereof) of the atoning dimensions of Jesus' death, let the reader note that the passage as it stands in Acts tends rather to emphasize the "humiliation" of the unnamed sufferer and perhaps also his vindication.

The key word here is "humiliation" (*tapeinōsis*), found in the middle of the citation, a term that refers to a "social position within Mediterranean society" that "was severely reprobative" (Braun 1995, 50; Lucian, *Somn.* 9; cf. also 13; Pollux, *Onom.* 5.162–164). It is not surprising that the eunuch, whose access to wealth is tenuous at best and ironically dependent upon his socially debased position, should be drawn to this figure in Isaiah who, like the eunuch, is described as being in a state of "humiliation" and from whom, like the eunuch, "justice was withheld" (Acts 8:33).

Furthermore, this figure in Isaiah is not only socially marginalized, but also depicted as unclean or polluted (see Spencer 1992a, 159). The Isaianic figure is identified as a slaughtered lamb and a shorn sheep (Acts 8:32). Both similes on the Jewish map of purity evoke images of pollution. Dead bodies, whether carcasses or corpses, were unclean and taboo to the touch (see Lev 11:24–40; 21:1–4). Likewise, priests were required to follow certain regulations regarding shaving their bodies (Lev 21:5; cf. also Num 6:1–21; Acts 21:21–26). Again, the eunuch in Luke's narrative would have closely identified with the Isaianic figure since both are depicted as ritually unclean. He, too, is like a lamb before its "cutter," reduced to silence in humiliation (Acts 8:32–33).

But the passage from Isaiah may not limit its vision to a description only of the servant's debased status. Rather, there may be allusions to a radical reversal of social status, although these are at most ambiguous. The first hint of reversal may come in the phrase in Acts 8:33, "justice was denied him," which might be rendered more accurately as a vindication: "judgment was removed from him" (on Luke's use of this term as "judgment," see Luke 10:14; 11:31–32). The next phrase is likewise ambiguous: "Who can list his descendants?" Is this a lament over the fact that the servant is cut off from his descendants or a note rejoicing the "indescribable generation" too many to number? Finally, the last phrase in the scripture citation also has a double meaning: "for his life was taken up from the earth" (8:33). Here again, the reference may be either to the figure's death or his "lifting up" in exaltation, symbolized in Jesus' ascension in Acts 1:9. How much hope the eunuch sees in this passage is difficult to say, but he is surely drawn to this Isaianic figure as one whose social status, like his own, is tenuous at best and marginalized at worst.

The ambiguous nature of the scripture requires a Christian interpreter. The eunuch asks: **About whom does the prophet say this, about himself or about someone else?** So **Philip began to speak** (cf. 8:32b) and **starting with this (passage of) scripture, he preached the good news about Jesus to him** (8:34–35). This good news, no doubt, included the vindication as well as the suffering of Jesus and what may have been ambiguous in the scripture is now made clear in its Christian exposition.

The messianic exegesis of Christians was not unique because they saw the Messiah foretold in the scriptures (their Jewish contemporaries saw that as well; cf. *Tg. Isa.* 52:13; *b. Sanh.* 98b); the uniqueness lay in the fact that they believed this Messiah had already come in the person of Jesus Christ. And for the eunuch, this Jesus figure becomes the source of hope for social and spiritual transformation. All that is needed now is a ritual to symbolize his status transformation.

8:36–39. Convinced of the truth of Philip's message, the eunuch lets forth with the refrain of an unhindered gospel that runs throughout Acts: **Look, water! What is preventing me from being baptized?** (8:36; cf. Acts 10:47; 28:31; on the theme of the "unhindered" gospel, see comments on 28:31 and Stagg 1955). Until now, the eunuch could not undergo religious initiation rites; he could not be circumcised and could not be a proselyte to Judaism. But now because of the "good news about Jesus" proclaimed to him by Philip, nothing prohibits his transformation being ritualized through Christian baptism (see McVann 1991). The eunuch follows up his question with a command for the wagon to be stopped, and he is baptized by Philip (8:38). His work completed, Philip is caught up by the Spirit of the Lord (cf. 1 Kgs 18:12; 2 Kgs 2:16), and the eunuch went on his way, rejoicing (on the Lukan theme of joy as a proper response to divine activity, see Luke 1:14, 28; 2:10; 6:23; 10:17, 20; 13:17; 15:5, 7, 10, 32; 19:6, 37; 24:41, 52; esp. Acts 5:41 and 8:8; Johnson 1992, 157).

8:40. The story ends with Philip finding himself in Azotus and preaching the gospel to all the towns till he comes to Caesarea (8:40). More important than either the eunuch's ethnic identity as a Gentile or his racial identity as a person of color is his social status as a eunuch. Here the two stories of Philip in Acts 8 coalesce. Philip has explored the liminality of both the Jewish symbolic map of purity and the Greco-Roman cultural map of shame and honor. The Ethiopian eunuch would have been viewed by Luke's auditors as sexually ambiguous, socially ostracized, and morally evil (greedy and cowardly). Yet when the eunuch finds water and asks, "What is preventing me from being baptized," Luke's response is that surely neither the eunuch's physical condition, nor his place of origin, nor his likeness to a sheared sheep prevents his entrance into the eschatological community; this is therefore the fulfillment of the Abrahamic covenant to be a "blessing to all the nations," and as a member of a community in which "God shows no partiality" (Acts 10:34).

Philip is a man on a mission, pressing the boundaries. He preaches the gospel, and despised and unclean Samaritans and an ostracized eunuch, literally from the "end of the earth," are converted. The Jerusalem church, through Peter and John, finishes his Samaritan mission and eventually endorses (implicitly at least) his mission to the Gentiles. Later Paul finds Philip in Caesarea (21:8), where the narrator left him. But now Philip is not alone; he has four unmarried daughters "who had the gift of prophecy," and no doubt Philip's encouragement to exercise it. Not only is Philip's adventuresome spirit reaffirmed for the audience, his openness to the fresh winds of God's Spirit has been passed on to another generation.

Theological Issues

The story of the Ethiopian eunuch is the climax of a series of stories about the inclusion in the eschatological community, under the warrant of the Abrahamic covenant, of those who are physically disabled (see also comments on Acts 3; Parsons 2006). The bent woman (Luke 13) and Zacchaeus (Luke 19) were "daughter" and "son" of Abraham, respectively. In the course of explaining the significance of the lame man's healing, Peter quotes the Abrahamic blessing (Acts 3:25; cf. Gen 12:3; 22:18; 26:4). Although explicit reference to Abraham is missing in Acts 8:26–40, the story of Philip and the Ethiopian eunuch is the logical conclusion to Luke's interest in physiognomy and the Abrahamic covenant. A Gentile, who is both an Ethiopian and a eunuch, is converted to Christianity. The Abrahamic covenant's promise that Abraham's seed would be a blessing to all the nations is now fulfilled. Today we read and hear these ancient texts in a cultural context that knows, on the one hand, the "emancipation proclamation" embodied in the Americans with Disabilities Act of 1990, and, on the other, the reality of racial profiling in a post–9/11 world.

Thus the conversion of the Ethiopian eunuch is less the beginning of the Gentile mission per se in Acts and much more the culmination to Luke's argument that the "physically defective" or "ethnically inferior" (so judged by the prevailing culture) are in no way excluded from the body of the new

Abrahamic community. This explains why the story of the Ethiopian eunuch is never again mentioned in Acts. The Gentile mission proper in Acts commences with the story of Cornelius (Acts 10) and it is to that event that the narrative returns when the question of the Gentile emerges with full force in Acts 15. Thus the interest in the Ethiopian eunuch is less in establishing a proleptic fulfillment of Jesus' command to the disciples to take the gospel to the "end of the earth" and more in his role in establishing the inclusion into the eschatological community of those who might otherwise be excluded either because of their ethnic origins or their physical appearance or both.

Luke has made clear that the lowly who are exalted (cf. Luke 1:52) include those whose physical traits and limitations might cause others to label them as outcasts according to conventional physiognomic canons. Luke uses physiognomic conventions in order to subvert them. For the Lukan Jesus, one's moral character is *not* determined by the color, shape, size, or limitations of one's body. This fact explains why Luke does not give physical descriptions of other characters in his works (Jesus, the disciples, John the Baptist, the Pharisees, etc.), since to do so would be to reinforce the very connection between outer appearance and inner character that he so struggles to break.

Luke has radically redrawn the map of who is in and who is out. He has done so under scriptural warrant, based on his understanding of the implications of the Abrahamic covenant for those so often excluded, whether because of physical condition or ethnic and racial identity. For Luke, God's covenant people can only be a "blessing to the nations" by including those previously excluded in the community itself. Luke's vision of this Abrahamic community is based also on his understanding of the teachings of Jesus, which include holding up an otherwise despised Samaritan as an example to follow (Luke 10) and on his obedience to a God who "shows no partiality" (Acts 10:34). For Luke, finally, the covenant messianic community, the "whole" body of Christ, includes even, perhaps especially, those who do not themselves have, in the eyes of the larger culture, a "whole" body. The kingdom of God belongs to these, and they to God's covenant community.

Acts 9:1–31

Saul and Ananias: Conversion and Call

◲

Introductory Matters

After two verses describing Saul and his plans, 9:1–31 contains six scenes. The first three scenes (9:3–9; 10–17a; and 17b–19a) may be read chiastically:

A Saul sees the vision, is blinded, and fasts (9:3–9).
   B Ananias sees a vision (9:10).
      C Ananias is commissioned to go to Saul (9:11–14).
         D Saul's mission is foretold by Christ (9:15–16).
      C′ Ananias goes to Saul (9:17a).
   B′ Ananias reports his vision (9:17b).
A′ Saul's sight is restored; he is baptized and eats (9:18–19a).

The theme of Saul's conversion from a persecutor of Christ to one persecuted for Christ holds together the entire segment of 9:1–31.

Acts 9:1–31 in the Narrative Flow

The people and places of the Jerusalem church (1–12)

The sense of a beginning (1–7)

Beyond Jerusalem: Philip, Saul, Peter, and others (8–12)

Philip: a man on a mission (8)

▶ Saul and Ananias: conversion and call (9:1–31)

The conversion of Saul (9:1–19a)

Saul's plans (9:1–2)

Saul's vision on the Damascus Road (9:3–9)

Ananias's vision in Damascus (9:10–17a)

Ananias and Saul (9:17b–19a)

From Damascus to Jerusalem (9:19b–31)

Tracing the Narrative Flow

The Conversion of Saul (9:1–19a)

Acts 9:1–19a is the first of three accounts in Acts of Paul's conversion (cf. Acts 22 and 26) and the only one to be told by the narrator of Acts; the other two accounts are retold by Paul (see Kurz 1993, 126–31). Thus this particular version carries a certain rhetorical and theological authority.

9:1–2. The reference in 9:1 to Saul's *still* breathing threats (cf. 3 Macc 2:24; 5:18; 5:37; 4 Macc 4:8; 7:2; 8:19) and murder against the disciples recalls his earlier appearances in 7:58 and 8:1, 3 and continues the character development begun there. Appearing in the background first as a bystander at the stoning of Stephen (7:58), and then as one assenting to the mob's actions (8:1), Saul's actions in the third scene (8:3) are in the context of the "great persecution," in which he himself participated. Acts 9:1 continues this description of Saul as the "arch persecutor" of the church who seeks permission to extend his persecution beyond Jerusalem to Damascus. In this sense, the description of Saul here recalls Stephen's invective against those who "always resist the Holy Spirit" (7:51–52). Likewise, the portrait of Saul who is breathing threats and murder recalls Stephen's description of his enemies as "murderers." Rather than a "friend of God" (*theophilos*), in the words of his teacher, Gamaliel (cf. 22:3), Saul is about to be exposed as one found "opposing God" (*theomachos*; 5:39). Saul is the active subject of all the verbs in 9:1–2. This emphasis on Saul as an active antagonist to the Christian movement is reported in vivid language, **voicing murderous threats** (9:1; see Acts 2 on ekphrastic language), and stands in sharp contrast to his passivity in the Damascus Road encounter that follows.

Just as the preaching of the gospel has moved outside Judea (cf. chap. 8), so Saul seeks to extend his persecution of the Way beyond Jerusalem into Damascus. To do so, he requests letters of recommendation (cf. 2 Cor 3:1; Rom 16; 3 John) from the high priest to take with him to the synagogues at Damascus **so that if he found anyone who belonged to the Way, he might bring (them) in chains—both men and women—to Jerusalem** (9:2).

9:3–9. The conversion account begins as **a light from the sky flashed around him** (9:3b; cf. 2:6; 26:12–13). This light from heaven brings the scene into focus and precipitates Saul's subsequent blindness. Light is characteristic in the OT of God's presence (Pss 4:6; 36:9; 56:13; 78:14; 89:15; 97:11; 104:2; Isa 2:5; 60:19; Wis 7:26; cf. also Acts 12:7). "Flashing" lightning (cf. 4 Macc 4:10) is especially a feature of OT theophanies (cf. Exod 19:16; 2 Sam 22:15; Pss 18:14; 77:18; 97:4; 144:6; Ezek 1:4, 7, 13; Dan 10:6; Johnson 1992, 163), as is the voice speaking in the light (cf. Exod 3:4; 19:16–20). Finally, the double vocative, **Saul, Saul** (9:3), is also recognizable as an OT echo to the audience familiar with the biblical idiom (Gen 22:11; 46:2; Exod 3:4; 1 Sam 3:4; cf. also Luke 8:24; 10:41; 22:31).

The typical response to the divine voice in the OT is for the auditor to identify himself ("Here am I!"). Such a response will have to wait until Ananias's vision (cf. 9:10). Here in our passage, Saul is not asked to identify himself but to be accountable for his actions: **Why are you persecuting me?** (9:4) The use of the word "persecute" is almost exclusively linked to the activities of Saul in the conversion accounts (Gaventa 1986, 58; in addition to 9:4–5; cf. 22:4, 7–8; 26:11, 14–15). The question contributes to the characterization of Saul as the archenemy of the church.

Saul responds to the question with another question: **Who are you, Lord?** (9:5). He is presented as recognizing for himself that he is involved in a theophany, but he is unsure at this point in the story as to the particular identity of this *kyrios*. Saul is also about to be forced to conclude that this Lord is none other than Jesus, and that the title "Lord," usually reserved in Jewish thinking for Yahweh God, may appropriately be applied to Jesus as well.

The Lord's identity is made forcefully known by the voice's response: **I am Jesus whom you are persecuting** (9:5b). The apparent identification of the church, the disciples of the Lord (9:1), with Jesus himself is striking. Saul's activities were not simply against a group of Jewish Christian opponents; he was persecuting Jesus. The suffering vocation of the Christ (cf. Luke 24:46) continues through the persecuted body of Christ, which embodies the work and mission of the risen Christ. Here we have the fulfillment in Acts of the prediction of Jesus in the Third Gospel: "whoever rejects you rejects me" (Luke 10:16). And once Saul joins this persecuted group, it will belong to his vocation to suffer as well (cf. 9:16). Any triumphalistic reading of Acts must always take into account this sobering note that as the Christ suffered, so must the church suffer (Moessner 1990). At this point Saul is directed to enter the city of Damascus to await further instructions (9:6).

The narrative is interrupted with a brief notice about Saul's traveling companions: **The men who were traveling with him stood (there) speechless, because they heard the voice but did not see anyone** (9:7). The role of these traveling companions changes in Paul's subsequent recounting of this event in Acts 22, and they are missing altogether in Acts 26. Is their experience in continuity with or in contrast to Saul's (Gaventa 1986, 59)? The notice is brief; Saul's companions stood speechless, heard a voice, and saw

---

Reduplication in Acts 9

Luke's focus on persecution is underscored by the use of the rhetorical figure of reduplication (*conduplicatio*), which is "the repetition of one or more words for the purpose of amplification or appeal to pity" (*Rhet. Her.* 4.28.38). For example: "You were not moved when his mother embraced your knees? You were not moved?" (*Rhet. Her.* 4.28.38). In the Damascus vision, the Lord repeats the charge of persecution, "Why do you persecute me?" (*ti me diōkeis*, 9:4), and "I am Jesus whom you are persecuting" (*hon sy diōkeis*, 9:5).

127

no one. Saul also fell to the ground and heard a voice, but was not speechless. Did he see someone?

"Seeing" is often related in Luke and Acts to perceiving God's activity (e.g., Luke 10:18; 24:37, 39; Acts 3:16; 7:56) or with understanding the significance of an event (Acts 4:13; 17:22; 21:20; 27:10; see Gaventa 1986, 60). The fact that Saul's companions do not see may imply that they were unaffected by the events. Underscoring this impression is the further contrast between these companions who "stood" and Saul who "fell to the ground." Thus they do not corroborate Saul's experience of seeing (or identifying) the Lord and therefore revelation eludes them (Marguerat 1995, 143); nonetheless, they are (presumably) those who did at least hear the voice and facilitate Saul's obedience to the instructions: **leading him by the hand, they brought him into Damascus** (9:8).

While his companions may have been unaffected by the christophany, Saul's character undergoes a radical transformation. Saul arose from the ground **but when he opened his eyes he could not see anything** (9:8). Several points about Saul's blindness are noteworthy. Luke uses the blindness/sight, darkness/light metaphor to make the point that Saul, though physically blind, has his eyes opened spiritually to "see the Lord" (in contrast to his companions). This point is emphasized later in the story when Barnabas reports to the Jerusalem church "how he [Saul] had seen the Lord" (9:27). The metaphorical use of light to describe the Christian mission will become more important in Saul's later retellings of his conversion. The counterpart to light, darkness, is highlighted here in Saul's blindness.

Is Saul's blindness the result of God's punishment, that is, a "punitive miracle" in the OT tradition (cf. Deut 28:28–29)? Hearing echoes of Isaiah help clarify Luke's point. In Isaiah, darkness/light and crooked/straight are used as images to describe the transformation of those opposing God: "I will lead the blind by a road they do not know, by paths they have not known I will guide them. I will turn the darkness before them into light, the rough places into level ground" (Isa 42:16; cf. 26:7; 35:5). Throughout Isaiah, then, a cluster of images is employed to contrast those who are resisting God's redemption with those who are following God's plan: unrighteous/righteous; darkness/light; blind/seeing; crooked/straight; deaf/hearing (Hamm 1990, 70). Saul's blindness, and later the opening of his eyes, is an appropriate symbol for this "enemy of God" who has attempted to reverse the plan of God (5:38–39; cf. Hamm 1990, 70; Pervo 1990, 34).

The use of the passive voice to describe Saul's eyes being opened also fits the radical transformation of Saul's character (Marguerat 1995, 142). This inactivity of Saul culminates in the notice that for **three days he could not see; and he neither ate nor drank** (9:9). Saul's blindness not only symbolizes his resistance to the straight way of the Lord; it also connotes his "symbolic death" (Horton 1995, 68–70). Loss of sight was certainly depicted as a necessary stage (linked with death) on the way "to the world beyond" in Jewish thought (cf. Pss 49:19; 58:8b; *m. Shabb.* 23.4–5). Sheol was depicted as a place of dark shadowy existence (cf. Job 17:13; Pss 23:4; 49:14; 88:6; Prov 7:27; cf. also the Egyptian *Book of the Dead* 3, 64, 66, 68, 69). Early Christian literature also used darkness as a symbol for death. Matthew employs the notion of "outer darkness" as an appropriate destination for the wicked (Matt 8:12; 22:13; 25:30). The time of Jesus' death is set within complete darkness (Mark 15:33; Luke 23:44). That Saul "neither ate nor drank" is also a sign of his lifelessness, his death, just as Jesus associated fasting with his suffering and death (Luke 22:15–16). The reference to Saul being blind and fasting for "three days" is likewise suggestive of the three days Jesus spent in a dark tomb (cf. Luke 24:46). The cumulative weight of these rhetorical elements and intertextual echoes suggests that at least at some level Luke's audience will understand that Saul's passivity, fasting, and blindness represent Saul's resistance, punishment, and symbolic death. All these factors will be reversed before this episode concludes.

9:10–17a. Saul is not the only character to receive a vision in this episode. The Lord also visits Ananias, a disciple in Damascus (9:10–14). Such a "double vision" was a frequently employed rhetorical device in a variety of writings from late antiquity (cf. Apuleius, *Metam.* 11.1–3, 6, 21–22, 26–27; Josephus, *Ant.* 11.327; Dionysius of Halicarnassus, *Ant. Rom.* 1.57.4; Herm. *Vis.* 3.1.2; *Jos. Asen.* 14–15; Heliodorus, *Aeth.* 3.11–12, 3.18; Chariton, *Chaer.* 1.12). The double revelation to Saul and Ananias highlights God's control of the action.

Furthermore, this second scene follows the form of a typical dream-vision in antiquity, which consists of: (1) scene-setting; (2) dream-vision terminology; (3) dream-vision proper (which can include a commissioning and dialogue); and (4) reaction/response (see Acts 16:6–10; 18:9–11; Dodson 2006, 93–99).

The encounter between the Lord and Ananias fits quite nicely into this pattern: (1) *Scene-setting*: **Now there was a disciple at Damascus named Ananias (9:10a).** (2) *Dream-vision terminology*: **The Lord said to him in a vision (9:10b).** (3) *Dream-vision proper*: **"Ananias!" And he replied, "Yes, Lord." Then the Lord (said) to him, "Go at once to the street called Straight, and at the house of Judah look for a Tarsian named Saul. For he is praying and he has seen [in a vision] a man named Ananias coming in and laying hands on him so that he may see again" (9:10b–12).** (4) *Reaction*: **But Ananias answered, "Lord, I have heard a lot of people talk about the many terrible things this man has done to your people in Jerusalem; and he has authority here from the chief priests to arrest all who call on your name." Then the Lord said to him, "Go, for I have chosen this man as an instrument to carry my name before the Gentiles, kings, and the people of Israel. I will show him how much he must suffer for the sake of my name." So Ananias left (his house) (9:13–17a).**

Ananias is commissioned to go to Saul who himself has had a vision that someone will come to heal him; the two scenes are interwoven together. Saul's healing will be mediated through the laying on of hands by Ananias. Regaining sight points beyond the reacquisition of physical sight to the revelation of spiritual insight. For Saul, this revelatory experience will come through Ananias. Within Ananias's reaction/response is found Saul's commission (9:14–15). Saul is to be "an instrument to carry my name before the Gentiles, kings, and the people of Israel," a role Saul fulfills in the subsequent narrative: he carries Christ's name before Gentiles (beginning in 13:44), kings (chap. 26), and the people of Israel (chap. 22).

Saul also "must suffer for the sake of my name" (9:16). This word reverses Ananias's complaint in 9:13–14; the one who did evil to those "who call on the name" will now suffer "on account of" Jesus' "name." Saul's call to the Gentile mission cannot be separated from his call to suffer; it is a divine necessity. His entire ministry throughout Acts is characterized by rejection and persecution (cf. 13:46–47; 20:19–21; 22:15–18). As such, he stands in the long line of persecuted prophets that extends from Moses to Jesus and more recently to Stephen (see Tannehill 1990, 114). But Saul does not have to wait until his "first" missionary journey to experience this suffering; his first preaching tour in Damascus ends with a narrow escape in a basket from his persecutors (Acts 9:25).

Not only is Saul's healing mediated through Ananias, but Saul's call to go to the Gentiles is revealed first to Ananias. The role of Ananias in this first account of Saul's conversion and call is unparalleled in the other two accounts. In fact, in Saul's autobiographical retellings, Ananias's role diminishes as Saul's role expands (Witherup 1992, 77). In Acts 22 Ananias tells Saul to receive his sight and that he will be a "witness" of all he has seen and heard. By Acts 26 Ananias drops out of the story completely.

Why does Ananias play a critical role in the healing/conversion/calling of Saul here in Acts 9? The opening notice about Ananias in 9:10a provides a clue. The audience is told that Ananias is a "disciple" and as such is representative of the Christian community at Damascus. The Lord chooses to reveal Saul's Gentile mission and the suffering nature of his vocation to a representative of the church (contra Gal 1:1).

Inflection in Acts 9

The emphasis on the role of the disciples in Saul's call/conversion is underscored by Luke's use of the rhetorical device of inflection (*klisis*; Theon, *Prog.* 74.24–35, ed. Patillon 1997, 33; 85.29–31; ed. Patillon 1997, 48; Quintilian, *Inst.* 9.1.34). In Acts 9, the term "disciple" (*mathētēs*) occurs six times in four cases and in both singular and plural: accusative plural, 9:1; nominative singular, 9:10; genitive plural, 9:19; nominative plural, 9:25; dative plural and nominative singular, 9:26. Again the inflection functions rhetorically to signal to the audience that whatever else the call/conversion of Saul may be about, it is in the first instance a narrative about the role of the disciples, the Christian community, in that call—an emphasis that all but drops out in Paul's subsequent retelling of the event in chapters 22 and 26.

This "ecclesial mediation" does not occur without some resistance (Marguerat 1995, 145). Ananias's own objection to his commission is instructive on this point. In the OT commissioning component of a dream-vision, the note of protest usually has to do with the unworthiness of the commissionee (cf. Exod 6:30; Judg 6:15). Here, Ananias does not protest because of his own lack of qualifications, but rather on the grounds that Saul is unworthy of the Lord's intervention through him: **Lord, I have heard a lot of people talk about the many terrible things this man has done to your people in Jerusalem** (9:13). This objection echoes the narrator's earlier description of Saul as enemy of the Way (cf. 8:3; 9:1), but does not take into account Saul's Damascus Road experience of which Ananias is evidently unaware, but about which the audience and narrator possess knowledge. Christ is the initiator, not only for Saul, but also for the church. The church (represented by Ananias) not only lags behind, but resists the divine initiative. If Acts 9:1–9 demonstrates the ease with which Christ overthrows the enemy (so Gaventa 1986), Acts 9:10–17a shows how much trouble Christ has in convincing his own followers of the efficacy of his plan (Marguerat 1995, 146). But that is about to change.

9:17b–19a. Both Ananias's words and his actions indicate his acceptance of his role and Saul's. Obedient to his commission, Ananias enters the house in which Saul waits and lays his hands on him (9:17b). His address, **Brother Saul**, is a familial term to indicate Ananias's shift from accusations against "this man" (9:13) to full-fledged affirmation of Saul as a fellow Christian.

The next phrase in his speech, **the Lord Jesus, who appeared to you on the road you traveled** (9:17c), suggests that Christ intervened against Saul's previous orientation, "the path down which he was traveling." Ananias reveals to Saul that he, unlike Saul's own traveling companions, is aware of the significance of the epiphany for Saul and the Christian community. Next, Ananias interprets his previous action of laying his hands on Saul: Ananias has been sent so that Saul may regain his sight and be filled with the Holy Spirit (9:17c). The gesture is appropriate, for in Acts the laying on of hands conveys, among other things, both healing (cf. Acts 5:12; 28:8) and the gift of the Spirit (Acts 8:17).

The narrator reports that **immediately, things like scales fell from his eyes; and he . . . was able to see again** (9:18). Employing the rhetorical figure of the simile (*imago*; *Rhet. Her.* 4.49.62), the reference to "things like scales" may be an intertextual echo to the book of Tobit in which a similar word is used to describe Tobit's healing from blindness (11:11–14). Tobit's response ("Blessed be God") makes it clear that the process of white film being peeled away and thus his healing are the results of God's action, as is also the healing of Saul: he "was able to see again."

The Scales Fell from His Eyes

Beyond the oft-noted connection to Tobit, we may consider also how the authorial audience, shaped by an ancient "physiognomic consciousness" that identified outer physical appearance with inner character (see Theological Issues on Acts 8) might have heard the text. In commenting on Acts 9:18, the Venerable Bede observed:

> *"Every dragon's body is said to be covered with scales. Therefore, because the Jews were called serpents and a brood of vipers, this man, who had been an eager follower of their lack of faith, covered over the eyes of his heart, so to speak, with a serpent's skin. With the falling of the scales from his eyes under the hands of Ananias, however, his face showed that he had received the true light in his mind."* (Comm. Acts 9.18, trans. L. Martin 1989)

Thus Saul is depicted as a Leviathan-like opponent of God, breathing murderous threats against the Christians (see especially Ps 104:26; cf. Job 7:12; 41:1; Ezek 32:2), whose conversion is marked by having something like scales dropping from his eyes (see Hartsock 2008).

There is certainly no indication that Saul's baptism or conversion is in any way defective (as with others, cf. Acts 19:1–8). If Saul's passivity and fasting were indicators of a symbolic death (Acts 9:3–9), then Saul's baptism is symbolic of his resuscitation/resurrection (see Rom 6:3–11). The taking of food was proof of Jesus' resurrection (Luke 24:36–43; Acts 1:3), and may be so symbolically understood here. Saul will become active again, this time in preaching the gospel (9:20). The radical reorientation of Saul's mission, at least at some level beneath the narrative's surface, is structured along a death-resurrection motif (Horton 1995, 91).

Acts 9:19b–31 in Context

Saul and Ananias: conversion and call (9:1–31)

  The conversion of Saul (9:1–19a)

    Saul's plans (9:1–2)

    Saul's vision on the Damascus Road (9:1–9)

    Ananias's vision in Damascus (9:10–17a)

    Ananias and Saul (9:17b–19a)

▶ From Damascus to Jerusalem (9:19b–31)

    Saul in Damascus (9:19b–22)

    Foiling the plot against Saul (9:23–25)

    Saul in Jerusalem (9:26–31)

From Damascus to Jerusalem (9:19b–31)

Taken together, the fourth (9:19b–22) and fifth (9:23–25) scenes, both of which occur in Damascus, form a twin narrative with the action in Jerusalem (9:26–31). The two stories recount suspenseful plots against Saul, and the parallels may be schematized as in table 3 (for a different surface structure, cf. Gill 1974, 546–48).

Table 3.
Parallels between the Damascus and Jerusalem Scenes in Acts 9

Damascus	Jerusalem
Saul is with disciples (9:19b).	Saul attempts to be with disciples (9:26a).
Saul preaches in the synagogues (9:20).	
Those who hear him are skeptical of Saul's conversion (9:21).	The disciples are skeptical of Saul's conversion (9:26b).
	Barnabas intervenes on Saul's behalf, bringing him to the apostles (9:27).
Saul increases in power (9:22a).	Saul preaches boldly (9:29a).
Saul confounds the Jews (9:22b).	Saul disputes against the Hellenists (9:29b).
The Jews plot to kill Saul (9:23).	The Hellenists seek to kill Saul (9:29c).
The disciples assist Saul's escape (9:25).	The disciples assist Saul's escape (9:30).

9:19b–22. The fourth scene (9:19b–22) begins with the comment that **Saul was with the disciples at Damascus,** thus indicating his full incorporation into the body of believers at Damascus (9:19b). It also indicates the acceptance finally of the Lord's plan for Saul as a "chosen instrument," despite initial resistance. **Right away, he began to proclaim Jesus in the synagogues, (saying), "This man is the Son of God"** (9:20). This is the only statement in 9:19b–25 without at least a thematic parallel in 9:26–30. "By having Saul begin in the synagogue, Luke establishes the pattern for Paul's preaching throughout the rest of the narrative: he always begins in the synagogues and only when rejected there moves to other venues (13:5, 13–16; 14:1; 16:13, 16; 17:1; 18:4; 19:8)" (Johnson 1992, 170).

The amazement expressed by Ananias at the radical reversal of Saul's mission is expressed again, now by **all who heard (him) [who] were amazed and were saying, "Isn't this the one who in Jerusalem tried to destroy those who called on this name? Hadn't he come here for this (very) purpose—that he might bring them in chains before the chief priests?"** (9:21). The verb *portheō* ("destroy" or "made havoc") is used in the LXX only in 4 Macc 4:23; 11:4 to describe the violence done against the Jews by Antiochus IV and his henchmen, though Paul himself uses it to describe his persecution of Christians (Gal 1:13, 23).

Despite the skepticism, **Saul was becoming more powerful and confounding the Jews who lived in Damascus by proving that Jesus is the Messiah (9:22).** Clearly more than physical strength is meant by the reference to Saul's "becoming more powerful." In some LXX texts the word connotes empowerment by the Spirit (see Judg 6:34; 1 Chr 12:18). Saul, who was zealous in his persecution of Christians, is now equally inspired in his debates with the Jews. Starting with a shared assumption that there was a Messiah, Saul "confounds" the Jews by "proving" or teaching that this Messiah was Jesus (see Acts 2:31–32).

9:23–25. When many days had passed (9:23), the first of several Jewish plots against Saul was hatched (see also 20:3, 19; 23:30). The danger and intrigue require the intervention of the Damascus disciples, who by lowering him over the city wall ingeniously deliver Saul in a basket. From the beginning, the threat of suffering for Christ's name is real for Saul (cf. Acts 9:16).

9:26–31. The emphasis on the suffering character of Saul's ministry continues in this next episode of Saul in Jerusalem (9:26–31). This time the rejection begins within the Christian community, as seen in attempts by Saul to join the Jerusalem disciples, which are thwarted because **they were all afraid of him because they did not believe that he was a disciple** (9:26). These fears echo the earlier concerns of Ananias. Intervention on Saul's behalf is again required.

This intervention comes in the person of Barnabas. According to Luke, Barnabas's name means "son of encouragement" (4:36), and this story is but one more snapshot of Barnabas fulfilling the role demanded by his name (4:32–5:11). Barnabas brings Saul to the apostles and speaks on his behalf.

Barnabas's role is the most significant variation between the plot story located in Damascus and the one here in Jerusalem. Just as Ananias had served earlier as ecclesial mediator for Saul's conversion and call, and as the unnamed disciples had intervened in his behalf at Damascus, and as the Jerusalem brethren would shortly do the same, so Barnabas intervenes in Saul's behalf before the Jerusalem apostles. Barnabas makes two points: (1) he confirms the genuineness of Saul's christophany: he **described to them how he had seen the Lord on the road, that he had spoken to him**; and (2) he asserts that **in Damascus he** [Saul] **had spoken boldly in the name of Jesus** (9:27). After Barnabas declares that Saul "has spoken boldly," Saul does just that, going in and out among them at Jerusalem **speaking boldly in the name of the Lord** (9:28). By preaching boldly, Saul matches the courage of the apostles (4:13, 29, 31; cf. Tannehill 1990, 123) and initiates a kind of rhetorical tone that will characterize his mission throughout the rest of Acts (see 13:46; 14:3; 19:8; 26:26; 28:31). This preaching boldly "in the name of Jesus" echoes Saul's commission to "carry my name" (9:15) and foreshadows that same command of the Lord that "he must suffer for the sake of my name" (9:16).

The possibility of suffering is precipitated when Saul again "disputes," this time with the Hellenists. Saul takes up the role (along with the threats of suffering and death that accompanied it) of the martyred Stephen in the debate with the Hellenists with whom he once associated. Later he will face accusations similar to those leveled against Stephen (21:28; cf. Tannehill 1990, 114).

The plot to kill Saul repeats the plot in Damascus (9:29 // 9:23). Again, believers come to the rescue. This time Saul is sent, via Caesarea, to Tarsus. He will remain there in his hometown (cf. 22:3) until Barnabas retrieves him (11:25).

Theological Issues

It would be difficult to overestimate the significance of the conversion and call of Paul for the narrative of Acts, or indeed, for the course of early Christian history. But there is debate as to whether the event was a "conversion" or a "call." In a highly influential essay, Krister Stendahl argues that Paul's "Damascus Road experience" as recounted both here in Acts (chap. 9, but also in chaps. 22 and 26) and Galatians (1:11–17) is best understood as a prophetic "call to mission rather than a conversion" (1976, 10–11). For Stendahl, "the term 'conversion' easily causes us to bring into play the idea that Paul 'changed his religion': the Jew became a Christian. But there is ample reason to question such a model. To begin with, people in those days did not think about 'religions.' And, furthermore, it is obvious that Paul remains a Jew as he fulfills his role as an Apostle to the Gentiles" (Stendahl 1976, 11). Despite its continuing influence among scholars, there is "ample reason" to question Stendahl's interpretation. There is, for example, considerable evidence that people in antiquity converted. Such conversion might entail a radical reorientation away from magic to cultic paganism (Apuleius, *Metam.* 11.1–30), or from ignorance to philosophy (Aulus Gellius, *Noct. Att.* 5.3.1–7), or from paganism to Jewish monotheism (*Jos. Asen.*), or from one form of Judaism to another (CD 1.8–21; Acts 9; cf. Talbert 2005, 83).

Thus Stendahl is correct in stating that Paul does not convert from one religion, Judaism, to another, Christianity. Nascent Christianity was considered a form of Judaism (Boccaccini 1991; Segal 1986), and this was certainly Luke's perspective (see Theological Issues on 9:32–11:18). But Luke's account in Acts *does* record a conversion from one form of Judaism (non-messianic Pharisaism) to another (the messianists or Christian Judaism), and it contains the components typical of a conversion narrative (Talbert 2005, 83–85). Likewise, this conversion narrative has at its heart Paul's commission to be a witness to the Gentiles. Thus Paul's Damascus Road experience, contra Stendahl, is presented as both a conversion *and* a call, both in his letters (see also Martyn 1997) and in Acts (Talbert 2005, 82–90). By the end of the episode the zealous persecutor of Christ and his church has been radically transformed and has become the zealous missionary persecuted in Christ's name and for his church.

Acts 9:32–11:18

Peter: His Words and Deeds

🔲

Introductory Matters

The next three scenes, the healing of Aeneas, the raising of Tabitha, and the conversion of Cornelius and his household, may all be grouped under the larger heading, "the acts of Peter." Theologically all three stories serve to reveal further the complex character of Peter, as well as underscore the inclusive nature of the gospel. Here Peter fulfills Jesus' commission (Acts 1:8) to be a witness in all Judea (9:32–35, 36–43) and to the end of the earth (10:1–11:18). Peter's acts parallel the earlier three stories of members of the Seven who also obey Christ's commission to be witnesses in Jerusalem (6:8–7:60), Samaria (8:14–25), and the end of the earth (8:26–40; see Talbert 2005, 74).

Tracing the Narrative Flow

Peter's Raising of Aeneas and Tabitha (9:32–43)

The parallels between the stories of Aeneas (9:32–35) and Tabitha (9:36–43) focus the spotlight on Tabitha. First let us note the similarities. These two stories share much in common in terms of intertextuality and structure: they echo the Elijah-Elisha cycles of 1 and 2 Kings, as well as events in the career of the earthly Jesus (Acts 9:32–35 // Luke 5:18–26; Acts 9:36–43 // Luke 8:40–56). Further, unlike most healing stories in Luke and Acts, the healed persons here are named (contra Luke 5:17–26; 11:14–23; 18:35–43; Acts 3:1–10; 14:8–18). Both Aeneas and Tabitha are healed through divine power (9:34, 40). Both healings result in many conversions to the faith in their respective locales (9:35, 42).

The two stories also share common vocabulary and grammatical constructions. Common words include "saints" (9:32, 41); "come" (9:32, 38); "Lydda" (9:32 and 35, 38); and "see" (9:35, 40). Both contain the construction "a certain man/disciple by the name of Aeneas/Tabitha" (9:33, 36; cf. 10:1); in both, Peter commands, "Aeneas/Tabitha, get up" or "be raised" (9:34, 40); both conclude with statements that observers "turned to" or "believed the Lord" (9:35, 42). Finally, these first two stories are held together with an *inclusio*; they begin and end with the phrase, "it happened" (9:32, 43).

9:32–35. As in Acts 8, Peter is on an "inspection tour" among some of the churches (cf. 8:14–25; Conzelmann 1987, 76); he is not establishing churches but rather comforting them in the Holy Spirit (cf. 9:31). His travels bring him to Lydda, a sizable town in Judea (Josephus, *Ant.* 6.130). While visiting the "saints" (cf. 9:13) in Lydda Peter encounters a paralyzed "saint" who had been bedridden for eight years.

Now for the second time, Luke recounts a story of Peter healing a lame man (see Acts 3:1–10; see also 5:15). As such Peter stands in continuity with Jesus and Paul, both of whom are depicted as healing lame men (Luke 5:17–26; Acts 14:8–12). Note especially the linguistic parallels with Luke 5:17–26 ("heal," Luke 5:17/Acts 9:34; "paralyzed," Luke 5:18, 24/Acts 9:33; "reclining (bedridden)," Luke 5:25/Acts 9:33).

The story is bare and unadorned with details, but it does contain the essential elements of a healing story: (1) *Encounter*: there he [Peter] found . . . Aeneas (9:33). (2) *Healing gesture or word*: Aeneas, Jesus Christ heals you! (9:34). (3) *Demonstration of the cure*: and immediately he [Aeneas] got up. (4) *Effects of the healing*: Everyone who lived in Lydda and Sharon saw him, and they turned to the Lord (9:35). Peter's work in Lydda spreads to the Sharon Plain, and those who saw the healed man "turned to the Lord" (9:35; cf. 9:31).

9:36–43. The second miracle story is set in Joppa (9:36–43), a port city near Lydda and predominately Jewish since Maccabean times (cf. 1 Macc 12:33; 13:11). By the time Acts was written, the audience would have known that Joppa had been a center of the Jewish revolt (Josephus, *BJ* 2.508–509).

The audience is led to empathize deeply with Tabitha and her mourners. Tabitha (which the narrator tells us means Dorcas or "Gazelle"—a name for female slaves in some rabbinic texts; cf. *y. Nid.* 2.49d; *Lev. Rab.* 19.4) is described as a **certain female disciple** (9:36). The word for "female disciple"

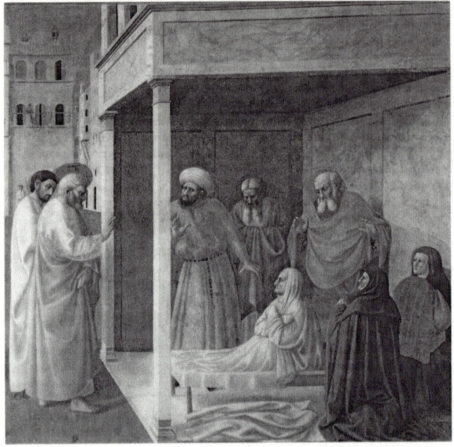

Figure 6. Tommaso Masolino, *St. Peter Raising Tabitha*, 1425–1427. Fresco. Brancacci Chapel, S. Maria del Carmine, Florence, Italy.
The Brancacci Chapel presents a fresco cycle from the life of St. Peter. Here Peter resuscitates Tabitha before some of those who had been mourning her death.

Scala / Art Resource, NY

(*mathētria*) occurs only here in the NT, though the grammatical construction, "a certain female disciple" (rather than "*the* female disciple"), suggests that Tabitha was not the only female disciple in Joppa (see Diogenes Laertius, *Vit. phil.* 4.2; 8.42, where the word is used of female disciples in philosophical schools; also Diodorus Siculus, *Hist.* 2.52.7; and *Gos. Pet.* 50, where it is used of Mary Magdalene).

The narrator continues in his characterization of Tabitha: **She was known for all the good deeds and charitable acts that she did** (9:36; cf. the description of Cornelius at 10:2). Tabitha is depicted as a benefactor, following the model of Jesus, whom Peter will later describe as one who went around "doing good" (10:38). The concept of "good works" was common in early Christian literature (cf. Rom 2:7; 13:3; 2 Cor 9:8; Eph 2:10; Phil 1:6; Col 1:10; 1 Tim

2:10; 5:10; 2 Tim 2:21; 3:17; Titus 1:16; 3:8; *Barn.* 4:9b–10) as well as the larger Greco-Roman culture (see Winter 1994).

If the term "good works" appealed to a larger Greco-Roman audience, the description applied to Tabitha ("known for . . . good deeds and charitable acts that she did," 9:36) has a rich tradition in Second Temple Judaism. Often taken as a specific reference to "almsgiving" (*1 En.* 38.2; *2 En.* 50.5; Tob 4:8–11), *eleēmosynē* could also have the more general meaning of "kind deeds." A passage from Tobit is instructive here:

> In the days of Shalmaneser I performed many acts of charity [*eleēmosynas*] to my kindred, those of my tribe. I would give my food to the hungry and my clothing to the naked; and if I saw the dead body of any of my people thrown out behind the wall of Nineveh, I would bury it. (Tob 1:16–18)

Here, "kind deeds" serves as a kind of umbrella for specific acts of Jewish piety, which include giving "clothing to the naked." So the audience of Acts might understand Tabitha's "acts of charity" as expressions of Jewish Christian piety, illustrated by, but not limited to, the garments she had made for the widows at Joppa.

The product of her benevolence is made explicit when the widows who are mourning her death show to Peter **the clothes and coats that Dorcas had made when she was with them** (9:39). Quite possibly, they are wearing the garments (the verb is in the middle voice); for the widows to lose Dorcas was to lose their benefactor (see Winter 1994). The problem of helpless Greek-speaking Jewish Christian widows resurfaces (cf. 6:1).

Although Luke knows of women of some independent means (see Acts 16:13–15), he consistently depicts widows in a weak socioeconomic state (Luke 18:1–5; 21:1–4; Acts 6:1). That Tabitha made these clothes herself argues against viewing her as a wealthy woman whose benefaction came out of her abundance, but rather supports the notion that she was a woman (if not a widow) who served as another "exegesis by example" of one who "out of her poverty put in all the living she had" (Luke 21:4). And though the narrator does not make the connection explicit, the audience might naturally see a cause and effect relationship between Tabitha's benefaction and the stark notice **in those days, she got sick and died** (9:37). Perhaps her ministry had literally cost her "all the living she had."

In an act of piety of their own, the believers ("saints" and "widows"; 9:41) washed her body (see *m. Shabb.* 23.5, though without anointing). Then, rather than burying her, they placed her corpse in an upper room, perhaps in the hopes of her resuscitation. In this regard another passage in Tobit is most interesting: "For almsgiving/acts of charity [*eleēmosynē*] delivers from death and keeps you from going into the Darkness" (Tob 4:10).

Knowing Peter was nearby, the disciples from Joppa sent two men who urge Peter: **come to us without delay** (9:38). Peter arrives and is escorted to the upper room. Perhaps moved by the widows' weeping and mute display of Tabitha's benefaction, Peter orders everyone outside (like Jesus, see Luke 8:51), kneels, prays, and commands, **Tabitha, get up!** (9:40). For auditors familiar with the Second Gospel, the command is reminiscent of Jesus' words in Mark 5:41, "Talitha [now Tabitha] cumi." She is raised, but not by Peter's power, a point indicated by the fact he prayed to a higher deity. Peter then presents Tabitha alive to the saints and widows (9:41). As with the healing of Aeneas, the raising of Tabitha **became known throughout all Joppa, and many believed in the Lord** (9:42).

The narrator then leaves Peter **for many days in Joppa with a certain Simon the Tanner** (9:43) until he was summoned by Cornelius's men (10:17–18). While some commentators downplay the significance of the occupation of Peter's host (see Conzelmann 1987, 77; Haenchen 1971, 340), the fact that Simon is a tanner is important to the story line. In almost every other instance where the narrator of Acts mentions a character's occupation, that occupation figures prominently in the story (see 8:9, 27; 10:1; 13:6–7; 14:13; 16:14, 16; 18:3; 19:24). Furthermore, the fact that Peter had taken lodging with Simon, a tanner, is mentioned twice more in the narrative (10:6, 32), indicating its significance for the narrator.

Occupation

Cicero includes occupation as a legitimate topic for an encomium (and presumably also an invective): "Under *manner of life* (*in victu*) should be considered with whom he was reared, in what tradition and under whose direction, what teachers he had in the liberal arts, what instructors in the art of living, with whom he associates on terms of friendship, *in what occupation, trade or profession he is engaged*, how he manages his private fortune, and what is the character of his home life" (*Inv.* 1.24.35, emphasis added; cf. also Theon, *Prog.* 110, trans. Kennedy 2003, 50). Theon, when discussing the role of occupation in encomia/invectives, even gives this example: "It is also worth admiring a workman or someone from the lower class who makes something good of himself, as they say Simon the leather worker (*skytotomos,* 'leather cutter') and Leontium the courtesan became philosophers. For virtue shines brightest in misfortune" (*Prog.* 111–12, trans. Kennedy 2003, 52).

Thus, even though Luke does not use Simon's occupation in an explicit invective against him (9:43), it is likely, given the general disdain for leatherworkers, that Luke intends Simon's occupation to create an ironic dissonance in the audience between the vision and its setting in a tanner's house.

A tanner was one who participated in a "trade which required the use of urine for processing leather, hence an unclean or mean trade" (Malina and Neyrey 1991, 88). While not, strictly speaking, a "chronically unclean" occupation (contra Johnson 1992, 179), later rabbis did despise the occupation as "dirty" and "smelly"; it was a socially ostracized trade (Artemidorus, *Onir.* 4.56). This particular tanner lived by the seaside (Acts 10:6). Simon's geographical location may be explained by the fact that tanners used sea water in their trade or that the sea breeze helped ameliorate the odor of the hides (Polhill 1992, 248, 249 n. 63). On Acts' social map of places, however, Simon's locale on the literal edge of town by the sea may also symbolize his liminal and marginalized place on the social map of persons. Peter has, then, taken a first step by taking up lodging with an ostracized tanner. We should not miss the irony of Peter's reticence to receive the vision of what is ritually clean and unclean in the very home of such a person. Only a conversion of the most radical sort will allow Peter's attitude to catch up with his setting.

The Conversion of Cornelius and Peter (10:1–11:18)

Equally important in Acts as the conversion of Cornelius and his household is the "conversion" of Peter to a new point of view, namely, that salvation knows no human boundaries and that "God shows no partiality" (10:34). The chapter division between 10 and 11 is misleading. The episode actually divides into seven scenes (see Haenchen 1971, 357–59), interlinked by much repetition (the vision of Cornelius is reported four times; Peter's vision is thrice related; and all of chap. 11 is basically a summary of chap. 10).

This is the fourth conversion story within three chapters, following the conversions of the Samaritans (8:4–25), the Ethiopian eunuch (8:26–40), and Saul (9:1–31). All these prepare the audience for this conversion story, the conversion of Cornelius and his household, and ultimately for the "official" inauguration of the Gentile mission by Paul. But Cornelius is not the only one converted in this story. In addition to Peter's "conversion" (noted above), the narrator clearly notes that the entire household of Cornelius is saved (11:14). Thus the story is also the first of four "household conversion" stories in Acts (see also 16:11–15, 25–34; 18:1–11; Matson 1996).

10:1–8. In 10:1–8, the scene shifts from Joppa to Caesarea, from a primarily Jewish center to a city populated mostly by Gentiles.

Acts 10:1–11:18 in Context

Peter: his words and deeds
(9:32–11:18)

   Peter's raising of Aeneas and
   Tabitha (9:32–43)

▶ The conversion of Cornelius and
   Peter (10:1–11:18)

     Cornelius's vision in Caesarea
     (10:1–8)

     Peter's vision in Joppa (10:9–17a)

     Cornelius's men in Joppa
     (10:17b–23a)

     Peter in Caesarea (10:23b–33)

     Peter's speech (10:34–43)

     The Gentile Pentecost
     (10:44–48)

     Reporting to the Jerusalem
     church (11:1–18)

Caesarea has already been mentioned in the narrative of Acts: Philip had been left there, preaching (8:40), and Paul had stopped there on his journey to Tarsus (9:30). And the city will figure prominently again in Acts' story (see 12:19; 18:22; 21:8, 16; 23:23, 33; 25:1, 4, 6, 13). The authorial audience recognizes Caesarea as a coastal town that had been built on the site of Straton's Tower (Pliny the Elder, *Nat.* 5.69; Strabo, *Geogr.* 16.2.27), rebuilt by Herod the Great (with some stunning buildings, including a new port; see Josephus, *Ant.* 15.331–341), and used as a Roman military headquarters under Vespasian during the Jewish War (Josephus, *BJ* 3.409–413).

Living in Caesarea were Cornelius, **a centurion of what was known as the Italian Cohort** (10:1), and his household (on the historical problems of the presence of the Italian Cohort in Caesarea at this time, see Broughton 1933, 441–43). The audience is expected to have rudimentary knowledge of the Roman military in late antiquity. Centurions, unlike higher ranking Roman military leaders (see comments on Claudius Lysias at Acts 23), were favorably depicted in Luke and Acts (see Luke 7:1–10; Acts 27:43–44). Centurions were commanders of a hundred men, a subunit of a cohort (composed of six centuries), which in turn was a unit of a legion (composed of ten cohorts, about six thousand soldiers; see Broughton 1933, 427–29). Centurions were drawn from the ranks of the enlisted soldiers, were Roman citizens, were well paid, and, of course, were Gentiles. Like the centurion in Luke 7, Cornelius had both wealth at his disposal and subordinates under his authority.

Cornelius is given a rather full and favorable characterization reminiscent of Tabitha. Cornelius and his household are described by Luke as ones who are **devout and fear God**, and Cornelius specifically is depicted as one who practiced traditional Jewish piety and **did many charitable acts . . . and prayed to God regularly** (10:2; see Tob 12:8; cf. Tabitha, who was "full of good works and acts of charity," 9:36). Much like the centurion in Luke 7 (who loved the Jewish nation and had built a synagogue for them, 7:5), the piety of the Gentile Cornelius had material benefits for the **people** (*laos* is regularly used in Acts for the Jewish people; though see Acts 15 for a significant exception).

Despite being depicted as a benefactor of the Jews and a Gentile practitioner of Jewish piety, the opening characterization of Cornelius as "devout" and one who "feared God" has universalizing overtones as well. Though there has been much debate about the status, and even existence, of the God-fearers in the first century, in Luke's narrative world it is quite clear that they did exist and that they were Gentiles (cf. Acts 11:18). Further, this notion of one who "feared God" had deep cultic roots in the traditions of the OT and postbiblical Judaism. In postexilic Judaism, especially in the book of Proverbs (see 1:7; 3:7; 9:10), the notion of "fearing God" had lost its cultic associations, and wisdom teachers "universalized the concept of allegiance to Yahweh," rooted in the creation theology of wisdom tradition (Clements 1990, 213). "The fear of God is the beginning of wisdom" (Prov 9:10). In this context, "fearing God"

Character Delineation

The description of Cornelius as pious in faith and practice is an example of a figure of thought known as character delineation (*notatio*; Greek *ethopoeia*), which "consists in describing a person's character by the definite signs which, like distinctive marks, are attributes of that character" (*Rhet. Her.* 4.50.63, trans. Caplan 1954, 387; cf. Cicero, *De or.* 3.53.204). This figure could be used to praise or blame a character, although the examples pseudo-Cicero cites are negative. In either case, character delineations "describe the qualities proper to each man's nature" and "carry very great charm, for they set before our eyes a person's whole character"; "in short, by such delineation any one's ruling passion can be brought into the open" (*Rhet. Her.* 4.51.65, trans. Caplan 1954, 395).

The character of Cornelius is further enhanced by the use of the rhetorical figure of synonymy (*interpretatio*), a "figure which does not duplicate the same word by repeating it, but replaces the word that has been used by another of the same meaning" (*Rhet. Her.* 4.28.38, trans. Caplan 1954, 325). Pseudo-Cicero cites an example: "You have impiously beaten your father; you have criminally laid hands upon your parent" (ibid.). In the case of Acts 10:2 (cf. 10:22), these descriptors, "devout," "feared God," "did many charitable acts," and "prayed to God regularly" are virtual synonyms used to praise Cornelius. (The commentary discusses any slight variation in meaning.)

"described the requisite attitude of life in which a truly Jewish morality and piety could flourish in a Gentile setting" (Clements 1990, 215). As a "God-fearer" Cornelius was associating with that tradition of Jewish piety, which already had universalizing tendencies (see below on Acts 10:34–35).

The description of Cornelius as "devout" lends support to this view. While *eusebēs* and its cognates denote Jewish reverence (see Sir 11:17; 13:17; 27:11; 2 Macc 12:45), the verb form occurs in Acts 17:23 in which Paul seeks to convince the Athenians that the "unknown god" they worship (*eusebein*) is the God of Israel. Paul also appeals here to the wisdom tradition of creation ("The God who made the universe and all that is in it," 17:24). Cornelius is a Gentile attracted to the universalizing stream of first-century Judaism, most commonly found in wisdom traditions.

Following this extended description of his character, Cornelius has a vision. Again, the elements reinforce Cornelius's piety. The vision occurs at the **ninth hour of the day** (10:3), which Luke has already identified as "the hour of prayer" (see Acts 3:1). In this vision an "angel of God" reinforces the view of Cornelius's piety: **Your prayers and charitable acts have gone up as a memorial before God** (10:4). Though the time of prayer remains the same in Acts, the setting has changed from the temple (in Acts 3:1) to a house (implied here at 10:3, but made explicit at 10:30). The shift from temple to house reinforces the characterization of Cornelius as one who can engage in traditional acts of piety quite apart from a traditional cultic context. The shift also contributes to Luke's argument that the house and not the temple (or the synagogue) is the appropriate socio-religious institution for expressions of piety to God (cf. Acts 7:44–50).

The commissioning of Cornelius is reported in the form of a vision. The story has most of the traditional elements typical of a dream-vision (see the comments on Acts 9:10–17a; Dodson 2006, 93–99): (1) *Scene-setting*: **Now, a certain man in Caesarea named Cornelius** (10:1–2). (2) *Dream-vision terminology*: **He saw clearly in a vision . . . an angel of God** (10:3). (3) *Dream-vision proper* (which can include a commissioning and dialogue): **He stared at him and was terrified. He said, "What is it, Lord?" And he said to him, "Your prayers and charitable acts have gone up as a memorial before God. Now send men to Joppa and summon a certain Simon, who is called Peter"** (10:4–6). (4) *Reaction*: **He called two of (his) personal servants and a devout soldier from among those who served him. After explaining everything to them, he sent them to Joppa** (10:7–8).

Two variations in the details of the dream-vision are noteworthy. First, the dream-vision in 10:5–6 is incomplete. Cornelius is not told why he should send for Peter, only that he should. Peter's vision (in the next scene) is likewise incomplete (see below). The divine "promptings" of both Cornelius and Peter are only understood after further reflection and interaction with other human characters (see Tannehill 1990, 128–29).

The incompleteness of the dream-vision makes the other variation even more striking. Even though Cornelius is given only the barest of details about Peter, he does not resist the vision. Without further question Cornelius complies by dispatching from his household two personal servants and a "faithful" soldier to fetch Peter (10:7–8). Cornelius's unquestioning obedience stands in sharp contrast to the resistance of Peter in the next scene (and earlier the objections of Ananias at 9:13). His loyalty, from Luke's perspective, is due less to being a "good soldier" and more to his genuinely pious character.

10:9–17a. The temporal change to **on the next day, at about noon** (10:9) notes a shift in scene. Further, there is a change in participants as the focus shifts from the messengers from Cornelius's house who **were traveling and getting close to the city** to Peter who **went up on the roof to pray** (10:9b). The sixth hour (noon) was not the usual time for Jewish prayers or meals. It was a common time in Luke's narrative world for divine guidance (see Acts 22:6; possibly 8:26). It may also indicate Peter's piety in praying at an undesignated time. Likewise, roofs were a typical site for prayer in the biblical tradition (see 2 Kgs 23:12; Neh 8:16; Jer 19:13; Zeph 1:5).

The audience is left to fill the gap left by the narrator's brief note that **while they were preparing the meal, he went into a trance** (Acts 10:10b). Did Peter call out from the roof to his host about his hunger? Does the "they" include

Simon and his servants or fellow Christians? While the audience ponders the understated hospitality of Simon and his household, the narrator moves on to what is more important: Peter's vision (which also follows the pattern of a dream-vision: scene-setting, 10:9–10a; dream-vision terminology, 10:10b–12; dream-vision proper (including instructions and dialogue), 10:13–16; reaction/response, 10:17a).

Peter, like Cornelius, experiences a vision while at prayer (10:10), in an example of a "double vision." In this vision, Peter sees the **sky opened** (10:11), recalling the scene at Jesus' baptism (Luke 3:21) and more recently Stephen's vision (7:56). The opened heaven is a typical element in visions (see Isa 64:1; 3 Macc 6:18; 2 Bar. 22.1; Corp. Herm. 13.17; John 1:51).

Peter sees **an object, like a large sheet, descending and being lowered to the ground by its four corners** (10:11). The word translated here "object" often refers to a container, and some have seen symbolic value with the "four corners" of the sheet perhaps representing the four corners or ends of the earth (see Isa 11:12; Ezek 7:2; Rev 7:1; 20:8), thus pointing to a worldwide mission (see Polhill 1992, 254; Pesch 1986, 1:338). If this symbolism is intended it is not close to the surface of the text.

More important are the contents of the sheet: **On it were all kinds of four-footed animals and reptiles and birds** (10:12). The passage echoes Gen 1:24, as well as 6:20; 7:14; and 8:19. It reflects the divisions of the animal world, including from a Jewish perspective presumably clean and unclean animals. A voice (cf. the baptism of Jesus again in Luke 3) issues a command: **Get up, Peter! Slaughter and eat!** (10:13). This phrase violates Jewish food laws (see Lev 11:47), but echoes Deut 12:15. The word for "slaughter" is used in Luke and Acts in reference to religious or cultic "sacrifice" (see Luke 22:7; Acts

---

Transplacement

In Acts 10:11–12, 16, Luke employs the rhetorical figure of transplacement (*traductio*), which "makes it possible for the same word to be frequently reintroduced not only without offense to good taste, but even so as to render the style more elegant, as follows . . . 'You call him a man, who, had he been a man, would never so cruelly have sought another man's life'" (*Rhet. Her.* 4.14.20, trans. Caplan 1954, 279). The word "sky" or "heaven" (*ouranos*) not only introduces the vision but is repeated to describe part of the content of the vision ("birds of the sky") and the conclusion of the vision, "the object was immediately taken (back) up into the sky/heaven" (Acts 10:11–12, 16). The same figure is used to describe the phenomenon in which "the same word is used first in one function, and then in another" (*Rhet. Her.* 4.14.21). Here Luke may intend the first and last occurrence of *ouranos* to have apocalyptic overtones, typical of heavenly visions, while the middle occurrence, "birds of the sky," may simply refer to their domain; cf. Acts 1:6–11.

14:13, 18), but may also have a more general meaning of "kill," while retaining ritualistic overtones of "slaughter" (see Luke 15:23, 27, 30).

If the divine voice intends that Peter's ritual slaughtering of the animals will render them fit for consumption (see Deut 12:21–22), Peter misses those allusions altogether, hearing only a command to disobey dietary regulations: **Certainly not, Lord! For I have never eaten anything that is impure and contaminated!** (10:14). Why could Peter not choose one of the "clean" animals from the sheet? As the narrative unfolds, the audience (as well as Peter) will be led to conclude that the clean animals were polluted by their association with the unclean animals and will apply that insight to social interaction among persons. At this point, Peter thinks he knows what is clean and unclean, and he refuses to eat what is unclean.

The voice addresses Peter, now for a second time: **That which God has made pure, do not call impure** (10:15). This declaration is repeated twice more in the course of the narrative and though the words are the same, the statement accrues in meaning and nuance over the larger narrative stretch 10:1–11:18. Here, it is simply a statement that Peter should not call any animal unclean because God has cleansed it.

The dream-vision scene concludes: **This happened three times, and then the object was immediately taken (back) up into the sky** (10:16). The ambiguous referent, "this," surely refers to the exchange between Peter and the voice, with Peter thrice refusing to eat. The sheet is finally taken up into heaven from whence it came, and the vision is over.

This vision may be over, but, like Cornelius's vision, it is still very much incomplete. Three times Peter is shown a sheet with all kinds of animals on it and is commanded to eat. Three times Peter refuses, claiming, "Certainly not, Lord! For I have never eaten anything that is impure and contaminated!" (10:14). Echoes of Jesus' baptism scene may recall for the audience the subsequent temptation of Jesus who was hungry but refused to turn stones to bread. The authorial audience, familiar with Mark, will also hear echoes of Jesus' teaching regarding

Commutatio in Acts 10

The rhetorical figure employed in 10:14–15 is "reciprocal change" (*commutatio*), which occurs "when two discrepant thoughts are so expressed by transposition that the latter follows from the former although contradictory to it, as follows: 'You must eat to live, not live to eat'" (*Rhet. Her.* 4.28.39, trans. Caplan 1954, 325). Furthermore, the chiastic structure in the example cited by pseudo-Cicero (eat/live . . . not live/eat) is similar to that found in Acts 10:14–15 ("For I have never eaten anything that is impure [*koinon*] and contaminated [*akatharton*]! . . . That which God has made pure [*ekatharisen*], do not call impure [*koinon*]!") and is commended by the author of *Ad Herennium*: "One cannot deny that the effect is neat when in juxtaposing contrasted ideas the words are also transposed" (*Rhet. Her.* 4.28.39).

clean and unclean foods (Mark 7:14–23, missing in Luke's Gospel)—a message ("Thus, he declared all foods clean," Mark 7:19) that Peter evidently failed to understand the first time around.

Peter's resistance stands in sharp contrast to Cornelius's unquestioning obedience. What remains unclear is the point of this vision. Is Peter to disregard Jewish dietary laws or is something else at stake? The audience is not the only one left pondering. The third scene begins with Peter **wondering what the vision that he had seen could possibly mean** (10:17a).

10:17b–23a. At that moment Cornelius's emissaries arrive in Joppa (10:17b). After having inquired about the specific location of Simon the tanner's house (they had been told only that it was "by the sea"; cf. 10:32), the messengers stand by the gate (*pylōnos*; used also of a residential abode in Luke 16:20; Acts 12:13). Perhaps they do not enter because they are aware that as Gentiles they would contaminate a Jewish home, even the home of a tanner. Or perhaps the smell of the tanner's trade, infamous in antiquity (cf. Pliny the Elder, *Nat.* 23.140) encouraged them to observe Jewish purity codes. In any case, from this position beside the gate, Cornelius's messengers cry out and ask, **Is Simon, who is called Peter, staying here?** (10:18; on translating the verse as direct discourse, see Newman and Nida 1972, 210).

While he is still **thinking about the vision,** the Spirit directs Peter in his next action: **Three men are looking for you! Go right down and go with them, without hesitation, for I have sent them** (10:19–20). The rhetorical device of ambiguity (*ambiguum*), in which "a word can be taken in two or more senses, but yet is taken in that sense which the speaker intends" (*Rhet. Her.* 4.53.67), creates some intriguing tension in the word translated "without hesitation" (*diakrinō*). In the active voice, the word means to "make a distinction" (see Acts 15:9). In the middle or passive (as it is here), it may mean "doubt" or "hesitate" (cf. also Jas 1:6; 2:4). The primary connotation is for Peter to go "without hesitation," but the sense of "without discrimination" cannot be far from the surface (cf. 11:12). The puzzled Peter, then, is still obedient enough to respond to the Spirit's call to go with these men "without hesitation" *and* "without discrimination" (10:20). As pseudo-Cicero says, "Even as we must avoid those ambiguities which render the style obscure, so must we seek those which produce an emphasis of this sort. It will be easy to find them if we know and pay heed to the double and multiple meanings of words" (*Rhet. Her.* 4.53.67, trans. Caplan 1954, 401).

Peter descends from the roof and speaks to the men, saying, **I am the one you are looking for. Why have you come?** (10:21). The reply of Cornelius's messengers begins to unlock Peter's puzzling vision and is the first of three times when Cornelius's vision will be repeated. The messengers' answer reinforces the characterization of Cornelius at the beginning of the unit: **Cornelius, a centurion who is a just man and who fears God and is respected by the whole nation of Jews** (10:22; cf. 10:1). Still, there are some subtle variations between this version and the earlier one that begin to reduce the role of Cornelius (on this see Witherup 1993, 55). No reference is made to Cornelius's practices of alms-giving or prayer, and the "angel of God" (10:3) has become simply a "holy angel." Furthermore, the messengers add a dimension to their version of the vision that was entirely missing from the narrator's, namely that Cornelius is to send for a certain Simon Peter **to summon you to his house and to listen to what you [Peter] say** (10:22; emphasis added). This reduction of Cornelius's role will continue in the third and fourth repetitions of the vision and is similar to the fading of Ananias in the subsequent retellings of Paul's conversion (see comments on chaps. 22, 26).

Peter responds by extending hospitality to these Gentile visitors and giving them a night's lodging (Arterbury 2005, 169). Though table fellowship was less of a problem when Jews entertained Gentiles (Polhill 1992, 257), this act of hospitality to Gentiles by Peter already begins to blur the distinctions between "insider" and "outsider," which many observant Jews would wish to maintain (see *Jub.* 22.16; *Jos. Asen.* 7.1). Cornelius is not the only one awaiting a conversion experience. The way for Peter's conversion is being gradually but thoroughly prepared, and this act of hospitality is a significant step in that direction.

10:23b–33. Again the scene change is marked by a temporal shift: **The next day he got up and went with them, and some of the believers from Joppa went along with him** (10:23b). The presence of these "believers from Joppa" gives the following scenes a public, ecclesiastical context—this is no isolated encounter between two individuals—and they will become important validating witnesses later in the story (see 10:45; 11:12). Another temporal notice, **on the following day** (10:24), ends the two-day journey from Joppa to Caesarea and pushes the story into its fourth day.

The narrator reports that Cornelius was waiting for Peter to arrive, and in preparation had **called together his relatives and close friends** (10:24). The extended household mentioned in 10:2 is brought back into focus and will be an important element in the subsequent narrative. Finally, the two protagonists meet: **When Peter arrived, Cornelius met him** (10:25a). In a reverential and subordinating gesture, Cornelius falls at Peter's feet and worships him (cf. comments on Acts 4:35).

Lest Cornelius's action be mistaken as more than reverential respect (as in Xenophon, *Ephes.* 1.1.3; 1.2.7; 1.12.1), Peter raises him up and declares his own mortality: **Get up! I myself am also (just) a man** (10:26; cf. 14:15). For the second time, the narrator emphasizes that Peter has entered Cornelius's house: **Then, as he talked with him, he went in and found many people had gathered** (10:27).

Peter takes his next step toward conversion and correctly interpreting his vision when he sees the crowd of Gentiles gathered in Cornelius's house and says: **You yourselves know how it is socially unacceptable for a Jew to associate**

Table 4.
Synopsis of Cornelius's Vision

Acts 10:1–8	Acts 10:22	Acts 10:31–33	Acts 11:13–14
Perspective: Narrator of Acts	*Perspective: Cornelius's Messengers*	*Perspective: Cornelius*	*Perspective: Peter*
(3) and <u>saying</u> to him,		31 And he <u>said</u>,	(13) and <u>saying</u>,
"Cornelius."		"Cornelius,	
4 He stared at him and was terrified. He said, "What is it, Lord?" He answered,			
"<u>Your prayers</u> and <u>charitable acts</u> have gone up as a <u>memorial before God</u>.		<u>God</u> has listened to <u>your prayer</u> and <u>he is aware</u> of <u>your charitable acts</u>.	
5 Now, <u>send</u> men <u>to Joppa</u>		32 So <u>send</u> (someone) <u>to Joppa</u>	'Send to Joppa
and <u>summon</u> a certain Simon, who is called Peter;	to <u>summon you</u>	and <u>summon</u> <u>Simon</u>, who is called Peter.	and bring <u>Simon</u>, who is called Peter;
6 <u>This man is staying</u> with a certain <u>Simon</u> <u>the Tanner</u>, whose <u>house</u> is by <u>the sea</u>."		<u>He is staying</u> in the <u>house</u> of <u>Simon</u> <u>the Tanner</u> by <u>the sea</u>."	
7 When the angel who had been speaking to him left, he called two of (his) personal servants and a devout soldier from among those who served him.			
8 After explaining everything to them, he sent them to Joppa		33 Therefore, I immediately sent (someone) to you	
	to his <u>house</u>	and you have done well by coming. So, all of us are now here in God's presence	14 he will give you a message by which you and your entire <u>household</u> will be saved.'
	and <u>to listen to</u> what <u>you say</u>.	<u>to hear</u> all that the Lord has instructed <u>you</u> (to say).	

Double underlining = verbatim agreement (in the Greek text)
Single underlining = near verbatim agreement
Dotted line = conceptual, but not verbal, agreement

with or visit a foreigner; but God has shown me that no one should call a person impure or contaminated (10:28). Peter's statement makes two moves toward interpreting his vision, one dramatic, one subtle. The dramatic move is that Peter perceives that his vision was about more than clean and unclean foods; it involves proper social interaction with persons—"no one should call a person impure or contaminated." Gentile hostility toward Jews was rooted in part in Jewish adherence to dietary regulations and purity customs (Tyson 1987, 627). This view is born out by *Jub.* 22.16: "Keep yourself separate from the nations, and do not eat with them; and do not imitate their rites, nor associate yourself with them" (for a Gentile's perspective, see Juvenal, *Sat.* 14.104–105; Tacitus, *Hist.* 5.5). Thus to move from the issue of food to persons would have seemed natural to the audience.

The other change from the original vision evident in Peter's statement is more subtle. It violates social custom, Peter says, for a Jew to associate with or visit an unclean Gentile (or foreigner), because such contact would defile the Jew. Whereas Peter had equated "common" and "unclean" in the original vision ("Certainly not, Lord! For I have never eaten anything that is impure *and* contaminated"), here he distinguishes between the two, saying, "God has shown me that no one should call a person impure *or* contaminated." The shift from "and" (*kai*) in 10:14 to "or" (*ē*) here at 10:28 is significant in extending Peter's understanding of the vision. There are two categories of defilement. The logic of his statement can be drawn out in the following parallelism: the Jew who is defiled by association with a Gentile is "common," while the Gentile is by diet and lifestyle "unclean" (see Klawans 1995, 285–312). So Peter claims God has revealed to him that he is to refrain from calling any Jew "common" for associating with Gentiles, or any Gentile "unclean" because of diet (see Parsons 2000).

Peter understands that Jews are not polluted by contact with Gentiles, because God has cleansed them. This is the point he will make later to the circumcised believers at Jerusalem who are concerned about his table-fellowship with the uncircumcised (see 11:4–12). But here Peter has pressed beyond the vision in another way. Not only has he extended the vision from food to persons; he has extended the statement of the divine voice to include Gentiles. God has also cleansed the Gentiles, so Peter should refrain from calling them "unclean." Later he will make the very bold move of declaring Gentiles clean before a Jewish audience (see 15:9).

Peter takes a great step forward toward understanding that his vision entails more than food; he has made it into an allegory about persons. Further, the vision has not only declared Jews (like Peter) who were made "common" by association with Gentiles to be "clean," but also includes God's cleansing of Gentiles, who were "unclean" because of diet and lifestyle.

Peter concludes his address by affirming that he came with Cornelius's messengers **without any objection** and now asks (for a second time; cf. 10:21): **May**

I ask, then, why you sent for me? (10:29). Cornelius responds by recounting (now for the third time) his vision (10:30–33). While the substance of the vision is the same, Cornelius does introduce some interesting variations. The role of Cornelius is further reduced, continuing the pattern begun in the second report (see 10:22). Missing is any description of Cornelius's piety. Instead, Cornelius simply reports: **Four days ago, at this very hour, I was praying the ninth hour prayer in my house** (10:30a). No longer is the angel described as "an angel of God" (10:3) or a "holy angel" but simply a **man in shining clothing** (10:30b). Cornelius's version of the vision, **Cornelius, God has listened to your prayer and he is aware of your charitable acts** (10:31), strips the statement of any cultic or sacrificial connotation ("prayers and charitable acts have gone up as a *memorial* before God") and heightens the role of God's divine guidance in the episode.

An additional comment from Cornelius changes the emphasis of the scene: **So all of us are now here in God's presence to hear all that the Lord has instructed you (to say)** (10:33). The emphasis is on the *entire* household of Cornelius gathered to hear *all* that God has commanded. Cornelius's speech serves to set the stage for Peter's kerygmatic declaration in the fifth scene by employing a variety of rhetorical devices (see Soards 1994, 71): (1) the use of "now" (*nyn*) marks a major turning point in Acts (cf. 3:17); (2) the phrase "in God's presence" suggests that God is present through his emissary, Peter, and that it is God, ultimately, who serves as host in this hospitality scene; (3) the phrase "all of us are now here . . . to hear" affirms that Cornelius's household is prepared to do what other speeches have demanded, namely, "hear" (cf. 2:22); (4) the words "all that the Lord has instructed you (to say)" reinforce the notion that the following speech by Peter ultimately has God as its source.

10:34–43. After Cornelius recounts his vision Peter responds to Cornelius's invitation to address the assembly (10:34–43). His epideictic speech focuses on belief (Kennedy 1984, 122–23; cf. the sidebar "Species of Ancient Rhetoric" in the introduction) and falls into three parts, the introduction (10:34–35), the kerygma (10:36–42), and the conclusion (10:43). The speech begins with a solemn notice: **Then Peter opened (his) mouth and said** (10:34a), indicating the importance of his speech (cf. Acts 8:35; 18:14; also Exod 4:12; Num 22:28; Judg 11:36; Ezek 33:22; Dan 3:25 LXX; 10:16). Peter's conversion to this new perspective of Gentile cleanness is continued in the opening line of this speech: **I have truly come to understand that God does not show favoritism** (10:34b). Each phrase is significant. Five of the seven occurrences in the NT of the phrase translated "in truth" or "truly" (*ep alētheias*) are in Luke and Acts (Luke 4:25; 20:21; 22:59; Acts 4:27; 10:34), and all occur in speeches confirming the truthfulness (theological or historical) of the statement that follows. Peter's understanding continues to grow from his accepting hospitality from a tanner, a marginalized Jew, to extending hospitality to Gentile strangers, to entering the house of a Gentile, to expressing his understanding that he is not to call anyone "impure or contaminated."

Now Peter expresses his conviction that this understanding is ultimately rooted in God's own character: "God shows no partiality" (10:34). Other early Christian writers also argue, as Peter does here, that God does not discriminate (cf. Rom 2:11; Eph 6:9; Col 3:25; *1 Clem.* 1.3; *Barn.* 4.12; Pol. *Phil.* 6.1) and that it is wrong for humans to do so (Jas 2:1, 9). Though the arguments of these writers are subtly nuanced (see Bassler 1985, 546–52), they are grounded in the OT (cf. especially Deut 10:17–18).

The speech continues: **Rather, in every nation the one who fears him and does what is right is acceptable to him** (10:35). Peter has come to accept the pious characterization of Cornelius as one "who fears God" (10:2, 22) and who is "just" (10:22) and is now willing to generalize by saying "in every nation, the one" who may be characterized in these ways "is acceptable" to God. The use of the word "acceptable" is interesting here. Originally associated with the sacrificial cult (in the Greek versions of Exod 28:38; Lev 1:3–4; 17:4; 19:5 *et passim*), the wisdom traditions had extended its meaning to refer to a life pleasing to God (in the Greek versions of Prov 10:24; 11:1; 12:22; 16:7; Sir 2:5). Peter's speech continues to draw upon the same universalizing tendencies of the Jewish wisdom tradition that the narrator had utilized at the beginning of the unit.

Peter asserts: **This** [namely, that God shows no partiality] **is the word that he sent to the children of Israel, preaching good news of peace through Jesus Christ—He is Lord of all** (10:36; on this translation see Krodel 1986, 196). This translation has the advantage of removing the phrase "He is Lord of all" from a disruptive and intrusive phrase (placed in parentheses in the RSV) to the centerpiece of the thought unit. Both God, who "does not show favoritism," and Jesus, who is "Lord of all" (cf. Acts 2:36), support Peter's perspective on the radically inclusive nature of the gospel. Peter states that this good news of impartial peace conveyed through Jesus Christ was "sent to the people of Israel." Luke (like Paul) knows that this gospel was given "to the Jew first and also the Greek," and so even the message of radical inclusion begins as part of the larger narrative of Israel's story.

The speech continues: **You know what happened throughout all of Judea, beginning in Galilee with the baptism that John proclaimed** (10:37; cf. 1:4–5, 22). Peter's use of "you know" is either a rhetorical gesture to endear the listener to the speaker (giving the auditors credit for knowing what in fact they do not) or assumes that these events are public knowledge and known even to a Gentile audience in Caesarea.

Peter further notes **how God anointed him with the Holy Spirit and with power** (10:38a). This phrase recalls not only the baptism of Jesus, at which the Holy Spirit descended upon Jesus (cf. Luke 3:20–22), but also Jesus' inaugural speech at Nazareth, during which he claimed, "The Spirit of the Lord is upon me, because he has anointed me" (Luke 4:18; cf. 4:14).

The outline that follows in Peter's speech characterizes Jesus' ministry as one of benefaction: **who went around doing good and healing all who were oppressed by the devil** (10:38b). This image of benefaction translates the Isaianic passage in which the anointing is for preaching "good news to the poor," "release to the captives," "recovery of sight to the blind," and "freedom for the oppressed" (cf. Luke 4:18–20; Isa 61:1–2). Benefaction is a particularly appropriate image for a Gentile audience familiar with patronage and especially the audience in Cornelius's house, which no doubt had personally enjoyed the benefits of Cornelius's benefaction. Luke has already described the apostle's healing ministry as a "benefaction" (see Acts 4:9) and placed the miracles of Christian missionaries in stark contrast to the magic practiced by the agents of Satan (see Acts 8:4–25). He now argues, through Peter's speech, that Jesus' healing ministry was itself the act of a generous benefactor engaged in a struggle against demonic forces by "healing all who were oppressed by the devil" (10:38b). The word "oppress" is found in the NT only here and at Jas 2:6, in which it refers to the poor being oppressed by the rich, a connotation found also in the LXX (see Exod 1:13; 21:17; Neh 5:5; Jer 7:6; 22:3; Ezek 18:7; Amos 4:1; 8:4). Thus Luke employs the economic terminology of the Greco-Roman patronage system and also of the Jewish scriptures to interpret Jesus' ministry as engaged in fulfilling the Isaianic vision.

Peter claims Jesus was able to engage in this ministry of healing and benefaction **because God was with him** (10:38c; an enthymeme according to Kennedy 1984, 123). Luke has already used this phrase in Stephen's speech to characterize Joseph, who was rescued from all his afflictions because "God was with him" (7:9). Similar words are used to depict the presence of God with Mary (Luke 1:28), John the Baptist (Luke 1:66), Christian missionaries in Antioch (Acts 11:21), and Paul (18:10). The phrase was also a favorite one in the LXX to describe God's protection and empowerment of his servants (Gen 21:20, 22; 39:2; Exod 3:12; Isa 58:11). So, too, Jesus is empowered by God to fulfill his prophetic vocation (see also Acts 2:22).

In Acts 10:39–42, Peter returns to familiar themes of apostolic witness and the kerygma of Jesus' death and resurrection. Peter asserts: **we are witnesses of all the things he did both in the Jews' region and in Jerusalem** (10:39a). Apostolic witness is a Lukan theme (see Acts 1:8, 22; 2:32; 3:15; 5:32; 13:31; 22:15; 26:16), and the reference here to being witnesses of Jesus' ministry fulfills the first qualification Peter earlier claimed was necessary for anyone who was part of the circle of the Twelve (see Acts 1:1, 21–22).

Peter then focuses attention on one particular aspect of Jesus' activity, namely his death and resurrection: **He whom they killed by crucifixion, this is the one whom God raised on the third day and caused to be revealed** (10:39b–40). This kerygmatic formula is found with some variation throughout the early speeches in Acts (see 2:23–24; 3:13–15; 4:10; 5:30–31), as well as some of the subsequent addresses by Paul (13:28–31; 26:22–23). The amplification that Jesus was put to death "by hanging on a tree" clearly recalls the language of Deut 21:23, "Cursed by God is everyone who hangs on a tree" (cf. Acts 5:30). The shameful death of Jesus is in sharp contrast to God who "raised [him] on the third day."

The death of Jesus is inseparable from his resurrection. Suffering is an integral part of exaltation; this is true not only for Christ but also for the church (see Moessner 1990). Furthermore, God is the one responsible for the resurrection of Jesus: it is God who acts to raise him from the dead. Peter goes on to say that God was also responsible for the postresurrection appearances ("and [God] caused [Jesus] to be revealed"; cf. Acts 2:27 and 13:35, quoting Ps 15:10 LXX).

Peter then resumes the theme of witness: God allowed Christ to appear **not to all the people, but only to the witnesses who had been chosen in advance by God—to us, who ate and drank with him after he rose from the dead** (10:41). Noting that God chose the apostles to be "witnesses" is consistent with the theocentric focus of this speech. The reference to those witnesses who "ate and drank" with Christ after his resurrection fulfills the second qualification stipulated by Peter for electing a replacement for the Twelve ("one of these to become a witness of the resurrection with us"; Acts 1:22) and calls to mind those passages in which the resurrected Christ did, indeed, eat with his followers (Luke 24:30, 41–43; Acts 1:4; cf. John 21).

The resurrected Christ **commanded us to proclaim to the people** (10:42; cf. 1:8). This note that the message must go first to the Jewish people (*laos*) has been struck before (Acts 3:26) and will be sounded again (Acts 13:46). Once again Peter claims that the apostles have been called to bear witness, this time specifically to the fact that Christ **is the one who was appointed by God as the judge of the living and the dead** (10:42b). The sovereignty of God is emphasized by the phrase "the one appointed by God" and recalls the "fixed intention" of God in Acts 2:23 (cf. 4:28). The role of Christ as judge recurs in Paul's Areopagus speech in 17:31: "He [God] is going to judge the world according to the standard of righteousness by the man he has appointed." That Christ is judge "of the living and the dead" makes the same universalizing point of Peter's earlier claim that Jesus is "Lord of all" (10:36; Tannehill 1990, 141).

In the concluding element of his speech, Peter appeals to another common Lukan theme, the witness of the OT prophets: **All the prophets testify** (10:43a; see Luke 24:27, 44; Acts 3:24; 26:22). While Peter may have avoided direct quotations from the OT because of his Gentile audience (as will be the case later with Paul in Acts 13 and 17), this entire episode and specifically Peter's address are replete with OT echoes and allusions, at least some of which the audience might have been expected to catch.

Peter's conclusion recapitulates important concepts for Luke: believing in Christ (5:14; 8:12; 9:42; 11:17; 13:39; 16:34; 18:8; 19:4; 24:14; 26:27; 27:25); forgiveness of sins (2:38; 3:19; 5:31; 13:38; 22:16; 26:18); and the efficacy of Christ's name (2:38; 3:16; 4:10, 12; 21:13). Just as significant is the *inclusio* that the theme of universality forms with the beginning of the speech: **everyone who believes in him receives forgiveness of sins through his name** (10:43b). Nothing in the speech indicates that the apostles are themselves responsible for a Gentile mission; they are called to "proclaim to the (Jewish) people." Still Luke knows that this proclamation is a necessary part of the Gentile mission (see Acts 13:46), and Peter is here affirming that the story of the Jewish Messiah has universal significance for Gentiles as well. The subsequent events in the next scene confirm Peter's insight and push him toward the last step in his "conversion" process that the story of Jesus is a word of salvation for Cornelius and his household (see Tannehill 1990, 141–42).

10:44–48. Before Peter could finish speaking, a second Pentecost occurs (10:44–48; the rhetorical technique of the "interrupted speech" in 10:44 occurs also at 2:36; 17:32; 22:22; 23:7; 26:24; cf. 11:15). Both the untimely nature of the Spirit's arrival (during Peter's speech and before baptism) and the amazement of the circumcised believers emphasize the surprising initiative of God, who is still directing these actions.

This "Gentile Pentecost" is the fourth outpouring of the Holy Spirit in Acts (Acts 2:1–4; 4:31; 8:17). The phenomenon is experienced by **all those who heard the message** (10:44b), recalling Peter's address. The focus has now shifted from the individual character, Cornelius, to his household. Cornelius has disappeared totally from the story (Matson 1996, 113). When this scene is recounted in Acts 15 by Peter and James, they relate the conversion of a group, not an individual. The corporate nature of the experience is continued in the next verse: **The circumcised believers who had come with Peter were amazed because the gift of the Holy Spirit had even been poured out upon the Gentiles** (10:45). That the Holy Spirit is described as a "gift" fits the context of hospitality. Gift-giving by the host to the guest was customary in ancient hospitality and often marked the transition from a temporary to a permanent hospitality relationship (see Homer, *Od.* 1.311–318; 8.430–32; Longus, *Daphn.* 3.9.4.6; Virgil, *Aen.* 8.152–169; Tob 10:10–11; Josephus, *Ant.* 5.281–282; cf. Arterbury 2005, 170).

And as in the first Pentecost, the gift of the Spirit is confirmed for the "circumcised believers" when **they heard them [the Gentiles] speaking in tongues and magnifying God** (10:46). So the scene now brings to the foreground those believers who had accompanied Peter to Caesarea (10:23) and the household of Cornelius (10:2, 24); both groups had remained silently in the background until this moment. The rather unusual idiom for "Jewish believers" (literally "the faithful from the circumcision"; cf. Culy and Parsons 2003, 215; similarly Gal 2:12; Col 4:11; Titus 1:10) emphasizes the contrast between Peter's Jewish companions and the Gentiles upon whom the Spirit has now been poured. This emphasis on the communal nature of the event continues until the end of the scene.

Speaking in tongues is an "irrefutable legitimation for the acceptance of the Gentiles into the community" (Esler 1992, 136). In light of this demonstrable evidence, Peter asks, **Surely no one is going to withhold water in an effort to keep these people, who have received the Holy Spirit like us, from being baptized?** (10:47). Just as earlier nothing could hinder the Ethiopian eunuch from being baptized (8:36) and later not even prison could hinder Paul from preaching the gospel (28:31), so now the barrier of Gentile uncleanness could no longer hinder the inclusion of Gentiles into the kingdom, though it would be the subject of one more debate (see chap. 15). Continuing the theme of the household's conversion, Peter then commands **them to be baptized in the name of Jesus Christ** (10:47b). The scene ends on the familiar note of hospitality (**Then they asked him to stay for several days**; 10:48). The conversion of this Gentile household occupies center stage in the conflict presented in the next and final scene of this episode (11:1–18).

11:1–18. The change in scene is marked by a shift in locale and participants: **Now, the apostles and other believers throughout Judea heard that the Gentiles had also accepted the message of God** (11:1). Word of the happenings at Cornelius's house travels back to Judea to the apostles and believers, who together comprise the entire Jerusalem congregation. Neither the leaders nor the rank and file evidently had any problem with the conversion and baptism of the household since the word "accepted" is used several times (cf. Acts 8:14; 17:11).

But the Jerusalem church did have objections, which they expressed when Peter returned to Jerusalem: **(some of) those (believers) who were circumcised started arguing with him** (11:2). These "(believers) who were circumcised" are not part of a specific "party" or "faction" but rather refer to the whole congregation of Jewish Christians who stand in contrast to the "uncircumcised" men with whom Peter has had social interaction (cf. 10:45). Luke makes full use of the polyvalence of the word translated here "arguing" (see 10:19b–20). Earlier the same word had been used by the voice that instructed Peter to accompany Cornelius's messengers without doubt/discrimination, and later in this scene will be so used again. "What the Spirit forbade Peter to do toward the Gentiles, namely 'debate/make distinctions/doubt,' these fellow Jews are now doing toward him!" (Johnson 1992, 197).

They level specific charges against Peter: **You visited men who were uncircumcised and ate with them!** (11:3). Peter is charged with the taboo of eating with unclean Gentiles (cf. 2 Macc 5:27; Luke 5:30). Peter's table-fellowship with Gentiles is not mentioned explicitly in the preceding narrative, but it is reasonable to infer from Peter's stay in Cornelius's house "for

Clarity

Clarity is an important (perhaps the most important) aspect of narrative, according to Theon, and one way clarity is achieved is through the "arrangement" (*taxis*) of the subject matter: "Guard also against confusing the times and the order of the events. . . . For nothing confuses the thought more than these things" (*Prog.* 80.26–29, trans. Patillon 1997, 41). By "order" in the narrative, Theon (like Acts 11:4) does not imply any kind of strict historical or chronological order. Theon does seem to distinguish between unintentionally "mixing up . . . the order of events" (*to mē synchein . . . tēn taxin tōn pragmatōn*), which he says "one must guard against" and the elementary exercise of intentionally "changing the order of events," of which he does approve (*Prog.* 86.9–87.13, trans. Patillon 1997, 48–50).

several days" that they did share meals (see Acts 10:48). Nor does Peter deny the charge in his defense speech.

Peter does have a response, however, which falls into four parts. First, he recounts his vision at Joppa (11:4–10), then he gives his version of Cornelius's vision (11:11–14); next he recounts the Pentecost experience (11:15–16), and finally he concludes his address with a question (11:17) that forces his audience to share in his conclusion (11:18). Peter's address contains certain elements typical of a defense speech (cf. Plato, *Phaedr.* 266D–E; Aristotle, *Rhet.* 1345b): narration (*narratio*), which dominates the response; proof (*probatio*) in the form of witnesses (11:12) and signs (11:15); and a conclusion (*peroratio*) in the form of a rhetorical question (11:17).

The narrator also notes that Peter began to explain "in order" or "step by step" (*kathexēs*, 11:4). The modern audience expecting the story to be told in chronological sequence will be surprised to hear that Peter begins by reversing the order of presentation of the visions: his own vision precedes that of Cornelius. But the word "in order" (cf. Luke 1:1–4) has little to do with chronological or linear order. Rather, Peter (and in a larger sense the narrator) is seeking to present the events in a manner which his audience will find rhetorically persuasive. (See the sidebar "Clarity.")

Peter begins by recounting his vision (11:5–10; cf. 10:9–16), and there are significant variations in the retelling. This second version truncates the first: **I was praying in the city of Joppa and saw a vision while in a trance (11:5a).** Any reference to Simon the tanner (cf. 10:5, 17, 32) is entirely missing, perhaps an effort on Peter's part to avoid further distressing his circumcised audience with news of his lodging with an objectionable Jew. There is no reference to Peter's hunger or food being prepared. Further, though the report of the great sheet is nearly verbatim—**an object descending, like a large sheet that was being lowered (11:5b)**—the direction emphasized changes from something "being

Table 5.
Synopsis of Peter's Vision

Acts 10:9–21	Acts 10:28–29	Acts 11:4–12
Perspective: *Narrator of Acts*	*Perspective:* *Peter before Cornelius and his household*	*Perspective:* *Peter before the Jerusalem believers*
9 On the next day, at about noon, while they were traveling and getting close to the city,		4 Peter began (speaking) and explained (everything) to them in an orderly manner,
Peter went up on the roof <u>to pray</u>.		5 "I was <u>praying</u> in the city of Joppa,
10 He became hungry and wanted to eat; but while they were preparing the meal,		and saw a vision while
he went into a <u>trance</u>.		in a <u>trance</u>,
11 He saw the <u>sky</u> standing open and <u>an object like a large sheet descending</u>,		<u>an object descending, like a large sheet</u>
and <u>being lowered</u> to the ground <u>by its four corners</u>.		that was <u>being lowered</u> from the <u>sky</u>, <u>by its four corners</u> and it came right down to me.
		6 As I stared at it I began to look carefully and saw
12 On it were all kinds		
of <u>four-footed animals</u>		<u>four-footed animals</u>, wild animals,
and <u>reptiles</u>		<u>reptiles</u>,
and <u>birds</u>.		and <u>birds</u>.
13 Then a <u>voice</u> (said) to him,		7 Then I heard a <u>voice</u> saying to me,
"Get up, Peter!		'Get up, Peter!
<u>Slaughter and eat</u>."		<u>Slaughter and eat</u>.'
14 But Peter <u>replied</u>,		8 But I <u>said</u>,
"<u>Certainly not, Lord! For</u>		'<u>Certainly not, Lord! For</u>

Acts 10:9–21	Acts 10:28–29	Acts 11:4–12
Perspective: Narrator of Acts	*Perspective: Peter before Cornelius and his household*	*Perspective: Peter before the Jerusalem believers*
I have never eaten anything	28 He <u>said</u> to them, "You yourselves know how it is forbidden for a Jewish man to associate with or to visit a foreigner; but God has shown me that no one should call a person	
that is <u>impure</u> and <u>contaminated</u>."	<u>impure or contaminated</u>.	nothing <u>impure or contaminated</u>
		has ever entered my mouth.'
15 Then the <u>voice</u> (spoke) to him again, <u>a second time</u>,		9 Then the <u>voice</u> spoke from heaven <u>a second time</u>."

Double underlining = verbatim agreement
Single underlining = near verbatim agreement

lowered *to the ground* by its four corners" (10:11) to the sheet being lowered **from the sky** (11:5). This change allows Peter to streamline his presentation, omitting the reference to the "the sky standing open" (10:11), while maintaining that the vision did indeed originate in heaven.

Peter also adds several details of a personal and intimate nature: **and it [the sheet] came right down to me. As I stared at it, I began to look carefully** (11:5b–6a). These details not only add color, they draw the hearer into the account and form part of Peter's strategy in narrating his story "in order," that is, in a way that helps his hearers follow the logic of his thinking and ultimately convinces them to accept the truth of what he says.

The expansion from a three- to a fourfold classification introduces a variety of animals, "beasts of prey" or "wild animals" (*thēria*), that can be used quite generically, (Gen 1:25; cf. Ps 148:10 LXX), but in Acts the phrase "wild animals" introduces a sinister element into the story. Near the end of Acts, the viper that bites Paul on Malta (28:1–6) is twice called a *thērion* (see Diodorus Siculus, *Hist.* 20.42.2; Galen, in Kühn 1821, 4:779). The words of the divine voice reported by Peter here are verbatim those recorded earlier by the narrator: **Get up, Peter! Slaughter and eat** (11:7 // 10:13). And the beginning of Peter's response is likewise repeated verbatim: **Certainly not, Lord!** (11:8 // 10:14). But the remainder of his reply contains several interesting and important variations. First, there is a shift in subject. In 10:14, Peter claims, "I have never eaten anything that is impure and contaminated!" but here in 11:8, he says, **For nothing impure or contaminated has ever entered my mouth!** This change forefronts the words "impure or contaminated" and removes the specific reference to Peter eating.

159

There is also the change from the connective "impure *and* contaminated" to the disjunctive "impure *or* contaminated." This change had already occurred in Peter's earlier elliptical reference to his vision: "God has shown me that no one should call a person impure *or* contaminated" (10:28). Peter now differentiates between common and unclean in a way that he had not done in the initial vision in which "common" and "unclean" were essentially synonyms. Here in chapter 11 Peter's subsequent reflection on the meaning of the vision has shaped his retelling of it.

When the voice responds at 11:9 (in verbatim agreement with 10:15), **that which God has made pure, do not call impure**, Peter intends his audience to come to the same conclusion that he eventually reached. The vision is not just about diet; it is about the very issue of Jew/Gentile associations with which these circumcised believers are so concerned. Further, the divine voice insists that Jews who associate with Gentiles have been cleansed by God and should not be called "common." Peter is able to make this point a bit more emphatically simply by changing the conjunction "and" to the disjunctive "or." And he is able to reinterpret the vision in its retelling without having to offer explicit interpretation as he did in 10:28. This strategy also allows Peter to avoid for the moment the more objectionable conclusion for Jewish hearers that he had earlier shared with a Gentile audience, namely that Gentiles should not be called "unclean" either (but cf. 15:9). By employing these rhetorical strategies, Peter hopes to move his audience to reach the same conclusion, perhaps sooner than he did himself.

After reporting that the vision occurred three times before **everything was drawn back up into the sky again** (11:10; cf. 10:16), Peter next recounts the visit of three men. References to Cornelius and the tanner are avoided. They were **sent from Caesarea** (not from Cornelius) and stood **(outside) the house where we were staying** (11:11; not Simon's house; see 10:17). Echoing 10:20, Peter reports that **the Spirit told me to go with them without any questions** (11:12). The event in Caesarea was divinely prompted. Peter continues: **These six believers also went with me and we entered the man's house** (11:12). These fellow circumcised believers are also "culpable" of the charge of entering the house of uncircumcised men, an accusation originally leveled against Peter alone (11:3).

Peter then recounts Cornelius's vision (though Cornelius is again left unnamed). **He informed us of how he had seen an angel standing in his house and saying, "Send (someone) to Joppa and summon Simon, who is called Peter. He will tell you how you, along with your whole household, can be saved"** (11:13–14). The multiple layers of narration are interesting: Luke says that Peter says that Cornelius says that the angel says (see Acts 2). Still, the angel maintains an authoritative voice through "direct speech."

Again the speech of the angel reported by Peter (summarizing Cornelius) contains truncations and expansions. There is no reference to Cornelius's pious acts; even his name is omitted again. Rather, the entire speech focuses on Peter and his message of salvation for the household (Witherup 1993, 57). The significance of the entire event has been boiled down to the salvation of a Gentile household. The narrative "flow" from Jew-Gentile table-fellowship to the question of the salvation of the Gentiles is exactly opposite that of the flow of chapter 15, which moves from the soteriological question to the issue of table-fellowship.

That salvation, Peter argues, was confirmed by the gift of the Holy Spirit: **Then, just as I was starting to speak [to them], the Holy Spirit fell upon them just as [he fell] upon us at the beginning** (11:15). Peter here connects this Pentecost experience with the first Pentecost, in which many in his audience had no doubt participated. He had made a similar connection earlier (see 10:47). What is new here is found in the next verse: **And I remembered the words of the Lord, how he had said, "John baptized with water, but you will be baptized with the Holy Spirit"** (11:16). The experience, Peter reveals (for the first time), prompted a memory and a new application of a dominical saying (possibly from a gospel no longer extant, but see especially Acts 1:5; cf. Luke 3:16): not only did the Jerusalem church receive a baptism in the Holy Spirit, but that work continues.

The conclusion of Peter's defense is a sharply stated question: **If, then, God gave the same gift to them as to us, who have believed in the Lord Jesus Christ, who was I to try to stop God?** (11:17). Familiar themes are sounded again: the Holy Spirit as a gift (Acts 2:38); the parallels between the first Pentecost in Jerusalem and this "Gentile Pentecost" (God gave them the same gift he gave us; cf. 10:47; 11:15); and, most notable, the motif of the "unhindered" gospel ("who was I to try to stop God?" 8:36; 10:47; 28:31).

This question is not intended to be "merely rhetorical," and the silence is finally broken when these Jewish Christians from Jerusalem praise God saying, **Perhaps God has also given the repentance that leads to life to the Gentiles** (11:18). The issue of Gentile inclusion in the church is by no means resolved, as Acts 15 demonstrates, but at least Peter's conversion is as complete as Cornelius's. For him, at least, God has "made no distinction between them [Gentiles] and us [Jews]" (15:9). Further, these two individuals are joined in their conversion by two groups: the Jerusalem church, which rejoices with Peter that **God has also given the repentance that leads to life to the Gentiles** (11:18), and the household of Cornelius, which increasingly becomes the focus of this story as the recipients of a message by which they shall be saved.

Theological Issues

Luke's view of the relationship of the Christian movement to Judaism is much debated in current scholarship. The view that Luke portrays Christianity as a universal, superior, and separate religion and Judaism as inferior and particularistic (a view with roots in critical scholarship as far back as F. C. Baur) is an anachronistic description of Acts in general and an inaccurate reading of the Cornelius episode in particular (pace Brawley 1987).

This point becomes all the more important when we realize that the book of Acts presents the "Christian" movement (known variously in Acts as the "Way," the "sect of the Nazarenes," the "Christians") as one Jewish movement among several. This view of Christianity as a movement within pre-70 Judaism is the perspective of Christian, Jewish, and Roman characters in Acts, as well as the narrator himself.

Christian perspective: That members of the Way, or Christians, were still practicing Jews is demonstrated through their actions (Peter and John are found going up to the temple to worship in Acts 3), as well as their speeches. Twice Paul makes the claim, "I am a Jew" (21:39; 22:3). Later, he claims that he has "lived in accord with the strictest sect of our religion" (26:5; cf. also 24:14).

Jewish perspective: Tertullus, the Jewish advocate for the high priest before Felix, claims: "For we have found this man (to be) a troublemaker and one who incites rebellion among all the Jews throughout the world, and a ringleader of the sect of the Nazarenes" (24:5). The Jews in Rome say to Paul: "So we think it best to hear from you what you think, for regarding this sect we are aware that it is spoken against everywhere" (28:22).

Roman perspective: Festus reports to Agrippa about Paul: "His accusers . . . brought no accusation of the horrible things that I had suspected. Instead, they had certain disagreements with him about their own religion" (25:18–19). Claudius Lysias, in his letter to the governor, Felix the tribune: "I found him [Paul] accused with respect to matters of their law, but he had no charge (against him) that was worthy of death or imprisonment" (23:29).

Narrator's perspective: The narrator or storyteller portrays the Christians as Jews: "But some from the sect of the Pharisees, who were believers, stood up and said, 'It is necessary to circumcise them and to order (them) to keep the law of Moses'" (15:5). Therefore, to view the Christian movement, at its earliest stages, as a religion, discrete and separate from Judaism, is inaccurate and anachronistic. For this reason some scholars prefer to speak of these earliest Christians as "Messianists"—a term that has its own problems, since other Jewish groups expected a messiah or messiahs.

It is important, however, when speaking about the Christian Way in the first few decades, to understand that the conflicts with other Jewish groups (Pharisees, Sadducees) were part of an "intra-Jewish" debate about who was the "true Israel." Nonetheless, these first Christians—or at least some of them—redrew the "maps of purity," arguing for the inclusion of people, places, and foods that otherwise fell "outside" the boundaries on most (though not all—think of the God-fearers) Jewish symbolic maps of purity. For Luke, the reconstitution of the people of God to include Gentiles was done under the authority of the Abrahamic covenant and for the purpose of presenting Christians (followers of "the Way") as the true heirs of Israel. Ultimately, with the success of the Gentile mission, the fall of Jerusalem, and the redefinition of Judaism by the rabbis (Pharisees), Christianity was, in fact, recognized by Jews, Christians, and Romans as a separate religion sometime toward the end of the second or beginning of the third century (see Boccaccini 1991; Segal 1986).

Acts 11:19–12:25

Barnabas, Peter, and Herod

⊡

Introductory Matters

Luke employs the rhetorical device of the chain-link interlock to make the transition between major text segments (see Introductory Matters for Acts 8 and the comments on Acts 8:1–3). Acts 11:27–12:25 forms such a chain-link, interlocking the first half of Acts, with its focus on Peter and the Jerusalem church (chaps. 1–12), and the second half, with its focus on Paul and the Gentile mission (chaps. 13–28). The chain-link may be diagrammed as in table 6.

Table 6.
Chain-Link Interlock at Acts 11:27–12:25
(Longenecker 2005, 187)

TEXT-UNIT "A"	INTERLOCKED "b" (anticipatory)	INTERLOCKED "a" (retrospective)	TEXT-UNIT "B"
Acts 1:1–12:25	Acts 11:27–30/12:25	Acts 12:1–24	Acts 13–28

In Acts 11:27–30, the church at Antioch commissions Barnabas and Saul to deliver a financial collection to relieve the suffering, caused by famine, of believers in the Jerusalem church, thus shifting the focus from Peter and the Jerusalem church to Barnabas and Paul, major protagonists of the second half of Acts. This anticipatory note is continued in 12:25: "Barnabas and Saul returned from Jerusalem, after completing their ministry, and took John, who was called Mark, along." Inserted in between these interlocking texts is a rather lengthy retrospective unit that concludes the story of Peter, major protagonist of the first half of Acts.

Tracing the Narrative Flow

The Church at Antioch (11:19–30)

In addition to serving as part of the chain-link interlock between Acts 1–12 and 13–28, Acts 11:27–30 is also part of the textual unit 11:19–30 (Longenecker 2005, 240–41). This unit has two parts (11:19–26, 27–30) that are further divided into three subsections (see Krodel 1986, 205–6).

11:19–26. The account of the first Christian missions to Antioch begins with (1) the mission to Jews and Gentiles in Antioch carried out by unnamed believers who had been scattered by persecution (11:19–21), after which (2) Barnabas is sent from Jerusalem and encourages the believers there (11:22–24). (3) Barnabas then finds Saul and together they teach the "Christians" in Antioch (11:25–26).

1. Acts 11:19–26 begins with an echo of the report (11:19–21) of "those who were scattered" in Acts 8:4: **those who had been scattered as a result of the trouble that had happened because of Stephen** (11:19). Of course, for the audience much has transpired in the narrative between these two notices: Philip's ministry to the Samaritans and struggle against Simon; the conversion of the Ethiopian eunuch; the conversion and call of Saul; and the healing ministry of Peter. There is nothing to suggest, however, that the events recorded in 11:19–21 occurred after, or because of, the conversion of Cornelius and his household in 10:1–11:18 (Tannehill 1990, 147).

These "scattered" believers traveled **as far as Phoenicia, Cyprus, and Antioch** (11:19). The narrative will focus on the last of these places, Antioch, but the others play some role in Acts as well. The audience of Acts most likely considered both Joppa (cf. Pliny the Elder, *Nat.* 5.69) and Caesarea (see Josephus, *Ant.* 15.333) to be parts of Phoenicia and thus understood that the ministry of Philip and Peter had already penetrated the Phoenician territory. The major cities of Phoenicia—Tyre (21:3, 7) and Sidon (27:3)—were north of Caesarea (see Pliny the Elder, *Nat.* 5.75–78) and are a natural extension of

---

Acts 11:19–12:25 in the Narrative Flow

The people and places of the Jerusalem church (1–12)

The sense of a beginning (1–7)

Beyond Jerusalem: Philip, Saul, Peter, and others (8–12)

   Philip: a man on a mission (8)

   Saul and Ananias: conversion and call (9:1–31)

   Peter: his words and deeds (9:32–11:18)

▶ Barnabas, Peter, and Herod (11:19–12:25)

   The church at Antioch (11:19–30)

    First missions to Antioch (11:19–26)

     1. "Scattered" believers (11:19–21)

     2. The mission of Barnabas (11:22–24)

     3. Barnabas and Saul (11:25–26)

    Agabus and Christian benefaction (11:27–30)

   Herod: unmasking the powers (12:1–25)

Inflection in Acts 12 and 28

The rhetorical practice of inflection or *klisis* (inflecting the subject in the various Greek cases; see comments on Acts 9:1–30) may also indicate a major shift in action. Theon (*Prog.* 74.24–25) suggests inflecting the subject in only the oblique cases (genitive, dative, accusative).

In light of this comment another interesting pattern emerges in Acts 12. God (*theos*) is inflected in the accusative case (12:5), genitive case (12:22), dative case (12:23), and genitive case again (12:24). In one instance, God (*theos*) is used to refer to "a god," and not Yahweh God (12:22). Strikingly we find a similar phenomenon in Acts chapter 28. God (*theos*) is inflected again only in the oblique cases: accusative (28:6); dative (28:15); genitive (28:23); and genitive again (28:31). Again, *theos* is used once to refer to "a god" and not the God (28:6). Furthermore, it is God in chapter 12, and not Herod or Peter, and God in chapter 28, and not Paul, who is so inflected and thus presumably the subject of each respective passage. Furthermore, "God" occurs in the last verse of each chapter. Not only is this observation significant for the interpretation of each passage, but it may provide further textual and rhetorical evidence for the overall structure of Acts. If our analysis of the inflection is correct, then the audience would have been prepared for such a major shift by the rhetorical markers left not only by the device of the chain-link interlock, but also by the oblique inflection of God.

those missionary activities (Johnson 1992, 203). Likewise, Cyprus was featured as the home of Barnabas (4:36) and the place to which he returns several more times (see 13:4; 15:39; cf. Mnason of Cyprus in 21:16). In a pattern that will become familiar by the end of Acts, these dispersed believers were **telling the message to no one but Jews** (11:19c).

A subgroup of the "scattered" believers begins to address Gentiles as well: **But (*de*) there were certain men among them, who were from Cyprus and Cyrene, who went to Antioch and began speaking to the Greeks as well, preaching the good news of the Lord Jesus** (11:20). Luke is drawing a contrast between the "Jews" of Antioch (11:19) and the Gentiles to whom some of the men of Cyprus and Cyrene proclaimed the "Lord Jesus." Perhaps these "scattered" believers, who themselves had grown up in the Gentile environment of Cyprus and Cyrene, were sensitive to the cultural background of the Antiochenes and spoke not of Jesus as the Jewish Messiah, but rather proclaimed "the *Lord* Jesus" (11:20), a title those Gentiles would find more comprehendible.

The narrator ends this first subsection with a note about the growth of the church, a note steeped in the language of the OT: **The hand of the Lord was with them and a large number, who had believed, turned to the Lord** (11:21).

Something similar to the expression, "the hand of the Lord was with them," is commonly found in the LXX (Exod 9:3; 1 Sam 5:3, 6, 9; 2 Sam 3:12; 1 Kgs 18:46; Isa 59:1; 66:14; Ezek 1:3). This rhetorical figure, known as *synecdoche*, through which "the whole is known from a small part" (*Rhet. Her.* 4.33.44; cf. 11:30; Culy and Parsons 2003, 225), is used here to indicate that the power of God was with the person or group involved (cf. Acts 4:28, 30; 13:11; also Luke 1:66). That the church continues to grow (11:21) through the ministry of those who had been dispersed because of persecution is no less ironic now than it was when it was first mentioned in 8:1, 4.

2. The next subsection (11:22–24) introduces the mission of Barnabas. **The news about them reached the church in Jerusalem, and they sent Barnabas to Antioch** (11:22). The concept of the Jerusalem church serving a "confirming role" is not new (Acts 8:14), though two differences stand out. In Acts 8, it is the apostles who "hear" and "send"; here it is the "church in Jerusalem." Further, apostles, Peter and John, are sent as emissaries of the Jerusalem church; here it is an important but nonapostolic representative, Barnabas. The lack of reference to the apostles is probably not to be taken as a sign of eroding apostolic authority, but rather to give center stage once again to an important character in Acts, Barnabas.

Barnabas, like some of those nameless evangelists who preached to the Antiochene Gentiles, was himself a native of Cyprus and was a natural choice to serve as emissary of the Jerusalem church. When Barnabas arrived in Antioch and **saw the grace** (*charin*) **of God, he rejoiced** (*echarē*; 11:23a). The interplay of "grace" and "rejoice" is not only an artful use of rhetoric (assonance or paronomasia), it also "signals the perception of God's activity in the world" (Johnson 1992, 204; cf. Luke 1:14, 28; 6:23; 10:20; 13:17; 15:5, 32; 19:6, 37; Acts 5:41; 8:39). The Christians at Antioch are exhorted to **remain loyal to the Lord** (see Wis 3:9) **with determination** (11:23c; on "determination" as moral purpose, see Epictetus, *Diatr.* 1.21.2; 3.25.1; 4.6.26). As a result, the narrator reiterates the growth of the church: **And a substantial crowd turned to the Lord** (11:24).

But the middle portion of this subunit, 11:23b–24a, actually focuses more on the character of Barnabas than the Christians at Antioch. In this section, the narrator uses both "showing" and "telling" to describe Barnabas. First, Luke "shows" something of the character of Barnabas: he **began urging them all** (11:23b). The use of "urge" recalls Acts 4:36, where the narrator says that Barnabas was called a "son of encouragement/exhortation." In 11:24, the narrator uses the telling mode; that is, he employs direct commentary to give a positive evaluation of Barnabas: **For he was a good man, full of the Holy Spirit and faith.** The phrases echo previous descriptions: like Joseph of Arimathea, Barnabas was "a good man" (Luke 23:50); like Stephen, he was "full of the Holy Spirit and faith" (Acts 6:5; for more on Barnabas, see comments on Acts 4:36–37). This faithful, Spirit-filled Barnabas, who is (not blindly) loyal to the apostles and a continuing source of encouragement to the community (see also 15:36–40), stands in sharp contrast not only to the story of Ananias and Sapphira but also to the following story about Herod.

3. The collaboration of Saul with Barnabas is introduced in 11:25–26. Barnabas **left for Tarsus to look for Saul** (11:25), where the narrator had left him cooling his heels. When he had found him they returned to Antioch and **for an entire year they met with (the believers) in the assembly and taught a substantial crowd** (11:26). This passage is one of several in which the church at Antioch is described in ways strikingly similar to the description of the Jerusalem church (see Tannehill 1990, 147–50):

1. Both the Jerusalem (2:41, 47; 5:14) and Antioch (11:24) congregations add to their numbers.
2. Both the Jerusalem (2:42) and Antioch (11:26) congregations devote themselves to the teaching of their leaders.
3. Both the Jerusalem (2:44–45; 4:32–37; 6:1) and Antioch (11:29) congregations express their concern for the needy by giving aid, and Barnabas plays an important role in each congregation's decision to share its possessions (cf. 4:32–37; 11:30).

One significant variation between the two congregations is the narrator's concluding note to this unit that **it was in Antioch that the disciples were first called "Christians"** (11:26). Though the narrator does not explicitly say so, most readers have concluded that the name "Christians" was given as a pejorative title to the followers of Jesus by outsiders. The only other time the word occurs in Acts, it is on the lips of an outsider to the community, King Agrippa (26:28). Further, the authorial audience was aware that both Jewish and Roman writers used the term "Christians" to designate followers of Jesus (Josephus, *Ant.* 18.64; Tacitus, *Ann.* 15.44; Pliny the Younger, *Ep.* 10.96–97; Suetonius, *Nero* 16.2; Lucian, *Alex.* 25.38; *Peregr.* 11, 12, 14, 16). Not until the writings of Ignatius, second-century bishop of Antioch, is the term found as a Christian self-designation (see Ign. *Eph.* 11.2; *Rom.* 3.2; *Magn.* 10.3; *Pol.* 7.3; cf. Taylor 1994). The use of the name here may indirectly reflect the predominantly Gentile character of the Antiochene congregation and evidence of "a 'Gentile mission' larger than the initiative of Peter yet preceding Paul's own work" (Johnson 1992, 203).

11:27–30. The account of Agabus and Christian benefaction (11:27–30) begins when (1) unnamed prophets arrive in Antioch from Jerusalem (11:27). After (2) Agabus gives a specific prophecy about an impending famine (11:28), (3) the Christian community in Antioch determines its action of benefaction for the believers in Judea (11:29–30).

1. After the church was established and then encouraged and confirmed by Barnabas and Paul (11:22–26), **prophets went down to Antioch from Jerusalem**

(11:27). Rarely does Luke use the term "prophet" of Christian leaders. Jesus is occasionally referred to as a prophet (Luke 4:24; 7:16, 39; 13:33–34; 24:19; Acts 3:22–23; 7:37), as is John the Baptist (Luke 1:76; 7:26, 28; 20:6). Most frequently it is a title reserved for figures from Israel's past, who either engage in prophetic activities or write prophetic books (see, e.g., Luke 1:70; 3:4; 4:17, 27; 6:23; 9:8, 19; 10:24; 11:47, 49, 50; 13:28; 16:16, 29, 31; 18:31; 24:25, 27, 44; Acts 2:16, 30; 3:18, 21, 24). But here and at Acts 13:1, 15:32, and 21:10 (cf. also 2:17, 18; 19:6; 21:9) Luke uses the term "prophets" to describe a traveling group within the Christian community (cf. *Did.* 11.3–12; Herm. *Mand.* 11.1–21) who make predictions (Johnson 1992, 205).

> ### Acts 11:27–30 in Context
>
> The church at Antioch
> (11:19–30)
>
> > First missions to Antioch
> > (11:19–26)
> >
> > ► Agabus and Christian bene-
> > faction (11:27–30)
> >
> > > 1. Unnamed prophets ar-
> > > rive (11:27)
> > >
> > > 2. Agabus prophesies fam-
> > > ine (11:28)
> > >
> > > 3. Antiochene benefac-
> > > tion for Judean believers
> > > (11:29–30)

2. Agabus is one of these Jerusalem prophets and makes here the first of his two appearances in Acts (cf. 21:10–14). In both instances, Agabus engages in a predictive activity; here he indicated **through the Spirit that a severe famine was about to occur throughout the entire Empire** (11:28). That this utterance is divinely inspired is indicated by the phrase "through the Spirit" (see 21:4). The phrase, *holēn tēn oikoumenēn*, is better translated "empire" than "world," because "empire" reflects Luke's interest in the political nature of this term (see Luke 2:1; 4:5; Acts 17:6; 24:5; Johnson 1992, 206).

The narrator goes on to claim that this prediction was fulfilled **during Claudius's reign** (11:28). Food shortages during Claudius's reign (41–54 AD) are well documented in ancient sources (Suetonius, *Claud.* 18; Tacitus, *Ann.* 12.43; Josephus, *Ant.* 20.101; 3.320–321).

3. The Christian benefaction that the Antioch church undertook in response to the famine is remarkable given the pattern of benefaction practiced in the larger culture of the eastern portion of the Roman Empire (Winter 1994, 73). A wealthy Antiochene Christian (such as Mnason) might have been conscripted as *curator annonae* to provide relief for the food shortage. Rather, the narrator reports that **each of the disciples, in accordance with his financial ability, decided to send (something) as a contribution to the believers living in Judea** (11:29). The role of benefactor is shared by all members of the Christian community (Winter 1994, 76), a remarkable point given the chronic problem of overpopulation of Antioch (Josephus, *BJ* 3.29; 7.41–62; Stark 1991, 192), and the numerous disasters it had experienced during the previous century (c. 51 BC–AD 70; cf. Stark 2001, 206). If Antioch conjured images of filth, disease, and suffering for the ancient audience, then Luke's depiction of these Christians' act of benefaction is all the more remarkable. In the midst of their own

suffering, the Antiochene Christians reached out to those in need, not out of their plenty but out of their want.

When the disciples decide to send relief "to the believers living in Judea" (11:29) they send it **by the hands of Barnabas and Saul** (11:30). The church at Antioch seized the opportunity to minister to the believers in the church at Jerusalem, a clear sign that those first missioners encouraged mission *with* and not simply *to* the Antiochenes.

Herod: Unmasking the Powers (12:1–25)

With the note of true Christian benefaction ringing in their ears, the audience is introduced to the manufactured "benefaction" of a tyrant, Herod. In between is sandwiched the story of Peter's deliverance from prison. Both these episodes draw upon larger cultural and literary type-scenes familiar to the audience. This chapter demonstrates Luke's understanding of the nature and location of true power. The contrasts between displays of divine and earthly power are striking, as are these other contrasts (modifying Krodel 1986, 214):

1. James is executed by Herod (12:2); Peter is miraculously delivered by God (12:6–11).
2. Herod exercises brute force against the Christians (12:1–3), but is unable to withstand the power of the Christians' God at the end (12:20–23).
3. Herod hatches an elaborate scheme to keep Peter in prison (12:4–6); God gives specific instructions that lead to his release (12:6–11).
4. The church prayed for Peter (12:5b) but found it difficult to accept that its prayers had been answered (12:12–17).
5. Peter is passive and drowsy (12:6–7); the angel of God is quick and decisive (12:6–10).
6. Peter's release is secured with precision and haste (12:6–10); the church is slow and confused in its comprehension of his release (12:12–17).
7. Herod curried the favor of the Jews (12:3); he lost the favor of God (12:23).
8. Peter was "struck" to life and and freedom by an angel (12:7); Herod was "struck" to death by an angel of the Lord (12:23).

These contrasts not only enliven the story; they "give it theological depth" (Krodel 1986, 214).

Peter's deliverance from prison needs to be set against a broader canvas. Such miraculous prison-escape stories would no doubt have been very familiar to the audience (see Homer, *Il.* 5.749; Virgil, *Aen.* 6.81–82; Philostratus, *Vit. Apoll.* 7.38; Ovid, *Metam.* 3.690–700; Artapanus, *Jud.* frag. 3b; *Acts Paul* 7; *Acts Thom.* 162–163; also *Yoma* 39b and *y. Yoma* 43c.6).

The story also partakes of the death-resurrection motif noted elsewhere (see 9:32–43). Parallels between this passage and the passion of Jesus contribute to the audience's expectation that Peter is to experience a fate similar to that of Jesus. The beheading of James by Herod serves as a dark omen for Peter, much like the beheading of John the Baptist by another Herod (Luke 9:9) foreshadowed the death of Jesus. Though Peter does not experience physical death, three stock elements in the story—imprisonment, the night, and sleep—underscore Peter's symbolic death (see Horton 1995, 67–68). Psalm 107:10 LXX describes prisoners as those who live "in darkness and in gloom." Darkness, too, was a symbol of death (see Pss 49:19; 58:8b). Sleep, likewise, is a common euphemism in biblical idiom for death (Acts 7:60; 13:36; also Deut 31:16; 2 Sam 7:12; 1 Kgs 1:21; 2:10; 11:21; 15:8; 2 Kgs 8:24; 13:9; 2 Chr 9:31; 26:23; Ps 13:3; Jer 51:57).

Miraculous Escape

The original audience of Acts would have been familiar with escape stories in Greek literature. Euripides' *The Bacchae* records the miraculous escape of some young maidens:

> "As for the bacchant women you have restrained, arresting and chaining them up in the public prison, they are gone: free of their bonds they skipped off toward the mountain glades, calling on the god Bromios. The chains were loosed from their feet of their own accord, and keys opened doors with no mortal hand to turn them."
> (*Bacch.* 443–448, trans. Kovacs 2002)

This "death" imagery stands in sharp contrast with the "new life" Peter receives. An angel "suddenly . . . appeared" (12:7; cf. Luke 24:4), "woke him up" (*ēgeiren*), and commanded him to "get up quickly" (*anasta*, 12:7). The parallels between the risen Jesus and Peter are also striking (see Horton 1995, 72–73; Johnson 1992, 218–19):

1. A woman reports having seen Peter (12:14); women report seeing Jesus (Luke 24:10).
2. The recipients of this good news refuse to believe it (Acts 12:15/Luke 24:11).
3. Peter is mistaken for an angel (12:15); Jesus is mistaken for a ghost (Luke 24:37).
4. Both Peter and Jesus explain to the disciples what has happened (Acts 12:17/Luke 24:46) and issue a commission (Acts 12:17/Luke 24:47–49).
5. Both Peter and Jesus make a mysterious departure (Acts 12:17/Luke 24:51).

Peter's deliverance from prison demonstrates the continuing power of Jesus' resurrection (Johnson 1992, 219). It also provides the basis for exposing the fraudulent claims to power of a petty dictator.

12:1–5. This scene is connected to the previous action by the phrase **about that time** (12:1a), so that the famine relief mission of Barnabas and Saul frames the events recorded in chapter 12 (see 12:25). In particular, the event occurring about the same time is the persecution of Jerusalem Christians by the king: **King Herod arrested some members of the church in order to mistreat them** (12:1b). This political leader, Agrippa I, is named by the narrator simply as "King Herod." Agrippa I was the grandson of Herod the Great (also mentioned in Luke 1:5) and father of Agrippa II (later mentioned in Acts as simply "Agrippa"; see Acts 25:13–26:32). Of the extant literature dealing with Agrippa I, only in Acts is Agrippa I called simply "King Herod." To identify Agrippa I with the Herod the Tetrarch, enemy of Jesus in the Third Gospel (Luke 3:1, 19; 8:3; 9:7–9; 13:31; 23:7–15) recalls the similarity in the actions of the two in opposing Jesus and his followers.

This point was made clearly in the community prayer in Acts 4:23–31, in which the details of Ps 2:1–2 are used to interpret both the passion of Jesus and the persecutions of the Jerusalem church: the Gentiles = the Roman soldiers; the peoples = the people of Jerusalem; the kings = Herod the Tetrarch; the rulers = Pilate; and the anointed of the Lord = Jesus (Darr 1992, 167). This typology forces the audience of Acts to reassess the roles of Herod and Pilate in the trial of Jesus. Gone from Acts is any positive reference to Herod (or Pilate) finding Jesus innocent (see Luke 23:6–12). Rather, in Acts, the title "Herod" represents the archetypal "antagonist of the divine agenda" (Darr 1992, 167). So here in Acts 12, King Herod postures himself in opposition to the servants of the Lord.

Herod's opposition here, however, moves beyond "threats" (see Acts 4:29) into action. Specifically, Herod **had James, the brother of John, executed by the sword** (12:2). Compared to the narrative recording the martyrdom of Stephen, this notice of James's martyrdom is quite brief; it still serves its purpose of heightening the dramatic quality of the following story of Peter. No less importantly, it underscores the fact that not all of Christ's followers are divinely rescued; in this case, it is James, brother of John, one of the first of Jesus' followers to be called (Luke 5:10), one of the Twelve (Luke 6:14; Acts 1:13), and one of Jesus' "inner circle" (Luke 8:51; 9:28, 54) who meets his death. The church suffers along with its suffering Messiah. The authorial audience will hear echoes of Jesus' prediction of the martyrdom of James (and John) in the Synoptic tradition: "The cup that I drink you will drink;

and with the baptism with which I am baptized you will be baptized" (Mark 10:39; Matt 20:23; but missing in Luke).

The narrator reports that James's death **pleased the Jews** (12:3). The authorial audience familiar with Jewish tradition would know that beheading was considered "the most shameful of all deaths" (see *m. Sanh.* 7.2) and was reserved not only for murderers, but also for "the people of an apostate city" (*m. Sanh.* 9.1). Further, the "inhabitants of an apostate city" were to have no place in the next life. Seeing that this act curried the favor of the Jews, Herod determined to serve them Peter as well. Perhaps aware of Peter's reputation as an "escape artist" (see 5:19–26), Herod placed Peter under close around-the-clock watch (12:4; four squads possibly working on three-hour shifts— see Philo, *Flacc.* 111; Vegetius, *Epit.* 3.8). This reference to four squads of soldiers (a total of sixteen men) again increases the miraculous nature of Peter's deliverance.

In an aside, the narrator notes that the arrest of Peter occurred during the **feast of Unleavened Bread** (12:3), a temporal reference reinforced by reference to the "Passover" in 12:4. This detail is important for several reasons (see Tannehill 1990, 152–54). First, it explains why Peter did not immediately suffer the same fate as John; Herod wished to avoid a tumult of the people during the festival (see 12:4). Second, this setting parallels the passion of Jesus, which also occurred during the festival of Unleavened Bread (Luke 22:1, 7). The word used for Peter's "arrest" occurs also in reference to Jesus (Luke 22:54; also Acts 1:16). Likewise, Herod's intention **to present him to the people (for execution)** (12:4) echoes Pilate's presenting Jesus to the people (Luke 23:13). Other details in the text connect the two stories. The word "killed" is also used of Jesus in Luke 22:2; 23:32 (cf. Acts 2:23; 10:39; 13:28). Herod "delivers" Peter to the soldiers, just as Jesus is "delivered" to those who will kill him (Luke 9:44; 18:32; 23:25; 24:7, 20). Finally, the setting creates the biting irony of Peter in chains during the very festival that celebrates the deliverance of Israel from bondage in Egypt (see Pervo 1990, 41). This should not be surprising to the audience since Luke had already described the passion of Jesus as an "exodus" in his first volume (Luke 9:31; see Tannehill 1990, 154–55).

This first scene ends on the note that **Peter was kept in prison, but prayers were fervently being offered to God on his behalf by the church** (12:5). Luke reminds the audience that Peter was surrounded not only by walls and guards, but also by the protective prayers of his community (Krodel 1986, 218; on the church as a community of prayer, see 1:14, 24; 2:42; 3:1; 4:23–30; 6:6; 8:15; 9:11, 40–41; 10:4, 9; 13:3; 16:25; 20:36; 21:5; 22:17; 28:8).

12:6–19. Acts 12:6–19 is the second of three prison-escape stories in Acts (see Acts 5:17–21; 16:25–28), though clearly the prison escape itself is more important here than are the other two. The scene divides into three parts: (1) Peter's deliverance from prison (12:6–11); (2) his subsequent appearance

Figure 7. Raphael, *The Liberation of St. Peter from Prison*, 1514. Fresco. Stanze di Raffaello, Vatican Palace.

Working within the confines of a peculiarly shaped space, the Italian Renaissance master Raphael depicts the freeing of Peter from prison in a narrative sequence of three scenes. In the middle scene, the angel awakens Peter with a tap on the side. On the viewer's right, Peter and the angelic guide make their way out of the cell, past slumbering guards. On the opposite side, the guards are rudely awakened to find that their prisoner has miraculously escaped.

before the believers at the home of Mary, mother of Mark (12:12–17); and (3) Herod's response (12:18–19).

1. Each element of this opening verse contributes to the drama of Peter's release: **Now on the night before Herod was going to bring him before (the people for execution), Peter was sleeping between two soldiers. He had been bound with two chains and there were guards in front of the (prison) gate guarding the prison (12:6).** "The night before" is evidently a reference to the night of the Passover, which in some Jewish traditions (see, e.g., *Exod. Rab.* 12.42) "was expected to be a night of messianic deliverance" (Barrett 1994, 1:577, who also notes that this understanding was continued in the early church; see *Ep. apost.* 15). Likewise, details of the heightened security (Peter "bound in two chains," "between two soldiers," and "guards in front of the door") increase the wonder of Peter's deliverance.

The story continues: **Suddenly, an angel of the Lord appeared and a light shone in the prison cell. He tapped Peter on the side and woke him up, saying,**

"Get up quickly," and his chains fell off of his hands. The angel said to him, "Get dressed and put on your sandals." And he did so. Then he said to him, "Put on your coat and follow me" (12:7–8). The use of "suddenly," the verb "appeared" (see Acts 23:11; cf. Luke 2:9), and the angel's "tap" on Peter's side (see below on 12:23) highlight the startling nature of the angel's appearance. The accompanying light makes it quite clear that this angel is a divine, rather than human, emissary. This sudden and dramatic entry stands in sharp contrast to the pedantic instructions given Peter by the angel: "Get up!" "Get dressed!" "Put on your sandals!" "Put on your coat!" "Follow me!" These commands bring the still sleepy Peter's befuddlement into bold relief and make crystal clear just who is in charge. As in the Cornelius episode, everything is directed "from above" by an angel of the Lord, who even instructs Peter on how to dress himself (Pervo 1990, 62).

The Passover setting is also very important in understanding this scene. The exodus imagery is particularly evident in Luke's choice of language: "the night before" (12:6; Exod 12:12); "Get up quickly" (12:7; Exod 12:11); "put on your sandals" (12:8; Exod 12:11); "the Lord . . . rescued" (12:11; Exod 18:4, 8–10). Beyond demonstrating Peter's confusion, "it happens that the commands also correspond to the regulations for Passover. The Israelites who are about to be rescued must be ready for the journey that will follow. They must eat the Passover with their loins girded and sandals on their feet" (Tannehill 1990, 155).

Peter's passivity is further emphasized by the fact that he thought what was happening was another vision, not reality. He does at least respond again to the call, "Follow me" (12:8). Clearly, this is the story of Peter's *divine* deliverance from bondage (like the Israelites), not *his* escape. And the irony of Peter's deliverance by an angel is not lost on the audience, which knows that one important character group in the story, the Sadducees, did not even believe in the existence of angels (see 23:8).

The miracle continues as the angel guides Peter past two layers of guards to an iron gate leading into the street (12:10a). As in other stories of this nature, the gate **opened for them by itself** (12:10b). The parallel with the miraculous delivery of Moses from prison reported in Artapanus's fragment (preserved by Eusebius, *Praep. ev.* 9.27.23) is especially striking, given the exodus language that permeates this episode:

> When the king learned this, he confined him [Moses] in prison. But when night came, all the doors of the prison opened of themselves, and some of the guards died, while others were relaxed by sleep and their weapons were broken. Moses came out and went to the royal chambers. (*Jud.*, frag. 3b, trans. OTP 2:901)

Likewise, when the angel and Peter had passed through the miraculously opened gate, **they went out and had walked down (just) one street** (12:10c).

The angel then departs as suddenly as he had appeared. Peter finally **came to himself** (12:11a) and, as with the Cornelius episode, begins the process of reflecting upon what has happened to him: **Now I know for certain that the Lord sent his angel and rescued me from Herod's hands and from everything that the Jewish people were anticipating** (12:11b). This language is also reminiscent of the exodus from Egypt. Peter's claim that "the Lord . . . rescued me from Herod's hands" recalls God's words to Moses: "I have come down to rescue them from the hand of the Egyptians" (Exod 3:8). The hand of Herod is here coupled with "everything that the Jewish people were anticipating" (12:11).

2. In 12:12–17, realizing finally the reality of his deliverance, Peter goes to the house of Mary, mother of John Mark (who will assume a significant role in the narrative of chap. 13), where the believers have gathered to pray (12:12). Naming a woman as the head of a household is unusual but not unprecedented in Luke and Acts (see Luke 10:38–42; Acts 16:14–15). Peter will soon discover that his fellow believers have even more difficulty in comprehending his release than he had. This scene is filled with drama and punctuated with irony and comic relief.

Peter encounters a second gate, only this time it does not open miraculously (12:13a). Vulnerable to anyone who might see him, Peter knocks and a maidservant named Rhoda (Rose) comes to answer. In Luke and Acts, this is Peter's second encounter with a maidservant (cf. Luke 22:56–57), neither of which is very successful. Rhoda is so overjoyed at recognizing Peter's voice that she runs inside to tell the others, leaving Peter standing at the gate (12:14; cf. the use of *antistrophe*, the repetition of the same word, here *pylōn*, at the end of successive phrases; *Rhet. Her.* 4.13.19; cf. comments on 1:11; 3:2–3).

The believers who presumably had gathered to pray for Peter (see 12:5, 12) refuse to believe that their prayers have been answered. Rather, they inform Rhoda that she is out of her mind and suggest that what she has seen is not Peter, but rather his ghost. This is evidently another sign that they did not trust that God would deliver Peter since in popular Jewish tradition it was believed that each person had a "guardian angel" (see Gen 48:16; Tob 5:4–6, 22; *T. Jac.* 1.10; *LAB* 59.4). The appearance of the guardian angel would signal Peter's death.

Meanwhile, as the believers are debating poor Rhoda's testimony, Peter continues to knock. Finally they open the gate and find him there, much to their amazement (12:16). Upon entering, **he motioned to them with his hand to quiet down** (12:17; on this same gesture, see Acts 13:16; 21:40; 26:1). He then **related to them how the Lord had brought him out of the prison** (12:17b). Like the previous episode about Cornelius and his household, the story is repeated, but unlike that account there is no direct discourse and no multiple repetitions of the story.

The key part of Peter's speech, however, is given in direct discourse: **Report these things to James and the other believers** (12:17c). This James is the brother of Jesus mentioned but unnamed in 1:14. This unit ends with the cryptic remark that Peter **left and went somewhere else** (12:17d). Peter will make only one more appearance—before the Jerusalem Council (Acts 15)—before disappearing from the stage altogether. In that episode, the transition of leadership in the Jerusalem church from Peter to James is completed.

3. In 12:18–19, the story returns to the "scene of the crime" on the morning after: **there was great anxiety among the soldiers regarding what could have become of Peter** (12:18). Luke again uses litotes ("not a little anxiety"; see *Rhet. Her.* 4.38.50) to understate the turmoil and dismay of the soldiers (for other examples of Lukan litotes, see comments on Acts 1:5; 4:20; 5:26; 12:18; 14:28; 15:2; 17:4, 12; 19:11, 23, 24; 20:12; 21:39; 25:6; 26:19, 26; 27:14, 20; 28:2). Why they should be so upset is revealed in the next verse: **Herod, after searching for him and not finding him, questioned the guards and then ordered them to be taken away (for execution)** (12:19). The rhetoric here is juridical. The verb "questioned" often occurs in trial scenes (see Acts 24:8; 28:18; also Plato, *Symp.* 201E) and might best be translated "cross-examine." When conducted by tyrants, such questioning might also involve torture (Chariton, *Chaer.* 5.1–2; Pliny the Younger, *Ep.* 10, 96, 8). Though the Greek literally reads that Herod ordered them "to be taken away," the NRSV has correctly rendered it "to be put to death." The later Code of Justinian (9.4.4) stated that a Roman guard would suffer the same punishment that the escaped prisoner was scheduled to receive (thus explaining the Philippian jailer's anxiety in Acts 16:27). Such vindictiveness is not unexpected in Luke's narrative world either by tyrants in general (see Luke 12:46; 19:27) or this tyrant in particular (see 12:2, 21). Further, Luke uses the same word to describe Jesus being "led away" to his execution (Luke 23:26). The execution of these soldiers serves to justify further the divine punishment that Herod is about to receive. Herod, like Peter, departs, though his destination, Caesarea (still within the Roman province of Judea), is specified and becomes the locale for the next and final scene involving Herod.

Metonymy

In Acts 12:20, Luke uses the rhetorical figure of *metonymy*, "which draws from an object closely akin or associated an expression suggesting the object meant, but not called by its own name" (*Rhet. Her.* 4.32.43, trans. Caplan 1954, 335). Specifically, pseudo-Cicero cites the following example: "'Italy cannot be vanquished in warfare nor Greece in studies'; for here instead of Greeks and Italians the lands that comprise them are designated" (*Rhet. Her.* 4.32.43). Similarly, Luke's assertion that Herod is furious with Tyre and Sidon refers to the inhabitants of those countries and not their representatives or leaders (contra Barrett 1994, 1:589).

12:20–25. As the new scene opens, Herod has already killed James, imprisoned Peter with the intention of putting him to death, and presumably executed the four squads of guards (sixteen men) who had watched over him. Now he cuts off food supplies from the people of Tyre and Sidon (on this economic dependency, see 1 Kgs 5:11; Ezek 27:17), because he is angry with them for some unspecified reason (12:20).

So they went to him together and by persuading Blastus, the king's personal assistant, (to let them speak to the king) they began asking for peace (12:20b). Blastus appears only here in Acts, but he is a key figure in the negotiations (on the access of a chamberlain to royal power, see Epictetus, *Diatr.* 1.19.17–23; 3.33.15; 4.7.1–19). A "peace" between the king and the Phoenician citizens is evidently brokered by Blastus, and a celebration is held for the king to receive the people's praise for his benefaction, which, of course, is only necessary because of Herod's own tyrannical actions.

Luke does not specify the **appointed day** (12:21) for the celebration, but it may have coincided with the spectacles in Caesarea that Herod observed in honor of Caesar (Josephus, *Ant.* 19.343). At any rate, **after Herod had dressed in his royal clothing and sat down on the judgment seat, he began to deliver a speech to them** (12:21). His speech garnered the people's favor and they **started shouting, "This is the voice of a god, not of a man!"** (12:22).

When Herod accepts this praise without protest and without giving **glory to God** he receives his own "tap" from an angel: **Immediately, an angel of the Lord struck him down . . . and he was eaten by worms and died** (12:23; see 12:7; the word "struck" is typically used of God "smiting" his enemies; cf. Exod 2:12; Judg 1:5; Pss 3:8 LXX; 77:66 LXX; also Luke 22:49–50; Acts 7:24). Herod thus meets the fate he intended for Peter.

Herod's death shares similarities with other accounts of tyrants who die a grisly, worm-infested death (see especially the death of Antiochus Epiphanes recorded in 2 Macc 9:5–9; also Jdt 16:17; and Herod's death, described in these terms by Josephus, *Ant.* 17.169; *BJ* 1.656; cf. also Herodotus, *Persian Wars* 4:205; Pliny the Elder, *Nat.* 7.172; Lucian, *Alex.* 59; *Apoc. Pet.* 27). The reason for Herod's death, that he accepted the deifying praise of the crowd, also has precedent in the biblical tradition (see Isa 14:12–20; Ezek 28:1–10).

The conclusion to this unit also serves as a transition, concluding this first half of Acts, which chronicles the growth of the church in and beyond Jerusalem, and introducing the second half of Acts, which takes the activities of Saul as its primary focus: **So the message of God spread widely. Meanwhile, Barnabas and Saul returned from Jerusalem** (see Dupont 1956, 275–303), **after completing their ministry, and took John, who was called Mark, along** (12:24–25). Acts 12:24 is the last summary statement describing the Jerusalem church (see Acts 2:47; 4:4; 6:7; 9:31; 11:24). Like the seed sown on good earth (see Luke 8:4–15), the "message of God spread widely" in the face of opposition and continued to produce a remarkable yield, just as it did at the beginning of this section (see 6:7). The reference to Barnabas and Saul in 12:25 recalls the beginning of this unit (11:27–30) and reminds the audience once again of the nature of true benefaction (in contrast to the preceding story of Herod). It also anticipates the events of Acts 13–14, which will involve Saul, Barnabas, and to some extent John Mark (13:5, 13). The "message of God" has indeed grown and multiplied and is now ready to spread throughout the empire.

Theological Issues

The story of Peter is the second of three rescues from prison and the demise of Herod is the third punitive miracle through which the opponent of God is struck down (see Judas and Ananias and Sapphira). These stories "unfold in inverse symmetry" (Pervo 1990, 43). The result is that the earthly powers, here represented by Herod, are unmasked for the impostors they are (see Wink 1986), and the power of God is demonstrated through the Antioch church, Barnabas, and Peter.

Kings who abused their power—tyrants—were so common in the ancient world that rhetoricians developed a commonplace, or topos, against a tyrant. To cite one example, Aphthonius, in his topos against a tyrant, argues in a *synkrisis* that the violence of a tyrant is worse than that of a murderer: "A murderer is a dreadful thing but a tyrant is a greater evil. The former does wrong against some ordinary person, but the other alters the whole fortune of the city. Thus, to the extent that causing grief on a small scale falls short of shedding the blood of all, to that extent murder is a lesser thing than tyranny" (*Prog.* 19R, trans. Kennedy 2003, 107). Thus Herod's actions move beyond simply taking the life of James, but represent the violence of a tyrant, an even "greater evil."

Furthermore, the portrait of Herod in Acts 12 is of a tyrant who is not only violent and evil but self-aggrandizing. This tendency of tyrants toward self-praise is captured again by Aphthonius in his commonplace against tyrants, who depicts the tyrant contemplating his superiority to the multitude: "Since I am clearly superior to the common people, shall I put up with being constantly treated as the equal of others and allow Fortune to bestow wealth upon me in vain? If I am subject to the same conditions as the many and the poor join together in judgment of me, whatever seems best to the many becomes a law for me. . . . I shall seize the acropolis and put aside the laws, curse them, and thus I shall be a law to the many, not the many to me" (*Prog.* 34, 19R, trans. Kennedy 2003, 106–7).

The demise of Herod not only echoes tyrants who engaged in self-aggrandizement (see above); it is a chilling illustration of Mary's Magnificat found in the Third Gospel: "He has brought down the powerful from their thrones" (Luke 1:52). Luke's positive attitude toward the state (see Acts 13:4–12;

18:12–17; 19:23–41; 23:10, 12–33; 26:32; 27:42–43) is balanced here by his criticism of rulers "who exalt themselves to the place of God and who act hostilely towards the church" (see Talbert 1984, 54–55). Thus the evidence fails to support attempts to view Luke's global purpose either as a defense before the Romans for the politically "innocuous" nature of the Christian community (Haenchen 1971; Conzelmann 1987) or as an apology for the Christian community to the Roman government (here represented by the puppet king, Herod; see Esler 1987).

This episode in Acts also recalls Luke's version of the Last Supper, in which a dispute arose among the disciples as to who was to be regarded as the greatest. In Luke 22:25–26, Jesus says, "The kings of the Gentiles lord it over them; and those in authority over them are called benefactors. But not so with you; rather the greatest among you must become like the youngest, and the leader like one who serves." In a sense, this episode (11:19–12:25) provides an exegesis by example of this saying. As Richard Pervo has observed: "The initial and concluding references to the offering from Antioch frame the account with Christian benefaction, strongly contrasted to the supposed 'benefactions' of tyrannical despots, who, having concocted a dispute, resolve it by accepting bribes and then rejoice to be hailed as saviors and benefactors" (Pervo 1990, 43). Luke makes clear that the unjust policies and practices of governing leaders who act out of their own self-interests rather than that of their constituents will not go unpunished.

Paul's Mission to the Gentile World

The next major division of Acts (chaps. 13–19) narrows the vision from the activities of the Twelve and the Seven to focus in its first section on the Gentile mission of Paul and his apostolic company (13–14). The second section revolves around the controversy surrounding Paul's missionary efforts and its resolution (15:1–16:5). The next three sections focus on Paul in Macedonia (16:6–17:15), in the Achaean cities of Athens and Corinth (17:16–18:17), and in Ephesus (18:18–19:41). The shift, then, is from persons (chaps. 5–12) to places (chaps. 13–19), but the spread of the gospel remains the central theme.

Acts 13–19 in Context

The people and places of the Jerusalem church (1–12)

The sense of a beginning (1–7)

Beyond Jerusalem: Philip, Saul, Peter, and others (8–12)

The missionary activities of Paul (13–28)

▶ Paul's mission to the Gentile world (13–19)

Paul's initial missionary campaign (13–14)

The conference in Jerusalem and its consequences (15:1–16:5)

Paul in Macedonia (16:6–17:15)

Paul in Achaia (17:16–18:17)

Paul in Ephesus (18:18–19:41)

Paul's farewell journey (20–28)

181

Acts 13–14

Paul's Initial Missionary Campaign

Introductory Matters

Acts 13–14 recounts Paul's first missionary campaign. The efforts at spreading the gospel among the Gentiles do not come without conflict and suffering, as can be seen from the narrative flow of the material. Each chapter divides into three units (modifying Spencer 1997, 131). The opening and closing scenes record Paul's commission in and return to Antioch. In between, each scene is marked by conflict and, in some cases, violence. Paul's ministry begins with a contest with the Jewish sorcerer, Elymas, in Cyprus. His preaching in Pisidia results in his expulsion from the region. Nearly stoned in Iconium, he *is* stoned and left for dead in Lystra. Ananias, through the Spirit, had predicted that in order to fulfill his commission as the "chosen instrument" to carry the gospel to the Gentiles he would suffer for Jesus' name (Acts 9:15–16), and this initial campaign is the narrative fulfillment of that prophecy.

Acts 13–14 in the Narrative Flow

The people and places of the Jerusalem church (1–12)

The missionary activities of Paul (13–28)

Paul's mission to the Gentile world (13–19)

▶ Paul's initial missionary campaign (13–14)

Commissioning at Antioch (13:1–3)

Contest on Cyprus (13:4–12)

Preaching and expulsion in Pisidia (13:13–52)

Success and division in Iconium (14:1–7)

Healing and stoning in Lystra (14:8–20)

Strengthening the disciples (14:21–28)

Tracing the Narrative Flow

Commissioning at Antioch (13:1–3)

Acts 13 begins with the commissioning of Paul and Barnabas by the church at Syrian Antioch (13:1–3): **Now there were many prophets and teachers in the local church at Antioch** (13:1). The importance of the Christian community at Antioch has already been noted at 11:19. The leadership of this congregation consists of teacher-prophets, who give Spirit-inspired exhortation and instruction (on the combination of prophets and teachers, see also *Did.* 15.1). Prophets from Antioch (though not necessarily these) had already been mentioned at Acts 11:27, and though this is the first mention in Acts of "teachers," the verb "teach" occurs frequently (1:1; 4:2, 18; 5:21, 25, 28, 42; 15:1, 35; 18:11, 25; 20:20; 21:21, 28; 28:31), most notably at Acts 11:26, in which Barnabas and Saul are depicted as teaching the Antiochene congregation.

Two things are noteworthy about the list of five prophet-teachers given in Acts 13:2–3 (now the fourth in Acts; see 1:13, 23; 6:5). The diversity of the Antiochene church is evidenced by this short list. **Barnabas** is already familiar to the audience as a Levite and native of Cyprus (cf. Acts 4:36). Like Joseph Barsabbas called Justus (Acts 1:23), and John called Marcus (Acts 12:12), **Simeon** is another Jewish Christian with a Latin surname, **Niger** (Johnson 1992, 220). "Niger" is the Latin term for "black," and it is possible this Simeon was from North Africa (though cf. Barrett 1994, 1:603). **Lucius** is originally from Cyrene and perhaps among those broad-minded enough to evangelize among the Gentiles (see 11:20). **Manaen** was of aristocratic Jewish stock, having been brought up in the court of Herod Antipas (see Luke 3:1; Acts 4:27; and comments on Acts 11:27–30). Members of this group of prophet-teachers, rounded out by **Saul** of Tarsus (referred to as a "prophet" only here), are no less diverse in their social and economic backgrounds than were the Twelve whom Jesus originally called.

The second important feature is the role of Holy Spirit in the commissioning: **While they were serving the Lord and fasting** (13:2). The "they" here could refer either to these aforementioned leaders (so Barrett 1994, 1:604), but more probably refers to the larger Antioch congregation (so Polhill 1992, 290), since in other situations the entire community ratifies decisions (Acts 1:15; 6:2, 5; 14:27; 15:22; Krodel 1986, 228). The term for "serving the Lord" clearly draws on the parlance of the LXX to refer to service of the Lord in worship (Exod 28:31, 39; Num 1:50; 4:33; 18:6; Deut 17:12; 18:7; 1 Sam 2:11; Ezek 40:46; 45:5; cf. also Luke 1:23; Heb 1:7; 8:2, 6; 9:21; *Did.* 15.1).

Luke wants to make it clear that just as the Holy Spirit was involved in the beginning of the public ministry of both Jesus (Luke 3) and the apostles (Acts 1), the Antiochene church sets Saul and Barnabas apart under the direction of the Holy Spirit (13:2): **the Holy Spirit said (to them), "Set apart for me Barnabas and Saul for the work to which I have called them"** (13:2). For only the third time in Acts (see Acts 8:29; 10:19), the Holy Spirit is depicted as speaking in direct discourse as a character in the narrative, as opposed to other characters reporting what the Spirit said (cf. Acts 11:12; 21:11) or the narrator reporting that the Spirit spoke through someone else (see Acts 21:4). Earlier the Spirit had spoken directly to an individual (Philip and Peter, while in a trance); for the first (and only) time in Acts, the Spirit here speaks to a group in direct discourse (the verb "set apart" is a second-person plural aorist imperative). This verb "set apart" has a rich sense in the LXX of "separate/make holy" (see Exod 13:12; 29:26–27; Lev 13:4; Num 18:24; 2 Sam 8:1; Isa 52:11).

The "work" for which Saul and Barnabas are to be set apart recurs at the end of the missionary journey when Paul and Barnabas return to Antioch to be "commended for the *work* that they had completed" (14:26). References to "work" then form an *inclusio* to this unit (pace Polhill 1992, 290) and events recorded in between in chapters 13 and 14 clarify that this work is related to opening "a door of faith for the Gentiles" (14:27). That Saul and his company have been "divinely called" to perform this "work" of the Gentile mission will later be reinforced by the reference in Acts 16:10 that Paul and his companions sought to cross over to Macedonia, convinced that "God had 'called' us to proclaim the good news to them [the residents of Macedonian Philippi and Thessalonica]."

The Antioch believers respond with three actions before sending Saul and Barnabas to fulfill their work: they **fasted, prayed, and laid (their) hands on them** (13:3a). Prayer and fasting are common expressions of Jewish (Neh 1:4; Jer 14:12; Matt 6:5, 16; *Jos. Asen.* 10.17–12.12; *T. Sim.* 2.12–3.4) and Christian piety (see Pol. *Phil.* 7.2; 2 *Clem.* 16.4; *Did.* 8.1–2; Johnson 1992, 221). Further, fasting was observed in some mystery cults (see Sallustius, *De deis* 4). While corporate prayer is quite common in Acts (1:24; 6:6; 8:15; 12:12; 14:23; 21:5), there are only three references to fasting, two here (13:2, 3), and one in 14:23. All three refer to the church at Antioch fasting in connection with the appointment of church leaders. The church that selflessly gave to relieve fasting imposed by famine (11:27–30) now engages in fasting for religious purposes. Finally, the Antiochenes "laid their hands" on Saul and Barnabas, a gesture of transmitting authority (see Acts 6:6; 8:17–19; 9:17; cf. God's instructions to Moses for the laying on of hands for the Levite priests in Num 8). In the case of Acts 13, it is the authority of Saul and Barnabas specifically to undertake the work associated with the Gentile mission. Though other Gentiles (the Ethiopian eunuch and the household of Cornelius) had converted already to Christianity, and while Saul and Barnabas would regularly proclaim the Christian message in Jewish synagogues, here in Acts 13:1–3 they are commissioned to the full-time and intentional pursuit of the Gentile mission. As such it marks a major division in the story of Acts. The emphasis, however, is on the purpose of the commission and not on some ritualistic pattern associated with it (see Theological Issues).

The commissioning of Saul and Barnabas echoes the beginnings of the missions of both Jesus and the apostles (see Tannehill 1990, 161). Like the mission of Jesus and the apostles, the mission of Saul and Barnabas is preceded by prayer (13:2a; cf. Luke 3:21; Acts 1:14) and directed by the Spirit (13:2b; cf. Luke 3:22; Acts 2:1–4). Fasting is also an important element in the preparation for Jesus' mission (Luke 4:1–2; cf. Acts 13:1, 3, though it is missing from the apostles' mission).

Contest on Cyprus (13:4–12)

The parallels between Paul and Jesus continue in the next scene (13:4–12). Saul and Barnabas are sent out by the Holy Spirit (13:4) after their commissioning as was Jesus (see Luke 4:1). **So they, after being sent out by the Holy Spirit, went down to Seleucia and from there sailed to Cyprus** (13:4). The passage begins with the emphatic use of the personal pronoun "they," drawing attention to the identity of Barnabas and Saul without naming them. The area of Cyprus is, of course, familiar ground to Barnabas, who is a native of that island (see 4:36), as well as to the audience who knows that Christian missionaries had already been there (see Acts 11:19).

But the narrator makes no mention of Barnabas and Saul visiting already established churches; rather, the narrative continues: **While they were in Salamis, they proclaimed the message of God in the Jewish synagogues** (13:5a). A large Jewish population on Cyprus is well-attested in sources from late antiquity (see 1 Macc 15:23; Philo, *Legat.* 282; Josephus, *Ant.* 13.284). Salamis was a port city on the eastern coast of Cyprus, and here the two engage in a practice that would characterize the rest of Saul's missionary career; they preached the word of God in the synagogues of the Jews (cf. 13:14; 14:1; 17:1, 10, 17; 18:4, 19; 19:8).

The narrator makes no mention of the results of the missionary preaching to the Jews of Salamis, but he does at this point add the note: **and they had John as their assistant** (13:5b). The audience is right in identifying this John with the John Mark of 12:12 and 25. He is here described as an "assistant." While this word has a wide and varied usage in Luke and Acts (see especially Luke 1:2, "servants of the Word"; and Paul's description of himself as "servant and witness" at Acts 26:16), here the word seems to have the more nondescript meaning of "helper." John Mark has consistently been depicted in a subordinate role (see Acts 12:25) or left out altogether. He is not counted with Barnabas and Saul in the listing of the "prophets and teachers" at Antioch, though presumably, given this current statement, he was present. And in the next scene, the encounter with Bar-Jesus, he drops from focus again (see 13:7). Further, Acts 13:5b "explicitly says that John Mark was present as an assistant, neither to the Holy Spirit (cf. 13:2, 4) nor to the Lord (cf. 26:16) nor to the word (cf. Luke 1:2), but to Barnabas and Saul" (Black 1998, 243). John Mark is a servant of the servants of God (cf. also 5:22, 26; 13:5; 20:34; 24:23); his departure in Acts

13:13b is being subtly prepared for in his mundane description here.

The narrator notes in a brief dispatch that Barnabas and Saul (and John Mark) traversed the length of the island to **Paphos** on the other coast (13:6a). **Here they found a man, a magician and Jewish false prophet, who went by the name Bar-Jesus** (13:6b).

Though the specific terms "magician" and "false prophet" are new to Acts, the negative sentiment expressed is certainly not. For the second time in Acts, a Christian missionary confronts a magician who represents the forces of evil (see the comments on 8:4–25). Further, the narrator's positive evaluation of the various roles of "prophet" throughout Acts makes clear the denigrating assessment of a "false prophet." Indeed, it was not uncommon for Gentiles to connect Jewish propagandists with magic (see Strabo, *Geogr.* 16.2.39; 16.2.43; Pliny the Elder, *Nat.* 30.2.11; Apuleius, *Apol.* 90). Certainly, the proximity of Acts 13:1, in which Barnabas and Saul are listed as "prophets" set apart by the Spirit, pits these two against this false prophet. Both roles of magician and false prophet will provide background later for Paul's invective in 13:10 (see below). Though issues

---

Describing Bar-Jesus

Using the rhetorical device of *appositio,* that is, the addition of adjacent explanatory or descriptive elements (cf. Quintilian, *Inst.* 8.6.40–41), Luke gives a lengthy description of Bar-Jesus as a "magician," a "false prophet," and a "Jew" (13:6). The stringing together of such descriptors is typically discouraged in rhetoric. Quintilian argues that style "is overloaded when a large number [of epithets] are employed. For then it becomes long-winded and cumbrous, in fact you might compare it to an army with as many camp-followers as soldiers, an army, that is to say, which has doubled its numbers without doubling its strength" (8.6.42, trans. Butler 1921). Such description moves beyond mere ornamentation, and is therefore justified, when it "adds something to the meaning" (8.6.40). Clearly here the descriptors of Bar-Jesus are critical to understanding the conflict between him and Paul as it unfolds in the narrative.

---

revolving around the name of this magician will grow more complicated in a moment (see 13:8), the audience will not miss the irony of the underlying Aramaic meaning of this Jewish magician's name—Bar-Jesus, "son of Jesus"; Paul certainly did not (see comments on 13:10).

The narrator reports almost incidentally that Bar-Jesus was in the service of a leading Roman official, **Sergius Paulus**, described here as a **proconsul**, the appropriate term for the administrator of a senatorial province such as Cyprus; imperial provinces were overseen by military "procurators" like Pilate, Felix, and Festus. The narrator's description of Sergius Paulus is as positive as the depiction of Bar-Jesus was negative. The proconsul was **an intelligent man who summoned Barnabas and Saul and sought to hear the message of God** (13:7). "Intelligence" was widely recognized as one of the cardinal

The Meaning of "Bar-Jesus"

Some early readers of Acts noted the significance of Bar-Jesus' name, but their resistance to the name destroyed its ironic value. The Venerable Bede, for example, refuses even to recognize the name, claiming rather:

"Barjesu is a corrupt reading, for it ought to read Berieu, that is, wrongdoer, or in evil. I believe that the name Jesus could be written with the identical letters, but with a mark placed above it. It is not suitable for an infamous man and a sorcerer to have been called the son of Jesus, that is, of the savior. On the contrary, Paul applied to him the son of the devil." (Comm. Acts 13.6, trans. L. Martin 1989, 117; citing Jerome, Nom. Hebr. 72.144.25–26)

virtues (Aristotle, *Eth. Nic.* 1.13.20; Diogenes Laertius, *Vit. phil.* 7.126; Philo, *Mos.* 1.154). Sergius Paulus will demonstrate his wisdom later in his choice to follow Paul's message rather than Bar-Jesus. While not all Roman officials are as receptive to the Christian message as some commentators have suggested (see, e.g., 18:1–7; 22:29; 23:23–30; 24:22; 25:23–27), certainly Sergius Paulus here demonstrates his openness to religion and philosophy, first through his employment of a magician as court adviser (see Philo, *Spec.* 3.100; ps.-Callisthenes, *Alex.* 1.1–12) and finally through his acceptance of the Christian message (cf. 13:12).

The real focus here is on the conflict between Bar-Jesus and Saul: **but the magician Elymas—yes, that is how his name is translated—opposed them by trying to turn the proconsul away from the faith** (13:8). The opposition is emphasized by the use of the rhetorical figure of *adiunctio* (or *epizeugma*), "when the verb holding the sentence together is placed not in the middle, but at the beginning or end" (*Rhet. Her.* 4.27.38). Here the word "opposed" occurs at the beginning of the sentence: "resisted them, did Elymas the magician" (cf. *Rhet. Her.* 4.27.38, which gives the example: "Fades physical beauty with disease or age"). The narrator also informs the audience that "Bar-Jesus the magician" is "Elymas the magician," but this phrase is fraught with problems. One may press the connection of Elymas with the Aramaic word *haloma*, which means "interpreter of dreams" and may invoke a faint echo of Jeremiah's encounter with the dreamer prophet, Shemaiah the Nehelamite (cf. Jer 36:29–32), but that remains only a possibility, and the audience may need to be satisfied with understanding Elymas as an "alias" for Bar-Jesus, especially if the word is taken not in the technical sense of "translate," but rather with the broad connotation of "understood to mean" (Johnson 1992, 223; cf. Acts 4:36). Bar-Jesus' opposition recalls the prediction of Jesus that his followers would face just such opposition (Luke 21:15; cf. Acts 6:10).

Bar-Jesus not only opposes Barnabas and Saul but also attempts to turn the proconsul away ("turn away" is frequently used in the LXX to refer to the perverting of the people and distorting of the truth by false prophets;

see Num 15:39; 32:7) from "the faith" (cf. 6:7, where the same phrase refers to the Christian movement), which incurs the wrath of Saul: **Saul, who was also (known as) Paul, and who was filled with the Holy Spirit, looked right at him and said, "You are full of all deceit and every kind of wrongdoing, you son of the devil! You are an enemy of every kind of righteousness! Will you never stop making the straight paths of the Lord crooked?"** (13:9–10). The invective makes the nature of the confrontation explicit: this is a conflict between the agent of God, Paul, and the agent of Satan, Bar-Jesus. Paul has been commissioned by the Holy Spirit and was "filled with the Holy Spirit"; Bar-Jesus is "full of all deceit and every kind of wrongdoing." The phrase "full of all deceit" draws on its use in the LXX, especially Sir 1:30, in which the fall of those who exalt themselves is predicted (Garrett 1989, 150). Further, in an ironic twist, Paul discloses the real identity of this Bar-Jesus, this "son of Jesus," to be in truth a "son of the devil" (made even more striking by the presence of Barnabas, "son of prophecy," or as Luke insists, son of [Christian] encouragement). The confrontation is also between Paul, a true prophet, and the false prophet, Bar-Jesus, who seeks to undo the work of another true prophet, John the Baptist, by "making crooked the straight paths of the Lord" (13:10; cf. Luke 3:4), and echoes the conflict between Jesus and Satan at the beginning of Jesus' public ministry (Luke 4).

Paul's invective leads to his curse of blindness on Elymas: **Now, the hand of the Lord is against you! You will be blind, unable to (even) see the sun for a time!** (13:11). This was an especially fitting curse: as an idolator who serves as an agent of Satan, Elymas is cursed to the darkness from which he has come. Note also the irony here. Paul has himself just made the transition from darkness to light (chap. 9) and was called to open blind Gentile eyes, but now Paul pronounces a curse that seems to reverse his experience and mission and leads to **a dark mist, which causes** Bar-Jesus **to search for someone to lead him by the hand** (13:11). The curse echoes Deut 28:28–29, in which Moses gives a list of punishments that await the Israelites who forsake Yahweh for idolatrous allegiance to other gods: "The Lord will afflict you with madness, blindness, and confusion of mind; you shall grope about at noon as blind people grope in darkness, but you shall be unable to find your way" (cf. also 1QS 2.11–19; Garrett 1989, 82–83). Bar-Jesus' punishment for his idolatrous activities as a "son of Satan" and an agent of darkness is to be confined to the darkness itself (cf. Luke 8:3), the realm of Satan cut off from the light and life found only in God (cf. Garrett 1989, 83). The Lukan symbolism of light and sight, so familiar from other passages (cf. comments on 9:8), now probes the underside of darkness and blindness, and the blinding of Bar-Jesus is a stark reminder of the negative portion of Jesus' saying recorded in Luke 11:34: "Your eye is the lamp of your body. If your eye is healthy, your whole body is full of light; but if it is not healthy, your body is full of darkness" (see Parsons 2006).

The comparison and contrast between Paul and Bar-Jesus could not be more striking: both had sought to hinder the spread of the gospel, both are blinded and both must be led "by the hand." Paul, in his efforts to imprison and persecute Christians, had been a "one-time servant of the devil" (Garrett 1989, 84). But whereas Bar-Jesus was said to "make straight paths crooked," Paul is led to a "street called Straight" (9:11). And though Bar-Jesus is blinded by mist and darkness, Paul is blinded by a great light (22:11; 26:13). And finally, Paul's blindness is a stage on the way to a radical reorientation of his life; Bar-Jesus is left in blindness. The two paths diverge in directions as different as night and day (see Garrett 1989, 84). As was the case with Simon the magician, the fate of this individual agent of Satan is of less interest to Luke than the demonstration of Paul's authority over Satan. The point of this scene for the ministry of Paul is crucial: like Jesus, Paul has demonstrated his authority over the forces of Satan and thus has proven himself worthy of the mission set before him. The conversion and commission of Paul, which began in chapter 9, is now complete, and from this point on Saul is consistently identified as Paul (see 13:9; see Garrett 1989, 85). With the fulfillment of his change in status from one who opposed God to one who now serves him comes a change in name and status (from this point, with only a few exceptions—14:12, 14; 15:12, 25—Paul's name occurs first in the list of those involved in the Gentile mission; for Paul and Barnabas, see 13:43, 46, 50; 15:2, 22, 25, 35; for Paul and other companions, see 13:13; 16:17, 25, 29; 17:4, 10).

The scene concludes with this note: **Then, when the proconsul saw what had happened, he believed because he was completely astounded at the teaching about the Lord** (13:12). That the central focus of the passage is on the subduing of Satan and his agent does not detract from the closing note that the church also gains a prominent convert in Sergius Paulus as an important by-product of this encounter.

Preaching and Expulsion in Pisidia (13:13–52)

This next scene (13:13–52) has three parts: the setting (13:13–15); the speech (13:16–41); and the aftermath (13:42–52). Each section will be taken up in turn.

13:13–15. After a whistle stop in Perga, Paul and his company come to Antioch of Pisidia. Not all of Paul's companions continue with him: **but John deserted them and returned to Jerusalem** (13:13b; on the translation that

Alliteration in Acts 13:13

In Acts 13:13, Luke uses the compositional device of alliteration or *homoeoprophoron*, the repetition of the initial letter, to alert the audience to a scene change: "After sailing from Paphos, Paul and his companions came to Perga in Pamphylia" (Greek, *"Anachthentes de apo tēs Paphou oi peri Paulon ēlthon eis Pergēn tēs Pamphylias"*; in English, something like: "Sailing from Paphos, the people with Paul came to Perga in Pamphylia"). Rhetoricians warn against excessive use of alliteration; for example, pseudo-Cicero gives the example "O Tite, tute, Tati, tibi tanta, tyranne, tulisti" (*Rhet. Her.* 4.22.18; in English, "Thyself to thyself, Titus Tatius the tyrant, thou tookest those terrible troubles"). Luke's repetition of the "p" sound at this pivotal point from one pericope to the next pericope is probably purposeful.

John "deserted" them, see comments on Acts 15:36–41). Paul and the rest of his company continue on to Antioch in Pisidia. They **went into the synagogue on the Sabbath day and sat down** (13:14). In an echo of Jesus' first public address (Luke 4), and in what would prove to be his pattern in Acts, Paul enters the synagogue on the Sabbath. **After the reading of the Law and Prophets** (13:15; see Luke 4; Acts 15:21), the **leaders of the synagogue** (cf. Luke 8:41, 49; 13:14; Acts 18:8, 17) invite Paul to speak a **word of encouragement** (cf. Heb 13:22). Paul then delivers the first of his three major missionary addresses in Acts (cf. Acts 17:22–31; 20:18–35).

13:16–41. While in the synagogue, **Paul stood up, motioned with his hand, and** spoke (13:16a). The posture and gesture are typical of speakers in Acts (on standing to speak, see 1:15; 5:34; 6:9; 11:28; 13:16; 15:5, 7; 23:9; 25:18; 27:21; on waving the hand, see 12:17; 13:16; 19:33; 21:40; 26:1) and suggest the activity of a Greek orator (esp. waving the hand; see Apuleius, *Metam.* 2.21). The gestures, however, may not all carry the same meaning in each instance, nor may the lector have been expected to use the same motion (see Shiell 2004). In Acts 12:17, Peter gestures to silence an amazed crowd; in 13:16, Paul signals to alert the audience that a word of exhortation is about to commence (see Quintilian, *Inst.* 11.3.96–100; on the particular gesture expected, see Shiell 2004, 145–48).

Not only is the gesture appropriate to a Greek orator; the speech itself reflects a structure easily recognized by an audience familiar with conventions of ancient rhetoric: 13:16b, a brief *exordium* or introduction establishing audience favor; 13:17–25, a review of Israelite history in the form of a *narratio* or narration, a statement of the "facts" of the case; 13:26, the *probatio* in which the speaker states a proposition (in this case, 13:26, in which the proposition is introduced by the phrase "my brothers" and declares that the "message of salvation" is being proclaimed to Jews and God-fearers), which he intends to demonstrate (here in 13:27–37 by arguing that salvation can be preached to Israel because God has vindicated Jesus by raising him from the dead); and finally, 13:38–41, the *peroratio* or epilogue, in which the hearers are urged to accept this salvation (slightly modifying Kennedy 1984, 118–19). The terminology and number of rhetorical divisions vary among the rhetorical handbooks; the analysis above follows the divisions of Quintilian (*Inst.* 3.9.1–5), who, contra Cicero (*Inv.* 1.14.19), does not consider the *partitio* (the central claim of the *narratio*) as a separate section.

This is not to argue that Luke or his audience knew only the categories of Quintilian or that the speech cannot be analyzed using other rhetorical categories from antiquity (see Kennedy 1984, 118–19), but rather to make the general point that the structure of Paul's speech here as well as most of the others in Acts should be examined in light of rhetorical conventions known to be practiced in late antiquity. In this case, the rhetorical markers of the speech itself suggest a division similar to Quintilian's proposal. Each rhetorical unit (with the exception of the *narratio*) is introduced with a form of direct address ("You Israelites," 13:16b; "my brothers," 13:26; "my brothers," 13:38). These direct addresses make it clear that Paul is addressing Jews ("you Israelites") and those who are deeply interested in Judaism ("others who fear God"). While Paul's speech at Antioch of Pisidia does not fit the specific pattern of a forensic, deliberative, or epideictic speech (see Aristotle's discussion of these three types of oratory in *Rhet.* 3.13–19; also Quintilian, *Inst.* 3.7.1–6; 3.8.6–13; 3.9.1–5), there is evidence from late antiquity that these speech forms often overlapped and were modified to meet the requirements of a specific case (see Quintilian, *Inst.* 7.10.11–13).

The *exordium* or introduction (13:16b) is very brief. Paul addresses his audience as **Israelites** (literally, "men, Israelites"; a similar greeting is used elsewhere in Acts at 2:22; 7:2; 15:13; 22:1; 26:3). The other group addressed by Paul, the **God-fearers,** are mentioned again at 13:26 and may be taken to be identical to the "devout converts to Judaism" mentioned in 13:43, both signifying in a nontechnical way Gentiles who had aligned themselves with the worship and practices of the Jewish synagogue (for more on God-fearers in Acts, see comments on 10:2).

The second part of the speech, the *narratio* (13:17–25), is similar to Stephen's speech in that it recounts Israel's history; its emphasis, however, differs by focusing not on Israel's rebelliousness, but rather on God's faithfulness. In fact, the first words of this part of the speech are "the God of this people Israel" (echoing the epithet "God of Israel," familiar from the Greek translations of Pss 40:14; 58:6; 67:8, 35; 68:9; 71:18; cf. also Luke 1:68). God is the subject of most of the verbs in this section: God "chose" (13:17); God "made them a great people" (13:17b); God "led them out" (13:17c); God "put up with them" (or "cared for," 13:18; see sidebar); God "overthrew" seven nations in the land of Canaan (13:19a); God "gave their land (to our ancestors)" (13:19b); God "provided" them judges (13:20); God "gave" them Saul (13:21);

God "removed" Saul (13:22); God "raised up David to be their king" (13:22b); God "spoke" (13:22); God "brought" (13:23). In addition, several of these verbs are used elsewhere of divine activity: to choose (13:17; cf. 1:24b–25); to make great (cf. 2:33; 5:31); to lead out (cf. 7:40).

The divine activity described by Paul moves from the exodus to the enthronement of David. Paul's description of that segment of Israelite history at the discourse level is instructive. He begins: **The God of this people Israel chose our ancestors and made them a great people during the time they lived as foreigners in the land of Egypt. In a powerful way he led them out of Egypt** (13:17). The reference to "this people Israel" strikes several familiar Lukan themes. The name "Israel" occurs three times in Paul's speech (here in 13:17 as well as 13:23, 24) as it does in Stephen's speech (7:23, 37, 42; see Johnson 1992, 230). Israel as the "people of God" is a theme that recurs throughout both Luke and Acts (Luke 1:16, 54, 68, 80; 2:25, 32, 34; 4:25–27; 7:9; 22:30; 24:21; Acts 1:6; 2:36; 4:10, 27; 5:21, 31; 9:15; 10:36; 28:20).

The events are telescoped in Paul's reference to God's choosing the "ancestors," which is much briefer than the treatment of Abraham in Stephen's speech (see 7:2–8) and gives quickly away to the statement that God had "made them a great people during the time they lived as foreigners in the land of Egypt" (again treated much more fully by Stephen in 7:9–34). In addition to the two places in Acts in which "made great" refers to the resurrection of Jesus, the word "exalt" is used in the reversal statements of Luke 1:52; 14:11; 18:14 (see Johnson 1992, 231). Reference to the "stay" in Egypt again echoes Stephen's speech in which the same word is used at 7:6, 29. Mention of the Exodus is likewise brief (again cf. 7:35–36): "In a powerful way he led them out of Egypt" (13:17c). In Stephen's speech, Moses is the one who performs "signs and wonders" in effecting the Israelites' release (7:36); here, in Paul's speech and in keeping with the emphasis on divine activity, it is literally God's "uplifted arm" (echoing the imagery used in the LXX to depict the power of God: Exod 6:1, 6; 32:11; Deut 3:24; 4:34; 6:21; 7:8; 9:26; Ps 135:12; Isa 26:11; Jer 39:17; Ezek 20:34; cf. Luke 1:51), which leads the people out of Egypt. Israel's wilderness wanderings are also mentioned briefly: **he put up with them for about forty years in the wilderness** (13:18).

Paul next touches on the conquest narrative: **He overthrew seven nations in the land of Canaan and gave their land (to our ancestors)—(all this took place over) about 450 years** (13:19–20a). Paul provides no more detail about the conquest than does Stephen (see 7:45), though there is one slight difference in emphasis. In Stephen's recounting, the conquest is the effort of both the ancestors and God ("Our ancestors inherited it and brought it with Joshua when they took possession of the nations that God drove out from the presence of our ancestors"). In Paul's speech, however, God is given full credit for overcoming the "nations" of Canaan and giving the Israelites the land as an inheritance (on the land as inheritance, see 7:3–5). The reference to the "seven" nations echoes Deut 7:1, in which the nations are listed (see also Josephus, *Ant.* 5.88; 1QM 11.8–9). Mention of specific time intervals is characteristic of Paul's speech (see 13:18, 20, 21; and also Stephen, see 7:6, 23, 30, 36, 42). Here the explicit reference to "450 years" is missing from the OT, but not inconsistent with Luke's rendering of this time period: four hundred years of bondage in Egypt (Acts 7:6), forty years of wilderness wanderings (7:36; 13:18), and an implied ten years of conquest.

Paul also quickly moves over the period of the judges, but unlike the previous material of Paul's speech (which was the focus of considerable attention on the part of Stephen), the portion of the speech dealing with the judges has no parallel in Stephen's speech: **After these things, he provided judges until (the time) of Samuel the prophet** (13:20b). In the reference to the judges may be heard a faint echo of several of those judges whom "the Lord raised up . . . for the Israelites, who saved them" (Othniel, Ehud; Judg 3:9, 15), which may, for the discerning audience, point forward in the speech to the description of Jesus as savior (13:23). Samuel is also depicted as a transitional figure earlier in Acts 3:24: "All the prophets who spoke, including Samuel and those who came after him, also announced these days."

The shift in subject from God to the Israelites in 13:21 introduces a negative element into Paul's recital of Hebrew history (and echoes the antimonarchical texts of the OT; see, e.g., 1 Sam 12:1–25): **After that, they asked for a king and God gave them Saul son of Kish, a man of the tribe of Benjamin** (see 1 Sam 10–12). That Paul views the request for a king negatively is seen in the next phrase, **after removing him** [Saul] (13:22a; cf. 1 Sam 15:23; 16:1). This note on Saul's forced removal from office (on "removal from office," see Dan 2:21; also Euripides, *Iph. Taur.* 775) causes the audience, which might know

Textual Variants in Acts 13:18

There is a notoriously difficult textual problem revolving around whether Luke wrote "cared for" (*etrophophorēsen*) or "put up with" (*etropophorēsen*), both having substantial support in the manuscript tradition. The issue is not resolved by appeal to the Greek version of Deut 1:31, because both readings appear there as well. On the whole, it is more likely scribes changed "put up with" to "cared for" because of the context and because of a reluctance to make God the subject of such an "unseemly" verb. But no conclusive decision is forthcoming, since either word could have been introduced into the manuscript tradition due to faulty transcription (the two words are near homonyms, differing by only one letter; see Culy and Parsons 2003, 253–54). Even accepting the "more difficult" reading of God "putting up" with Israel in the desert, the part of Stephen's speech describing the wilderness wanderings is much longer and more polemical than this brief notice (see 7:39–43).

that Paul himself was of the tribe of Benjamin (Rom 11:1; Phil 3:5), to revise any idea that Paul mentions Saul's tribe out of excessive pride in his ancestry. Saul's forty-year reign is mentioned nowhere in the OT, though it is consistent with Josephus's rendering (see *Ant.* 6.378; although cf. *Ant.* 10.143, in which Josephus records a twenty-year reign for Saul).

After God removed Saul from the throne, Paul reports, God **raised up David to be their king** (13:22a). The word "raised" is the word typically associated with the resurrection of Jesus, as it is later in the speech at 13:30 (cf. also Acts 3:15; 4:10; 5:30; 10:40). In the rest of verse 22, Paul depicts God as giving testimony about David, echoing the prominent "witness" theme of Acts (see 1:8, 22; 2:32, 40; 3:15; 4:33; 5:32; 6:13; 7:44, 58; 8:25; 10:22, 39, 41, 42, 43; 13:22, 31; 14:3; 15:8; 16:2; 18:5; 20:21, 23, 24; 22:5, 12, 15, 18, 20; 23:11; 26:5, 16, 22; 28:23; on God as "witness" see 10:43; 15:8; for a separation of the *marty-* cognate word group, see Soards 1994, 24): **He said, as a testimony, "I have found David son of Jesse (to be) a man after my heart who will carry out all my plans"** (13:22b). The testimony itself is a catena of scripture quotations taken from Ps 89:20 ("I have found David"), 1 Sam 13:14 ("a man after my own heart"), and Isa 44:28 ("who will do everything I want him to do"; the phrase "son of Jesse" may come from 1 Sam 16:1). Messianic interpretations of Davidic passages are also found in the Qumran community (see 4QFlor 1.10). God's speech not only testifies to David's obedience, but also to the providence of God, who has a will or plan.

After this brief summary of Israel's history from the ancestors to David, the central claim of the *narratio* (what some ancient rhetoricians would call the *partitio*) is made in 13:23: **From the descendants of this man, God brought a savior to Israel, Jesus, in accord with (his) promise.** Paul then cites the words of John the Baptist as corroborating evidence to support his claim that God's faithfulness has climaxed in Jesus.

That Jesus is the fulfillment of God's promises to Israel is worked out in more detail in the second part of Paul's speech (13:26–37). Having appealed to the content of Jewish history (13:17–22) and the witness of John the Baptist, Paul now employs two favorite scriptures (Pss 2 and 16) and the rules of Jewish messianic interpretation (see Juel 1988). But Christian messianic exegesis once again takes a startling turn (see Acts 3:20); this Messiah whom God promised and to whom the scriptures point has already come in the person of Jesus (13:32–33). That the psalmist is speaking of Jesus (who did not experience "decay") and not David (who did experience "decay") is made clear through the use of the rhetorical figure of *antistrophe*, in which the last word in successive phrases is repeated (*Rhet. Her.* 4.13.19). In this case, "decay" is repeated: **Now, that he raised him from the dead to no longer be on the verge of decay. . . . Therefore, it also says in another (psalm), "You will not allow your holy one to experience decay."** For David, after serving his own generation in accord with

God's purpose, died, was buried with his ancestors, and experienced decay. But the one whom God raised did not experience decay (13:34–36).

The conclusion of the sermon is twofold. First, Paul extends an invitation for the hearers to receive the forgiveness of sins, which can come only through Jesus, not through the law of Moses (13:38–39). He also issues a prophetic warning (quoting Hab 1:5; cf. 1QpHab 2.1–10) that to reject Paul's message is to reject God's salvation and to be condemned to play the part of **scoffers** whose fate is to **be destroyed** (13:41).

Paul's inaugural speech is remarkably similar to Jesus' inaugural address in Luke 4 and Peter's first major speech recorded in Acts 2 (see Tannehill 1990, 160). All three speeches use scripture to interpret the mission (Luke 4:18–19; Acts 2:17–21; 13:47) and include Gentiles in God's salvation (Luke 4:25–28; Acts 2:39; 13:45–48).

13:42–52. Immediately following the sermon, the people urge Paul and Barnabas to return the next Sabbath, and in the meantime the people follow these Christian missionaries who continue to exhort them (13:42–43). The rest of this unit falls into two parallel scenes (44–48; 49–52), summarizing Paul's ministry in Antioch (Krodel 1986, 246–47):

A The whole city gathered to hear the word of the Lord (13:44)
  B The rejection of unbelieving Jews (13:45)
    C Response of Paul and Barnabas: turning to the Gentiles (13:46–47)
      D The Gentiles rejoice (13:48)
A′ The word of the Lord spread throughout the region (13:49)
  B′ Unbelieving Jews stir up persecution against Paul and Barnabas (13:50)
    C′ Response of Paul and Barnabas: shaking off the dust from their feet (13:51; the action recalls Luke 9:5; 10:11, although the verb "shook off" occurs only in the parallel passage of Matt 10:14)
      D′ The disciples rejoice (13:52)

The emphasis on the Gentile mission here is underscored by the rhetorical figure of reduplication, in which one or more words is repeated for the purpose of amplification (*Rhet. Her.* 4.28.38). Within a span of three verses, the word "Gentiles" occurs three times, twice on the lips of Paul and Barnabas, and once reported by the narrator: But both Paul and Barnabas replied boldly, ". . . Since you reject it and do not consider yourselves worthy of eternal life, we are turning (our attention) to the *Gentiles*! For this is the command the Lord has given to us: 'I have appointed you as a light for the *Gentiles*, so that you might bring salvation to the end(s) of the earth.'" When the *Gentiles* heard (this) they rejoiced and spoke highly of the Lord's message (13:46–48a).

Noteworthy also is the fact that this pattern continues to the end of Acts: (1) the proclamation of the gospel, which leads to (2) division among those listening, (3) rejection by the unbelievers, (4) withdrawal by the Christian missionaries, and finally (5) Luke's report of the progress, despite the opposition. And it will be repeated in the very next scene of Paul and Barnabas in Iconium. Despite the opposition, this scene ends with the note that **the disciples were filled with joy and the Holy Spirit** (13:52).

Success and Division in Iconium (14:1–7)

Acts 14:1–7 is a tightly woven summary narrative, organized in an ABCDC'B'A' pattern (slightly modifying Nelson 1982, 60; Talbert 2005, 123).

A They entered . . . spoke (14:1a).

  B Jews and Gentiles believed (14:1b).

    C Jews stirred up Gentiles (14:2).

      D They preached and performed "signs and wonders" (14:3).

    C' People of city were divided (14:4).

  B' Gentiles and Jews attempted to stone them (14:5).

A' They fled. . . . They preached (14:6–7).

Paul and his circle arrive at Iconium (for historical information on the city see Kee 1997, 170–71; the apocryphal *Acts of Paul and Thecla* also refers to a visit by Paul to Iconium; *Acts Paul* 1.1). Immediately **they entered the synagogue of the Jews as usual** (14:1a; on the translation see Culy and Parsons 2003, 271; Barrett 1994, 1:667). This verse invites comparison with other scenes in which Paul and company enter the synagogues of other cities. In those instances, Paul is opposed by Jews in the synagogue. The description of the scene in Iconium, however, prevents the audience from reducing Paul's ministry to the simple formula of rejection by the Jews and success among the Gentiles (Tannehill 1990, 176). Rather, Luke reports that **a large number of both Jews and Gentiles believed** (14:1b). Furthermore, the Jews who opposed Paul **turned the hearts of the Gentiles against the believers** (14:2). In the midst of this strife, the apostles nonetheless **stayed for a considerable amount of time and spoke boldly about the Lord who confirmed the message about his grace by causing signs and wonders to be performed through them** (14:3). The apostles speaking "boldly" is another reference to what the rhetoricians call "frankness of speech," in which "when, talking before those to whom we owe reverence or fear, we yet exercise our right to speak out, because we seem justified in reprehending them, or persons dear to them, for some fault" (*Rhet. Her.* 4.36.38, trans. Caplan 1954, 349; cf. sidebar at 4:13). Those involved in the Gentile mission perform signs and wonders, a phrase that links their mission to that of the Seven (6:8; 8:6), the apostles (4:30; 5:12), and Jesus (2:22), underscoring Luke's point that the Christian movement consists of the true "heirs" of Moses, who also performed signs and wonders (7:36; see the discussion on 2:19).

The city is split, not along ethnic lines between Jews and Gentiles, but between those who hear the word and accept it and those who reject the message and persecute the messenger: **Now the population of the city was divided, some siding with the Jews and others with the apostles. When both the Gentiles and Jews, along with their rulers, decided to mistreat and stone them (14:4–5).** Thus Paul's words in 13:46–47 are not to be understood in any rigid sense; division is not always along ethnic lines, certainly not in Iconium. When the apostles learned about their plans, **they fled to the cities of Lycaonia—Lystra and Derbe—and the surrounding region. There they continued to preach the good news (14:6–7).**

Healing and Stoning in Lystra (14:8–20)

The scene in Lystra (14:8–20) begins with Paul healing a man lame from birth (14:8–10), recalling the scene in Acts 3:1–10 in which Peter heals a lame man (cf. also Luke 5:18–26). As such, it follows the typical form of a healing story (but, as we shall see, with some significant variations): statement of the ailment (14:8); the cure (14:9–10); the reaction(s) (14:11–20).

14:8. The description of the ailment (14:8) serves to highlight the miraculous nature of the healing. Luke employs the rhetorical figure of *interpretatio*, in which a word or phrase "that has been used" is replaced "by another of the same meaning" (*Rhet. Her.* 4.28.38). Here **a man who could not use his feet** is replaced with **he had been lame since birth and had never walked** (14:8). The figure serves to focus on the extent of the man's plight and thus to highlight the miraculous nature of the subsequent healing. As pseudo-Cicero states, with *interpretatio* "the hearer cannot but be impressed when the force of the first expression is renewed by the explanatory synonym" (*Rhet. Her.* 4.28.38).

14:9–10. Two elements in the description of the cure prepare the audience for the Lycaonians' identification of Paul and Barnabas as gods (Strelan 2000). First, Luke notes that Paul **looked directly at him** (14:9). This "stare" recalls the ancients' belief that the gods "stare" straight

---

Acts 14:8–20 in Context

Paul's initial missionary campaign (13–14)

  Commissioning at Antioch (13:1–3)

  Contest on Cyprus (13:4–12)

  Preaching and expulsion in Pisidia (13:13–52)

  Success and division in Iconium (14:1–7)

▶ Healing and stoning in Lystra (14:8–20)

    Statement of the ailment (14:8)

    The cure (14:9–10)

    Reactions (14:11–20)

  Strengthening the disciples (14:21–28)

ahead without blinking (Heliodorus, *Aeth*. 3.13.2–3). That Paul's stare has, for Luke, some elements of "paranormal vision" is demonstrated by the fact that Paul is able to "see" that the lame man **had faith to be healed** (14:9; on such "sight," see also the comments on physiognomy at Acts 3:1–10). Second, Paul speaks **in a loud voice** (14:10), echoing the view in antiquity that gods spoke with frightfully loud voices (cf. Homer, *Il*. 20.375–380; *Od*. 24.529–535; Apollonius Rhodius, *Argon*. 4.640–662; Lucian, *Icar*. 23; Silius Italicus, *Pun*. 9.306–308; a view found also in Jewish literature; cf. Exod 19:19; 1 Sam. 7:10; Pss 18:7–15; 29:3–5; 46:6; Ezek. 9:1; Strelan 2000, 495–96). Given these clues, the Lycaonians' identification of Paul and Barnabas as gods would have been quite understandable to the authorial audience. That this identification is a misunderstanding, however, is clarified as the narrative unfolds.

14:11–20. Reactions to the healing of the lame man vary from the Lycaonians to Paul and Barnabas to the Jews from Antioch and Iconium. As noted, when the Lycaonian crowds **saw what Paul had done, they shouted in the Lycaonian language, "The gods have taken on human form and come down to us!"** (14:11). In addition to (mis)apprehending the "clues" of Paul's "divine" stare and "loud voice," the Lycaonians were especially prone to mistake Paul and Barnabas as gods because of the widely attested and well-known story that Zeus and Hermes visited this region incognito and, after being rejected by many residents of the region, were finally given hospitality by the elderly couple, Philemon and Baucis (Ovid, *Metam*. 8.611–725). Perhaps the hasty conclusion reached here by the Lycaonians was an attempt to avoid making the same mistake twice. That Luke's audience would have recognized this intertextual echo is seen in the next verse, in which the Lycaonians specifically identify Barnabas and Paul as Zeus and Hermes: **They began calling Barnabas "Zeus" and Paul "Hermes," since he was the main speaker** (14:12).

But more seems to be going on with this story (for what follows, see Béchard 2000; 2001). Paul is the chosen instrument to carry Christ's name to the Gentiles (9:15). Yet only twice in Acts is Paul's missionary preaching aimed at an exclusively non-Jewish audience: here in 14:15–17, and later in the Areopagus speech in Athens (17:16–34). The contrast between these two "Gentile" settings, however, could not be more drastic. In Athens, Paul faces a sophisticated and skeptical audience in what was still recognized as the cultural center of the ancient world (cf. Cicero, *Flac*. 26.62: "There are present men from Athens, where men think civilization, learning, religion, agriculture, justice and laws were born and spread thence into every land. . . . Its prestige is so great that the present enfeebled and shattered renown of Greece is sustained by the reputation of this city").

Lycaonia, on the other hand, was regularly reckoned as one of those rural regions whose inhabitants typified the "superstitious and uncivilized" behavior of rustic mountain-dwellers. According to Strabo, for example, the Lycaonians (or many of them) lived in remote "mountain caves," ate food "unmixed with salt," and were ignorant of the sea (where most urban sophisticates dwelt; see *Geogr.* 12.6.5; 14.5.24). Beyond locating the setting of this healing in a recognizably "rustic" context, Luke provides several other hints of the remote nature of the region. He notes that the crowd speaks in the Lycaonian dialect (14:11; this is the only time that Luke refers to a local dialect). Strabo again views the persistence of unevolved dialects as one of the signs of a "primitive" culture (*Geogr.* 8.1.6; 13.1.25). Luke also refers to a single priest of Zeus joining in the praise (14:13). The word for the "gates" of the temple is used by Luke elsewhere in relation to a domestic structure (Luke 16:20; Acts 10:17; 12:13). This description suggests that the temple of Zeus in Lystra was hardly an imposing structure served by a "college of priests," but was rather a rural temple-shrine, which was "an unassuming building just slightly larger than a private dwelling," served by a single priest (Béchard 2001, 92).

The unbridled and uncritical reaction of the crowds in declaring Paul and Barnabas "gods" is confirmed by the priest who is all too willing to transfer to Paul and Barnabas the accoutrements of what was evidently some festival in progress: **together with the crowds, the priest of Zeus brought bulls and garlands to the city gates, wanting to offer sacrifices (to them)** (14:13). Later their gullibility resurfaces when Jews from Antioch and Iconium convince them to join in the stoning of one whom they had only recently mistaken for a god (14:19). Certainly the unreflective response by these remote and rural mountain dwellers stands in sharp contrast to Luke's description of the agora in urban Athens, populated by skeptical representatives of the philosophical schools of the Epicureans and Stoics. But why present the story this way?

Many critics of Christianity in the second century accused the movement of being populated by credulous and uneducated "rustics." Lucian, for example, charged, "If any charlatan or trickster, able to profit by occasions,

Attributing Divine Status

Lucian of Samosata, in his satire *Alexander the False Prophet*, provides further corroboration that local inhabitants of the rural highlands of Asia Minor were especially ready to confer divine status on any stranger with a special skill:

> *"Whenever a man but turned up with someone at his heels to play the flute or the tambourine or the cymbals, telling fortunes with a sieve, as the phrase goes, they were all agog over him on the instant and stared at him as if he were a god from heaven."* (*Alex.* 9, trans. Béchard 2001, 98)

How easy, then, for the crowd at Lystra to mistake for gods Paul and Barnabas (14:11), who, in the healing of a lame man, had done something far more sensational than playing the flute or telling fortunes!

comes among them, he quickly acquires sudden wealth by imposing upon such simple folk" (*Peregr.* 13). Such characterization of Christianity as a movement drawing primarily on the *hoi polloi* extends back even into the first century (cf. 1 Cor 1:26–31). In this scene Luke defends Paul (and other Christian missionaries) "against the charge of manipulating the uncritical naiveté of rural folk" (Béchard 2001, 86). In order to do so he employs (with variation) the literary topos of the self-disclosing sage whose commitment to wisdom and truth compels him to full disclosure in order to guard against misimpressions regarding his powers, especially among a particularly susceptible "rustic" audience.

The response of Paul and Barnabas to the Lycaonians' adulations is three-fold (cf. Béchard 2001, 96–97): (1) **they tore their garments** (14:14a); (2) **rushed out to the crowd** (14:14b); and (3) shouted, **"Men! Why are you doing these things? We too are men, with the same natures as you"** (14:15a). These actions correspond closely to the literary topos of what the sage should do who finds himself the object of a crowd's excessive admiration. Dio Chrysostom has summarized the desired response (*Cel. Phryg.* 35.9–10; cf. Béchard 2001, 97):

1. He should tear his garments.
2. He should leap forth naked upon the public highways.
3. Thus he will prove to all the world that he is no better than any other man.

The tearing of the garments and rushing out is obviously a symbolic gesture of "self-disclosure," and an "ocular demonstration" (cf. *Rhet. Her.* 4.55.68) that the sage has nothing to hide. But Paul's speech makes clear that more is at stake here than Paul and Barnabas's self-disclosure as messengers **who preach the good news to you to turn from these useless things** (14:15). Rather, Paul organizes his speech along the lines of God's own self-disclosure as the **living God who made the sky, the earth, the sea, and all that is in them** (14:15b). The emphasis on natural theology here anticipates a major theme developed in the Areopagus address (17:24–26). But several other points seem relevant for this particular Gentile audience. Although God had **allowed all the nations to go their own way** (14:16; cf. Rom 1:28–31), nonetheless **he did not leave himself without a witness** (14:17a). Rather, he **did good things (for you)** (14:17b); specifically **he gave you rain from heaven and fruitful seasons** (14:17c). There is epigraphic and iconographic evidence that older Hittite fertility gods of weather and vegetation were worshiped in local Zeus cults in Asia Minor, including Lycaonia, during the Roman imperial period (Breytenbach 1996, 69–73; idem. 1993, 396–413). The effect of this part of the speech, then, is to declare to the Lycaonians that the "living God," whom Paul and Barnabas serve, is the true "weather" God, and not Zeus, for whom they have mistaken Barnabas. This God, not Zeus (nor Paul and Barnabas), has **satisfied (your** bodies) with food and your hearts with gladness (14:17d). So enthusiastic is the crowd, however, that even by saying these things, they barely prevented the crowd from sacrificing to them (14:18).

The story ends with one last twist on the topos of the self-disclosing sage. Dio Chrysostom had ended his advice to the true sage by recommending that if someone were following at the heels of the sage, claiming to be his pupil, the teacher must drive him away, even pelting him with stones if necessary (*Or.* 35.10). At Lystra, Paul and Barnabas do not take up stones in order to deflect excessive admiration; rather, Jews came from Antioch and Iconium, and after winning over the crowd and stoning Paul, they dragged him outside the city because they thought he was dead (14:19). This inversion of the stoning motif (cf. Lucian, *Alex.* 45; *Peregr.* 15) highlights the theme of Paul's suffering for Christ's name, foretold to Ananias in an epiphany (9:16), that now becomes a painful reality, and is a note struck repeatedly in this chapter (see below on 14:22). Is Paul ritually (and actually) stoned to death (suggested by Strelan 2004, 243–53)? Whether dead or only left for dead, efforts to destroy Paul are in vain: when the disciples gathered around him, he got up and went into the city (14:20a). This symbolic (or actual) death and resurrection bear witness again to the "unhindered" nature of the gospel. Strengthened by the disciples, Paul now turns to strengthen the disciples.

Strengthening the Disciples (14:21–28)

This last unit (14:21–28) begins with a reference to Paul preaching the good news in that city [Derbe] (14:21a), thus connecting to the previous story, which ends with Paul and Barnabas in Derbe (14:20). Not only do Paul and Barnabas preach the gospel in Derbe, they are also involved in making a substantial number of disciples (14:21b). The word translated "making . . . disciples" occurs elsewhere in the NT only in Matthew, most notably Matt 28:19 (cf. also 13:52; 27:57). The authorial audience, familiar with Matthew, would hear echoes of the Great Commission, in which Jesus instructs his followers to "make disciples of all the nations." Making disciples for Luke as well as Matthew involved more than evangelism and baptism (Detwiler 1995, 33–41). For the Matthean Jesus, "discipling" involved "teaching them whatsoever I have commanded you"; for the Lukan Paul, it involved "strengthening the souls of the disciples" (14:22a).

In order to strengthen the disciples (14:22a), Paul (1) clarifies the role of suffering as an inevitable part of God's rule and (2) appoints leaders to continue the pastoral ministry of nurture and care for the believers (Spencer 2004, 161). What then are the implications of Paul's emphasis on suffering and succession?

According to Paul, suffering is a way to strengthen the disciples (14:22). Exhorting the Asian Christians to remain in the faith, Paul reminds them that we will inevitably pass through many trials prior to entering the kingdom of

God (14:22b). The phrase "through many trials" is "forefronted" and upsets the expected Greek word order of verb-subject-object in order to draw attention to or place emphasis upon the word or phrase being forefronted (Culy and Parsons 2003, 282). The focus on suffering is underscored also by the shift from indirect to direct discourse; "*we* will inevitably pass through many trials." The "we" here should not be mistaken as evidence of a "we" source or Luke's presence at this point in the narrative, but rather indicates that Paul includes himself in this suffering, a point made all the more poignant by the fact that it is addressed to believers who have only recently witnessed Paul's persecution at the hands of his opponents, culminating in his stoning in Lystra (Moessner 1990, 193–94). Paul returns to these cities in which he has so recently been badly mistreated "not in order to overwhelm his foes, but in order to attend pastorally to his communities" (Johnson 1992, 256).

If Luke seeks to establish continuity between the founder and followers by means of reference to miracles ("signs and wonders"; see comments on 14:3), he also establishes continuity between Moses and his "true heirs" through suffering: Moses was forced into exile, having been rejected by his own as "ruler and judge" (Acts 7:28–29); Jesus the Messiah suffers a martyr's death (Luke 23; cf. 24:46–47; Acts 17:3); the apostles are persecuted (Acts 5:40–41); Stephen, one of the Seven, is martyred (Acts 7:54–60); and Paul is stoned and left for dead (Acts 14:19–20; cf. 9:15–16). So suffering is also inevitable for the Gentile believers who hope "to remain in the faith" and "enter the kingdom of God." In other words, no cross, no crown. This continuity is made more explicit by appeal to the literary convention of succession in the next verse.

Paul also strengthens the disciples by **appointing elders for them in each church** (14:23). The language and convention of a succession narrative, found in ancient Greco-Roman, Jewish, and early Christian writings, is used here (Stepp and Talbert 1998, 173–75). These succession stories typically used language of transfer and also were comprised of three components: (1) that which was being passed on is named; (2) symbolic acts accompany the transfer; and (3) confirmation that the succession has taken place (Stepp and Talbert 1998, 167). Luke uses "appoint," one of the terms of transfer found in succession narratives (*P.Herc.* 1018 [7.7]; *P.Herc.* 1021 [8.10]; Josephus, *Ant.* 13.2.2, 45; Stepp and Talbert 1998, 151). He also employs two of the constituent elements of a succession narrative and implicitly refers to the third: (1) that which is being transferred to the elders in Acts 14 is the pastoral care and nurture of the churches (cf. Acts 20:28, in which this same function is labeled "shepherding"); (2) prayer and fasting are the ritual acts accompanying the transfer (14:23b); (3) the "very existence of the Lukan narrative" provides implicit confirmation that the elders have been faithful in strengthening the believers who face tribulations (Stepp and Talbert 1998, 173).

This context of succession also sheds light on two other elements of the story. First, Luke refers to "elders" to describe those appointed to succeed

Paul in the task of pastoral care. In his undisputed letters, Paul variously describes church leaders as "overseers" (Phil 1:1) or "deacons" (Rom 16:1; Phil 1:1). The Pastoral Epistles, however, do refer to "elders" (1 Tim 5:17, 19; Titus 1:5). More important for our understanding of the term in Acts is its repeated use to describe a category of Jewish leaders (e.g., Acts 4:5, 8, 23; 6:12; 22:5; 23:14; 24:1; 25:15). Even in a mixed congregation in the Diaspora Luke chooses to use this term with clear Jewish connotations, thus maintaining "certain structural associations" with nonmessianic Judaism (Spencer 2004, 161). This point is strengthened by the fact that Luke also uses the verbal form of "synagogue," which means "to gather together," when he reports that Paul **gathered the church together** (14:27a) in Pisidian Antioch (cf. also 15:30). The term "elders" is used in Acts of Christian leaders both before (cf. 11:30) and after (20:17; 21:18) this narrative. It is used next in the story in tandem with "apostles" (15:2, 6, 22), which brings us to our other point.

We have delayed until now discussion of a conundrum of Acts 14 that has long puzzled interpreters. Twice in Acts 14 (14:4, 14), Paul and Barnabas are referred to as "apostles." Elsewhere in Acts, this term is limited to those who had served with Jesus during his earthly ministry (1:21–22), and indeed was synonymous with the "Twelve." Two solutions are regularly cited: (1) Luke's source uses the term and Luke does not bother to correct it (Fitzmyer 1998, 526); (2) the term in Acts 14 refers simply to Paul and Barnabas being "sent out" (*apostellō*) as missionaries and has no technical sense (Barrett 1994, 1:671–72). In light of the fact that the term is used twice in a chapter that culminates with a succession narrative, we may offer another explanation. Like the apostles (Luke 6:13; Acts 1:2, 24), Paul is "chosen" by Christ (Acts 9:15) and like them (Acts 10:41) was "appointed" by God (Acts 22:14). Thus he is explicitly labeled an "apostle" here, and for the purposes of succession, Paul and Barnabas carry the apostolic authority necessary to transfer their pastoral ministry to the elders.

At the end of this unit, Luke narrates Paul and Barnabas continuing to retrace their steps, finally making their way back to Syrian Antioch where the episode began, thus forming a literary *inclusio*. In Antioch, **they reported all that God had done with them** (14:27b). The phrase "with them" may seem a bit odd but similar phrases occur elsewhere in Acts: God was "with Joseph" (Acts 7:9), as well as "with Jesus" (Acts 10:38). Theologically, the phrase is more closely analogous to 1 Cor 3:9 ("we are co-laborers with God"). Paul and Barnabas also report that God **had opened a door of faith among the Gentiles** (14:27c). Not only does this image of the door pick up on the language of "entering" the kingdom of God, found earlier in 14:22; it also echoes an idiom that in the NT is distinctively Pauline (1 Cor 16:9; 2 Cor 2:12; Col 4:3). Very shortly, however, some in the church would seek to close that door or at least severely limit its access. The episode ends with the note that **they stayed for** a considerable amount of time with the disciples (14:28; a litotes, "no little time"; see comment on Acts 1:5).

Theological Issues

The reception history of two details in Acts 13–14 deserves further comment here. Acts 13:1–3 is considered a key text (along with Acts 6:1–6; 1 Tim 4:14; 5:22; 2 Tim 1:6) for denominations seeking a biblical "foundation" for the ritual of ordination, and, to a certain extent, the language of Acts 13:1–3 lends itself to this kind of application. Saul and Barnabas are "set apart" for work to which the Holy Spirit has "called" them; hands are "laid" upon them and they are "sent." Probing this text a bit further, however, suggests that Luke did not intend to prescribe a ritual or ceremony for conferring "permanent and portable" authorization for church leaders (Dowd 2002, 216). First, we should note that elsewhere in Acts leaders are sent out without congregational ratification through the laying on of hands (Acts 8:14; 11:22, 30). Furthermore, Ananias's imposition of hands on Saul (9:15–19) can hardly be construed as an "ordination," and commentators rarely, if ever, do so. Acts 14:26 states that Paul and Barnabas returned to Antioch, "where they had been commended to the grace of God for the work which they had (now) completed." This text suggests "that the ceremony described in 13:1–3 was a commissioning for a specific task that has been completed after they report to the sending church" (Dowd 2002, 212). Later Paul leaves Antioch, once again "after being commended to the grace of the Lord by the believers" (15:40). All this suggests that Acts 13:1–3 records a specific commissioning for a specific task, and not, for Luke, an "ordination" to a permanent position. The same may be said of Acts 14:23 (in which Paul and Barnabas appoint elders for each church). Luke's concern here is on reporting how Paul strengthened the churches through legitimate succession, not on laying down a ceremonial pattern of ordination that must be repeated in subsequent generations.

The second point has to do with Paul's so-called missionary journeys. I fondly remember being fascinated as a child with the "Bible maps" that sat in my Sunday school classrooms and to which my teachers made frequent reference. I was particularly impressed by the map labeled "The Missionary Journeys of St. Paul." On this map were three lines of different color and length, which together charted the so-called three missionary journeys of Paul.

I also remember—less fondly—being required in college to memorize the cities and sequence of each missionary journey (see Parsons 1992, 28–29). Then, while a seminary student, I was utterly dumbfounded at an off-handed comment by one of my NT professors that Luke makes no mention of "*three missionary journeys*" by Paul to and from one centralized place from which he received spiritual and financial support. Rather, the professor suggested,

Luke conceived Paul moving from one mission center to another, often staying several months or even years in one particular locale, hardly qualifying for what we would consider a "journey." Today, in fact, some commentators have suggested the narrative "more naturally coheres around two expeditions," one in the Mediterranean region and the other in the territory of the Aegean Sea (Spencer 1997, 130).

After recovering from the shock of the hours lost in memorizing the details of three missionary journeys that do not exist, I wondered when this notion developed. John Townsend observes that the first reference to "three Pauline missionary journeys" occurs in J. A. Bengel, *Gnomon Novi Testamenti* (1742) and, further, that the concept of Paul's missionary journeys was "created" as part of the propaganda developed by the Society for Promotion of Christian Knowledge (founded 1698) and the Society for the Propagation of the Gospel in Foreign Parts (founded 1701). Paul's "missionary journeys" provided a biblical pattern for missionaries going out from a central location to the "ends of the earth" and then returning periodically for spiritual renewal, administrative guidance, and financial support (Townsend 1986, 99–104). The mythical journeys of Paul provided the biblical foundation necessary to persuade believers to support these missionary causes, and the romantic appeal of the three journeys is seen in their stubborn resistance as they continue to hold a place of prominence in Bible atlases, introductory NT textbooks, and classroom lectures and discussions in both church and academy. While Paul's mission to the Gentiles certainly occupies a central place in the second half of Luke's narrative, it may not fit the familiar pattern of "Paul's missionary journeys," no matter how attractive the map.

This conclusion does not mean that contemporary communities of faith must cease observing ordination rituals for their clergy or refrain from missionary endeavors. Both examples do serve, however, as a cautionary tale against using the text as a pretext for our particular agendas and concerns, no matter how worthy the cause. Further, they suggest that modern-day denominations, especially those claiming to follow the "NT church," might be more circumspect in acknowledging ecclesial biases and the influence of postcanonical developments on the church structure and practices (Garland 2003, 25).

Acts 15:1–16:5

The Jerusalem Conference

⌘

Introductory Matters

Acts 15 is widely recognized as standing at the center of the book of Acts both literarily and theologically (Haenchen 1971, 461–62; Marshall 1980, 242; Johnson 1992, 280; Witherington 1998, 439). Finally the issue of Gentile inclusion into the family of God is addressed and resolved. The episode divides into seven scenes: a description of the nature of the conflict (15:1–5); the debate in Jerusalem focusing on the speeches by Peter (and Paul and Barnabas) (15:6–12) and James (15:13–21); the solution (15:22–29); the report to Antioch (15:30–35) and the aftermath in which Paul and Barnabas separate (15:36–41); and Paul taking on Timothy and continuing to disseminate the decision of the council throughout the cities (16:1–5).

Tracing the Narrative Flow

The rhetorical situation of the council is "deliberative," in which the speakers seek "to

---

**Acts 15:1–16:5
in the Narrative Flow**

The people and places of the Jerusalem church (1–12)

The missionary activities of Paul (13–28)

Paul's mission to the Gentile world (13–19)

Paul's initial missionary campaign (13–14)

▶ The Jerusalem conference (15:1–16:5)

The conflict (15:1–5)

Peter, Paul, and Barnabas speak (15:6–12)

James speaks (15:13–21)

The solution (15:22–29)

The report distributed (15:30–35)

Transition: Paul and Barnabas separate (15:36–41)

The report distributed (16:1–5)

---

persuade" the audience "to take some action in the future" (Kennedy 1984, 19), in this case, to allow Gentiles into the Christian community without requiring circumcision.

The Conflict (15:1–5)

The opening unit (15:1–5) is arranged in a chiastic pattern (Talbert 1984, 62):

A People from Judea teach circumcision is necessary for the Gentiles' salvation (15:1)

  B Paul and Barnabas (and others) are sent to Jerusalem to discuss the matter (15:2)

    C On the way they relate the conversion of the Gentiles to believers in Phoenicia and Samaria (15:3)

  B' When they arrive in Jerusalem, they are welcomed by the church (15:4)

A' Some Pharisaic Christians say circumcision and keeping the law are necessary for Gentiles (15:5)

The outer frame of the chiasm suggests that the conflict in Acts 15 has interrelated but ultimately distinct soteriological and social dimensions.

The success of Paul and Barnabas reported in Acts 13 and 14 prompted some unnamed individuals to travel from Judea to Antioch to assert the official position of the Jerusalem church: **Now some people came down from Judea and began teaching the believers, "Unless you are circumcised in accord with the Mosaic custom, you cannot be saved"** (15:1). The status of Gentiles was a much debated topic in Judaism, and the apostolic council must be understood in its light. At one end of the Jewish spectrum stands the witness of the book of *Jubilees*, a sectarian Jewish document from the first century BC, which claims: "And anyone who is born whose own flesh is not circumcised on the eighth day is not from the sons of the covenant which the Lord made for Abraham, since (he is) from the children of destruction. And there is therefore no sign upon him so that he might belong to the Lord because (he is destined) to be destroyed and annihilated from the earth . . . because he has broken the covenant of the Lord our God" (*Jub.* 15.26–27). This position virtually eliminates the possibility of Gentile conversion. In this light, the appeal of *Jubilees* elsewhere to the Noahic commandments (*Jub.* 7.20–21; cf. Gen 9:9–18) is clearly intended "to provide *Jubilees* with a legal warrant for condemning the Gentiles" (Segal 2001, 71).

At the other end of the spectrum, some Jewish traditions allow that "righteous Gentiles" can be saved *as* Gentiles without conversion to Judaism. According to *t. Sanh.* 13.2, Rabbi Joshua, in a debate over the meaning of Ps 9:17

("the wicked shall go into Sheol, and all the nations that forget God") with Rabbi Eliezer (who held a view similar to that of *Jubilees*), claimed: "If the verse had said, 'The wicked shall go into Sheol with all the nations,' and had stopped there, I should have agreed with you, but as it goes on to say 'who forget God,' it means there are righteous men among the nations who have a share in the world to come" (on the reliability of the tradition reflecting a first-century Jewish view, cf. Segal 2001, 67–68). Most of those holding a place for the "righteous Gentile" would still have expected converts to Judaism to undergo circumcision (cf. Segal 2001, 68), a viewpoint that had biblical warrant to support it (Gen 17:10–14; 34:15–24). Those who come from Judea (15:1) espouse this viewpoint.

Josephus, however, reports that a Jewish merchant, Ananias, instructs Izates, king of Adiabene, a potential Gentile proselyte, that monotheism was superior to circumcision, implying that circumcision was therefore not necessary (Schwartz 1996). Another Jewish teacher, Eleazar, however, insisted that circumcision was necessary to enter the Jewish covenant community, and thus Ananias was overruled (*Ant.* 20.2.3–4; 34–46; Barrett 1998, 2:699; Talbert 2005, 128–29). Finally, there existed a minority view that no one, Jew or Gentile, was required to be circumcised in order to be saved. This was apparently the view of the "radical allegorizers" described (and criticized) by Philo (*Migr.* 89–93). Peter's perspective (see below) most closely resembles that of Ananias, and his comments regarding the soteriological place of the Gentiles must be read in light of these perspectives. We must also hear his description of the "righteous Gentile" in light of this debate.

The use of litotes (see 12:18) and a doublet ("no small dissension and debate") underscore the seriousness of this dispute (Culy and Parsons 2003, 286). Thus delegates, including Paul and Barnabas, were ordered **to go up (and meet with) the apostles and elders in Jerusalem concerning this point of disagreement** (15:2). The major players are introduced: the circumcision party (to whom Luke refers again in 15:5), which has no individual spokesperson but rather speaks as a group; the apostles, who will be represented by Peter; and the elders, who will be represented by James. The only group missing is that of the "Hellenists," and Luke may intend for the audience to understand that Paul and Barnabas have been appointed by the Antioch church to represent their concerns (15:2; cf. 13:1). As they pass through Phoenicia and Samaria on their way to Jerusalem, Paul and Barnabas relate **the conversion of the Gentiles (as they went), and brought great joy to all the believers** (15:3). Upon arriving in Jerusalem, initially at least, **they were welcomed by the church, the apostles, and the elders and they reported all that God had done with them** (15:4).

No sooner had they arrived than **some from the sect of the Pharisees, who were believers, stood up** (15:5a). Some Christians from the sect of the Pharisees (but not all; consider, e.g., Paul, Acts 23:6) raise a second, related issue: must Gentiles convert to Judaism (be circumcised and observe the Torah) in order to live with and among Jews? They give a resounding "Yes!" **It is necessary to circumcise them and to order (them) to keep the law of Moses (15:5b).** The issue here is not about the Gentiles' salvation but whether Gentiles and Jews can commingle without the Jews' being defiled by association with Gentiles, who are by nature unclean (see discussion at 11:1–18 and below). This is a social, not a soteriological, question. Again, a variety of opinions existed in middle Judaism (see Talbert 2005, 129). According to 1 Maccabees, during the Jewish revolt against Antiochus Epiphanes, Gentiles in regions inhabited and controlled by Jews faced compulsory circumcision (1 Macc 2:46), a policy continued under the Hasmoneans (Josephus, *Ant.* 13.9.1.257). These Pharisaic Christians insisted on circumcision and Torah-observance for Gentiles as a condition of residence among them (cf. Josephus, *Vita* 113). Leviticus 17–18, which also presumes a social context of a Gentile minority living within the environs of a Jewish majority, mandates that "resident aliens," while they did not have to be circumcised, should observe certain of the ritual and moral laws of the Mosaic covenant in order to engage in social intercourse with Jews.

Finally, there are remnants in pre-Christian Jewish texts of an emerging understanding of the Noahic commandments, a doctrine more fully espoused in later rabbinic Judaism (cf. *t. Abod. Zar.* 8.4; *b. Sanh.* 56b). In these texts, the rules incumbent upon the "righteous Gentiles" are derived neither from the rituals of the temple cultus nor from strict observance of Mosaic law; rather, they emerge from and function somewhat like the concept of "natural law," which "any just person can be expected to follow by observation and reason" (Segal 2001, 69). In the first-century AD Jewish *Sibylline Oracles*, for example, we find the following injunctions placed upon righteous Gentiles:

> Happy will be those of [hu]mankind of earth who will love the great God, blessing him before drinking and eating, putting their trust in piety. They will reject all temples when they see them, altars too, useless foundations of dumb stones (and stone statues and handmade images) defiled with blood of animate creatures, and sacrifices of four-footed animals. They will look to the great glory of the one God and commit no wicked murder, nor deal in dishonest gain, which are most horrible things. Neither have they disgraceful desire for another's spouse or for hateful and repulsive abuse of a male. (*Sib. Or.* 4.24–34, trans. OTP 1:384–385; cf. *Jub.* 7.20–21; *Ps.-Phoc.* 228–230)

These rules emerge in the context of Diaspora Judaism, in which the Jews themselves, in a kind of role reversal from the situation imagined in Lev 17–18, are the "resident aliens," living as minorities in Gentile populated areas. "In these situations, the concept of a righteous Gentile, who eschewed sin but did not explicitly take up the special rules of Judaism, would have a positive value" (Segal 2001, 75). In these cases, Jews could, without defiling themselves by such association, interact with these "righteous Gentiles," who adhered to a minimum code of ethics. This position will be adopted and modified by James (whose opinion, according to Luke, the church ultimately follows). James's speech and the Apostolic Decree should be read in light of the various Jewish views on the social interaction with Gentiles.

Peter, Paul, and Barnabas Speak (15:6–12)

The other representatives are then allowed to present their position in a public assembly. Peter speaks first. By recounting briefly the Cornelius story (but without mentioning his name), Peter appeals to his own experience to justify including without restrictions the Gentiles within the family of God. Peter's argument, however, is not *just* an autobiographical argument; it is a theological argument (Tannehill 1990, 184). The speech throughout describes what God was doing in those events: Peter stood up and said to them, "Fellow believers, you know that long ago God chose me from among you so that through my mouth the Gentiles would hear the message of the gospel and believe. And God, who knows the heart, has provided evidence for them by giving (them) the Holy Spirit just as (he gave him) to us. He made no distinction between them and us regarding our faith, but cleansed their hearts (as well as ours) (15:7–9). God is the subject of most of the verbs and participles in this speech: God made a choice; God knows the human heart; God testified to them [Gentiles]; God gave them the Holy Spirit; God cleansed their hearts; God has made no distinction between them and us. The upshot is that God, not Peter (or Paul), is responsible for the inclusion of the Gentiles.

Earlier, in Acts 11, Peter had claimed that Jews who associated with Gentiles were not defiled. Now he makes the very bold move of declaring Gentiles clean before a Jewish audience (see 15:9). This interpretation has the advantage of explaining why in the narrative flow of Acts the Jerusalem Council in Acts 15 was necessary. The Cornelius episode had resolved for the Jerusalem church the problem of Jews associating with Gentiles. Peter proclaimed that his vision justified such social interaction because God would cleanse the Jew who had been rendered "defiled" by social intercourse with an unclean Gentile.

The more radical conclusion that neither were Gentiles to be called unclean—a conclusion that Peter had shared with his Gentile audience in 10:29—is withheld from a Jewish audience until the Jerusalem Council of Acts 15. The Jerusalem believers, not content with the claim that God could cleanse Jews contaminated by social contact with Gentiles, begin insisting that the Gentiles who wish to become Christians must follow Torah regulations, symbolized by their circumcision (15:2). At this point Peter is forced to make explicit the implications of the Cornelius episode: "he cleansed their hearts (as well as ours)" (15:9).

While the council will ultimately choose a less radical solution, the so-called Apostolic Decree in which Gentiles agreed to observe certain sexual mores and dietary regulations, Peter's speech indicates that his own conversion is finally complete. God does not discriminate between Jew and Gentile; both have been declared clean. As such, on the sociological level, Peter claims Gentiles need not be circumcised in order to interact with Jews. While the audience might surmise that Peter (and Paul and Barnabas) expect the Gentiles to behave in a way consistent with the ethical practices of this new Christian community (cf. 2:45; 4:32, 34)—embodying what Paul calls in Galatians the "fruit of the Spirit" (Gal 5:22) or the "law of Christ" (Gal 6:2)—Peter does not explicitly impose any other kind of observance of Jewish moral or ritual rules (e.g., as in Lev 17–18) or even a kind of "natural law" (e.g., the Noahic commandments). On the soteriological level, Peter identifies with the Jewish point of view that claims the "righteous Gentile" does not have to be circumcised in order to enter into God's covenant community and into "the world to come." But how are Gentiles made "righteous"?

In certain Jewish views (see Rabbi Eliezar's view expressed in *Tosefta Sanhedrin* above), some Gentiles were capable of remembering God and God's way and thus acting in a righteous or just manner. Such a view is based on an "optimistic anthropology" in which persons were capable of observing the law, whether natural or Mosaic. Peter shares with *Jubilees* (not to mention Paul) a basically pessimistic anthropology (see Talbert 2001, 20). He claims that it is not right to place a **yoke on the disciples' necks that neither our ancestors nor we ourselves have been able to bear** (15:10). Rather, salvation is an act of God's grace, not the result of human effort, which, however noble, on its own is bound ultimately to fail. Righteousness, in other words, is effected by grace through faith: **we believe that we are saved through the grace of our Lord Jesus in the very same manner as these people!** (15:11, cf. 15:9; on the grammar and translation, see Culy and Parsons 2003, 290). The emphasis is on salvation through grace, which is, of course, a very common theme in Paul's letters (cf. e.g., Rom 3:24), but it is also found in the message of the Lukan Paul. At the end of his synagogue speech in Antioch, Paul asserts, "everyone who believes is justified" (13:38–39). Peter holds the pessimistic anthropology of certain sectarian Jews: Gentiles cannot keep the Noahic commandments.

Contrary to the view of *Jubilees*, however, Peter thinks that "righteous Gentiles" can, in fact, enter the world to come. In this regard, he resembles the viewpoint of Rabbi Eliezar. He departs from Eliezar's view (which is based on an optimistic anthropology), however, in his conviction that such righteousness (whether for Jew or Gentile) is available only through the enabling "grace of our Lord Jesus." Peter's words reduce the assembly to silence (15:12a). Paul and Barnabas support Peter by relating all **the signs and wonders that God had done through them among the Gentiles** (15:12b).

James Speaks (15:13–21)

Following Paul and Barnabas's speech, James, the representative of the Jerusalem elders, addresses the assembly. As Peter had offered a theological argument for Gentile inclusion in part on the basis of his personal experience,

James offers a theological argument based on another source of authority: scripture. James begins his speech with a reference to Peter's: **Simeon has explained how God first acted and took a people from among the Gentiles for himself** (15:14). The Greek word for "people" is used elsewhere in Luke and Acts exclusively for the Jews, but here it unmistakably identifies believing Gentiles with God's chosen "people." In James's opinion, circumcision is not necessary for the Gentiles to be saved. On the soteriological question, James agrees with Peter (and Paul and Barnabas). But whereas Peter makes the argument on the basis of God's gift of the Holy Spirit to the Gentiles, making no distinction between Jew and Gentile, and Paul and Barnabas appealed to the signs and wonders performed by God through them among the Gentiles, James makes his argument from scripture (Bauckham 1995, 1:452).

James argues that **with this the words of the prophets agree** (15:15), namely that the Gentiles are included in the people of God: **After these things I will return, and I will restore the tent of David, which had fallen. I will rebuild its ruins and restore it in order that the rest of humankind may seek the Lord, even all the nations whom I have called by my name, says the Lord who made these things known long ago** (15:16–18). James employs an exegetical method similar to the *pesharim* found at Qumran. In this method, what "appears to be merely a quotation of a scriptural text turns out to be in fact also an interpretation of the text" (Bauckham 1995, 1:453; cf. Stowasser 2001). Depicting the Jewish Christian, James, as a skilled exegete, familiar with the intricacies of *pesharim*, is another example of *ethopoeia* or "speech-in-character," in which the author attributes to a person words that "are suitable to the speaker and have an indisputable application to the subject discussed" (Theon, *Prog.* 115, trans. Kennedy 2003, 47; cf. sidebar on p. 32). Furthermore, Theon argues that "one should have in mind . . . to whom the speech is addressed . . ." (Theon, *Prog.* 115, trans. Kennedy 2003, 47). As we shall see, James's audience is well disposed toward his speech and ultimately follows his counsel.

James argues that the "dwelling of David," which God will build, is the eschatological temple, composed not of mortar and bricks but rather formed by the Gentiles together with Jews (Bauckham 1995, 1:454–55). Several features of the scriptures cited support this claim (for what follows, see Bauckham 1995, 1:454–58). James offers an intricate exegesis based on Amos 9:11–12. But in the opening and closing frame of the text he draws also on allusions to other prophetic texts (Jer 12 and Isa 45, both noted in the margins of NA[27]), hence the opening reference to "the words of the prophets." The first three Greek words of the quotation, "after these things, I will return," do not appear in Amos; rather, they allude to Jer 12:15–16:

> And *after* I have plucked them [the Gentile nations] up, I *will again* have compassion on them. . . . And then, if they will diligently learn the ways of my people, . . . *they shall be built up* in the midst of my people.

Jeremiah refers both to the conversion of the Gentiles and "their being built up" as the eschatological temple.

The conclusion of James's citation, "who made these things known long ago," also departs from Amos (which in the LXX has simply "who does these things"; cf. Culy and Parsons 2003, 294). "Known long ago" is an allusion to Isa 45:21, part of another prophecy that the Gentiles will turn to God and be saved (Isa 45:20–22). Thus these allusions, "which frame the main quotation from Amos put the latter in a context of prophecies which associate the eschatological conversion of the Gentile nations with the restoration of the temple in the Messianic age" (Bauckham 1995, 1:455).

> ### Alliteration in Acts 15:16
>
> While it is possible to argue that the Lukan James is following a variant LXX tradition to explain the use of *anastrepsō* for *epistrepsō* (which Codex D "corrects"), it is more likely that James has employed in 15:16 the rhetorical figure of *homoeoprophoron* or alliteration, the repetition of the initial sound (*Rhet. Her.* 4.22.18; see sidebar on 13:13), detectable even in the English translation: *anastrepsō* ("I will return"); *anoikodomēsō* (twice; "I will rebuild"); *anorthōsō* ("I will restore").

The quotation from Amos itself, however, is necessary to support James's interpretation. Other prophetic texts that predict the inclusion of the Gentiles into God's people *could* be interpreted to mean that these Gentiles would first become proselytes to Judaism and thus undergo circumcision (Isa 19:25; Zech 2:11). But Amos (assisted by allusions to Isa 45 and especially Jer 12) states that the nations *as nations* belong to God. The phrase **all the nations whom I have called by my name** (15:17; Amos 9:12) is a literal rendering of a Hebrew idiom that elsewhere expresses ownership, especially God's ownership of the people of Israel (Deut 28:10; 2 Chr 7:14; Jer 14:9; Dan 9:19; see Bauckham 1995, 1:457). To these now belong also the Gentiles, and there is no mention here, explicitly or implicitly, of the Gentiles being circumcised or obeying the Mosaic law in order to be called by God's name. Furthermore, in Amos, these Gentiles do not enter the eschatological temple; they, along with remnant Israel, *are* the temple. Therefore, James concludes that scripture confirms Peter's experience that the Gentiles should not have to become Jews in order to become Christians: **we should not trouble those among the Gentiles who turn to God** (15:19). On the soteriological question, James agrees with Peter: circumcision is *not* necessary for Gentile salvation.

On the sociological issue, however, James does go one step further toward compromise with the "sect of the Pharisees" by suggesting that the council write to the Gentiles, instructing them to observe certain Jewish regulations. **Instead, (we should simply) write them a letter in order that they might abstain from things defiled by idols, from sexual immorality, from (eating the meat of** animals that have been) strangled, and from (eating/drinking) blood (15:20). These stipulations echo the regulations required of the "resident aliens" in Lev 17–18, a kind of application of Noahic stipulations (see above). Why are the Gentiles instructed to observe these regulations? James explains: **since ancient times the law of Moses has been proclaimed from city to city as it is read in the synagogues each and every Sabbath day** (15:21; cf. Philo, *Spec.* 2.62; Josephus, *Ant.* 16.2.3.43; *C. Ap.* 2.28.175). "The Gentile Messianists are to behave in this way not because the law says so but because it is the minimum that will allow Jews who observe the law to associate with Gentiles who do not" (Talbert 2005, 133).

The Solution (15:22–29)

The council is persuaded by James's words and adopts a less radical social solution than that proposed by Peter. They agree with Peter that Gentiles need not be circumcised in order to be saved; they agree with James that Gentiles must observe certain Noahic food laws in order to have social interaction with Jews. They then decide to communicate their decision to the Gentile believers in Antioch, Cilicia, and Syria in a letter: **Then the apostles and elders, along with the whole church, decided to send (some) chosen men to Antioch with Paul and Barnabas—Judas, who was called Barsabbas, and Silas, men who were leaders among the believers. They sent (this) letter with them** (15:22–23a). Both the form and the content of the letter are of interest. First, we note the significance of communicating the apostles and elders' decision through a letter, which has a salutation—**The apostles and elders, [your] fellow believers, to the believers among the Gentiles, in Antioch, Syria, and Cilicia. Greetings** (15:23b)—and closing ("Farewell") typical of Hellenistic letters (cf. letters 17, 18, 20 in Horsley 1981; 2 Macc 11:16, 21). Much debate has revolved around the authenticity of this letter and the one in Acts 23:26–30 (Cadbury 1927, 191; Lüdemann 1989, 168; Judge 1981). It would seem more plausible for Luke to have access to an internal church document like the Apostolic Decree than a military/legal communication such as Lysias's letter in Acts 23. The issue of the "historicity" of the letters in Acts, however, is ultimately irresolvable, since the rhetoricians give evidence both for inventing letters and for quoting proceedings, as necessity demands (cf. Quintilian, *Inst.* 3.8.52; 9.2.4). What is usually missing from this debate is the rhetorical function of the letter within the narrative.

About letters, the Hellenistic rhetorician Demetrius commented, "The letter, just as the dialogue, should have a strong use of characterization. For everyone, more or less, writes a letter as an image of his or her own soul. It is also possible to see the character of the writer in every other form of written-communication, but in none so clearly as in the letter" (*Eloc.* 4.227; cf. Cicero, *Quint. fratr.* 1.45). Like speeches, letters were intended to reflect the character of the writer/speaker, another vehicle for *ethopoeia* or speech-in-character (cf. Hermogenes, *Prog.* 20, trans. Kennedy 2003, 84; Aphthonius, *Prog.* 34 R, trans. Kennedy 2003, 115; called *prosopopoeia* by Theon, *Prog.* 115, trans. Kennedy 2003, 47; see also the sidebar on p. 32). In fact, the progymnasmatists suggested that in addition to speeches, letter writing was an appropriate medium through which to explore *ethopoeia*. Nicolaus writes in his chapter on *ethopoeia*, "To me, it seems also to exercise us in the style of letter writing, since in that there is need of foreseeing the character of those sending letters and those to whom they are sent" (Nicolaus, *Prog.* 67, trans. Kennedy 2003, 166; cf. also Theon, *Prog.* 115, trans. Kennedy 2003, 47). In fact, fictive epistolography was a minor genre of the Second Sophistic period (second and third centuries AD).

There exist collections of fictive letters by Alciphron, Aelian, and Philostratus. *Ethopoeia* often took the form of inventing a speech in response to a question, for example, "What words would a man say to his wife when leaving on a journey? Or a general to his soldiers in time of danger?" (Theon, *Prog.* 115, trans. Kennedy 2003, 47). In these letter collections, letters rather than speeches were composed to answer such questions as, "What did the fisherman's daughter in love say to her mother?" (see Rosenmeyer 2001, 260; Alciphron, *Letters* 1.11.1–4). Alciphron has 123 extant fictional prose letters in four books, categorized under farmers, fishermen, parasites, and courtesans (Rosenmeyer 2001, 260). These fictive letters were designed to reveal something of the "character" associated with the stock characters to whom they are attributed. We should not be surprised to find that the letters in Acts 15 and 23 also reveal something about the character of their senders.

Whether invented or quoted (perhaps from an "Antiochene source"; cf. Fitzmyer 1998, 563) or "something in between" (see the sidebar below on embedded letters; cf. Rosenmeyer 2001, 60), when placed in the larger context of Acts 15, the Apostolic Decree contributes to the characterization of its senders, especially James. The prohibitions listed in the decree echo James's conclusion in 15:20 and solidify his position not only as a competent messianic exegete of scripture, but also as the acknowledged leader not only of the elders but of "the apostles and elders," indeed of all the "fellow believers" (15:23). This position as leader of the Jerusalem church is reiterated when Paul visits Jerusalem and presents himself to James, along with the elders of the church (21:18); once again Paul is reminded of the contents of the letter (21:25). But the letter does more than contribute to James's characterization.

The letter also amplifies the decision-making process to include the Holy Spirit: **It seemed best to the Holy Spirit and to us** (15:28a). Not explicitly mentioned in the deliberations of 15:1–21 (though see 15:8), the Holy Spirit's inclusion in the letter contributes to the characterization of the Holy Spirit's pivotal role in the Gentile mission. The Spirit directs Philip to the Ethiopian eunuch (8:29) and Peter to Cornelius (11:12). The gift of the Spirit to Cornelius and his household provides the testimony Peter needs to baptize them (10:44,

46). After the council the Holy Spirit continues to guide the mission; in fact, Paul gives his final words in Acts over to the Holy Spirit who proclaims through the prophet Isaiah, "Therefore, let it be known to you that this salvation from God has been sent to the Gentiles; and they will listen" (28:28). Thus the addition of the Holy Spirit adds authoritative weight to the church's decision.

Acts 15:23–29 is "embedded" in a larger literary context, thus resembling other letters in antiquity that were embedded into a larger narrative, whether history, novel, tragedy, or biography (see Aune 1987, 128; Rosenmeyer 2001; Klauck 2006, 420–29; Howell 2009), in both Jewish (e.g., 1 Macc 10; 11; 13; 2 Macc 1; 11; 3 Macc 3:11–29; Josephus, *Ant.* 16.162–173) and Greco-Roman writings (inter alia, Herodotus, *Hist.* 3.40; Thucydides, *Hist.* 7.11–15; and Sallust, *Bell. Cat.* 35.1–6; 445). Pseudo-Callisthenes's *Alexander Romance* (second or third century AD?)—which is described as "antiquity's most successful

Embedded Letters

Patricia Rosenmeyer has written helpfully about the function of letters embedded in historical narrative:

"Both Herodotus and Thucydides, by including letters in their historical narratives, reveal the affinity of letters with other forms of fictional narration: letters, whether documentary, freely invented, or something in between, reflect the invention of a self, a story, a plot in both senses of the word. Herodotus uses letters to enliven his narrative, Thucydides to bolster his historical arguments; both include letters as a kind of external reassurance, to persuade their readers of the quality of their work." (Rosenmeyer 2001, 60)

Likewise, Josephus defends his decision to cite a series of Roman decrees:

"Now it was necessary for me to cite these decrees since this account of our history is chiefly meant to reach the Greeks in order to show them that in former times we were treated with all respect and were not prevented by our rulers from practicing any of our ancestral customs." (*Ant.* 16.174)

Luke, in addition to employing the embedded letter to advance the plot and build characterization, also uses the Apostolic Decree as a kind of documentary "proof," an added authoritative testimony to the story he narrates. The use of a formal Greek period in 15:24–26 (see Polhill 1992, 334) and language typical of assemblies, for example, "it seemed best" or "we resolved" (*edoxe*; cf. "the senate and the people have decreed," Diogenes Laertius, *Vit. phil.* 2.142; Josephus, *Ant.* 16.163) lend solemnity to the letter. The repetition of the term *edoxe*, once in the narrative (15:22) and twice in the letter (15:25, 28), is also an example of the rhetorical figure of *reduplication* (*Rhet. Her.* 4.28.38), for the purpose of escalating the level of authority invoked and likewise accentuating the letter's gravitas.

novel," with a "popularity and diffusion exceeded only by the Bible" (Dowden 1989, 650)—employs over thirty embedded letters for a variety of purposes: military communications, exchanges with enemies on the eve of war, letters home, and others (see Rosenmeyer 2001, 169–92). In the Greek novels, embedded letters were often used to reveal the character of the sender as well as to move the plot along (see Chariton, *Chaer.* 4.4.7–10; 8.4.3, 4; Achilles Tatius, *Leuc. Cli.* 1.3.6).

The *Rhetorica ad Alexandrum* argued that a proper use of rhetorical techniques such as amplifications, minimizations, and recapitulations allows one to acquire a "great facility both in speaking and writing" (28.2–4). The Apostolic Decree, as embedded letter, contains all three techniques and serves also to contribute to the plot development of the role of the Gentiles and the Gentile mission in the newly constituted people of God. On the one hand, the debate between Peter and the apostles, James and the elders, and the Pharisaic Christians has been minimized in the letter; in fact, reference to any internal conflict has been reduced to the phrase "becoming [rather than "being"] all of one accord." Focus is on the amplification of the "external pressures" that precipitated the letter's writing (further on amplification see comments above on the addition of the Holy Spirit to the decree). The letter has been sent because the apostles and elders and fellow believers have heard that **some people have gone out from among us, whom we did not send, and upset you with (their) message and troubled your hearts** (15:24). The upsetting message, namely that "circumcision was necessary in order to be saved," is refuted by the letter's report of the decision **to lay no greater burden on you than these necessary (things)** (15:28), which does not include circumcision as a soteriological necessity. What then is the decision of the council?

Here Luke uses the rhetorical convention of recapitulation (see above) to state again the prohibitions that the Gentiles are required to observe: **to abstain from (eating) meat offered to idols, from blood, from (the meat of animals that have been) strangled, and from sexual immorality. If you keep yourselves from these things, you will do well** (Acts 15:29). The prohibitions echo those regulations mandated for "resident aliens" in Lev 17–18. Depending on how one counts, there are a dozen or so prohibitions mentioned in Lev 17–18 (Talbert 2005, 132). So why does the Apostolic Decree mention only these four? From the perspective of the authorial audience, the answer may not be very clear since there are no other lists that single out these particular four prohibitions (Witherington 1998, 465). From a compositional perspective, however, it is interesting to note that Jer 12:16, alluded to at the beginning of James's scripture citation (15:16), ends with the reference to the Gentiles being "built in the midst of my people." The phrase "in the midst of my people" has the advantage of shifting the focus from Gentiles living in the land of Israel (clearly in view in Lev 17–18) to Gentiles living among Jews, without specifying a locale (the diasporic context of the early church described by

Textual Variants in Acts 15

Text-critical problems with the prohibitions in James's speech and the Apostolic Decree (as well as 21:25) are well known (see the table in Strange 1992, 88). It is common to view the Western text's replacement of the reference to blood with a version of the Golden Rule (see, e.g., Codex D) as a move, as the church became increasingly Gentile, from a ritual to an ethical code. William Strange, however, has cautioned against that conclusion, arguing: "To see the development of early Christian thought as a drift from 'ritual' to 'ethics' is an oversimplification. It was quite possible for early Christian teaching to include elements which might be described as 'ritual' alongside those which might be called 'ethical': The *Didache* includes not only teaching on the 'Two Ways' (2–5), but also clear instruction on not eating food offered to idols (6)" (Strange 1992, 96, who also cites the evidence of Aristides' *Apology* 15 and *Ps.-Clem.* 7.4.2–4). Thus, given the ethical implications of ritual regulations, it is possible, even preferable, to view these ritual prohibitions of the decree as a way to address the moral pollutions of Gentiles (see Bauckham 2005, 127). Still, few have accepted Strange's solution of adopting a text that omits both the term *pniktōn* ("what is strangled") and the Golden Rule, a reading that is poorly attested (see Strange 1992, 104–5).

Luke). For Luke the Gentiles are living "in the midst of the people" as part of the eschatological temple, comprised of persons and not "made with hands" (cf. comments above on Acts 15:16).

This phrase, "in the midst of my people," is used five times in Lev 17–18 (Hebrew text) to modify four of the prohibitions (Lev 17:8, 10, 12, 13; 18:26; the phrase is repeated in 17:8 and 17:10 on the one prohibition against eating blood; Bauckham 1995, 1:459–61; idem, 1996, 154–84). These very same four prohibitions are repeated, in that order, in the Apostolic Decree (explaining the variation in order between James's speech and the decree): (1) "meat sacrificed to idols" (cf. Lev 17:7–9). Leviticus 17:7 assumes that sacrifices not offered to Yahweh in the tabernacle are offered to "goat idols." (2) Eating "blood" is prohibited by Lev 17:8–10. (3) "Things strangled" are prohibited by Lev 17:13 (cf. Philo, *Spec.* 4.122). (4) "Sexual immorality" refers to the various sexual relations specified in Lev 18:6–23 and described in 18:26 as "detestable things" from which the "resident alien in your midst" must abstain.

These four requirements are "all basically ritual requirements aimed at making fellowship possible between Jewish and Gentile Christians" (Polhill 1992, 331). This view is supported further by other clues in the text. In 16:1–3, Timothy (whose mother is Jewish and father Greek) is circumcised by Paul, not to ensure his salvation, but to remove any obstacle that would hinder fellowship with the Jews with whom he came into contact. Further, these regulations are recalled again in 21:21, in which Paul is accused of leading Jews living among Gentiles to "forsake Moses." There the situation has changed: "The problem is no longer the demands being made on Gentiles to become Jews but the pressure being felt by Jews to conform to a Gentile way of life" (Tannehill 1990, 191). But the problem is still basically a social one of fellowship between Jewish and Gentile Christians. These prohibitions are chosen "because these customs are the minimalist concession that communal spirit demands to enable ethnic Jews and Gentiles, all of whom have become believers in Jesus the Messiah, to live together in unity" (Talbert 2005, 135).

The Report Distributed (15:30–35)

The appointed delegation (Paul, Barnabas, Judas Barsabbas, and Silas) departs, and the letter is delivered and read to the church at Antioch (15:30–31a). Reactions to letters varied in antiquity. Pseudo-Callisthenes' *Alexander Romance* records a whole range of responses by the recipients of letters. Sometimes a letter prompted an immediate written reply (*Alex.* 3.25); sometimes the recipient was moved to smile (*Alex.* 3.26); once the epistolary audience was so angry they crucified the messengers bearing the message (*Alex.* 1.35). One recipient was even moved to kiss the letter of a lost love (Chariton, *Chaer.* 8.5). The Apostolic Decree achieves the desired results: **they rejoiced because of its encouragement!** (15:31).

The bearers of the letter also play an important role, invested as they are both in the decision and its outcome. Two of the couriers, Paul and Barnabas, are recommended to the Antiochenes as "men who have risked their lives for the name of our Lord Jesus Christ" (15:26). Along with them are Judas and Silas, who were instructed to "inform you orally of these same things (which we have written)" (15:27). In addition to fulfilling the instructions of the letter, their report was also in keeping with the expected role of courier (*P.Col.* 3.6; *P.Lond.* 42; 1 Macc 12:23; cf. Epp 1991, 46). Judas and Silas repeat and clarify the decision: **Judas and Silas, who were also prophets themselves, spoke for a long time and encouraged and strengthened the believers** (15:32). The Gentile mission has won a significant dispute, and equally important for Luke, the church has resolved another major conflict in an orderly and peaceable fashion. Church unity has been restored. Thus Judas and Silas **were sent off in peace by the believers (to return) to those who had sent them** (15:34), while **Paul and Barnabas remained in Antioch and, along with many others, taught and preached the message of the Lord** (15:35).

Transition: Paul and Barnabas Separate (15:36–41)

Acts 15:36–16:5 functions as a "bridge paragraph" with an A/a + b/B pattern, which facilitates transition from one subject (A) to another (B) (Longenecker 2005, 36). Here the transition is from the story of Barnabas (A), who plays a significant role in Acts up to this point (see comments on 4:35–36), but is not mentioned again after 15:36–41, to (a) the story of Timothy, who is first introduced in 16:1–5 and (b) continues to play a significant role in the subsequent narrative (B) (cf. 17:14–15; 18:5; 19:22; 20:4; Longenecker 2005, 227). The first unit of the bridge paragraph is framed by Paul's request to return to the site of previous missionary activity (15:36) and the narrator's report that this is exactly what Paul does (15:41).

Following the conference, **Paul said to Barnabas, "Let's go back and visit the believers in each and every city where we proclaimed the message of the Lord (to see) how they are"** (15:36). This plan does not materialize at first because of a dispute about whether John Mark should accompany them (on the historical issues involved in reconciling this account with Gal 2:11–14, see Wedderburn 2002, 291–310). The rest of the paragraph forms a chiasm (Johnson 1992, 282; Talbert 2005, 136):

A Barnabas's desire (15:37)
  B Paul's perception (15:38)
    C The split (15:39a)
  B′ Barnabas's action (15:39b)
A′ Paul's action (15:40)

Now, Barnabas wanted to take along John, who was called Mark, but Paul thought it best not to take someone who had deserted them in Pamphylia and not accompanied them in their work (15:37–38). Combined with other details earlier in the narrative, a close reading of Mark's final appearance here in Acts 15 is unflattering to John Mark (see Black 1993). The use of the harsh word "desert" or "abandon" (cf. Acts 5:37–38) in relation to the "work" (a reference to the Gentile mission; see comments on 13:2 and 14:26) clarifies the rather ambiguous terms used earlier of John Mark's actions (see 13:13). The phrase "someone who had deserted them" is forefronted for emphasis (Culy and Parsons 2003, 304) and is an example of *hyperbaton*, in which the expected word order is upset for emphasis or rhetorical flourish (*Rhet. Her.* 4.32.44).

This description also contributes to the finality of an overall negative portrait of John Mark. After the conversion of Sergius Paulus, Luke records that John Mark "left" and "returned to" Paul and his company (13:13b), a passage in which the verbs describing John's departure may be construed as having rather neutral connotations (see Luke 1:56; 9:39; Acts 1:12). In their wider usages, however, both words were employed in military contexts to speak of "withdrawal" after a defeat (Thucydides, *Hist.* 2.89) or "retreat" under fire (Homer, *Il.* 5.581; 12.71; Herodotus, *Hist.* 7.211; 9.14; Thucydides, *Hist.* 3.24). In fact, "return" in several places in Luke may reflect this usage (Luke 11:24;

23:48). John's implicit rejection of the Gentile mission in Acts 13:13 is made explicit here at 15:38. Other details support this conclusion.

First, note John Mark's close allegiance with Jerusalem (12:12, 25; 13:13b) and possibly the Jerusalemites who insist on circumcision for Gentile converts to Christianity (cf. 15:1). Second, Mark is not mentioned in the commissioning scene at Antioch, where Barnabas and Saul are set aside for the work (i.e., the Gentile mission) to which God has called them (13:1–3), but rather appears in the role of an assistant in their proclamation of the gospel in the synagogues of Salamis.

The conflict escalates to a critical point: **They had such a strong disagreement that they separated from each other (15:39a).** That **Barnabas took Mark and sailed for Cyprus (15:39)** may also be a muted criticism, because in a sense Barnabas is returning to his homeland of Cyprus (4:36), thus himself abandoning the "work," taking Mark with him (Luke is silent on the familial relationship between Barnabas and John Mark and the possible reconciliation between Paul and Barnabas; cf. 1 Cor 9:6; Col 4:10; Johnson 1992, 283). Paul, meanwhile, **chose Silas and departed (15:40).** He continues on his original plan to return to the sites of his previous missionary efforts, and he **traveled through Syria and Cilicia and strengthened the churches (15:41).** Thus with regard to the Gentile mission the conflict ultimately produces a positive result.

The Report Distributed (16:1–5)

Paul's choice of Timothy as a traveling companion (16:1–3) is understood best in light of his earlier choice of Silas as a traveling companion (15:40). Both deserve comment at this point. Silas, along with Judas, was one of the "leading men" of the Jerusalem church (15:22) who had been chosen to bear the Apostolic Decree to the Gentile churches. In Antioch, Silas had shown his mettle by saying much "to encourage and strengthen the believers" (15:32). In fact, Luke identifies him as a "prophet" (15:32). Rather than exclude the Jerusalem church from further participation in the mission because they were on the losing side of the debate, Paul chooses to include Silas in his apostolic company (15:40).

Timothy also represents the interests and concerns of the Jewish Christians. Some might have questioned the Jewish ethnicity of **the son of a believing Jewish woman and a Greek father (16:1),** since matrilineal descent can be firmly established only at a later date (see Cohen 1986, 251–68). The Lukan Paul, however, clearly viewed Timothy as a Jewish believer, a disciple who **was respected by the believers in (both) Lystra and Iconium (16:2).** Already a believer, Timothy's circumcision has nothing to do with the soteriological issue resolved at the Jerusalem Council; he is not circumcised to enter the world to come. Rather, his circumcision is an attempt on Paul's part to accommodate Jewish sensitivity and to ensure Timothy's acceptability among the Jews with whom he will work: **Paul wanted him to go with him, so he took him and had** him circumcised because of the Jews who were in that place (16:3; Johnson 1992, 284; Talbert 2005, 137). Silas and Timothy, therefore, embody Paul's commitment to Jewish sensitivities without sacrificing anything essential in the Gentile mission.

This unit refers again to the dissemination of the Apostolic Decree: **As they went through the towns, they passed on to them the rules that the apostles and elders in Jerusalem had decided on so that they could follow them (16:4).** It is significant that the "they" includes both a Jewish Christian member of one of these Diaspora churches and a Jewish Christian member of the Jerusalem congregation. As a result of such a strategy, the churches grew daily both qualitatively ("in the faith") and quantitatively ("in numbers"): **So the churches were strengthened in the faith and grew in number every day (16:5).**

Theological Issues

What is the relationship between the Jerusalem Council in Acts 15 and the decision reached regarding the Gentile mission reported by Paul in Gal 2? Scholars of Acts and of Paul have struggled with the difficult historical issues involved in this question. For example, Paul does not mention the prohibitions of the Apostolic Decree (Acts 15:22–29); Luke says nothing here of the collection for the poor (Gal 2:10). The role of James in Acts seems in conflict with his role in Galatians (for a list of the problems, see Witherington 1998, 441). These apparent discrepancies cannot and should not be quickly glossed over, and have led to various solutions, including identifying the meeting described in Gal 2 not with Acts 15, but the brief account mentioned in Acts 11:30; 12:25 (see Witherington 1998, 442; Bauckham 2005, 135–42). Still, "only the most intransigent skeptic would deny that behind the different and sometimes conflicting reports of Luke (Acts 15) and Paul (Gal 2) there was a real and significant series of events. The discrepancies in the two sources are of interest, after all, because of their general agreement. . . . By the standards of sane historiography, there is much more here that is certain than uncertain" (Johnson 1996, 73–74). Furthermore, the conclusion reached by the council, that circumcision is not required for Gentiles to enter "the world to come" through faith in Christ, was remarkably successful. "[T]here is virtually no evidence after this date [the Jerusalem conference] of Jewish Christians who thought Gentile Christians should be circumcised and obey the whole law of Moses" (Bauckham 2005, 139).

We would do well also, rather than to rehearse again the historical reconstructions regarding Galatians and Acts, to ponder the implications of the decision-making process described in Acts that led to this remarkable result. Acts 15 "is unique in the New Testament for the fullness of the attention it gives to the decision making process" (Johnson 1996, 68–69). Key to this process is the role of testimony (on the importance of testimony in philosophical and theological discussions, see Coady 1992). Peter gives testimony to the activity of God in his narrated experience (Acts 15:7–9). Likewise Barnabas and Paul bear witness to the "signs and wonders God had done through them among the Gentiles" (15:12). James corroborates Peter's testimony (15:14) and further introduces the testimony of scripture, which agrees with and further corroborates Peter's witness (15:15–18). Furthermore, testimony regarding the activity of God in the community's experience had already been introduced before the assembly gathered together. On their way to Jerusalem, Paul and Barnabas had been "relating the conversion of the Gentiles (as they went)" (15:3), underscoring a second important aspect of the narrative, namely that the decision was the result of a long process and series of earlier events and decisions.

The decision reached in Acts 15 is the "climax to a story beginning in Acts 10" (Johnson 1996, 89). In other words, the decision to include Gentiles in the covenant people of God without requiring their circumcision begins with the first decision (again based on the testimony of Peter, Cornelius, and the Holy Spirit) to baptize the Gentile Cornelius and his household (10:1–48). That decision is defended in a second series of events by Peter in Jerusalem (11:1–18), and finally opposed and resolved in the events leading to and including the Jerusalem Council (14:26–15:35; cf. Johnson 1996, 98–106). In other words, decision making is "a theological process—that is, an articulation of the church's faith in the living God"; that theological process is discernment (Johnson 1996, 109).

The process of discernment in decision making certainly involves bearing testimony to God's activity in our narrated experience, but it also and equally involves listening to the testimony of scripture and the experience of others. For example, Acts 15 regularly serves as a test case or model for contextualization or missiology (Kraft 1979; Hesselgrave and Rommen 1989; Wagenaar 2003). Along those lines, Justo González, writing from the perspective of the recipients rather than the initiators of missionary efforts, presents some remarkably insightful comments on Acts 15, certainly worth hearing in full:

> The Hispanic Church is a result of missionary adventures of the past. Some of them were more violent than others, and some more benevolent than others. But in all of them we learned to receive. We received missionaries. We received doctrines. We received ideas. We received money. In the midst of so much receiving, we are tempted to believe that we are somehow inferior: the important church is elsewhere, the place where the missionaries come from; the books worth reading are only those that come from over there; the models that we should imitate are the ones that have proven valuable in that other place. We, poor little folk, must forever be receiving.
>
> But no! The case of Paul, a Pharisee of Pharisees (23:6) and his contrast with these other Christians, equally Pharisees from Jerusalem, presents the matter

in a different way. The place where we are, at the apparent edge, is where God is doing new things. And those who daily see the new things that God is doing in the world have the obligation toward God and toward the rest of the Church to go back to the old centers, which often have lost much of their vision, taking to them our renewed vision of what God is doing today. (González 2001, 179–80)

Perhaps one of the greatest challenges to the church in the West in the twenty-first century is not so much in the undertaking of new missionary enterprises, but rather to prepare ourselves to receive with joy this testimony of the new things being done by God being brought to us from "the apparent edge."

Acts 16:6–17:15

Paul in Macedonia

🌀

Introductory Matters

With Silas and Timothy, his new traveling companions, Paul initiates his second missionary campaign, an "Aegean expedition" that "takes him further west to several major urban centers around the Aegean Sea" (Spencer 2004, 169). This second campaign follows a pattern familiar to the audience from Paul's first missionary expedition reported in Acts 13:1–16:5. During the outreach portion of his travels, Paul visits Philippi (16:11–40), Thessalonica (17:1–9), Berea (17:10–15), Athens (17:16–34), Corinth (18:1–17), and Ephesus (18:18–21). His "return" visits include Antioch (18:22), Galatia and Phrygia (18:23), and Ephesus (18:24–19:41). Of the episodes that receive more than passing reference (Philippi, Thessalonica, Berea, Athens, Corinth, and Ephesus), four—Philippi, Thessalonica, Corinth, and Ephesus (with slight variation)—follow a similar pattern of events, or type-scene, of "public accusation" (Tannehill 1990, 201–3; cf. Spencer 2004, 169–70). The pattern includes:

1. Christians are forcefully brought before officials or a public assembly (16:19; 17:5; 18:12; 19:29).
2. They are accused, and this accusation is highlighted by direct quotation (16:20–21; 17:6–7; 18:13; 19:25–27).
3. We are told the result of this attempt to curb the Christian mission (16:22–24; 17:8–9; 18:14–16; 19:29, 34–36).

In two of the scenes (Philippi and Ephesus), the accusers are Gentiles; in the other two (Thessalonica and Corinth), they are Jews (Tannehill 1990, 202–3). The Jewish response in Berea (17:10–14) and the Gentile response in Athens (17:15–34), while not altogether positive, stand in contrast to these heated, often violent, reactions.

Table 7.
Parallels between Paul's First
and Second Campaigns
(adapted from Talbert 2005, 138)

13:1–3	Divine inauguration	16:6–10
14:4–28	Outreach	16:11–18:21
15:1–35	To Jerusalem	18:22
15:36–16:5	Return	18:23–19:41

Tracing the Narrative Flow

In this section Paul brings the Christian message to a new region. The pattern of epiphany, resistance, incarceration, and release in 16:6–40 is similar to other "resistance myths" in antiquity, which are about the resistance mounted against the transfer and establishment of religious movements or "foreign gods" into a new region (Weaver 2004). Often connected to the Dionysian "resistance myths" (Euripides, *Bacchai*; Ovid, *Metamorphoses*), this pattern is certainly not limited to them (on the role of epiphany in the introduction of "foreign gods" in Greek and Roman regions, see Julian, *Or.* 5.159a; Plutarch, *Marc.* 17.9; Cicero, *Leg.* 2.37; Demosthenes, *Or.* 19.281). After his "Macedonian vision" in Troas (16:6–10), Paul travels to Philippi and converts Lydia and her household (16:11–15); he exorcises a slave girl, which leads to his arrest (16:16–23); he converts his jailer and his household, then confronts the local police and magistrates over their unlawful imprisonment (16:24–40). In each of these sections there are similarities and discontinuities with the overall cultural and rhetorical pattern of this resistance myth. This unit concludes with accounts of Paul's preaching activities in two other cities of Macedonia: Thessalonica (17:1–9) and Berea (17:10–15).

The Macedonian Vision (16:6–10)

Divine epiphanies are regularly reported to justify the establishment of a religious movement in a new region (Weaver 2004, 53–54; Dodson 2006, 47–52). This unit begins with an epiphany to Paul, commissioning him to evangelize Macedonia. The "commission" is in the form of a dream-vision narrative (16:6–10): scene-setting (16:6–8); dream-vision terminology (16:9a); dream-vision proper, which includes a commissioning/invitation for assistance (16:9b); and reaction/response, which can include a process of discerning the vision's meaning (16:10) (cf. Philostratus, *Vit. Apoll.* 4.34; Plutarch, *Luc.* 12.1; *Eum.* 6.4; discussed in Hanson 1980, 1400–1413; cf. Dodson 2006, 171).

An Outline of Acts 16:6–10

The Macedonian vision (16:6–10)

Scene-setting (16:6–8)

Dream-vision terminology (16:9a)

Dream-vision proper (16:9b)

Reaction/response (16:10)

16:6–8. Luke does not avoid reporting the limitations and failures of Paul's mission: **They went through the region of Phrygia and Galatia because the Holy Spirit prevented them from speaking the message in (the province of) Asia. When they had come as far as (the province of) Mysia, they tried to enter (the province of) Bithynia but the Spirit of Jesus would not allow them** (16:6–7). Luke twice reports that Paul was forbidden by the Spirit, first from speaking the word in Asia and then next from entering into Bithynia (Breytenbach 2004, 157–69). The floundering mission is finally given focus when **having arrived at Mysia they went down in Troas** (16:8; cf. Jewett 1997, 1–21; Jewett 2000, 74–90).

16:9a. **Paul saw a vision during the night** (16:9a). The term for "vision" here was part of the common vocabulary of ancient dream theory (Macrobius, *Comm. somn.* 3.9; cf. Acts 10:9). The night vision may describe a dream (Pilch 2004, 116), though no sharp distinctions were drawn in antiquity either in theory or practice between dreams and visions. Both were considered to be aspects of what could be labeled "altered states of consciousness" (Pilch 2004, 1–5).

16:9b. This dream-vision is an "audio-visual" event, having both the appearance of a figure and the figure's verbal message (Hanson 1980, 1412–13; for examples of such audio-visual dream-visions, see Chariton, *Chaer.* 2.9.6; Longus, *Daphn.* 2.23.1–24.2; 2.26.5–28.1; 3.27.2–28.1; 4.34.1–3). In this case, the vision is a plea in which **a Macedonian man was standing and calling him, saying, "Come over to Macedonia and help us!"** (16:9b). Luke establishes divine validation for the introduction of the Christian movement in Macedonia.

16:10. Paul describes the vision, but understanding its meaning is the result of group discernment (on first-person narration, see Theological Issues): **We immediately sought to go into Macedonia because we concluded that God had**

called us to preach the good news to them (16:10). Part of the discernment included the judgment that the vision was of divine origin. For Paul and his company, the divinely approved Aegean campaign has commenced.

Conversions and Imprisonments (16:11–40)

The audience is certainly not disappointed in the adventures of Paul here. Another household conversion story (16:11–15; cf. Acts 10–11), an exorcism (16:16–23), and the third rescue from prison (16:24–40) follow.

16:11–15. Paul and his companions pass quickly through Samothrace and Neapolis (16:11) to **Philippi, which is a main city in that district of Macedonia and a (Roman) colony (16:12).** The historical difficulties in labeling Philippi a "main city" hardly warrant the majority of the United Bible Society committee's replacing *prōtē* with the poorly attested reading *prōtēs* (rendering the reading "a city of the first district of Macedonia"; cf. Metzger 1994, 446). The nomenclature may be a remnant of "civic pride" (Ascough 1998, 93–103). At any rate, once in Philippi, true to their Jewish identity (*Jub.* 2.19–20) and in keeping with their typical missionary pattern (13:5, 14 *et passim*), Paul and the others went looking for the local worshiping community of Jews: **On the Sabbath day we went outside the city to a river where we thought there would be (a place for) prayer (16:13a).** While "place for prayer" could indicate a synagogue proper (Josephus, *Vita* 54.277, 280; Levinskaya 1996, 208–25), it seems unlikely to be what Luke had in mind since he typically uses the term "synagogue" to designate a structure (especially in the proximate context; cf. Acts 13:5; 17:1, 10, 17; 18:19). But it was not unreasonable to search for a Jewish community near water; Josephus observed that Jews "may make their places of prayer at the seaside, according to the customs of their fathers" (*Ant.* 14.10.23). What they do find is a gathering of worshiping women, presumably God-fearers (16:13).

An Outline of Acts 16:11–40

Conversions and imprisonments (16:11–40)

  The conversion of Lydia (16:11–15)

  Local witness and resistance (16:16–23)

  Imprisonment and release (16:24–40)

    1. The prison setting (16:24–25)

    2. The earthquake (16:26–27)

    3. Paul's intervention (16:28–34)

    4. The aftermath (16:35–40)

Chief among them is a **woman named Lydia, a dealer in purple cloth from the city of Thyatira, who worshiped God (16:14a).** Scarcely more is known than her name, her occupation, her place of origin, and something of her faith. Lydia was a native of Thyatira, a city in the province of Lydia. Hence, she is "Lydia of Lydia." On the basis (among other things) of the "symbolic richness" of her name, some have recently conjectured that Lydia is a fictional character (Matthews 2004, 131; MacDonald 2004, 109–10). This need not

229

be the case, however, as it was not uncommon for slaves and freedmen (and women) to take the name of their homeland. Strabo, for example, mentions "Lydus" as an appropriate name for a slave purchased in the region of Lydia (*Geogr.* 7.3.12).

If "Lydia of Lydia" were so called because she was formerly a slave and is now a freed woman, we might learn something more about her social status and economic level. Traditionally she has been grouped with those "leading women" who respond favorably to Paul's message in the ensuing episodes in Thessalonica (17:4) and Berea (17:12). Certainly this is one way to construe Lydia's occupation as a "dealer in purple cloth." She belonged by virtue of this trade to the category of "women of means" (Witherington 1998, 492).

It may be important, however, to distinguish between "purple-*wearers* and purple-*weavers*" (Spencer 2004, 148). Plutarch, for example, claimed: "often we take pleasure in a thing, but we despise the one who made it. Thus we value aromatic salves and purple clothing, but the dyers and salve-makers remain for us common and low craftspersons" (*Per.* 1.3–4). Lydia's location outside the city and near a river would support the inference that she was involved in both the production and the distribution of purple cloth. If so, the authorial audience would have understood her as a "common craftsperson," perhaps even despised, given the fact that dye works, like tanneries, not only required an abundant water supply but were considered dirty and smelly operations (Richter Reimer 1995, 107). Nonetheless, she is successful enough to be a householder (16:15). Perhaps, then, it is best to locate her somewhere between those who view her as among the urban elites (Gill 1994, 115–17), on the one hand, and those who count her among the "poorest of the poor," on the other (Schottroff 1993, 131–37). She appears, rather, to belong to that category of persons in Acts "of low status but (relatively) high income" (Matthews 2004, 126), such as the Ethiopian eunuch and, more notably, Simon the tanner (see comments on 9:43; Spencer 2004, 149).

Whatever her specific social standing, Lydia of Thyatira holds the prominent place in Luke's narrative of being the first Christian convert in this new region of Macedonia: **the Lord opened her heart so that she paid close attention to what Paul was saying** (16:14b). Once again, there is emphasis on the divine nature of the conversion, thus validating the movement.

But she is not alone in her conversion. **She and her household** (16:15) were baptized. This is the second of four household conversion stories in Acts (see Acts 10–11; 16:11–15, 25–34; 18:8). Each conforms to the pattern of the household mission established in the Third Gospel in the mission of the Seventy(-Two) in Luke 10:5–7 (see Matson 1996). There Jesus instructs his disciples (1) to enter the house (10:5a); (2) deliver the salvific message to the household (10:5b–6); and (3) remain in the house (10:7). The story of Lydia contains two of the elements; only the first is suppressed, perhaps because of the irregular circumstances of meeting at the "place of prayer" by the river

(Matson 1996, 145–46). The break in the pattern also allows the story to end on a note of hospitality: she [Lydia] **invited us (to her home). She said, "If you have concluded that I am faithful to the Lord, come and stay in my house." And she persuaded us** (16:15). Thus she adopts the role of a gracious Christian hostess and patroness (see Rom 12:13; Heb 13:2; 3 John 5–8) in opening her home to and sharing her possessions with Paul and his company. At the end of the next episode, they will visit with Lydia once again (16:40).

16:16–23. During their time with Lydia, Paul and his companions encountered a slave girl whose fortune-telling was very lucrative for her owners, and from whom they eventually exorcise a spirit (on this and other "slave girl" stories in Luke 22:56 and Acts 12:13–15, see Spencer 1999, 133–55): **Now as we were going to (the place of) prayer, a slave girl met us who was possessed by a "Python spirit." She made a lot of money for her owners by telling fortunes** (16:16).

The reference to a "Python" (or "Pythian") spirit evokes for the audience cultural associations with the oracle at Delphi (Strabo, *Geogr.* 9.3.12; Pausanias, *Descr.* 2.7.7). That oracle was often associated with the introduction of a new cult (especial Dionysus cults) to a city (Weaver 2004, 235). Pausanias connects Delphic oracular pronouncements with the founding of Dionysus cults at Athens (1.2.5), Corinth (2.27), Sicyon (2.7.6), Sparta, and Patrae (7.19.6–10), among other places.

The slave girl's pronouncement is ambiguous (Kauppi 2006, 33–37). Elements of her proclamation might be interpreted as having veiled polytheistic overtones (Witherington 1998, 494–95). However, ancient oracles, especially those of the Delphic Pythian, were notoriously ambiguous (Herodotus, *Hist.* 1.53; Aeschylus, *Prom.* 661–662; Plutarch, *Garr.* 17; Pausanias, *Descr.* 8.11.10–12; cf. Weaver 2004, 250), and this fact should not completely efface the generally positive nature of her pronouncement: **She followed Paul and (the rest of) us, shouting, "These men are servants of the Most High God, who are proclaiming to you the way of salvation!"** (16:17). Thus the appearance in Acts 16 of a "Python spirit" to validate the introduction of the Christian movement into the Roman colony of Philippi meets the cultural and rhetorical conventions expected of a religious movement at the point of its transfer to a new region. Such external validation was necessary to counter the resistance to the movement on the part of the inhabitants of the new region.

So why does Paul exorcise the spirit? Nowhere in this story is the "Python spirit" labeled unclean or evil or demonic. This fact sets the scene apart from other exorcism stories to which this one has been compared, especially Luke 8:26–39 (see Hintermaier 2000, 152–75, esp. 155; Klutz 2004, 228–36). Here her incessant mantic activity, not the misleading nature of her message, so annoys Paul that he exorcises the spirit to get a little peace and quiet. **The Pythia went on doing this for many days. (Finally) Paul became really annoyed and turned around and said to the spirit, "I command you in the name of Jesus Christ to** come out of her!" And it came out of her at that very moment (16:18). The exorcism also demonstrates the power of Paul's God over the Pythian spirit, which has recognized the "Most High God."

The exorcism creates its own economic crisis. With the departure of the Spirit went also the fortune of the slave girl's owners: **Now, when her masters saw that their hope of making money was gone, they grabbed Paul and Silas and dragged them before the authorities in the public square** (16:19). Whatever the reason for the exorcism, clearly it demonstrates the lack of concern on the part of Paul and company for the monetary value of the slave girl's divining power. This lack of interest stands in sharp contrast to the "real" motives of the slave owners, disclosed here to the audience: "their hope of making money was gone." It also stands in contrast to "one of the most widespread stereotypes of new religious movements in the ancient world: their desire for money" (Weaver 2004, 259). The exploitation of the rich by new religious movements was widely reported (and parodied) in antiquity (see Apuleius, *Metam.* 8.24–30; Josephus, *Ant.* 18.82–83; Juvenal, *Sat.* 6). Thus the slave owners' desire for financial gain indirectly absolves Paul and Silas, who show no interest in using their religion to seek financial gain (Weaver 2004, 259).

The owners then drag Paul and Silas into the marketplace before the authorities and hide their rage at economic loss behind weightier political charges: **After bringing them before the magistrates, they said, "These men, who are Jews, are stirring up trouble in our city and are advocating customs that are unlawful for us either to accept or to practice, since we are Romans"** (16:20–21). While the accusations against Paul and his company are specifically about their being Jews, these charges amount to accusing Paul and his company of introducing foreign customs (whether Jewish or otherwise) in the Roman world, a stock charge in the ancient polemic against migratory religious movements (cf. Tacitus, *Ann.* 2.85; Suetonius, *Tib.* 36.1; Seneca, *Ep.* 108.22; Dio Cassius, *Hist. Rom.* 53.2; Livy, *Hist.* 39.16.8–9). "The charges against Paul and Silas in Acts 16 are understandable as conventional slurs against new or foreign cults, which could be invoked at any time, regardless of the basis for the charges" (Weaver 2004, 232).

Both the crowds and the magistrates join in the hostilities against the Christian missionaries: **The crowd joined the attack against them, and after the magistrates had caused the clothes to be torn off them they gave orders to beat them** (16:22). The resistance motif reaches its violent nadir. Far from normal Roman procedure (contra Rapske 1994, 121–29), the scene here is one of hostility out of control. As in other tales of resistance to the foundation of a new religious movement, the local authorities publicly shame the Christian missionaries by having their clothes ripped off (on the opposition of local authorities to the transfer of a religious movement, see Tacitus, *Hist.* 4.84; Ovid, *Metam.* 15.645). The violence escalates as orders to have them beaten are followed with gusto: **After severely beating them they threw them into** prison and ordered the jailer to carefully guard them (16:23). The actions of the Philippian opponents are not only violent, they are illegal.

16:24–40. Acts 16:24–40 is the third of three prison release episodes in Acts (cf. chaps. 5, 12). All three contain a miraculous release from prison; in all three, jailers play an important role (to varying degrees), and, perhaps most importantly, in all three the release is not only *from* prison but *for* proclamation (Weaver 2004, 265). Nonetheless, the divergences from the pattern are significant in Acts 16. The prison episode divides into four parts: (1) the prison setting (16:24–25); (2) the earthquake and its effects on the jailer (16:26–27); (3) Paul's loud shout and his effect on the jailer (16:28–34); and (4) the aftermath of the earthquake (16:35–40).

1. Acts 16:24–25 gives the setting. The jailer complied with the magistrates' orders and took **them into the inner part of the prison and fastened their feet in stocks** (16:24). While in prison, Paul and Silas broke out into a midnight hymn sing! **Now at midnight Paul and Silas were praying and singing hymns to God and the other prisoners were listening to them** (16:25). Such prison praises were commended in pagan (Epictetus, *Diatr.* 2.6.26–27), Jewish (*T. Jos.* 8.5), and Christian texts (*Martyrdom of Pionius* 18.12; Talbert 2005, 146).

2. The earthquake and its effects occupy 16:26–27. Unlike Acts 5 and 12, in which an angel is responsible for the prison release, here in Acts 16 an earthquake is responsible for the liberation (on the [non]influence of the *Bacchae* on Acts, see Weinreich 1929, 169–464, and Vögeli 1953, 415–38): **Suddenly, there was an earthquake that was so strong that it shook the foundations of the prison. Right away, all of the doors opened and the chains of all (the prisoners) came loose** (16:26). It would be a mistake, however, to draw the conclusion that the first two prison releases were "miraculous," while the third was a "natural" phenomenon; all three are the result of divine activity. Earthquakes were associated with theophanies (1 Kgs 19:11–12; Ps 18:7–9; Mic 1:4; for other texts, cf. Horst 1989, 44–45), and Luke is familiar with this convention (Acts 4:31). When the jailer awakens to discover the prison doors opened, he draws his sword to take his own life before the local authorities can (16:27; cf. 12:18–19).

Given the prisoners' presumed escape, the jailer thought it best to take his own life before the local authorities could (cf. 11:18–19), despite the fact that Justinian made allowances for such prison escapes that were effected by "acts of God" (Justinian, *Dig.* 12.48.3; cf. Haenchen 1971, 497). In any case, Luke's focus of attention on the jailer (and his household) will continue to the end of the episode.

3. In 16:28–34, Paul's loud shouting has a dramatic effect. Another departure from most ancient prison escape scenes is that the prisoners do not, in fact, seek to escape. Rather, **Paul shouted loudly, "Don't harm yourself! We're all here!"** (16:28). Speaking in a loud voice was also a typical feature of divine epiphany (for texts, cf. comments on 14:10; Strelan 2000, 488–503; Weaver 2004, 267). Paul's "loud voice" (*megalē phōnē*) recalls and parallels

233

the "great earthquake" (*seismos megas*). The jailer, first made despondent by the earthquake, is now motivated by fear by Paul's utterance. **After asking for lights, he rushed in and fell down before Paul and Silas trembling (16:29).** The fear is followed by an inquiry of faith: **Then he took them outside and said, "Sirs, what must I do to be saved?" (16:30).**

Paul and Silas respond with the kerygma in a nutshell: **"Believe in the Lord Jesus and you will be saved—you and your household." Then they told him, along with all those in his household, the message of the Lord (16:31–32).** What follows then is a recounting of the third household conversion scene in Acts (see above on 16:11–15; Matson 1996, 254–68; for verbal parallels between the two scenes, see Hintermaier 2003, 258–61): **(The jailer) took them, at that very hour of the night, and cleaned their wounds. Then he and his whole family were immediately baptized. (After that) he brought them into (his) house and fed them; and he was full of joy because he, with his entire household, had come to believe in God (16:33–34).** Both parties receive cleansing waters, one for wounds, the other for baptism, and the jailer sets food before them. Like Lydia, the jailer demonstrates the authenticity of his faith by acting as the proper host. Most importantly, with this focus on the conversion of the jailer and his household, "the prison epiphany propagates the Christian cult by catalyzing the cult's further expansion into the social structures of the Macedonian *polis*" (Weaver 2004, 274). Furthermore, by gaining ground via the household the Christian movement poses a challenge not only to the temple cult (see Elliott 1991, 211–40) but also to the Roman Empire, which regarded itself as a household with the emperor as *paterfamilias* (Green 2002, 37) and for which the household functioned as "the seed-bed of the state" (Cicero, *Off.* 1.53–55).

4. The aftermath is described in 16:35–40. In the morning, **the magistrates sent (a message to the jailer with some) police officers, saying, "Release those**

Jailers in Antiquity

The reactions of Paul and the jailer are remarkable, especially given the widespread reputation for cruelty on the part of those who guarded prisoners. For example, Philo wrote:

"Everyone knows well how jailors are filled with inhumanity and savagery. For by nature they are unmerciful, and by practice they are trained daily toward fierceness, as to become wild beasts. They see, say, and do nothing good, not even by chance, but instead the most violent and the most cruel things. . . . Jailers, therefore, spend time with robbers, thieves, burglars, the wanton, the violent, corrupters, murderers, adulterers, and the sacrilegious. From each of these they draw and collect depravity, producing from that diverse blend a single mixture of thoroughly abominable evil." (Ios. 81, 84, trans. Skinner 2003, 82–83)

men" (16:35). While the reason for the release is unstated in the text, Codex D makes it explicit; the magistrates were "fearful because they recalled the earthquake that had occurred." After receiving the message from the magistrates' officers, Paul replied, **They beat us publicly without a trial, even though we are Roman citizens, and threw us into prison** (16:37a). This disclosure of citizenship comes too late in the story to offer protection, but it does set the stage for later encounters with political authorities when Paul's Roman citizenship becomes important again (22:25). Paul continues: **And now they want to send us away secretly? Certainly not! They themselves must come and let us out!** (16:37b). The aftershock of the "epiphanic earthquake" extends to the local magistrates who, though falling short of repentance, do nonetheless apologize to Paul and Silas for what amounts to illegal action on their part (16:38b–39). The local authorities' resistance to the transfer of the Christian cult into Macedonia is overcome by divine epiphany and timely rhetoric; the leaders meekly accept the validity of the Christian messengers and their God. Before departing as requested, Paul visits Lydia, and **when they saw the believers (there) they encouraged them and left** (16:40). With the Christian community firmly established in the households of Lydia and the jailer, Paul and company depart for their next destination.

Mission in Thessalonica and Berea (17:1–15)

In the first half of Acts 17, Paul continues his Macedonian ministry. This section (17:1–15) is comprised of two units: (1) the mission in Thessalonica (17:1–9) and (2) the mission in Berea (17:10–15). Both are compressed and "stylized summaries" similar in pattern to Acts 14:1–7 (see Talbert 2005, 147).

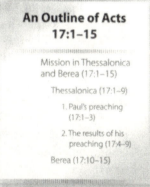

An Outline of Acts 17:1–15

Mission in Thessalonica and Berea (17:1–15)

Thessalonica (17:1–9)

1. Paul's preaching (17:1–3)

2. The results of his preaching (17:4–9)

Berea (17:10–15)

17:1–9. The first unit subdivides into two scenes: (1) Paul preaching in the Thessalonian synagogue (17:1–3); and (2) the ensuing results (17:4–9).

1. Passing through **Amphipolis** and **Apollonia**, Paul and Silas make their first stop in Thessalonica (17:1). According to Livy (*Hist.* 45.29), Amphipolis was the capital city of the first district of Macedonia, and Apollonia lay farther inland (45.28); both lay along the Egnatian Way. In Thessalonica, there was a **Jewish synagogue** (17:1; on Jewish presence in Thessalonica, see Malherbe 1987, 6; Levinskaya 1996, 154–57). **As was Paul's custom, he went in (to the synagogue) with them and had a discussion with them about the scriptures on three Sabbath days** (17:2). Thus he has not yet abandoned the Jewish mission. Given that these discussions occurred during a period of three Sabbaths, Luke summarizes Paul's argument rather than giving it in direct discourse. The argument is

introduced by noting that Paul **explained** (literally, "opened"; cf. Luke 24:31) **(the scriptures) and tried to demonstrate (to them)** (17:3). The term "demonstrate" was often used to indicate persuasion by the marshaling of rhetorical proofs (Lucian, *Rhet. praec.* 9; Josephus, *Vita* 6; Dio Chrysostom, *Or.* 17.10; Johnson 1992, 305).

These terms signal that Paul's argument is in the form of Hellenistic rhetoric. The specific form of rhetoric employed is the enthymeme, a proof in which one of the premises is omitted or suppressed (Kurz 1980, 179–80). Theon's *Progymnasmata* demonstrates that the enthymeme was common in Hellenistic school exercises and was understood to be an argument with one premise missing or truncated (contra Aune 2003). Theon gives this example of a *chreia* in the form of an enthymeme: "When his acquaintance Apollodorus said to him, 'The Athenians have unjustly condemned you to death,' Socrates broke into a laugh and said, 'Were you wanting them to do so justly?' We need to add a proposition that it is better to be condemned unjustly than justly, which seems to have been omitted in the chreia but is potentially clear" (Theon, *Prog.* 99–100, trans. Kennedy 2003, 18). In Acts 17, Paul argues **that it was necessary for the Christ to suffer and to rise from the dead. (He told them,) "This Jesus, whom I am proclaiming to you, is the Christ"** (17:3). The major premise, "it was necessary for the Christ to suffer and rise from the dead," leads to the conclusion that "this Jesus . . . is the Christ." The authorial audience can readily fill in the missing or truncated minor premise—namely, that Jesus did, in fact, suffer and rise again—from the reference to Jesus, "whom I am proclaiming to you," which echoes the cross-resurrection kerygma explicated more fully elsewhere in Acts (cf., e.g., 13:28–31). While the form is Hellenistic, the content of the message is thoroughly Jewish (Juel 1988), reminiscent of earlier statements by the Lukan Jesus (Luke 24:26, 46) and Peter (Acts 3:18).

2. Rhetoric is intended to persuade, and the result of Paul's "proofs" was that **some of them . . . were persuaded and joined Paul and Silas** (17:4a). The converts included presumably some of the Jews in the synagogue but also **a large group of pious Greeks and many prominent women** (17:4b). Though Luke has consistently given attention to the role of women in the Christian community (e.g., 1:14; 5:14; 8:12), they receive even greater attention in chapters 16–18 (cf. 16:13–14, 16; 17:4, 12, 34; 18:2, 18, 26). The notice of leading women in the Macedonian churches is "very much in keeping with inscriptional evidence that in Macedonia women had considerable social and civic influence" (Polhill 1992, 361). Even more important for the role of women in these churches, no doubt, was the gospel of freedom and radical inclusion that Paul preached.

A familiar pattern emerges in Acts 17:5: **The Jews became jealous, gathered some worthless bums (from the marketplace), formed a mob, and started a riot in the city.** When their searching fails to turn up Paul, they settle for Jason and some other believers: **Then they showed up at Jason's house and were** trying to find (Paul and Silas) and drag them before the assembly of citizens. But when they did not find them (there) they dragged Jason and some other believers before the city officials, shouting, "These men who have caused trouble throughout the world have now come here!" (17:5b–6). The compressed style of the narrative here precludes gleaning much detail regarding this Jason, but evidence from later in Acts (18:1–3) and inscriptional evidence related to Thessalonica (see Ascough 1997, Appendix 1; 2000) suggests that Jason was a Gentile and a fellow artisan of Paul's (Malherbe 1987, 14), making the reference to "worthless bums" (e.g., lower-class artisans) not a little ironic.

Knowing that religious differences will matter little to the city authorities (cf. Acts 18:14–15), the opponents hurl political charges again (see 16:21), claiming that the Christians "have caused trouble throughout the world" and that all of them are violating the decrees of Caesar by saying there is another king, (called) Jesus (17:7). The specific referent of the "decrees of Caesar" has eluded interpreters (though see Judge 1971). That the Thessalonian officials would have been particularly sensitive to disruptive political dissent seems clear not only from the recently issued expulsion of Jews from Rome "because of a certain Chrestus [Christus?]" in AD 48/49 (Suetonius, *Claud.* 25.2; cf. Acts 18:2), but also from what the authorial audience may have known of the imperial cult in Thessalonica and the rhetoric of Paul's Thessalonian correspondence. Numismatic evidence from Thessalonica demonstrates that, beginning about 27 BC, the Thessalonians replaced the head of Zeus with that of Augustus on their coins and acclaimed Caesar as a god, seeking to curry the favor of the Roman emperor (Hendrix 1984, 173, 253).

Although only the barest of summaries of Paul's argument are available in Acts, his first letter to the Thessalonians bears clear anti-imperial rhetoric that would substantiate the political charges against them (Donfried 1985, 344–52). The early principate program of "peace and security" (*pax et securitas*) seems under direct attack in 1 Thess 5:3: "When they say, 'There is peace and security,' then sudden destruction will come upon them, as labor pains come upon a pregnant woman, and there will be no escape!" Furthermore, as has been frequently noted, the language of the preceding verses also contains loaded political language (Donfried 1985, 344): *parousia* ("coming"; 1 Thess 4:15) and *apantēsis* ("meet"; 1 Thess 4:17), which both relate to the "visit of" or "meeting with" a military or political dignitary; and *kyrios* (4:16) with its associations to the emperor cult. Thus Paul, in his letter, challenges the cozy relationship between the Thessalonians (including evidently some in his congregation) and the imperial cult; ultimately only God in Christ can provide the "peace and security" for which they yearn. If the authorial audience knows this argument from 1 Thessalonians, then they will not be surprised to see the charge of "preaching another king, Jesus," brought against Paul and his associates (Donfried 1985). The officials are disturbed, but choose only to fine Jason and the others before releasing them (17:8–9).

17:10–15. Meanwhile Paul and Silas are carried off to Berea (17:10–15). Again the scene is compressed and stylized in the pattern in which initial success in the synagogue is repeated (17:10–12), followed by persecution of the leaders (17:13–15). The believers immediately sent Paul and Barnabas away to Berea during the night. When they arrived they went to the Jewish synagogue (17:10). But Luke reports that the people there were more willing to learn than those in Thessalonica. They were extremely eager to receive the message and each day would carefully examine the scriptures (to determine) whether the things (the apostles were saying) were true (17:11). Whereas only "some" Jews believed in Thessalonica, Luke reports that in Berea many of them believed—in particular, quite a few respected Greek women and men (17:12; litotes, literally "not a few respected"; see Acts 1:5).

Although the Berean Jews were receptive, the Thessalonian Jews were equally persistent; thus the opposition that comes is "external" to Berea: When the Jews from Thessalonica learned that Paul had also proclaimed God's message in Berea, they went there too to stir up the crowds (17:13; cf. 14:19–20). The Berean Christians respond quickly: Without delay the believers sent Paul away to the seacoast, and both Silas and Timothy remained there. Those who escorted Paul took him as far as Athens (17:14–15a). After these believers receive a command for Silas and Timothy to come to Paul as quickly as possible, they left (17:15b). Paul has arrived at the cultural center of the Roman world, the ancient city of Athens.

Theological Issues

Within this larger unit, 16:6–17:15, we encounter the first of the so-called "we" passages (16:10–17), in which the narrator participates in the events (cf. also 20:5–15; 21:1–18; 27:1–29; 28:1–16). The approaches to the phenomenon have been well rehearsed elsewhere. Stanley Porter has provided a convenient summary of proposed solutions:

> To summarize, the four major proposals are: (1) they indicate the author's personal presence as an eyewitness (this is the traditional solution); (2) they reflect a diary or literary source, perhaps from the author but more likely from another writer (this is the source-critical solution); (3) they are some form of redacted document, reflecting the author's imaginative editorial manipulation (this is the redaction-critical solution); (4) they are a literary creation, reflecting the author's creation of a larger fictive narrative work patterned after contemporary literature, or his use of a literary convention for telling of sea voyages in the first-person plural (this is the so-called literary solution). (Porter 1999, 10; cf. Praeder 1987, 193–218; Hemer 1989, 308–34)

From a compositional point of view, the problem has proven intractable and unsolvable (Talbert 2005, 140; Johnson 1992, 297). But what is the rhetorical function of such eyewitness testimony, whatever its source? Again modern suggestions are numerous. The "we" passages create a sense of "intimacy" (Pervo 1990, 56), or "urgency" (Gaventa 2003, 230), or "legitimacy" (Spencer 2004, 172–73).

From the ancients' point of view, this kind of eyewitness testimony, *autopsia*, was an indispensable ingredient to gaining information about the past, even preferable to written sources and oral tradition (see Polybius, *Hist.* 12.25d.1; Quintilian, *Inst.* 10.1.34). In the "we" passages, Luke combines references to all three—written sources (primarily the OT, but also letters), oral tradition (possibly including speeches), and eyewitness testimony—to "make the writing persuasive by providing it with a forceful diachronic rhetoric" (Byrskog 2003, 280). The use of details and local color in these passages add to the story's realism. That Luke was successful in using the "we" passages to give authority to his narrative is seen from one of the earliest recorded references to these passages by Irenaeus, who was clearly impressed by Luke's details and local color (on these details, see Hemer 1989, 329–34):

> But that this Luke was inseparable from Paul, and his fellow-labourer in the Gospel, he himself clearly evinces, not as a matter of boasting, but as bound to do so by the truth itself. For he says that when Barnabas, and John who was called Mark, had parted company from Paul, and sailed to Cyprus, "we came to Troas;" and when Paul had beheld in a dream a man of Macedonia, saying, "Come into Macedonia, Paul, and help us," "immediately," he says, "we endeavoured to go into Macedonia, understanding that the Lord had called us to preach the Gospel unto them. Therefore, sailing from Troas, we directed our ship's course towards Samothracia." And then he carefully indicates all the rest of their journey as far as Philippi, and how they delivered their first address: "for, sitting down," he says, "we spake unto the women who had assembled;" and certain believed, even a great many. And again does he say, "But we sailed from Philippi after the days of unleavened bread, and came to Troas, where we abode seven days." And all the remaining [details] of his course with Paul he recounts, indicating with all diligence both places, and cities, and number of days, until they went up to Jerusalem; and what befell Paul there, how he was sent to Rome in bonds; the name of the centurion who took him in charge; and the signs of the ships, and how they made shipwreck; and the island upon which they escaped, and how they received kindness there, Paul healing the chief man of that island; and how they sailed from thence to Puteoli, and from that arrived at Rome; and for what period they sojourned at Rome. As Luke was present at all these occurrences, he carefully noted them down in writing, so that he cannot be convicted of falsehood or boastfulness, because all these [particulars] proved both that he was senior to all those who now teach otherwise, and that he was not ignorant of the truth. (*Haer.* 3.14.1, trans. *ANF*)

Thus from a rhetorical viewpoint we recognize the overall function of the "we" passages as providing additional authority to the story, while acknowledging that, from a compositional perspective, the source of this authority is now inaccessible to us. By employing such a strategy Luke would have been open to sharp criticism should he have been unable to validate the eyewitness testimony if called upon to do so. But that Luke's authorial audience would have heard the "we" passages in just this way is equally clear:

> From the beginning, this [Luke's participation in the events of the narrative] is the only way in which readers . . . could have understood the "we" passages. "We" therefore appears in travel accounts because Luke simply wanted to indicate he was there. However, his personal experiences are uninteresting. Paul remains the focal point. (Hengel 1979, 66)

Acts 17:16–18:17

Paul in Achaia

⊟

Introductory Matters

This episode takes place in the region of Achaia, specifically in the cities of Athens (17:16–34) and Corinth (18:1–17). Earlier (Acts 14:15–17), Paul had addressed the naive Gentile "rural rustics" of Lycaonia; in Athens, Paul speaks to the sophisticated and sceptical inhabitants of an advanced civilization of a coastal city (see Strabo, *Geogr.* 13.1.25; Béchard 2000, 381). Paul next spends an extended period of time in Corinth. Both cities were well known in the ancient world. Though it had faded from its period of prominence (fourth–fifth century BC), Athens was still highly regarded as the cultural and intellectual center of the Roman Empire (Cicero, *Flac.* 26.62), and Corinth had emerged as the largest, most cosmopolitan city in Greece. Thus in Achaia Paul continues his pattern of evangelizing in significant urban centers.

> **Acts 17:16–18:17 in the Narrative Flow**
>
> The people and places of the Jerusalem church (1–12)
>
> **The missionary activities of Paul (13–28)**
>
> Paul's mission to the Gentile world (13–19)
>
> Paul's initial missionary campaign (13–14)
>
> The Jerusalem conference (15:1–16:5)
>
> Paul in Macedonia (16:6–17:15)
>
> ▶ Paul in Achaia (17:16–18:17)
>
> Paul in Athens (17:16–34)
>
> Paul in Corinth (18:1–17)

Figure 8. The Parthenon.
The Parthenon was the widely recognized symbol of Athens, still a major cultural center in the first century AD.

Tracing the Narrative Flow

Paul in Athens (17:16–34)

The scene in Athens (17:16–34) divides into three parts: the setting leading up to the sermon is described in some detail (17:16–21); the sermon itself is the centerpiece of the time in Athens (17:22–31); and the scene ends with a report of the responses to Paul's message (17:32–34).

17:16–21. While waiting for Silas and Timothy to join him, Paul has the opportunity to see the city of Athens (cf. 1 Thess 3:1): **While Paul was waiting for them in Athens he became very troubled when he saw that the city was full of idols** (17:16). Athens was well known in antiquity to have an abundance of cult statues (cf. Livy, *Hist.* 45.27). Luke's picture of Paul's "sightseeing" among the cult statues in an urban center was a motif familiar to his audience (Moxnes 1995, 123) and the subject of ancient guide literature, the most famous of which was Pausanias's *Description of Greece* (second century AD). Paul's response to these statues, however, is that of a sectarian minority. Rather than being impressed by its magnificent art and architecture, Paul is "troubled" to see the city full of "idols"; both terms reflect a negative "Jewish judgment on Greek piety" (Johnson 1992, 312; cf. Philo, *Decal.* 66; Josephus, *C. Ap.* 2.34.239–241; 1 Cor 10:20). Paul will tone down his reaction when addressing the Athenians for the purpose of engaging them in an intellectual discussion (17:23; see Moxnes 1995, 123).

Paul follows the normal pattern in Acts of conversing with the Jews in the synagogue (see 13:5, 14, 43; 14:1; 17:1, 10, 17), but there is no report of opposition from the Athenian Jews or their sympathizers (Fitzmyer 1998, 604). Luke goes on to say that Paul engaged in debate also in the marketplace each and every day with whomever happened to be there (17:17b), especially Epicurean and Stoic philosophers: Some of the Epicureans and Stoic philosophers debated with him (17:18a). The Epicureans and Stoics represented two of the leading philosophical schools of the day (see Zeller 1962; Long 1986; Brunschwig 1995): the Epicureans were committed to an ethical system that tolerated the existence of gods but gave them no vital role (see Diogenes Laertius, *Epicurus* 10.1–21); the Stoics were pantheists who held a more dynamic view of the gods, believing that the divine "spark" was present in all of creation (Diogenes Laertius, *Zeno* 7.1–160). Paul will allude several times in his speech to certain views of these philosophers.

Paul's debate elicits two kinds of responses. The first is derogatory: some were saying, "What is this foolish babbler trying to say?" (17:18b). Referring to Paul as a "babbler" (*spermologos*, lit. "seed picker") was obviously a term of ridicule, referring to those who acquire "bits and pieces of relatively extraneous information" (L&N §27.19) and pass it off as their own (Barrett 1998, 2:930). Dio Chrysostom criticizes the Cynics who "gather at street-corners and in alley-ways and at temple gates and con youngsters and sailors and crowds made up of that sort, stringing together rough jokes and much babbling [*spermologian*] and that rubbish of the marketplace" (*Alex.* 9; Lucian, *Peregr.* 3–4; Horace, *Sat.* 2.3; Epictetus, *Diatr.* 3.22.26–30; Apuleius, *Metam.* 8.24; 11.8; Talbert 2005, 151).

The second response is more positive: Others (said), "He seems to be a herald of foreign deities." (They said this) because he was preaching about Jesus and the resurrection (17:18c). Athens was well known in antiquity for "promoting new cults throughout the Greek world" and giving "them a prominence which greatly facilitated their subsequent elevation to the rank of Panhellenic deities" (Garland 1992, 8). Evidently, the Athenians heard Paul introducing "new gods": Jesus (which in Greek is grammatically masculine) and his consort, "Anastasia" ("resurrection," which in Greek is grammatically feminine), an understanding that extends back at least to John Chrysostom, *Hom. Act.* 38.1).

The Athenians took Paul to the Areopagus to present his new ideas: Then they grabbed him and brought him to the Areopagus, saying, "We would like to know, what is this new teaching that you have been talking about? For you are bringing some strange things to our ears, and we want to know what these things mean" (17:19–20). There is some debate whether Luke means that Paul

Figure 9. Mars Hill.

This marble outcropping located between the Acropolis and the Agora (marketplace) is the traditional site of Paul's address to the council of Athens. It was the seat of the criminal court of Athens.

was taken to a hill located beneath the Acropolis and above the Agora called the Areopagus (see, e.g., 17:22 KJV, "Mars' hill") or whether he had in mind the court that was known by that name (for the modern reader, an analogy is Wall Street, which may refer to the place or the stock exchange named after the street). If, in fact, the Athenians think Paul is introducing "new gods" for the purpose of securing them a place in the Athenian Pantheon (Winter 1996, 83), then the reference is most probably to the council and not the place, since the council of the Areopagus (along with the *Demos*) was the governmental body responsible for adding any new deities to the pantheon of gods (see *SIG*[3] 814, lines 29–30, 44–51 [28th Nov., AD 67]; Winter 1996, 76). For this reason, Bruce Winter suggests translating the last statement as a courteous request to the herald, a person of standing, bringing the request for official recognition of the deities, "We therefore wish to make a judgment on what is being claimed (or decreed) these things are" (1996, 83).

The setting ends with a description of the Athenians' "curiosity": **Now, all the Athenians and the foreigners living among them spent their time in nothing other than (trying) either to say or to hear something novel (17:21).** This interest, certainly true of ancient Athens (Demosthenes, 4 *Philip.* 10; Aristophanes, *Eq.* 1260–1263; Thucydides, *Hist.* 3.38.4–7), was generally characteristic of urban culture in coastal cities, which, according to Strabo, were marked by an

Paul and Socrates

Parallels have long been noted between Paul's experience and the trial of Socrates (Plato, *Apol.*; see, e.g., Gärtner 1955, 52–65; Sandnes 1993, 13–26). The accusation that Socrates had "introduced" other "new gods" (Plato, *Apol.* 24B) may be echoed in the description of Paul introducing a "new teaching" (17:19), which had earlier been identified as "foreign deities" (17:18). Paul, of course, here escapes the fate of Socrates, and one does not have to posit a formal trial before the Areopagus to acknowledge the parallels with Socrates's trial.

"openness" to "new things" in terms of language, social and political customs, modes of life, and dwelling places (*Geogr.* 13.1.25; Béchard 2000, 382; for a negative interpretation of Athenian curiosity, see Gray 2005, 113–16). "This observed curiosity establishes the rhetorical situation for the speech that follows, in which Luke cleverly reverses the expectation of his readers by allowing Paul to demonstrate that in proclaiming the true identity of the 'unknown God' he presents something far from new" (Béchard 2000, 383).

17:22–31. The Areopagus sermon is the fullest and most dramatic speech of Paul's missionary career. Anticipated by the shorter address in Lystra (14:15–17) and consistent with the kerygma Paul presents to the Gentiles in his letters (cf. Rom 1–3; 1 Thess 1), this address provides a window into how Paul dealt with the Gentiles in other places. Just as the Lystra address conformed to and challenged local conceptions of deities (see comment on 14:15–17), so the Areopagus speech reflects and challenges the language and concepts of the Epicureans, and especially the Stoics (Klauck 2000, 81–95). The speech fits the general form of Hellenistic oratory: *exordium* (17:22–23a); *propositio* (17:23b); *probatio* (17:24–29); and *peroratio* (17:30–31) (Zweck 1989, 94–103). In terms of content, the speech is composed of five couplets following a chiastic pattern (slightly modifying Polhill 1992, 37).

A Introduction: evidence of the ignorance of pagan worship (17:22–23)

   B The object of true worship is the one Creator God (17:24–25)

      C Proper relationship between humanity and God (17:26–28)

   B′ The objects of false worship are the idols of gold, silver, or stone (17:29)

A′ Conclusion: the time of ignorance is now over (17:30–31)

A. The sermon begins with a typical convention of ancient rhetoric, the *captatio benevolentiae*, in which Paul attempts to curry the favor of his audience with a compliment (though the term "religious" is somewhat ambiguous;

cf. Gray 2005, 109–10): **Paul stood up in front of the Areopagus (Council) and said, "Athenians! I see that you are very religious in every way"** (17:22; cf. Pausanias, *Descr.* 1.17.1; Josephus, *C. Ap.* 2.12.130). His evidence is taken from his tour of the city: **For as I walked around and carefully observed your objects of worship, I even discovered an altar upon which had been inscribed, "To an unknown god"** (17:23a; on inscriptions to "unknown gods," see Pausanias, *Descr.* 1.1.4; Philostratus, *Vit. Apoll.* 6.3.5; Horst 1989, 1426–56). Paul uses the inscription as a point of departure for the remainder of his speech; within the compliment is an implicit criticism: **that which you worship in ignorance, this is what I am proclaiming to you** (17:23b). The Athenians had been worshiping an object, not a personal God, a "what," not a "whom."

B. Paul then claims that this unknown God is none other than the Creator God: **The God who made the universe and all that is in it, the one who is Lord of heaven and earth, he does not live in temples made by human hands, nor is he tended to by human hands as if he needs something, since he himself gives life and breath and everything else to all (people)** (17:24–25). The concept of a creator deity was not unknown to the Greeks (see Epictetus, *Diatr.* 4.7.6; cf. Schneider 1982, 239). There is no other god worthy of worship; indeed, Paul would argue there is no other God. Though Paul does not quote scripture, his monotheism is biblically grounded (cf. 1 Kgs 8:27; 2 Chr 6:18; Isa 42:5; on the OT intertextual echoes throughout the speech, see Litwak 2004, 199–216). This emphasis on God the Creator (who is separate from the created order) also echoes earlier speeches in Acts: 4:24; 7:48–50; 14:15. The statement that God has "need of nothing" echoes both Jewish ("the Deity stands in need of nothing"; Josephus, *Ant.* 8.4.3.111) and pagan philosophical ("God has need of nothing"; Euripides, *Herc. fur.* 1345–1346) views of God's self-sufficiency. Furthermore, that such a God is not to be worshiped in human-made temples also resonates both with Jewish (Isa 57:15; Bel 5; Josephus, *Ant.* 8.3.2.114) and pagan (Lactantius, *Inst.* 6.25; Lucian, *Sacr.* 11) traditions. The argument here also specifically echoes some Stoic (and possibly Epicurean; cf. Witherington 1998, 525) teaching: "It is Zeno's teaching that one should not build temples of the gods" (Plutarch, *Mor.* 1034B). As we shall see, however much Paul wishes to identify with his audience, in the end he proclaims a distinctively Christian message.

C. The central portion of the speech (17:26–28) begins with God's creation of humanity: **From a single person he made every race of people** (17:26a). Once again Paul's argument sounds a deep double entendre that Greek and Jewish ears would have heard differently. Paul says that God made every race from, literally, "the one" (on Codex D's reading of "from one blood," see Barrett 1998, 2:842); this notion of the "one" and the "many" was part and parcel of Platonic cosmology (Plato, *Resp.* 596a). Furthermore, some pagan philosophical traditions held to the divine origin of the human race (Seneca, *Ep.* 44.1; Dio Chrysostom, *Charid.* 26). Despite these connections, Paul is echoing not the Platonic, philosophical "one," but rather the "one man" Adam from whom the human race descended (Gen 2:7; see Luke 3:23–38), a point to which Paul will momentarily return (see 17:31 below).

This same God also **established orderly seasons and boundaries (17:26b)**. This claim as well resonates with a Greco-Roman understanding (Cicero, *Tusc.* 1.28.68–69, claims seasons and zones are proof of the divine's existence; cf. Talbert 2005, 156), but it also is grounded in Jewish understanding of God's creative work in separating "space and time in orderly fashion" (Johnson 1992, 315, citing Gen 1:24; Deut 32:8; Ps 73:17 LXX; Wis 7:17–19; cf. also 1QM 10.12–16; *1 En.* 2.1–5.3). Humanity is created **to live (17:26b)** within this cosmos and **to seek God (17:27a**; taking both infinitives as purpose; cf. Culy and Parsons 2003, 338–39). "Seeking God" is a biblical theme (Isa 51:1; Pss 26:8 LXX; 104:4 LXX; Prov 16:8 LXX; 28:5 LXX; Sir 2:16). The next phrase expands on the nature of our seeking: **If only they might really search hard for him and find (the one) (17:27a)**. The sense of "search hard" is that of the blind person groping in darkness (cf. Homer, *Od.* 9.416). The outcome of this search, while perhaps not utterly futile (as Wis 13:6 and Philo, *Spec.* 1.32–40 suggest), is in doubt as the Greek grammar suggests (fourth class conditional sentence, cf. Culy and Parsons 2003, 339). That God **is not far from any one of us (17:27b)** is not only found in pagan (Seneca, *Ep.* 41.1–2) and Jewish (Josephus, *Ant.* 8.4.2.108) literature; it is a cause for hope (Barrett 1998, 2:845). In fact, the book of Acts, with its various epiphanies of God's voice, Spirit, angel, and Anointed One (Acts 2; 9; 10–11; 12; 13; 16 *et passim*), confirms Paul's claim of God's immanence (Tilborg 2001, 86–104). But does the experience of the divine come through human fumbling and groping after it or is it God who enables our apprehension of his presence?

In anticipation of such a question, Paul claims: **For in him we live and move and exist (17:28a)**. The triad of live, move, and exist underscores the fact that our very existence depends utterly and absolutely on God. In God we live, move (search?), and exist. Paul's natural theology is grounded in the enabling presence of God (see Theological Issues). Paul's argument then pivots, not on an OT quotation, but rather a citation from **some of your own poets who have said, "For we too are his offspring" (17:28b)**. The quotation is presumably from the Stoic philosopher Aratus (*Phaen.* 5; cf. Clement of Alexandria, *Strom.* 1.19.91), and fits within a rhetorical strategy that seeks to quote authorities as a kind of proof or testimony. Quintilian describes authority as

opinions which can be attributed to nations, peoples, wise men, distinguished citizens, or famous poets. Even common sayings and popular beliefs may be useful. All these are in a sense testimonies, but they are actually all the more effective because they are not given to suit particular causes, but spoken or given by minds free of prejudice and favor for the simple reason that they seemed either very honorable or very true. (*Inst.* 5.11.37–38, trans. Butler 1921)

Thus, at this point in the *probatio* (proofs) section of the speech, quoting "the poets" is an appropriate kind of "testimony" to Paul's Athenian audience. Nonetheless, the underlying sense of the quotation has a biblical grounding, picking up the allusion above to the "one": through Adam, the "son of God" (cf. Luke 3:38). That is, we are God's offspring, created in God's image (cf. Gen 1:26; a similar argument is made by the second-century BC Jewish apologist, Aristobulus, preserved in Eusebius, *Praep. ev.* 13.12.6).

B'. Building on his last statement, Paul contrasts the object of true worship (17:24–25) with an account of the false worship of idols: **Therefore, since we are God's offspring, we should not think that the divine one is like gold or silver or stone, (like) an image (made) by a person's skill and creativity (17:29).** Here then is the basis for Paul's attack on idolatry, which follows: since we are God's offspring, and humans are the true image of God, then no image made "by a person's skill and creativity" could possibly be anything other than a distortion of the image of the one, true God (17:29). The condemnation of idolatry is standard in Jewish polemic (Deut 4:28; Pss 113:12 LXX; 134:15 LXX; Isa 40:18; 44:9–20; Wis 13:5, 10; 15:16–17; Ep Jer 8, 24, 26, 34–40; cf. Acts 7:41–43), but is not altogether missing in pagan philosophy (Dio Chrysostom, *Dei cogn.* 80–83).

A'. In the *peroration*, or conclusion (17:30–31), Paul ends his sermon by announcing that the time of ignorance is over and calling for eschatological repentance: **So then, although God overlooked the times of (their) ignorance, he is now commanding people—everyone, everywhere—to repent. For he has set the day on which he is going to judge the world according to the standard of righteousness by the man he has appointed, and he has provided proof (of this) for all by raising him from the dead (17:30–31).** Now Paul's purpose is clear. He does not seek to add a new god to the Athenian Pantheon; rather, he seeks the Athenians' repentance (Winter 1996, 85). God will no longer "overlook" this ignorance (cf. 14:16; Rom 3:25); now is the time for repentance (17:30). Just as God had made all the nations to inhabit the whole earth from one man (17:26), so God will judge the world through the one man whom God appointed (cf. Rom 5). That this man is Jesus is confirmed when Paul says that God raised him from the dead (17:31). Paul has deferred the misunderstood subject of resurrection (17:18) until the end of his speech. This rhetorical strategy of deferral, known as the "subtle approach" (*insinuatio*), was appropriate for controversial or difficult issues (Quintilian, *Inst.* 4.1.42–50). The sermon ends with God as the main actor: God overlooks, commands, sets the day, judges the world, and provides proof through the resurrection.

17:32–34. The response to Paul's sermon is mixed (17:32–34). Attempts to align the skeptical response with the Epicureans and the cautious reserve with the Stoics (Croy 1997, 21–39) have failed to convince; rather, it is more reasonable that the authorial audience concluded that individuals from both groups identified with one or the other response (Klauck 2000, 78–79). The

The Rhetoric of the Areopagus Speech

The Areopagus speech (17:22–31) is rhetorically polished and packed with figures. Paul employs "inflection" (*polyptoton* or *klisis*), in which the subject is inflected in all cases (Theon, *Prog.* 74.24–35, ed. Patillon 1997, 33; 85.29–31, ed. Patillon 1997, 48; Quintilian, *Inst.* 9.1.34; see sidebar on Acts 7:2). The five occurrences of "God" are inflected in four cases within a matter of a few verses: dative, 17:23; nominative, 17:24; accusative, 17:27; genitive, 17:29; and nominative, 17:30. This inflection would suggest that the topic of Paul's Areopagus speech was God, not so surprising since this speech is well known for its preference of general revelation over christological formulation. That God is "sovereign over all" is seen in the parallel use of "everything" (*pas*) eight times, singular (17:24, 25, 26) and plural (17:22, 24, 25, 30, 31), and in three cases (genitive, 17:26; dative, 17:25, 31; accusative, 17:22, 24, 25, 26, 30; cf. Morgenthaler 1993, 331–34).

The Areopagus speech is also unusually "lyrical" and euphonic. As Dionysius of Halicarnassus remarked: "The science of public oratory is, after all, a kind of musical science" (*Comp.* 11.124.20; cf. Quintilian, *Inst.* 1.10.9). The Lukan Paul here uses specific rhetorical figures: assonance (the repetition of internal vowel sounds in neighboring words; cf. Demetrius, *Eloc.* 28–29): *zōēn kai pnoēn*, 17:25; alliteration (the repetition of the initial sound; *Rhet. Her.* 4.22.18): *pantos prosōpou*, 17:26; *pistin paraschōn pasin*, 17:31; reduplication ("the repetition of one or more words for the purposes of amplification"; *Rhet. Her.* 4.28.38): *genos*, 17:28, 29; antistrophe (the repetition of the last word in successive phrases; *Rhet. Her.* 4.13.19): *esmen/esmen*, 17:28; litotes (affirming by negating the opposite; *Rhet. Her.* 4.38.50): *ou makran*, 17:27; and paronomasia (similar sounding words with dissimilar meanings; *Rhet. Her.* 4.21.29): *theōrō/anatheōrōn*, 17:22, 23; *pantas/pantachou*, 17:30; *estēsen/anastēsas*, 17:31. These rhetorical flourishes reinforce Luke's picture of Paul as a "man of letters" and able to hold his own against the Athenian intelligentsia.

Athenian audience has no problem with the concept of a divine eschatological judgment. Justin noted: "When we assert that the souls of the wicked living after death will be sensibly punished . . . we believe the same things as your poets and philosophers" (*1 Apol.* 20; cf. Lucian, *Jupp. conf.*; Talbert 2005, 156). What they cannot accept is the claim about the resurrection: **When they heard about the resurrection from the dead some started laughing** (17:32a; cf. Acts 23:6–7; 1 Cor 1:23; Aeschylus, *Eum.* 647–648), while others pledge to hear Paul again: **We would like to hear you (speak) about this matter again** (17:32b). To view the Areopagus speech as a total failure would be a mistake (contra Dibelius 1939). Some pledge to hear Paul speak again (17:32); others **joined him and believed, among whom was Dionysius the Areopagite** and a **woman named Damaris, and others with them** (17:34; on the [in]frequency of the names Dionysius and Damaris in Athenian prosopography, see Gill 1999,

483–90). Neither Paul nor the gospel failed in Athens; only those who heard the good news and did not respond in faith failed.

Paul in Corinth (18:1–17)

Acts 18:1–17 divides into four stylized scenes: Paul with Aquila and Priscilla (18:1–4); rejection at the synagogue and the conversion of Crispus's household (18:5–8); Paul's dream-vision (18:9–11); and the public accusation before Gallio (18:12–17). The last three scenes each echo earlier material in form and substance, in what have been called type-scenes, that is, "when a basic situation, with similar characters and plot elements, recurs several times in a given literature" (Tannehill 1990, 202, 221–29). These three scenes underscore "three important pronouncements (by Paul, v. 6; by the Lord, vv. 9–10; and by Gallio, vv. 14–15)" (Tannehill 1990, 221).

18:1–4. In the opening section (18:1–4), **Paul left Athens and went to Corinth** (18:1; on Corinth, see Murphy-O'Connor 1983). There he meets Aquila and Priscilla, Jews who had recently come to Corinth from Italy. These two characters are mentioned elsewhere in Paul's letters (cf. Rom 16:3; 1 Cor 16:19; 2 Tim 4:19). That they are Jews is significant, given the recent and mounting resistance to Paul in Macedonia (cf. Acts 16); Aquila and Priscilla give evidence that not all Diaspora Jews sought to persecute Paul (Spencer 2004, 187). Luke explains that these two Jews had come to Corinth from Italy **because Claudius had ordered all Jews to leave Rome** (18:2). Although Luke does not explicitly state it, Claudius's edict suggests that Aquila and Priscilla were Jewish Christians. Suetonius reports: "Since the Jews were continually making disturbances at the instigation of Chrestus, he [Claudius] expelled them from Rome" (*Claud.* 25.4). Most likely this Chrestus "is a garbled spelling of Christus and the disturbances referred to are the results of conflicts in synagogues between Messianists and non-Messianists" (Talbert 2005, 159). Thus Priscilla and Aquila were accustomed to the same kind of conflict that Paul had been experiencing in the synagogues and marketplaces.

Like Paul, Aquila and Priscilla were also tentmakers: **Since he practiced the same trade (as they did), he stayed with them and worked—for they were tentmakers by trade** (18:3). The term "tentmaker" may refer more generally to "leather-workers" (Bruce 1990, 392). This characterization of Paul as an artisan who worked with his hands coheres with the picture Paul paints of himself in his letters (1 Cor 4:12; 9:6; 1 Thess 2:9; 2 Thess 3:6–8). If the Paul of the letters viewed such manual

---

An Outline of Acts 18:1–17

Paul in Corinth (18:1–17)

  Paul with Aquila and Priscilla (18:1–4)

  Rejection at synagogue, conversion of Crispus (18:5–8)

  Paul's dream-vision (18:9–11)

  The accusation before Gallio (18:12–17)

    1. Compelled to appear (18:12)

    2. The accusation (18:13)

    3. The outcome (18:14–17)

---

labor negatively (so Hock 1978, 555–64; but cf. now Still 2006, 781–95), there is no indication he does so in Acts (cf. also Acts 20:34–35). Paul stayed and worked with Aquila and Priscilla. Paul moves from intellectual debate with Athenian philosophers to manual labor with Corinthian artisans, and in so doing "becomes all things to all people" (1 Cor 9:22). His economic self-sufficiency was no doubt important, not only given the length of his stay (eighteen months; cf. 18:11), but also because of Corinth's reputation for hosting philosophical charlatans and other "peddlers" who sold their intellectual "wares" to the highest bidders. Dio Chrysostom, a contemporary of Luke, described the scene at the Isthmian games in Corinth:

> That was the time, too, when one could hear crowds of wretched Sophists around Poseidon's temple shouting and reviling one another, and their disciples, as they were called, fighting with one another, many writers reading aloud their stupid works, many poets reciting their poems, while others applauded them, many jugglers showing their tricks, many fortune-tellers interpreting fortunes, lawyers innumerable perverting judgment, and peddlers not a few peddling whatever they happened to have. (*Or.* 8.9, trans. Cohoon 1971)

It is little wonder, then, for an audience familiar with such practices that Luke would characterize Paul as engaging in work for self-support in order to distinguish himself from these hucksters in much the same way that Paul in writing to the Corinthians would seek to distance himself from "so many who are peddlers of God's word" (2 Cor 2:17). Gainfully employed during the week, Paul **debated in the synagogue every Sabbath, and tried to persuade both Jews and Greeks** (18:4), thus following his established pattern of synagogue debate (13:14, 43–44; 17:2, 17).

18:5–8. Luke reports that **Silas and Timothy came down from Macedonia** only to find Paul **completely absorbed with the message and testified to the Jews that the Christ was Jesus** (18:5). The movement from a discussion of the "Christ" to his identification with "Jesus" is typical of "messianic exegesis" (Acts 2:29–31; 8:34–35; 17:3; Juel 1988) and provides the setting for a "synagogue rejection" type-scene (18:5–8) in which Paul turns to the Gentiles in the face of Jewish rejection: **they opposed (him) and slandered (him)** (18:6). There are three such scenes in Acts (Haenchen 1971, 729; Tannehill 1990, 222). The first scene is found in Pisidian Antioch (13:44–47); the third occurs in Paul's speech to the Jews in Rome (28:23–28). In each instance, Paul makes a speech in which he announces that from that point on he is turning to the Gentiles: **he shook out his clothes and said to them, "Your blood is on your (own) head(s); I am clean. From now on, I will go to the Gentiles"** (18:6; cf. 13:46; 19:6; 28:28). Why does Paul continue to preach to the Jews in the face of such resistance? His prophetic act of shaking the dust from his clothes (cf. 13:51; Luke 9:5) combines with his prophetic words, "Your blood is on your own head(s)" (see Ezek 33:4), to demonstrate that Paul is fulfilling his responsibility as witness to the Jews; they are responsible for their reaction. His symbolic shift is completed with his literal move from synagogue to house: **So he left there and went into the house of a certain man named Titius Justus who worshiped God (and) whose house was next door to the synagogue** (18:7). The scene ends on a hopeful note: **Crispus, the leader of the synagogue, believed in the Lord along with his whole household** (18:8a). The conversion of Crispus and his household (cf. 1 Cor 1:14–16) echoes the earlier household conversions of Cornelius (Acts 10–11), Lydia (16:11–15), and the Philippian jailer (16:25–34). That the conversion of the household of Crispus, the leader of the synagogue, occurs after Paul enters the house of Titius Justus "indicates that the household mission has not rejected the Jews as such; they, too, can constitute the people of God alongside believing Gentiles" (Matson 1996, 181; cf. 18:19, in which Paul once again enters the synagogue, this time in Ephesus). Evidently, as a result of the conversion of Crispus's household, **many of the** (presumably Gentile) **Corinthians who heard believed and were baptized** (18:8b), thus contributing to

Dream-Visions

Compare the dream-visions in Acts with these two examples. The first is from the OT:

Scene-setting: *"From there he [Isaac] went up to Beer-sheba."*

Dream-vision terminology: *"And that very night the Lord appeared to him"*

Dream-vision proper: *"and said, 'I am the God of your father Abraham; do not be afraid, for I am with you and will bless you and make your offspring numerous for my servant Abraham's sake.'"*

Reaction/response: *"So he built an altar there, called on the name of the Lord, and pitched his tent there. And there Isaac's servants dug a well."* (Gen 26:23–25)

The second comes from the larger Hellenistic context:

Scene-setting: *"The day before yesterday, when I [Leukippe] was crying because I was going to be butchered,"*

Dream-vision terminology: *"Artemis appeared, standing above me in my sleep,"*

Dream-vision proper: *"and said, 'Do not be sad, you shall not die, for I will stand by you and help you. You will remain a virgin until I myself give you away as a bride. No one but Kleitophon will marry you.'"*

Reaction/response: *"Of course I was upset at the postponement but very glad of our expectations."* (Achilles Tatius, *Leuc. Cli.* 4.1.5–8, trans. Reardon 1989, 222)

the diversity of the congregation, namely, "synagogue rulers, Roman centurions, female purple-merchants, and prison wardens within the one household of God" (Spencer 2004, 189).

18:9–11. The second type-scene (18:9–11) is that of a dream-vision. Other dream-visions, with explicit dream-vision vocabulary, occur in Acts at 9:10–18; 10:3–8, 10–17; 16:6–10 (see comments on 16:6–10). This one consists of the typical features: (1) *Scene-setting*: **one night . . . the Lord said to Paul** (18:9a). (2) *Dream-vision terminology*: **in a vision** (18:9a). (3) *Dream-vision proper*: **Do not be afraid, but speak and do not keep silent. For I am with you and no one will attack you or harm you, because I have many people in this city** (18:9b–10). (4) *Reaction/response*: **So he stayed and taught the word of God among them for one year and six months** (18:11).

As in the example from Achilles Tatius (see accompanying sidebar), the emphasis of the vision here is on reassurance ("Do not be afraid"; "no one will attack or harm you"). Unlike some of the other dream-visions, which include instructions to "go" (Ananias is told to go find Saul, Acts 9:10–18; Cornelius is instructed to send men to Peter in Joppa, Acts 10:3–8; Paul is entreated to come over to Macedonia, 16:6–10), Paul is emboldened to stay where he is in order to speak and not keep silent (18:9b). Paul can continue his teaching mission in Corinth in the confidence that the Lord is present with him (God is also declared to be with Joseph, 7:9, and Jesus, 10:38). The reality of this presence is felt (and needed) in the next scene.

18:12–17. The third type-scene has been identified as a public accusation before an official, here Gallio (18:12–17). Twice already the audience has encountered this pattern (16:19–24; 17:5–7; cf. also 19:23–40), which has three elements (Tannehill 1990, 202): (1) Christians are compelled to appear before an official person or body (18:12); (2) Christians are accused of wrongdoing (18:13); (3) the outcome is reported (18:14–17).

1. **While Gallio was the proconsul of Achaia, the Jews attacked Paul together and brought him to the judgment seat** (18:12). The "judgment seat" (*bēma*) was a raised platform on which the magistrate could make a public address or judgment before the assembly, located in the center of the Corinthian marketplace or agora (and still visible today in the ruins of ancient Corinth).

2. The Christians are accused of wrongdoing: **They said, "This man is inciting people to worship God in a way that is against the law"** (18:13). The term "incite" (*anapeithō*), when used elsewhere in legal settings, has the sense of "operating out of deceit to mislead others" (see *P.Magd.* 14; *P.Ryl.* 114; Winter 1999, 216). They are being "misled" to break the "law," but is the law that is being violated Jewish or Roman (cf. Witherington 1998, 552; Talbert 2005, 162)? The term "worship" in Acts is not exclusive to Jews or even God-fearers (cf. 19:27, in which it is used to describe those who worship Diana). Thus the reference to those "people" being misled is probably inclusive of all

Gallio

Although never mentioned by Paul in his letters, Luke's account of Paul's appearance before Gallio "has become the most important item in the study of Pauline chronology and missionary activity" (Fitzmyer 1998, 621). Much of this confidence rests on a fragmentary Greek inscription once displayed in a temple of Apollo in Delphi and dealing with the depopulation of Delphi. The key parts of the (reconstructed) inscription as related to Gallio's proconsulship are:

> *"Tiberius Claudius Caesar Augustus Germanicus, invested with tribunician power for the 12th time, acclaimed imperator for the 26th time. . . . I have always supported the cult of Pythian Apollo, but now since it is said to be destitute of citizens, as L. Junius Gallio, my friend and proconsul, recently reported to me."* (Oliver 1970, 239–40; Fitzmyer 1998, 621)

Figure 10. The Gallio Inscription.

This fragmentary Greek inscription, once displayed in a temple of Apollo in Delphi, deals with the depopulation of Delphi. Its mention of Gallio, together with other information we possess concerning Claudius and Gallio, allows us to date his proconsulship to AD 52–53.

Considering this inscription in tandem with other information about Claudius and Gallio, we can date Gallio's proconsulship to AD 52–53. This letter report was written between January and August in AD 52, and Paul made his appearance before Gallio between late spring and early fall of 52 (Fitzmyer 1998, 623). Fitzmyer concludes that the Gallio inscription "supplies a rare peg on which to hang . . . absolute chronology" (Fitzmyer 1998, 621).

the inhabitants of the Roman colony of Corinth, Jews and Gentiles, Roman citizens and noncitizens.

These points suggest that the violated law refers to Roman regulations, specifically concerning the Jews (Fitzmyer 1998, 629; Winter 1999, 217–18). Jews were given certain privileges and exemptions in the Roman Empire by

Julius Caesar: "Similarly do I forbid other religious societies but permit these people [Jews] alone to assemble and feast in accordance with their native customs and ordinances" (Josephus, *Ant.* 14.214–216) that continued beyond Caesar's death. These benefits were used later (beyond our period) to establish Judaism as a *religio licita*, a "legal religion" (Tajra 1984, 107–23), but some concessions were current in the first century or before. When the Roman Senate in 64 BC abolished voluntary associations or guilds because their frequent meetings had fostered seditious activities (Asconius, *Pis.* 8), the Jews were still allowed to gather for weekly synagogue meetings without being labeled as a *collegium illicitum*, or illegal association, guilty of political sedition (Cicero, *Flac.* 66; cited in Cotter 1996, 77). According to Josephus, Claudius issued this decree to Alexandria in behalf of the Jews (with implications for all Diaspora Jews): "It is right, therefore, that the Jews throughout the whole world under our sway should also observe the customs of their fathers without let or hindrance" (Josephus, *Ant.* 19.290; though see Dio Cassius, *Hist. Rom.* 60.6.6). Should the Jews cause trouble, however, of course they were not exempt from imperial wrath, as Claudius's expulsion of Jews (and Christians?) from Rome demonstrates (cf. 18:2). Thus if the Jews could persuade Gallio that Paul's meetings in the home of Titius Justus (18:7), given their ethnic mixture, were not Jewish and therefore not worthy of "protected Jewish status," then Gallio could rule the Christians an illegal voluntary association.

3. Luke reports the outcome: **When Paul was about to respond, Gallio said to the Jews, "If there were some crime or terrible wrongdoing, I would be patient with you Jews in this matter. But since the disputes are about a statement, names, and your own law, you must deal with it yourselves. I do not care to be a judge of these things"** (18:14–15). Gallio refuses to take the bait. He finds nothing politically illegal ("crime" or "wrongdoing") in Paul's activity. These debates about words, names (titles?), and laws were, in Gallio's opinion, the upshot of an intra-Jewish debate, for which he did not "care to be a judge." In effect, Gallio rules that the Christian movement and Paul's activities, in the eyes of the Romans, constitute a sect within Judaism, so that they are entitled to the privileges and immunities afforded to the Jews by the Romans in Achaia. "Whether Jewish Christians or Gentile Christians, Roman citizens, or provincials, they were all seen as 'a party' operating under the Jewish umbrella" (Winter 1999, 222; see Theological Issues on Acts 9:32–11:18).

This scene differs from the others in the outcome because rather than beating and imprisoning (16:19–24) or fining (17:5–7) Paul and company, **he** [Gallio] **drove them away from the judgment seat** (18:16). But neither Rome nor Gallio should be construed in this text as a "friend" of the Jews. The term often translated "dismissed" is here rendered "drove away" to capture the potential violence of the word. Presumably this act ordered by Gallio created a skirmish that quickly got out of hand. **Then, after they had all seized Sosthenes, the leader of the synagogue, they beat him in front of the judgment seat** (18:17a).

It is not clear who "they" are (though Codex D identifies them as "the Greeks") or whether this Sosthenes, who presumably was the spokesperson for the opposition to Paul, is Crispus's replacement or part of a consortium of synagogue leadership. Nor does Luke give any indication that this Sosthenes is a follower of Christ (cf. 1 Cor 1:14–16). The violence may have its roots partially in the general Gentile hostile attitudes against Jews (cf. Tacitus, *Hist.* 5.4.1; Philostratus, *Vit. Apoll.* 5.33) despite (or perhaps partially because of) the legal concessions that the Roman government made to the Jews. But given the implication that "all" here includes Jews as well, who are swept up in the mob violence, the scene may also plausibly be read as yet another example of "urban unrest" in the Roman Empire (see Hubbard 2005, 416–28).

Any number of actions could spark a "spontaneous expression of popular indignation" (Cicero, *Dom.* 12): famine (Philostratus, *Vit. Apoll.* 1.15; *Vit. soph.* 526); an irritating poet (Petronius, *Sat.* 90); a teacher accused of fraud (Lucian, *Peregr.* 15.19); a prank (Philo, *Flacc.* 36–40); and an unwelcome verdict from a judge (ps.-Socrates, *Ep.* 14; Hubbard 2005, 420). Gallio responds by not responding, perhaps in an act of self-preservation. Plutarch's statement, while hyperbolic, nonetheless has a grain of truth: "Men engaged in public affairs [are] compelled to live at the caprice of a self-willed and licentious mob" (*Mor.* 589A; cf. Suetonius, *Claud.* 18; *Rhet.* 6). **But none of these things were of any concern to Gallio** (18:17b). In any case this scene proves the truthfulness of the previous unit; at least in Corinth, no one lays a hand on Paul.

Theological Issues

Commentators have seen an irreconcilable difference between the Paul of the letters and of Acts in the area of "natural theology" (Vielhauer 1966, 36–37; Haenchen 1971, 528–30; Kümmel 1973, 182–83). Generally speaking, those who argue for disjuncture between the two see natural theology, especially of a Stoic variety, to be the dominant theme of Acts 17 and foreign to anything genuinely "Pauline" (Dibelius 1956, 57–77). We must begin, however, by distinguishing between "natural theology" and the biblical doctrine of general revelation. Bertil Gärtner has argued persuasively that the Stoic doctrine of "natural theology" is fundamentally different from the doctrine of what he terms "natural revelation," found in the OT and NT (Gärtner 1955, 73–116). In biblical "natural revelation," "knowledge of God is imparted by revelation coming from God, i.e., it has a transcendent source; the Stoics, on the other hand, achieved this knowledge by the exercise of the intellect, and it therefore has its mainspring in man, in something immanent in the cosmos" (Gärtner 1955, 115).

With this distinction in mind, a comparison of Paul's letters, especially (but not exclusively) Rom 1–2, with the Areopagus speech of Acts 17 reveals striking similarities.

1. Acts 17:16 relates that Paul was provoked at the idols in Athens, and Rom 1 is a blanket condemnation of idolatry; despite Paul's apparently accommodating tone in the Areopagus speech, the underlying reason is similar in content and character to Paul in the letters (cf. 1 Thess 1:9–10).
2. "Natural revelation" is assumed in both passages: God the Creator can be known in some manner from his works.
3. The kindness and generosity of God are assumed (Rom 2:4; Acts 17:30).
4. The command now is to repent (Rom 2:4; Acts 17:30).
5. The climax to both passages is eschatological (Rom 2:16; Acts 17:31).

Both the "epistolary Paul" and the "Lukan Paul" reflect the Jewish view that God reveals himself through creation (while being distinct from it), rather than the Stoic view that human intellect is the source of apprehension of the divine (Gärtner 1955, 144–46). In other words, both Romans and Acts lay emphasis on the divine initiative in God revealing himself in and through creation. And in both, human ability to apprehend this natural revelation is divinely enabled. In Romans, Gentiles know what they know about God, because "God has shown it to them" (1:19). In Acts, the God whom humans "feel after" is not "far from us"; in fact, in that God we live and move and exist (17:27–28). Within that enabling existence, we can know God. God reveals himself in the natural order and enables humankind to apprehend God in the natural order. But this knowledge of God is not saving knowledge; in both the letters and in Acts, humankind must repent (Rom 2:4; Acts 17:30).

The substantive difference comes primarily with the understanding of humans' and God's actions. In Romans, people are "without excuse" and, therefore, God responds by handing them over to their passions (repeated three times for emphasis). In Acts, people are led to the truth, and God has overlooked their ignorance to this point (17:30). Commentators attempting to reconcile these two passages generally do so on the basis of the divergent contexts of the pagan, philosophically minded audience of Acts 17 and the committed Jewish and Gentile Christian audience of Romans (Hemer 1989, 250–55). Do the dissimilar contexts so alter the message that the audience hears a profound disjuncture? Conforming the Areopagus speech to the theme of ignorance is not surprising, since ignorance is a theme in Luke/Acts (Luke 23:34; Acts 3:17; 13:27), but the ignorance is subsumed to a greater divine will. The context in Romans is the explanation of why all people, Gentiles and Jews, are guilty and in need of redemption.

The point of both is, of course, salvation. In both Romans and in Acts, then, Paul is provoked by idolatry and emphasizes natural revelation within an eschatological framework. In Romans, misguided knowledge of God leads to idolatry and immorality. There Paul is addressing an ethnically mixed Christian community, so both points are significant. In Acts, only the first point of idolatry is taken up (17:23–24), since Paul is laying the groundwork for proclaiming the gospel to a pagan audience that stands outside the Christian community. Given the strikingly different contexts, the similarities are more remarkable than the tensions. Hearing the common components, the audience would probably hear the difference as primarily one of context, and having heard the Areopagus speech and Romans, they would have samples of the Paul who could be all things to all people in hopes of winning as many as possible.

Acts 18:18–19:41

Paul in Ephesus

🗗

Introductory Matters

The final episode (18:18–19:41) of this division (chaps. 13–19) focuses on the city of Ephesus. As such, this episode represents the "climax of the Pauline mission in terms of both its position in the Acts narrative and its content" (Shauf 2005, 124). The unit divides into the following scenes: (1) Paul visits Ephesus, Jerusalem, and Antioch (18:18–23); (2) Apollos and "certain" disciples in Ephesus (18:24–19:7); (3) Paul teaching in the synagogue and the Hall of Tyrannus (19:8–10); (4) Paul and the sons of Sceva in Ephesus (19:11–20); and (5) Paul's resolve and the riot in Ephesus (19:21–41). The last unit is arranged in a chain-link interlock to connect the third division in Acts (chaps. 13–19) to the final and fourth division (chaps. 20–28). As such it functions in much the same way as the interlock at the previous "seams" in the narrative at Acts 8:1–3 and 11:27–12:25.

Table 8.
Chain-Link Interlock at Acts 19:21–41
(Longenecker 2005, 200)

TEXT-UNIT "A"	INTERLOCKED "b" (anticipatory)	INTERLOCKED "a" (retrospective)	TEXT-UNIT "B"
Acts 13:1–19:41	Acts 19:21–22	Acts 19:23–41	Acts 20:1–28:31

In Acts 19:21–22, Paul's resolve to travel through Macedonia and Achaia to Jerusalem and Rome anticipates Paul's travels to those very areas beginning with his return to Macedonia (Acts 20), his journey to Jerusalem (Acts 21), and his final voyage to Rome (Acts 27–28). Likewise, the riot at Ephesus (19:23–41) retrospectively completes the cycle of stories related to Paul's ministry in Ephesus in Acts 19:1–20 (Longenecker 2005, 199–205). Furthermore, this arrangement serves to connect the first (chaps. 13–19) and second (chaps. 20–28) parts of the second half of Acts.

Tracing the Narrative Flow

Paul Visits Ephesus, Jerusalem, and Antioch (18:18–23)

The first scene (18:18–23) is transitional and could just as easily be included at the end of the preceding section. Luke first notes: **When Paul had stayed for a number of days more with the believers, after saying good-bye, he sailed off to Syria (18:18a).** He next makes a quick stop in Ephesus where he left Priscilla and Aquila **while he himself went into the synagogue and debated with the Jews** (18:19). Paul returns to **Antioch** where he began these missionary endeavors (18:22b; cf. 15:35–41). Thus this passage looks back to Antioch where Paul began his missionary career and forward to Ephesus where he will spend his last three years as a free man. Paul's purpose in retracing his steps is the same as his earlier return trip, to nurture new converts: **After staying for a certain time he left and traveled from place to place in the region of Galatia and Phrygia, strengthening all the disciples** (18:23; cf. 14:21–23).

Three details stand out in this travel summary. First is the mention of **Priscilla and Aquila** (18:19b), who accompany Paul to Ephesus. When they were introduced earlier, Aquila was mentioned first (18:2). The alternating of names may be taken as a sign of their mutual partnership in marriage and business (cf. 18:2–3; Spencer 2004, 188). However, given Luke's attention to name order (cf. the inversion of "Barnabas and Paul" in 13:2, 7 to "Paul and Barnabas" in 13:43, 46, 50) and the fact that Priscilla is listed first again in their only other mention in Acts (18:26), the order may indicate Priscilla's rising prominence in the Christian movement (Talbert 2005, 164; cf. the Pauline letter tradition, in which Prisca [the proper form of the diminutive "Priscilla"] is mentioned before Aquila in two of the three occurrences; Rom 16:3–5; 2 Tim 4:19; cf. 1 Cor 16:19; Spencer 2004, 188).

The second detail is that Paul cuts **his hair at Cenchreae because of a vow he had taken** (18:18c), presumably a Nazirite vow (see Num 6:1–21; cf. Mishna tractate *Nazir*). The Nazirite vow typically took place in the temple, although later tradition (which may reflect earlier practice) allowed for the shaving of the head to take place outside Jerusalem (*m. Naz.* 6:8; cf. Koet 1996, 138). In Second Temple Judaism the Nazirite vow signified "a life specially dedicated to God" (Koet 1996,

Transplacement

That 18:18–23 characterizes a "man on the move" is seen in Luke's use of the rhetorical figure of *traductio* or transplacement (*Rhet. Her.* 4.14.20; see Acts 10:10). Here the term *erchomai*, "go" (including forms thereof), occurs four times in a span of five verses (18:19, 22, 23). As pseudo-Cicero observed, "The frequent recourse to the same word is not dictated by verbal poverty; rather there inheres in the repetition an elegance which the ear can distinguish more easily than words can explain" (*Rhet. Her.* 4.14.21, trans. Caplan 1954, 281).

134; cf. 1 Macc 3:49; Josephus, *Ant.* 19.292–294; *BJ* 2.313–314). Despite the historical difficulties and complexities involved in this account (cf. Koet 1996; Neusner 1999; Tomes 1995), Luke's purpose in reporting the vow is clear: Paul continues to be a practicing Jew despite charges to the contrary (see Acts 18:13; 21:21).

Narrative Flow in Acts 18

In terms of the narrative flow of the argument in Acts, there is certainly no major division between 18:22 and 18:23 (contra Fitzmyer 1998, 633, 636). The use of *kai* in 18:23 implies a continuation of the same series of events. The use of a participial clause with an initial participle to introduce 18:23 and the failure to use a full noun phrase to refer to Paul in 18:23 all indicate that no boundary should be perceived after 18:22 (Levinsohn 1992, 214; Culy and Parsons 2003, 354). Nonetheless, this verse, with its brief notice of Paul's visit to Jerusalem, has taken on historical significance beyond its import in the narrative. John Knox attached considerable importance to this verse, identifying it with Paul's Jerusalem visit recounted in Gal 2:1–10 (1950, 68–69). Knox has been followed by numerous scholars of Pauline chronology (Lüdemann 1984; Hurd 1967; for critique see Bruce 1988, 357). Such historical reconstruction is not inappropriate, but it illustrates the difference of approach between critics who mine the text for historical and chronological "nuggets" and those interested in reading the final form of the text for its rhetorical argument and theological message.

The third detail is that when Paul **landed in Caesarea he went up and greeted the church (at Jerusalem)** (18:22). Luke mentions Paul's visit to the Jerusalem church in a rather understated fashion, but his point is nonetheless important: Paul's visit to the Jerusalem church indicates his continuing "loyalty to and unity with the Jerusalem community" (Johnson 1992, 330). The tie between the Gentile mission and the Jerusalem church remains unbroken.

Apollos and Certain Disciples (18:24–19:7)

Each of the subunits of 18:24–19:7, which focuses on Apollos, is marked by reference to Apollos's location: in Ephesus (18:24a, introducing 18:24b–27b); in Achaia (18:27c, introducing 18:27d–28), and in Corinth (19:1a, introducing the next unit, 19:1b–7).

18:24–27b. Acts 18:24b–26 falls into an ABA' structure (modifying Talbert 2005, 164–65):

A Apollos was instructed in the *way* of the Lord and taught *accurately*, though knowing only the baptism of John (18:24b–25)

  B Apollos spoke with boldness in the synagogue (18:26a)

A' Priscilla and Aquila instructed Apollos in the *way* of God *more accurately* (18:26b)

In the first scene Luke does a rare thing (cf. 15:36) by shifting the spotlight away from Paul to a **Jew from Alexandria named Apollos** (18:24a; cf. 1 Cor 1:12; 3:4–6, 22; 4:6; 16:12). Alexandria was widely known as an intellectual and cultural center (cf. Parsons 1989). Thus it is no surprise to see Apollos described in glowing terms, especially with regard to his learning and eloquence in the Bible: **He was an eloquent man who knew the scriptures well** (18:24b). That Apollos is literally a "man with words" can be taken to refer to his knowledge or his rhetorical ability or, preferably, both (underscored also by reference to his "power in the scriptures" and his speaking "with great enthusiasm" and "boldly"). Though ethnically a Jew, Apollos had **been trained in the way of the Lord** (18:25a). The "way of the Lord" recalls not only the teaching of John the Baptist (Luke 3:4), but also echoes Luke's references to the "way" of salvation (16:17) and the Christian movement as the Way (9:2; cf. 19:9, 23; 22:4; 24:14, 22). Furthermore, **he spoke with great enthusiasm** (18:25b). The phrase "with great enthusiasm" (lit., "boiling spirit") is an example of the rhetorical figure, *energia* (Quintilian, *Inst.* 8.3.61; 9.2.40) or ocular demonstration in which

An Outline of 18:24–19:7

Apollos and certain disciples (18:24–19:7)

Apollos in Ephesus (18:24–27b)

Apollo in Achaia (18:27c–28)

Certain disciples in Ephesus (19:1–7)

"an event is so described in words that the business seems to be enacted and the subject to pass vividly before our eyes" (*Rhet. Her.* 4.45.68, trans. Caplan 1954, 405). Here it refers to the way Apollos spoke (Culy and Parsons 2003, 356) and not to Apollos himself (contra Barrett 1998, 2:888; Bruce 1988, 402). Apollos also **accurately taught things about Jesus** (18:25b). In light of what follows (18:26), this statement must mean that Apollos accurately taught everything he knew about Jesus although his knowledge was limited.

The thing lacking in Apollos was that he **only knew the baptism of John** (18:25c). John's baptism was for repentance for the forgiveness of sins (Luke 3:3). In an implicit *synkrisis* comparing Apollos to Paul, Luke suggests that there is something missing in Apollos's knowledge (Käsemann 1982, 147–48), though he does not specify what.

> ## Letters of Recommendation
>
> Letters of recommendation were common in Jewish (Acts 9:2; 22:5; *y. Hag.* 1.8), Christian (Rom 16:1–2; 1 Cor 16:10–11; 2 Cor 3:1–3; 8:23–24; 3 John 12), and pagan circles (ps.-Demetrius, *Eloc.* 2; Pliny the Younger, *Ep.* 9.21; *P.Oxy.* 1.32.4–15; 2.292.5–7; *P.Oslo* 2.55.7–9; cf. Malherbe 1988, 32–33). Given the prevalence of these letters in the ancient world, Luke's authorial audience would have been familiar with the form and content of Apollos's letter, despite the briefness of his mention of it (Acts 18:27b).

Thus he **began to speak boldly in the synagogue** and **when Priscilla and Aquila heard him they took him aside and explained the way of God to him more accurately** (18:26). In light of the references to the Way in the subsequent scene (19:9, 23), the sense seems to be that Priscilla and Aquila's "more accurate" instruction includes information about the development of the Christian movement, the Way, since Christ's death/resurrection/ascension (cf. Acts 1:22). Whatever his shortcomings, he is not required to receive baptism in the name of the Lord Jesus (cf. 19:5), thus suggesting Apollos's knowledge is less inadequate than that of the twelve disciples in Ephesus (see 19:1–7).

After receiving instruction from Priscilla and Aquila, Apollos **wanted to travel to Achaia** (18:27a). He receives both encouragement and endorsement: **The believers encouraged him and wrote to the disciples so that they would welcome him** (18:27b). These Ephesian believers write a letter of recommendation for Apollos to carry with him to the church in Achaia. The purpose of the letter is for the Corinthian Christians to "welcome" or "receive" Apollos, the vocabulary of hospitality and a regular feature of letters of recommendation (Kim 1972). The authorial audience, familiar with 1 Corinthians, would know that both the letter to and Apollos's ministry among the Corinthian Christians were successful.

18:27c–28. The brief unit in 18:27c–28 is once again marked by Apollos's location: **After he arrived (in Achaia)** (18:27c). His ministry there was twofold. Like Paul, he administers pastoral care within the church, strengthening the believers (cf. 14:23; 18:23): **he greatly helped those who had believed through grace** (18:27d). And, like Paul, he engages in disputes with the Jews over his messianic exegesis of scripture (cf. 9:22; 13:32–33; 17:3): **For he vigorously refuted the Jews in public by demonstrating through the scriptures that the Christ was Jesus** (18:28).

19:1–7. The connection to Apollos is made with the third of three "locators" of Apollos (this time to indicate his absence from, rather than his presence in, 19:1–7): **While Apollos was in Corinth, Paul . . . came to Ephesus** (19:1a–b). What sort of city did the name "Ephesus" evoke in the authorial audience? Philostratus describes ancient Ephesus thus:

> Who would desire to deprive Ephesus of her salvation, a city which took its beginnings from that purest of beings, Atthis, and which grew in size beyond all other cities of Ionia and Lydia, and stretched herself out to the sea, on the promontory over which she is built, and is filled with studious people, both philosophers and rhetoricians, thanks to whom the city owes her strength, not to her cavalry, but to the tens of thousands of her inhabitants in whom she encourages wisdom? (*Vit. Apoll.* 8.7.8)

Its economic, commercial, and cultural significance were widely attested (Strabo, *Geogr.* 14.1.24; cf. Thomas 1995, 81–117). Ephesus eventually became a major center for early Christianity as well (Oster 1987; Lampe 1992; Koester 1995).

The rest of the unit fits a chiastic pattern (modifying Shauf 2005, 145; Talbert 2005, 167):

A Paul finds "some" disciples (19:1b)
  B Question and answer regarding Holy Spirit (19:2)
    C Question and answer regarding baptism (19:3)
      D Paul teaches about John's baptism and John's relationship to Jesus (19:4)
    C′ Disciples are baptized into Jesus' name (19:5)
  B′ Disciples receive Holy Spirit and concomitant gifts (19:6)
A′ There are twelve disciples (19:7)

We may begin by inquiring as to the identity of **some disciples** (19:1b) found by Paul in Ephesus. The very reference to them as "disciples" would suggest that they belong to the Christian movement known as the Way, since elsewhere in Acts the term *always* refers to Christian disciples (Acts 6:1, 2, 7; 9:1, 10, 19, 25, 26 [twice], 38; 11:26, 29; 13:52; 14:20, 22, 28; 15:10; 16:1; 18:23, 27; 19:9, 30; 20:1, 30; 21:4, 16 [twice]; cf. Shauf 2005, 107). However, the plural term "disciples" is used only here in Acts without the article (Dunn

1970, 84). Thus the phrase "some disciples" (or "certain disciples") introduces a note of ambiguity when viewed in light of the other references. Even more compelling, however, is the use of the word "believe" in Paul's question: "Did you receive the Holy Spirit when you believed?" (19:2). The absolute use of *pisteuō* in Acts always refers to Christian believers (Acts 8:12–13; 15:5; 18:27; 19:18; 21:20, 25; Backhaus 1991, 199; Shauf 2005, 147). Taken together, this evidence points not to a group of disciples of John (contra Käsemann 1982, 136–48, and others following him) but rather to a group of Christian believers whose relationship with the Way is tenuous. The rest of the story explores and resolves that ambiguity.

The story proceeds (19:2) with a "Q and A" session between Paul and the disciples. Theon lists questions and dialogue as alternative ways to set out a narrative (*Prog.* 87, trans. Kennedy 2003, 35). About dialogue he writes: "If we wish to use a dialogue form, we shall suppose some people talking with each other about what has been done, and one teaching, the other learning, about the occurrences" (*Prog.* 89, trans. Kennedy 2003, 37). Theon also makes clear that questions are part of the dialogue form: "we shall continue asking and answering in accordance with the rules of dialogue" (*Prog.* 90, trans. Kennedy 2003, 38; cf. *Rhet. Her.* 4.52.65). Paul asks: **Did you receive the Holy Spirit when you believed?** (19:2a), to which they rather surprisingly respond: **We have not even heard whether there is a Holy Spirit** (19:2b). This answer has troubled interpreters at least since the scribes of P[38] (ca. AD 300) and D (fifth century) changed the text to read: "We have not heard *that anyone has received* the Holy Spirit." This change suggests the disciples are referring specifically to the Pentecost event and is a favorite interpretation among modern commentators, even among those who do not follow the variant reading (Bauernfeind 1980, 229; Bruce 1988, 363; Polhill 1992, 398–99). The text as we have it, however, suggests a basic ignorance of the Holy Spirit, although whether it is in terms

We Haven't Even Heard Whether There Is a Holy Spirit

In Acts 19:2, Paul uses the interrogative particle *ei* to introduce a direct question, which, strictly speaking, is unnecessary, even "unclassical" (a Hebraism? cf. BDF 440.3). It is used again by the Ephesians as a "marker of an indirect question as content" (BDAG 277.2) or in an indirect question to indicate "whether" (BDAG 278.5b). The two functions provide an example of the rhetorical figure of *antanaklasis*, "which occurs when the same word is used first in one function, and then in another as follows . . . 'I would leave this place, should the Senate give me leave' (*Veniam ad vos, si mihi senatus det veniam*)" (*Rhet. Her.* 4.14.21, trans. Caplan 1954, 281). In Acts 19:2, the figure serves to highlight the uncertainty and lack of knowledge of the Holy Spirit on the disciples' part: "We haven't even heard whether there is a Holy Spirit!"

of the disciples' knowledge or experience (or both) is, at this point, impossible to tell.

This difficulty does not stop Paul. He presses on with a second question in the dialogue: **How then were you baptized?** (19:3a). Paul's question can be taken literally, "Into what, then, were you baptized?" The response would have the logical sense of "Into John's baptism." Or the question can be understood to express purpose: "What then was the point of your baptism?" In this case, the disciples' response would mean something like, "To follow John's way of baptism" (see Culy and Parsons 2003, 360). The former sense is more natural; the disciples respond: **With John's baptism** (19:3b). Thus Paul's question connects the Holy Spirit with baptism at the level both of experience and knowledge. If they had been baptized, they should have received the Holy Spirit; if they have been baptized, they should have at least heard about the Holy Spirit (Shauf 2005, 151). These disciples have evidently done neither; their faith is somehow defective.

Paul moves in the dialogue from learner to teacher (see Theon above). In a "resolving utterance" (Levinsohn 1992, 132), he instructs them on the purpose of John's baptism: **John baptized (using) a baptism of repentance and told the people that they should believe in the one who was coming after him—that is, in Jesus** (19:4). The audience might have expected Paul to echo John himself and contrast John's baptism "with water" with Jesus' baptism "with the Holy Spirit and with fire" (Luke 3:16). Instead, Paul instructs the disciples regarding the preparatory nature of John's baptism and ministry. His baptism was for repentance; his ministry was to prepare people for the one who was coming after him, namely Jesus. As such, Paul is echoing points he had already made about John's baptism of repentance and ministry as forerunner in a speech he gave at Antioch: "John had preached, prior to his coming, a baptism of repentance to all the people of Israel. But when John was about to complete his mission, he had said, 'What do you think I am? I am not that. But a person is coming after me whose sandals I am not worthy to untie!'" (Acts 13:24–25). Chrysostom, long ago, captured the sense of this passage: "John's baptism did not have this effect [e.g., giving prophecies] and was therefore incomplete. Rather, it prepared them beforehand so that they would be deemed worthy of such a thing. So this was the intent of John's baptism, that they should believe in the one who was to come after him" (*Hom. Act.* 40).

With this explanation Luke proceeds to record the remedy of the disciples' deficiencies, first in terms of baptism and then in terms of the Holy Spirit: **When they heard (this), they were baptized in the name of the Lord Jesus** (19:5). Baptism in the "name of Jesus" is mentioned only three other times in Acts (2:38; 8:16; 10:48). The first occurrence in Peter's Pentecost address is programmatic: "Repent, and be baptized, each of you, in the name of Jesus Christ for the forgiveness of your sins and you will receive the gift of the Holy Spirit." The connection between baptism in Jesus' name and the gift of the

Holy Spirit is clear, and the lack of knowledge of and experience with the Holy Spirit on the part of disciples, who know only John's baptism of repentance, is understandable. But as the other occurrences demonstrate, the connection between baptism and the gift of the Spirit is not causal; the latter is never caused by the former (Shauf 2005, 155). In Acts 8:15–16 the Holy Spirit falls on the Samaritans after Peter and John pray and lay hands on them; in Acts 10:47–48 Cornelius and his household are baptized *after* they receive the Holy Spirit. Thus we should not be surprised when, as in the case of the "Samaritan Pentecost," the Holy Spirit only comes with baptism in the name of Jesus and the imposition of hands.

The final remedy of the disciples' deficiency occurred when **Paul placed his hands on them, the Holy Spirit came on them, and they began speaking in tongues and prophesying** (19:6). At last, baptized in Jesus' name and recipients of the laying on of hands, these disciples receive the Holy Spirit, along with the gifts of glossolalia and prophecy that accompany that gift. Their transformation and full incorporation into the community are complete.

Interpreters are divided as to whether the number **twelve** (19:7) lacks any symbolic overtones (Fitzmyer 1998, 644; Polhill 1992, 400) or is symbolic, and if so whether it symbolizes the twelve apostles (Walaskay 1998, 177) or the twelve tribes of Israel (Talbert 2005, 167; Johnson 1992, 338). In either case, this story is about "how Paul removed the deficiencies of a fringe group, thereby bringing them into the group marked by the proper understanding of and faith in Jesus, baptism in Jesus' name, and the gift of the Holy Spirit. The initial status of the twelve may be in question, but their final status is not" (Shauf 2005, 149).

Bede on Acts 19:7

The Venerable Bede connects the "apostolic" number to an earlier passage, Acts 16:6, in which Paul and company are forbidden to go at that point into Asia (and presumably Ephesus):

"Behold, Asia, which not long before was unworthy to be visited by the apostles [Acts 16:6], now consecrated by the apostolic number [i.e., twelve] and exalted by a prophetic gift! And it should be noted that the Holy Spirit showed signs of his coming both here in the twelve disciples, and earlier in the hundred and twenty [Acts 1:15] (which is the number twelve multiplied ten times). I believe that the former [manifestation occurred] in Jerusalem, and this one in Ephesus, which is a Greek city, to show that whether the one who believes is from the Jews or the Gentiles, he [the Spirit] fills only those who share in the unity of the catholic and apostolic church." (Comm. Acts 19.7, trans. L. Martin 1989)

Chrysostom on Apollos and the Ephesian Disciples

The early commentator John Chrysostom also picked up the syncritic elements of comparison/contrast between Apollos and the Ephesian disciples:

"And how is it that they who received the Spirit did not teach, but Apollos did when he had not yet received the Spirit? Because they were not so fervent or even so instructed. He, on the other hand, was instructed and very fervent. It seems to me that great was the man's boldness. But even if he taught the things concerning Jesus accurately, [Apollos] still needed more accurate teaching. So, though he did not know everything, by his enthusiasm he drew to himself the Holy Spirit, as did Cornelius and his companions."
(Hom. Act. 40, trans. Martin and Smith 2006, 232)

With Acts 18:24–19:7, we have another *synkrisis* ("language setting the better or worse side by side"; cf. Theon, *Prog.* 112, trans. Kennedy 2003, 52), this time between Apollos and the twelve disciples at Ephesus. Apollos is depicted much more favorably than the "disciples" encountered by Paul. The disciples, on the one hand, were not only limited to the baptism of John; they had not heard that there was a Holy Spirit! (19:2). Apollos, on the other hand, spoke with "fervent enthusiasm" (18:25). Further, these Ephesian disciples had to be instructed about the meaning of John's baptism for the coming of Jesus, while Apollos, limited as he was to John's baptism, is still able to teach "accurately the things concerning Jesus" (18:25). With a little fine-tuning instruction from Priscilla and Aquila (note a woman instructing an evangelist here in a post-Pauline document; cf. 1 Tim 2:12), Apollos is able to secure a letter of recommendation from the Ephesians to continue his ministry in Corinth (18:27–28; 19:1). These contrasts explain why the Ephesian disciples needed to receive baptism in the name of Jesus and the gift of the Holy Spirit (confirmed again by glossolalia; cf. 2:1–4; 10:44–48) while Apollos did not, even though both knew only the baptism of John.

Summary: Two Years at Ephesus (19:8–10)

Acts 19:8–10 is a condensed summary that echoes previous episodes, but with some noteworthy differences. After entering the synagogue, Paul spoke boldly over the course of three months, debating and trying to convince (them) about the kingdom of God (19:8). The language ("entering the synagogue" and "debating") is reminiscent of Paul's earlier encounter with the Ephesian Jews (18:12–21), in which he promised to return to them (although if this passage is to be taken as fulfillment of that promise, it is subtly done). The language used to describe Paul's activities in 19:8 is also typical of (but not unique to) Paul's behavior elsewhere: he "spoke boldly" (cf. 9:27, 28; 13:46; 14:3; 19:8; 26:26);

he is "debating" (17:2, 17; 18:4, 19; 19:9; 20:7, 9; 24:12, 25); and he is "trying to convince" (13:42; 18:4; 28:23). The subject of his activity, "the kingdom of God," is likewise a typical topic for Christian proclamation in Acts (cf. 1:3; 8:12; 14:22; 28:23, 31). The results of his synagogue disputation are likewise conventional; the Jews reject him and his movement, the Way: **certain men became stubborn and refused to believe, and (even) denounced the Way in front of the crowd** (19:9a; cf. 13:14–52; 14:1–2; 17:1–9, 10–15; 18:4–11).

There are, however, significant variations to the repeated pattern here (Shauf 2005, 165–68). First, there is the relatively long period, "three months," of Paul's disputation in the synagogues. Luke lists a time frame for only two of the previous five synagogue scenes: Paul debates for two Sabbaths in Antioch of Pisidia (13:14–46) and three in Thessalonica (17:1–9). While not a mark of unqualified success, the time period does suggest a much more intense and prolonged period of dialogue with his fellow Jews.

That the dialogue was at least partially successful is indicated by the use of the indefinite pronoun, "certain" or "few," suggesting, at least indirectly, that not all were opposed to Paul's teaching. Paul's success in the synagogue is hinted at also by Luke's note that when **he left them,** Paul **took the disciples** with him (19:9b). Presumably, this group of disciples included those Jews who became believers during his three-month ministry at the Ephesian synagogue.

Further, this opposition, unlike other scenes, does not lead to Paul's "turning to the Gentiles" (cf. 13:46–48; 18:6–7). In fact, Paul is not forced to leave the city as he was in all other synagogue disputes, except Corinth (13:50; 14:3–6; 17:5–10, 13–14). Instead, Paul **began speaking daily in the lecture hall of Tyrannus so that all those living in Asia, both Jews and Greeks, heard the message of the Lord** (19:9c–10). Thus over the ensuing two years Paul engages in a preaching activity in a typical lecture hall in which pupils and teachers met (cf. Aristotle, *Pol.* 1313b; Plutarch, *Alex.* 7.3; Dionysius of Halicarnassus, *Isocr.* 1; *Dem.* 44) that "seems to be good for both Jews and Gentiles" (Shauf 2005, 168).

Paul and the Sons of Sceva (19:11–20)

As in the portrayal of Philip, Paul's healing ministry (19:11–12; cf. 8:6–7; also 5:15) confirms his message regarding the "kingdom of God" (19:8) and, as in the story of Philip, is one of the ways Luke distinguishes the mighty works of God from the activities of Satan: **God performed extraordinary miracles through the hands of Paul so that even handkerchiefs and belts (he had used) were taken from him to the sick and the sickness left them and the evil spirits went away** (19:11–12). By healing illnesses and casting out unclean spirits, Paul confirms the Christian kerygma that the authority of Satan has been overturned (on this passage, see Garrett 1989, 89–99). Paul uses litotes (lit., "not ordinary"; see Acts 12:18–19; *Rhet. Her.* 4.38.50) to describe the miracles God performs through Paul. Important to Luke's argument here is that these

"extraordinary miracles" are performed by God "through the hands of Paul";
God is the actor, Paul is the agent, and the explication of Paul's teaching (the
"kingdom of God"; 19:8) is the goal.

Although the reference to the "handkerchiefs and belts (or aprons)" is often
understood to refer to Paul's tent-making attire of "sweat-rags" and "aprons"
(Bruce 1988, 467), the context of Paul's teaching in the hall of Tyrannus more
readily suggests that these garments represent the "accepted dress of an orator" (Strelan 2003, 157). While the "handkerchiefs" (*soudaria*) could refer
to a variety of clothing worn in multiple contexts, it was used specifically to
refer to a cloth used by orators to mop the brow (Suetonius, *Nero* 25.3, 51;
Quintilian, *Inst.* 6.3.60; 11.3.118) and "was worn and used for effect as much
as it was for practical purposes" (Strelan 2003, 155). The *sēmikinthia* probably refers to a belt or sash rather than an apron (cf. Petronius, *Sat.* 94.8), and
belts were often thought to symbolize life-giving power (Pliny the Elder, *Nat.*
28.9; Strelan 2003, 157). It is God working through the *body* of Paul (on the
power of bodies to heal, see Plutarch, *Pyrrh.* 3.4–5; *Mart. Pol.* 17–18), who is
an agent of God (and not the garments themselves), who, by virtue of that
role, possesses the power to cure illnesses and cast out demons. Just as Philip
the miracle-worker was superior to Simon the magician because his extraordinary deeds were done to demonstrate his teaching about the rule of God
rather than self-aggrandizement, so Paul's "exorcisms at a distance" provide
divine testimony to the authenticity of his message, in sharp contrast to the
practices of some of the itinerant Jewish exorcists who attempted to invoke
the name of the Lord Jesus over those who had evil spirits saying, "I order
you by Jesus whom Paul preaches (to come out)" (19:13).

As with the case of Philip versus Simon (Acts 8) and Paul versus Elymas
(Acts 13), we have here a struggle between an agent of God and agents of
Satan, here seven sons of Sceva, a Jewish chief priest (19:14), although the
specific battleground here is exorcism, not magic (on Jewish exorcists, see
Josephus, *Ant.* 8.2.5.45–49). Earlier in Luke's Gospel, Jesus had turned the false
accusation made against him that he was casting out demons "by Beelzebul, the
ruler of the demons" (Luke 11:15) against his accusers ("If I cast out demons
by Beelzebul, by whom do your exorcists cast them out?"; 11:19). Instead, Jesus
suggests that he is performing exorcisms "by the finger of God" in order to
demonstrate that "the kingdom of God has come to you" (11:20). So here in
Acts 19, the "finger of God" works through the "hands of Paul" once again to
cast out demons and to demonstrate that the "kingdom of God" has come.

In this context, the failed attempt of the Jewish exorcists functions as a
parody of an exorcism. In their adjuration, Sceva's seven sons attempt to
manipulate the "name of the Lord Jesus," whom they presumably know only
through Paul's preaching, with the result that an evil spirit answers with a
question of his own: I know Jesus, and I know about Paul, but who are you?
(19:15). The demon does not know them, that is, does not acknowledge their

authority, and therefore refuses to obey them. The demon's response indicates at least one aspect of the Jewish exorcists' failure: unlike Jesus (Luke 8:26–39) and Paul (Acts 16:16–18), they do not possess the stature to effect the exorcism, a stature that for Luke, as we have seen, comes with functioning as an agent for God and his rule. The demon then literally adds injury to the insult: **Then the man who had the evil spirit in him jumped on them. He overpowered them all and defeated them so that they ran away from that house naked and wounded** (19:16). Both the vivid, ekphrastic language (*Rhet. Her.* 4.50.68; cf. Acts 2:4; 8:6) and the foregrounding in Greek of the phrase "naked and wounded" heightens the sense of the humiliation that the exorcists suffer (Klutz 1999, 264). Hence, the reversal of the exorcism is complete; the Jewish exorcists, unlike Paul, are unable to complete the task (Talbert 2005, 169). And the prediction of Jesus is fulfilled, at least in spirit if not in letter: "Whoever is not with me is against me, and whoever does not gather with me scatters," and, "Then it [the unclean spirit] goes and brings seven other spirits more evil than itself, and they enter and live there; and the last state of that person becomes worse than the first" (Luke 11:23, 26).

While the episode is primarily about exorcism, one should not dismiss connections between exorcism and magic in this episode (contra Shauf 2005, 177–224). The language used to describe the activities echoes magical practices of antiquity, especially the term "adjure," which, as Susan Garrett correctly notes, is not used by Jesus or his disciples in any exorcism story. Rather, the term is frequently used in magical incantations in a double command: "I adjure X by [the authority of] Y." The adjuration is an attempt to manipulate both the object of adjuration and the deity whose authority is invoked. Thus in Mark 5:7 the words of the Gerasene demoniac to Jesus ("I adjure you by God") are an attempt to manipulate and control both Jesus and God (Garrett 1989, 154). That these exorcists are using the formula "the Jesus whom Paul preaches" probably implies that they, like Simon Magus, had mistaken Christian miracles for feats of magic. Thus they try to use Jesus' name in a way typical of magical technique, but Luke makes it clear that Jesus' name is not some magical talisman vulnerable to manipulation.

The connection between magic and exorcism is seen also in those who (mistakenly) identified Paul's garments as the vehicle through which the dismissal of evil spirits was effected. Garments were occasionally used in magical incantations, as in this adjuration, presumably attributed to Isis, preserved in a sixth–seventh AD text: "I invoke you (pl.) by your names, *by your garments*, by the places in which you dwell" (London Hay 10391 in *ACM* no. 127). Finally, that the story moves beyond exorcism into the realm of magic is seen by the response of the Ephesians: **This (incident) became known to all who lived in Ephesus, both Jews and Greeks. They were all afraid, and the name of the Lord Jesus was greatly honored** (19:17). The defeat of the sons of Sceva makes the accomplishments of Paul's exorcisms even more impressive, a fact

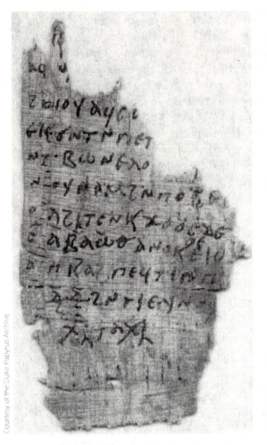

Figure 11. A Magical Text.

Scholars believe that the books gathered for burning at Ephesus may have resembled the Coptic magical texts that archaeologists have recovered in Egypt. Depicted is P.Duk.inv. 256, which mentions "Sabaoth" and contains magical symbols.

not lost on the Ephesians. Luke's language ("greatly honored" or "extolled," and "afraid" or "awestruck") is intimately associated with conversion (cf. 9:31; 10:46). This incident demonstrates that the name of Jesus cannot be manipulated and therefore is worthy of praise: Jesus' name is to be extolled, not adjured.

Further, these Jews and Greeks had already heard the word of the Lord (19:10) and seen the defeat of Satan confirmed in the healing ministry of Paul (19:11–12). Now they reckon with the fact that magic itself is obsolete: **And many of those who had believed were coming and openly confessing what they had done. A substantial number of those who had practiced magic gathered (their) books and then burned them before everyone. They added up the value of the books and found (that they had been worth) 50,000 silver coins** (19:19). Book burning was a fairly common event in antiquity (see Josephus, *Ant.* 10.6.2; Diogenes Laertius, *Vit. phil.* 9.52; Livy, *Hist.* 39.16.8; Augustine, *Bapt.* 5.1; cf. Talbert 2005, 169; Pease 1946, 145–60). In this case, the burning of the magical books is to be viewed as the act of believers who, as a result

272

of this incident, forsook their belief in and practice of magic and became believers (cf. Diogenes Laertius, *Vit. phil.* 6.95; ps.-John of Damascus, *Vit. Barl.* 32.302; Talbert 2005, 170). Rather than perish with their silver (as Peter had warned, Acts 8:20), the Ephesian magicians "make the better choice from a Lukan perspective, giving up their profitable trade to save their lives and secure their place in the kingdom of God" (Spencer 2004, 197).

Furthermore, as we noted earlier (see on 12:24) the phrase that concludes this section—**In this powerful way, the message of the Lord spread and prevailed** (19:20)—is one way Luke refers to the addition of believers to the church (see also 6:7). Ironically, the victory of the demon over Sceva's sons is actually a defeat for the devil, because both sides serve Satan (Garrett 1989, 98). Satan's kingdom is divided and thus doomed (Luke 11:18), and the word of the Lord continues to grow.

Paul's Resolve and the Riot at Ephesus (19:21–41)

The chain-link function of 19:21–41 in the overall structure of Acts was discussed above under Introductory Matters. It remains to interpret the text in its immediate context, a passage long and often noted to be a "literary gem" (Duffy 1994, 8) and "among the most brilliant bits of word-painting in Acts" (Foakes-Jackson 1931, 179).

This scene shares similarities with previous public accusations (in chaps. 16, 17, and 18). Here, as in the first scene in Philippi, the accusers are Gentiles (Jews are accusers in Thessalonica and Corinth; see Tannehill 1990, 202–3), making it a mistake to view opposition to the Christian movement as only and characteristically Jewish. Rather, both "Jews and Gentiles view the mission as a threat to the customs that provide social cohesion, to the religious basis of their cultures, and to political stability through Caesar's rule" (Tannehill 1990, 203). The scene also bears remarkable similarity to the riot in the Jerusalem temple (21:27–36). Especially similar is the reason for the riot in both instances: "Members of an established religion are protesting the effect that Paul's mission is having on their religion and its temple" (Tannehill 1990, 242).

19:21–22. In 19:21–22, Luke anticipates the rest of Paul's ministry as it is recorded in Acts: **After these things had happened, Paul decided to travel through Macedonia and Achaia and go to Jerusalem. He said (to himself), "After I have been there, I must also see Rome." He sent two of those who helped him—Timothy and Erastus—(ahead) to Macedonia, while he himself stayed for a while longer in Asia** (19:21–22). Thus Paul resolves in the Spirit (19:21) to go

> **An Outline of Acts**
> **19:21–41**
>
> Paul's resolve and the riot at Ephesus (19:21–41)
>
> Paul's resolve (19:21–22)
>
> Demetrius's speech and the shrines of Artemis (19:23–27)
>
> The riot (19:28–34)
>
> The town clerk ends the riot (19:35–41)

through Macedonia and Achaia (see 20:1–12), to visit Jerusalem once again (see 21:15–38), and finally to go to Rome (see 28:14–16). The language is quite strong; Paul says that he "must" (*dei*) see Rome, a word characteristically used in Acts to describe divine purpose. As such it is reminiscent of Jesus' resolve to go to Jerusalem (Luke 9:51). And though suffering is not mentioned explicitly here, there is good reason to see that the parallels between Jesus' journey to Jerusalem and Paul's journey to Rome include the dimension of suffering. For Paul, this insight becomes clearer the farther he journeys (20:22–24), but here we have the first step taken by Paul in understanding his divine destiny to travel to Rome.

19:23–27. The scene quickly shifts: **At that time there was a serious disturbance concerning the Way (19:23).** Though Paul is largely absent from this scene, he remains at the center of controversy. The unit opens with **a certain man named Demetrius, a silversmith, making silver shrines of Artemis (19:24),** addressing his fellow artisans: **"you have seen and heard how this Paul has persuaded and misled a substantial crowd, not only in Ephesus but in nearly all of Asia, by saying that these things that are made by (human) hands are not gods" (19:26).** Although Paul is not recorded as criticizing the pagan religion in Ephesus, there is no reason to doubt Demetrius's description, given Paul's teachings against idols made with hands elsewhere (Acts 14:15–17; 17:22–31).

Demetrius had accurately perceived that Paul's invectives against idols would be bad for business: **You know that our prosperity comes from this business (19:25)** of making silver shrines for Artemis; **there is a danger for us that this business will be seriously criticized (19:27a).** Not only was the temple of Artemis considered one of the architectural wonders of the world (Antipater, in *AG* 9.58; Pausanias, *Descr.* 7.5.4; Philo of Byzantium, *Sept.* 6.1); it was also a preeminent financial center. Paulus Fabius Persicus, for example, noted that the temple of Artemis was "the ornament of the whole province because of its size, its antiquity, and *the abundance of its revenues*" (*I.Eph.* Ia.18; Horsley 1992, 147–48; cf. also Dio Chrysostom, *Rhod.* 54). Thus Demetrius's economic concerns were well-founded. Pliny, in his letter to the emperor Trajan in the early second century AD, wrote of measures he took to reverse the negative economic effects that Christianity had wrought in Bithynia: "the temples, which had been almost deserted, begin now to be frequented . . . [and] there is a general demand for sacrificial animals, which for some time past have met with few purchases" (*Ep. Tra.* 10.96). Luke uses the rhetorical figure of litotes (cf. Acts 12:18–19; *Rhet. Her.* 4.38.50)—"not a little disturbance" (19:23) and "no little profit" (19:24)—to show that "the extent of the disturbance is in proportion to the extent of the perception of the loss of the workers' profit" (Shauf 2005, 252).

To this economic argument Demetrius adds a religious one: **The temple of the great goddess Artemis will be considered unimportant, and even that one whom the whole of Asia and the world worship will soon be thrown down** from her greatness! (19:27b). The status attributed to Artemis by Demetrius is supported by epigraphic and numismatic evidence (Oster 1979; Trebilco 1994, 332–36). Consider, for example, the claims made in this inscription from the mid-second century AD:

> Since the goddess Artemis, leader of our city, is honoured not only in her own homeland, which she has made the most illustrious of all cities through her own divine nature, but also among Greeks and also barbarians, the result is that everywhere her shrines and sanctuaries have been established, and temples have been founded for her and altars dedicated to her because of the visible manifestations effected by her. (*I.Eph.* Ia.24.B.5–15)

Whether the remarkable success of Paul in Ephesus (19:1–20) could have at this point in the development of the movement known as the Way rendered Artemis as "unimportant" or "thrown down from her greatness" is debatable (but cf. from a century later, the apocryphal *Acts of John*, 37–47, in which just such an event is, in fact, imaginable). Placing this perception on the lips of an opponent of the Way, however, gives the position a rhetorical force that it would have otherwise missed had it been placed on the lips of Paul or one of the other Christian characters.

19:28–34. Certainly the force of Demetrius's words is not lost on his audience: **When they heard (this) they too were filled with rage and began shouting, "Great is Artemis of the Ephesians!"** (19:28). Demetrius is so successful that **the city was filled with confusion, and (the mob) rushed together into the theater** (19:29a). In the ancient city, the theater (and Ephesus had a large one, able to accommodate as many as 25,000) was the typical location for legal assemblies, although this "assembly" had degenerated into a mob before it began. The riot is due to the impact the Way in general has had on Ephesus (and not simply on the effects of Paul); thus the mob seizes two members of the movement, **dragging Gaius and Aristarchus, who were Macedonians and traveling companions of Paul** (19:29b). The situation was too dangerous to allow Paul to enter: **Paul wanted to go in to (the theater to address) the citizen assembly, [but] the disciples would not let him** (19:30). Significantly, some of the most elite of the community join in the admonition for Paul to stay out of the theater, another indication of Paul's success across the socioeconomic strata of Ephesian society (Shauf 2005, 249–50): **Even some of the Asiarchs, who were his friends, sent (a message) to him and urged him not to venture into the theater** (19:31; on the use of the term "friends," see Theological Issues on Acts 27–28).

The scene is mass confusion: **So then, some were shouting one thing, others were shouting something else. For the assembly was confused and most of them did not (even) know why they had come together** (19:32). In the midst of the confusion, **some people from the crowd gave instructions to Alexander** after the Jews had put him forward (19:32). Here the verb *sumbibazō*, with a direct object, has the meaning of "advise by giving instruction" (L&N §33.298; cf. Culy and Parsons 2003, 377).

But why have the Jews become involved in this incident? And when **Alexander waved his hand (to show that) he wanted to present a defense to the people** (19:33), what is the nature of his "apologia"? Rather than disassociating the Jews from the Christians (so Bauernfeind 1980, 234; Bruce 1988, 419; Fitzmyer 1998, 660), Alexander joins with members of the Way to defend monotheistic (both Jewish and Christian) rejection of idols (Dunn 1996, 264). In this case Jews stand with Christians against pagan idolatry because it violates their shared religious convictions. Alexander is not permitted to speak because they **recognized that he was a Jew** (19:34a). Pagan hostility to Jews was widely recognized (Josephus, *Ant.* 16.2.3–4; cf. Acts 16:20; 18:17) and inhospitality to Jewish speakers was particularly offensive to Jews (Philo, *Flacc.* 4.24; Talbert 2005, 172–73). The Ephesians drown out Alexander by joining in an extended "praise chorus" to Artemis: **one cry arose from all those who were shouting, for about two hours: "Great is Artemis of the Ephesians!"** (19:34b).

19:35–41. A speech by Demetrius began the riot; finally a speech by the town clerk ends it (Tannehill 1990, 243). With appropriate rhetorical flourish (cf. 17:23), the town clerk, an important local civic official, begins by identifying with the point of view of the crowds by asking a rhetorical question (Quintilian, *Inst.* 9.2.7): **Ephesians! Is there anyone anywhere who does not know that the city of Ephesus is the keeper of the temple of the great Artemis and the stone from the sky?** (19:35). The clerk appeals to the special relationship that the city has with Artemis as the "keeper" or "guardian" of her temple, a relationship for which there is also numismatic evidence (Friesen 1993, 53–54). The clerk's reference to the "stone from the sky" is an indirect response to Demetrius's report of the criticisms of Paul. Paul did not insult Artemis because hers is the sacred stone that fell from the sky and was not made by human hands (see González 2001, 230). **These things,** the clerk declares, **are undeniable** (19:36a).

On this basis he urges the crowd: **you must restrain yourselves and not do anything rash** (19:36b). He also exonerates Paul's companions: **For you led these men (here) who are neither temple robbers nor blasphemers of our goddess** (19:37). He then provides instructions for the proper handling of the situation: **So then, if Demetrius and the craftsmen with him have a legal complaint against someone, the courts are in session and there are proconsuls (available). Let them bring charges against one another (there). And if you want to deal with anything else, it will have to be resolved in a legal assembly** (19:38–39). In all this, the clerk seems rather Gamaliel-like (see Acts 5:33–40), with one notable difference. The clerk is able to deny blasphemy charges against the Christian missionaries only because he has made Artemis and her "fallen from the sky" image immune to the critique of Paul, a move that neither the Lukan

Calvin on Acts 19:35–40

John Calvin understood the "disconnect" between the Ephesus town clerk's argument and the reality of the situation as understood by Luke and the Lukan Paul:

"Luke showeth in this place that the tumult was so appeased, that yet, notwithstanding, superstition prevailed with the people, and the truth of God was not heard. . . . If Paul had been in the common place at that time, he would rather have suffered death an hundred times than have suffered himself to be delivered from danger paying so dear for it. For though the town-clerk had not been by him commanded to speak thus, yet it should have been treacherous dissimulation in a public witness and preacher of heavenly doctrine. The scribe affirmeth that the image which the Ephesians did worship came down from heaven, and that Paul and his company spake no blasphemy against their goddess. Could he have holden his peace . . . ? And this had been to shake hands with idolatry. Therefore, it was not without cause that Luke said before that Paul was kept back by the brethren, and not suffered to enter into the common place." (Calvin, *Commentary upon the Acts of the Apostles* 2:230–31; Shauf 2005, 257)

Paul nor Luke nor the authorial audience would be prepared to accept (Shauf 2005, 257). Rather, it is an argument that can be convincing only to the clerk's pagan audience—and evidently it is. After chastising the mob for engaging in near riot, he sends them home: **"For we are in danger of being accused of rioting for (what has happened) today, since there is no cause we can offer as an explanation for this commotion." After saying these things, he dismissed the assembly** (19:40–41). The riot subsides, order is restored, and Paul is prepared to make his farewell journey to Jerusalem and Rome (Acts 20–28).

Theological Issues

About Acts 19:11–12, Scott Shauf has noted "the embarrassment with which many commentators have viewed the passage on the outstanding character of Paul's miracles, especially concerning the use of Paul's garments without his active involvement" (Shauf 2003, 111). No doubt this embarrassment is due, in part, to the multiple examples of abusive misinterpretation of the verses. Consider, for example, the exploitations of various televangelists who have employed "prayer cloths" as part of a mass mailing campaign to fleece the pockets of the faithful. Such abuses are noted by Justo González: "The reference to Paul's handkerchiefs and aprons has provided some supposed evangelists with an opportunity to make money by selling handkerchiefs and other items they have blessed" (González 2001, 222).

Other (Protestant) commentators on Acts 19:11–12 have noted "this practice often strikes the modern mind as too close to the relic worship that plagued the medieval church" (Polhill 1992, 402). In so doing, they echo the criticisms of the Protestant reformers who objected to the abuses of the sale of relics as part of the indulgence system. This system was widespread, very lucrative, and subject to much abuse in medieval Christianity (see Brown 1981; Abou-El-Haj 1994). In his commentary on Acts 19, John Calvin wrote: "The Papists are more blockish, who wrest this place unto their relics; as if Paul sent his handkerchiefs that men might worship them and kiss them in honour of them. . . . Yea, rather, he did choose most simple things, lest any superstition arise by reason of the price or pomp" (*Commentary upon the Acts of the Apostles*, 2:215).

We might balance these obvious instances of abuse by noting other examples of "mediated grace," which are more in keeping with the Lukan purpose of demonstrating the "extraordinary deeds" of God. The use of "devotional cloths" goes back to the very beginnings of the Pentecostal movement. R. Marie Griffith has collected testimonies by American Pentecostal women in the 1930s, published in several different denominational weekly organs, the *Evangel* (Church of God of Cleveland, Tennessee), *The Advocate* (Pentecostal Holiness Church), and the *Whole Truth* (African-American, Memphis-based Church of God in Christ) (Griffith 2002, 188–89). She writes: "A common practice reported in the letters printed in Pentecostal devotional materials, whether the audience was predominately white or black, was the use of 'anointed handkerchiefs' in procuring physical healings. This practice found scriptural basis in the nineteenth chapter of Acts (11–12)" (Griffith 2002, 197). Griffith cites several examples (Griffith 2002, 197–98):

> I received the letter and anointed cloths from you, for which I thank the Lord. My heart rejoiced and the power of God came upon me as I applied the cloth to my breast. I could feel the affected part being drawn, and when I applied the second cloth it completely left. I have not felt the hurting any more. I thank the Lord for being healed. (Sister L. Banks, *Whole Truth*, May 9, 1933, 2)

> I received the letter with the anointed handkerchief and wonderful blessings I received after I placed one to my body. . . . I surely do feel so much better. (Mrs. Minnie Johnson, *The Advocate*, Nov. 9, 1933, 15)

More often than not, these handkerchiefs came from other Pentecostal women (and not necessarily, or even often, from the hands of powerful Pentecostal preachers). For example, Della Turtle sent out this simple request: "Will somebody send me a handkerchief?" (*The Advocate*, May 7, 1931, 13). Furthermore, there was rarely money involved, except perhaps to cover mailing costs. Sister Maxwell's offer was typical: "Many write us that they have been wonderfully blest by application of the anointed handkerchiefs. Please remember to send stamps to pay for mailing same. It is not necessary for you to send handker-chiefs, as we have the thin soft material cut in sizes suitable for mailing. We can put a dozen of these in a letter if needed" (Sister Berta Maxwell, *The Advocate*, May 23, 1935, 7). However one evaluates these testimonies, their tone and intent are markedly different from the corruptions more commonly associated with the kind of modern mass mailings of televangelists referenced by González above. As Griffith notes: "The handkerchiefs themselves are just the most ordinary of objects. We use them to wipe away tears or sweat, or blow our noses—just the most ordinary kinds of bodily stuff. But even as these are objects of divine grace, they are also objects of human kindness and generosity. You can see the power of asking someone for a handkerchief out of desperation—when you have tuberculosis or some degenerative disease—and all these handkerchiefs flood into you from this widespread community of people you may never have met before" (http://www.materialreligion.org/journal/handkerchief.html [accessed March 28, 2007]).

Even closer to the Lukan account are the testimonies regarding the healing efficacies associated with the cult of the saints in late antiquity, especially prior to their intimate association with the abuses of medieval indulgences (although in the case cited below, Ambrose's transfer of the martyrs' remains to the altar of the cathedral did no doubt help consolidate his episcopal authority in Milan; see Brown 1981, 36–37). Consider, for example, Ambrose's report to his congregation regarding the discovery of the remains of the martyrs Gervasius and Protasius in AD 386. He comments on the healing efficacy of the martyr's remains:

> You know—nay, you have yourselves seen—that many are cleansed from evil spirits, that very many also, having touched with their hands the robe of the saints, are freed from those ailments which oppressed them; you see that the miracles of old time are renewed, when through the coming of the Lord Jesus grace was more largely shed forth upon the earth, and that many bodies are healed as it were by the shadow of the holy bodies. How many napkins are passed about! How many garments, laid upon the holy relics and endowed with healing power, are claimed! All are glad to touch even the outside thread, and whosoever touches will be made whole. (*Letter* 22.9, trans. *NPNF*² 10:438)

Ambrose also reports on a miracle that occurred to a blind butcher, Severus, during the transfer of the remains for burial. Severus, Ambrose relates, was able to call as witnesses those who had previously known him.

> They [the Arians] deny that the blind man received sight, but he denies not that he is healed. He says: I who could not see now see. He says: I ceased to be blind, and proves it by the fact. They deny the benefit, who are unable to deny the fact. The man is known: so long as he was well he was employed in the public service; his name is Severus, a butcher by trade. He had given up his occupation when

> this hindrance befel him. He calls for evidence those persons by whose kindness he was supported; he adduces those as able to affirm the truth of his visitation whom he had as witnesses of his blindness. He declares that when he touched the hem of the robe of the martyrs, wherewith the sacred relics were covered, his sight was restored. (*Letter* 22.17, trans. *NPNF*² 10:439)

St. Augustine, a professor at Milan at the time, also knows this story and adds the detail that the butcher touched his handkerchief to the body of the martyr and then to his eyes, achieving instantaneous recovery of sight (*Conf.* 9.7.16).

About reported miracles associated with relics, and this account by Ambrose in particular, Ronald Kydd observed: "One must avoid rank credulity when faced with these accounts. Nonetheless, I find it difficult to state categorically that nothing extraordinary ever happened. The story of Ambrose's butcher who received his sight back is remarkable by any standard" (Kydd 1998, 129).

In response to criticisms, the Council of Trent, in its twenty-fifth session (December 1563), issued a call for reform "in the invocation of saints, the veneration of relics, and the sacred use of images" in that "every superstition

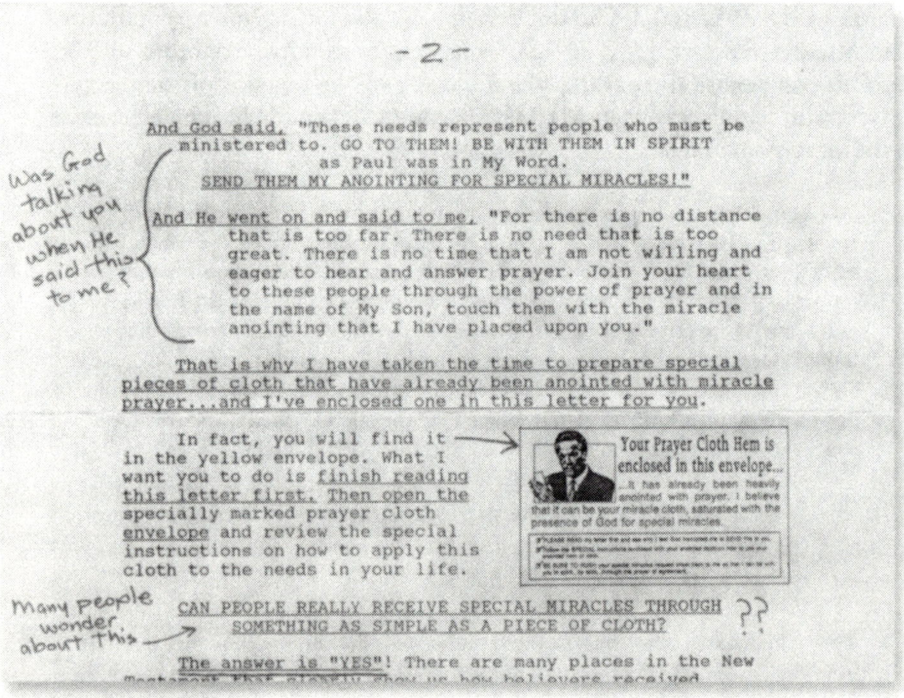

-2-

And God said, "These needs represent people who must be ministered to. GO TO THEM! BE WITH THEM IN SPIRIT as Paul was in My Word. SEND THEM MY ANOINTING FOR SPECIAL MIRACLES!"

Was God talking about you when He said this to me?

And He went on and said to me, "For there is no distance that is too far. There is no need that is too great. There is no time that I am not willing and eager to hear and answer prayer. Join your heart to these people through the power of prayer and in the name of My Son, touch them with the miracle anointing that I have placed upon you."

That is why I have taken the time to prepare special pieces of cloth that have already been anointed with miracle prayer...and I've enclosed one in this letter for you.

In fact, you will find it in the yellow envelope. What I want you to do is finish reading this letter first. Then open the specially marked prayer cloth envelope and review the special instructions on how to apply this cloth to the needs in your life.

Your Prayer Cloth Hem is enclosed in this envelope...

Many people wonder about this

CAN PEOPLE REALLY RECEIVE SPECIAL MIRACLES THROUGH SOMETHING AS SIMPLE AS A PIECE OF CLOTH? *??*

The answer is "YES"! There are many places in the New

Figure 12. What Would Luke Think?

This excerpt from a letter from a mid-twentieth-century evangelist shows how popular Christian faith in "prayer cloths," based on NT texts such as Acts 19:11–12, has been exploited for fund-raising purposes.

shall be removed, all filthy lucre be abolished; finally, all lasciviousness be avoided." The Council of Trent also clarified the relationship between the relics and the martyrs themselves in a way consistent with Luke's emphasis that the healing bore testimony to the "extraordinary deeds" of God and not to the efficacy of the cloth or even the saint: "Also, that the holy bodies of holy martyrs, and of others now living with Christ,—which bodies were the living members of Christ, and the temple of the Holy Ghost, and which are by Him to be raised unto eternal life, and to be glorified,—are to be venerated by the faithful; through which (bodies) many benefits are bestowed by God on men" (Session 25, December 1563; Martin Luther makes a similar distinction calling the "sufferings" of the martyrs the "true relics"; cf. *Luther's Works*, 31:226).

Abuses and superstitions, past and present, make it difficult, perhaps impossible, for modern interpreters to hear Acts 19:11–12 without a certain amount of skepticism, and naive credulity is no doubt to be avoided. Differences abound; no money exchanged hands in Acts 19, in contrast to Simon's actions in Acts 8, medieval indulgences, and modern mass mailings. Further, unlike the cult of relics, God works through Paul's "holy body" while he is still alive. However, if we are able to "suspend disbelief" even momentarily, we might ponder in wonder and perhaps even be edified by the "extraordinary deeds" wrought by God through Paul to underscore the efficacy of God's benevolent rule.

Paul's Farewell Journey

This last division (Acts 20–28) narrates Paul's farewell journey to Jerusalem and Rome. The unit consists of four episodes: Paul's last journey to Jerusalem (20:1–21:16); Paul in Jerusalem (21:17–23:35); Paul on trial before Felix, Festus, and Agrippa (chaps. 24–26); and Paul's sea voyage to Rome (27–28). For much of this part of the story Paul is under arrest, and the narrative is punctuated with Paul's defense speeches. Paul's major interlocutors in these episodes are the Romans and the Jews, and the characterization of each group is rather complex (Polhill 1992, 440–43). The Romans are both Paul's protectors (21:33; 23:27) and his persecutors (21:33; 22:24). They are more concerned at times with their own interests than in getting to the "truth" about Paul (24:25–26), despite

---

Acts 20–28 in Context

The people and places of the Jerusalem church (1–12)

  The sense of a beginning (1–7)

  Beyond Jerusalem: Philip, Saul, Peter, and others (8–12)

The missionary activities of Paul (13–28)

  Paul's mission to the Gentile world (13–19)

▶ Paul's farewell journey (20–28)

  Paul's last journey to Jerusalem (20:1–21:16)

  Paul in Jerusalem (21:17–23:35)

  Paul before Felix, Festus, and Agrippa (24–26)

  The sea voyage to Rome (27–28)

protests otherwise (cf. comments on 23:27). As judge, Festus asserts Paul's innocence (25:25), and yet tries to curry favor with the Jews (25:9). These Romans are hardly perfect examples of rendering justice.

The portrait of the Jews in these final chapters is also complex. Certainly there is no lack of Jewish opposition to Paul and his company (21:31, 36; 23:12–15; 24:5; 25:3), but there are also laudatory examples of Jewish piety (21:20; 22:12; 26:9–11). The major division among the Jews in these chapters is a theological debate about resurrection between the Pharisees (and Paul) and the Sadducees (23:6; 24:21; cf. 23:29; 25:19). In the final scene, some of the Jews are convinced by Paul's preaching while others disbelieve (28:24).

Acts 20:1–21:16

Paul's Last Journey to Jerusalem

Introductory Matters

In chapter 20, Paul gives encouragement to fellow believers through his words (20:1–6, 17–38) and his actions (20:7–12). In 21:1–16, Luke focuses on the warnings to Paul not to go to Jerusalem in the midst of a travel summary (21:1–6) and the prediction of his suffering, should he decide to do so, in his encounter with Agabus in Caesarea (21:7–16).

Tracing the Narrative Flow

Acts 20:1–21:16 describes the beginning of Paul's journey to Jerusalem (20:1–16), recounts his farewell address to the Ephesians (20:17–38), and records the resolve of Paul to continue to Jerusalem despite several warnings otherwise (21:1–16). Throughout the section, Paul exchanges good-byes with those whom he thinks he will never see again.

Acts 20:1–21:16 in the Narrative Flow

The people and places of the Jerusalem church (1–12)

  The sense of a beginning (1–7)

  Beyond Jerusalem: Philip, Saul, Peter, and others (8–12)

The missionary activities of Paul (13–28)

  Paul's mission to the Gentile world (13–19)

  Paul's farewell journey (20–28)

  ▶ Paul's last journey to Jerusalem (20:1–21:16)

    The beginning of the farewell journey (20:1–16)

     From Ephesus to Troas (20:1–6)

     Paul resuscitates Eutychus (20:7–12)

     From Troas to Miletus (20:13–16)

     Paul's farewell address to the Ephesians (20:17–38)

     Warnings to avoid Jerusalem (21:1–16)

285

The Beginning of the Farewell Journey (20:1–16)

Paul's farewell journey begins (20:1–16) with travel from Ephesus to Troas (20:1–6), the episode involving Eutychus (20:7–12), and further travel from Troas to Miletus (20:13–16).

20:1–6. The scene begins: **After the riot had ended, and Paul had sent for the disciples and encouraged (them), he said good-bye and then left for Macedonia (20:1).** Luke makes clear that the purpose of Paul's travels is encouragement: **After traveling through those regions and sharing many words of encouragement, he came into Greece and stayed (there) for three months (20:2–3a).** External opposition to him has not ceased (cf. 23:12–15): **When there was a plot by the Jews against him as he was about to set sail for Syria, he decided to return (instead) through Macedonia (21:3b).**

Luke then recounts that Paul is accompanied by seven named companions who represent various areas of the Gentile mission: **Sopater the son of Pyrrhus, a Berean, accompanied him, as did Aristarchus and Secundus from Thessalonica, Gaius from Derbe, Timothy, and Tychicus and Trophimus, (two) Asians (20:4).** Several of these coworkers are mentioned also in the Pauline letter tradition: Sopater (Rom 16:21?), Aristarchus (Col 4:10; Phlm 24), Timothy (Rom 16:21; 1 Cor 4:17; 16:10; 2 Cor 1:1, 19 *et passim*), Tychicus (Eph 6:21; Col 4:7; 2 Tim 4:12; Titus 3:12), and Trophimus (2 Tim 4:20). The coworkers total seven, and the number indicates both the Gentile mission and a certain completion or fullness of the same (cf. the Seven appointed to represent the concerns of the Hellenists in Acts 6). Luke further reports that [a]**fter going on ahead, these men waited for us in Troas (20:5).** Thus another of Paul's companions reappears here when the narrator employs the first-person narration, the second such "we" passage in Acts (cf. 16:17).

Luke concludes the travel summary with these words: **After the days of unleavened bread, we sailed from Philippi and after five days caught up to them in Troas, where we stayed for seven days (20:6).** The passing reference to the "days of unleavened bread" provides a temporal anchor in the Jewish calendar and implies that Paul, contrary to impending accusations (cf. 21:21), is an observant Jew (Talbert 2005, 176). After a brief separation in Philippi the group reconvenes in Troas. This brief travel summary characterizes Paul's farewell ministry by the continued opposition of the Jews to Paul's witness (20:3) and Paul's encouragement of the believers (20:2).

20:7–12. Paul's encouragement is given further detail in the next scene, in which Paul resuscitates Eutychus. On its surface, the paragraph is a typical miracle story (Talbert 2005, 176). A lad named Eutychus ("Lucky") had the misfortune of falling asleep and then falling out of a window of the upstairs room where they had met (20:9). Pronounced dead by the time Paul gets to him, Paul takes the boy in his arms (2 Kgs 4:34) and announces that he is still alive (20:10). Like Jesus (Luke 7:11–17) and Peter (Acts 9:36–42) before him, Paul now restores to life one who was presumably dead.

At a deeper level, the story served primarily a parenetic, and secondarily, a legitimating function for the authorial audience. In terms of its parenetic function, we note first the chiastic structure of the story (Arterbury 2009):

A On the first day of the week, after we had gathered to break bread, Paul addressed them, because he was about to leave the next day, and he prolonged the conversation until midnight. There were a number of lamps in the upstairs room where we had gathered. (20:7–8)

    B A young man named Eutychus, who was sitting on the window sill (20:9a)

    C falling into a deep sleep as Paul spoke on and on (20:9b)

    C′ was overcome by sleep (20:9c)

    B′ and fell down from the third story. When they picked him up he was dead. But Paul went down and knelt over him. Then, he put his arms around him and said, "Don't worry! He's still alive!" (20:9d–10)

A′ And so, after he had gone (back) upstairs, broken bread and eaten, and then talked (with them) for a long time—until dawn—he left. (20:11)

Verse 12 functions as an epilogue.

The outer ring of the structure A (20:7–8) and A′ (20:11) depicts Paul's interaction with the believers gathered for worship in Troas. There are references to the upper room, the breaking of bread, Paul's preaching, and his departure (Arterbury 2009). The inner ring, B (20:9a) and B′ (20:9d–10), describes Eutychus before and after falling asleep—perched in and falling out of the window and later being resuscitated by Paul. At the center of the ring structure, C (20:9b) and C′ (20:9c), Luke reports twice that sleep has overcome Eutychus.

Is this "sleep" symbolic, and if so, what does the "sleep" symbolize (for what follows, see Arterbury 2008)? In Greek literature especially, "sleep" (*hypnos*) was a deity who brought slumber to humans (and sometimes other gods) with the touch of a branch or sleep-inducing liquid (Homer, *Il.* 14.357–360; 16.451–54; Hesiod, *Theog.* 211–212, 758). "Sleep" was also used metaphorically to refer to divine inactivity (cf. Pss 44:23; 78:65; *b. Sotah* 48a; Homer, *Il.* 1.6.11). Of course sleep functioned euphemistically for death in pagan (cf. *Il*.11.241; *Aen.* 6.1211), Jewish (1 Kgs 2:10; 11:43; 14:20), and Christian literature (John 11:11–13; 1 Cor 15:51; 1 Thess

---

Don't Worry!

Paul's "Don't worry!" (20:10) before his raising of the "sleeping" Eutychus echoes a similar scene in Mark's Gospel in which Jesus asks the crowd, "Why are you worrying?" before raising the "sleeping" daughter of Jairus (Mark 5:39). The term "worry" is missing from the Lukan parallel in Luke 8:52. This passage is another instance of the rich intertextual connections between Acts and the synoptic tradition, especially Mark.

4:13–18; 5:10; *1 Clem* 26.2). "Sleep" could also function metaphorically to refer to irresponsible human behavior. This view is found in pagan literature (*Epic of Gilgamesh* 2.45–49; Homer, *Od.* 10.548–560; Virgil, *Aen.* 5.1100–1141). In his defense speech, Socrates acknowledges that his divine vocation is annoying because he has been called to rouse his fellow citizens from sleep, that is, a kind of moral or philosophical laxity: "But you . . . might . . . easily kill me; then you would pass the rest of your lives in slumber, unless God, in his care for you, should send someone else to sting you" (Plato, *Apol.* 31A).

This image of sleep representing moral laxity was prevalent also in biblical (Judg 16:14–20; Jonah 1:1–9; Nah 3:18a) and postbiblical Judaism (*T. Reu.* 3.1–9). The author of *Psalms of Solomon*, for example, argues: "When my soul slumbered, (I was far away) from the Lord, wretched for a time; I sank into sleep, far from God. For a moment my soul was poured out to death; (I was) near the gates of Hades with the sinner. Thus my soul was drawn away from the Lord God of Israel, unless the Lord had come to my aid with his everlasting mercy. He jabbed me as a horse is goaded to keep it awake; my savior and protector at all times" (16.1–4).

"Sleep" also functioned as a symbol for spiritual dullness in early Christian literature (Rom 13:11; *Barn.* 4:13). Paul writes: "But you, beloved, are not in darkness, for that day to surprise you like a thief; for you are all children of light and children of the day; we are not of the night or of darkness. So then let us not fall asleep as others do, but let us keep awake and be sober" (1 Thess 5:4–6).

Luke knows the use of "sleep" as a euphemism for death (Acts 7:60) and possibly for divine inactivity (cf. Luke 11:5–8), but he also uses it metaphorically to refer to those who are spiritually dull (cf. Luke 22:39–46). Conversely, Jesus' warnings to "stay awake" and "be watchful" represent the other side of this metaphorical coin (Luke 21:34–36). The authorial audience listening to Acts 20:7–12, then, would naturally hear echoes of moral laxity or spiritual negligence in the references to Eutychus being overcome by sleep (Arterbury 2009). Like the sleeping disciples in Gethsemane, Eutychus succumbs to temptation and falls asleep. His physical condition betrays the laxity of his spiritual state. Eutychus "falls away from the community that breaks bread on the Sabbath in an upper room while waiting for the dawn to arrive and dies" (Arterbury 2009). Paul's ministry of reconciliation then is to restore the "fallen" Eutychus to wholeness—physical and communal—by raising him back to life and reintegrating him into the worshiping congregation—**they brought the child (home)** (20:12a; Bulley 1994, 171–88). At the level of parenesis, the story of Eutychus functions as an "exegesis-by-example" of what Paul will later warn in his farewell address to the Ephesian elders only a few verses later: "Guard yourselves and all the flock . . . fierce wolves will come to you after my departure and will not spare the flock. . . . Therefore, be alert!" (20:28–31).

Why Did Eutychus Fall?

It is not altogether clear from Luke's story (20:7–11) whether Eutychus's spiritual dullness is the result of his own negligence or whether his downfall is caused by some external force (see Arterbury 2009). Support for both views is found in the early exegetical traditions associated with this text. The Venerable Bede, for example, wrote: "It is harder work to revive those who sin through negligence than it is to revive those who do so through weakness. The former is represented by Eutychus, the latter by Tabitha" (Bede, *Comm. Acts* 20.10, trans. L. Martin 1989). Here Bede clearly understands the moral fault to lie with Eutychus's own negligence of spiritual matters.

The *Acts of Paul* suggests a different interpretation in a passage that some scholars think is a retelling of Acts 20:7–12 (Lüdemann 1989, 224). A certain Patroclus sits in a window, listening to Paul speak:

> "But since the wicked devil was envious of the love of the brethren, Patroclus fell from the window and died, and the news was quickly brought to Nero. But Paul, perceiving it in the spirit, said: 'Brethren, the evil one has gained an opportunity to tempt you. Go out, and you will find a youth fallen from a height and already on the point of death. Lift him up, and bring him here to me!' So they went out and brought him. And when the crowd saw (him), they were troubled. Paul said to them: 'Now, brethren, let your faith be manifest. Come, all of you, let us mourn to our Lord Jesus Christ, that this youth may live and we remain unmolested.' But as they all lamented the youth drew breath again, and setting him upon a beast they sent him back alive with the others who were of Caesar's house." (*Acts Paul* 11.1, trans. *NTA* 2:261)

In this version, it is the devil who defeats a morally vulnerable youth and causes him to "fall." Paul's call to remain faithful and "unmolested" is, however, no less clear. In either case, whether by spiritual neglect or vulnerability to "wolves" among them, Paul exhorts believers then and now to remain watchful.

On an auxiliary level, this story also functions "as a legitimation device for Lord's Day worship" to counter "charges of nocturnal assemblies and associated immoralities" that "were a cultural commonplace among and within religious groups of the ancient Mediterranean world" (Talbert 2005, 179). Nocturnal meetings led to charges of immorality, especially of a sexual nature (for examples of pagan, Jewish, and Christian charges, see Talbert 2005, 177–79). Justin Martyr notes the pagan belief that during worship, Christians "extinguish the lights and indulge in unbridled sensuality" (Justin Martyr, *Dial.* 10; cf. Theophilus of Antioch, *Autol.* 3.4; Origen, *Cels.* 6.40). Luke deflects such charges by noting that "there were a number of lamps in the upstairs room" (20:8). Child sacrifice was also a charge leveled against nocturnal Christian meetings (Minucius Felix, *Oct.* 9.5; Origen, *Cels.* 6.27; Tertullian, *Apol.* 7.13–8.5). Luke counters charges of child-killing by relating rather the story of a child restored to life (Talbert 2005, 179).

The story ends with Luke's report that the Troas believers gladly received him and **were extremely comforted** (20:12; a litotes, "not a little encouraged"), picking up reference to the word used to describe Paul's ministry throughout Macedonia and Greece (20:2). The encouragement here derives from the integrity between Paul's word through preaching and sacrament (20:11) and his deed in raising Eutychus.

20:13–16. This episode ends with a brief summary of Paul's travels from Troas to Miletus: **We went on ahead to the boat and sailed to Assos where we were going to pick up Paul. For he had made such arrangements, since he himself was intending to go by land. When he met us in Assos, we took him aboard and went to Mitylene. After sailing from there, on the next day we arrived off Chios. On the following day we crossed over to Samos; and on the day after that we came to Miletus** (20:13–15). The audience learns that a temporal goal had been added to Paul's spatial goal; he wants to reach Jerusalem by Pentecost: **For Paul had decided to sail past Ephesus in order to avoid spending time in Asia. He was hurrying so that it might be possible for him to be in Jerusalem for the day of Pentecost** (20:16).

Paul's Farewell Address to the Ephesians (20:17–38)

Sandwiched between the report of the arrival of the Ephesian elders (20:17) and Paul's parting from them (20:36–38) is the speech given by Paul to them (20:18–35). Before examining the structure and content of the speech itself, it may help the reader to place the speech in a couple of contexts.

First, in the context of Acts, this speech is the third by the Lukan Paul. The first in Antioch of Pisidia (Acts 13:16–41) is addressed to Jews; the second is the Areopagus speech delivered to the Greeks in Athens (17:22–31); this speech in Acts 20 is aimed at fellow Christians. Later (chaps. 22, 24, 26) he will deliver forensic speeches before the civic authorities. The audience partly determines the shape and content of these first two speeches and this is no less true for this last speech, which is addressed to the Christian leaders from Ephesus who had gathered in Miletus to hear Paul. But this speech, perhaps more than any of the others attributed to Paul in Acts, has numerous echoes of the language and thought associated with the traditional Pauline corpus (see Witherington 1998, 610). As such, this speech reflects Luke's attempt at *ethopoeia*, that is, attributing words to a character that "are suitable to the speaker and have an indisputable application to the subject discussed" (Theon, *Prog.* 115, trans. Kennedy 2003, 47; cf. Acts 2).

Second, in form the speech shares many similarities with the ancient genre of the farewell address. Farewell speeches were common in biblical and post-biblical Judaism (Gen 49; Josh 23–24; 1 Sam 12; Tob 14; *As. Mos.*; *T. 12 Patr.*)

and early Christianity (Mark 13; Luke 22:14–38; John 13–17; 2 Tim 3:1–4:8; 2 Peter) and shared certain constituent elements: (1) the assembling of the speaker's family or friends, (2) notice that the speaker is about to leave or die, and (3) a speech exhorting the listener to emulate desired behavior and predicting events that will follow the speaker's departure or death (Polhill 1992, 423). The Miletus address reflects all these features.

The similarities in content with other farewell addresses in antiquity has led to the conclusion that the speech reflects epideictic rhetoric (Watson 1994); the speech, however, is lacking in the topics most usually addressed in the most common forms of epideictic—the funeral oration and the festival panegyric (Menander, *Epid.* 2.5–2.9; cf. Kennedy 1984, 75–76). Paul appeals to his past behavior among the Ephesians, giving the speech an apologetic or "forensic cast," but these appeals are to serve a purpose that is, overall, deliberative (Witherington 1998, 612). Paul seeks to persuade his audience; indeed he warns them (cf. Cicero, *De or.* 40.138; Aristotle, *Poet.* 19.1456b) to take particular actions in the future to avoid falling prey to heretical teachings after his departure (on the mixing of rhetorical species, see Quintilian, *Inst.* 7.10.11–13; Kennedy 1984, 19). This speech "involves not the rhetoric of praise or blame of the great man, but rather the rhetoric of advice and consent, of what is useful and imitable, appropriate for the deliberations of an assembly" (Witherington 1998, 613).

For the structure of the speech (modifying Nielsen 2000, 145–50), see the accompanying outline.

An Outline of Acts 20:17–38

Paul's farewell address to the Ephesians (20:17–38)

Setting and first retrospective/prospective narrative 1 (20:17–24)

1. Paul's way of life in Ephesus (20:18–21)

2. Paul's future trip to Jerusalem (20:22–24)

Second retrospective/prospective narrative (20:25–31)

1. Paul's ministry among the Ephesians (20:25–27)

2. The Ephesians' future (20:28–31)

Conclusion and farewell (20:32–35)

Parting from the Ephesians (20:36–38)

20:17–24. Given the fact that the audience is well known to him, Paul dispenses with the expected *exordium* (otherwise designed to curry the favor of the audience) and moves directly into a *narratio*. In this narrative, Paul (1) recalls the how, where, to whom, and what of his ministry in Asia (20:18–21; cf. Phil 4:15; 1 Thess 1:5; 2:1–2), then (2) looks ahead to the uncertain outcome of his travel to Jerusalem (20:22–24).

1. In 20:18–21, Paul first addresses the manner or "how" of his ministry: **You yourselves know how I lived during the whole time I was with you, from the first day that I set foot in Asia** (20:18). Specifically, he claimed that they knew **how I served the Lord with great humility and sorrow (in the midst of) the trials that happened to me because of the plots of the Jews** (20:19). The

claim that Paul had suffered with "great humility and sorrow" the "trials" that came because of the plots of the Jews resonates with what the authorial audience knows of Paul from Acts (9:23, 29; 13:50; 14:5, 19; 17:5, 13; 18:12; 20:3) and also from the Pauline letter tradition: Paul serves the Lord (Rom 1:1; 12:11; 14:18; Phil 2:22; Col 3:24; 1 Thess 1:9); he is humble-minded (2 Cor 7:6; 10:1; 11:7; 12:21; Phil 2:3; 4:12; Col 3:12; 1 Thess 2:6); he sheds tears (2 Cor 2:4); he is the target of Jewish plots against him (2 Cor 11:24, 26; 1 Thess 2:15; Titus 1:10, 14).

Second, in terms of the "where" or location of his ministry, Paul asserts that **I held back nothing that was useful** (cf. 2 Cor 4:2; Gal 4:16), **lest I fail to announce to you and teach you both in public and from house to house** (20:20; cf. Rom 16:5; Col 4:15; Phlm 2). Aristotle remarked: "Both those who give advice in private and those who speak in the assembly invariably either exhort or dissuade" (*Rhet.* 1.3.3). This distinction between public and private points to the social reality of public and private space in antiquity as embodied in the city and the household. Philo observed: "Organized communities are of two sorts, the greater of which we call cities and the smaller which we call households" (*Spec.* 3.171). The Ephesians knew that Paul had the social standing to speak both in a "public" place such as the hall of Tyrannus (19:8–10) or in a "private" space, such as a house meeting in Troas (20:7–12).

So Paul served and taught with humility and sorrow in both public and private places, but whom did he teach? Again Paul reminds the Ephesians that **I testified to both Jews and Greeks** (20:21a). This allusion to salvation history again resonates both with Acts (13:23, 38) and with the Pauline letter tradition, in which Paul claims the gospel was given for both Jew and Gentile (Rom 1:16; 10:12; 1 Cor 1:24; 9:20; 10:32; 12:13; Gal 3:28; Col 3:11). Finally Paul turns to the content of his preaching ministry, which was **about repentance toward God and faith in our Lord Jesus** (20:21b). Paul employs the term "repentance" infrequently but it is not altogether missing either in Acts (cf. 13:24; 26:20) or the Pauline corpus (Rom 2:4; 2 Cor 7:9, 10). The same is true of the phrase "faith in our Lord Jesus" (cf. esp. Acts 24:24; Eph 1:15; cf. Rom 10:9–13).

2. The preceding brief retrospective of the how, where, and what of his Ephesian ministry is the groundwork for Paul's reflection in 20:22–24 on his impending journey to Jerusalem (chaps. 22–24): **And now, since I have been bound by the Spirit, I am going to Jerusalem even though I do not know what will happen to me there. (I only know) that the Holy Spirit, in every city, keeps testifying to me and saying that prison and suffering await me** (20:22–23; on Paul's uncertainty regarding his future, see Rom 15:30–32). The Holy Spirit is directing Paul in this journey (cf. Acts 13:4; 16:6, 7; 19:21) and bears witness to the sufferings that await him (cf. Acts 9:16). No "theology of glory" here! Rather, the humility and sacrifice that characterized his Ephesian ministry will serve Paul in his Jerusalem sojourn: **But on no account do I regard my life as precious for myself so that I might finish my race and the ministry that**

I received from the Lord Jesus (20:24a). The athletic imagery, while missing elsewhere in Acts, is familiar to the authorial audience that knows its "Pauline" writings (1 Cor 9:24; 2 Tim 4:7). The goal of Paul's journey and concomitant suffering is **to testify to the good news of God's grace** (20:24b).

20:25–31. Paul turns again to (1) his ministry among the Ephesians (20:25–27) and (2) his immanent separation from them (20:28–31).

1. **And now I know that none of you among whom I traveled, preaching about the kingdom, will see my face again!** (20:25). Preaching about the "kingdom" is characteristic of the Lukan Paul's message (Acts 14:22; 19:8; 28:23, 31). Paul further declares himself morally innocent: **I am innocent of the blood of all people** (20:26; cf. 18:6; also 1 Sam 12:2–5; *T. Sim.* 6.1; *T. Levi* 10.1–2). This claim is based on the completion of his ministry: **For I did not hold back (anything) lest I fail to announce to you the whole plan of God** (20:27). The "whole plan of God" is not limited only to Paul's, or even the Ephesians', situation; rather, it refers to the divine plan that encompasses human history from David (Acts 13:36), to Jesus (Acts 2:22), to the church (Acts 4:28; 5:38), and even includes those who are found opposing God's plan (Luke 7:30; cf. Paul's analogous use of the "will of God" in 1 Cor 1:1; Gal 1:4; Johnson 1992, 362). Its content within the farewell address may be seen in the parallel phrase in 20:20–21: "how *I held back nothing* that was useful . . . to both Jews and Greeks about repentance toward God and faith in our Lord Jesus." This is the "whole plan of God."

2. Once again, Paul turns his thoughts to the future, this time to the future of the Ephesians in his absence. His call is one of vigilance: **Guard yourselves and all the flock among whom the Holy Spirit has placed you as overseers to guide the church of God, which he purchased with his own blood** (20:28). Like Eutychus, if the Ephesians are unprepared, they will find themselves vulnerable to those who would cause them to fall away from the community. The authorial audience recalls Jesus' description in the synoptic tradition of the people who are like sheep without a shepherd (Matt 9:36; Mark 6:34; but not in Luke). Paul puts it this way: **I know that fierce wolves will come to you after my departure and will not spare the flock** (20:29). The defenselessness of lambs against the wolf is well known (Homer, *Il.* 22.263; *Epig. Gr.* 1038.38 [in AG 105]; Philostratus, *Vit. Apoll.* 8.22; Justin, *1 Apol.* 58.2; Didymus, *In Gen.* 86.18). Certainly the metaphor is common in Jewish literature (cf. Isa 11:6; 40:11; Ezek 34:11–31; Philo, *Praem.* 86). "What does a wolf have in common with a lamb? No more has a sinner with the devout" (Sir 13:17). "The devout of God are like innocent lambs among them" (*Pss. Sol.* 8.23; cf. *4 Ezra* 5.18; *Tanhuma Toledot* 5; for the term "flock" used elsewhere figuratively in reference to a sophist's pupils, see Libanius, *Or.* 58.36; in reference to the people of Israel, see Jer 13:17; Zech 10:3; and in reference to the church, see 1 Pet 5:2–3; *1 Clem* 44.3; 54.2; 57.2). The Lukan Jesus also appeals to this image in his commission of the Seventy(-Two) (Luke 10:3; cf. also Matt 7:15).

The imagery gains further nuance by considering the culturally conditioned meaning of the imagery of the wolf in the ancient world (Parsons 2006). According to Polemo, the wolf is "bold, treacherous, vicious, plundering, greedy, harmful, deceitful, offering help in order to harm" (*Physiogn.* 172; also *Anon. Lat.* 126; *Arrian's Discourses of Epictetus* 1.3.7; Homer, *Il.* 16.156–166; cf. 4.472). Of course, the imagery of lambs and wolves also echoes Isaiah's "the wolf will lie down with the lamb" (11:6; 65:25), though that eschatological vision seems not quite fulfilled in Paul's warnings! In the ancient world, wolves connoted people who behaved badly in particular ways: they were, among other things, faithless, treacherous, impious, and bloodthirsty. Luke communicates an environment of danger and hostility that awaits his followers and presumes that the symbol of the "wolves" will communicate that picture effectively.

Equally disturbing is Paul's suggestion that such hostility may rise from within the ranks of the community itself: **Even from among yourselves men will rise up who will say misleading things in order to draw away disciples after themselves** (20:30). These predictions function at two levels. In the narrative world of Acts these predictions are fulfilled within the course of the development of the plot. Thus within the narrative itself there is good reason to view those external opponents as Jews who in the very next episode are found in opposition to the church (21:27–28), and the internal opponents as Jewish Christians or Gentiles influenced by Judaism (21:20–21). On the historical level these predictions have already come to pass in Luke's community. There is ample historical evidence for heresy in the early church (especially Ephesus) at the end of the first century (see Eusebius, *Hist. eccl.* 3.32.7–8). The crisis faced here is how, in the face of internal and external pressures, to ensure that the Christian traditions are preserved in the passing from one generation to the next. Although the level of danger will rise with Paul's departure, these warnings are not altogether new: **Therefore, be alert and remember that for three years, night and day, I never stopped warning each one of you with deep concern** (20:31).

20:32–35. In the conclusion, Paul turns to **entrust you to God and to the message about his grace, which is able to build you up and give you an inheritance among all those who have been sanctified** (20:32). Paul then returns to his past ministry, offering himself as a model for the Ephesian elders: **I never wanted anyone's silver or gold or clothing. You yourselves know that these hands (of mine) took care of my needs and those who were with me. In everything (I did), I showed you that in this way, by working hard, it is necessary to help the weak** (20:33–35a). The call to imitation was widespread in antiquity (see Talbert 2005, 182–83). Dio Chrysostom observed: "That is precisely, it seems, what the pupil does—by imitating his teacher and paying heed to him he tries to acquire his art" (*Hom. Socr.* 4.4–5; cf. Xenophon, *Mem.* 4.1.1). Already Paul's self-sufficiency demonstrates the "true" character of his ministry compared to so many "peddlers of God's word" (see comments on Acts 18:3); now he claims the fruits of his labor extend to the "weak" as well. The farewell address to the Ephesian elders functions as a succession narrative (see comments on 14:23). Paul transfers the pastoral care of the flock to these "overseers," a care that includes spiritual vigilance and economic independence.

Paul ends with an appeal to **remember the words of the Lord Jesus. (Remember) that he himself said, "It is more blessed to give than to receive"** (20:35b). In so doing, he grounds his exhortation in a dominical tradition (O'Toole 1994, 329–49). This agraphon is missing from the (canonical) Gospels (though see *1 Clem.* 2.1; *Did.* 1.5), although it may have been part of one of the "many" gospels that Luke references in the preface to his Gospel, no longer extant. This saying has the character as of "divine testimony" (see the "*Topoi*" sidebar at Acts 2:18). As Cicero notes: "The testimony of the gods is covered thoroughly enough by the following: first, utterances, for oracles get their name from the fact that they contain an utterance (*oratio*) of the gods" (*Top.* 20.76). Appeals are made to divine testimony in order to persuade the audience to accept his argument. Whether a free-floating tradition or a quotation from a lost gospel, the saying here is invoked by Paul as the divine testimony of Jesus to complete Paul's description of pastoral care for the flock as "working hard to help the weak"; such self-giving ministry is not only "necessary" (20:34), it is, according to the Lord Jesus, a "blessing."

20:36–38. The scene ends on an emotional note: **After he had said these things he knelt with all of them and prayed. There was a lot of weeping among all of them and they began embracing Paul and kissing him. They were upset most by his statement that they were not going to see him again. Then they escorted him to the ship** (20:36–38).

Inflection in Paul's Speech in Acts 20

The intimate nature of the conclusion to the Miletus address does not come as a surprise for the attentive authorial audience. Paul has used the rhetorical device of inflection or *klisis* to highlight the importance of the Ephesian recipients of Paul's address (Theon, *Prog.* 74.24–35, ed. Patillon 1997, 33; 85.29–31, ed. Patillon 1997, 48; Quintilian, *Inst.* 9.1.34; see above, pp. 91, 130). In the farewell address, Paul appeals twelve times to his audience with "you" (*hymeis*), the emphatic plural personal pronoun. Within the first three verses, the pronoun occurs in all four cases—nominative, 20:18; genitive, 20:18; dative, 20:20; and accusative, 20:20. In the subsequent eight occurrences over the rest of the speech, the pronoun is inflected again in all four cases: nominative, 20:25; genitive, 20:30; dative, 20:26, 27, 35; accusative, 20:28, 29, 32. Luke uses grammatical inflection to highlight Paul's rhetorical focus on his audience and prepare the authorial audience for the emotionally charged response at the end of the speech by those who have been the focus of Paul's sustained attention throughout the speech.

Warnings to Avoid Jerusalem (21:1–16)

Acts 21:1–16 divides into two parts: a travel summary (21:1–6), followed by an account of Paul's sojourn in Caesarea (21:7–16). In both, Paul is warned to avoid Jerusalem.

21:1–6. With tears and farewells, Paul and his company are ready to sail again: **When we set sail, after leaving them, we followed a straight course and came to Cos. On the next day (we sailed) to Rhodes, and from there (we sailed) to Patara. After finding a ship that was crossing to Phoenicia, we went aboard and set sail. When we had sighted Cyprus and passed it on our left, we sailed on to Syria and landed at Tyre, because the ship was going to unload its cargo there** (21:1–3). In Tyre, Paul and company **located (some) disciples and stayed there for seven days** (21:4a). The passing reference to a stay of "seven days" implies that Paul and company were there long enough to share in the weekly Christian worship meeting (see Acts 20:6–7; cf. 28:14). These believers **kept telling Paul through the Spirit not to go to Jerusalem** (21:4b). This is their first warning not to go to Jerusalem, probably because they, like Paul, knew that suffering and persecution were awaiting him there (cf. 20:23). In spite of this weighty testimony to the contrary, Paul persists in continuing his journey to Jerusalem: **When we had finished our time (there), we left and went on our way** (21:5a).

At Tyre Paul again visits a congregation with which he is familiar, but which he did not found (cf. Acts 15:3). In fact, this congregation was presumably started by a "pre-Pauline" mission as a result of persecutions in which Saul (now Paul) was a central leader (9:1–2; 11:19; cf. 8:1–3). Given their prior history, their response to Paul is nothing less than a remarkable display of Christian hospitality: **All of them, along with (their) wives and children, escorted us until we were outside the city. After we had knelt upon the shore and prayed, we said good-bye to one another. Then we boarded the ship and they returned to their own homes** (21:5b–6). Paul, who had previously dragged men and women in chains from nearby Damascus to Jerusalem, kneels and prays on the shore with men, women, and their children who are now fellow believers (Spencer 2004, 206). He boards a ship, voluntarily headed to suffer the same kind of persecution in Jerusalem that he himself once meted out.

21:7–16. After a brief stop in Ptolemais (21:7), Paul and his company arrive in Caesarea and encounter several characters already familiar to the authorial audience. First they meet Philip the evangelist (Acts 8): **We went to the house of Philip the evangelist, who was a member of the Seven, and stayed with him** (21:8). Philip, the authorial audience now learns, had **four unmarried daughters who prophesied** (21:9). While it is unclear whether Paul will make it to Jerusalem by Pentecost, it is clear that already in Caesarea he is seeing evidence of the fulfillment of Pentecost prophecies, in this case, that "sons and daughters shall prophesy" (Acts 2:17).

Paul also meets with the prophet Agabus, who had prophesied a famine in Judea (11:27–30): **After we had stayed (there) many days, a prophet came down from Judea, named Agabus (21:10).** Through Agabus, the Holy Spirit again describes the persecution awaiting Paul in Jerusalem (cf. 20:23). Like an OT prophet (cf. Jer 19:1–3; Ezek 4:1–7), Agabus combines a prophetic sign, binding his own hands and feet with Paul's belt, with a prophetic warning: **Here is what the Holy Spirit says: "This is the way that the Jews in Jerusalem will tie up the man to whom this belt belongs and hand him over to the Gentiles"** (21:11). The believers interpret this sign as a warning to Paul not to continue the journey to Jerusalem: **When we heard these things both we and the local residents begged him not to go up to Jerusalem (20:12).** In the face of this third prediction of his passion (20:23; 21:4, 11), Paul remains resolute: **What are you doing, crying and breaking my heart? For I am ready not only to be tied up, but even to die in Jerusalem for the sake of the name of the Lord Jesus (20:13).** Unlike Peter, who made a similar promise (Luke 22:33) but failed to fulfill it (at least in the narrative of Luke), Paul remains true to his oath. Seeing **he could not be persuaded** the believers **gave up and said, "The Lord's will be done!"** (21:14). In language that echoes Luke 22:42, Paul is depicted here as facing his own Gethsemane, where he, like Jesus, finally prays, "Not my will, but yours be done." Given the angst surrounding Paul's journey to Jerusalem, the narrator's conclusion is something of an anticlimax: **After this time, we packed up and headed to Jerusalem (21:15).** The scene concludes with this note: **Some of the disciples from Caesarea went with us in order to bring us to the one with whom we were to stay, Mnason, who was a Cypriot and an early disciple (21:16).** In so doing, Luke brings the story full circle: Paul and his (now considerable) entourage are again extended Christian hospitality, this time in Jerusalem by Mnason, a "Cypriot and early disciple," perhaps one of those missionaries from Cyrene and Cyprus who had originally preached the gospel in Phoenicia (11:20).

Theological Issues

The intimate and emotional tone of Paul's farewell address to the Ephesian elders should not be allowed to efface the profound theological character of the speech. While it would be anachronistic to speak of a "trinitarian" theology here, Paul's sustained appeal to God, Spirit, and Jesus is nonetheless noteworthy (on NT passages that reference Father, Son, and Spirit together and their significance in the development of the doctrine of the Triune God, see Humphreys 2006, 285–303). There are five references to God, three to the Spirit, and three to the Lord Jesus (although omitted from Table 9, the reference to Paul serving the "Lord" in 20:19 is presumably also a reference to Jesus; cf. Fitzmyer 1998, 676).

Table 9.
References to God, Spirit, and Jesus
in Paul's Farewell Address to the Ephesians

God
repentance toward God (20:21)
the good news of God's grace (20:24)
the whole plan of God (20:27)
the church of God (20:28)
I entrust you to God (20:32)

Spirit
I have been bound by the Spirit (20:22)
the Holy Spirit . . . keeps testifying to me (20:23)
the Holy Spirit has placed you as overseers (20:28)

Jesus
faith in our Lord Jesus (20:21)
the ministry that I received from the Lord Jesus (20:24)
remember the words of the Lord Jesus (20:35)

There is no apparent strict "division of labor" among God, Spirit, and Jesus; rather, there is considerable overlap between and among them. In terms of ecclesiology, the church is of God (20:28); the Holy Spirit has placed overseers in the church (20:28); and Jesus has given Paul his ministry (20:24). Both the Spirit and Jesus bear witness to the sacrificial nature of Christian ministry: the Spirit testifies concerning Paul's suffering; Jesus' words, "It is more blessed to give than to receive," are to be remembered. In terms of divine providence, Paul speaks both of the "plan of God" (20:27) and being "bound by the Spirit" (20:22). The "good news of God's grace" (20:24) calls for "repentance toward God" (20:21) and "faith in our Lord Jesus" (20:21). It is easy to see how this language would later bear the fruit of trinitarianism in the early church.

The roles come together in the most complex way in 20:28: "Guard yourselves and all the flock among whom the Holy Spirit has placed you as overseers to guide the church of God, which he acquired with his own blood." The difficult idea that God had "blood" evidently led to a change from the "church of God" to the "church of the Lord" in some manuscripts ($\mathfrak{P}^{74}$, a, A, C, D, E, et al.), in which "Lord" presumably refers to Jesus (as it does elsewhere in this speech, 20:21, 24, 35), thus easing the difficulty a bit by making Jesus (and not God) the referent of "his blood" (Metzger 1994, 426). Still others have resolved the problem in translation by rendering the phrase as "the blood of his Own" (NRSV note) or "his own Son" (RSV, NRSV, NJB), although syntactically the more natural reading is "of his own blood." However we render the text and its translation, Joseph Fitzmyer has rightly noted: "In any case, one should not miss the triadic nuance of this verse: the explicit mention of 'God,' 'the Spirit,' and the 'blood,' which implies the Son. It is a trinitarian dimension that

Luke associates with the Christian community and its governance" (Fitzmyer 1998, 680).

This verse in particular has been a *crux interpretum*, both among ancient and modern interpreters. How does one speak meaningfully about God having "blood"? Fundamentally, we may say that when Christ shed his blood on the cross "he was acting as the representative of God; he was God's way of giving life, blood, for the world" (Barrett 1998, 2:977). This is surely what lies behind Tertullian's rather cryptic formulation: "we are not our own, but bought with a price; and what kind of price? The blood of God" (*Ux.* 2.3). This idea was developed in the doctrine of *communicatio idiomatum* ("interchange of properties") "by which properties or actions belonging to one nature of Christ may be attributed to, or predicated of, the other nature, because of the unity of the single person of the God-man" (Pelikan 2005, 221). Leo the Great articulated the classic formulation of the idea in his address to the Council of Chalcedon: "It does not belong to the same nature to weep out of deep-felt pity for a dear friend, and to call him back to life again at the word of command (John 11:35–44)" (*Tome of Leo* 9, CCF 1:117–18), "since only the human nature could do the first and only the divine nature could do the second and yet the actions are both attributed to the single person of the incarnate Logos" (Pelikan 2005, 222). Thus the two natures of Christ are acknowledged as evidence of "One and the same Christ, son, Lord, Only begotten, acknowledged in two natures which undergo no confusion, no change, no division, no separation" (Definition of Faith of the Council of Chalcedon 16–18 [CCF 1:180–81; Pelikan 2005, 222]). Similarly, the Venerable Bede claims: "He did not hesitate to say 'the blood of God,' because of the oneness of person in two natures of the same Jesus Christ" (*Comm. Acts* 20.28b, trans. L. Martin 1989). John Calvin also knows and affirms this doctrine in his commentary on Acts 20:28:

> But because the speech which Paul useth seemeth to be somewhat hard, we must see in what sense he saith that God purchased the Church with his blood. For nothing is more absurd than to feign or imagine God to be mortal or to have a body. But in this speech he commendeth the unity of person in Christ; for because there be distinct natures in Christ, the Scripture doth sometimes recite that apart by itself which is proper to either. But when it setteth God before us made manifest in the flesh, it doth not separate the human nature from the Godhead. Notwithstanding, because again two natures are so united in Christ, that they make one person, that is improperly translated sometimes unto the one, which doth truly and indeed belong to the other, as in this place Paul doth attribute to God; because the man Jesus Christ, who shed his blood for us, was also God. This manner of speaking is called, of the old writers, *communicatio idiomatum*, because the property of the one nature is applied to the other. (Calvin, *Commentary on Acts*, chap. 20, trans. Beveridge, 2:256–57)

We may wish to leave behind the subsequent exegetical tradition of this passage as irrelevant and argue rather that Luke was simply expressing the idea that "Christ has acquired his people by blood (that is, by atoning death)" (Barrett 1998, 2:977). However, this formula cuts against the grain of much critical Lukan scholarship since Hans Conzelmann. Conzelmann, in fact, rejected the notion that Luke had any sense of the atoning death or vicarious suffering of Jesus. Concerning Luke's redaction, Conzelmann (echoing Cadbury and Dodd) concludes: "The most important finding in this connection for our purpose is that there is no trace of any Passion mysticism, nor is any direct soteriological significance drawn from Jesus' suffering or death. There is no suggestion of a connection with the forgiveness of sins" (Conzelmann 1960, 201). Conzelmann has been followed in this line of interpretation by numerous commentators and exegetes.

Whatever one makes of Conzelmann's interpretation of the "atoneless" Lukan passion narrative, one must still reckon with the claim in Acts 20:28 by the Lukan Paul that God "purchased" the church "with his own blood." Conzelmann himself recognized the problem when he wrote that Acts 20:28 "probably adopts a turn of phrase current in the Church (perhaps to give a speech a Pauline stamp?)" (Conzelmann 1960, 201). Conzelmann does not deny that the passage indicates the atoning significance of Christ's death, only that it can be dismissed as a kind of "Paulinism," which Luke himself would not embrace! Certainly the economic language of God "purchasing" the believer or the church through Christ's sacrifice is Pauline (1 Cor 6:19–20). However, it is hardly acceptable by redaction-critical criteria, much less more recent literary models, to dismiss the passage as an errant tradition that slipped past Luke and does not represent his point of view. More theologically and rhetorically satisfying is to try to understand the passage within the whole argument of Luke and Acts. At the least, Acts 20:28 calls for the interpreter to reconsider Luke's overall portrait of the death of Jesus and to ask how this view of Jesus' vicarious suffering fits within that view. We may admit that Luke does not emphasize Jesus' atoning death in the same way as Paul or Mark, but we need not conclude that vicarious atonement is missing altogether from Luke. Rather, it seems that Luke has put together the material in a way that connects Jesus' suffering and death and the forgiveness of sins in a key that may be different but still plays the same soteriological song (see also comments on Acts 8). The farewell address in Acts 20 is at once an intimate portrayal of the affection shared between the Apostle and the Ephesian congregation and, at the same time, a profound theological probing of the work of God, the Spirit, and Jesus to create and sustain the "church of God, which he purchased through his own blood."

Acts 21:17–23:35

Paul in Jerusalem

Introductory Matters

The time of Paul's much anticipated (and in some ways dreaded) journey to Jerusalem finally arrives. To emphasize the importance of Paul's arrival in Jerusalem the narrator uses a rhetorical strategy similar to "dwelling on the point" (*commoratio*), a rhetorical figure in which "one remains rather long upon, and often returns to, the strongest topic on which the whole cause rests" (*Rhet. Her.* 4.45.58, trans. Caplan 1954, 375). The author of *Ad Herennium* was unable to give examples of this convention because, unlike other figures, "this topic is not isolated from the whole cause like some limb, but like blood is spread through the whole body of the discourse" (ibid.).

At this point in the narrative in Acts, Luke focuses on the significance and implications of Paul's visit in Jerusalem by, in effect, "slowing" narrative time (see Genette 1980); that is, Luke "dwells" on the events associated with Paul's arrival by narrating those events in some detail (see Polhill 1992, 445; Spencer 2004, 212). In the second half of Acts, which recounts Paul's mission (chaps. 13–28), Acts 21:17–23:35 is the longest episode, containing more than 1,800 Greek words. Yet the time period covered is less than two weeks (cf. the time references in 21:18, 26, 27; 22:30; 23:11, 12, 23, 31–32).

To put this focus in perspective, consider how Luke has dealt with the episodes immediately preceding and following this one. The preceding episode (20:1–21:16) contains approximately 1,000 Greek words and is punctuated with summaries that quickly recount days, weeks, even months (cf. 20:3) of Paul's travel from place to place (20:1–6; 20:13–16; 21:1–8, 15–16), and the following episode (chaps. 24–26) contains approximately 1,600 Greek words and takes place during a period of two years (24:27). Luke clearly wants to take his time in narrating these events in Jerusalem. Ultimately the point on which Luke dwells is, as the Lukan Paul himself makes clear, not only the vindication of Paul per se, but rather the "hope in the resurrection from the dead" (23:6). This claim, as we shall see, has both religious and political ramifications.

Tracing the Narrative Flow

Paul's Arrival and Arrest in Jerusalem (21:17–40)

Acts 21:17–40 further divides into two units: Paul and the Jerusalem elders (21:17–26) and Paul's arrest in the temple area (21:27–40).

21:17–26. When Paul and his company **arrived in Jerusalem, the believers (there) welcomed us gladly** (21:17). Like Mnason, the Jerusalem believers "welcomed" Paul "gladly," recalling again the ancient practice of hospitality (Arterbury 2005). Paul's fear of a hostile reception among the Jerusalem Christians is alleviated for the moment (cf. Rom 15:31). **On the following day, Paul went with us to (visit) James, and all the elders were present** (21:18). Presumably this group of leaders is distinct from the unnamed believers in 21:17, since now Paul is depicted as greeting them: **After he had greeted them, he began explaining in detail each of the things that God had done among the Gentiles through his ministry** (21:19). The scene here is reminiscent of the earlier scenes in chapter 11 and especially chapter 15 (Johnson 1992, 379; Talbert 2005, 185–86):

1. Paul is welcomed by the church and its leaders (21:17–18; cf. 15:3–4).
2. Paul recounts what "God had done among the Gentiles through his ministry" (21:19; cf. 15:4, 12).
3. In response, **those who heard glorified God** (21:20a; cf. 11:18).
4. The Apostolic Decree is repeated (21:25; cf. 15:23–29).

James and the Jewish elders respond with a deliberative speech that falls into two parts (for the rhetorical strategy of assigning a single speech to several leaders to indicate a "community decision," see Thucydides, *Hist.* 1.68). The proem sets out the need for action (21:20–22), followed by counsel, with a rationale (21:23–24; Kennedy 1984, 134). First, the need for action is specified: **Brother, you can see how many thousands of believers there (now) are among the Jews, and all (of them) are strongly devoted to (keeping) the law. But they have been told about you that you teach all the Jews throughout the nations to abandon (the law of) Moses by saying that they should not circumcise their children or live according to (our) customs. So what should we do? They will certainly hear that you have come (21:20b–22).** The Jewish believers have been told that Paul was teaching Jews living among Gentiles to forsake Moses and abandon Jewish customs (21:21).

This is the third church conflict involving Jewish-Gentile relations (see Tannehill 1990, 268). First the question of baptizing (and eating with) Gentiles was resolved in Acts 11. Then the controversy over requiring Gentiles to be circumcised was addressed in Acts 15. The problem before the church now has to do with pressure, real or perceived, on Jewish Christians to forsake their Jewish customs, values, and practices. And Paul is at the center of this problem. The authorial audience knows that the charges are patently false. Paul has circumcised Timothy (16:3), taken a Nazirite vow (18:18), and observed the Jewish feasts (20:6, 16). In other words, he has been a Torah observant Jew and nowhere in Acts has he taught his fellow Jews to do otherwise. Nonetheless, because Paul is the leader of the Gentile mission, he has created a social situation that is not particularly supportive of Jewish Christians who wish also to honor their Jewish heritage. As the Gentile mission continues to be successful and the Jewish population in the church becomes more and more of a minority, this problem intensifies.

The solution proposed by James and the elders is for Paul to demonstrate tangibly his support for Jewish Christians to live as Jews: **Therefore, you must do what we tell you. We have four men who have taken a vow. Take them and have yourself purified with them. Also, pay their expenses so that they may have their heads shaved. Then everyone will know that there is no (truth) to the things they were told about you, but that you yourself also live according to custom by keeping the law (21:23–24).** Paul is to join four Jewish believers who are under a vow in going through a seven-day rite of purification in the temple (21:23–24). The four men have evidently made a Nazirite vow; they are to have their heads shaved (cf. comments on Acts 18:18; Num 6:9). It is not clear whether Paul, too, is being asked to make a Nazirite vow (which did include a prohibition against "uncleanness"; cf. *m. Naz.* 6.5) or whether Paul would undertake a ritual purification required of those passing through "unclean" lands (*m. 'Ohal.* 2:3; 17:5; 18:6; Haenchen 1971, 612). After all, Paul had been in contact with "unclean" Gentiles (e.g., Trophimus the Ephesian, cf. 21:29) and had recently come into contact with a corpse (e.g., Eutychus, 20:7–12). Paul is also expected to pay for the purification, a not-so-inexpensive procedure (cf. Num 6:21; Josephus, *Ant.* 19.294). This is not the first time in this episode that Paul is presumed to have money (cf. also 24:26), perhaps from the collection of alms and offerings he has taken up for his nation (on the collection in Paul's writings, see 1 Cor 16:1–4; 2 Cor 8–9; Gal 2:10). Whatever the nature of the purification and the payment, these actions will, according to the elders, provide the evidence needed to dispel the rumors about Paul. Further, the elders argue, this solution in no way compromises the agreement reached at the Jerusalem conference regarding the Gentiles: **And regarding Gentile believers, we sent word (to them), after reaching a decision, that they should avoid (eating) meat offered to idols, blood, (the meat of animals that have been) strangled, and sexual immorality (21:25).** The expectations regarding the way the Gentile believers are to relate to the law remain intact.

Paul, despite all the Spirit's previous warnings of persecution and suffering, agrees and engages in the very public act of temple purification: **Then, on the following day, after Paul had taken the men and been purified with them, he entered the temple in order to announce the time when the period of purification would be complete, at which time a sacrifice would be offered for each one of them (21:26).** Paul thus "acts in an accommodating way to foster the unity of the church" (Talbert 2005, 186).

21:27–40. While Luke reports nothing of the response by Jewish believers to Paul's acts, he has much to say about the reaction of the Jewish community. The reception of Paul in Jerusalem has moved from a glad-hearted welcome from the Jerusalem believers (21:17) to a more cautious reception on the part of James and the elders (22:19–25) to outright hostility on the part of Diaspora Jews, specifically from Asia (cf. 20:18–19), perhaps in Jerusalem for the feast of Pentecost (cf. Acts 2:5; 20:16; Josephus, *Ant.* 14.13.4; 17.10.2): **When the seven days were almost over, after spotting him in the temple, the Jews from Asia stirred up the whole crowd. They grabbed him and shouted (21:27–28a).** From the point when these Diaspora Jews seize Paul until his departure for Rome (and perhaps beyond; cf. 27:1), "Paul is never again a free man" (Skinner 2003, 110). Their charges echo those leveled earlier against Stephen: "This man never stops saying things against the holy place and the law" (6:13): **Israelites, help! This is the man who teaches everyone everywhere against (our) people, (our) law, and this (holy) place (21:28b).** Even more volatile in a festival period is their accusation that Paul has defiled the temple (cf. Josephus, *Ant.* 15.417; *BJ* 5.193–194): **Furthermore, he has even brought Greeks into the temple and defiled this holy place! (21:28c).** Prohibitions against bringing foreigners into the temple were well known and grounds for "death without appeal" (Philo, *Legat.* 31.212; cf. Josephus, *BJ* 5.193–194; *Ant.* 15.11.5). Herod's temple evidently contained a warning that read something like: "No one of another nation may enter within the fence and enclosures round the temple. Whoever is caught shall have himself to blame that his death ensues" (*OGIS* 598; Fitzmyer 1998, 698). The accusation was patently false and based on a hasty conclusion:

Lukan Rhetoric in the Temple Scenes

The importance of these actions in and around the temple setting is underscored by Luke's rhetoric. Luke uses the rhetorical convention of *polyptoton* or *klisis* (Theon, *Prog.* 74.24–35, ed. Patillon 1997, 33; 85.29–31, ed. Patillon 1997, 48; Quintilian, *Inst.* 9.1.34; see p. 91 above), in which a term, here "temple," is inflected in the various Greek cases. Although the term *hieron*, "temple," never occurs in the nominative case in Acts (or the entire NT for that matter), the word does occur here in the genitive (21:30), dative (21:27), and accusative (21:26, 28, 29). The multiple use of a term in such close proximity is also similar to the rhetorical figure of *reduplication* (*Rhet. Her.* 4.28.38; cf. 9:6). The focus on the temple is emphasized by the use of synonymy (*interpretatio*), a "figure which does not duplicate the same word by repeating it, but replaces the word that has been used by another of the same meaning" (*Rhet. Her.* 4.28.38, trans. Caplan 1954, 325). Twice in Acts 21:28, Paul's opponents use the term "place" (or "holy place"), *topos*, in their accusations regarding Paul's teaching against and defilement of the temple (cf. Acts 3:2–3, in which Luke uses the rhetorical figure of speech called *antistrophe*, repeating "temple" at the end of successive lines for emphasis; *Rhet. Her.* 4.13.19).

For earlier they had seen Trophimus the Ephesian in the city with him, and they thought that Paul had brought him into the temple (21:29). Perhaps these "Asian Jews" recognized Trophimus from Paul's extended ministry in Ephesus. At any rate, the results, given the previous accounts of mob violence (cf. Acts 7:54–59; 13:50; 16:19–23; 17:5–6; 18:17; 19:29), are predictable, especially in light of festival sentiments of religious and political nationalism (cf. Josephus, *BJ* 1.88–89; 2.8–13; 2.42–48; 2.169–174 *et passim*; cf. Johnson 1992, 381): **The whole city was in an uproar and a mob of people formed. After seizing Paul, they dragged him outside the temple, and immediately the gates were closed (21:30).** The closing of the temple gates is ominous; never again in Acts will they be opened to Paul.

Only the intervention of a Roman tribune prevents Paul from meeting his death: **As they were trying to kill him, news that all of Jerusalem was in turmoil reached the commander of the cohort (stationed there). He immediately took soldiers and centurions and ran down to them. When they saw the commander and the soldiers, they stopped beating Paul (21:31–32).** The Roman tribunal delivers Paul "in the nick of time, from nothing less than death" (Skinner 2003, 111). Still, Paul is arrested and bound (cf. Agabus's prophecy in 21:11) before any attempt is made to determine Paul's identity: **Then the commander came up and arrested him and ordered him to be bound with two chains. He asked who he could possibly be and what he had done (21:33).** Even then, efforts by the tribune to learn Paul's identity are thwarted by the uproar of the crowd: **Now, some among the crowd were shouting one thing and some another. So when he was unable to determine what had really happened, because of the turmoil, he ordered that (Paul) be brought into the barracks** (21:34). The pursuing mob became so violent that Paul had to be carried away by Roman soldiers: **When he reached the steps (of the barracks), Paul had to be carried by the soldiers because the crowd was so violent** (21:35). While the consequence of this act was to rescue Paul from the angry mob, the intent was rather to avoid a riot and to get Paul to a more private place where he could be interrogated, with torture if necessary, as a possible insurrectionist (cf. 22:24). Paul is carried away in the midst of shouts of **"Away with him!"** (21:36), the very cry of the crowds who called for Jesus' death (Luke 23:18).

While Jesus went to his death with no defense speech, Paul requests to speak, first to the tribune: **Then, as he was about to be taken into the barracks, Paul said to the commander, "May I say something to you?"** (21:37a). Surprised, the Roman officer asks, perhaps condescendingly: **Do you understand Greek?** (21:37b). Evidently the commander had jumped to a few conclusions of his own. **Then you are not the Egyptian who started a rebellion some time ago and led four thousand terrorists out into the desert?** (21:38; cf. Josephus, *BJ* 2.261–263). Paul identifies himself to the Roman tribune as a Jew from a leading city: **I am a Jew from Tarsus of Cilicia, a citizen of an important city** (21:39a). Paul's understatement (on *diminutio*, see *Rhet. Her.* 4.37.50) in the form of a litotes (on litotes, see the sidebar on p. 27) was a discreet, but well-founded rejoinder to the commander: Tarsus (cf. Acts 9:30; 11:25) was indeed "no mean city," recognized as both a cultural (Strabo, *Geogr.* 14.5.13–15) and philosophical center (Dio Chrysostom, *1 Tars.* 48; *Grat.* 3). He then requests to speak to the crowd: **I beg you to allow me to speak to the people** (21:39b). **After the commander had given him permission, Paul stood on the steps and motioned with his hand to the people. When it was completely quiet, he addressed them in the Hebrew language** (21:40). The "Hebrew language" here most likely means Aramaic (see Acts 1:19; 22:2; 26:14).

Paul Addresses the Crowd and the Tribune (22:1–29)

Acts 22:1–29 is the first of three defense speeches in Acts 22–26 (cf. 24:1–23, and 26:1–32); in fact, here Paul explicitly calls his speech a defense or "apology" (*apologia*, 22:1), even though the setting is hardly an official judicial proceeding. The verb form, *apologeomai*, occurs elsewhere in Luke/Acts only in Luke's Gospel, when Jesus predicts that his followers would be called upon to make their defense before the authorities with the aid of the Holy Spirit (Luke 12:14) and Jesus himself (Luke 21:14). Paul's speech here and in the subsequent chapters fulfills this prediction: Paul defends himself and the gospel. As with many other ancient narratives that record forensic speeches, Paul's speech in Acts 22:1–21 corresponds roughly to what the rhetorical manuals expect of

Orators' Gestures

Acts 21:40 is one of six passages in Acts that refer to a gesture made prior to a deliberative or judicial speech (12:17; 13:16; 19:33; 21:40; 24:10; 26:1; cf. Shiell 2004, 139). The NRSV renders 21:40 as "[He] motioned to the people for silence," perhaps influenced by the crowd's response ("it was completely quiet") or the earlier reference in 12:17, in which the gesture is explicitly for silence. Here, though, the gesture would have been understood by the authorial audience as the orator (perhaps also performed by the lector) gesturing to alert the audience that his speech is about to begin (and thus a different gesture than the one signaling the beginning of the *exordium* proper; cf. 26:1).

These rhetorical gestures were part of a fixed convention of gestures described in the rhetorical handbooks and depicted visually in manuscripts and in decorative art. Quintilian advised the orator to extend thumb, index, and middle fingers while closing the remaining two into the palm (Quintilian, *Inst.* 11.3.98). Apuleius describes this same gesture in *Metamorphoses*: "He leaned on his elbow at the table and sitting up on his right hand, and in the way of orators shaped it with the two smaller fingers closed and stretching out the others with the opposed thumb sticking up. Then he began to speak" (*Metam.* 2.21; Shiell 2004, 52). This gesture apparently had a long history, and is seen in Greek works of art as early as the sixth century BC (Shiell 2004, 151).

Photograph © 2008 Museum of Fine Arts, Boston

Figure 13. I'm Going to Say Something Now.
In this amphora from the sixth century BC, which depicts Achilles and Ajax, Ajax (on the right) is making the hand gesture recommended by Hellenistic rhetoricians for a person beginning a speech.

Thus the NRSV translation of 21:40 is misleading; it is better to understand Paul's gesture as calling the audience to attention rather than an explicit gesture for silence. That the crowd responds in silence indicates both the breadth of chaos current on the steps of the military barracks and the level of respect the audience gives to Paul—at least for the moment.

a juridical speech; it consists of an *exordium* or introduction (22:1–3) and an extended *narratio*, a narrative summarizing past events or a statement of facts concerning the case (22:4–21). Luke's report of the responses to Paul's speech follows (22:22–29).

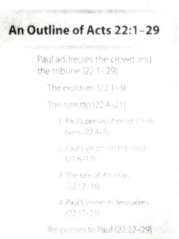

22:1–3. The *exordium* in a forensic speech was aimed to gain the favorable attention of the audience (*Rhet. Her.* 1.7; Cicero, *Inv.* 1.20; Quintilian, *Inst.* 4.1.5). One could secure this attention simply by asking the audience for it directly, or as pseudo-Cicero says, "bidding them listen attentively" (*Rhet. Her.* 1.7). Paul chooses this direct approach: **Brothers and fathers, listen now to my defense to you!** (22:1). Not only does he seek to connect with the audience by using familial language of "brothers and fathers," he is also **addressing them in the Hebrew language** (22:2a), a strategy that is immediately effective, as Luke notes in a narrative aside: **they became even quieter** (22:2b). Further, in an *exordium*, the speaker could choose to speak about himself, his opponent(s), the audience, or the case itself (Quintilian, *Inst.* 4.1.6–11). Paul chooses to speak about himself. This brief biographical sketch reflects several of the topics considered essential by the rhetoricians when recounting a "life," in the preferred sequential order of origins, nurture/training, deeds, and comparison (Hermogenes, *Prog.* 15–16, trans. Kennedy 2003, 81–82; Nicolaus, *Prog.* 50–52, trans. Kennedy 2003, 156–58; see Martin 2008, 18–41). In particular, the number and order of the topics chosen for Paul's "biography" closely resemble Aphthonius's list (minus the prologue and epilogue, which are not appropriate to the defense speech here) of origin, nurture/training, deeds, and comparison (Aphthonius, *Prog.* 22R, trans. Kennedy 2003, 108):

Origins: **I am a Jew who was born in Tarsus of Cilicia** (22:3a). Here national origins are mentioned before the city of origins as pseudo-Hermogenes and Nicolaus specify.

Nurture and training: **I was raised in this (very) city and trained at the feet of Gamaliel in accord with the precise nature of (our) ancestors' law** (22:3b). The first phrase, "raised in this (very) city," serves as a bridge between city of origins (on Tarsus as a praiseworthy city, see Strabo, *Geogr.* 14.5.12–15) and nurture ("I was raised"). Paul refers to his training under Gamaliel, a well-known Pharisee (cf. 5:34; *m. Peah* 2.6; *m. Orlah* 2.12; *m. Sheqal.* 6.1; Johnson 1992, 99), "in accord with the precise nature" of the Jewish law. This treatment bears a striking resemblance to Aphthonius's model encomium of Thucydides, in its treatment of nurture/training. There Aphthonius describes Thucydides' training under Athens' praiseworthy law: "Born from such circumstances [= in Athens], he is nurtured under a constitution and laws that are by their nature better than others" (*Prog.* 37). Paul and his audience would no doubt have agreed on the superiority of the "praiseworthy" nature of the Jewish law for purposes of moral training.

Deeds or virtues: **I am deeply devoted to God** (22:3c). Here the expected Greek virtues of "courage" or "prudence" (cf. *Prog.* 36) are replaced with reference to Paul's Jewish piety.

Comparison: **Just as all of you are today** (22:3d). This last element in Aphthonius's list compares Paul favorably with his audience and is designed to win their favorable attention, though clearly this is not Paul's ultimate goal. Luke's authorial audience would have expected such topics to be touched upon in an *exordium* that gives a biographical summary.

Topics Not Covered

The comments on 22:1–3 point out topics from the rhetorical tradition that Paul uses in his *exordium*. Equally important are some of the subtopics that are missing, for example, marvelous occurrences at birth, parentage, wealth, children, and bodily goods (e.g., physical beauty), or (obviously) death (cf. Theon, *Prog.* 109). In part, these differences can be accounted for by the fact that Paul is giving an autobiography and some topics might be inappropriate (e.g., marvelous occurrences at birth or mention of wealth). Others might be accounted for by historical circumstance (omission of reference to children, cf. 1 Cor 7:8, or physical beauty, 2 Cor 10:10). Still one wonders about the lack of reference to, say, parentage. Of course Paul could again, at this point, have been trying to appeal to his audience, in effect following the advice of the *progymnasmata*. Nicolaus writes that "origin" involves

> "consideration of nationality, native city, and ancestors. Either all of these are applicable or we shall use those that are; for example, if the city is illustrious and of high repute, then we shall spend more of the speech on that than on nationality, but if we have nothing notable to say about the city, then we shall take refuge in the nation. If we are unable to say anything worthwhile about either, then we shall begin straight off with the ancestors, and then add whatever can be said about the other things mentioned earlier, I mean nationality or native city." (Nicolaus, *Prog.* 50, trans. Kennedy 2003, 156)

We should not necessarily conclude that Paul's parents were an embarrassment to him (he was, after all, a "son of Pharisees," Acts 23:6, and a "Hebrew born of Hebrews," Phil 3:5), but rather that an appeal to his ethnicity/nationality, and cities of origin and training, were more conducive to currying the favor of his audience (with whom he shared these topics) than would have been mention of his parents.

22:4–21. Although Paul has been accused of teaching against the law and defiling the temple (21:28), these hardly amount to formal charges. Further, Paul is presumably unaware of the inadvertent role Trophimus has played in the upheaval (21:29); at any rate, the crowd cannot finally agree on what exactly he has done wrong (cf. 22:33b–34). Thus Paul dispenses with the expected rebuttal of charges (*refutatio*), so common in defense speeches in ancient narrative, especially ancient historiography (cf. Xenophon, *Hell.* 2.3.24–47; Dionysius of Halicarnassus, *Ant. Rom.* 9.29–32; Appian, *Hist. Rom.* 40.9.15; 11.4–9; 12.7–15.10; Curtius Rufus, *Hist. Alex.* 6.9.16–19; Tacitus, *Ann.* 6.8; 13.21; 16.31; Josephus, *Ant.* 16.109–112; *BJ* 1.627–628; 1.629–633; see Hogan 2006, 154 *et passim*). Rather, he turns to the *narratio*, the statement of facts. Although there is no rebuttal of any specific charges, Paul is aware of the criticisms that he has been teaching fellow Jews not to observe the Jewish rites and customs (21:21). Thus Paul's appeal to topics in the *exordium* intended to reassure his Jewish audience continues in a more subtle way in the *narratio*.

The *narratio* in Acts 22:4–21 addresses four topics: (1) Paul's persecution of Christians (22:4–5); (2) Paul's vision on the road to Damascus (22:6–11); (3) the role of Ananias in Paul's conversion (22:12–16); and (4) Paul's vision in Jerusalem (22:17–21). And although the *narratio* does not rise to the level of proofs against specific charges leveled against him, in each section, Paul makes appeal to his authentic "Jewishness" and those around him as well as to the grounding of his mission in a divine call by Israel's God.

1. The transition from *exordium* to *narratio* is marked by the change in verb tense from present to aorist (Hogan 2006, 154). Paul refers to his previous experience as a persecutor of Christians: **I persecuted the Way, even to the point of having them killed, by binding both men and women and delivering them to prison, as even the high priest and all the elders can attest for me** (22:4–5a). On one level, Paul's account of his previous life as a persecutor of the Way continues to appeal to his audience. That the high priest and elders can confirm these activities likewise would have reassured the crowd, at least temporarily. But obviously such appeasement is not Paul's ultimate goal. Paul had received orders to travel to Damascus to extend his persecution of the believers there: **(They are the ones) from whom I also received letters to fellow Jews in Damascus, and I was going (there) in order to take those (Christians) who were there (22:5b)**. Paul's purpose was to bring the Damascus Christians **in chains to Jerusalem so that they might be punished**. Ironically, this is the predicament in which Paul currently finds himself, a Christian in Jerusalem, bound in chains, and on the verge of punishment.

2. In 22:6–11, Paul recounts his conversion experience in the form of a dream-vision (cf. Philostratus, *Vit. Apoll.* 4.34; Plutarch, *Luc.* 12.1; *Eum.* 6.4; see comments on 16:6–10). This is the second time Paul's conversion is narrated in Acts (see Acts 9:1–18), and there are both significant similarities and differences between the two accounts (and the third to be related later in

chap. 26). This could be simply a matter of Luke's "paraphrasing" the story to make different points for different parts of the narrative (on paraphrasing, see Theon, *Prog.* 108P, trans. Kennedy 2003, 70; see Theological Issues on Acts 7). Once again the four typical elements are present: (1) *Scene-setting*: **Now, as I was on my way and nearing Damascus at about noon** (22:6a). Luke's earlier account of Paul's conversion (9:2) is missing this reference to the time of day (cf. the comments on 10:9; here the term is unambiguously a temporal reference). (2) *Dream-vision terminology:* **A bright light from the sky suddenly flashed around me! I fell to the ground and heard a voice** (22:6b–7a). The bright light flashing and the voice are typical features of a dream-vision epiphany (cf. 9:3–4). (3) *Dream-vision proper*, including instructions for action: **"Saul, Saul, why are you persecuting me?" I answered, "Who are you, Lord?" And he said to me, "I am Jesus, the Nazarene, whom you are persecuting." Those who were with me saw the light but did not hear the voice of the one who was speaking to me. Then I said, "What should I do, Lord?" And the Lord said to me, "Go at once into Damascus and there you will be told all that you have been assigned to do"** (22:7b–10). The dialogue between Paul and Jesus is a nearly verbatim repetition of the previous account (compare with 9:4–5). The addition of "the Nazarene" to Jesus' name (22:8) is appropriate for a Jewish audience. Luke also uses the rhetorical figure of *antistrophe*, in which the last word is repeated in successive phrases (*Rhet. Her.* 4.13.19; cf. Quintilian, *Inst.* 9.3.31): in the Greek the word "persecute" occurs at the end of 22:7 and 8. It is startling that the Lord identifies Paul's persecution of the church with persecution of himself ("Why do you persecute me?" // "I am Jesus whom you are persecuting"). The church in Acts is called to complete the sufferings of Christ for the sake of the gospel and in behalf of the world (cf. Moessner 1990). (4) *Reaction/response*: **When I could not see, because of the brilliance of the light, I entered Damascus with those who were with me leading me by the hand** (22:11). The "brilliance" of the light might also be translated the "glory" of the light; it indicates "God's effective presence in the world" (Johnson 1992, 389; cf. Luke 2:9, 14, 32; 9:31–32). Paul's spiritual blindness is now reflected in his physical blindness (cf. Hartsock 2007). He enters Damascus where he is totally dependent on others for his mobility.

3. With Ananias's role in Paul's conversion (22:12–16) we find the most significant variation from the earlier account of Paul's conversion. First Ananias restores Paul's sight. **Now a certain Ananias, a devout man by the law's standards and respected by all the Jews who lived there, came to me, stood beside me and said, "Brother Saul, see again!" And at that very moment I looked up at him** (22:12–13). The description of Ananias as a pious Jew (22:12) rather than as a devout Christian (as in 9:10) again helps Paul establish his Jewishness, and the Jewishness of those with whom he associated, with this temple mob.

Next Ananias tells Paul of his mission. **Then he said, "The God of our ancestors has chosen you to know his will and to see the Righteous One and** hear his voice. For you will be his witness to all people of the things you have seen and heard. So now, what are you waiting for?" (22:14–15). This is the heart of the *narratio*, but the force of Paul's commission at this point is somewhat muted. In Acts 9:10–17, the account of Ananias is reported in the form of a commissioning story. Here the role of Ananias is slightly diminished (cf. 9:10–17). No longer is Ananias the recipient of his own vision; rather, he simply reports that the God of Israel has chosen Paul "to know his will and to see the Righteous One and hear his voice." Indeed, Paul will be a "witness to all people," but gone now are Ananias's objections, the divine prediction of Paul's suffering for Christ's sake, and the explicit reference to Paul being the instrument to carry Christ's name before the Gentiles (now effaced in the bland reference to "all people").

Finally, Ananias urges Paul to receive baptism: **Be baptized and have your sins washed away as you call on his name** (22:16). Likewise, the account of Paul's baptism and subsequent strengthening (Acts 9:17–19a) are reduced to Ananias's exhortation to baptism. An important element in explaining the differences is that Paul, not an omniscient narrator (as in chap. 9), is recounting the story and thus Paul relates events as they unfolded to him.

4. Acts 22:17–21 follows the pattern of a dream-vision and parallels the dream-vision on the road to Damascus (22:6–11), although, as we shall see, the last element, the reaction/response, is omitted. (1) *Scene-setting*: **Now, after I had returned to Jerusalem, while I was praying in the temple** (22:17a). Dream-visions often occur in a temple or cultic setting (Luke 1:8–23; cf. 1 Kgs 3:1–5; *Jub.* 32.1–2; *T. Levi* 8.1–19; *2 Bar.* 34.1–43.3; Josephus, *Ant.* 11.326–328; and various Asclepian inscriptions [e.g., IG IV² 1, 513, 561]). Paul, as an observant Jew, is praying in the temple, thus continuing the emphasis on his "Jewishness" before the crowd. (2) *Dream-vision terminology*: **I fell into a trance** (22:17b). "Trance" is typical language of a dream-vision (cf. Acts 10:10; 16:6–10). (3) *Dream-vision proper*: **And I saw (the Lord) saying to me, "Hurry, you must leave Jerusalem quickly because they will not accept your testimony about me!"** (22:18). Now for the first time, Paul reveals to the crowd Christ's prediction that from the beginning those in Jerusalem would not accept Paul's message about Christ. Dream-visions can include a dialogue between the vision figure and the recipient of the vision (see Acts 9; 10; cf. Gen 20:3–8; 31:10–13; 46:2–6; Homer, *Od.* 4.786–841; 20.1–55; *Il.* 23.64–119). Such is the case here. Paul continues by rehearsing his previous participation in the persecution of the Christians: **I replied, "Lord, they themselves know that (I went) from synagogue to synagogue imprisoning and beating those who believe in you"** (22:19). He then specifically recalls his role in the martyrdom of Stephen: **And when the blood of Stephen, your witness, was shed, I myself was standing there, approving (of what was happening) and guarding the outer garments of those who were killing him** (22:20; cf. Acts 7:58). The

brief mention of Stephen's stoning prepares the authorial audience for the response of the incensed crowd.

Christ speaks once again to Paul, this time issuing a command: **Then he said to me, "Go (now), for I will be sending you far away to the Gentiles!"** (22:21). The prophetic commissioning to the Gentiles (cf. Isa 6:10) was earlier mediated through Ananias (22:14–15; cf. 9:15–16). Now Ananias's rather muted report that Paul is to be "a witness to all people" is clarified and amplified and given directly to Paul. Once Paul explicitly mentions the Gentile mission, the mob is once again stirred against him.

22:22–29. Taking the explicit mention of Gentiles as confirmation that Paul is guilty of "forsaking Moses," the crowd interrupts Paul's speech (cf. 23:7; 26:24; Horsley 1986), and the last element of the dream-vision, the reaction/response, is omitted: **Now they were listening to him until this statement, but (when they heard it) they shouted, "Away from the earth with such a person! For it is not right for him to live!"** (22:22). Such interruptions are not uncommon in speeches embedded in ancient narrative (cf. Appian, *Bell. civ.* 3.51–61; Curtius Rufus, *Hist. Alex.* 6.9.2–24; 7.1.10–40; Tacitus, *Ann.* 16.31; pace Hogan 2006, 156–57; contra Dibelius 1956, 160–61). These shouts were accompanied by frenzied gestures (22:23): **they were yelling** (cf. 7:57; 14:14); **throwing off their outer garments** (cf. 14:14; 18:6); **and flinging dirt into the air** (cf. 13:51). In this sense, Paul's "defense" is a failure; his efforts to prove his "Jewishness" to the crowd finally give way to his conviction that he is called to be an apostle to the Gentiles. While these two convictions—authentic Jewishness and openness to Gentiles—were not incompatible for Paul (and other Pharisaic Jews; cf. comments on Acts 15), they are oxymoronic to the crowd.

Once again the tribune, perhaps ignorant of Aramaic and unable to understand exactly what has transpired (see Witherington 1998, 677), intervenes and decides to get to the bottom of this conflict by literally beating the answers out of Paul (for examples of interrogation by torture, cf. Chariton, *Chaer.* 1.5.2; 3.4; Pliny the Younger, *Ep.* 10.96; Achilles Tatius, *Leuc. Cli.* 7.12.2–3; Quintilian, *Inst.* 5.4.1; Talbert 2005, 193): **The commander ordered him to be brought into the barracks and said that he should be interrogated using a whip so that he might learn the precise reason why they were shouting at him in this way** (22:24). Suddenly the military barracks, so recently a refuge for Paul to escape beating and death, are to become a torture chamber (Skinner 2003, 116–18). The soldiers **tied him up with straps (to be beaten)** (22:25). But just before he is to receive lashes—and with a flair for the dramatic—Paul reveals to the centurion what the authorial audience already knows (16:37), namely that Paul is a Roman citizen: **Paul said to the centurion who was standing (there), "Is it lawful for you to beat a man who is a Roman citizen and has not been tried?"** (22:25). Flogging a Roman citizen was presumably not an acceptable practice (see, e.g., Cicero, *Verr.* 2.5.66; see also Fitzmyer 1998, 589, 712, for other comparative material). Alarmed, the centurion in charge immediately reports to the commander: **When the centurion heard (this) he went to the commander and reported it, saying, "What are you about to do? This man is a Roman citizen!"** (22:26).

The tribune responds immediately: **So the commander went (to Paul) and said to him, "Tell me, are you a Roman citizen?" And he replied, "Yes, (I am)"** (22:27). Perhaps out of suspicion that Paul is lying, the commander presses on: **"My citizenship cost me a lot of money!" But Paul replied, "I was born (a citizen)"** (22:28). Purchasing Roman citizenship is attested by, among others, Dio Cassius (*Hist. Rom.* 60.17.4–9). Paul's inherited citizenship gives him a superior social standing to the tribune, whose citizenship was purchased, despite the fact that Lysias, as a tribune, holds a rank of significant social status (Lentz 1993, 44–46). The soldiers' response is sudden and decisive; no one wants to be responsible for torturing a Roman citizen: **Immediately, those who were about to interrogate him moved away from him, and the commander was also afraid because he knew that he had bound a Roman citizen** (22:29). Realizing he has bound and nearly flogged a Roman citizen, the tribune looks for an alternative plan for finding out the nature of the differences between Paul and the Jewish opponents. This will not be the last time that the tribune's actions betray an element of self-preservation (cf. 23:26–30).

Paul before the Sanhedrin (22:30–23:11)

The next scene (22:30–23:11) consists of two parts: Paul confronts the high priest (22:30–23:5), and Paul addresses the Sanhedrin (23:6–11).

22:30–23:5. Seeking to put the dispute to an end, the tribune brings Paul before the Sanhedrin (on Roman officials convening the Sanhedrin, see Tajra 1989, 91): **The next day, because (the commander) wanted to know the facts—(specifically) why (Paul) was being accused by the Jews—he released him and ordered the chief priests along with the entire council to assemble. Then he had Paul brought in and had him stand before them** (22:30). Paul begins with an assertion: **Paul looked directly at the council and said, "Brothers, up until this day I have lived in accord with God's standards with a completely clear conscience"** (23:1). He is saying, in effect, that he has been obedient to God by fulfilling his calling to the Gentile mission (cf. 26:19).

The high priest simply cannot accept that Paul's mission is indicative of his obedience to God: **The high priest Ananias gave orders to those standing next to him to slap his mouth** (23:2). Paul immediately responds with a sharp retort, **"God is about to strike you, you whitewashed wall! Do you (dare) sit there judging me according to the law and yet order me to be slapped even though it is against the law?"** (23:3). Several rhetorical figures are employed in these two verses. In Acts 23:2–3, Luke uses transplacement (*traductio*; *Rhet. Her.* 4.14.20; cf. Acts 10:10 and 18:18–23) by repeating the word "strike" or "slap" (*tuptō*) three times, drawing attention to the offensive and illegal nature of this act against Paul (cf. Deut 28:22). The Lukan Paul also employs frankness of speech (*Rhet. Her.* 4.36.38; see 4:13) when he addresses his assailant as a "white-washed wall" and accuses him of judging Paul "according to the law" while he himself treats Paul as a criminal even before his case is heard, an act that is also "against the law" (Deut 1:16–17; *Exod Rabbah* 21.3; *m. Sanh.* 3.6–8).

Those standing next to Paul protest, "Do you dare insult God's high priest?" (23:4). **Paul replied, "I did not know, brothers, that he was the high priest! For it is written, 'You must not speak evil of your people's ruler'"** (23:5). It is unlikely that Paul would not have recognized Ananias as the high priest (for whose organization he previously worked), and therefore his response should not be understood as a straightforward apology (contra Levinsohn 1987, 32; pace Marshall 1980, 363–64; Culy and Parsons 2003, 460). Rather, given Paul's bold speech, the authorial audience would recognize Paul's prophetic critique of a corrupt leader and his ironic use of Exod 22:28 to make the point that he did not recognize the high priest because he was not acting like one might expect the leader of the people to act.

23:6–11. Paul then notices that both Sadducees and Pharisees are present on the council, and he attempts to redirect the focus of the debate from whether Paul is an observant Jew to a weighty theological issue, the question of the resurrection of the dead: **When Paul realized that part (of the group) was Sadducees and part Pharisees, he shouted out in the council, "Brothers, I am a Pharisee, a son of Pharisees, (and) I am being tried for (my) hope in the resurrection from the dead!"** (23:6). Paul is attempting to do more, however, than simply start a controversy among members of the Sanhedrin. Rather, his concern about "hope and resurrection" raised here continues to be an important theme throughout the defense even when it no longer creates controversy (see 24:15, 21; 28:20; see Tannehill 1990, 286–87).

Nonetheless, Paul's words about resurrection spark a debate between the Sadducees, who deny the doctrine of resurrection (as well as the existence of angels and spirits), and the Pharisees, who affirm it: **When he said this, an argument began between the Pharisees and the Sadducees, and the group was divided. For the Sadducees say that there is no resurrection, or angels, or spirits; but the Pharisees profess them all** (23:7–8). Note that Paul here is speaking about a final eschatological **resurrection** of the dead (plural), which Sadducees were widely known to deny (Josephus, *BJ* 1.163–165; *Ant.* 13.297–298; 18.16–17; *Sanh.* 90b; Luke 20:27–38), not specially of the resurrection of Christ. What Luke meant by the Saducean rejection of "angels" and "spirits" is less clear (cf. Parker 2003, 344–65). **Angels** may refer to "angel speculation," since angels were often viewed as agents of divine providence (cf. 1 Kgs 22:22–23; Dan 3:25, 6:22; *b. Nid.* 16a). Sadducees were known to reject determinism in favor of a radical view of free will, while the Pharisees allowed for a combination of fate and free will (Josephus, *Ant.* 13.171–173; 18.13; *BJ* 2.162–165), and presumably were less antagonistic toward the view of angels as agents of divine providence (Parker 2003, 360–61). **Spirits** may refer to belief in the survival of the disembodied soul after death, another doctrine that the Sadducees evidently denied (Josephus, *Ant.* 18.1.4; *BJ* 2.164–165) and the Pharisees affirmed (Josephus, *Ant.* 6.332; *Sanh.* 102b; *Lev. Rab.* 18.1).

The Lukan Paul (and Luke) here seeks to emphasize the similarities between the Christian sect and other segments of Judaism, and thus lay the groundwork for more explicit claims later about the resurrection of Jesus (26:23). The Pharisees proclaim Paul's innocence (23:9), much as Pilate, Herod, the penitent thief, and the centurion pronounced Jesus innocent (cf. Luke 23): **So there was a lot of shouting, and some of the scribes, who were members of the Pharisees, stood up and began strongly protesting, saying, "We find nothing wrong with this man. Did an angel or spirit (actually) speak to him? (Perhaps one did!)"** (23:9). Whether or not the Pharisees are suggesting that an angel of divine providence or the disembodied spirit of a deceased person was speaking to Paul (and therefore in effect "interfering" with and redirecting Paul's actions), their question was surely designed to irritate and annoy the Sadducees.

Once again, the tribune, fearing for Paul's safety, has him delivered back to the barracks: **When a terrible argument ensued, the commander became afraid that they would tear Paul to pieces so he ordered the troops to go down and take him away from them and then bring him (back) to the barracks** (23:10). Three times between now and the end of the chapter, Luke mentions the barracks in which Paul is held in custody (cf. also 23:16, 32). In fact, all six occurrences of the term "barracks" occur between Acts 21:34 and 23:32 (cf. also 21:37 in addition to the other citations here). Here, as before (21:34; 22:24), the military barracks are a kind of "uneasy" place of refuge for Paul against mob violence (see Weaver 2004, 116).

In Custody

Ulpian (third-century AD jurist) lists a spectrum of possibilities for custody in the Roman Empire (in Justinian, *Dig.* 48.3.1; cf. Rapske 1994, 20–35): the most severe is a prison, a building constructed or renovated specifically for incarceration (cf. Pausanias, *Descr.* 6.13.1; Juvenal, *Sat.* 4.313), followed by a military barracks or camp, under military guard (Tacitus, *Ann.* 1.21; 12.66; 13.15), and finally, house arrest, reserved for persons of high social status (cf. Cicero, *Verr.* 2.5.68, 76). Luke locates Paul in all three custodial settings: the prison or jail (Acts 16:23); the military barracks, here in Acts 21–23, the Fortress Antonia (cf. Josephus, *Ant.* 18.91–92); and finally Paul's apparent house arrest here (23:35) as well as the house arrest with which the book of Acts ends (28:16–31). In all these contexts of Roman custody, Paul continually shows himself to be a person of great influence and divine empowerment.

This scene ends with Paul as the recipient of yet another dream-vision, this time in abbreviated form (see Dodson 2006, 172–73): **The next night, the Lord stood beside him and said, "Have courage! For just as you have testified about me in Jerusalem, in the same way you must also testify in Rome"** (23:11). (1) The *scene-setting* is minimal: "The next night." It is noteworthy that, in contrast to the more conventional setting of the temple in the earlier dream-vision, this one occurs in a military barracks. (2) There is no *dream-vision terminology*, although the posture of the dream figure is conventional: "the Lord stood beside him." (3) The function of the *dream-vision proper* is twofold: "(a) to encourage Paul in his present circumstance and (b) to foretell Paul's eventual arrival and testimony in Rome" (Dodson 2006, 172). The reason for the divine necessity for Paul to go to Rome is made clear: he is to "bear witness" there as he has in Jerusalem. The foreshadowing of Paul's impending journey and testimony in Rome, given its connection to his current circumstance in Jerusalem, is foreboding. (4) Prisoner that he is, Paul has no immediate *response/reaction* to the dream-vision, but the point is that it will ultimately be fulfilled.

An Ambush Avoided (23:12–35)

The remainder of chapter 23 recounts a foiled plot against Paul's life. First Luke narrates the hatching of the plot (23:12–15), then its exposure by Paul's nephew (23:16–22), and finally the intervention of Roman officials to save Paul's life (23:23–35).

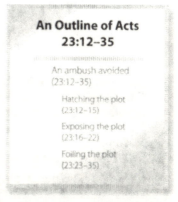

An Outline of Acts 23:12–35

An ambush avoided
(23:12–35)

   Hatching the plot
   (23:12–15)

   Exposing the plot
   (23:16–22)

   Foiling the plot
   (23:23–35)

23:12–15. The resolve of the Jerusalem Jews against Paul is demonstrated by the next scene: **When it was day, the Jews made a plan and bound themselves (to it) with an oath, saying that they would neither eat nor drink until they had killed Paul. There were more than forty who formed this conspiracy** (23:12–13). Unnamed Jews (presumably distinct from the Sanhedrin) approached the temple establishment (Sadducean chief priests and elders) with a plan to take Paul by ambush (the absence of the more sympathetic Pharisees from this conspiracy is noteworthy): **They went to the chief priests and elders and said, "We have bound ourselves with an oath to consume nothing until we have killed Paul. So now, you must report to the commander, along with the council, so that he will bring him down to you as if you are going to examine his case more thoroughly. And we will be ready to kill him before he arrives!"** (23:14–15). Such "death oaths," while extreme, were not impossible in first-century Judea (cf. Josephus, *Vita* 201–203; *BJ* 2.418–422; 4.129–134; Johnson 1992, 404). They successfully seek to engage members of the Sanhedrin in the plot.

23:16–22. The plan is thwarted by Paul's nephew, the son of his sister, both of whom we hear about now for the first time: When Paul's nephew heard about the ambush, he went and entered the barracks and informed Paul (23:16). Access to prisoners in barracks was evidently not forbidden (Lucian, *Peregr.* 12–13; Phil 2:25; 2 Tim 1:16–17; *Acts Andr.* 14; *Acts Paul* 18–19; Johnson 1992, 404): Then Paul called one of the centurions and said, "Take this young man to the commander, for he has something to report to him." So the one who took him brought him to the commander and said, "The prisoner (named) Paul called me and asked me to bring this young man to you, who has something to say to you." After the commander had taken him by the hand and moved away, he asked him privately, "What is it that you have to report to me?" (23:17–19). Paul, although a prisoner, still has the influence to summon a centurion. He replied, "The Jews have agreed to petition you in order that you might bring Paul down to the council tomorrow as if they are going to ask more thoroughly about something concerning him. Therefore, don't pay attention to them, for more than forty of their men are lying in ambush for Paul. They have bound themselves with an oath not to eat or drink until they have killed him, and now they are ready and waiting for your decision." Then the commander sent the young man away after giving him the following order: "Tell no one that you have reported these things to me" (23:20–22). The young man reports the conspiracy to the tribune with detailed accuracy (cf. Lysias's less accurate letter, below).

23:23–35. The tribune again acts decisively on Paul's behalf: Then he summoned two of (his) centurions and said, "Have two hundred soldiers, along with seventy horsemen and two hundred spearmen, ready to go to Caesarea by nine o'clock tonight." He also said to provide horses for Paul to ride so that they could take him safely to Felix the governor (23:23–24). Remarkable resources are deployed in "Operation Paul" (Pervo 1987, 32–33). In addition, the tribune drafted a letter to be delivered to Felix (23:25–30). This missive is a "letter of report" (*dimissoria littera*), sent to a higher jurisdiction and containing the results of previous inquiries and interrogations along with reasons justifying the remission of the prisoner to a higher court (see Ulpian in Justinian, *Dig.* 49.6.1; Tajra 1989, 106; cf. also Acts 25:26–27): Claudius Lysias, to the most excellent Governor Felix. Greetings. This man had been seized by the Jews and was about to be killed by them; but I arrived (on the scene) with (my) soldiers and rescued him, (after) learning that he was a Roman. And since I wanted to determine the reason why they were accusing him, I had him brought down to their council. I found him accused with respect to matters of their law, but he had no charge (against him) that was worthy of death or imprisonment. When it was reported to me that there would be a plot against this man, I immediately sent (him) to you and also ordered his accusers to state the charges against him before you (23:26–30). This is the second "embedded letter" in Acts (see 15:23–29). Lysias's letter not only recapitulates the events leading up to and including Paul's arrest (with the requisite amplifications and omissions; cf. *Rhet. Alex.* 28.2–4), but also reveals something of the character of Claudius Lysias (and perhaps more than Lysias himself would have preferred).

Lysias is a complex figure. He has acted decisively on Paul's behalf, thrice intervening in life-threatening situations (21:31–36; 23:10; 23:23–25). He has also been persistent in his investigations to learn the facts about Paul, and he has been willing to change previous impressions about Paul (accepting that he was not an Egyptian insurrectionist; that he was a Roman citizen; and that there was a Jewish conspiracy to kill him). Thus he accurately reports that the conflict between Paul and his opponents was an intra-Jewish dispute "with respect to matters of their law." And he rightly concludes that Paul "had no charge (against him) that was worthy of death or imprisonment" (see Howell 2009).

But in this letter the audience also learns that Lysias is willing to rearrange and suppress the facts to put himself in a better light. In the letter to Felix, Lysias suggests that he intervened in Paul's behalf *because* he was a Roman citizen (23:27); from this account Paul presumably would not have been bound or imprisoned (because Lysias found no charge worthy "of imprisonment"). But the audience knows that Lysias had at first thought Paul was a revolutionary and learned of Paul's citizenship only after he had placed him in chains and nearly had him flogged, a point Lysias conveniently omits. "In both instances, the discrepancies suggest that Roman officials need to present a public image that partially conceals the truth about their actions and motives" (Tannehill 1990, 295). Lysias's self-assurance in decision-making is marred with interests of self-protection.

The plot ends as secretly as it began: **So the soldiers, in accord with the orders that had been given to them, took Paul and brought him to Antipatris during the night. The next day, after dismissing the mounted soldiers to go on with him, (the other soldiers) returned to the barracks** (23:31–32). Paul is placed before the Roman governor who quickly assesses the situation and renders a decisive edict: **When they had entered Caesarea and delivered the letter to the governor, they also turned Paul over to him. When (the governor) had read (the letter), asked what province he was from, and discovered that (he was) from Cilicia, he said, "I will hear your case when your accusers have also arrived"** (23:33–35a). Meanwhile Paul was kept under house arrest in Herod's headquarters (23:35b). It will be quite some time before a Roman official again acts so expeditiously on Paul's behalf.

Theological Issues

Ernst Haenchen contends that while Paul is a great miracle-worker in Acts, Paul in the letters did not "overcome all obstacles by miraculous means—an apostle must plunge into the depths of suffering and *there* experience the help of Christ" (Haenchen 1971, 113–14, citing 2 Cor 12:10). The narrative of Acts, however, did not describe Paul using miracles magically to "overcome all obstacles," but rather to evoke faith and to legitimate his position, as Paul does in the letters. In the case of suffering, as well, we see also a confluence of the author of the letters with the figure in Acts.

In his letters Paul employs forms of *paschō* (Rom 8:17–18; 1 Cor 12:26; 2 Cor 1:3–8; Gal 3:4; Phil 1:29; 3:10; 1 Thess 2:2, 14) and, more often, *thlipsis* (Rom 5:3; 8:35; 12:12; 2 Cor 1:3–8; 6:4; 7:4; 8:2; Phil 1:17; 4:14; 1 Thess 1:6; 3:3, 7) for suffering. The latter term was commonly used in the LXX for various types of affliction, but "its theological significance arose from the fact that it predominantly denotes the oppression and affliction of the people of Israel or of the righteous who represent Israel" (Schlier 1965, 3:139–48). The term is always used in the NT for people of the church, members of the body of Christ, who therefore share in the sufferings of his body, and sometimes explicitly in the sense of eschatological tribulation (Schlier 1965, 3:143–44). It shared this eschatological sense with Judaism (Dan 12:1; *As. Mos.* 8.1; *4 Ezra* 13.16–19).

The epistolary Paul describes his suffering in some detail. "Poorly clothed and beaten and homeless" are only a few of his struggles (1 Cor 4:11); he is also in danger from the Jews, from the Gentiles, and at sea (2 Cor 11:23–33). One interpretative option for Paul's "thorn in the flesh" (2 Cor 12:7) has been his apostolic sufferings at the hands of his enemies (cf. Barré 1980, 216–17). These trials are crucial to and expected in apostleship, and Paul does not discuss this suffering outside the topic of his service to God (2 Cor 6:4–10). The afflictions are necessary because they are part of the suffering of Christ, to the point that Paul can say that the missionaries carry in the body the death of Jesus (2 Cor 4:10; cf. Phil 1:17). The true followers, then, will share in the apostolic sufferings as well.

> Blessed be the God and Father of our Lord Jesus Christ . . . who consoles us in all our affliction [*thlipsei*]. . . . For just as the sufferings of Christ are abundant for us [*pathēmata*], so also our consolation is abundant through Christ. If we are being afflicted [*thlibometha*], it is for your consolation and salvation; if we are being consoled, it is for your consolation, which you experience when you patiently endure the same sufferings [*pathēmatōn*] that we are also suffering [*paschomen*]. . . . You share in our sufferings [*pathēmatōn*]. (2 Cor 1:3–8; cf. 1 Thess 1:6)

Paul himself, moreover, connects closely in his own letters the active power of the Holy Spirit with suffering as proof of apostleship that is worthy of imitation:

> Our message of the gospel came to you not in word only, but also in power [*dynamei*] and in the Holy Spirit and with full conviction; just as you know what kind of persons we proved to be among you for your sake. And you became

imitators of us and of the Lord, for in spite of persecution [*thlipsei*] you received the word with joy inspired by the Holy Spirit, so that you became an example to all the believers in Macedonia and in Achaia. (1 Thess 1:5–7)

Not only apostles, then, but also all believers will suffer and must remain firm in faith. Paul sent Timothy to Thessalonica to establish the believers in their faith, "that no one would be shaken by these persecutions (*thlipsesin*). Indeed, you yourselves know that this is what we are destined for. In fact, when we were with you, we told you beforehand that we were to suffer perse-cution (*thlibesthai*); so it turned out, as you know" (1 Thess 3:3–4). Suffering has the positive role of producing endurance for the path (Rom 5:3), but can never separate the believer from the love of Christ (Rom 8:35). The believers, therefore, must be "patient in affliction (*thlipsei*) and constant in prayer" (Rom 12:12). Suffering is necessary. True followers follow faithful models and become models themselves.

Listening to Acts, the audience quickly receives a picture of suffering apostle-ship within which to understand the Paul of the epistles. Not only does Jesus proclaim that he himself must suffer and die (Luke 9:22; 18:31–33, etc.) but, for Jesus' followers in Acts, suffering for the gospel is established as necessary long before the account of Paul begins to dominate the narrative (Acts 4:1–3; 5:17–18; 6:12; 7:54; 8:3; 12:1–5). The audience is, in fact, introduced to Paul in the midst of the profound suffering of Stephen, and is repeatedly reminded of Paul's role in the suffering of the church (7:60–8:3; 9:1–2; 22:4–5; 26:9–11).

The narrative of Acts fills out Paul's experiences of suffering and expands the knowledge of the audience with specific examples of his endangerment by Gentiles (14:5; 16:19–24 *et passim*), Jews (13:50; 14:2, 19 *et passim*), and his travels at sea (27:13–44). The terms Paul employs in the epistles move through Acts in an intriguing way. Forms of *paschō* are used in reference to the necessity of Christ's suffering, first proclaimed by Peter (3:18), then twice by Paul (17:3; 26:23). In between, God applies the term to the necessity of Paul's suffering in his instructions to Ananias (9:16). Though this reference is almost mysteriously cryptic at this point in the narrative, the audience who knows Paul's letters already understands its crucial importance to Paul's discipleship.

The audience hears the term *thlipsis* first in Stephen's speech, concerning Joseph: "but God was with him and rescued him from all his afflictions" (*ek pasōn tōn thlipseōn*; 7:9–10). The fathers suffered great affliction (*thlipsis megalē*) as well by the famine in Egypt and Canaan (7:11). Later they hear that those believers "who were scattered because of the persecution (*thlipseōs*) that took place over Stephen traveled as far as Phoenicia, Cyprus, and Antioch, and they spoke the word to no one except Jews" (11:19). Soon *thlipsis* recurs with reference to the next "questionable" inheritors of the true tradition, Paul and Barnabas. Paul is stoned and left for dead outside the city and then, with near-miraculous strength and courage, gets up and reenters the city. When Paul and Barnabas "had proclaimed the good news to that city and had made many disciples," they returned to Lystra, Iconium, and Antioch, "confirming the souls of the disciples, and exhorting them to continue in the faith, and that we must through much tribulation (*dia pollōn thlipseōn*) enter into the kingdom of God. And after they had appointed elders for them in each church, with prayer and fasting they entrusted them to the Lord in whom they had come to believe" (14:21–23). Later, the term recurs on Paul's own lips in his farewell address to depositors of the tradition, the Ephesian elders: "the Holy Spirit testifies to me in every city that imprisonment and persecutions (*thlipseis*) are waiting for me" (20:23). He continues immediately with the importance of accomplishing his ministry, using an athletic metaphor (20:24).

Predictions of Paul's suffering in Jerusalem come to fulfillment in our passage, Acts 21:17–23:35. Paul is attacked by a riotous mob, which drags him from the temple and beats him with intent to kill (21:30–32). He is then bound with chains (21:33) and prepared for interrogation by torture at the hands of the Roman military (22:24–25). He is slapped by the high priest (23:2). Forty Jews take an oath to kill him through ambush (23:12), a plot barely foiled by Paul's resourceful nephew (23:16–25). In an act of self-serving preservation, Lysias covers up his part in Paul's imprisonment and suffering (23:30–35).

In Paul's final recounting of his call in Acts 26, moreover, his apostolic vocation as the apostle who suffers for Christ has strong parallels with his own self-understanding as disclosed in his letters. His description of his life in Judaism focuses on his own persecution of the church (Gal 1:13; Acts 26:10–11) and his zeal for Jewish traditions (Acts 26:4; cf. Phil 3:5–6).

In Acts, he was "set apart" (26:15), in Galatians, "appointed" (1:15). In Acts, Christ says that he is appearing to Paul for his mission to the Gentiles (26:16–18); in Galatians, Paul describes Christ as revealed to him for his mission to the Gentiles (1:16). The Acts narrative, then, develops for the audience what they already know in part from the letters: Paul was right that afflictions are a necessary part of his vocation as an apostle. The expansion in areas of detail shows that Paul fits the pattern of the suffering ones who belong to the suffering Messiah. As C. K. Barrett points out, Luke moves "between two motivations, on the one hand to show how much Paul was prepared to suffer for Christ, on the other to show the power of God to deliver him from suffering" (1994, 1:457). Contra Haenchen, the picture of an apostle who "must plunge into the depths of suffering and *there* experience the help of Christ" resonates with both Acts and Paul's Epistles.

Acts 24–26

Paul before Felix, Festus, and Agrippa

⊡

Introductory Matters

This section is filled with legal scenes and defense speeches. Here Paul confronts the political establishment—the Roman officials, Felix and Festus, and the Jewish king, Agrippa. But a close reading of these passages reveals that Paul is not the only one "on trial"; he is joined by the Christian gospel. Paul not only defends himself; he bears witness to the Christian faith whether before the Jews, their king, or the Roman procurators. "Far from a low point, it was in many respects the high point of Paul's career" (Polhill 1992, 440). The unit has three episodes: Paul before Felix (chap. 24); Paul before Festus, leading to an appearance before Agrippa (chap. 25); and the longest, and in a sense climactic episode, Paul's trial before Agrippa (chap. 26).

Tracing the Narrative Flow

Paul before Felix (24)

Paul's Caesarean "trial" before Felix (chap. 24) consists of three parts: Tertullus and the "charges" against Paul (24:1–9), Paul's defense (24:10–21), and Felix's response(s) (24:22–27).

24:1–9. After a lapse of five days, **the high priest Ananias came down with some elders and a lawyer named Tertullus, and they presented charges against Paul to the governor (24:1).** The word *rhētōr*, used only here in the whole NT, may refer simply to "speaker" (Lucian, *Rhet. praec.* 1), but here it seems to have the technical use of "lawyer" (Dio Chrysostom, *Consuet.* 4; Josephus, *Ant.* 17.226.19, 208). As expected, Tertullus begins his charges against Paul with an *exordium*: **Since we are experiencing much peace through you and since reforms are taking place in this nation through your foresight, we welcome this in all ways and in every place, most excellent Felix, with great gratitude (24:2b–3).** There are several interesting points about this part of Tertullus's speech. He begins by flattering the judge (for similar rhetorical strategy, see Chariton, *Chaer.* 5.6.5; 5.7.1; Josephus, *Ant.* 16.105–108). Tertullus uses all the right phrases to curry Felix's favor, and as Quintilian advises, he links the flattery of the *exordium* to the furtherance of the case (*Inst.* 4.1.16; cf. Hogan 2006, 162). Felix has brought much "peace" to the Jews. He has enacted "reforms" that grew out of his "foresight," thus highlighting Felix's competence to judge such matters as stand before him now (24:2). Later Tertullus will accuse Paul of being a "troublemaker" and thus a potential threat to the peace and reform that Felix has brought and further linking the *exordium* to the "facts" of the case (24:5). Tertullus continues that all Jews everywhere and in every way are grateful to Felix for his benevolence (24:3), a claim that fades for the authorial audience in the face of the rebellion against Felix by disgruntled Jews (Josephus, *Ant.* 20.181–182).

Quintilian also suggests that the attention of the judge may be secured by an assurance of brevity on the speaker's part (*Inst.* 4.1.34), and Felix ends his *exordium* with a promise of brevity: **But so that I might not trouble you further, I urge you to listen to us briefly out of your graciousness (24:4).** And he fulfills his promise, but not without a rhetorical price. The *exordium* (also known as the *captatio benevolentiae*) in which Felix is praised is nearly as long as the charges lodged against Paul (24:2–4). Quintilian criticizes a disproportionately lengthy exordium by likening it to a head that is too large for its body (*Inst.* 4.1.62). Thus while Tertullus begins in his *exordium* with a promising rhetorical flourish, he delivers a "very lame and impotent conclusion" (Bruce 1954, 467).

The *narratio* follows the *exordium*. In this statement of facts, Tertullus levels two charges against Paul. First, he asserts: **For we have found this man (to be) a troublemaker and one who incites rebellion among all the Jews throughout**

Flattery

Flattery was so common in antiquity that Plutarch penned an essay, *How to Tell a Flatterer from a Friend*, in which he warned against being seduced by false praise. Although the essay is framed with regard to the protocols of friendship (in which one should expect and encourage "frank speech" as opposed to "flattery"), he does venture opinions about the dangers of political leaders falling prey to excessive flattery. Flattery, he claimed,

> "all but subverted and destroyed the character of the Romans in those days, by trying to extenuate Antony's luxuriousness, his excesses and ostentatious displays, as 'blithe and kind-hearted actions due to his generous treatment at the hands of Power and Fortune.' What else was it that fastened the mouthpiece and flute upon Ptolemy? What else set a tragic stage for Nero, and invested him with mask and buskins? Was it not the praise of his flatterers? And is not almost any king called an Apollo if he can hum a tune, and a Dionysus if he gets drunk, and a Heracles if he can wrestle? And is he not delighted, and thus led on into all kinds of disgrace by the flattery? For this reason we must be especially on our guard against the flatterer in the matter of his praises." (*Adul. amic.* 56, trans. Babbitt 1969)

The authorial audience, with even a rudimentary knowledge of the facts of Felix's reign, will recognize that, despite Tertullus's claims (24:2–3), Felix's procuratorship was badly flawed. Tacitus writes that Felix "practiced every kind of cruelty and lust, wielding the power of a king with all the instincts of a slave" (*Ann.* 12.54; cf. *Hist.* 5.9). The authorial audience will see through this poorly veiled attempt to influence Felix through flattery.

the world, and a ringleader of the sect of the Nazarenes (24:5). This accusation has taken a decidedly political direction from the complaints lodged earlier in 21:21. The charge of political sedition is appropriate for criminal proceedings (cf. Cicero, *Inv.* 2.516–8.28; *Rhet. Her.* 2.3.3–3.4). This charge of sedition would not be taken lightly by Felix, in light of the previous Jewish riots in Felix's territory of Judea (see Josephus, *BJ* 6.124–128). The second charge is that he also tried to desecrate the temple, so we arrested him (24:6). The charge that Paul is profaning the temple may have been the more offensive one to the Jews, but Tertullus combines it with the accusation of insurrection because the political charge is, from Felix's point of view, more serious.

Tertullus concludes his speech with what rightly may be called a *peroratio*: By questioning (him) concerning all these things, you yourself will be able to find out from him about the things we are accusing him of (doing) (24:8). What is missing in Tertullus's speech is the *probatio* (Quintilian, *Inst.* 5.1.1), or proofs that provide the basis for the accusations. The proofs seek to answer one or more of the following questions: Was the action committed? Did the

Tertullus's Faulty Speech

The claim that the authorial audience would have viewed Tertullus's speech (in 24:1–9) as defective because it omitted the *probatio* is supported by the textual evidence for this passage. The English reader will notice that 24:7 is missing altogether from most recent translations. Some manuscripts (E Ψ 33 36 181 307 Byz) have this reading (which extends into 24:8): "But Lysias the commander came along, and with much violence took him out of our hands, ordering his accusers to come before you." This reading suggests not only that Lysias had interrupted the "proceedings" of the Jews and ordered Paul's accusers to appear before Felix (and hence the need to "bother" Felix with the matter at all), but that Tertullus is inviting Felix to examine not Paul but Lysias (i.e., the "him" in the Byzantine text refers to Lysias, not Paul) to ascertain the facts of the case. Thus certain scribes have supplied the missing *probatio* by having Tertullus call Lysias to the stand (see Maxwell 2007).

action incur injury? Was it significant? Was it just (see Hogan 2006, 38)? Such proof can take the form of written testimony (documentation) or oral witnesses, who, for the prosecutor at least, may be either voluntary or conscripted (*Inst.* 5.7). According to Quintilian, the *probatio* is the only part of a forensic speech that cannot be omitted (*Inst.* 5). By inviting Felix to examine Paul for himself, Tertullus does not supply any supporting evidence or witnesses for his accusations (a point on which Paul will capitalize in his rebuttal), indicating the weakness of his case (Hogan 2006, 164–65).

The best Tertullus can do is produce other Jews who support his charges: **The Jews also joined in the attack by insisting that these things were true** (24:9). But this hardly rises to the level of proof or eyewitness testimony.

24:10–21. Rather than conduct his own investigation at this point, **the governor motioned to him [Paul] to speak** (24:10a; on the gesture see Shiell 2004, 151–53), which Paul does (24:10–21). Like Tertullus, Paul begins with an *exordium*: **Because I know that you have been a (good) judge for many years to this nation, I gladly defend myself** (24:10b). Unlike Tertullus, however, Paul limits his praise to the simple acknowledgment that Felix's judicial experience ought to qualify him to judge the veracity of the charges brought against Paul. Paul counters Tertullus's sweeping and ambiguous charges with a detailed narration of the events of twelve days ago. This *narratio* extends from 24:11 to 24:18a and takes the form of a ring structure (slightly modifying Hogan 2006, 166–67):

A Response to accusations (temporal marker followed by "they did not find"): **Since you are able to determine that I have had no more than** twelve days since I went up to worship in Jerusalem, and they neither found me in the temple disputing with anyone nor causing a crowd of the people (to gather), neither in the synagogues nor around the city (24:11–12).

B Declaration of innocence: nor are they able to provide proof to you concerning the things they are now accusing me of (doing) (24:13).

C Concession/confession: I (now) admit this to you that in accordance with the Way, which they call a sect, I serve (our) ancestral God and believe everything that is in accord with the law and that is written in the Prophets, and I have the same hope in God that these men themselves embrace, namely, that there will soon be a resurrection of both the righteous and the wicked (24:14–15).

B′ Declaration of innocence: With this in mind, I too strive to have a clear conscience before God and people at all times (24:16).

A′ Response to accusations (temporal marker followed by "they found"): After many years, I came to present money for the poor to my people along with offerings (to God). This is what I was doing when some Jews from Asia found me in the temple, ritually purified, associated with neither a crowd nor a disturbance (24:17–18a).

In the outer ring, A (24:11–12), Paul addresses first the charge that he is disrupting the peace. He denies "disputing with anyone" or "causing a crowd" to gather (a riot), either in the synagogue or around the city. In the corresponding ring, A′ (17–18a), Paul denies the charge of profaning the temple. Far from defiling the sacred precinct, he was in the temple "ritually purified" for the purpose of presenting a collection of money for the poor among his people, a conventional act of piety (see Philo, *Legat.* 216, 313). Now these very people are bringing charges against him. Nor, he claims, did he make a disturbance in the temple (pace 21:26), lest Felix mistakenly draw the conclusion that his actions in the temple, while not religiously offensive, were nonetheless politically suspect. Paul's case is made all the more plausible by giving the motives for the actions in question (as recommended by Quintilian, *Inst.* 4.2.52; cf. Hogan 2006, 167).

Rings B (24:13) and B′ (24:16) contain Paul's declaration of innocence and a clear conscience "before God and people at all times." Beyond that, however, Paul points to the lack of proof by his adversaries: Tertullus is unable to produce any eyewitnesses to the political and religious charges brought against him.

The heart of the ring structure, C (24:14–15), is in the rhetorical form of a concession (*concessio*; Quintilian, *Inst.* 9.2.51; *Rhet. Her.* 2.16.23; Cicero, *Inv.* 2.31), in which Paul "admits something that may at first seem unfavorable to him but does not actually hurt his case" (Hogan 2006, 167). Paul first admits to following the Way, which, Paul notes, his opponents refer to as a "sect" (24:5). While the term can refer generally (and more neutrally) to a "school" or "party" (cf. 5:17; 15:5; 26:5), his accusers appear to have used it in a pejorative sense (cf. 28:22). Paul thus chooses a more neutral term, the Way. The concession quickly turns into a confession in which Paul claims that he serves the same ancestral God as do they and believes "everything that is in accord with the law and that is written in the Prophets" (24:14). Furthermore, returning to what Paul believes is at the heart of the dispute (cf. 23:6; 24:21), he shares with his accusers (Sadducees notwithstanding) "the same hope in God . . . that there will soon be a resurrection of both the righteous and the wicked" (24:15).

After this rhetorically well-formed *narratio*, Paul proceeds to the *probatio* (24:18b–21). He reminds Felix again (cf. 24:13) that his accusers lack credible witnesses: Either these Asian Jews **should appear before you and state their accusations if they actually have anything against me. Or let these men here say what crime they found when I stood before (their) council** (24:19–20). Paul's proof consists in claiming that the prosecution lacks proof; otherwise Tertullus would bring forth witnesses from the Asian Jews (who are conspicuously absent) or from those with the high priest and elders to give firsthand testimony against Paul.

Paul then makes explicit the true nature of the charge against him. His crime was **in regard to this one thing that I shouted out when I stood among them: "I am being tried before you today concerning the resurrection of the dead!"** (24:21; cf. 24:15). What is at stake here, Paul claims, is the "resurrection of the dead," the "fundamental issue that unites Pharisaic Judaism with Christianity and divides non-Christian Judaism" (Krodel 1986, 441).

24:22–27. Felix evidently interrupts Paul before he can finish his speech with a summary or *peroratio* (on interrupted speeches in Acts, see Horsley 1986): **Felix, now that he had a more accurate knowledge of the Way, dismissed**

More Accurately

Most translators and commentators take the adverb "more accurately" (24:22) as elative or superlative and assume Felix possessed "more accurate knowledge of the Way" prior to his hearing with Paul (Bruce 1988, 482; Johnson 1992, 414; Fitzmyer 1998, 739; NRSV: "Felix, who was rather well informed about the Way"; cf. NJB, NIV). In this case, it is reasonable to assume he had gained this knowledge through his long procuratorship (24:10) or perhaps through his Jewish wife, Drusilla (24:24; cf. Johnson 1992, 414). It is possible, as my translation suggests, to take "more accurately" as a comparative adverb, implying that Felix acquired this knowledge of the Way through this present encounter with Paul (Witherington 1998, 713; Culy and Parsons 2003, 469; possibly ASV). Either way, he dismisses the case without rendering a judgment.

them, saying, "When commander Lysias comes down, I will decide your case" (24:22).

Felix's decision to postpone judgment until Lysias arrives appears at first reading to be a cautious and reasonable choice by a competent judge. Felix even gives Paul some freedom under a "lightened form of military custody" (Rapske 1994, 171–72) and arranges to hear him again: **He gave orders to the centurion to keep Paul in custody, to allow him some freedom, and not to prevent any of his friends from taking care of him** (24:23; see Acts 23:10). This favorable impression of Felix continues in the next verse: **Some days later, Felix arrived with his wife, Drusilla, who was a Jew. He sent for Paul and listened to him (speak) about faith in Christ Jesus** (24:24). It appears that Felix, along with his Jewish wife, Drusilla, wishes to hear more about Paul's Messiah, Jesus. Paul then draws out the ethical implications of his Christology (in categories familiar to Hellenistic moral philosophy; cf., e.g., Epictetus, *Diatr.* 4.1.10) by speaking **about righteousness, self-control, and the impending judgment** (24:25a). These terms resonate with a variety of contexts. First, they echo the teachings elsewhere of the "epistolary Paul": "righteousness" or "justice" (Rom 3:21–26; 9:30; 10:3; Gal 3:21–22; Phil 3:8–11), "self-control" (one of the "fruits of the Spirit"; Gal 5:23), and "impending judgment" (Rom 2:1–11; 5:16; 11:33; 13:11–14). These specific terms also reflect important themes elsewhere in Acts. Christ is the "Righteous One" (cf. Acts 3:14; 7:52; 22:14), whose "impending judgment" of the living and the dead (Acts 10:42) will be administered with "righteousness/justice" (Acts 17:31). The term "self-control" per se is absent, but its effects are certainly present in Acts. "Self-control" refers to the restraint of the passions or bodily impulses, understood usually in terms of sexuality or food (BDAG 274). The Christian community participates in fasting (Acts 13:2–3; 14:23) and continues to insist on certain food laws even among the Gentiles and a sexual code of conduct (Acts 15:20, 29; 21:25). Of course, not all vows of self-restraint are portrayed positively; consider the "encratic" vow of the Jews not to eat or drink until Paul is killed (Acts 23:12, 14, 21).

In its immediate context, the virtues practiced by followers of the Way may have struck uncomfortably close to home to Felix. And here the initially favorable impression of Felix's response to Paul begins to sour. By many accounts Felix was notoriously lacking in terms of "righteousness/justice" and "self-control." Recall Tacitus's comment that Felix "practiced every kind of cruelty and lust" (*Ann.* 12.54). Josephus records various miscarriages of justice in Felix's dealings with the Jews that finally led to a Jewish delegation pleading its case before Nero (*BJ* 2.13.2–7). Felix fares no better if we take "self-control" to refer specifically to sexual continence (cf. 1 Cor 7:9; *T. Naph.* 8.8; *Acts Paul* 4–6). Even if the accounts of the infelicities of Felix's marriage to Drusilla were embellished (cf. Canali de Rossi and Brenk 2001) the public perception of Felix's notorious passions was widespread. Josephus recounts disapprovingly Felix's seduction of and eventual marriage to Agrippa's sister,

Drusilla, who was already married to Azizos, King of Emesa (*Ant.* 20.139–144). Felix shows no propriety in matters of justice and no self-control in matters of sex and marriage (cf. Schneider 1982, 2:351–52). Felix's response in light of Paul's talk of an "impending judgment," coupled with the moral teachings of the Way with regard to "justice" and "self-control," is certainly understandable: **Felix became afraid and said, "For the time being, you may go. When I have more time, I will call for you"** (24:25b).

Any residual question for the authorial audience regarding Felix's own inadequacy in the area of justice and self-control is resolved by Luke's report that Felix was seeking bribe money, perhaps because of Paul's mention of a "collection for his people" (24:17): **Now, at the same time, he was also hoping that Paul would offer him a bribe** (24:26a). Evidently it is his desire to receive bribe money from Paul (for accounts of bribery in the ancient Mediterranean world, see Talbert 2005, 203), and not any sincere interest in learning more about the Way, that motivates frequent conversations between Felix and Paul: **For this reason, he frequently sent for him and conversed with him** (24:26b). His lack of justice is demonstrated in the final note of this scene: **When two years had elapsed, Felix was succeeded by Porcius Festus. And since he wanted to gain favor with the Jews, he left Paul in prison** (24:27). Far from using this extended period of time to determine the facts of Paul's case and render a judgment in it, he leaves Paul in prison until his own procuratorship ends in order "to gain favor with the Jews" (24:27). "Thus Roman justice is undermined by an unjust administrator" (Tannehill 1990, 302).

Paul before Festus (25)

The next scene (chap. 25) has three parts: the plot against Paul revived and resisted (25:1–5), Paul's "trial" (25:6–12), and Festus's (in)decision (25:13–27). In this scene Paul's destiny is sealed: he will journey to Rome.

Acts 25 in Context

Paul before Felix, Festus, and Agrippa (24–26)

Paul before Felix (24)

▶ Paul before Festus (25)

The plot revived and resisted (25:1–5)

Paul's trial (25:6–12)

Festus's (in)decision (25:13–27)

Paul before Agrippa (26)

25:1–5. Paul's opponents waste no time in renewing the charges against Paul before Festus: **Three days after Festus arrived in the province, he went up to Jerusalem from Caesarea, and the chief priests and (other) leaders of the Jews presented (charges) against Paul to him** (25:1–2a). Within three days of assuming office (AD 59/60), Festus traveled from Caesarea to Jerusalem (on Festus, cf. Josephus, *Ant.* 20.182–188; *BJ* 2.271–272). The opponents now are no longer described as "Jews from Asia," but rather consist of the "chief priests" and other "leaders" (literally, "first men"; cf. Acts 13:50; 28:17). The list of opponents may have altered over the ensuing two years but the hostilities remain the same. At the first opportunity Paul's opponents immediately revive their agenda with Festus, seeking this time not a trial but a favor: **They appealed to him and asked a favor that he might send Paul to Jerusalem because they were arranging an ambush to kill him along the way** (25:2b–3). They no doubt had come to expect this kind of favor from the Roman procurator through their dealings with Felix. Underlying the request to transfer Paul to Jerusalem was the old plot to ambush him along the way (cf. 23:14–15). Festus's reply raises hope that with this change in administration, justice might finally be served: **Then Festus responded that Paul was being kept in custody in Caesarea and that he himself was going there right away. "Therefore," he said, "let those among you who are influential go down with me and accuse him if this man has done anything improper"** (25:4–5).

25:6–12. Luke reports that after a stay of **eight or ten more days, he** [Festus] **went down to Caesarea** (25:6a), where Festus had determined to hear the charges against Paul: **On the following day, he sat on the judgment seat and ordered Paul to be brought** (25:6b). The "judgment seat" was the place where magistrates would hear cases and render legal judgment (Acts 12:21; 18:12, 16–17; cf. Josephus, *Ant.* 20.130; 2 Macc 13:26; Epictetus, *Diatr.* 4.10.21). The trial itself is condensed. There is no speech by the prosecution; rather, Luke reports that **those Jews who had come down from Jerusalem surrounded him and brought many serious charges against him that they had no way of proving** (25:7). Ominously, the antagonists "surrounded" Paul (cf. 2 Macc 14:9). While the charges are "many" and "serious," they are still unsubstantiated. They simply have no proof (cf. 24:13, 19).

Paul's speech is likewise abbreviated: **Meanwhile, Paul defended himself (by saying): "I have not done anything wrong against the law of the Jews or against the temple or against Caesar"** (25:8). The first two claims that he has done nothing wrong "against the law of the Jews" or "against the temple" echo the earlier charges of 21:28 and 24:5–6. The reference to Caesar (now Nero) is new (Johnson 1992, 421) and perhaps prompted by Paul's appearance at the Roman judgment seat; Paul has done nothing contrary to Roman law (Fitzmyer 1998, 744).

Festus responds by asking Paul if he wishes to go to Jerusalem for trial: (Tannehill 1990, 306–7): **But Festus, since he wanted to gain favor with the Jews, answered Paul, "Would you like to go up to Jerusalem so that you can stand trial there before me concerning these matters?"** (25:9). Earlier Festus had rebuffed the Jews' request for a "favor" with regard to Paul; now he wishes to "gain favor" with them. It appears that within the eight or ten days Festus had spent in Jerusalem he had evidently learned the political necessity of doing favors for the Jews (Tannehill 1990, 306–7).

Paul's response is no little shock: rather than a simple yes or no, Paul again asserts his innocence: **I am (now) standing before the judgment seat of Caesar, where I should be judged. I have not wronged the Jews in any way, as you well know** (25:10). Paul's impatience begins to show. There is no reason to return to Jerusalem for trial; the "judgment seat of Caesar" is where he should be judged. Furthermore, no matter how abbreviated the report of the proceedings, Festus has heard enough to know that Paul is innocent of wronging the Jews ("as you well know").

It appears as though Paul gives up, employing the figure of surrender (*permissio*), which, according to *Ad Herennium*, "is used when we indicate in speaking that we yield and submit the whole matter to another's will, as follows: 'Since only soul and body remain to me, now that I am deprived of everything else, even these, which alone of many goods are left me, I deliver up to you and to your power'" (*Rhet. Her.* 4.29.39, trans. Caplan 1954, 327). Paul claims: **Therefore, if I am guilty and have done something worthy of death, I do not refuse to die** (25:11a). He stops short, however, of total surrender to Festus's will because he has placed his willingness to die under the condition of guilt. So once again he returns to the lack of substance of the accusations against him: **But if there is no merit to the things of which these men are accusing me, no one has the right to hand me over to them** (25:11b). Paul knew about the previous plot to kill him en route from Caesarea to Jerusalem; mention of a trial in Jerusalem further raises his suspicion, seen clearly in the Greek. Festus had sought to do the Jews a "favor" (*charin*); Paul claims that no one—not even Festus—"can grant me to them as a favor (*charisasthai*)" (Tannehill 1990, 307).

Only now he introduces a new element into the proceedings, with his dramatic utterance **I appeal to Caesar!** (25:11c). Historically, the details of the appeal to the emperor, the *provocatio*, remain shrouded in mystery (see Polhill 1992, 491). Nonetheless, some things in our text are clear. With this utterance, "Paul makes the proceedings against him stop, for he has invoked authority higher than that of the provincial governor. It means that Paul has to remain in Roman custody and cannot be brought before the Sanhedrin" (Fitzmyer 1998, 745). By the first century (see the Augustan *Lex Iulia de vi publica et privata*), Roman citizens living in the provinces could appeal to Caesar and effectively suspend proceedings and prevent injury to the appellant until the case can be heard in Rome (cf. Tacitus, *Ann.* 16.10.2). Whether Paul thought he could have a fairer hearing before the emperor (Nero) than before Festus is probably less important than his desire to fulfill his destiny to bear witness to the gospel before the emperor in Rome (19:21; 23:11; 27:24).

Unwilling even on this point to make judgment alone, **Festus conferred with his council** (25:12a; a group of advisers, cf. 4 Macc 17:17; Philo, *Legat.* 254; Josephus, *Ant.* 16.163). Sensing an opportunity to rid themselves of a difficult case, they formally ratify his request with the terse judgment: **"You have appealed to Caesar; to Caesar you will go!"** (25:12b; on the historical questions of Festus's legal right to grant such a request, see Tajra 1989, 147–51).

25:13–27. Acts 25:13–27 could be taken as the introduction to the next episode, Paul's defense before Agrippa (so Johnson 1992, 427; Talbert 2005,

Epanaphora

The drama of Paul's appeal and Festus's response is intensified by Luke's use of the rhetorical figure of *epanaphora* in which "one and the same word forms successive beginnings ... as follows: 'Scipio razed Numantia, Scipio destroyed Carthage, Scipio brought peace, Scipio saved the state!'" (*Rhet. Her.* 4.13.19, trans. Caplan 1954, 277). In the Greek of Acts 25:12, Caesar appears first in two successive phrases and as the second term (following a necessary preposition) in the third: "*Caesar*, I call upon!" ... "*Caesar* you have called upon, to *Caesar* you shall go!" *Epanaphora* "has not only much charm, but also impressiveness and vigour in the highest degree" (*Rhet. Her.* 4.13.19).

205; Tannehill 1990, 309). Certainly Paul remains the focus of the narrative, and 25:13–27 allows Agrippa to hear a summary of Paul's case before hearing from Paul himself. This section, however, also focuses on the character of Festus. For more than half of the unit (25:13–23a) Paul steps offstage, a rarity in the second half of Acts. Furthermore, 223 of the 307 words (more than 70 percent) in this section are direct discourse attributed to Festus. Given the ancients' interest in *ethopoeia*, speech in character, it is necessary to attend to Festus's speech not only in terms of what it contributes to the plot of Paul's trial but also to the authorial audience's understanding of the characterization (and character) of Festus.

First, new characters are introduced: **After some days had passed, King Agrippa and Bernice arrived in Caesarea and greeted Festus** (25:13). This Agrippa is Herod Agrippa II, son of Agrippa I, mentioned in Acts 12 (cf. also Josephus, *BJ* 2.223; *Ant.* 19.360; 20.138). Bernice II was also the daughter of Agrippa I and sister of Agrippa II and Drusilla, wife of Felix (Acts 24:24). After her husband, Herod of Chalcis, died, she took up residence with Agrippa II (Josephus, *Ant.* 20.7.3; *BJ* 2.1.5), which scandalized some in upper Roman circles (Juvenal, *Sat.* 6.156–160). Apparently a devout Jew (she would later intervene with the Roman governor Florus on behalf of the Jews; cf. Josephus, *BJ* 2.15.1), she also moved among the elite of Roman society, becoming involved with the Roman Titus (Suetonius, *Tit.* 7.1; Dio Cassius, *Hist. Rom.* 65.14.4; Tacitus, *Hist.* 2.2). Luke depicts a "thoroughly pro-Roman family" who "comes to pay its respects to the new governor in a state visit" (Johnson 1992, 425).

Festus takes advantage of their extended stay: **When they had been there for many days, Festus presented Paul's case to the king** (25:14a). Festus uses this opportunity to involve Agrippa in the proceedings against Paul and, of equal importance, to offer a public defense of his own actions. In these two speeches by Festus (25:14–22, 24–27), Luke subtly discloses Festus's hypocrisy without explicitly labeling it as such (for what follows, see Tannehill

1990, 310–15). Festus's report adds details to the case, providing, from his perspective, a fuller account of the proceedings, but in the process he also attempts to put himself in the best possible light before Agrippa. He begins: **There is a man (here) whom Felix left as a prisoner, concerning whom, while I was in Jerusalem, the high priest and elders of the Jews presented charges and requested a ruling against him** (25:14b–15). This description conforms well enough to the narrator's description in 25:2–3 (although it omits any reference to the Jews asking for a "favor"). Festus's reply adds details not necessarily in conflict with the narrator's description in 25:4–5: **I answered them that it is not the custom of the Romans to hand over any man before the one who is accused has met his accusers face to face and received an opportunity to defend himself against the accusation** (25:16). The Roman custom of justice is well documented (Appian, *Bell. civ.* 3.8.54; Josephus, *Ant.* 16.258). The language of Festus's claim "not to hand over/grant" (*charizesthai*), however, echoes his intention to grant a "favor" (*charis*) to Paul's accusers (25:9; cf. 25:11). "Festus cites the point in the narrative where he looked good. He guaranteed Paul a trial in Caesarea. However, his choice of words reminds us that he did not show the same commitment to justice when it came to the verdict" (Tannehill 1990, 311).

His next statement about conducting the interrogation without delay is likewise accurate but self-serving: **So after they came (back) here with (me), I did not delay at all, but on the next day I sat on the judgment seat and ordered the man to be brought** (25:17). The next part of Festus's report runs similarly: **But when his accusers stood up, they brought no accusation of the horrible things that I had suspected. Instead, they had certain disagreements with him about their own religion and about a man named Jesus who had died, whom Paul claimed to be alive** (25:18–19). Festus acknowledges that the accusers brought no charges of "horrible things" worthy of the death penalty in Roman law (cf. 25:25), but rather the disagreements were of an intra-Jewish religious nature. This charge resonates with earlier Roman judgments (18:14–15; 23:29), but raises the question for the authorial audience, "If Festus perceived this to be the case, why did he not say so at the trial and acquit Paul?" (Tannehill 1990, 311). Why, in other words, does he allow it to get to the point where Paul must appeal to Caesar for any chance of justice?

Festus's next statement stands in direct conflict with the earlier account provided by the narrator: **Since I was baffled by the dispute over these matters, I asked if he might want to go to Jerusalem and be tried there on these charges** (25:20). Festus's confession to being "baffled by the dispute over these matters" can be taken as admission to his lack of knowledge of and experience with matters of Jewish religion (cf. also 26:24). Thus he could be appealing for help from Agrippa, who is not only a Jew but acknowledged (later in the narrative by none other than Paul) to have expertise in Jewish matters (26:3, 26). But the authorial audience also knows that the public face of ignorance of things Judaic stands in conflict with the fact that Festus suggests Jerusalem as a venue for the trial, not because there are others there more familiar with Jewish customs who can ensure a fair trial for Paul, but because he wished "to grant a favor to the Jews" (25:9). Whether ignorant or calculating, Festus, in the eyes of the authorial audience, "has ceased to be a just judge" (Tannehill 1990, 313).

Festus then brings the account up to date with an accurate summary: **But when Paul requested that he be judged by the emperor, I ordered him to be kept in custody until I could send him up to Caesar (25:21).** Agrippa responds: **"I would like to hear this man myself" (25:22a).** Festus wastes no time in complying: **"Tomorrow," he replied, "you will hear him for yourself" (25:22b).**

The appointed time for the interview arrives: **So the next day, Agrippa and Bernice came with great pomp and entered the audience hall with both the commanders and the prominent men of the city (25:23a).** On the one hand, this description can be taken at face value: Agrippa and Bernice arrive with great fanfare and an impressive entourage. Such displays of power were not unexpected. In the dispute between Mithridates and Dionysius, Chariton describes the courtroom:

> When the appointed day came, the King took his seat. There is a special room in the palace which is designated as a law court, an unusually big and beautiful room. In the middle stands the King's throne; on each side are places for the King's friends, those who in rank and ability count among the very first in the land. Around the throne stand captains and commanders and the most distinguished of the King's freedmen. (*Chaer.* 5.4, trans. Reardon 1989, 80)

On the other hand, given the previous equivocating (if not downright improper and unjust) behavior toward Paul by the Romans and their sympathizers, Luke knows that, through Paul, God is once again about to "disarm the principalities and powers" and to "make a public example of them, triumphing over them" in Christ (Col 2:15).

Finally Paul reappears on the scene: **when Festus had given the order, Paul was brought (25:23b).** Festus continues with his self-serving report, this time before a public audience: **King Agrippa and all of you men present with us, you see this man concerning whom the entire Jewish populace appealed to me both in Jerusalem and here shouting that he must certainly not be allowed to live any longer (25:24).** Festus exaggerates the pressure he is under (Tannehill 1990, 313). He claims "the entire Jewish populace appealed" to him "both in Jerusalem" and in Caesarea. He portrays the situation as one of near mass chaos and a people on the verge of riot, enough to disturb any Roman official. However, the disturbance with the Jewish mob at the temple occurred before Festus arrived in Jerusalem and only "the high priests and prominent men of the Jews" made appeals to him in Jerusalem (25:2–3) and later in Caesarea (25:6–7). He has magnified the extent of the disturbance and his role in quelling it.

In this imagined riot, Festus depicts the crowd shouting that Paul must die; he, however, the just dispenser of Roman law, decreed: **I, on the other hand, realized that he had done nothing worthy of death; but since he himself appealed to the emperor, I decided to send him** (25:25). The authorial audience is left to wonder: if Festus is the great model of Roman justice, why does Paul invoke the *provocatio*, a provision usually reserved for Roman citizens who fear justice will not otherwise be served for them? If one takes Festus's remarks at face value, then Paul's request is incomprehensible. If, however, his speeches are understood as a cover-up, then Paul's appeal to Caesar to escape the incompetence if not corruption of this "judge" is understandable.

Festus ends his speech with an appeal for aid: **I do not have anything definite to write to my master about him. Therefore, I have brought him before you all, and especially before you, King Agrippa, so that after a hearing has occurred I will have something to write. For it seems ridiculous to me to send a prisoner without indicating the charges against him** (25:26–27). The mention of Festus writing the emperor refers to a "letter of report" (*dimissoria littera*), similar to the one Lysias had sent Felix. Such letters were sent when a judge or official determined to send a prisoner to a higher court. The letter was intended to present the results of previous inquiries and interrogations along with reasons justifying the remission of the prisoner to a higher court (see Ulpian in Justinian, *Dig.* 49.6.1; cf. also Acts 23:26–30). Festus, however, cannot justify charges against Paul and therefore cannot pen the letter. The decision to send Paul to Rome relieves one problem, but creates another. Festus is no longer responsible for rendering a judgment in Paul's case, but he must specify the charges against Paul in a letter to the emperor. Perhaps his motivation to include Agrippa is grounded in the desire to have someone share the responsibility should the authorities at Rome determine that the charges against Paul are of no substance, but rather are due to the incompetence of the local administration.

Speeches allow the writer to explore the character of the speaker through the rhetorical convention of *ethopoeia*, speech in character (cf. Theon, *Prog.* 115, trans. Kennedy 2003, 47; see the sidebar on p. 143). In the case of Festus, that personality is complex, even duplicitous. The actions and motives for actions shown to the audience by the narrator do not mesh with the public persona that Felix gives himself before Agrippa and Bernice and later their entourage. He seeks to portray himself as a competent Roman administrator, capable of meting out justice, but this portrayal stands in contrast to Luke's presentation, in which Festus's actions are at least partially "tainted by favoritism" (Tannehill 1990, 314). With literary finesse Luke uses the rhetorical strategy of the embedded letter (Acts 23:26–30), narrative (24:26), and speech

(25:14–21, 24–27) to characterize the ambiguous, conflicting, and even hypocritical responses of Roman authority to Paul and his message.

Paul before Agrippa (26)

This unit (chap. 26) begins with Paul's defense (26:1–23). The speech is then interrupted by Festus, followed by an exchange first with Festus and then with Agrippa (26:24–29). The episode concludes with another pronouncement of Paul's innocence and the judgment that he must be sent to Caesar (26:30–32).

26:1–23. Attention turns once again to Paul: **So Agrippa said to Paul, "You are granted permission to speak for yourself"** (26:1a). Indeed, Paul's speech in this scene allows him to fulfill the words of Jesus directed at his followers: "you will be brought before kings and governors because of my name" (Luke 21:12). Paul responds to Agrippa: **Then Paul gestured with his hand and began his defense** (26:1b). This is the only explicit gesture recorded as part of an actual defense speech. In an *apologia*, the same gesture was used for the *exordium*, *narratio*, and *argumentatio*, and most likely Paul is here signifying the beginning of the *exordium* (Shiell 2004, 153). The orator was to place "the middle finger against the thumb and extend the remaining three" (Quintilian, *Inst.* 11.3.92, trans. Butler 1921). In the *exordium*, the motion was deliberate and restrained (*Inst.* 11.3.159).

> ### Acts 26 in Context
>
> Paul before Felix, Festus, and Agrippa (24–26)
>
> Paul before Felix (24)
>
> Paul before Festus (25)
>
> ▶ Paul before Agrippa (26)
>
> Paul's defense (26:1–23)
>
> 1. *Exordium* (26:1–8)
>
> 2. *Narratio* (26:9–23)
>
> The exchange with Festus and Agrippa (26:24–29)
>
> Paul's innocence declared (26:30–32)

In its ancient performance, the lector would have been expected to imitate this gesture to alert the audience regarding the beginning of the *exordium* (Shiell 2004, 153–54).

The speech itself falls into two parts: (1) the *exordium*, in which Paul (again following convention) appeals to the favor of Agrippa and anticipates some of the major elements of the case (26:1–8); and (2) the *narratio* (26:9–23). As such, Paul's speech lacks a *refutatio* or refutation of the charges against him (pace Hogan 2006, 171; contra, e.g., Witherington 1998, 737–38). This omission has led commentators to label the speech defective (Johnson 1992, 441) or even "irrelevant in a Roman court of law" (Tajra 1989, 163). It is important to remember, however, that although Paul is described as "making a defense" the context is not a formal trial. Festus had already decided that the accusations did not reach the level necessary for a Roman trial (25:25). "Paul's speech, then, is not a usual defense speech in which he can refute the charges against him since those hearing the case are unsure how he should be charged" (Hogan 2006, 172). Rather, Paul gives an extended *narratio*, in which he summarizes his past in a way that makes clear that he is guilty of no crime.

337

1. Even if the rest of Paul's speech is judged incomplete, the *exordium* (26:1–8) is very full, touching on all the subjects Quintilian deemed suitable: the judge, the speaker, the opponent, and the case itself (*Inst.* 4.1.6–11; cf. Hogan 2006, 172–73). Regarding the judge, Paul begins with a simple but elegant *capitatio benevolentiae*: **King Agrippa, I consider myself fortunate to be about to make my defense before you today concerning all the things of which I am accused by the Jews. Therefore, I ask you, in particular, who are an expert in all the customs and disputes of the Jews, to listen to me patiently** (26:2–3). Unlike Festus (though cf. 24:10), Agrippa is not only a fellow Jew, but "an expert in all the customs and disputes of the Jews." Thus Paul speaks as Jew to Jew. Earlier Tertullus had asked Festus to hear him "briefly"; Paul asks Agrippa to hear him "patiently." Both were appropriate requests (cf. Luke 18:7). Paul considers himself "fortunate" or "blessed" to have such a judge so experienced in matters of Judaica.

Next Paul addresses the topic of the speaker (himself) and the opponents. **Now, all the Jews know how I lived since my youth, living among my own people from the beginning, and also in Jerusalem; and they have known me for a long time, if they care to testify, that I—(as) a Pharisee—lived in accord with the strictest sect of our religion** (26:4–5). He speaks of his life as a Jew living openly among fellow Jews from his youth (presumably in Tarsus), continuing to his time in Jerusalem (cf. 22:3–5). Furthermore, he lived as a Pharisee and a member of the "strictest sect of our religion." In this description of his Jewishness he insinuates that his fellow Jews are being dishonest in their accusations since they all know and could testify to his former manner of life, if they wanted to. Such insinuations regarding the accusers' integrity were appropriate for an *exordium* (Quintilian, *Inst.* 4.1.42–50).

Finally, Paul moves to the last topic of the *exordium*, the case itself (26:6–8). Once again, his opponents' objections notwithstanding, Paul claims that the issue was not the religious and political ramifications of his disregard for Jewish customs, but rather the resurrection (23:6; 24:15; 25:19): **And now I am standing trial because of my hope in the promise that God made to our ancestors** (26:6). Far from rejecting his Jewish heritage by embracing the resurrection, Paul claims here that such hope actualizes the promise made by God to the "ancestors." Furthermore, **our twelve tribes, by earnestly serving (God) day and night, themselves hope to receive this (same) promise; and this is the very hope of which the Jews are accusing me, Your Majesty!** (26:7). Paul here affirms both the continuity of the resurrection with the "promise of *our* ancestors" and the hope of "*our* twelve tribes," as well as the division that this resurrection hope brings: **How can you people find it unbelievable that God raises the dead?** (26:8). The *exordium* ends with this penetrating rhetorical question (on rhetorical questions, see Quintilian, *Inst.* 9.2.7; *Rhet. Her.* 4.15.22).

2. Paul's *narratio* (26:9–23) takes the form of a narrative. "Narration is the exposition of the matters under debate in the lawcourts in a way advantageous

to the speaker, while narrative is the report of historical and past happenings" (Nicolaus, *Prog.* 12; on the confusion of terms in the handbooks regarding this distinction, see Hermogenes, *Prog.* 4.9–15, trans. Kennedy 2003, 75; Theon, *Prog.* 60.5, trans. Kennedy 2003, 4–5). Here Paul provides a narrative or report in which he rehearses his work as persecutor of Christians (26:9–11; cf. 22:3–5); recounts his conversion, once again in the form of a dream-vision (26:12–20; cf. 22:6–11); and then recalls his efforts to bear witness to the prophecies of a suffering Christ and his resurrection (26:21–23). Across the entirety of the *narratio* Paul employs all the elements necessary to compose a "complete narrative," according to Theon (*Prog.* 78, trans. Kennedy 2003, 28; cf. Aphthonius, *Prog.* 22, trans. Kennedy 2003, 96–97; Nicolaus, *Prog.* 13, trans. Kennedy 2003, 137; modifying Hogan 2006, 173):

Person. On the surface, Paul himself, of course, is the central character of the narrative. The Lukan Paul, however, uses the now familiar rhetorical strategy of *klisis* or *polyptōton* to suggest another "subject" of this narrative (Theon, *Prog.* 74.24–35, ed. Patillon 1997, 33; 85.29–31, ed. Patillon 1997, 48; Quintilian, *Inst.* 9.1.34; cf. Acts 7:2). In Paul's defense speech, the word "God" occurs in the nominative (26:8), genitive (26:6, 22), dative (26:29), and accusative (26:18, 20). Thus while the narrative appears to be a defense of Paul's actions, in the end it is a defense of the actions of God, who works through Christ to appoint Paul apostle to the Gentiles.

Action. This includes what is "just or unjust, honorable or dishonorable" (Theon, *Prog.* 78, trans. Kennedy 2003, 28). In a movement from what, from Paul's point of view, was dishonorable to honorable, Paul describes his activities from bearing witness against and persecuting Christ's followers, to becoming a follower of Christ to bearing witness in behalf of Christ.

Place. Theon specifies places that were "near a city or town," whether "sacred or unhallowed," "deserted or inhabited," and "all similar things" (Theon, *Prog.* 79, trans. Kennedy 2003, 29). Paul describes action that moves from Jerusalem to Damascus back to Jerusalem and Judea and beyond, "foreign cities" and "among the Gentiles." The action occurs in "sacred" places (synagogues, the temple) and profane places (prisons, the audience chamber in Herod's palace); in cities and along a presumably uninhabited Damascus road.

Time. "To time," Theon asserts, "belong what has gone by, what is present, what is going to be . . . what is appropriate to life in our time, what in ancient times . . . during the night or by day" (*Prog.* 79, trans. Kennedy 2003, 28–29). Time in Paul's *narratio* moves from some undetermined point in the past to a specific point, "midday," on his journey to Damascus to the present. He refers to events in the remote past (what the prophets and Moses said), in the recent past (his persecution of Christians, his conversion, his mission to the Gentiles), and his current circumstances ("to this day"). He also alludes to the future time when the Gentiles would take their place among those sanctified by faith in Christ (26:18).

Manner of action. Theon described manner of action as having been done intentionally or unintentionally. If unintentionally, then the action was out of ignorance, accident, or necessity (*Prog.* 79, trans. Kennedy 2003, 29). Throughout the *narratio*, Paul describes his actions, past and present, as the result of "necessity." In fact, he moves from one necessity to another, from the necessity of "doing hostile things against the name of Jesus" (26:9) to the necessity of being a "servant and witness of the things" Paul has "seen" (26:16). Paul is "appointed" by Christ to "bear witness" to the Gentiles (26:16–17), and to this vision Paul dare not be "disobedient" (26:19). Thus Paul chooses to "obey" that which was "necessary" for him to do. As such, in the manner of *ethopoeia*, Paul's words here reflect his Pharisaic view that allowed for the interaction of fate and free will (Josephus, *Ant.* 13.171–173; 18.13; *BJ* 2.162–165; cf. comments on Acts 23:8–9). Obedience to that which is necessary also echoes the teaching of Luke elsewhere ("there is need of only one thing. Mary has chosen the better part," Luke 10:42), as well as the thought of the epistolary Paul ("If I proclaim the gospel, this gives me no ground for boasting, for an obligation is laid on me, and woe to me if I do not proclaim the gospel!" 1 Cor 9:16). In the larger Greco-Roman culture, actions that were done out of compulsion or necessity were regarded as the least praiseworthy kind of action (Theon, *Prog.* 111.18, trans. Kennedy 2003, 51–52). Within the Jewish worldview, however, a worldview shaped by Israel's scriptures (cf., e.g., Lev 4:2; 5:17; Dan 2:28–29), and which Paul shares with his principle auditors, Agrippa and his entourage, "the Creator God is in control of the affairs of the world, and one who submits totally to his plan is worthy of praise" (Bass 2008). Thus, like Jesus before him (cf., e.g., Luke 2:49; 4:43; 9:22; 13:33; *inter alia*), Paul's actions as a witness for God are commended because they are done under compulsion of divine necessity; he has "received help from God up until this day" (26:22; cf. Acts 23:11; 27:24). Obedience to God's will, for the Lukan Paul, may not reduce its necessity, but it may, counterculturally, increase its praiseworthiness.

Cause of action. "To the cause of actions," Theon asserts, "belongs whether it was done to acquire good things or for the sake of escape of an evil" (Theon, *Prog.* 79, trans. Kennedy 2003, 29). The cause of the action in Paul's *narratio* is so that Paul may "open their eyes so that they might turn from darkness to light and from the authority of Satan to God so that they might receive forgiveness of sin" (26:18).

Paul begins his *narratio* with an admission of his previous activities as persecutor. Acts 26:9–11 is one long Greek period, governed by Paul's opening description of the "necessity" of his actions (see above): **Now I myself thought that it was necessary to do many hostile things against the name of Jesus the Nazarene (26:9).** Reference to the "name of Jesus" echoes not only the first account of his conversion (9:15–16) but also earlier parts of the narrative (2:21, 38; 3:6, 16; 4:7, 10, 12, 17, 18, 30; 5:40; 8:12; cf. comments on 3:6). His persecution of Christ's followers is described as acts "against the name of Jesus the Nazarene." He then specifies the details of those "hostile things": And that is what I did in Jerusalem—after receiving authority from the chief priests to do so, I both locked up many of God's people in prison and cast my vote against them when they were condemned to death (26:10). This last item, that Paul cast his vote against those condemned to death, is new. The phrase is literally "I cast my pebble against them," and is employed to refer to vote casting, in which pebbles were used (Josephus, *Ant.* 2.163; 10.60). Paul is not depicted elsewhere in Acts or his letters as belonging to the Sanhedrin, so it is unlikely Luke meant the term to be taken in its technical sense. The idiom, however, does suggest that Paul was working as an agent of the religious authorities and a reminder that when the authorities stoned Stephen, Paul was there to "cast his pebble against" him too (Johnson 1992, 434). I punished them often in every last synagogue and forced them to blaspheme; and because I was absolutely furious with them I even pursued them to foreign cities (26:11). Another new detail is added here. In Acts 22:5, Paul travels to Damascus to arrest Christians and return them for punishment. Here Paul admits that he was punishing them (with synagogal floggings? cf. 2 Cor 11:24) in synagogues in order to make them blaspheme. As with later persecutions (cf. Pliny the Younger, *Ep.* 10.96.5), "blaspheme" here presumably refers to cursing or reviling Christ. Paul's use of the term reflects his thoroughly Christian orientation.

As in Acts 22:6–11, Paul recounts his conversion experience in the form of a dream-vision (see comments there and on 16:6–10).

Scene-setting: Meanwhile, as I was on my way to Damascus with authority and complete power from the chief priests, in the middle of the day along the road (26:12–13a). Paul's reference to having authority from the chief priests echoes earlier accounts (9:2, 14; 22:5). Missing are any reference to letters of recommendation (22:5), but Paul does refer to having the authorities' "complete power" or commission (cf. Josephus, *Ant.* 8.162).

Dream-vision terminology: Your Majesty, I saw a light from heaven, brighter than the sun, shining around me and those traveling with me. After all of us had fallen to the ground, I heard a voice saying to me in the Hebrew language (26:13b–14a). The description moves from a "light" (9:3) to a "great light" (22:6) to a light "brighter than the sun" (see comments on 9:3). The use of such ekphrastic language is common in theophanies and appeals to the eye more than the ear (cf. Theon, *Prog.* 118, trans. Kennedy 2003, 45; *Rhet. Her.* 4.50.68). Its function is to draw attention to the significance of the event (Krieger 1992, 7). The detail that the voice spoke in the "Hebrew language" (Aramaic) is new, and possibly explains why Paul is addressed by his Jewish name, "Saul."

Dream-vision proper (often including instructions for action): The voice addresses Paul: Saul, Saul, why are you persecuting me? (26:14b). The double vocative is an example of the rhetorical figure *epizeuxis* (Phoebammon, *Fig.*

1.3), in which a word is repeated with no intervening words for emphasis; it is typical of theophanies (Gen 22:11; 46:2; 1 Sam 3:4; *4 Ezra* 14.1; *2 Bar.* 22.2). The voice continues: **It is bad for you to kick against the goads!** (26:14c). This is another new element in Paul's conversion account. The saying is proverbial in Greek literature (Euripides, *Bacch.* 795; Aeschylus, *Prom.* 324–325; *Ag.* 1624; Pindar, *Pyth.* 2.94–95). The goad was a sharp stick used to move livestock; the sense is that Paul should not resist God who is pushing him toward the Way (on God using a goad to direct behavior, cf. *Pss. Sol.* 16.4; Philo, *Decal.* 87). This saying continues the general theme of the necessity, or in a sense the inevitability, of Paul following God's call to become a follower of the Way. The next exchange is nearly verbatim from the earlier accounts (see comments on 9:4–5). **Then I said, "Who are you, Lord?" And the Lord said, "I am Jesus whom you are persecuting"** (26:15).

The following verses represent the most significant variation from the previous accounts: **But get up and stand on your feet. For here is the reason that I have appeared to you: to choose you in advance to be a servant and witness of both the things you have seen and of the things I will reveal to you** (26:16). Ananias is missing entirely from this account of Paul's conversion, and the commission now comes directly to him. He is to be "servant and witness" to the Gentiles (cf. Luke 1:2, "eyewitnesses and servants of the word"). The theme of witness is prominent in Acts (Trites 1977); like the Twelve (1:22; 2:32; 10:39, 42) and the Seven (22:20), Paul is chosen to be a "witness" (cf. 22:15).

The commission continues with a promise from the Lord that he will protect Paul **by rescuing you from (your own) people and from the Gentiles to whom I am sending you** (26:17). The language here is reminiscent of Jer 1:7–8: "But the LORD said to me, . . . 'For you shall go to all to whom I send you, and you shall speak whatever I command you. Do not be afraid of them, for I am with you to deliver you, says the LORD.'" Paul's "own people," of course, refers to those who have been plotting against him, and the Gentiles to whom he is sent, some of whom may also oppose him (cf. Acts 19; Fitzmyer 1998, 761).

No longer blinded himself, Paul is sent **to open their eyes so that they might turn from darkness to light and from the authority of Satan to God so that they might receive forgiveness of sins and an inheritance among those who have been sanctified by faith in Christ** (26:18). The commission is cast in Isaianic language ("I am the LORD, I have called you . . . a light to the nations, to open the eyes that are blind," Isa 42:6–7; "I will turn the darkness before them into light," Isa 42:16). The language of transformation includes also turning from the authority of Satan to God; once again the issue of obedience to a higher authority is broached. By choosing to serve God as master, forgiveness of sins is possible and an inheritance is secured "among those who have been sanctified."

Reaction/response: **Therefore, King Agrippa, I did not disobey the heavenly vision. Instead I preached—first to those in Damascus and Jerusalem, and then in all the region of Judea and among the Gentiles—that they should** repent and turn to God, and do things that are consistent with repentance (26:19–20). Paul's reaction to the heavenly vision, in this account, is entirely unmediated. He is "obedient to the vision" (literally "did not disobey"; on litotes, see *Rhet. Her.* 4.38.50 and Acts 1:5) and preaches in Damascus and Jerusalem and Judea—and among the Gentiles—a message of repenting and turning to God (cf. Luke 3:8; Acts 3:19).

In 26:21–23, Paul is portrayed as a witness of the suffering and resurrected Christ (26:21–23). The *narratio* ends with Paul summarizing the recent past events in Jerusalem and claiming that they are a result of the change in his theological orientation: **Because of these things, after the Jews had seized me in the temple they were trying to kill me** (26:21). With this brief sentence, Paul addresses the charges brought against him, but he quickly turns to what he considers the main (and real) issue of contention: **Therefore, since I have received help from God up until this day, I stand and testify to all people, speaking about nothing besides those things that both the prophets and Moses said were going to happen. Was the Christ destined to suffer? Was he the first to rise from the dead? Then, of course, he is going to proclaim light to both the (Jewish) people and the Gentiles!** (26:22–23). Paul's preaching is an explication of what "the prophets and Moses said were going to happen" (cf. Luke 16:29–31; 24:25, 27, 44; Acts 2:16; 3:18, 24; 10:43; 13:15; 15:15; 24:14). How, then, can he be accused of abandoning his Jewish faith and practice? Beginning his speech with a reference to doing what he thought was necessary, Paul returns to that theme with a statement about the necessity of Christ's suffering and the evidence of Christ rising from the dead. In the illumination provided by Christ's death and resurrection, the message of Christ is proclaimed to both Jews and Gentiles.

26:24–29. Festus interrupts Paul: **As Paul was saying these things in his defense, Festus in a loud voice said, "You're crazy, Paul! Your great learning is**

If the Christ Was Destined to Suffer

Most modern translations render the clause in Acts 26:23 as a complement, equivalent to a *hoti* clause (cf. BDAG 278): "That the Messiah must suffer, and that, by being the first to rise from the dead, he would proclaim light both to our people and to the Gentiles" (NRSV; cf. also NIV). The construction used in both cases employs the Greek particle *ei* ("if" or "since"), which here could be taken to introduce either a conditional clause or a direct question (cf. 19:2). Although I have rendered the clauses as questions, the end result is essentially the same. The questions lead to the inference that follows ("Then, of course, he will proclaim"), much like the protasis of a conditional construction leads to the apodosis: "If the Christ was destined to suffer, [and] if he was the first to rise from the dead, [then] he would be eager to proclaim light to both the (Jewish) people and the Gentiles" (see Culy and Parsons 2003, 501).

Paul's Great Learning

There are several elements of rhetorical style that justify Festus's claim that Paul possesses "great learning" (26:24, lit. "knows his letters"; for a similar use of "letters" to indicate a higher level of education, see *Let. Aris.* 121). By way of contrast, see Acts 4:13, where Peter and John are described as being "without letters" (*agrammatoi*), i.e., uneducated. Paul reflects the classical use of the perfect tense as a present tense in 26:2 ("I consider"; *hēgēmai*); the rhetorical elegance and function of the *exordium* (see above); the use of the classical *isasi* ("have known") in 26:4 and "strictest" (*akrobestatēn*) in 26:5; the use of a Greek proverb in 26:14; genitive articular infinitives in 26:18; the use of litotes in 26:19 (cf. also 26:26); the Atticized use of "attempt" (*peirasthai*) in 26:21; the classical use of "must suffer" (*pathētos*) in 26:23 (Long 1982, 237–39; Witherington 1998, 737). In an ironic twist, Paul does not complete his inflection of "God" (see above), until his response to Agrippa (26:29) in which he uses *theos* in the dative case, confirming that he is, indeed, a man of "great learning," or at least knows enough to inflect the subject of his speech.

driving you insane!" (26:24). The virtues of a narrative are "clarity, conciseness, credibility" (Theon, *Prog.* 79, trans. Kennedy 2003, 29). For the authorial audience, Paul has achieved all three in his *narratio*. For Paul's audience in the narrative, however, there is some question at least about the "credibility" of his story. Festus accuses Paul of allowing his "great learning" to drive him "insane" (26:24).

For the first time in this scene, Paul addresses Festus: **I am not crazy, most excellent Festus** (26:25a). Denying he is mad, Paul claims to be **saying [what] is true and sensible** (26:25b; for a similar exchange see Justin, *Dial.* 39.4; cf. Dio Chrysostom, *Or.* 45.1). He then appeals to Agrippa, first indirectly and then later through direct address: **The king, to whom I also speak frankly, knows about these matters. For I am not convinced, by any means, that he is ignorant of any of these things** (26:26a). Speaking "in language derived from discussions by and about the moral philosophers of his day" (Malherbe 1989, 163), Paul has been "speaking frankly or boldly" (see Plutarch, *Adul. amic.* 71E; Lucian, *Demon.* 3; cf. sidebars on 4:13; 24:2–3). Likewise Paul employs Greco-Roman philosophical discourse to make the apologetic claim that the Christian movement is no secret society, ignorant of and irrelevant to world events and persons. Against charges that Christianity was an "obscure" religious sect, Paul counters by claiming that **this matter was not carried out in a corner** (26:26b). The idiom "in a corner" had been "used pejoratively, especially by orators or philosophers of rhetorical bent, of people, particularly philosophers, who did not engage in public life" (Malherbe 1989, 156). In his oration on friendship, Themistius wrote: "What you do not seem to me to have many opportunities to hear, however, are orations that can improve people's lives. This is no fault of yours; it is the fault of those so-called philosophers, who have assumed that it was enough for them to whisper their words to the young in some isolated corner" (*Or.* 22.265B–C).

Far from shrinking "in a corner," Paul claims that the teachings of Christianity prepared its adherents to engage in matters of public life and concerns no less effectively than other "philosophical" schools (Malherbe 1989, 155–56). In this regard the Lukan Paul resonates with the teaching of other ancient philosophers who claim philosophy prepared its followers especially for participation in public life (cf. Epictetus, *Diatr.* 1.29.36; 2.12.17).

Paul turns his attention back to Agrippa: **King Agrippa, do you believe the prophets? I know that you do** (26:27). Throughout the speech Paul addresses King Agrippa by name or by title five times (cf. also 26:2, 7, 13, 19). This is the rhetorical figure of *communicatio* and is employed on the part of the speaker to include one's audience overtly in a discourse (Cicero, *De or.* 3.53.204).

In a Corner

Epictetus frequently uses the idiom of "sitting in a corner" (cf. Acts 26:26) to describe those philosophers who have shirked their responsibility to engage in debate in the public arena. He admonishes his students to "apply" their learning to public matters of piety and justice:

"Shall the truly educated man pay attention to an uninstructed person when he passes judgment on what is holy and unholy, and on what is just and unjust?

"How great is the injustice committed by the educated in so doing! Is this, then, what you have learned here? Will you not leave to others, mannikins incapable of taking pains, the petty quibbles about these things, so that they may sit in a corner and gather in their petty fees, or grumble because nobody gives them anything, and will you not yourself come forward and make use of what you have learned? For what is lacking now is not quibbles; nay, the books of the Stoics are full of quibbles. What, then, is the thing lacking now? The man to make use of them, the man to bear witness to the arguments by his acts. This is the character I would have you assume, that we may no longer sue old examples in the school, but may have some example from our own time also." (Diatr. 1.29.55–57, trans. Oldfather 1967, 201; cf. Diatr. 2.13.24–26, trans. Oldfather 1967, 305)

Paul, too, defends the public character of his message and declares that King Agrippa cannot be unaware of these matters concerning the Christian movement.

Paul had earlier appealed to fulfillment of what the "prophets and Moses said were going to happen" (26:23); now again he appeals, through reasoning by question and answer (*ratiocinatio*; *Rhet. Her.* 4.16.23; see the sidebar on p. 39), to the scriptures of Israel in support of his argument. The "oracles" of the prophets function for Luke as divine witness to support his argument. As Cicero notes, "The testimony of the gods is covered thoroughly enough by the following: first, utterances, for oracles get their name from the fact that they contain an utterance (*oratio*) of the gods" (*Top.* 20.76). Such appeal to "divine testimony" was a rhetorical commonplace and could be expected to undergird the persuasiveness of the argument (see Acts 2:17; 20:35). **Then Agrippa (said) to Paul, "Are you trying to persuade me to become a Christian so easily?"** (26:28). Agrippa objects to Paul's implication that he (Agrippa) could experience such instantaneous transformation to the Christian point of view. The possibility of "instantaneous conversion" was an ongoing debate in ancient philosophical circles (see Malherbe 1989, 161), and Agrippa joined the side of those skeptical of such immediate change (cf. Plutarch, *Virt. prof.* 75C–E; Albinus, *Epit.* 30.2) over against those who allowed for the possibility of sudden conversion (Apuleius, *Dogm. Plat.* 2.20; Lucian, *Bis acc.* 17; *Nigr.* 1; Diogenes Laertius, *Vit. phil.* 4.16).

Paul replied to Agrippa: **(If it were up to me,) I would pray to God that whether "so easily" or with difficulty not only you, but also all those who hear me today would become just as I indeed am** (26:29a). Paul avoids the philosophical debate on the nature of conversion and rather ends his apology with a hortatory appeal that Agrippa, and indeed all of Paul's audience, would become, whether quickly or gradually, just as he is, a follower of Christ (cf. Justin's appeal: "I could wish that all should form a desire as strong as mine, not to stand aloof from the Savior's words"; *Dial.* 8.2). Paul's last phrase, **except for these chains** (26:29b), reminds the audience that, although he speaks boldly and "not in a corner," he is still a prisoner and thus without honor or dignity (Josephus, *BJ* 4.10.7.628–629; cf. Talbert 2005, 209).

26:30–32. But Agrippa has heard enough: **Then the king, along with the governor, Bernice, and those sitting with them, stood up, and as they were leaving they spoke to one another, saying, "This man has done nothing worthy of death or imprisonment"** (26:30–31). Like Jesus, Paul is declared innocent: by a Roman soldier (23:29; cf. Luke 23:47); then by Festus, a Roman governor (25:25; cf. Luke 23:4, 14, 22); and now, finally, by the Herodian family (26:31; cf. Luke 23:15). Agrippa confides to Festus: **This man would have been able to be released if he had not appealed to Caesar** (26:32). By now the response that Paul could have been set free if he had not appealed to the emperor (26:32) sounds more than a little hollow. The authorial audience has no reason to think that Festus and Agrippa would have released Paul, regardless of his innocence or his appeal. The voyage to Rome begins.

Theological Issues

There were a variety of views toward the state in the ancient world (see Talbert 2002, 295–96; Walton 2002). The majority view among Romans (e.g., Tacitus, *Hist.* 4.74; Plutarch, *Princ. iner.* 3), Jews (*Let. Aris.* 45; Josephus, *BJ* 5.366–368), and Christians (*1 Clem* 60.4; *Mart. Pol.* 10.2) held a positive assessment of the state. Romans 13:1–7 reflects this positive view. On the other hand, some Jewish (*Pss. Sol.* 1.4–25; 17; *Sib. Or.* 5.155–178; 8.65–72) and Christian (*Barn.* 2.1) authors viewed the Roman Empire as evil and oppressive. Revelation 13 reflects this view of the state.

Where does Acts fit within this spectrum? To answer that question, we begin with an overview of the various reasons for which Luke was thought to pen Acts (see Walton 2002). Until fairly recently the dominant view was that Luke was presenting an apology to Romans for the Christian movement as a politically harmless movement (Cadbury 1927, 308–15; Conzelmann 1960, 137–49; Bruce 1988, 8–13). This view rests primarily on the repeated judgments of innocence rendered by Roman officials, first in the case of Jesus and later in the trial of Paul. C. K. Barrett's oft-quoted judgment reflects the current scholarly skepticism of this view: "No Roman official would ever have filtered out so much of what to him would be theological and ecclesiastical rubbish in order to reach so tiny a grain of relevant apology" (Barrett 1961, 63).

At the other end of the spectrum are those who argue that Luke wrote an apology for Rome to the Christian community who were suspicious of the state (Walaskay 1983, 15–37). As we have seen, the Roman attitude toward and treatment of the Christians in Acts is mixed and often unfair (cf. Esler 1987); thus it seems unlikely that Luke is writing to defend the state to the Christian community (for other views and critiques, see Walton 2002).

The stance that Luke takes toward church-state relations in Acts is subtle and nuanced and stands somewhere between the positive (Rom 13) and negative (Rev 13) poles. Cornelius, a Roman centurion and the first public Gentile convert to the Christian movement, is certainly portrayed as a commendable character in Acts 10–11. Furthermore, Paul appeals to and relies on the state for protection in his missionary work (Acts 16:37–39; 18:12–17; 22:24–29; cf. Talbert 2002, 297). When arrested, Paul submits to trial by the Romans, and when on trial, he even appeals to Caesar for justice (25:11). Such positive treatment of Rome and Romans can also be found in the Third Gospel (cf. Talbert 2002, 297; Walton 2002). So, on the one hand, the Romans protect Paul and testify to his innocence. On the other, the political establishment presents a less consistent picture. In Acts 23–26, the Roman officials—Lysias, Felix, and Festus—are willing to distort the facts in order to portray themselves in the most favorable light. And both Felix and Festus withhold justice from Paul, despite his innocence. Earlier Herod Agrippa I is depicted as a tyrant who meets his grisly but deserved end (see Acts 12). Thus, Acts (and Luke) assumes a mediating position between Rom 13 and Rev 13.

There is also in Acts an explicit and implicit challenge to human authority. The explicit challenge is made by the apostles, when they are forbidden by the religious authorities to teach in Jesus' name (5:27–28). Peter and the apostles reply: "We are to obey God rather than humans" (Acts 5:29). There is an implicit challenge to human authority, and perhaps specifically to Roman imperial power, that is reflected in the language of Acts (see Walton 2002, 29–30). Luke refers to Jesus as "king" more than any other evangelist (Walton 2002, 29; cf. especially Luke 19:38). In Acts 17:7, Paul is accused in Thessalonica of preaching "another king, Jesus," a charge not altogether incompatible with either the context of Acts 17 or the epistolary Paul's argument in 1 Thessalonians. Such language has unmistakable political overtones to an ancient authorial audience living in the Roman Empire; Jesus is presented as a rival king to Caesar. So also Luke's favorite title for Jesus, "Lord" (*kyrios*), a common title for Caesar, is used some sixty times in Acts alone (see Dunn 1998, 241–53). "Savior" is another favorite Lukan term for Jesus that is associated with the emperor (cf. *SIG*[3] 760 in which Julius Caesar is described as "the god made manifest . . . and common savior of human life"; see Walton 2002, 30 n. 89 for other references). Steve Walton's conclusion is apropos: "The use of these three groups of words for Jesus so prominently suggests that Luke presents the early Christians as subversively using Caesar's titles for Jesus" (Walton 2002, 30).

In a sense, the overall structure of the book of Acts supports this "anti-imperial" reading (Wright 2003). The book begins with Jesus discussing with

Obeying God Rather than Humans

Acts 5:29 became important in later discussions regarding the limits of the state's legitimate claim on citizens' obedience. John Calvin, for example, ends the *Institutes* with this comment:

"But in that obedience which we have shown to be due the authority of rulers, we are always to make this exception, indeed, to observe it as primary, that such obedience is never to lead us away from obedience to him, to whose will the desires of all kings ought to yield, to whose majesty their scepters ought to be submitted.

"I know with what great and present peril this constancy is menaced, because kings bear defiance with the greatest displeasure.... But since this edict has been proclaimed by the heavenly herald, Peter—'We must obey God rather than men'—let us comfort ourselves with the thought that we are rendering that obedience which the Lord requires when we suffer anything rather than turn aside from piety." (John Calvin, *Institutes* 4.32, trans. McNeill 1960, 2:1520–21)

his disciples the restoration of the "kingdom" to Israel (1:6). That conversation is followed by Jesus' ascension, an event similar to, among other things, the Roman leaders who supposedly ascended to the heavens after their death (cf. Plutarch, *Rom.* 27; Minucius Felix, *Oct.* 22.7; Parsons 1987, 135–39). The first half of Acts (chaps. 1–12) ends with the punishment of a tyrant who had abused his power, persecuted Christians, and exploited his subjects' desire for peace. Because Herod "did not give God the glory, he was eaten by worms and died" (12:23). In the second half of Acts, Paul preaches "another king, Jesus," the resurrected one. He is arrested and detained without just cause. The book ends with Paul in Rome preaching the "kingdom of God" and Jesus the Messiah openly and unhindered in Caesar's backyard.

One final note about the "politics" of Paul's preaching in Acts 23–26: Paul had consistently maintained that "resurrection," not his fidelity to Jewish custom, was the true core of the accusations against him (23:6; 24:15; 25:19). This focus on resurrection moved from a general resurrection of the dead (23:6) to the resurrection of Jesus (26:23). The Roman officials evidently understood this subject to be an intra-Jewish point of religious dispute. When read in the larger context of Acts, however, the political implications associated with preaching Christ resurrected are revealed. In Peter's brief summary of the kerygma in Acts 10:38–42, he makes clear that the followers of Jesus were to bear witness to the vocation of the resurrected Jesus as "the one ordained by God to be judge of the living and the dead" (Acts 10:42). Thus when Paul preaches that Christ has been raised from the dead, he is also bearing witness to the resurrected Lord's vocation as judge. As Oliver O'Donovan has argued, "judgment" is the primary political act; it is what governments and rulers seek to do—to render decisions, which brings order to society (O'Donovan 1994). The resurrected Christ's vocation in dispensing judgment and justice is exactly what the Roman officials have either refused (so Gallio in 18:15) or failed (so Felix, 24:25–26; and Festus, 25:20) to do.

The challenge for modern Christians is urgent. N. T. Wright, bishop of Durham, England, made this very clear in his 2007 Easter homily preached at Durham Cathedral:

> We urgently need, as thinking Christians, to join up the debates and to think through the ways in which the resurrection of Jesus Christ from the dead establishes him, not any human institution, as the ultimate judge of the living and the dead. And to those who take fright at this, and warn about theocracy and extremism, we must reply that part of the point is that our judgments too, as followers of Jesus Christ, are partial and are themselves subject to sharp scrutiny; and that the objection sounds a little like special pleading when you see the way in which our present government, to look no further, is ramming through one policy after another which seem designed to provoke Christian opinion and, sooner or later, to force us to say that we must obey God rather than penultimate human authority. When that moment comes . . . we must

know as Christian people that we stand in this matter firmly on the ground of Easter itself, in which Jesus Christ is ordained by God as the sole and ultimate judge of the living and the dead. May we have courage and strength not only to believe the Easter message but to know how to apply it where it may be urgently needed. (http://www.ntwrightpage.com/sermons/Easter07.htm)

Paul's obligation to bear witness before the authorities to the suffering and resurrected "Lord and Judge of all" becomes our obligation as well. It is then "the task in particular of those who believe in Jesus Christ to announce his judgment both *in and through* particular and judicial decisions and also *upon* those decisions themselves, since they themselves partake systematically of the very injustice which they are trying to address" (http://www.ntwrightpage.com/sermons/Easter07.htm).

Acts 27–28

The Sea Voyage to Rome

⊡

Introductory Matters

In the last unit of Acts (chaps. 27–28) the long-awaited journey to Rome is narrated. Luke returns to his use of first-person narration in these chapters and much of the material shares common features with other sea voyage stories: shipwreck, narrow escapes, suspense, conflict, and high drama. This unit falls into two parallel pairs of panels, with the first and last panels being the most detailed:

A Paul journeys to Malta (27)
    B Paul on Malta (28:1–10)
A′ Paul journeys to Rome
    (28:11–16)
    B′ Paul in Rome (28:17–31)

Of course, Paul's stay at Malta is occasioned when he and his companions are shipwrecked, while his voyage to Rome has been an intentional destination for much of the second half of Acts.

Acts 27–28 in the Narrative Flow

The people and places of the Jerusalem church (1–12)

    The sense of a beginning (1–7)

    Beyond Jerusalem: Philip, Saul, Peter, and others (8–12)

The missionary activities of Paul (13–28)

    Paul's mission to the Gentile world (13–19)

    Paul's farewell journey (20–28)

        Paul's last journey to Jerusalem (20:1–21:16)

        Paul in Jerusalem (21:17–23:35)

        Paul before Felix, Festus, and Agrippa (24–26)

    ▶ The sea voyage to Rome (27–28)

        Paul journeys to Malta (27)

        Paul on Malta (28:1–10)

        Paul journeys to Rome (28:11–16)

        Paul in Rome (28:17–31)

Scholars have long debated whether Acts 27:1–28:16, along with the other "we" sections at 16:10–17, 20:5–15, and 21:1–18, are based on a travel diary (whether by the author himself or someone else) or are the result of Luke creating or imitating a literary convention employed in sea voyage sections to achieve certain rhetorical effects—for example, to give credibility to the narrative as an eye-witness account, or to create a sense of connection between Paul and the audience (see Fitzmyer 1998, 103; Porter 1999; Robbins 1978). Whatever the nature of the underlying source, our concern here is the function of the final form of the text. The unit functions to "indicate God's declaration of Paul's innocence" and "to show that nothing can hinder the unfolding of God's plan, in particular, Paul's bearing witness in Rome" (Talbert 2005, 210–11). To these two functions we may add a third. Through his portrayal of Paul as "in control," the narrator "is implicitly laying claim to a cultural territory [the sea] which many readers, both Greek and Judaeo-Christian, would perceive as inherently 'Greek'" (Alexander 2005, 85).

The setting of the sea is important for understanding the various functions of this passage. In Luke/Acts only Paul and his associates travel on the sea (rather than the Lake of Galilee; Robbins 1978, 216). In a way typical of sea voyage stories, Luke describes a variety of settings through which Paul and his fellow prisoners, the sailors, and Julius and his fellow soldiers pass: Sidon, Myra, Cnidus (or nearby), Fair Havens, and Malta. In the process, they pass near several other cities, regions, or islands: Cilicia and Pamphylia, Crete, Lasea, Phoenix, Cauda, and Syrtis. But the one setting that remains constant throughout this voyage is the sea (both the Mediterranean and the Adriatic). The sea, of course, played a prominent role in journey narratives in antiquity, from Homer's *Odyssey* to Virgil's *Aeneid* to the Greek romances of Chariton and Xenophon of Ephesus (see Alexander 2005, 69–86). Yet the epistolary Paul never uses the vocabulary of sailing to describe his extensive travels (not even in 2 Cor 11).

In both Jewish and Greek literature of antiquity, the sea was viewed sometimes as an evil or hostile place of chaos and confusion, sometimes as a vehicle through which divine forces punish wickedness. Homer tells how Odysseus's crew was killed in a shipwreck as punishment for destroying Helios's cattle (*Od.* 12.127–141, 259–446). In Chariton, evil persons are drowned at sea and the just are spared (*Chaer.* 3.3.10, 18; 3.4.9–10). In the OT, God uses the sea to reverse creation and judge evil humanity (Gen 6–8); God uses a sea to destroy the Egyptians and rescue the Israelites (Exod 14); God employs a storm to persuade a recalcitrant prophet to speak (Jonah 1). The same view is held in postbiblical Judaism. In the Babylonian Talmud, Rabbi Gamaliel is spared from the raging sea only after declaring his innocence before God (*b. Mezia* 58b–59). Thus both Greek and Jewish readers would understand the potential disasters involved here. If Paul perishes at sea, he is no doubt guilty of the charges leveled against him; if he is spared, then he has been honored with divine vindication.

Furthermore, the sea and its accompanying winds are no match for Paul's God. Despite contrary winds and devastating storms, nothing will hinder Paul from fulfilling his call to bear witness in Rome (27:23–25; cf. 23:11). Finally, the sea, for Luke (as in the ancient novels; cf. Chariton, *Chaer.* 7.5.8; 6.1–2; 8.2.12), is "Greek cultural territory" (Alexander 2005, 83–85). By depicting Paul as calm in the face of the storm, in control over the ship's captain, and as benefactor to the ship's crew, Paul demonstrates his authority, or rather the authority of the God he serves, over the final frontier of Greco-Roman dominance.

Tracing the Narrative Flow

Paul Journeys to Malta (27)

Acts 27, which narrates Paul's journey to Malta, consists of a prologue (27:1–12), an account of a storm at sea (27:13–38), and the story of the shipwreck on Malta (27:39–44).

27:1–12. Acts 27:1–12 is both a prologue and a summary, for in twelve verses, Luke describes Paul and the others on board setting sail for Italy and stopping at four ports along the way, culminating with Paul's warning not to continue past Fair Havens.

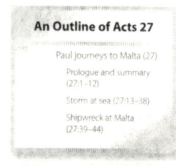

An Outline of Acts 27

Paul Journeys to Malta (27)

Prologue and summary (27:1–12)

Storm at sea (27:13–38)

Shipwreck at Malta (27:39–44)

The journey begins in Caesarea when Paul is entrusted to the custodial care of a centurion: **When it was decided that we should set sail for Italy, they handed Paul over, along with some other prisoners, to a centurion of the Augustan Cohort named Julius. We boarded a ship from Adramyttium that was about to sail to places along the coast of Asia, and set sail (27:1–2a).** The "we" reappears now for the first time since 21:18 and remains with Paul throughout the journey to Rome (27:1–8,

---

Synonymy in Acts 27

The emphasis on the sea voyage is underscored by Luke's use of synonymy (*interpretatio; Rhet. Her.* 4.28.38; see Acts 10:2). Within the first twelve verses of Acts 27, Luke uses four different nautical terms eleven times to express the act of "sailing." In addition, one of the terms, *pleō*, also appears in three different compound forms (*apopleō, hypopleō,* and *diapleō*). The use of this figure of speech has the advantage of avoiding the monotony of repeating the same word over and over while, at the same time, drawing attention to the voyage theme.

18–20, 37; 28:1–2, 7, 10; Spencer 2004, 241), though evidently the narrator does not count himself as one of the "other prisoners." Rather, the narrator is among those trusted friends who refuse to abandon Paul, even at the risk of their own lives (cf., e.g., the examples of Agathocles in Lucian, *Tox.* 18, and Polymarchus in Chariton, *Chaer.* 3.5; 4.3, each of whom sails with his friend at great peril). Another of Paul's former traveling companions also resurfaces: **Aristarchus, a Macedonian from Thessalonica, was with us** (27:2b; cf. 19:29; 20:4; Col 4:10; Phlm 24). Centurions, more than any other Roman official or officer, are depicted in a consistently favorable light in Luke and Acts (Luke 7:1–10; 23:47; Acts 10–11), and Julius is no different: **On the next day we landed at Sidon, and Julius acted kindly toward Paul and allowed him to go to his friends and receive care** (27:3). Julius is portrayed as acting "kindly" (*philanthrōpos*) toward Paul (who, as a prisoner bound for Rome, was under some duress; cf. Acts 28:2) by allowing him to visit "friends" and "receive care from them." Paul is surrounded by Christian friends (see Theological Issues).

Leaving Sidon, the group **set sail and sailed under the shelter of Cyprus because the winds were against us** (27:4). Unable to head directly for Rome in the open sea because of head winds (cf. Lucian, *Nav.* 7), they sailed north along the coast of Cyprus, protected partially from the severe winds by the land mass (Johnson 1992, 446). Luke continues with his summary of the voyage: **After sailing across the open sea off Cilicia and Pamphylia we arrived at Myra of Lycia** (27:5). The ship abandons its "coast-hugging route" and turns west across the "open sea," arriving in Myra, on the southern coast of Asia Minor and near Patara, where Paul had previously landed (21:1; cf. Pliny the Elder, *Nat.* 5.100). The unfriendly weather has created a kind of impromptu sailing scenario, as the crew and prisoners move from place to place in ad hoc fashion as the winds allow. In Myra **the centurion found an Alexandrian ship sailing to Italy and put us aboard it** (27:6). Presumably the vessel was a grain ship en route from Egypt to Italy; Egyptian grain was a significant source of food for Rome (cf. Josephus, *BJ* 2.386). Suetonius records efforts by the emperor Claudius to secure grain from Egypt, even in the winter, in order to anticipate the unavoidable food shortages in Rome and other urban areas (*Claud.* 18.2).

Inclement weather continues to impede their progress: **Over a period of many days we sailed along slowly, and with difficulty we made it as far as Cnidus—since the wind did not allow us to proceed** (27:7a). Cnidus, a port city on the tip of southwestern Asia Minor, was a well-known landmark among Alexandrian merchant ships (Thucydides, *Hist.* 8.24.35). Continuing their slow journey, they **then sailed under the shelter of Crete off Salmone**, on the northwest tip of Crete (27:7b; Strabo, *Geogr.* 10.4.2). Finally, **sailing along its coast we came with difficulty to a place called Fair Havens, which is near the town of Lasea** (27:8). Fair Havens (modern-day Kali Limenes) lay on the south side of Crete and provided, if not much else (cf. 27:12), safe harbor from the northern and western winds.

Luke next notes the lapse of time since their voyage began: **Since a lot of time had passed and the voyage was already unsafe because the Fast had already passed** (27:9a). Once again, Luke marks time by reference to the Jewish calendar (see the reference to Pentecost at 20:16). "The Fast" here refers to the Day of Atonement (Lev 16:29–31; Philo, *Spec.* 2.32.193–203; Josephus, *Ant.* 14.66; 18.94), which was celebrated around the time of the autumn equinox (Fitzmyer 1998, 775). Because severe weather rendered its waters unnavigable, the Mediterranean was considered a "closed sea" (*mare clausum*) during the winter months (about November to March) (Johnson 1992, 447; Fitzmyer 1998, 775). Luke also deepens the characterization of Paul as a Christian prophet and benefactor through a description, first of his words and later of his deeds. After taking harbor in Fair Havens, Paul predicts the dangers that lay before him and

> **Reduplication in Acts 27**
>
> Twice within two verses the word translated "with difficulty" occurs (27:7–8). "[T]he repetition of one or more words for the purpose of amplification" is the rhetorical figure of reduplication (*conduplicatio*) and is used to make "a deep impression upon the hearer" (*Rhet. Her.* 4.28.38). Here the figure reinforces the harsh weather conditions and foreshadows the impending shipwreck.

his fellow travelers: **Paul urged them, saying, "Men! I can see that this voyage is going to end in disaster and great loss of not only the cargo and the ship, but our lives as well!"** (27:9b–10). Paul's words are ignored by his audience: **But the centurion paid attention to the helmsman and captain rather than to what Paul had said** (27:11). Thus the "majority" (presumably of the crew responsible for the ship) made other plans to continue their voyage: **Since the harbor was not suitable for spending the winter, the majority made a plan to sail from there, (thinking that) somehow, if they could reach Phoenix—a harbor of Crete that faces southwest and northwest—they would be able to spend the winter (there)** (27:12). Luke does not state the reason that the harbor was "unsuitable" for wintering—perhaps it was unsuitably vulnerable to the harshness of winter weather or perhaps was lacking in "social amenities for the crew" (Barrett 1998, 2:1191). The location of Phoenix is disputed, but at any rate irrelevant, since they do not make that port. The remote possibility of reaching this destination is hinted at already in the use of *ei* with the optative mood (*ei pōs dunainto*; cf. Culy and Parsons 2003, 513).

27:13–38. Their journey begins in a promising way: **When a south wind began to blow gently, thinking that they had achieved their plan, they raised the anchor and were sailing as close as possible along (the coast of) Crete** (27:13). This gentle wind that would bring the ship safely to Phoenix soon shifts: **a very strong wind, called a northeaster, came down from (the direction**

of Crete) (27:14). Like many winds, modern and ancient, this one had a name (although otherwise unattested), a "Nor'easter," made from the compound of Euros, east, and Aquila, north (winds). Since the ship was **unable to face into the wind, we gave in (to the wind) and were carried along (27:15)**. Ships out of control and at the mercy of winds and waves were a common feature of ancient sea voyages (cf. Homer, *Od.* 9.82–84; Achilles Tatius, *Leuc. Cli.* 3.1–2; Petronius, *Sat.* 114; Lucian, *Tox.* 19; *Nav.* 7). They are afforded some temporary relief **under the shelter of a small island called Cauda (27:16a)** and engage in emergency measures before reemerging into the full force of the gale winds: **we were somehow able to gain control of the dinghy. After hoisting it aboard, they used ropes to undergird the ship (27:16b)**. The dinghy, or lifeboat, normally in tow behind the ship (Heliodorus, *Aeth.* 5.27.6), is taken into the ship to avoid its being damaged or lost completely in the storm. Ropes are used presumably to prevent the ship from breaking apart from the waves' force. Furthermore, **since they were afraid they would run aground on the Syrtis, they lowered the (drift) anchor and were carried along (27:17)**. Although they are still a considerable distance from the Syrtis (shallow waters of Cyrenaica), its treacherous reputation (Dio Chrysostom, *Lib. myth.* 5.8–11; Josephus, *BJ* 2.381) causes them to lower the drift anchor as a brake in an effort to slow them down.

During the next two days, the crew sought to lighten the ship's load, first by throwing over cargo and then the ship's tackle: **On the next day, since we were being battered by the storm, they began throwing things overboard. Then, on the third day, they threw the ship's gear overboard with their own hands (27:18–19)**. The ship's passengers begin to relent when the storm does not: **When neither sun nor stars appeared for many days, and a terrible storm persisted, finally all hope of our being saved was (slowly) taken away (27:20)**. Paul's prophecy is gradually coming to fulfillment.

A new element is introduced, when Luke reports that **they had gone without food for some time (27:21a)**, presumably not for lack of food (cf. 27:33–36), but rather due to seasickness, fear, or preoccupation with fighting the storm (Barrett 1998, 2:1199). Then **Paul stood up among them and said, "Men, you could have paid attention to me and not set sail from Crete, and thus avoided this damage and loss" (27:21b)**. Paul begins with a kind of "I-told-you-so" tone (Barrett 1998, 2:1199), but then shifts to a note of encouragement: **But now, I urge you to cheer up, for there will be no loss of life among you; only the ship (will be lost) (27:22)**. Paul's assurance is based on his report of a dream-vision, the last recorded in Acts.

The setting of the scene is brief: **For last night (27:23a)**. Dream-terminology per se is missing but is implied by the temporal reference ("last night") and the appearing of a messenger: **an angel of God, to whom I belong and whom I worship, stood by me and said (27:23b–24a)**. The dream proper, like other dream-visions (18:9–11; 23:11), provides encouragement (Dodson 2006, 174): **Don't be** afraid, Paul! It is necessary for you to stand before Caesar; and God graciously promises you that he will protect all those who are sailing with you! (27:24b). Included in the promise of God's protection for all passengers on the ship is the prediction of the "necessity" of Paul's appearing before the emperor (cf. 23:11). Although the authorial audience would have expected the dream-vision to be fulfilled, it is only partially so. All those sailing with Paul are, indeed, protected. The fulfillment of this divine promise that Paul would appear before Caesar, however, is not narrated in Acts (see comments on 28:17–31).

Paul's response is to declare his faith in the dream-vision: So, cheer up, men! For I believe God—that things will happen in exactly the way that I have been told (27:25). Paul's words echo expressions of faith found elsewhere in the Third Gospel (Luke 1:45; 2:20; 22:13) and are similar to pious expressions regarding divine providence at work in sea voyages and shipwrecks (cf. Homer, *Od.* 5.300–302; Aelius Aristides, *Hier. log.* 2.12–13; Johnson 1992, 449). Despite issuing words of assurance of their ultimate safety, Paul ends his speech with the bad news that they will not escape mishap altogether: But it is necessary for us to run aground on a certain island (27:26). This prophecy of Paul, too, will come to pass and is part of the process required for the deliverance of Paul and his company (cf. Acts 28:1).

Luke fast-forwards to the fourteenth night and reports that as we were being driven across the Adriatic Sea, in the middle of the night the sailors suspected that they were approaching land (27:27). This is the same location where Josephus says he was shipwrecked (*Vita* 3.15). Perhaps a change in the sound of the waves made them suspicious of approaching land (Fitzmyer 1998, 778). At any rate, their suspicions are confirmed: They took soundings and found (the depth to be) twenty fathoms. Then, after going a little farther and taking soundings again, they found (the depth to be) fifteen fathoms (27:28). The crew attempts to slow the pace of the ship: afraid that we might run aground somewhere at a rocky place they threw out four anchors from the stern (27:29a). As with Odysseus's shipwreck (*Od.* 9.151), these pagan sailors prayed for daylight (27:29b) and, no doubt, deliverance. "Their prayer was ultimately answered—not by their gods but by Paul's God" (Polhill 1992, 525).

Evidently the sailors doubt the efficacy of their prayers and take matters into their own hands: the sailors tried to flee from the ship and lowered the dinghy into the sea, as if they were going to lower anchors from the bow (27:30; cf. Achilles Tatius, *Leuc. Cli.* 3.3; Petronius, *Sat.* 102). This attempted deception does not fool Paul, who reports to the centurion and the soldiers, "Unless these men remain on the ship, you cannot be saved" (27:31). This is Paul's third edict regarding the fate of the ship and its passengers (cf. 27:10, 21–26), and this time the centurion heeds his words: Then the soldiers cut the ropes of the dinghy and allowed it to fall (27:32). Cutting the suspended dinghy is the most expedient way to follow Paul's advice. This action ensures that the crew will remain with the ship, even if the lifeboat is lost.

Paul continues to direct the actions on board ship, this time with a fourth edict, encouraging the passengers and crew to take sustenance: **Now, as the day was about to dawn, Paul started urging everyone to have some food, saying, "As of today, this is the fourteenth day you have been anxiously waiting and going without food, eating nothing at all. Therefore, I urge you to have some food, since you need it to survive. For not one of you will be harmed in any way"** (27:33–34). Paul remains calm in the crisis, even concerned about the well-being of the others (cf. Lucian, *Peregr.* 43–44; *Tox.* 20; Diogenes Laertius, *Vit. phil.* 9.68; Epictetus, *Diatr.* 4.1.92). Whether the two-week "fast" is hyperbole or literal (cf. Aelius Aristides, *Hier. log.* 2.68, for an account of shipwreck victims going without food for fourteen days), Paul urges them all to eat since they will "need it to survive." Paul's exhortation to eat is based on his prediction that none will be harmed (lit., "for a hair from the head of none of you will be lost"), echoing both the OT (1 Sam 14:45; 2 Sam 14:11) and Jesus (Luke 21:18). Following these words Paul **took (some) bread and gave thanks to God in front of them all. Then he broke it and began to eat** (27:35). Some have seen eucharistic overtones in the language of "taking bread," "giving thanks," and "breaking" (cf. Luke 22:17–19; Reicke 1948, 401–10; Schneider 1980, 2:396). It is scarcely a eucharistic ritual, however, since not all the participants are believers. Still, the actions echo other meal scenes in Luke (cf. Luke 9:15–17), and "the meal shared between Paul and his shipmates constitutes them as a community under God's protection" (McMahan 1987, 258; Tannehill 1990, 336). The point of Paul's actions is to encourage them to imitate him, and in this Paul is successful: **Then all of them were encouraged and also had (some) food themselves** (27:36). Luke adds a parenthetical note that there were **276** of them on the ship (27:37). The specific number may have been added to give verisimilitude to the account (although the scribal tendency to give a round [270, 275] or approximate [about 76 or about 70] number destroys that effect if intended), which claims to be that of an eyewitness (cf. Bovon 1985). If any symbolism is to be attached to 276 it is probably to be found in the fact that 276 is a "triangular number," the sum of the numbers 1 through 23; and here the significance is that 23 is *not* 24 (a similar phenomenon has been noted about the "seven sayings from the cross"; cf. Whitlark and Parsons 2006). In Luke's logic, 24, as a multiple of 12, represents the church (a common later view; cf. Tyconius, *Comm. Apoc.* 4.4), and 23 does not. Thus the 276 gathered on the boat with Paul do *not* represent the church, and the meal Paul shares with them is *not* the Eucharist, because 23 is *not* 24 (for more on this possible symbolism, see Parsons 2008).

Luke further reports: **When they had had their fill of food they began to lighten the ship by throwing the wheat overboard into the sea** (27:38). Whether the wheat was part of their provisions (Johnson 1992, 455) or cargo (Fitzmyer 1998, 779), the crew continues the process of unloading the ship (cf. 27:18–19) in preparation to make a run as far up the beach as possible (Polhill 1992, 528).

27:39–44. When daybreak finally arrived, the ship's crew **did not recognize the land but noticed a bay that had a beach onto which they decided to run the ship aground, if possible** (27:39). The identification of the island of Malta remains unknown to them, but they decide nonetheless to take refuge on the beach by running the ship aground there. To beach the ship, they undertook a series of steps, intended to guide them ashore: **So they abandoned the anchors and let them (sink) into the sea. At the same time they released the ropes that held the rudders, raised the (fore)sail to the wind, and headed for the beach** (27:40). They dropped the four stern anchors and at the same time released the pennants of the steering oars, which had been raised out

> **Reduplication in Acts 27**
>
> The reference to food here in 27:38 is the fourth use of the word in 27:33–38 and is an example of the rhetorical figure of *reduplication* (*Rhet. Her.* 4.28.38; see the sidebar on p. 74). The emphasis here is on encouragement, not the Eucharist, or as Beverly Gaventa observes: "This is not the bread of the eucharist, it is the bread of hope" (2003, 355).

of the water and tied down to prevent them from banging about, in order to steer the ship to land (Casson 1995, 228n17). Finally they raised the foresail and made for shore. Despite their efforts they did not reach their destination: **When they encountered a sandbar, they ran the ship aground. The bow got stuck and would not move, but the stern began to be broken up by the force of the waves** (27:41). The ship ran aground on a sandbar; on one end the bow was stuck in the sand and, on the other, the stern began to be broken apart by the waves. The ship is now all but lost, as Paul had foretold (27:10, 22).

There is nothing left to do now but abandon ship—every man for himself. Should they survive, however, the soldiers would be responsible for any escaped prisoners (cf. Acts 12:19; 16:27). So a plan is hatched to kill the prisoners: **Now, the soldiers' plan was that they would kill the prisoners so that no one would swim away and escape** (27:42). Luke reports that since the **centurion wanted to spare Paul, he prevented them from carrying out their plan and ordered those who were able to swim to be the first to jump overboard and head for land** (27:43). Once again, the centurion is portrayed in a favorable light (cf. 27:3), and the focus is on Paul's safety. Those traveling with Paul are spared as a by-product of the intent to spare Paul; thus Paul's dream-vision is fulfilled: "God will protect all those who are sailing with you" (27:24). The centurion further commands **the rest** (the nonswimmers) **to get to land by using boards and others using some of the other things from the ship** (27:44a). Rescue on planks featured prominently in other shipwreck stories (Homer, *Od.* 5.370f; Achilles Tatius, *Leuc. Cli.* 3.4, 5–6, 8). The *hous men* / *hous de* construction suggests two groups (some . . . others), and while it is possible that the "other things from the ship" may be taken as "people from the ship" (that is, the nonswimmers were carried on the backs of the swimmers; Barrett 1998, 2:1215), the text seems to suggest that the swimmers made their way to land first (Culy and Parsons 2003, 531). The shipwreck ends on a note of relief: **And in this way everyone made it safely to land** (27:44b).

Shipwreck stories were common in ancient writings (Seneca, *Con.* 7.1.4; 8.6; cf. Miles and Trompf 1976, 259–67) and contained common elements (cf. Talbert 2005, 212). Often the storm or shipwreck was attributed to the presence of some offending party on board, who had incurred divine wrath (cf. Jonah; Seneca, *Con.* 7.1). Thus ancient auditors might be tempted to view Paul's shipwreck as evidence of divine wrath and judgment upon him; certainly this was the initial view of the inhabitants of Malta (cf. 28:4). But not all shipwreck stories functioned this way. Luke's story of Paul's shipwreck (27:39–44) belongs to that category of storm and shipwreck stories that attribute the cause of the storm to natural causes and the outcome as the result of divine activity (for the taxonomy of shipwreck stories in antiquity, see Talbert 2005, 212–13). Thus Luke depicts a combination of the time of year (the Fast, 27:9), the impatience of the ship's owner and captain (27:11), and an unsuitable harbor as the cause of the storm and subsequent shipwreck (Talbert 2005, 215). In other words, "Paul's presence was in no sense responsible for the storm. . . . On the contrary, Paul's presence was responsible for their *deliverance* from the storm" (Polhill 1992, 530). Paul's innocence is vindicated by God and his witness before Rome is insured.

Luke also uses this sea voyage with all its colorful details and rich imagery to depict the symbolic death and resurrection of Paul, much as he narrates the imprisonment and release of Peter in Acts 12. Both prison and shipwreck are common metaphors for death in antiquity. Night, the disappearance of heavenly luminaries (27:20; cf. Luke 23:44–45), and the loss of hope (27:20; cf. Luke 24:21) all echo the passion of Jesus and allude to Paul's symbolic death. References to daylight, the third day (21:19), a shared meal (27:33–35; cf. Luke 24:30–31), and Paul's deliverance from the tomb of the sea (27:44) all point to a kind of symbolic resurrection.

Paul on Malta (28:1–10)

Paul and all his companions are delivered safely from the shipwreck and find themselves on the island of Malta (on historical issues related to Malta, see Bauckham 2006, 73–87): **When we had made it to safety, we then learned that the island was called Malta** (28:1). Though "barbarians," the Maltese inhabitants show Paul and company "philanthropy," one of the most prized of Greek virtues (see Theological Issues): **The local inhabitants showed us extraordinary kindness. They welcomed us all and built a fire because it had started to rain and was cold** (28:2; on the litotes, "not ordinary," see Acts 1:5).

Paul joins in the fire-building, and here the theme of Paul's vindication continues: **After Paul had gathered a bundle of firewood and was putting it** on the fire, a viper came out because of the heat and latched on to his hand (28:3). Just as nature was understood to be a vehicle of divine vindication or retribution, so was the animal kingdom in both Jewish (see *t. Sanh.* 8.3; *y. Ber.* 5.1) and pagan (*Anth. Pal.* 7.20) sources. The latter is of particular interest since it, too, combines shipwreck with snake bite:

> The shipwrecked mariner had escaped the whirlwind and the fury of the deadly sea, and as he was lying on the Libyan sand not far from the beach . . . naked and exhausted by the unhappy wreck, a baneful viper slew him. Why did he struggle with the waves in vain, escaping then the fate that was his lot on the land? (*Anth. Pal.* 7.20, trans. Paton 1919, 159)

Paul, too, survived the shipwreck, but will he survive the bite of the viper that fastens itself to his hand while he gathers firewood? The natives think not, assuming that he is being punished by the Greek goddess of justice (*Dikē*) for some heinous crime, like murder: **When the local inhabitants saw the creature hanging from his hand, they started saying to one another, "Surely, this man is a murderer! Although he escaped from the sea, Justice won't allow him to live"** (28:4). Like the shipwrecked mariner, he may have escaped the judgment of the sea, but he will not survive the viper's sting. The natives' judgment that Paul was a murderer reflects typical physiognomic thinking in which the viper "is a cruel, harmful, insidious animal, terrible when it decides to be, quick to flee when afraid, gluttonous. . . . Such men [who are like vipers] are murderers, bold, timid, devoted to evil-doing" (*Anon. Lat.* 128; André 1981). In an ironic twist, it appears the "murderous viper" has, by its bite, recognized a fellow "murderer"; it takes one to know one.

But, once again, Paul is vindicated by God: **Paul, though, shook the beast into the fire and suffered no harm. Now they were expecting him to become feverish at any time or suddenly to drop dead. But after they had waited a long time and seen nothing bad happening to him, they changed their minds and started saying that he was a god** (28:5–6). How quickly the Maltese inhabitants reverse their opinion! Interpreters sometimes find it disturbing that Paul does not correct the misperception that he "was a god," as he does at Lystra (14:11–15; cf. 10:25–26); however, that point is made implicitly in the next scene.

The final act of Paul on Malta denies the natives' conclusion that he was a god and rather confirms his role as a righteous representative of a beneficent God (28:7–10). Luke sets the scene: **The chief man of the island, named Publius, owned land in the areas around that place. He welcomed us and kindly treated us as guests for three days** (28:7). Publius was the "first man" of the island, probably a reference to his position as the leading local magistrate and civic leader. The language of Publius's actions toward Paul and company is that of ancient hospitality ("welcomed us," "kindly treated us as guests," even the note on "three days," 28:7; cf. *Did.* 11:1–3; the reference to "honor" and "many gifts," 28:10). When the father of Publius falls ill, **suffering with a fever and dysentery, Paul went to him and prayed, as he laid hands on him, and healed him** (28:8). Paul's act of praying makes clear he is no god, but rather the agent of God's healing power (Talbert 2005, 218). When word spread of the healing, **the rest of those on the island who had illnesses also started coming to (him) and were being cured** (28:9). In return, Paul the Christian benefactor is the recipient of great honor and provisions at the hands of the Maltese: **They also greatly honored us, and when we were ready to sail, they put on board the things we needed** (28:10). Christians, Luke seems to say, have no corner on hospitality and benefaction (see Theological Issues).

Paul Journeys to Rome (28:11–16)

With spring approaching Paul resumes his journey: **So after three months we set sail in an Alexandrian ship that had spent the winter at the island and had the "Heavenly Twins" as its emblem** (28:11). They catch another Alexandrian ship headed for Rome (cf. 27:6), itself wintering in Malta due to the inclement weather. Its name-device, whether carved or painted (Casson 1995, 344–45), was the "Heavenly Twins," or Dioscuri, the twin sons of Zeus, Castor and Pollux, who were protectors from the sea (cf., e.g., Epictetus, *Diatr.* 2.18.19; Lucian, *Nav.* 9; Aelius Aristides, *Hier. log.* 4.35–37; Diodorus Siculus, *Hist.* 4.43.1–2). Luke summarizes their progress: **We landed at Syracuse and stayed there for three days. From there we sailed around and arrived at Rhegium. After a day, a south wind came up and we came to Puteoli on the second day** (28:12–13). In Puteoli, they **found believers and were invited to stay with them for seven days** (28:14a). With rhetorical understatement, Luke reports the conclusion of the sea voyage: **So in this way we came to Rome** (28:14b). Paul thus takes the decisive step to fulfill the earlier theophanic prophecy ("Do not be afraid, Paul; it is necessary for you to stand before Caesar," 27:24).

Once again Paul is greeted by believers from the local area (cf. 28:14): **The believers from there had heard about our affairs and had come as far as Appius's Market and the Three Taverns to meet us** (28:15a). Luke does not say how Christians came to be in Rome, but that there was already a Christian community in Rome is confirmed by Paul's letter to the Romans (Rom 16:3–16). These Roman Christians had traveled a great distance (thirty or forty miles) to greet Paul (on the Three Taverns, cf. Cicero, *Att.* 2.10). The sight of them is a source of encouragement to Paul: **When Paul saw them, he gave thanks to God and took courage** (Acts 28:15b). The scene ends with a reminder that Paul, despite his immediate past heroism, is still a prisoner: **When we entered Rome, Paul was allowed to live by himself with the soldier who guarded him** (28:16). This verse anticipates the ending of Acts 28:30, in which Paul again is depicted as being under house arrest (see the sidebar on forms of Roman custody at 23:10). It is a reminder that Paul arrives to bear witness before the emperor *as a prisoner*.

Paul in Rome (28:17–31)

The end of a book is no less important than its beginning. Luke chooses to end this narrative neither with a confrontation between Paul and the emperor nor with a narration of Paul's martyrdom (see below), but rather by focusing on Paul's dialogue with the Roman Jews. The closing scene (28:17–31) divides into three parts: Paul's first (28:17–22) and second (28:23–28) encounters with the Jews, and the final summary statement about Paul's ministry in Rome (28:30–31).

28:17–22. In the first encounter with the Roman Jews, Paul recounts the events of Acts 22–26. In so doing, Luke preserves what is most important for the authorial audience to retain from that long stretch of narrative and speeches. This section consists of two speeches, one by Paul (28:17–20) and the other a response by his Jewish auditors (28:21–22). Luke first sets the scene: **After three days Paul called together the leading men of the Jews** (28:17a). His interest in speaking with the Jewish leaders in Rome indirectly attests to their influence in Roman matters (cf. Cicero, *Flac.* 28.66–69; Josephus, *Ant.* 17.11.1; *Vita* 3.13–16). Paul then reiterates his "Jewishness," a claim that has been made throughout the last chapters of Acts (21:23–26; 22:3; 23:6; 24:17–18; 26:5). Next he emphasizes his innocence, another theme resounding through the last chapters: **Fellow Jews, . . . I had done nothing against the people or our ancestral customs** (cf. 23:29; 25:18–19; 26:31–32). **I was handed over to the Romans as a prisoner from Jerusalem. After questioning me, they wanted to release me because there was no basis for imposing the death sentence (28:17b–18).** He then explains that his appeal to Caesar did not mean he intended to bring charges against his fellow Jews: **But when the Jews objected, I was forced to appeal to Caesar—though I did not have any reason to accuse my own people (28:19).** Rather, Paul insists that it was **for this reason I requested to see you**

Acts 28:17–31 in the Narrative Flow

The people and places of the Jerusalem church (1–12)
The sense of a beginning (1–7)
Beyond Jerusalem: Philip, Saul, Peter, and others (8–12)

The missionary activities of Paul (13–28)
Paul's mission to the Gentile world (13–19)
Paul's farewell journey (20–28)
Paul's last journey to Jerusalem (20:1–21:16)
Paul in Jerusalem (21:17–23:35)
Paul before Felix, Festus, and Agrippa (24–26)
The sea voyage to Rome (27–28)
Paul journeys to Malta (27)
Paul on Malta (28:1–10)
Paul journeys to Rome (28:11–16)
▶ Paul in Rome (28:17–31)
First encounter with Roman Jews (28:17–22)
Second encounter with Roman Jews (28:23–28)
Final summary statement (28:30–31)

and to speak to you. For I am wrapped in this chain because of the hope of Israel (28:20). Throughout this speech, Paul maintains that he has remained a loyal Jew and that his mission to the Gentiles is not based on an anti-Jewish foundation.

The Jews respond by saying that they had received no bad reports about Paul: We neither received letters concerning you from Judea, nor have any of (our) fellow Jews come (from there) and reported or said anything bad about you (28:21). They express a desire to hear more from Paul for themselves, since he represents the Christian "sect" about which they *have* received negative reports: So we think it best to hear from you what you think, for regarding this sect we are aware that it is spoken against everywhere (28:22).

28:23–28. The second encounter with the Roman Jews begins with a summary of Paul's preaching: After setting a day to meet with him, they went to him, to the place where he was staying, in even greater numbers. From early in the day until quite late he explained to them as he testified about the kingdom of God and tried to convince them about Jesus from both the law of Moses and the prophets (28:23). A familiar pattern emerges (28:24–28): Paul is first heard favorably by the Jews, and is then resisted; finally, he turns to the Gentiles (see 13:42–48; 18:5–7; 19:8–10). Once again, his proclamation of Jesus divides his audience: Some were convinced by what he said, but others would not believe. Since they disagreed among themselves, they began leaving (28:24–25a). This statement has a double effect; on the one hand, it demonstrates that there are still Jews who are responding positively to the message about Jesus (2:12–13; 4:1–4; 5:12–17; 6:8–14; 9:21–25; 13:42–45; 17:1–5; 18:4, 12–17; 19:8–10). On the other hand, this discord among the Jews stands in sharp contrast to the unity among the Christian community emphasized throughout Acts (1:14; 2:43–47; 4:32–35; 8:6; 15:25). In antiquity, unity was held to be the mark of a superior community or state, and discord as the sign of a failing or unhealthy community (Plato, *Ep.* 7.337; Polybius, *Hist.* 11.25.5). Several Jewish writers contrast the unity of Israel and its God (Philo, *Virt.* 35; Josephus, *C. Ap.* 2.179–181) over against the divisions among the Egyptians (Philo, *Flacc.* 17) or the Greeks (Josephus, *C. Ap.* 2.242–243). Thus the authorial audience, familiar with this literary topos, would understand the narrator's comment as a criticism leveled against the Jews as a *people* (Pao 2003).

This point is made clear in Paul's parting statement to them, in which he appeals both to the Holy Spirit and to the prophetic tradition: Paul said one (last) thing: "The Holy Spirit spoke appropriately through the prophet Isaiah to our ancestors" (28:25b). Paul then quotes Isa 6:9–10. Luke alone of all the NT writers who cite or allude to Isa 6:9–10 (cf., e.g., Matt 13:14–15; Mark 4:12; John 12:40; Rom 11:8) includes the introductory formula: Go to this people and say (28:26a). "The scope of the argument has changed from individuals (28:24) to collective declarations" about the "people" (Marguerat 1999, 300):

You will listen carefully, but will never understand. You will look carefully, but will never perceive. For the heart of this people has become insensitive, and their ears are plugged, and they have closed their eyes so that they might not see with their eyes, hear with their ears, perceive with their heart, and turn and I would heal them (28:26b–27). This Greek translation of Isa 6:9–10 reflects the rhetorical figure of *antithesis*, or the building on contraries (e.g., "When there is need for you to be silent, you are uproarious; when you should speak, you grow mute. Present, you wish to be absent; absent you are eager to return"; *Rhet. Her.* 4.15.21, trans. Caplan 1954, 283). Furthermore, 28:27 reflects a chiastic antithetical structure:

A Heart grown dull
 B Ears hard of hearing
  C Shut eyes
  C′ Look with eyes
 B′ Listen with ears
A′ Understand with heart

Just as Jewish belief in the gospel leads to the inclusion of Gentiles in God's people (cf. Acts 15:13–21), so also Jewish unbelief leads to the same result (cf. Acts 13:27–29). "It was a common cultural conviction that the divine purpose behind history that determines history's movement is effective not only in connection with human understanding and cooperation but also in spite of human misunderstanding and opposition" (Talbert 2005, 227). So for the third and final time, Paul turns to the Gentiles: Therefore, let it be known to you that this salvation from God has been sent to the Gentiles; and they will listen! (28:28; cf. 13:46; 18:6).

28:30–31. The book of Acts ends rather enigmatically with the notice that Paul spent the next two years living under house arrest at his own expense, preaching and teaching: So he lived (there) for two whole years at his own expense (28:30a). Mention of "two years" in Acts often refers to periods of special blessing (see 18:11; 19:10; though cf. 24:27; see Talbert 1984, 104). He welcomed everyone who came to visit him, and he boldly preached the kingdom of God and taught about the Lord Jesus Christ without hindrance (28:30b–31). This ending both provides a sense of closure by recalling themes introduced in Acts 1 and a sense of being unfinished by leaving other major themes incomplete or unstated. In terms of closure, the following points of linkage between chapters 1 and 28 should be noted (Parsons 1987, 156–59; Puskas 1980, 91–95):

1. There is an emphasis on the Kingdom of God. Four of the eight occurrences of "kingdom" are equally distributed in the opening (Acts 1:3, 6) and closing (28:23, 31) chapters of Acts.

2. There is an emphasis on the universal nature of the Christian mission in both Acts 1 ("you will be my witnesses . . . to the end of the earth," 1:8) and Acts 28 ("this salvation has been sent from God to the Gentiles," 28:28). If "the end of the earth" is taken as an implicit criticism of Rome (which most ancients understood to be the "center" or "navel" of the world), then Paul's arrival in Rome, the "center" of the Gentile world, may be seen as an ironic fulfillment of Jesus' commandment to be witnesses to the "end of the earth."

3. Both the beginning (1:1) and end (28:31) focus on the activity of teaching. By framing the narrative with references to teaching, the narrator has highlighted the parallel activities of Jesus and Paul; however, in Acts 28, Jesus is no longer the teacher, but the subject matter, no longer the proclaimer but the proclaimed.

4. The Holy Spirit is actively involved in the pronouncement of Jesus (1:2) and Paul (28:25). The anticipated empowering of the disciples by the Holy Spirit is presupposed in Acts 28.

Despite these points of contact between the beginning and ending of the story, there is much that is left unresolved, or at least unstated, by story's end. As such, Acts joins other writings from antiquity characterized by "suspended" ending (Magness 1986) or the "rhetoric of silence" (Marguerat 1999). Although less attention was paid to endings than to beginnings in ancient theory, there were those who maintained that the ending "is that which is inevitably or, as a rule, the natural result of something else but from which nothing else follows" (Aristotle, *Poet.* 7.21; cf. Dionysius of Halicarnassus, *Pomp.* 4.778, who claimed the historian is obligated to "end where nothing is left to be desired").

Nevertheless, the rhetorical effectiveness of the "unstated" was acknowledged by ancient rhetoricians ("Are there not in speech some details to be concealed, whether they must not be shown, or whether they cannot be expressed for the sake of dignity?" Quintilian, *Inst.* 2.13.12–13, trans. Butler 1921), and suspended endings are found in pagan (Homer, *Il.* 22.405; *Od.* 23.248–296; Virgil, *Aen.* 12.952; Herodotus, *Hist.* 9.114–121), Jewish (2 Kgs 25:27–30), and early Christian literature (Mark 16:1–8). Thus, despite attempts to explain the ending of Acts on historical grounds—Luke ran out of papyrus scroll (Spitta 1891) or information (Hemer 1989)—the ending is best understood, on literary grounds, as another example of a "suspended" ending.

In this light, the authorial audience would complete the story in the following ways (see

Chrysostom on the Ending of Acts

Chrysostom was one of the first interpreters to recognize the literary implications of the ending of Acts: "The author [Luke] conducts his narrative up to this point, and leaves the hearer thirsty so that he fills up the lack by himself through reflection" (*Hom. Act.* 15). How would the audience be expected to "fill up the lack"? By completing the story in accord with what has preceded (cf. Aristotle, *Poet.* 7.21; Marguerat 1999, 297).

Talbert 2005, 231). Paul's case was heard before Caesar (cf. 25:12; 27:24), and Paul was found innocent (23:29; 25:18–19; 26:31–32). Despite his innocence, Paul was not released but rather continued to suffer (9:15–16) and finally met his death in Rome (20:25, 38), perhaps as the result of corruption in the Roman judicial system (24:26–27; 25:9). Further, although Luke is uncertain or ambivalent about the future role of Israel in the new Christian community (or vice versa), the door to individual Jewish participation remains open (28:31).

The last word of the book is that Paul preached the kingdom of God (cf. 1:6) "unhindered" (28:31). The focus subtly shifts from Paul the messenger to the message he is proclaiming, the Christian gospel. Frank Stagg (1955) has persuasively demonstrated that this final word sums up the message of Acts: the gospel has overcome all human-made prejudice and every geographical, social, ethnic, gender, and theological barrier. In this regard, Richard Pervo's words are apropos: "Luke's own last word is a perfect summary of his writings, a one-word closure that is, at the same time, an opening, a bright and invigorating bid to the future, an assurance that 'the ends of the earth' is not the arrival at a boundary, but realization of the limitless promises of the dominion of God" (Pervo 1990, 96).

The gospel is unhindered because of the sovereignty of God who ultimately ensures its triumph in the face of adversity. But from Luke's perspective, this "unhindered" gospel remains an "unfinished" gospel. The gospel is unfinished because of the grace of God, who ultimately ensures that its completion can occur when all have had the opportunity to hear about the "kingdom of God" and the "Lord Jesus Christ." Unfettered yet unfinished, the gospel can be completed only when the audience takes up the challenge at the beginning of the first of Luke's two volumes proclaimed by John the Baptist, who also quotes the words of the prophet Isaiah: "*all flesh* shall see the salvation of God" (Luke 3:6).

Theological Issues

Three social customs from antiquity are featured conceptually and semantically in Acts 27–28: philanthropy, friendship, and hospitality. The ancients recognized philanthropy as a virtue (Demosthenes, *Or.* 19.225; Plato, *Euthyphr.* 3d; Plutarch, *Aem.* 39). According to Diogenes Laertius, Plato cataloged "philanthropy" into three categories: (1) offering greetings; (2) hosting dinners; and (3) offering benefactions, especially in times of trouble ("one is given to assisting everyone in distress"; see *Vit. phil.* 3.98). Philanthropic characters figure prominently in ancient literature (see Longus, *Daphn.* 1.3.1–20; Chariton, *Chaer.* 2.5.4), as do, conversely, misanthropic figures (cf. Menander, *Dysk.* 726.427–428; Dio Chrysostom, *Ven.* 7.56–58).

367

Philanthropy in Acts falls into the category of assisting those in distress (cf. also the Good Samaritan in Luke 10; Hock 1998, 132–37). After Paul's shipwreck, the inhabitants of Malta showed Paul and his company "unusual kindness" (*ou tēn tychousan philanthrōpian*) by welcoming them and kindling a fire (28:2). In Acts 27:3, Julius acts philanthropically toward Paul, allowing him to receive care from his "friends."

Although this is only the second occurrence in Acts of the term for "friends" (cf. 19:31), Luke was well aware of the cultural protocols and expectations associated with friendship in antiquity (see Parsons 2007, 54–61). In the Greco-Roman world, "friendship" was a very broad idea that covered "largely utilitarian relations of self-interest and advancement as well as those bonds which spring from family ties or social relations of true affection and commonality of character" (Fiore 1997, 73). Greco-Roman friendships tended to be based on the concept of *reciprocity*, which was expressed by such things as hospitality, gift giving, loyalty, honor, and political support (Garnsey and Saller 1987, 154; Stambaugh and Balch 1986, 63–64). Friends were expected both to provide help during times of need and publicly to acknowledge any help they had received from other friends.

The Greco-Roman writers made a distinction between public and private friendship. Public "friendships" involving a "patron" and a "client" were an important feature of political life. Public friendship often crossed social boundaries, and was closely tied to the idea of (asymmetrical) reciprocity. The exchange of goods and services that characterized Greco-Roman relationships thus made friendship a vital strand in the fabric of Greco-Roman society. Such public "friendships," however, were of a fundamentally different character than private, or "genuine," friendships. Indeed, one had to be careful to distinguish between friendships of advantage and true friendships (e.g., Cicero, *Amic.* 17.64). The former was considered a necessary evil while the latter was highly desirable.

In Greco-Roman society there was no better possession than private, genuine friendship (Plutarch, *Adul. amic.* 49F). Cicero considered friendship to be the most valuable gift, with the exception of wisdom, that the gods had granted to humans (*Amic.* 6.20). One of the key components of genuine friendship was commonality. True friends did not cling to their possessions as their own private property. Rather, friends shared everything, tangibly demonstrating their affection for and commitment to one another. The expression "friends have all things in common" dates back at least to the time of Aristotle (*Eth. Nic.* 9.8.2; see also Plutarch, *Adul. amic.* 65A).

Luke's use of the language of friendship reflects varying Hellenistic perceptions. In Luke 7:6, the term "friend" is used to describe subordinates: "When he [Jesus] was not far from the house, the centurion sent friends to say to him" (cf. John 4:5). In other places, "friend" functions as a patron: "Look, a glutton and a drunkard, a friend of tax collectors and sinners!" (Luke 7:34).

The Asiarchs in Acts 19:31, who are Paul's "friends," are likely functioning as his patrons (see Keener 2006). The term "friend" is used in relationship to presumed social equals: "When he [the shepherd] comes home, he calls together his friends and neighbors" (Luke 15:6; see 15:9, 29). The idea of intimate friendship is also present in Acts. Although the term is missing in earlier descriptions of the sharing of goods in the Christian community, the concept is certainly present (see comments on 2:44; Mitchell 1992). Here in Acts 27:3, as an expression of Christian friendship, Paul is the beneficiary of the shared nurture and care of these otherwise anonymous Sidonian Christians.

Travel appears to be the constant social context in scenes of ancient hospitality. Hospitality was a highly valued and presumably widely practiced custom among pagans, Jews, and Christians. Hosts were expected to provide food, shelter, amenities, and protection to these traveling strangers, who sometimes turned out to be gods incognito (Ovid, *Metam.* 8.626–724). In Greek culture, Zeus was celebrated as the god of hospitality (Homer, *Od.* 9.266–271; Heliodorus, *Aeth.* 2.22.2), and the practice of hospitality (among other things) separated high Greek civilization from the "barbarians" (but cf. comments on 28:7). Often these hospitality scenes ended with the host bestowing gifts upon the guest (Acts 28:10; cf. Homer, *Od.* 1.311–318; Chariton, *Chaer.* 5.97; Longus, *Daphn.* 3.9; 4.6; Dio Chrysostom, *Ven.* 7.21–22, 45, 57–58; Virgil, *Aen.* 8.152–169).

Jewish examples of hospitality also abound. The prime example in scripture, of course, is that of Abraham, who extends hospitality to three strangers (Gen 18:1–16; see also Gen 19:1–23; 24:10–61; 43:16–34; Exod 2:15–22; Josh 2:1–22; Judg 4:17–22; cf. Arterbury 2005, 55–86). The story of Abraham is reiterated in later Jewish stories, including, among others, Philo (*Abr.* 107–118), Josephus (*Ant.* 1.191–198), and the testamentary literature (*T. Ab.* 1.1–6). References to hospitality are also found in early Christian sources (cf. 1 Cor 16:5–12; 2 Cor 1:15–16; Phlm 22; 2 John 10–11; *Did.* 11, 12; *Acts Pil.* 14–16; cf. Arterbury 2005, 94–132).

Luke makes reference to hospitality in the Third Gospel (cf., *inter alia*, 7:36–50; 9:51–56; 10:38–42; 19:1–10) and Acts (9:11; 16:11–15; 17:5–7; 18:2–3; 21:7–16; 28:7–10). Gift-giving by the host to the guest is customary in ancient hospitality (28:10; see Homer, *Od.* 1.311–318; 8.430–432; Longus, *Daphn.* 3.9.4.6; Virgil, *Aen.* 8.152–169; Tob 10:10–11; Josephus, *Ant.* 5.281–282), and often precipitated the formation of permanent friendship.

In the ancient world, the protocols of these cultural conventions often overlap. Philanthropy, on the one hand, involved a moral obligation to accept "a limited number of responsibilities toward an unlimited number of people" (Hock 1998, 137). The language of philanthropy is frequently used in specific contexts of assisting the "other" *in duress* (victims of brigands or shipwreck or prisoners). Friendship, on the other hand, "calls for an unlimited number of responsibilities to a limited number of people" (Hock 1998, 137; cf. Chariton,

Chaer. 3.5). In Acts 27:3b, friendship was the basis of social exchange across ethnic and socioeconomic strata *within* the Christian community (cf. Acts 2:43–44). Thus in Acts 27–28 Luke uses philanthropy to describe acts of kindness by outsiders (natives of Malta) toward insiders, especially those under duress (28:2; cf. Luke 10; Acts 27:3a) and friendship to describe obligations of those in Christian community with each other (Acts 2:44; 27:3b).

Hospitality in Acts occurs in a context in which one person has traveled to another geographic region and, unlike philanthropy, seems to focus on household scenes. In Acts the host and guest may be insider/outsider or outsider/insider or both insiders. Thus hospitality in some instances overlaps with philanthropy, since hospitality is sometimes shown by outsiders to insiders (cf. Publius, who entertains Paul in Acts 28:7). Insiders may also serve the role of host, as Paul does when he "welcomes" everyone who comes to him in his rented quarters in Rome (28:30). Hospitality also overlaps with friendship, since Paul the traveler is entertained along his journey by a fellow insider (cf. Mnason of Cyprus, who entertains Paul in Acts 21:16).

This Lukan social ethic provides a solid foundation for Christian habits and practices both within the community (we have unlimited responsibilities to our Christian friends) and with the world (we are called to provide Christian philanthropy to those unlike us in nationality, faith, or ethnicity and assistance to those in immediate crisis). Christians are called to extend hospitality both as hosts and guests, and to fellow Christians and non-Christians alike. Such hospitality calls for personal and intimate engagement in a way that an insipid value such as "tolerance" does not. We are *not* called simply to "tolerate" or "endure" those not like us (see Conyers 2001); rather, the ancient "Christian virtues" of philanthropy and especially hospitality demand that we engage and interact with the "other," whether we are guest or host, and Christian friendship obligates us to practices that are mutually beneficial to the whole community, even when we may not always be in complete agreement with our Christian friends. Philanthropy, hospitality, and friendship are three Christian virtues well worth our consideration and cultivation as we go about preaching "the kingdom of God" and teaching "about the Lord Jesus Christ without hindrance" (28:31).

Bibliography

Abou-El-Haj, Barbara F. 1994. *The Medieval Cult of Saints: Formations and Transformations.* Cambridge: Cambridge University Press.

Aland, Kurt. 1966. "Neue Neutestamentliche Papyri." *New Testament Studies* 12:193–210.

Alexander, Loveday. 2005. *Acts in Its Ancient Literary Context: A Classicist Looks at the Acts of the Apostles.* London: T. & T. Clark.

Ambrose. 1982. *Epistularum liber decimus: Epistulae extra collectionem, Gesta concilii Aquileiensis.* Corpus Scriptorum Ecclesiasticorum Latinorum 82.3. Edited by M. Zelzer. Vienna: Austrian Academy of Sciences.

André, Jacques, ed. 1981. *Traité de physiognomonie: anonyme latin.* Paris: Les Belles Lettres.

Arterbury, Andrew E. 2005. *Entertaining Angels: Early Christian Hospitality in Its Mediterranean Setting.* Sheffield: Sheffield Phoenix.

———. 2009. "The Downfall of Eutychus: How Ancient Understandings of Sleep Illuminate Acts 20:7–12." In *Contemporary Studies in Acts*, edited by Thomas E. Phillips. Macon, GA: Mercer University Press.

Ascough, Richard S. 1997. "Voluntary Associations and Community Formation: Paul's Macedonian Christian Communities in Context." PhD diss., University of St. Michael's College.

———. 1998. "Civic Pride at Philippi: The Text-Critical Problem of Acts 16:12." *New Testament Studies* 44:93–103.

———. 2000. "The Thessalonian Christian Community as a Professional Voluntary Association." *Journal of Biblical Literature* 119:311–28.

Aune, David E. 1987. *The New Testament in Its Literary Environment.* Philadelphia: Westminster.

———. 2003. "The Use and Abuse of the Enthymeme in New Testament Scholarship." *New Testament Studies* 49:299–320.

Babbitt, F. C. 1969. *Plutarch: Moralia*. Loeb Classical Library. Cambridge, MA: Harvard University Press.

Backhaus, Knut. 1991. *Die Jüngerkreise des Täufers Johannes: Eine Studie zu den religionsgeschichtlichen Ursprüngen des Christentums*. Paderborn: Ferdinand Schöningh.

Balch, David L. 1985. "Acts as Hellenistic Historiography." *Society of Biblical Literature Seminar Papers* 24:429–32.

———. 1987. "Comparing Literary Patterns in Luke and Lucian." *Perkins Journal* 40/2:39–42.

———. 1990. "The Genre of Luke-Acts: Individual Biography, Adventure Novel, or Political History? *Southwestern Journal of Theology* 33:5–19.

———. 1995. "Paul in Acts: '. . . you teach all the Jews . . . to forsake Moses, telling them not to . . . observe the customs' (Act 21,21)." In *Panchaia: Festschrift für Klaus Thraede*, edited by Manfred Wacht, 11–23. Münster: Aschendorff.

———. 2003. "*Metabolē politeiōn*: Jesus as Founder of the Church in Luke-Acts: Form and Function." In *Contextualizing Acts: Lukan Narrative and Greco-Roman Discourse*, edited by Todd C. Penner and Caroline Vander Stichele, 139–88. Atlanta: Society of Biblical Literature.

Balch, David L., and John E. Stambaugh. 1986. *The New Testament in Its Social Environment*. Philadelphia: Westminster.

Barré, Michael L. 1980. "Qumran and the 'Weakness' of Paul." *Catholic Biblical Quarterly* 42:216–27.

Barrett, C. K. 1961. *Luke the Historian in Recent Study*. London: Epworth.

———. 1994–1998. *A Critical and Exegetical Commentary on the Acts of the Apostles*. International Critical Commentary. 2 vols. Edinburgh: T. & T. Clark.

Bass, Kenneth. 2009. "The Rhetorical Function of Necessity in Luke's Bios of Jesus." PhD diss., Baylor University.

Bassler, Jouette M. 1985. "Luke and Paul on Impartiality." *Biblica* 66:546–52.

Bauckham, Richard. 1995. "James and the Jerusalem Church." In *The Book of Acts in Its Palestinian Setting*, edited by Richard Bauckham, 415–80. Vol. 4 of *The Book of Acts in Its First Century Setting*, edited by Bruce W. Winter. Grand Rapids: Eerdmans.

———. 1998. "For Whom Were Gospels Written?" In *The Gospels for All Christians: Rethinking the Gospel Audiences*, edited by Richard Bauckham, 9–48. Grand Rapids: Eerdmans.

———. 2005. "James, Peter, and the Gentiles." In *Missions of James, Peter, and Paul*, edited by Bruce Chilton and Craig Evans, 91–142. Leiden: Brill.

———. 2006. "The Estate of Publius on Malta (Acts 28:7)." In *History and Exegesis: New Testament Essays in Honor of Dr. E. Earle Ellis for His 80th Birthday*, edited by Sang-Won Son, 73–87. New York: T. & T. Clark.

Bauernfeind, Otto. 1980. *Kommentar und Studien zur Apostelgeschichte*. Tübingen: Mohr Siebeck.

Béchard, Dean P. 2000. *Paul Outside the Walls: A Study of Luke's Socio-Geographical Universalism in Acts 14:8–20*. Rome: Pontificio Istituto Biblico.

———. 2001. "Paul among the Rustics: The Lystran Episode (Acts 14:8–20) and Lucan Apologetic." *Catholic Biblical Quarterly* 63:84–101.

Berding, Kenneth. 2002. *Polycarp and Paul: An Analysis of Their Literary and Theological Relationship in Light of Polycarp's Use of Biblical and Extra-Biblical Literature*. Leiden: Brill.

Bird, Michael F. 2007. "The Unity of Luke-Acts in Recent Discussion." *Journal for the Study of the New Testament* 29:42–48.

Black, C. Clifton. 1988. "The Rhetorical Form of the Hellenistic Jewish and Early Christian Sermon: A Response to Lawrence Wills." *Harvard Theological Review* 81:1–18.

———. 1993. "The Presentation of John Mark in the Acts of the Apostles." *Perspectives in Religious Studies* 20:236–54.

———. 1998. "John Mark in the Acts of the Apostles." In *Literary Studies in Luke-Acts: Essays in Honor of Joseph B. Tyson*, edited by Richard P. Thompson and Thomas E. Phillips, 101–20. Macon, GA: Mercer University Press.

———. 2001. *The Rhetoric of the Gospel: Theological Artistry in the Gospels and Acts*. St. Louis: Chalice.

Blass, F., and A. Debrunner. 1961. *A Greek Grammar of the New Testament and Other Early Christian Literature*. Translated and revised by Robert W. Funk. Chicago: University of Chicago Press.

Boccaccini, Gabriele. 1991. *Middle Judaism: Jewish Thought, 300 B.C.E.–200 C.E.* Minneapolis: Fortress.

Bock, Darrell L. 1987. *Proclamation from Prophecy and Pattern: Lucan Old Testament Christology*. Sheffield: JSOT Press.

———. 2007. *Acts*. Grand Rapids: Baker Academic.

Bockmuehl, Markus. 1995. "The Noachide Commandments and New Testament Ethics, with Special Reference to Acts 15 and Pauline Halakhah." *Revue biblique* 102:72–101.

———. 2005. "Why Not Let Acts Be Acts? In Conversation with C. Kavin Rowe." *Journal for the Study of the New Testament* 28:163–66.

———. 2006. *Seeing the Word: Refocusing New Testament Study*. Grand Rapids: Baker Academic.

Boismard, M. E., and A. Lamouille. 1984. *Le texte occidental des Actes des Apôtres: reconstitution et réhabilitation*. 2 vols. Paris: Editions Recherche sur les civilizations.

Bonz, Marianne P. 2000. *The Past as Legacy: Luke-Acts and Ancient Epic*. Minneapolis: Fortress.

Bovon, François. 2001. "Names and Numbers in Early Christianity." *New Testament Studies* 47:267–88.

Braun, Willi. 1995. *Feasting and Social Rhetoric in Luke 14*. Cambridge: Cambridge University Press.

Brawley, Robert L. 1987. *Luke-Acts and the Jews: Conflict, Apology, and Conciliation*. Atlanta: Scholars Press.

———. 1999. "Abrahamic Covenant Traditions and the Characterization of God in Luke-Acts." In *Unity of Luke-Acts*, edited by Jozef Verheyden, 109–32. Louvain: Leuven University Press.

Breytenbach, Cilliers. 1993. "Zeus und der lebendige Gott: Anmerkungen zu Apostelgeschichte 14:11–17." *New Testament Studies* 39:396–413.

———. 1996. *Paulus und Barnabas in der Provinz Galatien: Studien zu Apostelgeschichte 13f.; 16,6; 18,23 und den Adressaten des Galaterbriefes.* Leiden: Brill.

———. 2004. "Probable Reasons for Paul's Unfruitful Missionary Attempts in Asia Minor (A Note on Acts 16:6–7)." In *Apostelgeschichte und die hellenistische Geschichtsschreibung: Festschrift für Eckhard Plümacher zu seinem 65. Geburtstag,* edited by Cilliers Breytenbach und Jens Schröter, 157–69. Leiden: Brill.

Brodie, Thomas L. 1990. "Luke-Acts as an Imitation and Emulation of the Elijah-Elisha Narrative." In *New Views on Luke and Acts,* edited by Richard Earl, 78–85. Collegeville, MN: Liturgical Press.

Broughton, T. R. S. 1933. Repr. 1979. "The Roman Army." In *The Beginnings of Christianity,* edited by F. J. Foakes Jackson and K. Lake, 5:427–45. 5 vols. Grand Rapids: Eerdmans.

Brown, Peter. 1981. *The Cult of the Saints: Its Rise and Function in Latin Antiquity.* Chicago: University of Chicago Press.

Bruce, F. F. 1954. *Commentary on the Book of the Acts.* Grand Rapids: Eerdmans.

———. 1986. *The Acts of the Apostles.* New International Commentary on the New Testament. Grand Rapids: Eerdmans.

———. 1988. *The Book of the Acts.* Rev. ed. Grand Rapids: Eerdmans.

———. 1990. *The Acts of the Apostles: The Greek Text with Introduction and Commentary.* 3rd ed. Grand Rapids: Eerdmans.

Brunschwig, Jacques. 1995. *Études sur les philosophies hellénistiques: épicurisme, stoïcisme, scepticisme.* Paris: Presses universitaires de France.

Bulley, Alan D. 1994. "Hanging in the Balance: A Semiotic Study of Acts 20:7–12." *Église et théologie* 25:171–88.

Byrskog, Samuel. 2003. "History or Story in Acts—A Middle Way? The 'We' Passages, Historical Intertexture, and Oral History." In *Contextualizing Acts: Lukan Narrative and Greco-Roman Discourse,* edited by Todd C. Penner and Caroline Vander Stichele, 257–83. Atlanta: Society of Biblical Literature.

Cadbury, Henry J. 1920. *The Style and Literary Method of Luke.* Cambridge, MA: Harvard University Press.

———. 1927. *The Making of Luke-Acts.* New York: Macmillan.

Calvin, Jean. 1949. *Commentary upon the Acts of the Apostles.* Translated by Henry Beveridge. Grand Rapids: Eerdmans.

Canali de Rossi, Filippo, and Frederick E. Brenk. 2001. "The 'Notorious' Felix, Procurator of Judaea, and His Many Wives (Acts 23–24)." *Biblica* 82:410–17.

Caplan, Harry. 1954. *[Cicero:] Ad C. Herennnium de ratione dicendi (Rhetorica ad Herennium).* Loeb Classical Library. Cambridge, MA: Harvard University Press.

Carter, Warren. 1996. *Matthew: Storyteller, Interpreter, Evangelist.* Peabody, MA: Hendrickson.

Carver, William O. 1916. *The Acts of the Apostles.* Nashville: Broadman.

Casson, Lionel. 1995. *Ships and Seamanship in the Ancient World*. Baltimore: Johns Hopkins University Press.

Chatman, Seymour B. 1978. *Story and Discourse: Narrative Structure in Fiction and Film*. Ithaca, NY: Cornell University Press.

Clark, Albert C. 1933. *The Acts of the Apostles: A Critical Edition, with Introduction and Notes on Selected Passages*. Oxford: Clarendon.

Clark, David J. 2004. "A Not Infrequent Construction: Litotes in the Book of Acts." *Bible Translator* 55:433–40.

Clements, Ronald E. 1990. "The Old Testament Background of Acts 10:34–35." In *With Steadfast Purpose: Essays on Acts in Honor of Henry Jackson Flanders, Jr.*, edited by Naymond H. Keathley, 203–16. Waco: Baylor University Press.

Coady, C. A. J. 1992. *Testimony: A Philosophical Study*. Oxford: Oxford University Press.

Cohen, Shaye J. D. 1986. "Was Timothy Jewish (Acts 16:1–3)? Patristic Exegesis, Rabbinic Law, and Matrilineal Descent." *Journal of Biblical Literature* 105:251–68.

Cohoon, J. W. 1971. *Dio Chrysostom*. Loeb Classical Library. Cambridge, MA: Harvard University Press.

Conrad, Edgar W. 1991. *Reading Isaiah*. Minneapolis: Fortress.

Conyers, A. J. 2001. *The Long Truce: How Toleration Made the World Safe for Power and Profit*. Dallas: Spence.

Conzelmann, Hans. 1960. *The Theology of St. Luke*. Translated by Geoffrey Buswell. London: Faber & Faber.

———. 1987. *Acts of the Apostles: A Commentary on the Acts of the Apostles*. Edited by Eldon Jay Epp with Christopher R. Matthews. Translated by James Limburg, A. Thomas Kraabel, and Donald H. Juel. Philadelphia: Fortress.

Cotter, Wendy J. 1996. "The Collegia and Roman Law: State Restrictions on Voluntary Associations, 64 BCE–200 CE." In *Voluntary Associations in the Graeco-Roman World*, edited by John S. Kloppenborg and Stephen G. Wilson, 74–89. London: Routledge.

Cribiore, Raffaella. 2001. *Gymnastics of the Mind: Greek Education in Hellenistic and Roman Egypt*. Princeton, NJ: Princeton University Press.

Croy, N. Clayton. 1997. "Hellenistic Philosophies and the Preaching of the Resurrection (Acts 17:18, 32)." *Novum Testamentum* 39:21–39.

Culpepper, R. Alan. 1983. *Anatomy of the Fourth Gospel: A Study in Literary Design*. Philadelphia: Fortress.

Culy, Martin M., and Mikeal C. Parsons. 2003. *Acts: A Handbook on the Greek Text*. Waco: Baylor University Press.

Cumont, Franz. 1909. "La plus ancienne géographie astrologique." *Klio* 9:263–73.

Dahl, Nils Alstrup. 1976. "The Story of Abraham in Luke-Acts." In *Jesus in the Memory of the Early Church: Essays by Nils Alstrup Dahl*, 66–86. Minneapolis: Augsburg.

Danker, Frederick W. 1982. *Benefactor: Epigraphic Study of a Graeco-Roman and New Testament Semantic Field*. St. Louis: Clayton.

———. 1988. *Jesus and the New Age: A Commentary on St. Luke's Gospel*. Philadelphia: Fortress.

Darr, John A. 1992. *On Character Building: The Reader and the Rhetoric of Characterization in Luke-Acts*. Louisville: Westminster John Knox.

Dawsey, James M. 1986. *The Lukan Voice: Confusion and Irony in the Gospel of Luke*. Macon, GA: Mercer University Press.

Detwiler, David F. 1995. "Paul's Approach to the Great Commission in Acts 14:21–23." *Bibliotheca sacra* 152:33–41.

Dibelius, Martin. 1939. *The Message of Jesus Christ: The Tradition of the Early Christian Communities*. Translated by Frederick C. Grant. New York: Scribner.

———. 1956. *Studies in the Acts of the Apostles*. Edited by Heinrich Greeven. Translated by Mary Ling. New York: Scribner.

Dodson, Derek S. 2006. "Reading Dreams: An Audience-Critical Approach to the Dreams in the Gospel of Matthew." PhD diss., Baylor University.

Donfried, Karl P. 1985. "The Cults of Thessalonica and the Thessalonian Correspondence." *New Testament Studies* 31:336–56.

Dowd, Sharyn E. 2002. "'Ordination' in Acts and the Pastoral Epistles." *Perspectives in Religious Studies* 29:205–17.

Dowden, Ken. 1989. Introduction to "The Alexander Romance." In *Collected Ancient Greek Novels*, edited by B. P. Reardon, 650–54. Berkeley: University of California Press.

Downing, Gerald F. 1982. "Common Ground with Paganism in Luke and in Josephus." *New Testament Studies* 28:546–59.

Duffy, Maureen E. 1994. "The Riot of the Silversmiths at Ephesus (Acts 19:23–40): A Synchronic Study using Rhetorical and Semiotic Methods of Analysis." PhD diss., University of Ottawa.

Dunn, James D. G. 1970. *Baptism in the Holy Spirit: A Re-Examination of the New Testament Teaching on the Gift of the Spirit in Relation to Pentecostalism Today*. London: SCM.

———. 1996. *The Acts of the Apostles*. Valley Forge, PA: Trinity Press International.

———. 1998. *The Christ and the Spirit: Collected Essays of James D. G. Dunn*. 2 vols. Grand Rapids: Eerdmans.

Dupont, Jacques. 1956. "La mission de Paul 'à Jérusalem.'" *Novum Testamentum* 1:275–303.

———. 1961. "La destinée de Judas prophetisée par David (Actes 1:16–20)." *Catholic Biblical Quarterly* 23:41–51.

Eco, Umberto. 1992. "Overinterpreting Texts." In *Interpretation and Overinterpretation*, edited by Stefan Collini, 45–66. Cambridge: Cambridge University Press.

Ehrman, Bart D. 1993. *The Orthodox Corruption of Scripture: The Effect of Early Christological Controversies on the Text of the New Testament*. Oxford: Oxford University Press.

Eleen, L. 1977. "Acts Illustration in Italy and Byzantium." *Dumbarton Oaks Papers* 31:253–78.

Elliott, John H. 1991. "Temple versus Household in Luke-Acts: A Contrast in Social Institutions." In *The Social World of Luke-Acts: Models for Interpretation*, edited by Jerome H. Neyrey, 211–40. Peabody, MA: Hendrickson.

Epp, Eldon Jay. 1991. "New Testament Papyrus Manuscripts and Letter Carrying in Greco-Roman Times." In *The Future of Early Christianity*, edited by Birger A. Pearson et al., 35–56. Minneapolis: Fortress.

Esler, Philip F. 1987. *Community and Gospel in Luke-Acts*. Society for New Testament Studies Monograph Series 57. Cambridge: Cambridge University Press.

———. 1992. "Glossolalia and the Admission of Gentiles into the Early Christian Community." *Biblical Theology Bulletin* 22:136–42.

Fiore, Benjamin. 1997. "The Theory and Practice of Friendship in Cicero." In *Greco-Roman Perspectives on Friendship*, edited by John T. Fitzgerald, 59–76. Atlanta: Scholars Press.

Fitzmyer, Joseph A. 1989. *Luke the Theologian: Aspects of His Teaching*. New York: Paulist Press.

———. 1998. *The Acts of the Apostles*. Anchor Bible 31. New York: Doubleday.

Foakes-Jackson, F. J. 1931. *The Acts of the Apostles*. London: Hodder & Stoughton.

——— and Kirsopp Lake, eds. 1920–1933. *The Acts of the Apostles*. 5 vols. London: Macmillan.

Fossum, Jarl E. 1985. *The Name of God and the Angel of the Lord: Samaritan and Jewish Concepts of Intermediation and the Origin of Gnosticism*. Tübingen: Mohr.

Foster, Paul. 2006. "The Epistles of Ignatius of Antioch (Part 1)." *Expository Times* 117:487–95.

Fowler, Robert M. 1991. *Let the Reader Understand: Reader-Response Criticism and the Gospel of Mark*. Minneapolis: Fortress.

Friesen, Steven J. 1993. *Twice Neokoros: Ephesus, Asia, and the Cult of the Flavian Imperial Family*. Leiden: Brill.

Funk, Robert W. 1988. *The Poetics of Biblical Narrative*. Sonoma, CA: Polebridge.

Gaffin, Richard B. 1979. *Perspectives on Pentecost*. Grand Rapids: Baker.

Gamble, Harry Y. 1995. *Books and Readers in the Early Church: A History of Early Christian Texts*. New Haven: Yale University Press.

Garland, David E. 1993. *Reading Matthew: A Literary and Theological Commentary on the First Gospel*. New York: Crossroad.

———. 2003. "The Absence of an Ordained Ministry in the Churches of Paul." In *Baptists and Ordination*, edited by William H. Brackney, 25–37. National Association of Baptist Professors of Religion Special Studies 13. Macon, GA: The National Association of Baptist Professors of Religion.

Garland, Robert. 1992. *Introducing New Gods: The Politics of Athenian Religion*. Ithaca, NY: Cornell University Press.

Garnsey, Peter, and Richard Saller. 1987. *The Roman Empire: Economy, Society, and Culture*. Berkeley: University of California Press.

Garrett, Susan R. 1989. *The Demise of the Devil: Magic and the Demonic in Luke's Writings*. Minneapolis: Fortress.

Gärtner, Bertil E. 1955. *The Areopagus Speech and Natural Revelation*. Translated by Carolyn H. King. Uppsala: Gleerup.

Gasque, W. Ward. 1975. *A History of the Criticism of the Acts of the Apostles*. Tübingen: Mohr.

———. 1988. "A Fruitful Field: Recent Study of the Acts of the Apostles." *Interpretation* 42:117–31.

Gaventa, Beverly R. 1986. *From Darkness to Light: Aspects of Conversion in the New Testament*. Philadelphia: Fortress.

———. 2003. *The Acts of the Apostles*. Nashville: Abingdon.

Genette, Gérard. 1979. *Introduction à l'architexte*. Paris: Seuil.

———. 1980. *Narrative Discourse: An Essay in Method*. Translated by Jane E. Lewin. Ithaca, NY: Cornell University Press.

Gill, David H. 1974. "Structure of Acts 9." *Biblica* 55:546–48.

———. 1999. "Dionysios and Damaris: A Note on Acts 17:34." *Catholic Biblical Quarterly* 61:483–90.

Gill, David W. J. 1994. "Acts and the Urban Élites." In *The Book of Acts in Its Graeco-Roman Setting*, edited by David W. J. Gill and Conrad Gempf, 105–18. Vol. 2 of *The Book of Acts in Its First Century Setting*, edited by Bruce W. Winter. Grand Rapids: Eerdmans.

Gleason, Maud W. 1995. *Making Men: Sophists and Self-Presentation in Ancient Rome*. Princeton, NJ: Princeton University Press.

González, Justo L. 2001. *Acts: The Gospel of the Spirit*. Maryknoll, NY: Orbis Books.

Gray, Patrick. 2005. "Athenian Curiosity (Acts 17:21)." *Novum Testamentum* 47:109–16.

Green, Joel B. 2002. "'She and her household were baptized' (Acts 16.15): Household Baptism in the Acts of the Apostles." In *Dimensions of Baptism: Biblical and Theological Studies*, edited by Stanley E. Porter and Anthony R. Cross, 72–90. London: Sheffield Academic Press.

Gregory, Andrew F. 2003. *The Reception of Luke and Acts in the Period before Irenaeus: Looking for Luke in the Second Century*. Tübingen: Mohr Siebeck.

Griffith, R. Marie. 2002. "Female Suffering and Religious Devotion in American Pentecostalism." In *Women and Twentieth-Century Protestantism*, edited by Margaret L. Bendroth and Virginia L. Brereton, 184–208. Urbana: University of Illinois Press.

Haenchen, Ernst. 1971. *The Acts of the Apostles: A Commentary*. Translated by Bernard Noble and Gerald Shinn. Translation revised by R. McL. Wilson. Philadelphia: Westminster.

Hamm, M. Dennis. 1986. "Acts 3:1–10: The Healing of the Temple Beggar as Lucan Theology." *Biblica* 67:305–19.

———. 1990. "Paul's Blindness and Its Healing: Clues to Symbolic Intent (Acts 9; 22 and 26)." *Biblica* 71:63–72.

Hanson, John S. 1980. "Dreams and Visions in the Greco-Roman World of Early Christianity." *Aufstieg und Niedergang der Römischen Welt* 23.2:1395–1427. Part 2, *Principat*, 23.2. Edited by H. Temporini and W. Haase. Berlin/New York: Walter de Gruyter.

Harnack, Adolf von. 1907. *Luke the Physician, the Author of the Third Gospel and the Acts of the Apostles*. Translated by J. R. Wilkinson. Edited by W. D. Morrison. London: Williams & Norgate.

Harrison, P. N. 1936. *Polycarp's Two Epistles to the Philippians*. Cambridge: Cambridge University Press.

Hartog, Paul. 2002. *Polycarp and the New Testament: The Occasion, Rhetoric, Theme, and Unity of the Epistle to the Philippians and Its Allusions to New Testament Literature*. Tübingen: Mohr Siebeck.

Hartsock, Chad. 2008. *Sight and Blindness as an Index of Character in Luke-Acts and Its Ancient Cultural Milieu*. Leiden: Brill.

Hays, Richard B. 1989. *Echoes of Scripture in the Letters of Paul*. New Haven: Yale University Press.

Head, Peter M. 1993. "Acts and the Problem of Its Texts." In *The Book of Acts in Its Ancient Literary Setting*, edited by Bruce W. Winter and Andrew D. Clarke, 415–45. Vol. 1 of *The Book of Acts in Its First Century Setting*, edited by Bruce W. Winter. 5 vols. Grand Rapids: Eerdmans.

Hemer, Colin J. 1989. *The Book of Acts in the Setting of Hellenistic History*. Edited by Conrad H. Gempf. Tübingen: Mohr.

———. 1989. "The Speeches of Acts: Pt. 1: The Ephesian Elders at Miletus; Pt. 2: The Areopagus Address." *Tyndale Bulletin* 40:239–59.

Hendrix, Holland L. 1984. "Thessalonicans Honor Romans." ThD diss., Harvard Divinity School.

Hengel, Martin. 1979. *Acts and the History of Earliest Christianity*. Translated by John Bowden. Philadelphia: Fortress.

Hesselgrave, David J., and Edward Rommen. 1989. *Contextualization: Meanings, Methods, and Models*. Grand Rapids: Baker.

Hintermaier, Johann. 2000. "Grundlage und Entwicklung der paulinischen Mission am Beispiel von Apg 16,11–40." *Studien zum Neuen Testament und seiner Umwelt* 25:152–75.

———. 2003. *Die Befreiungswunder in der Apostelgeschichte: Motiv- und formkritische Aspekte sowie literarische Funktion der wunderbaren Befreiungen in Apg 5,17–42; 12,1–23; 16,11–40*. Berlin: Philo.

Hobart, William K. 1882. *The Medical Language of St. Luke*. Dublin: Hodges, Figgis & Co. Repr. Grand Rapids: Baker, 1954.

Hock, Ronald F. 1978. "Paul's Tentmaking and the Problem of His Social Class." *Journal of Biblical Literature* 97:555–64.

———. 1998. "Why New Testament Scholars Should Read Ancient Novels." In *Ancient Fiction and Early Christian Narrative*, edited by J. Bradley Chance, Ronald F. Hock, and Judith Perkins, 121–38. Atlanta: Scholars Press.

Hogan, Derek K. 2006. "Forensic Speeches in Acts 22–26 in Their Literary Environment: A Rhetorical Study." PhD diss., Baylor University.

Holmes, Michael W. 2006. "Polycarp of Smyrna, Letter to the Philippians." *Expository Times* 118:53–63.

Horsley, G. H. R., ed. 1981. *New Documents Illustrating Early Christianity*. Vol. 1. North Ryde, Australia: The Ancient History Documentary Research Centre Macquarie University.

———. 1986. "Speeches and Dialogue in Acts." *New Testament Studies* 32:609–14.

379

———. 1992. "The Inscriptions of Ephesos and the New Testament." *Novum Testamentum* 34:105–68.

Horst, Pieter W. van der. 1989. "The Altar of the 'Unknown God' in the Hellenistic and Roman Periods." *ANRW* 18.2:1426–56. Part 2, *Principat*, 18.2. Edited by H. Temporini and W. Haase. New York: de Gruyter.

———. 1989. "Hellenistic Parallels to Acts (Chapters 3 and 4)." *Journal for the Study of the New Testament* 35:37–46.

Horton, Dennis J. 1995. "Death and Resurrection: The Shape and Function of a Literary Motif in the Book of Acts." PhD diss., Baylor University.

House, Colin. 1983. "Defilement by Association: Some Insights from the Usage of κοινός/κοινόω in Acts 10 and 11." *Andrews University Seminary Studies* 21:143–53.

Howell, Justin R. 2009. "Embedded Letters and Rhetorical Auxesis in Sallust, Chariton, and Luke." In *Contemporary Studies in Acts*, edited by Thomas E. Phillips. Macon, GA: Mercer University Press.

Hubbard, Moyer V. 2005. "Urban Uprisings in the Roman World: The Social Setting of the Mobbing of Sosthenes." *New Testament Studies* 51:416–28.

Humphreys, Fisher. 2006. "The Revelation of the Trinity." *Perspectives in Religious Studies* 33:285–303.

Hurd, John C. 1967. "Pauline Chronology and Pauline Theology." In *Christian History and Interpretation: Studies Presented to John Knox*, edited by W. R. Farmer, C. F. D. Moule, and R. R. Niebuhr, 225–48. Cambridge: Cambridge University Press.

Jeremias, Joachim. 1969. *Jerusalem in the Time of Jesus: An Investigation into Economic and Social Conditions during the New Testament Period*. Translated by F. H. Cave and C. H. Cave. Philadelphia: Fortress.

Jewett, Robert. 1997. "Mapping the Route of Paul's 'Second Missionary Journey' from Dorylaeum to Troas." *Tyndale Bulletin* 48:1–22.

———. 2000. "Paul and the Caravanners: A Proposal on the Mode of 'passing through Mysia.'" In *Text and Artifact in the Religions of Mediterranean Antiquity: Essays in Honour of Peter Richardson*, edited by Stephen G. Wilson and Michel Desjardins, 74–90. Waterloo, ON: Wilfrid Laurier University Press.

Johnson, Luke T. 1977. *The Literary Function of Possessions in Luke-Acts*. Missoula, MT: Scholars Press.

———. 1979. "On Finding the Lukan Community: A Cautious Cautionary Essay." In *Society of Biblical Literature Seminar Papers*, edited by Paul J. Achtemeier, 87–100. Missoula, MT: Scholars Press.

———. 1989. "The New Testament's Anti-Jewish Slander and the Conventions of Ancient Polemic." *Journal of Biblical Literature* 108:419–41.

———. 1992. *The Acts of the Apostles*. Collegeville, MN: Liturgical Press.

———. 1996. *Scripture and Discernment: Decision Making in the Church*. Rev. ed. Nashville: Abingdon.

———. 1998. *Religious Experience in Earliest Christianity: A Missing Dimension in New Testament Studies*. Minneapolis: Fortress.

———. 2005. "Literary Criticism of Luke-Acts: Is Reception-History Pertinent?" *Journal for the Study of the New Testament* 28:159–62.

Judge, E. A. 1971. "Decrees of Caesar at Thessalonica." *Reformed Theological Review* 30:1–7.

———. 1981. "A State Schoolteacher Makes a Salary Bid." In *New Documents Illustrating Early Christianity*. Vol. 1, edited by G. H. R. Horsley, 72–78. North Ryde, Australia: The Ancient History Documentary Research Centre Macquarie University.

Juel, Donald. 1988. *Messianic Exegesis: Christological Interpretation of the Old Testament in Early Christianity*. Philadelphia: Fortress.

Karris, Robert J. 1985. *Luke, Artist and Theologian: Luke's Passion Account as Literature*. New York: Paulist Press.

Käsemann, Ernst. 1969. *Jesus Means Freedom*. Translated by Frank Clarke. Philadelphia: Fortress.

———. 1982. *Essays on New Testament Themes*. Philadelphia: Fortress.

Kauppi, Lynn Allan. 2006. *Foreign but Familiar Gods: Greco-Romans Read Religion in Acts*. London: T. & T. Clark.

Keathley, Naymond H., ed. 1990. *With Steadfast Purpose: Essays on Acts in Honor of Henry Jackson Flanders, Jr.* Waco: Baylor University Press.

Kee, Howard Clark. 1997. *To Every Nation under Heaven: The Acts of the Apostles*. Harrisburg, PA: Trinity Press International.

Keener, Craig S. 2006. "Paul's 'Friends' the Asiarchs (Acts 19:31)." *Journal of Greco-Roman Christianity and Judaism* 3:134–41.

Kelhoffer, James A. 2000. *Miracle and Mission: The Authentication of Missionaries and Their Message in the Longer Ending of Mark*. Tübingen: Mohr Siebeck.

Kennedy, George A. 1984. *New Testament Interpretation through Rhetorical Criticism*. Chapel Hill: University of North Carolina Press.

———, ed. and trans. 2003. *Progymnasmata: Greek Textbooks of Prose Composition and Rhetoric*. Writings from the Greco-Roman World 10. Atlanta: Society of Biblical Literature.

Kessler, Herbert L. 1973. "Paris Gr 102: A Rare Illustrated Acts of the Apostles." *Dumbarton Oaks Papers* 27:209–16.

———. 1979. "Scenes from the Acts of the Apostles on Some Early Christian Ivories." *Gesta* 18:110–19.

Kilgallen, John J. 1976. *The Stephen Speech: A Literary and Redactional Study of Acts 7,2–53*. Rome: Biblical Institute Press.

Kim, Chan-Hie. 1972. *Form and Structure of the Familiar Greek Letter of Recommendation*. Missoula, MT: Society of Biblical Literature for the Seminar on Paul.

Kittel, Gerhard, and G. Friedrich, eds. 1964–1976. *Theological Dictionary of the New Testament*. Translated by Geoffrey W. Bromiley. 10 vols. Grand Rapids: Eerdmans.

Klauck, Hans-Josef. 2000. *Magic and Paganism in Early Christianity: The World of the Acts of the Apostles*. Translated by Brian McNeil. Edinburgh: T. & T. Clark.

———. 2006. *Ancient Letters and the New Testament: A Guide to Context and Exegesis*. Waco: Baylor University Press.

Klawans, Jonathan. 1995. "Notions of Gentile Impurity in Ancient Judaism." *Association for Jewish Studies Review* 20:285–312.

Klutz, Todd E. 1999. "Naked and Wounded: Foregrounding, Relevance and Situation in Acts 19:13–20." In *Discourse Analysis and the New Testament: Approaches and Results*, edited by Stanley E. Porter and Jeffrey T. Reed, 258–79. Sheffield: Sheffield Academic Press.

———. 2004. *The Exorcism Stories in Luke-Acts: A Sociostylistic Reading*. Cambridge: Cambridge University Press.

Knox, John. 1950. *Chapters in a Life of Paul*. New York: Abingdon-Cokesbury.

Koester, Helmut. 1995. "Ephesos in Early Christian Literature." In *Ephesos: Metropolis of Asia*, edited by Helmut Koester, 119–40. Valley Forge, PA: Trinity Press International.

Koet, Bart J. 1996. "Why Did Paul Shave His Hair (Acts 18,18): Nazirate and Temple in the Book of Acts." In *The Centrality of Jerusalem: Historical Perspectives*, edited by M. Poorthuis and Ch. Safrai, 128–42. Kampen: Kok Pharos.

Kovacs, David. 2002. *Euripides: Bacchae; Iphigenia at Aulis; Rhesus*. Loeb Classical Library. Cambridge, MA: Harvard University Press.

Kraft, Charles H. 1979. *Christianity in Culture: A Study in Dynamic Biblical Christianity in Cross-Cultural Perspective*. Maryknoll, NY: Orbis Books.

Krieger, Murray. 1992. *Ekphrasis: The Illusion of the Natural Sign*. Baltimore: Johns Hopkins University Press.

Krodel, Gerhard. 1986. *Acts*. Minneapolis: Augsburg.

Kühn, Carolus Gottlob. 1821. *Claudii Galeni opera omnia*. 20 vols. in 22. Leipzig: Prostat in officina libraria Car. Cnoblochii.

Kümmel, Werner G. 1973. *The Theology of the New Testament According to Its Major Witnesses: Jesus-Paul-John*. Translated by John E. Steely. Nashville: Abingdon.

Kurz, William S. 1980. "Hellenistic Rhetoric in the Christological Proof of Luke-Acts." *Catholic Biblical Quarterly* 42:171–95.

———. 1993. *Reading Luke-Acts: Dynamics of Biblical Narrative*. Louisville: Westminster John Knox.

Kydd, Ronald A. N. 1998. *Healing through the Centuries: Models for Understanding*. Peabody, MA: Hendrickson.

Lake, Kirsopp. 1933. *The Text of the New Testament*. 6th ed. London: Rivingtons.

Lampe, Peter. 1992. "Acta 19 im Spiegel der ephesischen Inschriften." *Biblische Zeitschrift* 36:59–76.

Leaney, A. R. C. 1968. "Why There Were Forty Days between the Resurrection and the Ascension." In *Studia evangelica*, vol. 4, *Papers Presented to the Third International Congress on New Testament Studies Held at Christ Church, Oxford, 1965*, edited by F. L. Cross, 417–19. Berlin: Akademie-Verlag.

Lentz, John C. 1993. *Luke's Portrait of Paul*. Cambridge: Cambridge University Press.

Levinskaya, Irina. 1996. *The Book of Acts in Its Diaspora Setting*. Carlisle, PA: Paternoster.

Levinsohn, Stephen H. 1987. *Textual Connections in Acts*. Atlanta: Scholars Press.

———. 1992. *Discourse Features of New Testament Greek: A Coursebook*. Dallas: Summer Institute of Linguistics.

Litwak, Kenneth D. 2004. "Israel's Prophets Meet Athens' Philosophers: Scriptural Echoes in Acts 17,22–31." *Biblica* 85:199–216.

Long, A. A. 1986. *Hellenistic Philosophy: Stoics, Epicureans, Sceptics*. 2nd ed. Berkeley: University of California Press.

Long, W. R. 1982. "The Trial of Paul in the Book of Acts: History, Literary, and Theological Considerations." PhD diss., Brown University.

Longenecker, Bruce W. 2005. *Rhetoric at the Boundaries: The Art and Theology of New Testament Chain-Link Transitions*. Waco: Baylor University Press.

Longenecker, Richard N. 1995. *Acts*. Grand Rapids: Zondervan.

Lüdemann, Gerd. 1984. *Paul, Apostle to the Gentiles: Studies in Chronology*. Translated by F. Stanley Jones. Philadelphia: Fortress.

———. 1989. *Early Christianity According to the Traditions in Acts: A Commentary*. Translated by John Bowden. Minneapolis: Fortress.

MacDonald, Dennis R. 2003. *Does the New Testament Imitate Homer? Four Cases from the Acts of the Apostles*. New Haven: Yale University Press.

———. 2004. "Lydia and Her Sisters as Lukan Fiction." In *A Feminist Companion to the Acts of the Apostles*, edited by Amy-Jill Levine, 105–10. London: T. & T. Clark.

Magness, J. Lee. 1986. *Sense and Absence: Structure and Suspension in the Ending of Mark's Gospel*. Atlanta: Scholars Press.

Malherbe, Abraham J. 1987. *Paul and the Thessalonians: The Philosophic Tradition of Pastoral Care*. Philadelphia: Fortress.

———. 1988. *Ancient Epistolary Theorists*. Atlanta: Scholars Press.

———. 1989. *Paul and the Popular Philosophers*. Minneapolis: Fortress.

Malina, Bruce J., and Jerome H. Neyrey. 1991. "Honor and Shame in Luke-Acts: Pivotal Values of the Mediterranean World." In *The Social World of Luke-Acts: Models for Interpretation*, edited by Jerome H. Neyrey, 25–65. Peabody, MA: Hendrickson.

Marconi, Gilberto, and Gerald O'Collins, eds. 1993. *Luke and Acts*. Translated by Matthew J. O'Connell. New York: Paulist Press.

Marguerat, Daniel. 1995. "Saul's Conversion (Acts 9, 22, 26) and the Multiplication of Narrative in Acts." In *Luke's Literary Achievement*, edited by C. M. Tuckett, 127–55. Sheffield: Sheffield Academic Press.

———. 1999. "The Enigma of the Silent Closing of Acts (28:16–31)." In *Jesus and the Heritage of Israel: Luke's Narrative Claim upon Israel's Legacy*, edited by David P. Moessner, 284–304. Harrisburg, PA: Trinity Press International.

———. 2002. *The First Christian Historian: Writing the "Acts of the Apostles."* Translated by Ken McKinney et al. Cambridge: Cambridge University Press.

Marshall, I. Howard. 1980. *The Acts of the Apostles: An Introduction and Commentary*. Grand Rapids: Eerdmans.

———. 1990. "Luke's View of Paul." *Southwestern Journal of Theology* 33:41–51.

——— and David Peterson, eds. 1998. *Witness to the Gospel: The Theology of Acts*. Grand Rapids: Eerdmans.

Martin, Clarice J. 1989. "A Chamberlain's Journey and the Challenge of Interpretation for Liberation." *Semeia* 47:105–35.

Martin, Francis, and Evan Smith. 2006. *Acts*. Ancient Christian Commentary on Scripture. Downers Grove, IL: InterVarsity.

Martin, Lawrence T. 1989. *Bede: Commentary on the Acts of the Apostles*. Kalamazoo: Cistercian Publications.

Martin, Michael W. 2005. "Defending the 'Western Non-interpolations': The Case for an Anti-Separationist Tendenz in the Longer Alexandrian Readings." *Journal of Biblical Literature* 124:269–94.

———. 2008. "Progymnastic Topic Lists: A Compositional Template for Luke and Other Bioi?" *New Testament Studies* 54:18–41.

Martyn, J. Louis. 1997. *Galatians*. Anchor Bible 33A. New York: Doubleday.

Matson, David L. 1996. *Household Conversion Narratives in Acts: Pattern and Interpretation*. Sheffield: Sheffield Academic Press.

Matthews, Shelley. 2004. "Elite Women, Public Religion, and Christian Propaganda in Acts 16." In *A Feminist Companion to the Acts of the Apostles*, edited by Amy-Jill Levine, 111–33. London: T. & T. Clark.

Maxwell, Kathy. 2007. "Hearing between the Lines: The Audience as Fellow-Worker in Luke-Acts and Its Literary Milieu." PhD diss., Baylor University.

McConnell, James R. 2006. "The *Topos* of Divine Testimony and Its Use in Plutarch's *Lives* and Luke-Acts." Paper presented at Baylor University New Testament Colloquium. Waco, TX, February 2006.

McMahan, Craig T. 1987. "Meals as Type-Scenes in the Gospel of Luke." PhD diss., Southern Baptist Theological Seminary.

McNeill, John T., ed. 1960. *Calvin: Institutes of the Christian Religion*. Translated by Ford Lewis Battles. 2 vols. Philadelphia: Westminster.

McVann, Mark. 1991. "Rituals of Status Transformation in Luke-Acts: The Case of Jesus the Prophet." In *The Social World of Luke-Acts: Models for Interpretation*, edited by Jerome H. Neyrey, 333–60. Peabody, MA: Hendrickson.

Meier, John P. 1979. *The Vision of Matthew: Christ, Church, and Morality in the First Gospel*. New York: Paulist Press.

Menoud, Philippe H. 1962. "Pendant quarante jours (Actes 1:3)." In *Neotestamentica et Patristica: Eine Freundesgabe, Herrn Professor Dr. Oscar Cullmann zu seinem 60. Geburtstag überreicht*, 148–56. Supplements to Novum Testamentum 6. Leiden: Brill.

Metzger, Bruce M. 1970. "Ancient Astrological Geography and Acts 2:9–11." In *Apostolic History and the Gospel*, edited by W. Ward Gasque and Ralph P. Martin, 123–33. Exeter, UK: Paternoster.

———. 1994. *A Textual Commentary on the Greek New Testament: A Companion Volume to the United Bible Societies' Greek New Testament (3d ed.)*. 2nd ed. New York: United Bible Societies.

Miles, Gary B., and Garry W. Trompf. 1976. "Luke and Antiphon: The Theology of Acts 27–28 in the Light of Pagan Beliefs about Divine Retribution, Pollution, and Shipwreck." *Harvard Theological Review* 69:259–67.

Mitchell, Alan C. 1992. "The Social Function of Friendship in Acts 2:44–47 and 4:32–37." *Journal of Biblical Literature* 111:255–72.

Moessner, David P. 1990. "'The Christ Must Suffer,' the Church Must Suffer: Rethinking the Theology of the Cross in Luke-Acts." *Society of Biblical Literature Seminar Papers* 29:165–95.

————, ed. 1999. *Jesus and the Heritage of Israel: Luke's Narrative Claim upon Israel's Legacy*. Harrisburg, PA: Trinity Press International.

Moore, Stephen D. 1989. *Literary Criticism and the Gospels: The Theoretical Challenge*. New Haven: Yale University Press.

Morgan, David. 1999. *Protestants and Pictures: Religion, Visual Culture, and the Age of American Mass Production*. New York: Oxford University Press.

Morgenthaler, Robert. 1993. *Lukas und Quintilian: Rhetorik als Erzählkunst*. Zürich: Gotthelf.

Moxnes, Halvor. 1995. "'He saw that the city was full of idols' (Acts 17:16): Visualizing the World of the First Christians." In *Mighty Minorities? Minorities in Early Christianity, Positions and Strategies: Essays in Honour of Jacob Jervell on His 70th Birthday, 21 May 1995*, edited by David Hellholm, Halvor Moxnes, and Turid Karlsen Seim, 107–31. Oslo: Scandinavian University Press.

Murphy-O'Connor, J. 1983. *St. Paul's Corinth: Texts and Archaeology*. Wilmington, DE: Michael Glazier.

————. 1995. *Paul the Letter-Writer: His World, His Options, His Skills*. Collegeville, MN: Liturgical Press.

Nelson, Edwin S. 1982. "Paul's First Missionary Journey as Paradigm." PhD diss., Boston University.

Neusner, Jacob. 1999. "Vow-Taking, the Nazirites, and the Law: Does James' Advice to Paul Accord with Halakhah?" In *James the Just and Christian Origins*, edited by Bruce Chilton and Craig A. Evans, 59–82. Leiden: Brill.

Newman, Barclay M., and Eugene A. Nida. 1972. *A Translator's Handbook on the Acts of the Apostles*. London: United Bible Societies.

Neyrey, Jerome H. 1984. "The Forensic Defense Speech and Paul's Trial Speeches in Acts 22–26: Form and Function." In *Luke-Acts: New Perspectives from the Society of Biblical Literature Seminar*, edited by Charles H. Talbert, 210–24. New York: Crossroad.

————, ed. 1991. *The Social World of Luke-Acts: Models for Interpretation*. Peabody, MA: Hendrickson.

————. 1991. "The Symbolic Universe of Luke-Acts: 'They Turn the World Upside Down.'" In *The Social World of Luke-Acts: Models for Interpretation*, edited by Jerome H. Neyrey, 271–304. Peabody, MA: Hendrickson.

Nielsen, Anders E. 2000. *Until It Is Fulfilled: Lukan Eschatology according to Luke 22 and Acts 20*. Tübingen: Mohr Siebeck.

O'Day, Gail R. 1992. "Acts." In *The Women's Bible Commentary*, edited by Carol A. Newsom and Sharon H. Ringe, 305–12. Louisville: Westminster John Knox.

O'Donovan, Oliver. 1994. *Resurrection and Moral Order: An Outline for Evangelical Ethics*. Grand Rapids: Eerdmans.

Oldfather, W. A. 1967. *Epictetus*. Loeb Classical Library. Cambridge, MA: Harvard University Press.

Oliver, J. H. 1970. "The Epistle of Claudius which Mentions the Proconsul Junius Gallio." *Hesperia* 40:239–40.

Olyan, Saul M. 1998. "'Anyone Blind or Lame Shall Not Enter the House': On the Interpretation of Second Samuel 5:8b." *Catholic Biblical Quarterly* 60:218–27.

O'Reilly, Leo. 1987. *Word and Sign in the Acts of the Apostles: A Study in Lucan Theology.* Rome: Editrice Pontificia Università Gregoriana.

Oster, Richard E. 1979. *The Acts of the Apostles.* Pt. 2. *13:1–28:31.* Austin: Sweet.

———. 1987. *A Bibliography of Ancient Ephesus.* Metuchen, NJ: Scarecrow Press.

O'Toole, Robert F. 1994. "What Role Does Jesus' Saying in Acts 20,35 Play in Paul's Address to the Ephesian Elders?" *Biblica* 75:329–49.

Palmer, Darryl W. 1987. "The Literary Background of Acts 1:1–14." *New Testament Studies* 33:427–38.

Pao, David W. 2003. "Disagreement among the Jews in Acts 28." In *Early Christian Voices: In Texts, Traditions, and Symbols; Essays in Honor of François Bovon,* edited by David H. Warren, Ann Graham Brock, and David W. Pao, 109–18. Leiden: Brill.

Parker, Floyd O., Jr. 2003. "The Terms 'Angel' and 'Spirit' in Acts 23,8." *Biblica* 84:344–65.

Parsons, Mikeal C. 1986a. "A Christological Tendency in P^{75}." *Journal of Biblical Literature* 105:463–79.

———. 1986b. "Narrative Closure and Openness in the Plot of the Third Gospel: The Sense of an Ending in Luke 24:50–53." *Society of Biblical Literature Seminar Papers* 25:201–23.

———. 1987. *The Departure of Jesus in Luke-Acts: The Ascension Narratives in Context.* Sheffield: JSOT.

———. 1989. "Ancient Alexandria." *Biblical Illustrator* 15:30–34.

———. 1992. "What's 'Literary' about Literary Aspects of the Gospels and Acts?" In *1992 Society of Biblical Literature Seminar Papers,* 9:14–39. Atlanta: Scholars Press.

———. 2000. "'Nothing defiled AND unclean': The Conjunction's Function in Acts 10:14." *Perspectives in Religious Studies* 27:263–74.

———. 2001. "Who Wrote the Gospel of Luke?" *Biblical Research* 17/2:12–21, 54–55.

———. 2006. *Body and Character in Luke and Acts: The Subversion of Physiognomy in Early Christianity.* Grand Rapids: Baker Academic.

———. 2007. *Luke: Storyteller, Interpreter, Evangelist.* Peabody, MA: Hendrickson.

———. 2008. "Exegesis 'By the Numbers': Numerology and the New Testament." *Perspectives in Religious Studies* 35:25–43.

——— and Heidi J. Hornik. Forthcoming. *The Acts of the Apostles through the Ages.* Oxford: Blackwell.

——— and Richard I. Pervo. 1993. *Rethinking the Unity of Luke and Acts.* Minneapolis: Fortress.

——— and Joseph B. Tyson, eds. 1992. *Cadbury, Knox, and Talbert: American Contributions to the Study of Acts.* Atlanta: Scholars Press.

Patillon, Michel, and Giancarlo Bolognesi, eds. and trans. 1997. *Aelius Théon: Progymnasmata.* Paris: Belles Lettres.

Paton, W. R. 1919. *The Greek Anthology.* Loeb Classical Library. Vol. 2. New York: Putnam.

Pease, A. S. 1946. "Notes on Book Burning." In *Munera Studies,* edited by M. H. Shepperd, 145–60. Cambridge, MA: Episcopal Theological School.

Pelikan, Jaroslav. 2005. *Acts.* Grand Rapids: Brazos.

Pelikan, Jaroslav, and Valerie Hotchkiss, eds. 2003. *Creeds and Confessions of Faith in the Christian Tradition.* 4 vols. New Haven: Yale University Press.

Penner, Todd C. 2003. "Reconfiguring the Rhetorical Study of Acts: Reflections on the Method in and Learning of a Progymnastic Poetics." *Perspectives in Religious Studies* 30:425–39.

———. 2004. *In Praise of Christian Origins: Stephen and the Hellenists in Lukan Apologetic Historiography.* New York: T. & T. Clark.

Pervo, Richard I. 1987. *Profit with Delight: The Literary Genre of the Acts of the Apostles.* Philadelphia: Fortress.

———. 1990. *Luke's Story of Paul.* Minneapolis: Fortress.

———. 1999. "Israel's Heritage and Claims upon the Genre(s) of Luke and Acts: The Problems of a History." In *Jesus and the Heritage of Israel: Luke's Narrative Claim upon Israel's Legacy,* edited by David P. Moessner, 127–43. Harrisburg, PA: Trinity Press International.

———. 2006. *Dating Acts: Between the Evangelists and the Apologists.* Santa Rosa, CA: Polebridge.

Pesch, Rudolf. 1986. *Die Apostelgeschichte.* 2 vols. Zürich: Neukirchener Verlag.

Petzke, G. 1980–1983. "Εὐνοῦχος." In *Exegetisches Wörterbuch zum Neuen Testament,* edited by Horst Balz and Gerhard Schneider, 2:80–81. Stuttgart: Kohlhammer.

Phillips, Thomas E. 2006. "The Genre of Acts: Moving Toward a Consensus?" *Currents in Biblical Research* 4:365–96.

Pilch, John J. 2004. *Visions and Healing in the Acts of the Apostles: How the Early Believers Experienced God.* Collegeville, MN: Liturgical Press.

Polhill, John B. 1992. *Acts.* Nashville: Broadman.

Porter, Stanley E. 1999. *The Paul of Acts: Essays in Literary Criticism, Rhetoric, and Theology.* Wissenschaftliche Untersuchungen zum Neuen Testament 115. Tübingen: Mohr Siebeck.

Powell, Mark A. 1990. *What Is Narrative Criticism?* Minneapolis: Fortress.

———. 1991. *What Are They Saying about Acts?* New York: Paulist Press.

Praeder, Susan M. 1987. "The Problem of First Person Narration in Acts." *Novum Testamentum* 29:193–218.

Puskas, Charles B. 1980. "The Conclusion of Luke-Acts: An Investigation of the Literary Function and Theological Significance of Acts 28:16–31." PhD diss., St. Louis University.

Rabe, Hugo, ed. 2005. *Invention and Method: Two Rhetorical Treatises from the Hermogenic Corpus.* Translated by George A. Kennedy. Leiden: Brill.

Rabinowitz, Peter J. 1987. *Before Reading: Narrative Conventions and the Politics of Interpretation.* Ithaca, NY: Cornell University Press.

Ramsay, W. M. 1906. *Pauline and Other Studies in Early Christian History.* London: Hodder & Stoughton.

Rapske, Brian. 1994. *The Book of Acts and Paul in Roman Custody.* Carlisle, UK: Paternoster.

Reardon, B. P. 1989. *Collected Ancient Greek Novels*. Berkeley: University of California Press.

Reich, Keith. 2005. "The Church as Continuation of the 'Best' in Israel: Syncrisis in the Stephen Episode." Paper presented at Baylor University. Waco, TX, April 2005.

Reicke, Bo I. 1948. "Die Mahlzeit mit Paulus auf den Wellen des Mittelmeers: Act 27:33–38." *Theologische Zeitschrift* 4:401–10.

Rese, Martin. 1969. *Alttestamentliche Motive in der Christologie des Lukas*. Gütersloh: Gütersloher Verlagshaus G. Mohn.

Rhoads, David M., and Donald Michie. 1982. *Mark as Story: An Introduction to the Narrative of a Gospel*. Philadelphia: Fortress.

Richard, Earl. 1978. *Acts 6:1–8:4: The Author's Method of Composition*. Missoula, MT: Scholars Press.

———, ed. 1990. *New Views on Luke and Acts*. Collegeville, MN: Liturgical Press.

Richter Reimer, I. 1995. *Women in the Acts of the Apostles: A Feminist Liberation Perspective*. Translated by Linda M. Maloney. Minneapolis: Fortress.

Robbins, Vernon K. 1978. "By Land and by Sea: The We-Passages [in Acts] and Ancient Sea Voyages." In *Perspectives on Luke-Acts*, edited by Charles H. Talbert, 215–42. Danville, VA: Association of Baptist Professors of Religion.

Robbins, Vernon K., and Burton L. Mack. 1989. *Patterns of Persuasion in the Gospels*. Sonoma, CA: Polebridge.

Robertson, A. T. 1930–1933. *Word Pictures in the New Testament*. 3 vols. New York: Harper and Brothers.

Rohrbaugh, Richard L. 1991. "The Pre-Industrial City in Luke-Acts: Urban Social Relations." In *The Social World of Luke-Acts: Models for Interpretation*, edited by Jerome H. Neyrey, 125–49. Peabody, MA: Hendrickson.

Rosenmeyer, Patricia A. 2001. *Ancient Epistolary Fictions: The Letter in Greek Literature*. Cambridge: Cambridge University Press.

Rowe, C. Kavin. 2005. "History, Hermeneutics and the Unity of Luke-Acts." *Journal for the Study of the New Testament* 28:131–57.

———. 2007. "Literary Unity and Reception History: Reading Luke-Acts as Luke and Acts." *Journal for the Study of the New Testament* 29:449–57.

Ruthven, Jon. 1993. *On the Cessation of the Charismata: The Protestant Polemic on Post-biblical Miracles*. Sheffield: Sheffield Academic Press.

Sanders, James A., and Craig A. Evans, eds. 1993. *Luke and Scripture: The Function of Sacred Tradition in Luke-Acts*. Minneapolis: Fortress.

———, eds. 1998. *The Function of Scripture in Early Jewish and Christian Tradition*. Sheffield: Sheffield Academic Press.

Sandnes, Karl O. 1993. "Paul and Socrates: The Aim of Paul's Areopagus Speech." *Journal for the Study of the New Testament* 50:13–26.

Satterthwaite, P. E. 1993. "Acts against the Background of Classical Rhetoric." In *The Book of Acts in Its Ancient Literary Setting*, edited by Bruce W. Winter and Andrew D. Clarke, 337–79. Vol. 1 of *The Book of Acts in Its First Century Setting*. Edited by Bruce W. Winter. 5 vols. Grand Rapids: Eerdmans.

Schlier, H. 1965. θλίβω, θλῖψις. In vol. 3 of *Theological Dictionary of the New Testament*, edited by G. Kittel and G. Friedrich, 139–48. Translated by G. Bromiley. 10 vols. Grand Rapids: Eerdmans.

Schneider, Gerhard. 1980. *Die Apostelgeschichte: I. Teil, Einleitung, Kommentar zu Kap. 1,1–8,40*. Freiburg: Herder.

———. 1982. *Die Apostelgeschichte: II. Teil, Kommentar zu Kap. 9,1–28,31*. Freiburg: Herder.

Schoedel, William R. 1967. *Polycarp, Martyrdom of Polycarp, Fragments of Papias*. Camden, NJ: Nelson.

Schottroff, Luise. 1993. *Let the Oppressed Go Free: Feminist Perspectives on the New Testament*. Translated by Annemarie S. Kidder. Louisville: Westminster John Knox.

Schwartz, Daniel R. 1996. "God, Gentiles, and Jewish Law: On Acts 15 and Josephus' Adiabene Narrative." In *Geschichte—Tradition—Reflexion*, edited by Hubert Cancik, Hermann Lichtenberger, and Peter Schäfer, 263–82. Tübingen: Mohr Siebeck.

Scott, James M. 1994. "Luke's Geographical Horizon." In *The Book of Acts in Its Graeco-Roman Setting*, edited by David W. J. Gill and Conrad Gempf, 483–544. Vol. 2 of *The Book of Acts in Its First Century Setting*. Edited by Bruce W. Winter. 5 vols. Grand Rapids: Eerdmans.

Segal, Alan F. 1986. *Rebecca's Children: Judaism and Christianity in the Roman World*. Cambridge, MA: Harvard University Press.

———. 2001. "Acts 15 as Jewish and Christian History." *Forum* 4:63–87.

Shauf, Scott. 2005. *Theology as History, History as Theology: Paul in Ephesus in Acts 19*. New York: Walter de Gruyter.

Sheeley, Steven M. 1992. *Narrative Asides in Luke-Acts*. Sheffield: JSOT Press.

Shiell, William D. 2004. *Reading Acts: The Lector and the Early Christian Audience*. Boston: Brill.

Skinner, Matthew L. 2003. *Locating Paul: Places of Custody as Narrative Settings in Acts 21–28*. Leiden: Brill.

Snodgrass, Klyne. 1972. "Western Non-interpolations." *Journal of Biblical Literature* 91:369–79.

Soards, Marion L. 1994. *The Speeches in Acts: Their Content, Context, and Concerns*. Louisville: Westminster John Knox.

Spencer, F. Scott. 1992a. "The Ethiopian Eunuch and His Bible: A Social-Science Analysis." *Biblical Theology Bulletin* 22:155–65.

———. 1992b. *The Portrait of Philip in Acts: A Study of Roles and Relations*. Sheffield: JSOT Press.

———. 1994. "Neglected Widows in Acts 6:1–7." *Catholic Biblical Quarterly* 56:715–33.

———. 1997. *Acts*. Sheffield: Sheffield Academic Press.

———. 1999. "Out of Mind, Out of Voice: Slave-Girls and Prophetic Daughters in Luke-Acts." *Biblical Interpretation* 7:133–55.

———. 2004. *Journeying through Acts: A Literary-Cultural Reading*. Peabody, MA: Hendrickson.

Spencer, Patrick E. 2007. "The Unity of Luke-Acts: A Four-Bolted Hermeneutical Hinge." *Currents in Biblical Research* 5:341–66.

Spitta, Friedrich. 1891. *Die Apostelgeschichte, ihre Quellen und deren geschichtlichen Wert.* Halle: Verlag der Buchhandlung des Waisenhauses.

Squires, John T. 1993. *The Plan of God in Luke-Acts.* Cambridge: Cambridge University Press.

Stagg, Frank. 1955. *The Book of Acts: The Early Struggle for an Unhindered Gospel.* Nashville: Broadman.

Stambaugh, John E., and David L. Balch. 1986. *The New Testament in Its Social Environment.* Philadelphia: Westminster.

Stark, Rodney. 1991. "Antioch as the Social Situation for Matthew's Gospel. In *Social History of the Matthean Community: Cross-Disciplinary Approaches*, edited by David L. Balch, 189–210. Minneapolis: Fortress.

Stendahl, Krister. 1968. *The School of St. Matthew, and Its Use of the Old Testament.* Philadelphia: Fortress.

———. 1976. *Paul among Jews and Gentiles, and Other Essays.* Philadelphia: Fortress.

Stepp, Perry L., and Charles H. Talbert. 1998. "Succession in Mediterranean Antiquity, Part 2: Luke-Acts." *Society of Biblical Literature Seminar Papers* 37/1:169–79.

Sterling, Gregory E. 1992. *Historiography and Self-Definition: Josephus, Luke-Acts and Apologetic Historiography.* Supplements to Novum Testamentum 64. Leiden: Brill.

Sternberg, Meir. 1985. *The Poetics of Biblical Narrative: Ideological Literature and the Drama of Reading.* Bloomington: Indiana University Press.

Still, Todd D. 2006. "Did Paul Loathe Manual Labor? Revisiting the Work of Ronald F. Hock on the Apostle's Tentmaking and Social Class." *Journal of Biblical Literature* 125:781–95.

Stowasser, Martin. 2001. "Am 5,25–27; 9,11 f. in der Qumranüberlieferung und in der Apostelgeschichte: Text- und traditionsgeschichtliche Überlegungen zu 4Q174 (Florilegium) III 12/CD VII 16/Apg 7,42b–43; 15,16–18." *Zeitschrift für die neutestamentliche Wissenschaft und die Kunde der älteren Kirche* 92:47–63.

Strange, W. A. 1992. *The Problem of the Text of Acts.* Cambridge: Cambridge University Press.

Strauss, Mark L. 1995. *The Davidic Messiah in Luke-Acts: The Promise and Its Fulfillment in Lukan Christology.* Sheffield: Sheffield Academic Press.

Strelan, Rick. 2000. "Recognizing the Gods (Acts 14.8–10)." *New Testament Studies* 46:488–503.

———. 2003. "Acts 19:12: Paul's 'Aprons' Again." *Journal of Theological Studies* 54:154–57.

———. 2004. *Strange Acts: Studies in the Cultural World of the Acts of the Apostles.* Berlin: de Gruyter.

Swain, Simon, ed. 2007. *Seeing the Face, Seeing the Soul: Polemon's Physiognomy from Classical Antiquity to Medieval Islam.* Oxford: Oxford University Press.

Sylva, Dennis D. 1987. "The Meaning and Function of Acts 7:46–50." *Journal of Biblical Literature* 106:261–75.

Tajra, Harry W. 1989. *The Trial of St. Paul: A Juridical Exegesis of the Second Half of the Acts of the Apostles.* Tübingen: Mohr.

Talbert, Charles H. 1974. *Literary Patterns, Theological Themes, and the Genre of Luke-Acts.* Society of Biblical Literature Monograph Series 20. Atlanta: Scholars Press.

———. 1976. "Shifting Sands: The Recent Study of the Gospel of Luke." *Interpretation* 30:381–95.

———. 1977. *What Is a Gospel? The Genre of the Canonical Gospels.* Philadelphia: Fortress.

———. 1984. *Acts.* Atlanta: John Knox.

———. 1987. "Paul on the Covenant." *Review and Expositor* 84:299–313.

———. 1992. "Reading Chance, Moessner, and Parsons." In *Cadbury, Knox, and Talbert: American Contributions to the Study of Acts,* edited by Mikeal C. Parsons and Joseph B. Tyson, 229–40. Atlanta: Scholars Press.

———. 1997. *Reading Acts: A Literary and Theological Commentary on the Acts of the Apostles.* New York: Crossroad.

———. 1998. "Conversion in the Acts of the Apostles: Ancient Auditors' Perceptions." In *Literary Studies in Luke-Acts: Essays in Honor of Joseph B. Tyson,* edited by Richard P. Thompson and Thomas E. Phillips, 141–53. Macon, GA: Mercer University Press.

———. 2001. "Paul, Judaism, and the Revisionists." *Catholic Biblical Quarterly* 63:1–22.

———. 2002. *Reading Luke: A Literary and Theological Commentary on the Third Gospel.* Rev. ed. Macon, GA: Smyth and Helwys.

———. 2003. *Reading Luke-Acts in Its Mediterranean Milieu.* Supplements to Novum Testamentum 107. Boston: Brill.

———. 2005. *Reading Acts: A Literary and Theological Commentary on the Acts of the Apostles.* Rev. ed. Macon, GA: Smyth and Helwys.

Tannehill, Robert C. 1986–1990. *The Narrative Unity of Luke-Acts: A Literary Interpretation.* 2 vols. Philadelphia: Fortress.

Taylor, Justin. 1994. "Why Were the Disciples First Called 'Christians' at Antioch? (Acts 11, 26)." *Revue biblique* 101: 75–94.

Taylor, R. O. P. 1946. *Groundwork for the Gospels, with Some Collected Papers.* Oxford: Blackwell.

Thomas, Christine M. 1995. "At Home in the City of Artemis: Religion in Ephesos in the Literary Imagination of the Roman Period." In *Ephesos: Metropolis of Asia,* edited by Helmut Koester, 81–117. Valley Forge, PA: Trinity Press International.

Thompson, Richard P., and Thomas E. Phillips, eds. 1998. *Literary Studies in Luke-Acts: Essays in Honor of Joseph B. Tyson.* Macon, GA: Mercer University Press.

Tilborg, Sjef van. 2001. "Acts 17:27—'that they might feel after him and find . . .'" *Hervormde Teologiese Studies* 57:86–104.

Tomes, Roger. 1995. "Why Did Paul Get His Hair Cut? (Acts 18:18; 21:23–24)." In *Luke's Literary Achievement: Collected Essays,* edited by C. M. Tuckett, 188–97. Sheffield: Sheffield Academic Press.

Townsend, John T. 1986. "Missionary Journeys in Acts and European Missionary Societies." *Anglican Theological Review* 68:99–104.

Trebilco, Paul. 1994. "Asia." In *The Book of Acts in Its Graeco-Roman Setting*, edited by David W. J. Gill, 291–362. Vol. 2 of *The Book of Acts in Its First Century Setting*. Edited by Bruce W. Winter. 5 vols. Grand Rapids: Eerdmans.

Trites, Allison A. 1977. *The New Testament Concept of Witness*. Cambridge: Cambridge University Press.

Tyson, Joseph B. 1987. "The Gentile Mission and the Authority of Scripture in Acts." *New Testament Studies* 33:619–31.

———, ed. 1988. *Luke-Acts and the Jewish People: Eight Critical Perspectives*. Minneapolis: Augsburg.

———. 2006. *Marcion and Luke-Acts: A Defining Struggle*. Columbia: University of South Carolina Press.

Unnik, Willem C. van. 1966. "Luke-Acts: A Storm Center in Contemporary Scholarship." In *Studies in Luke-Act: Essays Presented in Honor of Paul Schubert*, edited by Leander E. Keck and J. Louis Martyn, 15–32. Nashville: Abingdon.

Verheyden, J., ed. 1999. *The Unity of Luke-Acts*. Leuven: Leuven University Press.

Vielhauer, Philipp. 1966. "On the 'Paulinism' of Acts." In *Studies in Luke-Acts: Essays Presented in Honor of Paul Schubert*, edited by Leander E. Keck and J. Louis Martyn, 33–50. Nashville: Abingdon.

Vögeli, Alfred. 1953. "Lukas und Euripides." *Theologische Zeitschrift* 9:415–38.

Wagenaar, Hinne. 2003. "'Stop Harassing the Gentiles': The Importance of Acts 15 for African Theology." *Journal of African Christian Thought* 6:44–54.

Walaskay, Paul W. 1983. *'And So We Came to Rome': The Political Perspective of St. Luke*. Cambridge: Cambridge University Press.

———. 1998. *Acts*. Louisville: Westminster John Knox.

Walker, William O. 1985. "Acts and the Pauline Corpus Reconsidered." *Journal for the Study of the New Testament* 24:3–23.

———. 1998. "Acts and the Pauline Corpus Revisited: Peter's Speech at the Jerusalem Conference." In *Literary Studies in Luke-Acts: Essays in Honor of Joseph B. Tyson*, edited by Richard P. Thompson and Thomas E. Phillips, 77–86. Macon, GA: Mercer University Press.

Walton, Steve. 2002. "The State They Were In: Luke's View of the Roman Empire." In *Rome in the Bible and the Early Church*, edited by Peter Oakes, 1–41. Grand Rapids: Baker Academic.

Warfield, B. B. 1918. *Counterfeit Miracles*. New York: Scribner.

Watson, Duane F. 1991. "Paul's Speech to the Ephesian Elders (Acts 20.18–38): Epideictic Rhetoric of Farewell." In *Persuasive Artistry: Studies in New Testament Rhetoric in Honor of George A. Kennedy*, edited by Duane F. Watson, 184–208. Sheffield: Sheffield Academic Press.

Weatherly, Jon A. 1994. *Jewish Responsibility for the Death of Jesus in Luke-Acts*. Sheffield: Sheffield Academic Press.

Weaver, John B. 2004. *Plots of Epiphany: Prison-Escape in Acts of the Apostles*. Berlin: Walter de Gruyter.

Wedderburn, Alexander J. M. 2002. "Paul and Barnabas: The Anatomy and Chronology of a Parting of the Ways." In *Fair Play: Diversity and Conflicts in Early Christianity; Essays in Honour of Heikki Räisänen*, edited by Ismo Dunderberg, Christopher Tuckett, and Kari Syreeni, 291–310. Leiden: Brill.

Weinreich, Otto. 1929. *Gebet und Wunder: Zwei Abhandlungen zur Religions- und Literaturgeschichte*. Stuttgart: Kohlhammer.

Westcott, Brooke F., and F. J. A. Hort. 1892. *The New Testament in the Original Greek*. Cambridge: Macmillan.

Whitlark, Jason, and Mikeal C. Parsons. 2006. "The 'Seven' Last Words: A Numerical Motivation for the Insertion of Luke 23.34a." *New Testament Studies* 52:188–204.

Wilder, Amos N. 1943. "Variant Traditions of the Resurrection in Acts." *Journal of Biblical Literature* 62:307–18.

Wilson, Stephen G. 1983. *Luke and the Law*. Cambridge: Cambridge University Press.

Wimsatt, William K., and Monroe C. Beardsley. 1954. *The Verbal Icon: Studies in the Meaning of Poetry*. New York: Noonday.

Wink, Walter. 1986. *Unmasking the Powers*. Philadelphia: Fortress.

Winter, Bruce W. 1994. *Seek the Welfare of the City: Christians as Benefactors and Citizens*. Grand Rapids: Eerdmans.

———. 1996. "On Introducing Gods to Athens: An Alternative Reading of Acts 17:18–20." *Tyndale Bulletin* 47:71–90.

———. 1999. "Gallio's Ruling on the Legal Status of Early Christianity (Acts 18:14–15)." *Tyndale Bulletin* 50:213–24.

Witherington, Ben, ed. 1996. *History, Literature, and Society in the Book of Acts*. Cambridge: Cambridge University Press.

———. 1998. *The Acts of the Apostles: A Socio-Rhetorical Commentary*. Grand Rapids: Eerdmans.

Witherup, Ronald D. 1992. "Functional Redundancy in the Acts of the Apostles: A Case Study." *Journal for the Study of the New Testament* 48:67–86.

———. 1993. "Cornelius Over and Over and Over Again: 'Functional Redundancy' in the Acts of the Apostles." *Journal for the Study of the New Testament* 49:45–66.

Zahn, Theodor. 1909. *Introduction to the New Testament*. Translated from the third German edition by John M. Trout et al. 3 vols. Edinburgh: T. & T. Clark.

Zeller, Eduard. 1962. *The Stoics, Epicureans, and Sceptics*. Translated by Oswald J. Reichel. New York: Russell & Russell.

Zweck, Dean W. 1989. "The Exordium of the Areopagus Speech: Acts 17:22, 23." *New Testament Studies* 35:94–103.

Zwiep, Arie W. 1996. "The Text of the Ascension Narratives (Luke 24:50–3; Acts 1:1–2, 9–11)." *New Testament Studies* 42:219–44.

Subject Index

Index of Modern Authors

Index of Scripture and Ancient Writings

Old Testament

Genesis

1:24   145, 247
1:25   159
1:26   248
2:7   247
6–8   352
6:20   145
7:14   145
8:19   145
9:1–4   68
9:9–18   208
10   38, 39
11   36, 90
11:26–12:4   91
12   91
12:2   70
12:3   37, 123
12:7   92
13:15   92
15   90
15:2   92
15:6   90
15:13   92
15:13–14   92
16:1   92
17:8   92
17:10–14   209
18:1–16   369

18:22   103
19:1–23   369
20:3–8   312
21:20 LXX   153
21:22 LXX   153
22:11   126, 342
22:18   37, 123
24:10–61   369
26:4   123
26:23–25   252
31:10–13   312
33:10   89
34:15–24   209
37–50   93
37:11   94
37:28   94
37:36   94
39:1 LXX   119
39:2 LXX   153
39:14 LXX   114
41–42   95
42:2   95
43:16–34   369
45:8   94
46:2   126, 342
46:2–6   312
48:4   92
48:16   176

49   290

Exodus

1:7–8   96
1:9–22   96
1:10   96
1:11   96
1:13 LXX   153
1:22   96
2:2   97
2:3–4   96
2:11–15   97
2:12   178
2:14   97
2:15–22   369
3:1–2   99
3:4   126
3:8   176
3:12   92–93
3:12 LXX   153
4:10   97
4:12   151
6:1 LXX   193
6:6 LXX   193
6:30   131
8:4 LXX   118
8:8   118

1 Samuel

2:11 LXX   184
3:4   126, 342
5:3 LXX   167
5:6 LXX   167
5:9 LXX   167
7:10   199
10–12   194
12   290
12:1–25   194
12:2–5   293
13:14   195
14:45   358
15:23   194
16:1   194, 195
25:24   73
25:41   73
29:9   89

2 Samuel

3:12 LXX   167
7:12   171
7:13   45
7:16   45
8:1 LXX   185
14:11   358
22:15   126
22:39   73

1 Kings

1:21   171
2:10   171, 287
3:1–5   312
5:11   178
8:27   246
11:21   171
11:43   287
14:20   287
15:8   171
18:12   122
18:46 LXX   167
19:11–12   233
22:22–23   315

2 Kings

2:9–11   27
2:16   122
4:34   286
8:24   171

13:9   171
23:12   144
25:27–30   366

1 Chronicles

12:18 LXX   133

2 Chronicles

6:18   246
7:14   214
9:31   171
26:23   171

Nehemiah

1:4   185
5:5 LXX   153
8:16   144
9:6–31   106

Esther

2:3   119
2:14   119
4:4–5   119

Job

7:12   132
17:13   129
41:1   132

Psalms

2   66, 195
2:1–2   172
3:8 LXX   178
4:6   126
8:6   73
9:17   208
13:3   171
15:10 LXX   154
16   45, 46, 195
18:4–6   16
18:7–9   233
18:7–15   37, 199
18:14   126
23:4   129
26:8 LXX   247
28:3 LXX   90
29:3–5   199

29:3–9   37
36:9   126
40:14   192
44:23   287
46:6   199
49:14   129
49:19   129, 171
56:13   126
58:6   192
58:8   129, 171
67:8   192
67:35   192
68:9   192
69:25   32
71:18   192
73:17 LXX   247
77   106
77:18   126
77:66 LXX   178
78:14   126
78:65   287
88:6   129
89:15   126
89:20   195
97:4   126
97:11   126
104   106
104:2   126
104:4 LXX   247
104:17 LXX   94
104:26   132
105   106
107:10 LXX   171
109:8   32
110   45, 46
110:1   70, 73
113:12 LXX   248
118:22   63
134:15 LXX   248
135   106
135:12 LXX   193
144:6   126
146:6   66
146:9   83
148:10 LXX   159

Proverbs

7:27   129
9:10   142
10:24   152
11:1   152

Deuterocanonical Books

New Testament

10:14 122
10:16 127
10:17 122
10:18 128
10:20 122, 167
10:24 169
10:25–27 68
10:38–42 176, 369
10:39 73
10:41 126
10:42 340
11:5–8 288
11:14–23 137
11:15 270
11:18 273
11:19 270
11:20 270
11:23 271
11:24 221
11:31–32 122
11:47 169
11:47–51 103
11:49 99, 169
11:50 169
12:11–12 62
12:14 306
12:46 177
13 123
13:10 68
13:10–17 88, 118
13:14 191
13:17 122, 167
13:28 169
13:31 172
13:33 340
13:33–34 169
13:34–35 103
14:1–6 88
14:11 193
15:5 122, 167
15:6 369
15:7 122
15:9 369
15:10 122
15:23 146
15:27 146
15:29 369
15:30 146
15:32 122, 167
16:16 169
16:20 147, 200
16:21 83

16:29 169
16:29–31 343
16:31 169
17:16 73
18:1–5 139
18:1–8 83
18:7 338
18:14 193
18:18 69
18:20 68
18:31 169
18:31–33 321
18:32 173
18:35–43 137
18:38 70
18:39 70
19 123
19:1–10 369
19:6 122, 167
19:23 83
19:27 177
19:28–40 29
19:29 29
19:37 29, 122, 167
19:38 348
20:6 169
20:21 151
20:27–28 315
20:41–44 46, 70
20:43 73
20:47 83
21:1–4 83, 139
21:4 139
21:5–6 88
21:12 337
21:14 306
21:14–15 87
21:15 188
21:18 358
21:24 88
21:27 28
21:34–36 288
21:36 104
21:37 29–30
22:1 173
22:2 173
22:3 31, 75
22:7 145, 173
22:12 30
22:13 3357
22:14–38 291
22:15–16 129

22:17–19 358
22:20 37, 70
22:21 83
22:21–22 31
22:22 31
22:25–26 180
22:27 84
22:30 193
22:31 31, 126
22:31–32 32
22:32 32, 41
22:33 297
22:34 31
22:39 29–30
22:39–46 288
22:40 30
22:42 297
22:47 31
22:49–50 178
22:53 31
22:54 173
22:54–62 31
22:56 231
22:56–57 176
22:59 151
22:66 87
22:69 103
23 203, 316
23:4 346
23:6–12 172
23:7 82
23:7–15 172
23:13 173
23:13–25 87
23:14 346
23:15 346
23:18 306
23:22 346
23:25 173
23:26 86, 177
23:27 113
23:32 173
23:34 104, 257
23:43 45
23:44 129
23:44–45 360
23:46 45, 104
23:47 346, 354
23:48 113, 221–22
23:49 30, 32
23:50 113, 167
23:50–56 68

415

Other Early Jewish, Christian, and Gnostic Corpora

435

Anonymous Ancient Works

CPSIA information can be obtained at www.ICGtesting.com
Printed in the USA
LVOW122041120313

323921LV00002B/387/P